Ran...
champson college
Lennoxville
Quebec

CANADIAN
EDITION

ESSENTIALS OF
Corporate Finance

Stephen A. Ross
Massachusetts Institute of Technology

Randolph W. Westerfield
University of Southern California

Bradford D. Jordan
University of Kentucky

Ernest N. Biktimirov
Brock University

Toronto   Montréal   Boston   Burr Ridge, IL   Dubuque, IA   Madison, WI   New York
San Francisco   St. Louis   Bangkok   Bogotá   Caracas   Kuala Lumpur   Lisbon   London
Madrid   Mexico City   Milan   New Delhi   Santiago   Seoul   Singapore   Sydney   Taipei

The McGraw·Hill Companies

McGraw-Hill
Ryerson

ESSENTIALS OF CORPORATE FINANCE
CANADIAN EDITION

ISBN-13: 978-0-07-095655-1
ISBN-10: 0-07-095655-3

1 2 3 4 5 6 7 8 9 10 QPD 0 9 8

Printed and bound in the U.S.A.

Care has been taken to trace ownership of copyright material contained in this text; however, the publisher will welcome any information that enables them to rectify any reference or credit for subsequent editions.

Editorial Director: Joanna Cotton
Senior Sponsoring Editor: Rhondda McNabb
Marketing Manager: Joy Armitage Taylor
Sponsoring Editor: Kimberley Redhead
Developmental Editor: Daphne Scriabin
Signing Representative: Allison Sigurdson
Editorial Associate: Stephanie Hess
Associate Developmental Editor: Alison Derry
Production Coordinator: Sheryl MacAdam
Senior Supervising Editor: Anne Nellis
Copy Editor: Susan James
Cover Design: Dianna Little
Interior Design: Dianna Little
Cover Image Credit: © Darwin Wiggett/FirstLight
Composition: Laserwords
Printer: Quebecor Printing Dubuque

Library and Archives Canada Cataloguing in Publication

    Essentials of corporate finance / Stephen A. Ross ... [et al.]. --
Canadian ed.

Includes bibliographical references and indexes.
ISBN: 978-0-07-095655-1

    1. Corporations--Finance--Textbooks. I. Ross, Stephen A.
HG4026.E88 2008   658.15   C2007-903239-7

About the Authors

Stephen A. Ross

Sloan School of Management, Franco Modigliani Professor of Finance and Economics, Massachusetts Institute of Technology

Stephen A. Ross is the Franco Modigliani Professor of Finance and Economics at the Sloan School of Management, Massachusetts Institute of Technology. One of the most widely published authors in finance and economics, Professor Ross is recognized for his work in developing the Arbitrage Pricing Theory and his substantial contributions to the discipline through his research in signaling, agency theory, option pricing, and the theory of the term structure of interest rates, among other topics. A past president of the American Finance Association, he currently serves as an associate editor of several academic and practitioner journals. He is a trustee of CalTech and of Freddie Mac.

Randolph W. Westerfield

Marshall School of Business, University of Southern California

Randolph W. Westerfield is Dean Emeritus of the University of Southern California's Marshall School of Business and is the Charles B. Thornton Professor of Finance.

He came to USC from the Wharton School, University of Pennsylvania, where he was the chairman of the finance department and a member of the finance faculty for 20 years. He is a member of several public company boards of directors including Health Management Associates, Inc., William Lyons Homes, and the Nicholas Applegate Growth Fund. His areas of expertise include corporate financial policy, investment management, and stock market price behaviour.

Bradford D. Jordan

Gatton College of Business and Economics, Professor of Finance and holder of the Richard W. and Janis H. Furst Endowed Chair in Finance, University of Kentucky

Bradford D. Jordan is Professor of Finance and holder of the Richard W. and Janis H. Furst Endowed Chair in Finance at the University of Kentucky. He has a long-standing interest in both applied and theoretical issues in corporate finance and has extensive experience teaching all levels of corporate finance and financial management policy. Professor Jordan has published numerous articles on issues such as the cost of capital, capital structure, and the behaviour of security prices. He is a past president of the Southern Finance Association, and he is coauthor (with Charles J. Corrado) of *Fundamentals of Investments: Valuation and Management,* 3rd edition, a leading investments text, also published by McGraw-Hill/Irwin.

Ernest N. Biktimirov

Faculty of Business, Brock University

Ernest N. Biktimirov, CFA, is Associate Professor of Finance and holder of the Chancellor's Chair for Teaching Excellence at the Faculty of Business, Brock University. He teaches both undergraduate and graduate finance courses, and conducts research on stock prices and financial education. Professor Biktimirov is the winner of numerous teaching awards, including the Academy of Finance Teaching Excellence Award (2006) and the Province of Ontario Leadership in Faculty Teaching Award (2007). His educational papers have won the best paper award at several conferences, such as the Financial Management Association (2002) and the Administrative Sciences Association of Canada (2006). Professor Biktimirov has conducted a large number of workshops on innovative teaching for different audiences across Canada.

From the Authors

We wrote the *Essentials of Corporate Finance,* Canadian Edition, because so many of our colleagues and students told us of challenges they face in an introductory finance course. Indeed, this can be a tough course both to teach and to take. One reason is that the course is usually required of all business majors, so it has students of widely varying backgrounds, learning styles, and motivations. It is not uncommon for a majority of the students to be non-finance majors. In fact, this may be the only finance course many of them will ever take. With these challenges in mind, our goal in *Essentials* is to convey the most important concepts and principles at a level that is approachable and attractive for the widest possible audience.

To achieve our goal, we have worked to distill the subject down to its bare essentials (hence, the name of this book), while retaining a decidedly modern approach to Canadian financial management. We have always maintained that the subject of corporate finance can be viewed as the working of a few very powerful intuitions. We also think that understanding the "why" is just as important as understanding the "how," especially in an introductory course.

By design, this book is not encyclopedic. As the table of contents indicates, we have a total of 18 chapters. Chapter length averages about 30 pages, so the text is aimed squarely at a single-term course, and most of the book can be realistically covered in a typical semester or quarter. Writing a book for a one-term course necessarily means some picking and choosing, with regard to both topics and depth of coverage. Throughout, we strike a balance by introducing and covering the essentials (there's that word again!) while leaving some more specialized topics to follow-up courses.

The other things we have stressed are readability and pedagogy. *Essentials* is written in a relaxed, conversational style that invites the students to join in the learning process rather than passively absorbing information. To motivate various topics and to appeal to different learning styles, we use a variety of learning tools, including attention grabbing chapter-opening vignettes, practical *Reality Bytes* and *Work the Web* boxes, illustrative *Calculator Hints* and *Spreadsheet Strategies* boxes, numerous examples, questions and problems, mini-cases, and engaging Web activities, among others. We have found that this approach dramatically increases students' willingness to read and learn on their own. Between larger and larger class sizes and the ever-growing demands on faculty time, we think this is an essential (!) feature for a text in an introductory course.

Throughout the development of this book, we have taken a hard look at what is truly relevant and useful. In doing so, we have worked to downplay purely theoretical issues and minimize the use of extensive and elaborate calculations to illustrate points that are either intuitively obvious or of limited practical use.

As a result of this process, three basic themes emerge as our central focus in writing *Essentials of Corporate Finance:*

An Emphasis on Intuition We always try to separate and explain the principles at work on a commonsense, intuitive level before launching into any specifics. The underlying ideas are discussed first in very general terms and then by way of examples that illustrate in more concrete terms how a Canadian financial manager might proceed in a given situation.

A Unified Valuation Approach We treat net present value (NPV) as the basic concept underlying corporate finance. Many texts stop well short of consistently integrating this important principle. The most basic and important notion, that NPV represents the excess of market value over cost, is often lost in an overly mechanical approach that emphasizes computation at the expense of comprehension. In contrast, every subject we cover is firmly rooted in valuation, and care is taken throughout to explain how particular decisions have valuation effects.

A Managerial Focus Students shouldn't lose sight of the fact that Canadian financial management concerns management. We emphasize the role of the Canadian financial manager as decision maker, and we stress the need for managerial input and judgment. We consciously avoid "black box" approaches to finance, and, where appropriate, we make the approximate, pragmatic nature of financial analysis explicit, describe possible pitfalls, and discuss limitations.

In *Essentials of Corporate Finance,* these three themes work together to provide a consistent treatment, a sound foundation, and a practical, workable understanding of how to evaluate financial decisions in the Canadian business environment.

Finally, throughout the development of this textbook, we have paid a great deal of attention to accuracy. Our goal is to provide the best Canadian textbook available on the subject. Therefore, we would like to hear from instructors and students alike. Please write and tell us how to make this a better text. Forward your comments to: Dr. Ernest Biktimirov, Faculty of Business, Brock University, 500 Glenridge Ave., St. Catharines, ON L2S 3A1; or e-mail your comments to *ebiktimirov@brocku.ca.*

Stephen A. Ross
Randolph W. Westerfield
Bradford D. Jordan
Ernest N. Biktimirov

Organization of the Text

We designed the Canadian edition of *Essentials of Corporate Finance* to be as flexible and modular as possible. There are a total of nine parts, and, in broad terms, the instructor is free to decide the particular sequence. Further, within each part, the first chapter generally contains an overview and survey. Thus, when time is limited, subsequent chapters can be omitted. Finally, the sections placed early in each chapter are generally the most important, and later sections frequently can be omitted without loss of continuity. For these reasons, the instructor has great control over the topics covered, the sequence in which they are covered, and the depth of coverage. Just to get an idea of the breadth of coverage in *Essentials,* the following grid presents selected highlights for each chapter.

Chapters	Selected Topics of Interest	Benefits to Users
PART ONE	**Overview of Financial Management**	
Chapter 1	Goal of the firm and agency problems.	Stresses value creation as the most fundamental aspect of management and describes agency issues that can arise.
	Ethics, financial management, and executive compensation.	Brings in real-world issues concerning conflicts of interest and current controversies surrounding ethical conduct and management pay.
	Security exchanges.	Defines different types of financial markets and discusses the TSX and the TSX Venture Exchange.
PART TWO	**Understanding Financial Statements and Cash Flow**	
Chapter 2	Cash flow vs. earnings.	Clearly defines cash flow and spells out the differences between cash flow and earnings.
	Market values vs. book values.	Emphasizes the relevance of market values over book values.
	Taxes.	Highlights the importance of marginal tax rate over average tax rate and illustrates the tax treatment of different kinds of income based on the latest Canadian tax code.
Chapter 3	Ratio analysis.	Thorough coverage of key financial ratios.
	Du Pont identity.	Explores interrelationships between operating and financial performances. An expanded Du Pont analysis for Magna International shows how to get and use real-world data, thereby applying key chapter ideas.

Learning Solutions

In addition to illustrating relevant concepts and presenting up-to-date coverage, *Essentials of Corporate Finance* strives to present the material in a way that makes it coherent and easy to understand. To meet the varied needs of the intended audience, *Essentials of Corporate Finance* is rich in valuable learning tools and support.

Each feature can be categorized by the benefit to the student:

- Real Financial Decisions
- Application Tools
- Study Aids

REAL FINANCIAL DECISIONS

We have included two key features that help students connect chapter concepts to how decision makers use this material in the real world.

Chapter Opening Vignettes with Functional Integration Links

Each chapter begins with a recent real-world event to introduce students to the chapter concepts. Since many nonfinance majors will use this text, a brief paragraph linking the vignette and chapter concepts to majors in marketing, management, and accounting is included.

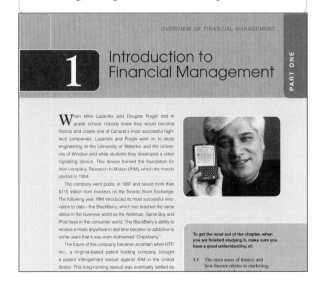

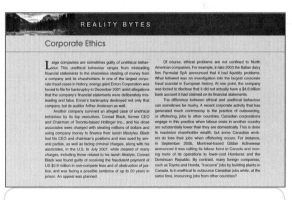

Reality Bytes Boxes

The majority of chapters include at least one *Reality Bytes* box, which takes a chapter issue and shows how it is being used in everyday financial decision making.

APPLICATION TOOLS

Realizing that there is more than one way to solve problems in corporate finance, we include many sections that will encourage students to learn different problem-solving methods, and also help them learn or brush up on their financial calculator and Excel spreadsheet skills.

Mini-cases

Located at the end of most parts, these mini-cases focus on hypothetical company situations that embody corporate finance topics. Each case presents a new scenario, data, and a dilemma. Several questions at the end of each case require students to analyze and focus on all of the material they learned from the chapters in that part. These are great for homework or in-class exercises and discussion.

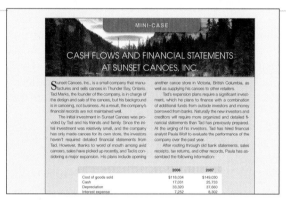

Work the Web

These boxes in the chapter material show students how to research financial issues using the Internet and how to use the information they find there to make business decisions.

Margin Web Links

These explanatory Web links are provided in the margins of the text. They are specifically selected to accompany text material and to provide students and instructors with a quick way to check for additional information using the Internet.

What's on the Web?

These end-of-chapter activities show students how to use and learn from the vast amount of financial resources available on the Internet.

Calculator Hints — Using a Financial Calculator

Although there are the various ways of calculating future values we have described so far, many of you will decide that a financial calculator is the way to go. If you are planning on using one, you should read this extended hint; otherwise, skip it.

A financial calculator is simply an ordinary calculator with a few extra features. In particular, it knows some of the most commonly used financial formulas, so it can directly compute things like future values.

Financial calculators have the advantage that they handle a lot of the computation, but that is really all. In other words, you still have to understand the problem; the calculator just does some of the arithmetic. In fact, there is an old joke (somewhat modified) that goes like this: Anyone can make a mistake on a time value of money problem, but to really mess one up takes a financial calculator! We therefore have two goals for this section. First, we'll discuss how to compute future values. After that, we'll show you how to avoid the most common mistakes people make when they start using financial calculators.

How to Calculate Future Values with a Financial Calculator Examining a typical financial calculator, you will find five keys of particular interest. They usually look like this:

For now, we need to focus on four of these. The keys labelled **PV** and **FV** are just what you would guess: present value and future value. The key labelled **N** refers to the number of periods, which is what we have been calling *t*. Finally, **I/Y** stands for the interest rate, which we have called *r*."

Calculator Hints

These are included in a self-contained section occurring in various chapters that first introduce students to calculator basics and then illustrate how to solve problems with the calculator.

Spreadsheet Strategies — How to Calculate Present Values with Multiple Future Cash Flows Using a Spreadsheet

Just as we did in our previous chapter, we can set up a basic spreadsheet to calculate the present values of the individual cash flows as follows. Notice that we have simply calculated the present values one at a time and added them up.

	A	B	C	D	E	F
1						
2			Using a spreadsheet to value multiple cash flows			
3						
4		What is the present value of $200 in one year, $400 the next year, $600 the next year, and $800 the				
5		last year if the discount rate is 12 percent?				
6						
7	Rate:	.12				
8						
9	Year	Cash flows	Present values	Formula used		
10	1	$200	$178.57	=PV($B$7,A10,0,-B10)		
11	2	$400	$318.88	=PV($B$7,A11,0,-B11)		
12	3	$600	$427.07	=PV($B$7,A12,0,-B12)		
13	4	$800	$508.41	=PV($B$7,A13,0,-B13)		
14						
15		Total PV:	$1,432.93	=SUM(C10:C13)		
16						
17	Notice the negative signs inserted in the PV formulas. These just make the present values have					
18	positive signs. Also, the discount rate in cell B7 is entered as $B$7 (an "absolute" reference) because					
19	it is used over and over. We could have just entered ".12" instead, but our approach is more flexible.					
20						
21						
22						

Spreadsheet Strategies

The unique Spreadsheet Strategies feature is also in a self-contained section, showing students how to set up spreadsheets to solve problems—a vital part of every student's education.

---

11. Growth Rates. The stock price of York Co. is $70. Investors require a 12 percent rate of return on similar stocks. If the company plans to pay a dividend of $4.25 next year, what growth rate is expected for the company's stock price?

12. Valuing Preferred Stock. E-Eyes.com has a new issue of preferred stock it calls 20/20 preferred. The stock will pay a $20 dividend per year, but the first dividend will not be paid until 20 years from today. If you require a 9 percent return on this stock, how much should you pay today?

13. Stock Valuation. Eldorado Corp. will pay a dividend of $3.75 next year. The company has stated that it will maintain a constant growth rate of 5 percent a year forever. If you want a 15 percent rate of return, how much will you pay for the stock? What if you want a 10 percent rate of return? What does this tell you about the relationship between the required return and the stock price?

14. Nonconstant Growth. Metallica Bearings, Inc., is a young start-up company. No dividends will be paid on the stock over the next six years, because the firm needs to plow back its earnings to fuel growth. The company will then pay a $7 per share dividend in year 7 and will increase the dividend by 5 percent per year thereafter. If the required return on this stock is 13 percent, what is the current share price?

15. Nonconstant Dividends. Three Creeks, Inc., has an odd dividend policy. The company has just paid a dividend of $12 per share and has announced that it will increase the dividend by $5 per share for each of the next four years, and then never pay another dividend. If you require a 12 percent return on the company's stock, how much will you pay for a share today?

Intermediate (Questions 14–26)

Spreadsheet Templates

Indicated by an Excel icon next to applicable end-of-chapter Questions and Problems, spreadsheet templates are available for selected problems on the Student Site of the Online Learning Centre at www.mcgrawhill.ca/olc/ross. These Excel templates are a valuable extension of the Spreadsheet Strategies feature.

STUDY AIDS

We want students to get the most from this book and their course and we realize that students have varied learning styles and study needs. We therefore present a number of study features to appeal to a wide range of students.

Learning Objectives

Each chapter begins with a number of learning objectives that are key to students' understanding of the chapter.

Pedagogical Use of Colour

The use of colour is a functional element to help students to follow the discussion. In almost every chapter, colour plays an important, largely self-evident role. A guide to the use of colour is found on the inside front cover.

Critical Thinking Questions

Every chapter ends with a set of critical thinking questions that challenge students to apply the concepts they have learned in that chapter to new situations.

Concept Questions

Chapter sections are intentionally kept short to promote a step-by-step, building-block approach to learning. Each section is then followed by a series of short concept questions that highlight the key ideas just presented. Students use these questions to make sure they can identify and understand the most important concepts as they read.

Numbered Examples

Separate numbered and titled examples are extensively integrated into the chapters. These examples provide detailed applications and illustrations of the text material in a step-by-step format. Each example is completely self-contained, so that students don't have to search for additional information. Based on classroom testing, these examples are among the most useful learning aids, because they provide both detail and explanation.

of the same risk as the warehouse project. Projects that have the same risk are said to be in the same risk class.

The WACC for a firm reflects the risk and the target capital structure of the firm's existing assets as a whole. As a result, strictly speaking, the firm's WACC is the appropriate discount rate only if the proposed investment is a replica of the firm's existing operating activities.

Summary Tables

These tables succinctly restate key principles, results, and equations. They appear whenever it is useful to emphasize and summarize a group of related concepts.

Sole Proprietorship

sole proprietorship
A business owned by a single individual.

A **sole proprietorship** is a business owned by one person. This is the simplest type of business to start and is the least regulated form of organization. For this reason, there are more proprietorships than any other type of business, and many businesses that later become large corporations start out as small proprietorships.

The owner of a sole proprietorship keeps all the profits. That's the good news. The bad news is that the owner has *unlimited liability* for business debts. This means that creditors can look to the proprietor's personal assets for payment. Similarly, there is no distinction between personal and business income, so all business income is taxed as personal income.

For more information on forms of business organization and how to start a business in Canada, visit **bsa.cbsc.org**.

The life of a sole proprietorship is limited to the owner's life span, and, importantly, the amount of equity that can be raised is limited to the proprietor's personal wealth. This limitation often means that the business is unable to exploit new opportunities because of insufficient capital. Ownership of a sole proprietorship may be difficult to transfer since this requires the sale of the entire business to a new owner.

Partnership

partnership
A business formed by two or more individuals or entities.

A **partnership** is similar to a proprietorship, except that there are two or more owners (partners). In a *general partnership*, all the partners share in gains or losses, and all have unlimited liability for *all* partnership debts, not just some particular share. The way partnership gains (and losses) are divided is described in the *partnership agreement*. This agreement

Key Terms

These are printed in colour the first time they appear and are defined within the margin.

Key Equations

These are identified by highlighted equation numbers and listed together in the end-of-chapter material.

current buying power to get the equivalent of $110, our real return is again 10 percent. Now that we have removed the effect of future inflation, this $110 is said to be measured in current dollars.

The difference between nominal and real rates is important and bears repeating:

> The nominal rate on an investment is the percentage change in the number of dollars you have.
>
> The real rate on an investment is the percentage change in how much you can buy with your dollars, in other words, the percentage change in your buying power.

The Fisher Effect

Our discussion of real and nominal returns illustrates a relationship often called the **Fisher effect** (after the great economist Irving Fisher). Because investors are ultimately concerned

Highlighted Phrases

Throughout the text, important ideas are presented separately and screened in colour to indicate their importance to the students.

SUMMARY AND CONCLUSIONS

This chapter has explored bonds and bond yields. We saw that:

1. Determining bond prices and yields is an application of basic discounted cash flow principles. Bond values move in the direction opposite that of interest rates, leading to potential gains or losses for bond investors.
2. Bonds have a variety of features spelled out in a document called the indenture.
3. Bonds are rated based on their default risk. Some bonds, such as Treasury bonds, have no risk of default, whereas so-called junk bonds have substantial default risk.
4. A wide variety of bonds exist, many of which contain exotic, or unusual, features.
5. Almost all bond trading is OTC, with little or no market transparency. As a result, bond price and volume information can be difficult to find.
6. Because of inflation, nominal rates are not equal to real rates, which reflect the percentage change in buying power.

www.mcgrawh

Chapter Summary and Conclusions

These paragraphs review the chapter's key points and provide the students with an overview of the chapter concepts.

Chapter Review and Self-Test Problems

Review and self-test problems appear after the chapter summaries. Detailed answers to the self-test problems follow immediately. These questions and answers allow the students to test their ability to solve key problems related to the content of the chapter.

CHAPTER REVIEW AND SELF-TEST PROBLEMS

6.1 Bond Values. A Mayflower Industries bond has a 10 percent coupon rate and a $1,000 face value. Interest is paid semiannually, and the bond has 20 years to maturity. If investors require a 12 percent yield, what is the bond's value? What is the effective annual yield on the bond?

6.2 Yields. A Canuck Corp. bond carries an 8 percent coupon, paid semiannually. The par value is $1,000, and the bond matures in six years. If the bond currently sells for $911.37, what is its yield to maturity? What is the effective annual yield?

■ Answers to Chapter Review and Self-Test Problems

6.1 Because the bond has a 10 percent coupon yield and investors require a 12 percent return, we know that the bond must sell at a discount. Notice that, because the bond pays interest semiannually, the coupons amount to

---

QUESTIONS AND PROBLEMS

Basic
(Questions 1–25)

1. **Calculating Liquidity Ratios.** Lodgepole Pine, Inc., has net working capital of $1,100, current liabilities of $4,180, and inventory of $1,600. What is the current ratio? What is the quick ratio?

2. **Calculating Profitability Ratios.** Nick's Bird Cages has sales of $43 million, total assets of $29 million, and total debt of $9.5 million. If the profit margin is 8 percent, what is net income? What is ROA? What is ROE?

3. **Calculating the Average Collection Period.** Bonds Lumber Yard has a current accounts receivable balance of $527,381. Credit sales for the year just ended were $4,386,500. What is the receivables turnover? The days' sales in receivables? How long did it take on average for credit customers to pay off their accounts during the past year?

4. **Calculating Inventory Turnover.** Windy Corporation has ending inventory of $865,371, and cost of goods sold for the year just ended was $4,378,650. What is the inventory turnover? The days' sales in inventory? How long on average did a unit of inventory sit on the shelf before it was sold?

5. **Calculating Leverage Ratios.** Victoria Golf, Inc., has a total debt ratio of .55. What is its debt-equity ratio? What is its equity multiplier?

6. **Calculating Market Value Ratios.** Niagara Cleaning, Inc., had additions to retained earnings for the year just ended of $380,000. The firm paid out $220,000 in cash dividends, and it has ending total equity of $5.5 million. If Niagara currently has 400,000 shares of common stock outstanding, what are earnings per share? Dividends per share? What is book value per share? If the stock currently sells for $32 per share, what is the market-to-book ratio? The price-earnings ratio?

7. **Du Pont Identity.** If Ottawa Legal has an equity multiplier of 1.70, total asset turnover of 1.45, and a profit margin of 9 percent, what is its ROE?

8. **Du Pont Identity.** Jiminy Cricket Removal has a profit margin of 11 percent, total asset turnover of 1.25, and ROE of 20.50 percent. What is this firm's debt-equity ratio?

9. **Calculating Average Payables Period.** For the past year, Miguaska, Inc., had a cost of goods sold of $41,682. At the end of the year, the accounts payable balance was

www.mcgrawhill.ca/ole/ross

End-of-Chapter Questions and Problems

Many students learn better when they have plenty of opportunity to practise. Extensive questions and problems are identified and segregated into three levels—Basic, Intermediate, and Challenge. Answers to selected end-of-chapter questions appear in Appendix B.

Comprehensive Teaching and Learning Package

We have made every effort to include the support material that is most critical for you and your students.

LYRYX FOR FINANCE

Lyryx Assessment for Finance is a leading-edge online assessment system designed to support both students and instructors. The assessment takes the form of a homework assignment called a Lab. The assessments are algorithmically generated and automatically graded so that students get instant grades and feedback. New Labs are randomly generated each time, providing the student with unlimited opportunities to try a type of question. After they submit a Lab for marking, students receive extensive feedback on their work, thus promoting their learning experience.

For the students, **Lyryx** offers algorithmically generated and automatically graded assignments. Students get instant grades and instant feedback—no need to wait until the next class to find out how well they did! Grades are instantly recorded in a grade book that the student can view.

Students are motivated to do their Labs for two reasons: first, because the results can be tied to assessment, and second, because they can try the Lab as many times as they wish before the due date, and only their best grade will be recorded.

Instructors know from experience that if students do their finance homework, they will be successful in the course. Recent research regarding the use of Lyryx has shown that when Labs are tied to assessment, even if worth only a small percentage of the total grade of the course, students WILL do their homework—and MORE THAN ONCE!

Please contact your *i*Learning Sales Specialist for additional information on the **Lyryx** Assessment Finance system. Visit **http://lyryx.com.**

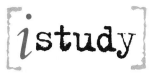

*i*Interact *i*Learn *i*Succeed

*i***Study** — Available 24/7: Instant feedback so students can study when you want, how you want, and where you want.

This online *i*Study space was developed to help students master the concepts and achieve better grades with all the learning tools they have come to expect, such as interactive quizzes with instant feedback and problems with full solutions, as well as new elements, including interactive financial simulations on key finance topics and video files for online viewing or as downloadable MP3 video files. *i*Study offers the best, most convenient way to Interact, Learn, and Succeed.

To see a sample chapter, go to the Online Learning Centre at www.mcgrawhill.ca/olc/ross. Full access to *i*Study can be purchased at the Web site or by purchasing a pin code card through your campus bookstore.

Instructors: Contact your *i*Learning Sales Specialist for more information on how to make *i*Study part of your students' success.

Student Online Learning Centre Prepared by Eric Wang, Athabasca University, this electronic learning aid, located at www.mcgrawhill.ca/olc/ross offers additional Web-based study aids created for this text, including: Multiple-Choice Quizzes, Excel templates, Internet Application Questions, annotated Web links, *Globe and Mail* Newsfeeds, video clips, and much more.

INSTRUCTOR'S SUPPLEMENTS

Instructor's Online Learning Centre (OLC)

The OLC at www.mcgrawhill.ca/olc/ross includes a password-protected Web site for Instructors. The site offers downloadable supplements for all instructor resources (except the Computerized Test Bank).

The Instructor's Resource CD-ROM contains the Instructor's Manual, Computerized Test Bank, PowerPoint® Presentation, and Solutions to Excel problems:

- **Instructor's Manual** Prepared by the author, the manual consists of three parts: (i) Instructor's Manual Solutions, which are the detailed solutions to all end-of-chapter problems, (ii) Case Solutions, and (iii) Instructor Outline, a teaching resource that integrates the PowerPoint® slides into chapter outlines.

- **Computerized Test Bank** Prepared by Elisabeth Carter, Douglas College, provides a variety of question formats including multiple-choice questions and open-ended questions. Each question is classified by: Type (Concept, Definition, Problem or Essay), Topic, and Level (Easy, Medium and Hard) to meet the instructor's testing needs.

- **PowerPoint® Presentation** Prepared by the author, the slides contain useful outlines, summaries, and exhibits from the text.

- **Image Bank** All figures and tables are available in digital format in the Instructor's CD.

- **Excel Templates** (with solutions) Prepared by Eric Wang, Athabasca University, Excel templates are included with solutions for the end-of-chapter problems indicated by an Excel icon in the margin of the text.

Integrated Learning Your Integrated Learning Sales Specialist is a McGraw-Hill Ryerson representative who has the experience, product knowledge, training, and support to help you assess and integrate any of our products, technology, and services into your course for optimum teaching and learning performance. Whether it's using our test bank software, helping your students improve their grades, or putting your entire course online, your *i*Learning Sales Specialist is there to help you do it. Contact your local *i*Learning Sales Specialist today to learn how to maximize all of McGraw-Hill Ryerson's resources!

www.blackboard.com

courses · campus · community

Create a custom course Website with **PageOut**, free with every McGraw-Hill Ryerson textbook.

To learn more, contact your McGraw-Hill Ryerson publisher's representative or visit www.mhhe.com/solutions

COURSE MANAGEMENT

PageOut is the McGraw-Hill Ryerson course management system. **Visit** www.mhhe.com/pageout to create a Web page for your course, using our resources. PageOut is the McGraw-Hill Ryerson Web site development centre. This Web page generating software is free to adopters and is designed to help faculty create an online course, complete with assignments, quizzes, links to relevant Web sites, and more—all in a matter of minutes.

In addition, content cartridges are available for course management systems such as **WebCT** and **Blackboard.** These platforms provide instructors with user-friendly, flexible teaching tools. Please contact your local McGraw-Hill Ryerson *i*Learning Sales Specialist for details.

We want to help bring your teaching to life, using our products and services. We do this by integrating technology, events, conferences, training, and more into services surrounding the textbook. We call it *i*Services. For more information, please contact your *i*Learning Sales Specialist.

TEACHING, LEARNING & TECHNOLOGY CONFERENCE SERIES

The educational environment has changed tremendously in recent years, and McGraw-Hill Ryerson continues to be committed to helping you acquire the skills you need to succeed in this new milieu. Our innovative Teaching, Learning & Technology Conference Series brings faculty together from across Canada with 3M Teaching Excellence award winners to share teaching and learning best practices in a collaborative and stimulating environment. Pre-conference workshops on general topics, such as teaching large classes and technology integration, will also be offered. We will even work with you at your own institution to customize workshops that best suit the needs of your faculty.

Acknowledgments

Our plan for developing the Canadian edition of *Essentials* revolved around the detailed feedback we received from many of our colleagues who regularly teach the introductory course. These dedicated scholars and teachers to whom we are very grateful are:

Mohamed Ayadi, *Brock University*

Elisabeth Carter, *Douglas College*

Merlyn Foo, *Athabasca University*

Ken Hartviksen, *Lakehead University*

Shahriar Hasan, *University College of the Cariboo*

Robert Ironside, *University of Lethbridge*

Dave Kennedy, *Lethbridge Community College*

Brian Korb, *Trinity Western University*

Marie Madill-Payne, *George Brown College*

Vanessa Oltmann, *Malaspina University College*

David Peters, *University of Western Ontario*

Judith Watson, *Capilano College*

Jun Yang, *Acadia University*

We owe a special debt to Merlyn Foo, Athabasca University, who not only provided invaluable comments, but also did outstanding work of technical proofreading, and in particular, careful checking of each calculation throughout the text.

We also thank our colleagues for their dedicated work on the supplements that accompany this text: Elizabeth Carter, Douglas College, for her work on the Test Bank, Jackie Shemko, Durham College, for her thorough checking of the solutions to the end-of-chapter problems and mini-cases, and Eric Wang, Athabasca University, for his development of the Student Online Learning Centre.

Finally, in every phase of this project, we have been privileged to have the complete and unwavering support of a great organization, McGraw-Hill Ryerson. Specifically, we are deeply grateful to the select group of professionals who served as our development team: Daphne Scriabin, Developmental Editor; Anne Nellis, Senior Supervising Editor; Alison Derry, Associate Developmental Editor; Susan James, Copy Editor; Joy Armitage Taylor, Senior Marketing Manager; Joanna Cotton, Editorial Director; and Lynn Fisher, Publisher. Others at McGraw-Hill Ryerson, too numerous to list here, have improved the book in countless ways.

Brief Contents

xix

Contents

CHAPTER **3**
Working with Financial Statements

PART **3**
VALUATION OF FUTURE CASH FLOWS

CHAPTER **4**
Introduction to Valuation: The Time Value of Money

PART 4

VALUING STOCKS AND BONDS

CHAPTER **6**

Interest Rates and Bond Valuation

PART 7
LONG-TERM FINANCING

CHAPTER **12**
Cost of Capital

CHAPTER **13**
Leverage and Capital Structure

CHAPTER **14**
Dividends and Dividend Policy

CHAPTER **15**
Raising Capital

PART 8
SHORT-TERM FINANCIAL MANAGEMENT

CHAPTER **16**
Short-Term Financial Planning

Chapter 17
Working Capital Management

List of Boxes

Introduction to Financial Management

1

When Mike Lazaridis and Douglas Fregin met in grade school, nobody knew they would become friends and create one of Canada's most successful high-tech companies. Lazaridis and Fregin went on to study engineering at the University of Waterloo and the University of Windsor and while students they developed a video signalling device. This device formed the foundation for their company, Research In Motion (RIM), which the friends started in 1984.

The company went public in 1997 and raised more than $115 million from investors on the Toronto Stock Exchange. The following year, RIM introduced its most successful innovation to date—the BlackBerry, which has reached the same status in the business world as the Walkman, Game Boy and iPod have in the consumer world. The BlackBerry's ability to receive e-mails anywhere in real time became so addictive to some users that it was even nicknamed "Crackberry."

The future of the company became uncertain when NTP, Inc., a Virginia-based patent holding company, brought a patent infringement lawsuit against RIM in the United States. This long-running lawsuit was eventually settled by RIM for US $612.5 million in March 2006. The rest of the year held brighter news for the company. RIM introduced Pearl, which received rave reviews, its co-chief executives, Mike Lazaridis and Jim Balsillie, won Canada's Outstanding CEO of the Year award, and the company was listed among the 50 fastest-growing Canadian tech companies.

Understanding Lazaridis and Fregin's journey from student entrepreneurs to corporate executives takes us into issues involving the corporate form of organization, corporate goals, and corporate control, all of which we discuss in this chapter.

To get the most out of the chapter, when you are finished studying it, make sure you have a good understanding of:

1.1 The main areas of finance and how finance relates to marketing, accounting, and management.

1.2 The basic types of financial management decisions and the role of the financial manager.

1.3 The financial implications of the different forms of business organization.

1.4 The goal of financial management.

1.5 The conflicts of interest that can arise between managers and owners.

1.6 How financial markets work.

To begin our study of financial management, we address two central issues. First: What is corporate, or business, finance and what is the role of the financial manager? Second: What is the goal of financial management?

1.1 | FINANCE: A QUICK LOOK

Check out the companion Web site for this text at **www.mcgrawhill.ca/olc/ross**

Before we plunge into our study of "corp. fin.," we think a quick overview of the finance field might be a good idea. Our goal is to clue you in on some of the most important areas in finance and some of the career opportunities available in each area. We also want to illustrate some of the ways finance fits in with other areas such as marketing, accounting, and management.

The Four Basic Areas

Traditionally, financial topics are grouped into four main areas:

1. Corporate finance
2. Investments
3. Financial institutions
4. International finance

We discuss each of these next.

For job descriptions in finance and other areas, visit **www.careers-in-business.com.**

Corporate Finance   The first of these four areas, corporate finance, is the main subject of this book. We begin covering this subject with our next section, so we will wait until then to get into any details. One thing we should note is that the term *corporate finance* seems to imply that what we cover is only relevant to corporations, but the truth is that almost all of the topics we consider are much broader than that. Maybe *business finance* would be a little more descriptive, but even this is too narrow because at least half of the subjects we discuss in the pages ahead are really basic financial ideas and principles applicable across all the various areas of finance and beyond.

Investments   Broadly speaking, the investments area deals with financial assets such as stocks and bonds. Some of the more important questions include:

1. What determines the price of a financial asset such as a share of stock?
2. What are the potential risks and rewards associated with investing in financial assets?
3. What is the best mixture of the different types of financial assets to hold?

Students who specialize in the investments area have various career opportunities. Being a stockbroker is one of the most common. Stockbrokers often work for large companies such as RBC Dominion Securities, advising customers on what types of investments to consider and helping them make buy and sell decisions. Financial advisers play a similar role, but are not necessarily brokers.

Portfolio management is a second investments-related career path. Portfolio managers, as the name suggests, manage money for investors. For example, individual investors frequently buy into mutual funds. Such funds are simply a means of pooling money that is then invested by a portfolio manager. Portfolio managers also invest and manage money for pension funds, insurance companies, and many other types of institutions.

REALITY BYTES

Three Magic Letters

Have you ever wondered what abbreviations such as CFA, CFP, and CTP mean? They refer to some of almost a dozen professional designations that we find in the finance profession. Different groups benefit from having professional designations. Employers use them as a low-cost screening tool for hiring the best candidates and promoting current employees. Clients look at professional designations to find knowledgeable and experienced professionals they can entrust with their capital. Finally, finance professionals proudly show their designations on business cards as an external validation of their competence.

Two of the most common designations in Canada are the Chartered Financial Analyst (CFA) and the Certified Financial Planner (CFP). While CFA is administered by the U.S.-based CFA Institute, it is one of the very few internationally recognized designations. Every year more than 100,000 candidates from over 150 countries write one of the three levels of CFA exams. The CFA program is primarily designed for people working in the investments area, but a growing number of CFA charterholders work in non-financial corporations, consulting firms, and government agencies. The CFA program accepts students who are still in the final year of a bachelor's degree program. Wilfrid Laurier University and Concordia University offer MBA programs with CFA options. Those who have earned a CFA charter are rewarded in the profession. According to a 2005 compensation survey in Canada, the median total compensation of CFA

charterholders with 10 years of experience or more reached $212,000, and was 35 percent higher than that of people in the same jobs who did not have a CFA charter. Interestingly, Canada has the largest number of CFA charterholders per capita in the world, and the Toronto CFA society is one of the largest CFA chapters.

CFP is designed for personal financial planners and is administered by the Financial Planners Standards Council (FPSC). Many countries have similar designations, but unlike the CFA charter, they are not transferable from one country to another. To qualify to write the CFP exam, candidates must complete an education program. Many universities and colleges offer these programs, such as the CFP Qualifying Program at the University of Victoria and the CFP Program at Centennial College in Toronto. In addition to passing the exams, both the CFP and CFA programs have work experience and code of ethics requirements for awarding the designations.

Other financial designations are most often applied in more specific finance fields, such as Certified Treasury Professional (CTP), Certified Business Valuator (CBV), and Fellow of the Canadian Institute of Actuaries (FCIA). To decide which designation is worth pursuing in your chosen field of finance, it is useful to talk to professionals from that area. They can advise you as to which professional designation will be most helpful for a successful career in that field.

Security analysis is a third area. A security analyst researches individual investments, such as stock in a particular company, and makes a determination as to whether the price is right. To do so, an analyst delves deeply into company and industry reports, along with a variety of other information sources. Frequently, brokers and portfolio managers rely on security analysts for information and recommendations.

These investments-related areas, like many areas in finance, share an interesting feature. If they are done well, they can be very rewarding financially (translation: You can make a lot of money). The bad news, of course, is that they can be very demanding and very competitive, so they are definitely not for everybody. To have a successful career, one should think about getting at least one of the many financial professional designations available. Our *Reality Bytes* box above discusses two of the most commonly found designations in Canada.

To learn more about the CFA and CFP designations visit **www.cfainstitute.org** and **www.cfp-ca.org**, respectively.

Financial Institutions Financial institutions are basically businesses that deal primarily in financial matters. Banks and insurance companies would probably be the most familiar to you. Institutions such as these employ people to perform a wide variety of finance-related tasks. For example, a commercial loan officer at a bank would evaluate whether a particular business has a strong enough financial position to warrant extending a loan. At an insurance company, an analyst would decide whether a particular risk was suitable for insuring and what the premium should be.

International Finance   International finance isn't so much an area as it is a specialization within one of the main areas we described above. In other words, careers in international finance generally involve international aspects of either corporate finance, investments, or financial institutions. For example, some portfolio managers and security analysts specialize in non-Canadian companies. Similarly, many Canadian businesses have extensive overseas operations and need employees familiar with such international topics as exchange rates and political risk. Banks frequently are asked to make loans across country lines, so international specialists are needed there as well.

Why Study Finance?

Who needs to know finance? In a word, you. In fact, there are many reasons you need a working knowledge of finance even if you are not planning a finance career. We explore some of these next.

Marketing and Finance   If you are interested in marketing, you need to know finance because, for example, marketers constantly work with budgets, and they need to understand how to get the greatest payoff from marketing expenditures and programs. Analyzing costs and benefits of projects of all types is one of the most important aspects of finance, so the tools you learn in finance are vital in marketing research, the design of marketing and distribution channels, and product pricing, to name just a few areas.

Financial analysts rely heavily on marketing analysts, and the two frequently work together to evaluate the profitability of proposed projects and products. As we will see in a later chapter, sales projections are a key input in almost every type of new product analysis, and such projections are often developed jointly between marketing and finance.

Beyond this, the finance industry employs marketers to help sell financial products such as bank accounts, insurance policies, and mutual funds. Financial services marketing is one of the most rapidly growing types of marketing, and successful financial services marketers are very well compensated. To work in this area, you obviously need to understand financial products.

Accounting and Finance   For accountants, finance is required reading. In smaller businesses in particular, accountants are often required to make financial decisions as well as perform traditional accounting duties. Further, as the financial world continues to grow more complex, accountants have to know finance to understand the implications of many of the newer types of financial contracts and the impact they have on financial statements. Beyond this, cost accounting and business finance are particularly closely related, sharing many of the same subjects and concerns.

Financial analysts make extensive use of accounting information; they are some of the most important end users. Understanding finance helps accountants recognize what types of information are particularly valuable and, more generally, how accounting information is actually used (and abused) in practice.

Management and Finance One of the most important areas in management is strategy. Thinking about business strategy without simultaneously thinking about financial strategy is an excellent recipe for disaster, and, as a result, management strategists must have a very clear understanding of the financial implications of business plans.

In broader terms, management employees of all types are expected to have a strong understanding of how their jobs impact profitability, and they are also expected to be able to work within their areas to improve profitability. This is precisely what studying finance teaches you: What are the characteristics of activities that create value?

You and Finance Perhaps the most important reason to know finance is that you will have to make financial decisions that will be very important to you personally. Today, for example, when you go to work for almost any type of company, you will be asked to decide how you want to invest your retirement funds. We'll see in a later chapter that what you choose to do can make an enormous difference in your future financial well-being. On a different note, is it your dream to start your own business? Good luck if you don't understand basic finance before you start; you'll end up learning it the hard way. Want to know how big your student loan payments are going to be before you take out that next loan? Maybe not, but we'll show you how to calculate them anyway.

These are just a few of the ways that finance will affect your personal and business lives. Whether you want to or not, you are going to have to examine and understand financial issues, and you are going to have to make financial decisions. We want you to do so wisely, so keep reading.

CONCEPT QUESTIONS

1.1a What are the major areas in finance?

1.1b Besides wanting to pass this class, why do you need to understand finance?

1.2 | BUSINESS FINANCE AND THE FINANCIAL MANAGER

Now we proceed to define business finance and the financial manager's job.

What Is Business Finance?

Imagine you were to start your own business. No matter what type you started, you would have to answer the following three questions in some form or other:

1. What long-term investments should you take on? That is, what lines of business will you be in and what sorts of buildings, machinery, and equipment will you need?

2. Where will you get the long-term financing to pay for your investment? Will you bring in other owners or will you borrow the money?

3. How will you manage your everyday financial activities, such as collecting from customers and paying suppliers?

These are not the only questions, but they are among the most important. Business finance, broadly speaking, is the study of ways to answer these three questions. We'll be looking at each of them in the chapters ahead.

The Financial Manager

For current issues facing CFOs, see www.cfo.com.

The financial management function is usually associated with a top officer of the firm, often called the chief financial officer (CFO) or vice president of finance. Figure 1.1 is a simplified organizational chart that highlights the finance activity in a large firm. As shown, the vice president of finance coordinates the activities of the treasurer and the controller. The controller's office handles cost and financial accounting, tax payments, and management information systems. The treasurer's office is responsible for managing the firm's cash and credit, its financial planning, and its capital expenditures. These treasury activities are all related to the three general questions raised above, and the chapters ahead deal primarily with these issues. Our study thus bears mostly on activities usually

FIGURE 1.1

A simplified organizational chart. The exact titles and organization differ from company to company.

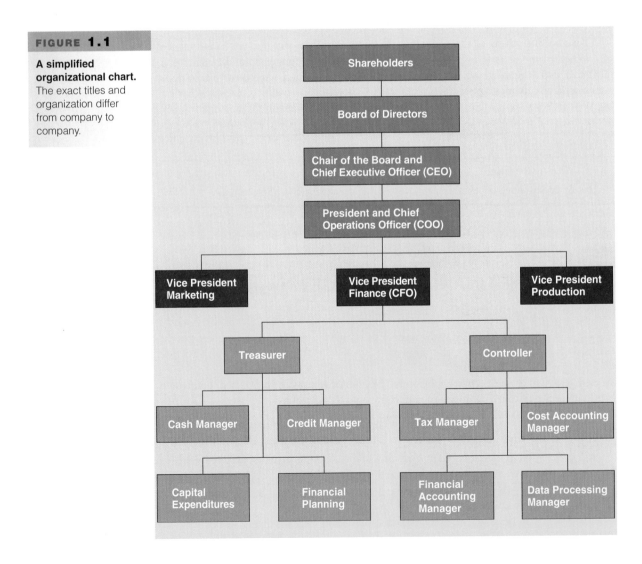

associated with the treasurer's office. In a smaller firm, the treasurer and controller might be the same person, and there would be only one office.

Financial Management Decisions

As our discussion above suggests, the financial manager must be concerned with three basic types of questions. We consider these in greater detail next.

Capital Budgeting   The first question concerns the firm's long-term investments. The process of planning and managing a firm's long-term investments is called **capital budgeting.** In capital budgeting, the financial manager tries to identify investment opportunities that are worth more to the firm than they cost to acquire. Loosely speaking, this means that the value of the cash flow generated by an asset exceeds the cost of that asset.

> **capital budgeting**
> The process of planning and managing a firm's long-term investments.

Regardless of the specific investment under consideration, financial managers must be concerned with how much cash they expect to receive, when they expect to receive it, and how likely they are to receive it. Evaluating the *size, timing,* and *risk* of future cash flows is the essence of capital budgeting. In fact, whenever we evaluate a business decision, the size, timing, and risk of the cash flows will be, by far, the most important things we will consider.

Capital Structure   The second question for the financial manager concerns how the firm obtains the financing it needs to support its long-term investments. A firm's **capital structure** (or financial structure) refers to the specific mixture of long-term debt and equity the firm uses to finance its operations. The financial manager has two concerns in this area. First: How much should the firm borrow? Second: What are the least expensive sources of funds for the firm?

> **capital structure**
> The mixture of debt and equity maintained by a firm.

In addition to deciding on the financing mix, the financial manager has to decide exactly how and where to raise the money. The expenses associated with raising long-term financing can be considerable, so different possibilities must be carefully evaluated. Also, corporations borrow money from a variety of lenders in a number of different ways. Choosing among lenders and among loan types is another job handled by the financial manager.

Working Capital Management   The third question concerns **working capital** management. The term *working capital* refers to a firm's short-term assets, such as inventory, and its short-term liabilities, such as money owed to suppliers. Managing the firm's working capital is a day-to-day activity that ensures the firm has sufficient resources to continue its operations and avoid costly interruptions. This involves a number of activities related to the firm's receipt and disbursement of cash.

> **working capital**
> A firm's short-term assets and liabilities.

Some questions about working capital that must be answered are the following: (1) How much cash and inventory should we keep on hand? (2) Should we sell on credit to our customers? (3) How will we obtain any needed short-term financing? If we borrow in the short term, how and where should we do it? This is just a small sample of the issues that arise in managing a firm's working capital.

Conclusion   The three areas of corporate financial management we have described— capital budgeting, capital structure, and working capital management—are very broad categories. Each includes a rich variety of topics, and we have indicated only a few of the questions that arise in the different areas. The chapters ahead contain greater detail.

1.3 | FORMS OF BUSINESS ORGANIZATION

Large firms in Canada, such as Royal Bank of Canada (RBC) and Imperial Oil, are almost all organized as corporations. We examine the three different legal forms of business organization—sole proprietorship, partnership, and corporation—to see why this is so.

Sole Proprietorship

sole proprietorship
A business owned by a single individual.

A **sole proprietorship** is a business owned by one person. This is the simplest type of business to start and is the least regulated form of organization. For this reason, there are more proprietorships than any other type of business, and many businesses that later become large corporations start out as small proprietorships.

The owner of a sole proprietorship keeps all the profits. That's the good news. The bad news is that the owner has *unlimited liability* for business debts. This means that creditors can look to the proprietor's personal assets for payment. Similarly, there is no distinction between personal and business income, so all business income is taxed as personal income.

For more information on forms of business organization and how to start a business in Canada, visit **bsa.cbsc.org.**

The life of a sole proprietorship is limited to the owner's life span, and, importantly, the amount of equity that can be raised is limited to the proprietor's personal wealth. This limitation often means that the business is unable to exploit new opportunities because of insufficient capital. Ownership of a sole proprietorship may be difficult to transfer since this requires the sale of the entire business to a new owner.

Partnership

partnership
A business formed by two or more individuals or entities.

A **partnership** is similar to a proprietorship, except that there are two or more owners (partners). In a *general partnership,* all the partners share in gains or losses, and all have unlimited liability for *all* partnership debts, not just some particular share. The way partnership gains (and losses) are divided is described in the *partnership agreement.* This agreement can be an informal oral agreement, such as "let's start a lawn mowing business," or a lengthy, formal written document.

In a *limited partnership,* one or more *general partners* will run the business and have unlimited liability, but there will also be one or more *limited partners* who do not actively participate in the business. A limited partner's liability for business debts is limited to the amount that partner contributes to the partnership. This form of organization is common in real estate ventures, for example.

Visit the Business Development Bank of Canada Web site at **www.bdc.ca** for more information on its services to small businesses.

The advantages and disadvantages of a partnership are basically the same as those for a proprietorship. Partnerships based on a relatively informal agreement are easy and inexpensive to form. General partners have unlimited liability for partnership debts, and the partnership terminates when a general partner wishes to sell out or dies. All income is taxed as personal income to the partners, and the amount of equity that can be raised is limited to the partners' combined wealth. Ownership by a general partner is not easily transferred because a new partnership must be formed. A limited partner's interest can be sold without dissolving the partnership, but finding a buyer may be difficult.

Because a partner in a general partnership can be held responsible for all partnership debts, having a written agreement is very important. Failure to spell out the rights and duties of the partners frequently leads to misunderstandings later on. Also, if you are a limited partner, you must not become deeply involved in business decisions unless you are willing to assume the obligations of a general partner. The reason is that if things go badly, you may be deemed to be a general partner even though you say you are a limited partner.

Based on our discussion, the primary disadvantages of sole proprietorships and partnerships as forms of business organization are (1) unlimited liability for business debts on the part of the owners, (2) limited life of the business, and (3) difficulty of transferring ownership. These three disadvantages add up to a single, central problem: The ability of such businesses to grow can be seriously limited by an inability to raise cash for investment.

Corporation

The **corporation** is the most important form (in terms of size) of business organization in Canada. A corporation is a legal "person" separate and distinct from its owners, and it has many of the rights, duties, and privileges of an actual person. Corporations can borrow money and own property, can sue and be sued, and can enter into contracts. A corporation can even be a general partner or a limited partner in a partnership, and a corporation can own stock in another corporation.

corporation
A business created as a distinct legal entity owned by one or more individuals or entities.

Not surprisingly, starting a corporation is somewhat more complicated than starting the other forms of business organization. Forming a corporation involves preparing *articles of incorporation* (or a charter) and a set of *bylaws*. The articles of incorporation must contain a number of things, including the corporation's name, its intended lifespan (which can be forever), its business purpose, and the number of shares that can be issued. This information must normally be supplied to regulators in the jurisdiction where the firm is incorporated. Canadian firms can be incorporated federally, under the *Canada Business Corporations Act,* or provincially, under the applicable provincial laws.

The bylaws are rules describing how the corporation regulates its own existence. For example, the bylaws describe how directors are elected. The bylaws may be amended or extended from time to time by the stockholders.

In a large corporation, the stockholders and the managers are usually separate groups. The stockholders elect the board of directors, who then select the managers. Management is charged with running the corporation's affairs in the stockholders' interests. In principle, stockholders control the corporation because they elect the directors.

As a result of the separation of ownership and management, the corporate form has several advantages. Ownership (represented by shares of stock) can be readily transferred, and the life of the corporation is therefore not limited. The corporation borrows money in its own name. As a result, the stockholders in a corporation have limited liability for corporate debts. The most they can lose is what they have invested.

The relative ease of transferring ownership, the limited liability for business debts, and the unlimited life of the business are the reasons why the corporate form is superior when it comes to raising cash. If a corporation needs new equity, it can sell new shares of stock and attract new investors. The number of owners can be huge; larger corporations have many thousands or even millions of stockholders. For example, Manulife Financial, a leading Canadian-based financial services company, has about 1.5 billion shares outstanding and more than 900,000 shareholders.

REALITY BYTES

Income Trusts Earn Our Trust

Income trusts. They are everywhere these days, and it seems everyone is talking about them. Even Carmela Soprano, a character in a popular TV series about a mob family "The Sopranos," urges her husband, Tony, to consider investing in income trusts in the opening episode of the fourth season. "There are these things called REITs," she tells Tony Soprano, based on the recommendation of her cousin, a financial advisor. Tony doesn't believe in equity markets. "We don't have those Enron-type connections," he replies.

While income trusts have not earned the trust of the fictional mafia boss, they have definitely succeeded with the Canadian investment public. The market capitalization of income trusts has ballooned from $2 billion at the end of 1994 to almost $190 billion in 2006 and makes up 9 percent of the market capitalization of the Toronto Stock Exchange.

As a rule, income trusts hold mature assets that produce stable income. A significant portion of this income is distributed to unitholders on a monthly basis. A large variety of income trusts exist. They can be classified into four major groups based on the type of businesses they own:

1. Real Estate Investment Trusts (REITs) have been around for more than 20 years. REITs generate income from different types of real estate, such as apartment complexes, office buildings, shopping centres and so on. Some REITs own a blend of income-producing real estate, while others specialize in specific sectors.

2. Royalty Trusts have been around for a long time as well. They exploit natural resources, such as oil, natural gas, coal, or iron ore. Royalty trusts usually offer the highest yields, but are also among the most volatile, as the underlying cash flow is affected by commodity prices.

3. Utility Trusts earn income from regulated public utilities, which include hydro, water, pipelines, and telecommunications. Within the income trust universe, they usually provide the most stable cash flow, and therefore distributions.

4. Business Trusts are the newest, largest and most diverse type of income trusts. They may hold any company that generates stable income. These businesses range from sugar to ice cream, from cold storage facilities to water heaters, from garbage collection to, well, beer.

One of the reasons for the surging popularity of income trusts has been their tax efficiency. Income trusts could usually avoid paying taxes on their earnings as long as most of the earnings were distributed to the unitholders. Thus, cash flows generated by underlying businesses were taxed only once, at the personal level, when they were paid out, not at the corporate level.

This tax advantage mostly disappeared on Halloween 2006, when federal Finance Minister Jim Flaherty announced plans to tax all income trusts, except REITs, like corporations. This rule would apply to newly created income trusts immediately, but would not affect existing trusts until 2011. The legislation passed and the new federal tax treatment has already effectively eliminated the incentive to convert corporations into income trusts.

Despite the recent tax changes, income trusts can still be attractive investments. If you become interested in investing in income trusts, you have several options. You can buy individual income trusts, which trade like stocks on the Toronto Stock Exchange with a ticker symbol extension of ".UN." To decrease the risk, you can spread your money across a large number of trusts through income trust mutual funds or closed-end funds. There are also two income trust exchange-traded funds, which trade under the ticker symbols XTR and XRE.

The corporate form has a significant disadvantage. Since a corporation is a legal person, it must pay taxes. Moreover, money paid out to stockholders in the form of dividends is taxed again as income to those stockholders. This is *double taxation,* meaning that corporate profits are taxed twice: at the corporate level when they are earned and again at the personal level when they are paid out.[1] A form of business organization that until recently could avoid double taxation is the income trust. See our *Reality Bytes* box above to learn more about income trusts.

---

[1] The dividend tax credit for individual shareholders reduces the "double taxation," but usually does not remove it entirely. The dividend tax credit is discussed in more detail in Chapter 2.

Company	Country of Origin	Type of Company	Translation	TABLE 1.1
Bayerische Motoren Werke (BMW) AG	Germany	Aktiengesellschaft	Corporation	**International corporations**
Dornier GmbH	Germany	Gesellschaft mit beschränkter Haftung	Company with limited liability	
Rolls-Royce PLC	United Kingdom	Public limited company	Public limited company	
Shell UK Ltd.	United Kingdom	Limited	Corporation	
Unilever NV	Netherlands	Naamloze Vennootschap	Limited liability company	
Fiat SpA	Italy	Società per Azioni	Public limited company	
Saab AB	Sweden	Aktiebolag	Joint stock company	
Peugeot SA	France	Société Anonyme	Joint stock company	

A Corporation by Another Name . . .

The corporate form has many variations around the world. Exact laws and regulations differ, of course, but the essential features of public ownership and limited liability remain. These firms are often called *joint stock companies, public limited companies,* or *limited liability companies.*

Table 1.1 gives the names of a few well-known international corporations, their countries of origin, and a translation of the abbreviation that follows the company name.

CONCEPT QUESTIONS

1.3a What are the three forms of business organization?

1.3b What are the primary advantages and disadvantages of sole proprietorships and partnerships?

1.3c What is the difference between a general and a limited partnership?

1.3d Why is the corporate form superior when it comes to raising cash?

1.4 | THE GOAL OF FINANCIAL MANAGEMENT

To study financial decision making, we first need to understand the goal of financial management. Such an understanding is important because it leads to an objective basis for making and evaluating financial decisions.

Profit Maximization

Profit maximization would probably be the most commonly cited business goal, but this is not a very precise objective. Do we mean profits this year? If so, then actions such as deferring maintenance, letting inventories run down, and other short-run cost-cutting measures will tend to increase profits now, but these activities aren't necessarily desirable.

The goal of maximizing profits may refer to some sort of "long-run" or "average" profits, but it's unclear exactly what this means. First, do we mean something like accounting net income or earnings per share? As we will see, these numbers may have little to do with what is good or bad for the firm. Second, what do we mean by the long run? As a famous economist once remarked, in the long run, we're all dead! More to the point, this goal doesn't tell us the appropriate trade-off between current and future profits.

The Goal of Financial Management in a Corporation

To find out about the services that Financial Executive International (FEI) Canada offers to its members who are senior financial officers of medium and large organizations, go to **www.feicanada.org.**

The financial manager in a corporation makes decisions for the stockholders of the firm. Given this, instead of listing possible goals for the financial manager, we really need to answer a more fundamental question: From the stockholders' point of view, what is a good financial management decision?

If we assume stockholders buy stock because they seek to gain financially, then the answer is obvious: Good decisions increase the value of the stock, and poor decisions decrease it.

Given our observations, it follows that the financial manager acts in the shareholders' best interests by making decisions that increase the value of the stock. The appropriate goal for the financial manager in a corporation can thus be stated quite easily:

> The goal of financial management is to maximize the current value per share of the existing stock.

The goal of maximizing the value of the stock avoids the problems associated with the different goals we discussed above. There is no ambiguity in the criterion, and there is no short-run versus long-run issue. We explicitly mean that our goal is to maximize the *current* stock value. Of course, maximizing stock value is the same thing as maximizing the market price per share.

A More General Financial Management Goal

Given our goal as stated above (maximize the value of the stock), an obvious question comes up: What is the appropriate goal when the firm has no traded stock? Corporations are certainly not the only type of business, and the stock in many corporations rarely changes hands, so it's difficult to say what the value per share is at any given time.

As long as we are dealing with for-profit businesses, only a slight modification is needed. The total value of the stock in a corporation is simply equal to the value of the owners' equity. Therefore, a more general way of stating our goal is:

> Maximize the market value of the existing owners' equity.

With this goal in mind, it doesn't matter whether the business is a proprietorship, a partnership, or a corporation. For each of these, good financial decisions increase the market value of the owners' equity and poor financial decisions decrease it.

Finally, our goal does not imply that the financial manager should take illegal or unethical actions in the hope of increasing the value of the equity in the firm. What we mean is that the financial manager best serves the owners of the business by identifying goods

For many Canadian resources for business ethics visit **www.businessethics .ca.**

REALITY BYTES

Corporate Ethics

Large companies are sometimes guilty of unethical behaviour. This unethical behaviour ranges from misleading financial statements to the shameless stealing of money from a company and its shareholders. In one of the largest corporate fraud cases in history, energy giant Enron Corporation was forced to file for bankruptcy in December 2001 amid allegations that the company's financial statements were deliberately misleading and false. Enron's bankruptcy destroyed not only that company, but its auditor Arthur Andersen as well.

Another company survived an alleged case of unethical behaviour by its top executives. Conrad Black, former CEO and Chairman of Toronto-based Hollinger Inc., and his close associates were charged with stealing millions of dollars and using company money to finance their lavish lifestyles. Black lost his CEO and chairman's positions and was sued by several parties, as well as facing criminal charges, along with his associates, in the U.S. In July 2007, while cleared of many charges, including those related to his lavish lifestyle, Conrad Black was found guilty of receiving the fraudulent payment of US$2.9 million in non-compete fees and of obstruction of justice, and was facing a possible sentence of up to 20 years in prison. An appeal was planned.

Of course, ethical problems are not confined to North American companies. For example, in late 2003 the Italian dairy firm Parmalat SpA announced that it had liquidity problems. What followed was an investigation into the largest corporate fraud scandal in European history. At one point, the company was forced to disclose that it did not actually have a $4.8 billion bank account it had claimed on its financial statements.

The difference between ethical and unethical behaviour can sometimes be murky. A recent corporate activity that has generated much controversy is the practice of outsourcing, or offshoring, jobs to other countries. Canadian corporations engage in this practice when labour costs in another country are substantially lower than they are domestically. This is done to maximize shareholder wealth, but some Canadian workers do lose their jobs when offshoring occurs. For instance, in September 2006, Montreal-based Gildan Activewear announced it was cutting its labour force in Canada and moving more of its operations to lower-cost Honduras and the Dominican Republic. By contrast, many foreign companies, such as Toyota and Honda, "insource" jobs by building plants in Canada. Is it unethical to outsource Canadian jobs while, at the same time, insourcing jobs from other countries?

and services that add value to the firm because they are desired and valued in the free marketplace. Our *Reality Bytes* box above discusses some recent ethical issues and problems faced by well-known corporations.

Sarbanes-Oxley Act

In response to corporate scandals involving companies such as Enron, WorldCom, Tyco, and Adelphia, the U.S. Congress enacted the *Sarbanes-Oxley Act* in 2002. The Act, which is better known as "Sarbox," is intended to strengthen protection against corporate accounting fraud and financial malpractice. In addition to U.S. corporations, Sarbox also applies to a large number of Canadian corporations that issue securities in the United States. Key elements of Sarbox took effect on November 15, 2004.

Sarbox contains a number of requirements designed to ensure that companies tell the truth in their financial statements. For example, the officers of a public corporation must review and sign the annual report. They must attest that the annual report does not contain false statements or material omissions and also that the financial statements fairly represent the company's financial results. In essence, Sarbox makes management personally responsible for the accuracy of a company's financial statements.

To find out more about Sarbanes-Oxley, go to: www.soxlaw.com.

Because of its extensive requirements, compliance with Sarbox can be very costly, which has led to some unintended results. For example, in 2003 about 200 public firms chose to "go dark," meaning that their shares would no longer be traded in the major stock markets, in which case Sarbox does not apply. Most of these companies stated that their reason was to avoid the cost of compliance. Ironically, in such cases, the law had the effect of eliminating public disclosure instead of improving it.

CONCEPT QUESTIONS

1.4a What is the goal of financial management?

1.4b What are some shortcomings of the goal of profit maximization?

1.5 | THE AGENCY PROBLEM AND CONTROL OF THE CORPORATION

We've seen that the financial manager in a corporation acts in the best interests of the stockholders by taking actions that increase the value of the firm's stock. However, we've also seen that in large corporations ownership can be spread over a huge number of stockholders. This dispersion of ownership arguably means that management effectively controls the firm. In this case, will management necessarily act in the best interests of the stockholders? Put another way, might not management pursue its own goals at the stockholders' expense? We briefly consider some of the arguments below.

Agency Relationships

The relationship between stockholders and management is called an *agency relationship*. Such a relationship exists whenever someone (the principal) hires another (the agent) to represent his or her interest. For example, you might hire someone (an agent) to sell a car that you own while you are away at school. In all such relationships, there is a possibility of conflict of interest between the principal and the agent. Such a conflict is called an **agency problem.**

agency problem
The possibility of conflict of interest between the owners and management of a firm.

Suppose you hire someone to sell your car and you agree to pay her a flat fee when she sells the car. The agent's incentive in this case is to make the sale, not necessarily to get you the best price. If you paid a commission of, say, 10 percent of the sales price instead of a flat fee, then this problem might not exist. This example illustrates that the way an agent is compensated is one factor that affects agency problems.

Management Goals

To see how management and stockholder interests might differ, imagine that a corporation is considering a new investment. The new investment is expected to favourably impact the stock price, but it is also a relatively risky venture. The owners of the firm will wish to take the investment (because the share value will rise), but management may not because there is the possibility that things will turn out badly and management jobs will be lost. If management does not take the investment, then the stockholders may lose a valuable opportunity. This is one example of an *agency cost.*

It is sometimes argued that, left to themselves, managers would tend to maximize the amount of resources over which they have control, or, more generally, business power or wealth. This goal could lead to an overemphasis on business size or growth. For example, cases where management is accused of overpaying to buy another company just to increase the size of the business or to demonstrate corporate power are not uncommon. Obviously, if overpayment does take place, such a purchase does not benefit the owners of the purchasing company.

Our discussion indicates that management may tend to overemphasize organizational survival to protect job security. Also, management may dislike outside interference, so independence and corporate self-sufficiency may be important goals.

Do Managers Act in the Stockholders' Interests?

Whether managers will, in fact, act in the best interests of stockholders depends on two factors. First, how closely are management goals aligned with stockholder goals? This question relates to the way managers are compensated. Second, can management be replaced if they do not pursue stockholder goals? This issue relates to control of the firm. As we will discuss, there are a number of reasons to think that, even in the largest firms, management has a significant incentive to act in the interests of stockholders.

Managerial Compensation Management will frequently have a significant economic incentive to increase share value for two reasons. First, managerial compensation, particularly at the top, is usually tied to financial performance in general and oftentimes to share value in particular. For example, managers are frequently given the option to buy stock at a fixed price. The more the stock is worth, the more valuable is this option. The second incentive managers have relates to job prospects. Better performers within the firm will tend to get promoted. More generally, those managers who are successful in pursuing stockholder goals will be in greater demand in the labour market and thus command higher salaries.

In fact, managers who are successful in pursuing stockholder goals can reap enormous rewards. For example, Hank Swartout, CEO of Calgary-based Precision Drilling Trust, had the highest compensation among the CEOs of Canadian companies in 2005, totalling almost $75 million. He was followed by Hunter Harrison, CEO of the Canadian National Railway Company, who earned more than $56 million. CEOs were not the only ones who enjoyed generous compensation in 2005: Frank Stronach, Chairman of Magna International Inc. was one of the top earners, receiving over $40 million.

Control of the Firm Control of the firm ultimately rests with stockholders. They elect the board of directors, who, in turn, hire and fire management. The mechanism by which unhappy stockholders can act to replace existing management is called a *proxy fight*. A proxy is the authority to vote someone else's stock. A proxy fight develops when a group solicits proxies in order to replace the existing board, and thereby replace existing management.

Another way that management can be replaced is by takeover. Those firms that are poorly managed are more attractive as acquisitions than well-managed firms because a greater profit potential exists. Thus, avoiding a takeover by another firm gives management another incentive to act in the stockholders' interests.

Sometimes it's hard to tell if a company's management is really acting in the shareholders' best interests. Consider the 2005 merger of software giants Oracle and PeopleSoft. PeopleSoft repeatedly rejected offers by Oracle to purchase the company. In November 2004, the board rejected a "best and final" offer, even after 61 percent of PeopleSoft's shareholders voted in favour of it. So was the board really acting in shareholders' best interests? At first, it may not have looked like it, but Oracle then increased its offer price by $2 per share, which the board accepted. So, by holding out, PeopleSoft's management got a much better price for its shareholders.

Conclusion   The available theory and evidence are consistent with the view that stockholders control the firm and that stockholder wealth maximization is the relevant goal of the corporation. Even so, there will undoubtedly be times when management goals are pursued at the expense of the stockholders, at least temporarily.

Agency problems are not unique to corporations; they exist whenever there is a separation of ownership and management. This separation is most pronounced in corporations, but it certainly exists in partnerships and proprietorships as well.

Stakeholders

Our discussion thus far implies that management and stockholders are the only parties with an interest in the firm's decisions. This is an oversimplification, of course. Employees, customers, suppliers, and even the government all have a financial interest in the firm.

stakeholder
Someone who potentially has a claim on the cash flows of the firm.

Taken together, these various groups are called **stakeholders** in the firm. In general, a stakeholder is someone who potentially has a claim on the cash flows of the firm. Such groups will also attempt to exert control over the firm, perhaps to the detriment of the owners.

CONCEPT QUESTIONS

1.5a   What is an agency relationship?

1.5b   What are agency problems and how do they arise? What are agency costs?

1.5c   What incentives do managers in large corporations have to maximize share value?

1.6 | FINANCIAL MARKETS AND THE CORPORATION

We've seen that the primary advantages of the corporate form of organization are that ownership can be transferred more quickly and easily than with other forms and that money can be raised more readily. Both of these advantages are significantly enhanced by the existence of financial markets, and financial markets play an extremely important role in corporate finance.

Cash Flows to and from the Firm

The interplay between the corporation and the financial markets is illustrated in Figure 1.2. The arrows in Figure 1.2 trace the passage of cash from the financial markets to the firm and from the firm back to the financial markets.

Suppose we start with the firm selling shares of stock and borrowing money to raise cash. Cash flows to the firm from the financial markets (A). The firm invests the cash in current and fixed (or long-term) assets (B). These assets generate some cash (C), some of which goes to pay corporate taxes (D). After taxes are paid, some of this cash flow is re-invested in the firm (E). The rest goes back to the financial markets as cash paid to creditors and shareholders (F).

A financial market, like any market, is just a way of bringing buyers and sellers together. In financial markets, debt and equity securities are bought and sold. Financial markets differ in detail, however. The most important differences concern the types of securities that are traded, how trading is conducted, and who the buyers and sellers are. Some of these differences are discussed next.

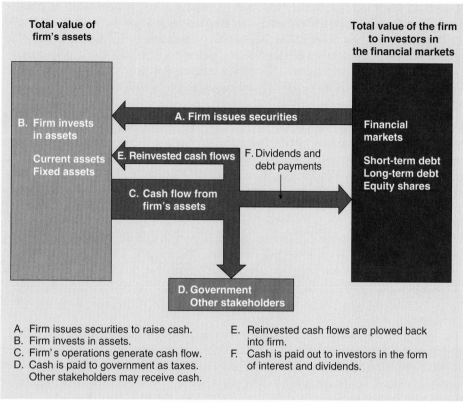

FIGURE 1.2

Cash flows between the firm and the financial markets

Total value of firm's assets

Total value of the firm to investors in the financial markets

A. Firm issues securities

B. Firm invests in assets

Current assets
Fixed assets

E. Reinvested cash flows

F. Dividends and debt payments

C. Cash flow from firm's assets

Financial markets

Short-term debt
Long-term debt
Equity shares

D. Government
Other stakeholders

A. Firm issues securities to raise cash.
B. Firm invests in assets.
C. Firm's operations generate cash flow.
D. Cash is paid to government as taxes. Other stakeholders may receive cash.

E. Reinvested cash flows are plowed back into firm.
F. Cash is paid out to investors in the form of interest and dividends.

Primary versus Secondary Markets

Financial markets function as both primary and secondary markets for debt and equity securities. The term *primary market* refers to the original sale of securities by governments and corporations. The *secondary markets* are those in which these securities are bought and sold after the original sale. Equities are, of course, issued solely by corporations. Debt securities are issued by both governments and corporations. In the discussion that follows, we focus on corporate securities only.

Primary Markets   In a primary-market transaction, the corporation is the seller, and the transaction raises money for the corporation. Corporations engage in two types of primary market transactions: public offerings and private placements. A public offering, as the name suggests, involves selling securities to the general public, whereas a private placement is a negotiated sale involving a specific buyer.

By law, public offerings of debt and equity must be registered with the provincial or territorial securities commissions. The Ontario Securities Commission (OSC) is considered the most significant because it has the largest number of companies and investors under its jurisdiction. Registration requires the firm to disclose a great deal of information before selling any securities. The accounting, legal, and selling costs of public offerings can be considerable.

Partly to avoid the various regulatory requirements and the expense of public offerings, debt and equity are often sold privately to large financial institutions such as life insurance companies or mutual funds. Such private placements do not have to be registered with the OSC and do not require the involvement of underwriters (investment banks that specialize in selling securities to the public).

primary market
The market in which new securities are originally sold to investors.

To learn more about the OSC, visit
www.osc.gov.on.ca.

secondary market
The market in which previously issued securities are traded among investors.

Secondary Markets   A secondary-market transaction involves one owner or creditor selling to another. It is therefore the secondary markets that provide the means for transferring ownership of corporate securities. Although a corporation is only directly involved in a primary-market transaction (when it sells securities to raise cash), the secondary markets are still critical to large corporations. The reason is that investors are much more willing to purchase securities in a primary-market transaction when they know that those securities can later be resold if desired.

Dealer versus auction markets   There are two kinds of secondary markets: *auction* markets and *dealer* markets. Generally speaking, dealers buy and sell for themselves, at their own risk. A car dealer, for example, buys and sells automobiles. In contrast, brokers and agents connect buyers and sellers, but they do not actually own the commodity that is bought or sold. A real estate agent, for example, does not normally buy and sell houses.

Dealer markets in stocks and long-term debt are called *over-the-counter* (OTC) markets. Most trading in debt securities takes place over the counter. The expression *over the counter* refers to days of old when securities were literally bought and sold at counters in offices around the country. Today, a significant fraction of the market for stocks and almost all of the market for long-term debt has no central location; the many dealers are connected electronically.

Auction markets differ from dealer markets in two ways. First, an auction market, or exchange, has a physical location (like Bay Street, or Wall Street). Second, in a dealer market, most of the buying and selling is done by the dealer, while the primary purpose of an auction market, on the other hand, is to match those who wish to sell with those who wish to buy. Dealers play a limited role.

Dealers and Brokers

dealer
An agent who buys and sells securities from inventory.

broker
An agent who arranges security transactions among investors.

Because most securities transactions involve dealers and brokers, it is important to understand exactly what is meant by the terms *dealer* and *broker.* A **dealer** maintains an inventory and stands ready to buy and sell at any time. In contrast, a **broker** brings buyers and sellers together, but does not maintain an inventory. Thus, as we said above, when we speak of used car dealers and real estate brokers, we recognize that the used car dealer maintains an inventory, whereas the real estate broker does not.

In the securities markets, a dealer stands ready to buy securities from investors wishing to sell them and sell securities to investors wishing to buy them. The price the dealer is willing to pay is called the bid price. The price at which the dealer will sell is called the ask price (sometimes called the asked, offered, or offering price). The difference between the bid and ask prices is called the spread, and it is the basic source of dealer profits.

Dealers exist in all areas of the economy, not just the stock markets. For example, your local university bookstore is probably both a primary- and a secondary-market textbook dealer. If you buy a new book, this is a primary-market transaction. If you buy a used book, this is a secondary-market transaction, and you pay the store's ask price. If you sell the book back, you receive the store's bid price, often half of the ask price. The bookstore's spread is the difference between the two prices.

In contrast, a securities broker arranges transactions between investors, matching investors wishing to buy securities with investors wishing to sell securities. The distinctive characteristic of securities brokers is that they do not buy or sell securities for their own accounts. Facilitating trades by others is their business.

Security Exchanges

There are four organized exchanges in Canada. Stocks are traded on the Toronto Stock Exchange (TSX) and the TSX Venture Exchange; derivative contracts are traded on the Montreal Exchange; and contracts on agricultural commodities on the Winnipeg Commodities Exchange. All Canadian exchanges operate as electronic auction markets.

Stocks that trade on an organized exchange (or market) are said to be *listed* on that exchange. In order to be listed, firms must meet certain minimum criteria concerning, for example, asset size and number of shareholders. These criteria differ for different exchanges.

The TSX is a senior exchange where shares of large, established companies are listed. To be listed on the TSX, a company is expected to have a market value for its freely tradeable shares of at least $4 million ($10 million for technology companies) and a total of at least 300 shareholders with at least 100 shares each. There are additional minimums on earnings, assets, and cash flow. In March 2007, 1597 companies were listed on the TSX. The TSX Venture Exchange has less stringent requirements, and, therefore, lists shares of small, emerging companies. Almost half of the 2271 companies listed on the TSX Venture Exchange were mining companies. Table 1.2 shows the market value and number of listed companies for the ten largest stock markets in the world, ranked by market value in March 2007. The TSX and the TSX Venture Exchange ranked seventh based on market capitalizations and had the largest number of listed companies among the top ten exchanges.

While listing on the TSX or the TSX Venture Exchange improves a company's ability to raise capital and increases its visibility and prestige, many large Canadian companies also choose to be listed on foreign exchanges. For example, in March 2007, 88 Canadian companies were listed on the New York Stock Exchange (NYSE). Canadian firms can derive several benefits from listing in the U.S., including access to larger capital markets and increased exposure. Similarly, some American companies are listed on the TSX. For example, shares of the U.S. company Magna Entertainment are traded on the TSX.

The United States has several stock exchanges and all of them, regardless of their location, are regulated by the same government agency—the Securities and Exchange Commission (SEC). The equity shares of most of the large firms in the United States trade in organized auction markets. The largest exchange in the world is the NYSE, which accounts for more than 85 percent of all the shares traded in auction markets. It has the most stringent listing requirements. Other auction exchanges include the American Stock Exchange (AMEX) and regional exchanges such as the Chicago Stock Exchange and the Pacific Stock Exchange.

For more information about the TSX and the TSX Venture Exchange go to **www.tsx.com.**

Markets	Market value of listed companies (in U.S. $ billions)	Number of listed domestic companies	Number of listed foreign companies
NYSE	15,467.7	1,798	451
Tokyo	4,737.5	2,388	25
Nasdaq	3,906.9	2,792	328
Euronext	3,882.2	953	246
London	3,842.6	2,598	647
Deutsche Börse	1,756.0	655	100
TSX and TSX Venture exchange	1,749.6	3,815	53
Hong Kong Exchanges	1,734.1	1,171	9
BME Spanish Exchanges	1,393.6	N/A	N/A
Shanghai	1,297.4	848	0

TABLE 1.2

Largest stock markets in the world by market value in March 2007

Information on world exchanges can be found at the World Federation of Exchanges Web site **www.world-exchanges.org.**

Source: Used with permission of the World Federation of Exchanges. *www.world-exchanges.org*

In addition to the stock exchanges, there is a large OTC market for stocks. In 1971, the National Association of Securities Dealers (NASD) made available to dealers and brokers an electronic quotation system called NASDAQ (NASD Automated Quotations system, pronounced "naz-dak"). There are roughly three times as many companies on NASDAQ as there are on NYSE, but they tend to be much smaller in size and trade less actively. There are exceptions, of course. Both Microsoft and Intel trade OTC, for example. Nonetheless, the total value of NASDAQ stocks is significantly less than the total value of NYSE stocks.

There are many large and important financial markets outside North America, of course, and U.S. and Canadian corporations are increasingly looking to these markets to raise cash. The Tokyo Stock Exchange and the London Stock Exchange are two well-known examples. The fact that OTC markets have no physical location means that national borders do not present a great barrier, and there is now a huge international OTC debt market. Because of globalization, financial markets have reached the point where trading in many instruments never stops; it just travels around the world.

CONCEPT QUESTIONS

1.6a What is a dealer market? How do dealer and auction markets differ?

1.6b What is the largest auction market in Canada?

1.6c What does *OTC* stand for? What is the large OTC market for stocks called?

SUMMARY AND CONCLUSIONS

1. Usually, financial topics are grouped into four main areas:
    a. Corporate finance
    b. Investments
    c. Financial institutions
    d. International finance

    A working knowledge of finance is important even if you are not planning a career in finance.

2. Business finance includes three main areas of concern:
    a. Capital budgeting. What long-term investments should the firm make?
    b. Capital structure. Where will the firm get the long-term financing to pay for its investments? In other words, what mixture of debt and equity should we use to fund our operations?
    c. Working capital management. How should the firm manage its everyday financial activities?

3. The corporate form of organization is superior to other forms when it comes to raising money and transferring ownership interests, but it has the significant disadvantage of double taxation.

4. The goal of financial management in a for-profit business is to make decisions that increase the value of the stock, or, more generally, increase the market value of the equity.

5. Conflicts between stockholders and management may arise in a large corporation. We called these conflicts agency problems and discussed how they might be controlled and reduced.

6. Financial markets function as both primary and secondary markets for debt and equity securities, and secondary markets can be organized as either dealer or auction markets. In Canada the shares of established companies are traded on the Toronto Stock Exchange (TSX), while the shares of emerging companies are traded on the TSX Venture Exchange.

Of the topics we've discussed thus far, the most important is the goal of financial management. Throughout the text, we will be analyzing many different financial decisions, but we always ask the same question: How does the decision under consideration affect the value of the equity in the firm?

CRITICAL THINKING AND CONCEPTS REVIEW

1.1 **Main Areas of Finance.** What are the four main areas of finance? What questions are addressed in the investments area?

1.2 **The Financial Management Decision Process.** What are the three types of financial management decisions? For each type of decision, give an example of a business transaction that would be relevant.

1.3 **Sole Proprietorships and Partnerships.** What are the four primary disadvantages to the sole proprietorship and partnership forms of business organization? What benefits are there to these types of business organization as opposed to the corporate form?

1.4 **Corporations.** What is the primary disadvantage of the corporate form of organization? Name at least two of the advantages of corporate organization.

1.5 **Corporate Finance Organization.** In a large corporation, what are the two distinct groups that report to the chief financial officer? Which group is the focus of corporate finance?

1.6 **Goal of Financial Management.** What goal should always motivate the actions of the firm's financial manager?

1.7 **Agency Problems.** Who owns a corporation? Describe the process whereby the owners control the firm's management. What is the main reason that an agency relationship exists in the corporate form of organization? In this context, what kinds of problems can arise?

1.8 **Primary versus Secondary Markets.** You've probably noticed coverage in the financial press of an initial public offering (IPO) of a company's securities. Is an IPO a primary-market transaction or a secondary-market transaction?

1.9 **Auction versus Dealer Markets.** What does it mean when we say the Toronto Stock Exchange is an auction market? How are auction markets different from dealer markets? What kind of market is Nasdaq?

1.10 **Not-for-Profit Firm Goals.** Suppose you were the financial manager of a not-for-profit business (a not-for-profit hospital, perhaps). What kinds of goals do you think would be appropriate?

1.11 **Ethics and Firm Goals.** Can our goal of maximizing the value of the stock conflict with other goals, such as avoiding unethical or illegal behaviour? In particular, do you think subjects such as customer and employee safety, the environment, and the general good of society fit in this framework, or are they essentially ignored? Try to think of some specific scenarios to illustrate your answer.

1.12 International Firm Goal.   Would our goal of maximizing the value of the stock be different if we were thinking about financial management in a foreign country? Why or why not?

1.13 Agency Problems.   Suppose you own stock in a company. The current price per share is $25. Another company has just announced that it wants to buy your company and will pay $35 per share to acquire all the outstanding stock. Your company's management immediately begins fighting off this hostile bid. Is management acting in the shareholders' best interests? Why or why not?

1.14 Agency Problems and Corporate Ownership.   Corporate ownership varies around the world. Historically, individuals have owned the majority of shares in public corporations in the United States. Canada has a similar situation, but a large group of companies are controlled by one or several majority shareholders, usually founding family members. In Germany and Japan, however, banks, other large financial institutions, and other companies own most of the stock in public corporations. Do you think agency problems are likely to be more or less severe in Germany and Japan than in Canada? Why? In recent years, large financial institutions such as mutual funds and pension funds have been becoming the dominant owners of stock in Canada, and these institutions are becoming more active in corporate affairs. What are the implications of this trend for agency problems and corporate control?

1.15 Executive Compensation.   Critics have charged that compensation to top management in Canada is simply too high and should be cut back. For example, focusing on large corporations, William Doyle of the Potash Corporation of Saskatchewan earned about $22 million in 2005. Is this amount excessive? In answering, it might be helpful to recognize that superstar athletes such as Steve Nash, top entertainers such as Ontario native Jim Carrey and British Columbia native Pamela Anderson, and many others at the top of their respective fields, earn at least as much, if not a great deal more.

WHAT'S ON THE WEB?

1.1 Finance careers.   Visit Careers in Business at **www.careers-in-business.com** and explore careers in finance. What are the different career opportunities available in finance? How does a career in corporate finance differ from a career in money management? Go to **www.financejobs.ca** and find a finance position opening close to your home. What are the required skills and experience?

1.2 Listing requirement.   This chapter discussed some of the listing requirements for the TSX and the TSX Venture Exchange. Find the complete listing requirements for these exchanges at **www.tsx.com**. Which has more stringent listing requirements? Why don't they have the same listing requirements?

1.3 Exchange listing.   In March 2007, 88 Canadian companies were listed on the NYSE. Go to the New York Stock Exchange at **www.nyse.com** and find out how many Canadian companies are listed there now. Why do you think some Canadian companies decide to list on the NYSE?

2

Financial Statements, Cash Flow, and Taxes

On January 1, 2004, investors in L'Oréal, the French cosmetics giant, received quite a shock. The company's net worth dropped from €8.1 billion to about €6.3 billion overnight. You would think it would take a major event to cause such a drop, and it did. On that date, over 7,000 companies in Europe, including L'Oréal, switched to new international accounting standards.

The new standards greatly changed the financial statements of other companies as well. For example, in 2003, Vodafone (part owner of Verizon Wireless) reported a net loss of £9 billion. But, under the new international accounting standards, the company would have reported a profit of £6 billion, a difference of £15 billion.

So, as a result of changes in accounting rules, was L'Oréal actually worth €1.8 billion less? Did Vodafone actually make £15 billion more? The answer to both questions: Probably not. This chapter shows that underneath all the accounting numbers lurks the financial truth. Our job is to uncover that truth by examining that all-important substance known as *cash flow*.

There are basically four things that you should be clear on when you have finished studying this chapter:

2.1 The difference between the book values on an accounting balance sheet and market values.

2.2 The difference between accounting net income as it is computed on the income statement and cash flow.

2.3 How to determine a firm's cash flow from its financial statements.

2.4 The difference between average and marginal tax rates, and tax treatment of dividends and capital gains.

In this chapter, we examine financial statements, cash flow, and taxes. Our emphasis is not on preparing financial statements. Instead, we recognize that financial statements are frequently a key source of information for financial decisions, so our goal is to briefly examine such statements and point out some of their more relevant features. We pay special attention to some of the practical details of cash flow.

As you read, pay particular attention to two important differences: (1) the difference between accounting value and market value and (2) the difference between accounting income and cash flow. These distinctions will be important throughout the book.

2.1 | THE BALANCE SHEET

balance sheet
Financial statement showing a firm's accounting value on a particular date.

The **balance sheet** is a snapshot of the firm. It is a convenient means of organizing and summarizing what a firm owns (its *assets*), what a firm owes (its *liabilities*), and the difference between the two (the firm's *equity*) at a given point in time. Figure 2.1 illustrates how the balance sheet is constructed. As shown, the left-hand side lists the assets of the firm, and the right-hand side lists the liabilities and equity.

Assets: The Left-Hand Side

Assets are classified as either *current* or *fixed.* A fixed asset is one that has a relatively long life. Fixed assets can either be *tangible,* such as a truck or a computer, or *intangible,* such as a trademark or patent. A current asset has a life of less than one year. This means that the asset will normally convert to cash within 12 months. For example, inventory would normally be purchased and sold within a year and is thus classified as a current asset. Obviously, cash itself is a current asset. Accounts receivable (money owed to the firm by its customers) is also a current asset.

Two excellent sites for company financial information are **ca.finance.yahoo.com** and **www.globeinvestor .com.**

Liabilities and Owners' Equity: The Right-Hand Side

The firm's liabilities are the first thing listed on the right-hand side of the balance sheet. These are classified as either *current* or *long-term.* Current liabilities, like current assets, have a life of less than one year (meaning they must be paid within the year), and they are

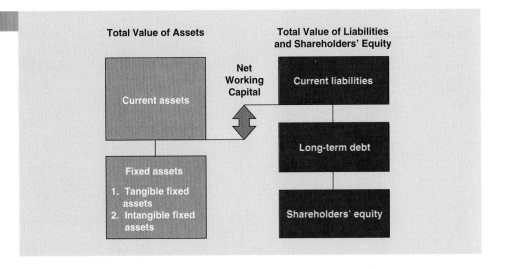

FIGURE 2.1

The balance sheet.
Left side: Total value of assets. Right side: Total value of liabilities and shareholders' equity.

listed before long-term liabilities. Accounts payable (money the firm owes to its suppliers) is one example of a current liability.

A debt that is not due in the coming year is classified as a long-term liability. A loan that the firm will pay off in five years is one such long-term debt. Firms borrow over the long term from a variety of sources. We will tend to use the terms *bonds* and *bondholders* generically to refer to long-term debt and long-term creditors, respectively.

Finally, by definition, the difference between the total value of the assets (current and fixed) and the total value of the liabilities (current and long-term) is the *shareholders' equity,* also called *common equity* or *owners' equity.* This feature of the balance sheet is intended to reflect the fact that, if the firm were to sell all of its assets and use the money to pay off its debts, then whatever residual value remained would belong to the shareholders. So, the balance sheet "balances" because the value of the left-hand side always equals the value of the right-hand side. That is, the value of the firm's assets is equal to the sum of its liabilities and shareholders' equity:[1]

$$\text{Assets} = \text{Liabilities} + \text{Shareholders' equity} \qquad \text{[2.1]}$$

This is the balance sheet identity, or equation, and it always holds because shareholders' equity is defined as the difference between assets and liabilities.

Royal Bank of Canada has a good investor site at **www.rbc.com.**

Net Working Capital

As shown in Figure 2.1, the difference between a firm's current assets and its current liabilities is called **net working capital.** Net working capital is positive when current assets exceed current liabilities. Based on the definitions of current assets and current liabilities, this means that the cash that will become available over the next 12 months exceeds the cash that must be paid over that same period. For this reason, net working capital is usually positive in a healthy firm.

net working capital
Current assets less current liabilities.

Building the Balance Sheet | EXAMPLE 2.1

A firm has current assets of $100, net fixed assets of $500, short-term debt of $70, and long-term debt of $200. What does the balance sheet look like? What is shareholders' equity? What is net working capital?

In this case, total assets are $100 + 500 = $600 and total liabilities are $70 + 200 = $270, so shareholders' equity is the difference: $600 − 270 = $330. The balance sheet would thus look like:

Assets		Liabilities and Shareholders' Equity	
Current assets	$100	Current liabilities	$ 70
Net fixed assets	500	Long-term debt	200
		Shareholders' equity	330
		Total liabilities and	
Total assets	$600	shareholders' equity	$600

Net working capital is the difference between current assets and current liabilities, or $100 − 70 = $30.

---

[1] The terms *owners' equity, shareholders' equity,* and *stockholders' equity* are used interchangeably to refer to the equity in a corporation. The term *net worth* is also used. Variations exist in addition to these.

TABLE 2.1

Balance sheets for
Loonie Corporation

LOONIE CORPORATION						
Balance Sheets as of December 31, 2007 and 2008						
($ in Millions)						
	2007	**2008**			**2007**	**2008**
Assets			**Liabilities and Owners' Equity**			
Current assets			Current liabilities			
Cash	$ 104	$ 160	Accounts payable		$ 232	$ 266
Accounts receivable	455	688	Notes payable		196	123
Inventory	553	555	Total		$ 428	$ 389
Total	$1,112	$1,403				
Fixed assets						
Net fixed assets	$1,644	$1,709	Long-term debt		$ 408	$ 454
			Owners' equity			
			Common stock and			
			paid-in surplus		600	640
			Retained earnings		1,320	1,629
			Total		$1,920	$2,269
			Total liabilities and			
Total assets	$2,756	$3,112	owners' equity		$2,756	$3,112

Table 2.1 shows a simplified balance sheet for the fictitious Loonie Corporation. There are three particularly important things to keep in mind when examining a balance sheet: liquidity, debt versus equity, and market value versus book value.

Liquidity

Annual and quarterly financial statements (and lots more) for most public Canadian corporations can be found in the SEDAR database at **www.sedar.com.**

Liquidity refers to the speed and ease with which an asset can be converted to cash. Gold is a relatively liquid asset; a custom manufacturing facility is not. Liquidity really has two dimensions: ease of conversion versus loss of value. Any asset can be converted to cash quickly if we cut the price enough. A highly liquid asset is therefore one that can be sold quickly without significant loss of value. An illiquid asset is one that cannot be quickly converted to cash without a substantial price reduction.

Assets are normally listed on the balance sheet in order of decreasing liquidity, meaning that the most liquid assets are listed first. Current assets are relatively liquid and include cash and those assets that we expect to convert to cash over the next 12 months. Accounts receivable, for example, represent amounts not yet collected from customers on sales already made. Naturally, we hope these will convert to cash in the near future. Inventory is probably the least liquid of the current assets, at least for many businesses.

Fixed assets are, for the most part, relatively illiquid. These consist of tangible things such as buildings and equipment that don't convert to cash at all in normal business activity (they are, of course, used in the business to generate cash). Intangible assets, such as a trademark, have no physical existence but can be very valuable. Like tangible fixed assets, they won't ordinarily convert to cash and are generally considered illiquid.

Liquidity is valuable. The more liquid a business is, the less likely it is to experience financial distress (that is, difficulty in paying debts or buying needed assets). Unfortunately, liquid assets are generally less profitable to hold. For example, cash holdings are the most liquid of all investments, but they sometimes earn no return at all—they just sit there. There is therefore a trade-off between the advantages of liquidity and forgone potential profits.

Debt versus Equity

To the extent that a firm borrows money, it usually gives first claim to the firm's cash flow to creditors. Equity holders are only entitled to the residual value, the portion left after creditors are paid. The value of this residual portion is the shareholders' equity in the firm, which is just the value of the firm's assets less the value of the firm's liabilities:

Shareholders' equity = Assets − Liabilities

This is true in an accounting sense because shareholders' equity is defined as this residual portion. More important, it is true in an economic sense: If the firm sells its assets and pays its debts, whatever cash is left belongs to the shareholders.

The use of debt in a firm's capital structure is called *financial leverage*. The more debt a firm has (as a percentage of assets), the greater its degree of financial leverage. As we discuss in later chapters, debt acts like a lever in the sense that using it can greatly magnify both gains and losses. So, financial leverage increases the potential reward to shareholders, but it also increases the potential for financial distress and business failure.

The home page for the Chartered Accountants of Canada is **www.cica.ca.**

Market Value versus Book Value

The true value of any asset is its *market* value, which is simply the amount of cash we would get if we actually sold it. In contrast, the values shown on the balance sheet for the firm's assets are *book values* and generally are not what the assets are actually worth. Under **Generally Accepted Accounting Principles (GAAP),** audited financial statements show assets at *historical cost*. In other words, assets are "carried on the books" at what the firm paid for them, no matter how long ago they were purchased or how much they are worth today.

Generally Accepted Accounting Principles (GAAP) The common set of standards and procedures by which audited financial statements are prepared.

For current assets, market value and book value might be somewhat similar since current assets are bought and converted into cash over a relatively short span of time. In other circumstances, they might differ quite a bit. Moreover, for fixed assets, it would be purely a coincidence if the actual market value of an asset (what the asset could be sold for) were equal to its book value. For example, a railroad might own enormous tracts of land purchased a century or more ago. What the railroad paid for that land could be hundreds or thousands of times less than what it is worth today. The balance sheet would nonetheless show the historical cost.

Managers and investors will frequently be interested in knowing the market value of the firm. This information is not on the balance sheet. The fact that balance sheet assets are listed at cost means that there is no necessary connection between the total assets shown and the market value of the firm. Indeed, many of the most valuable assets that a firm might have—good management, a good reputation, talented employees—don't appear on the balance sheet at all. To give one example, one of the most valuable assets for many well-known companies is their brand name. According to the 2006 "Best Canadian Brands by Value" Interbrand report, the name "Royal Bank of Canada" is worth almost $4 billion, and the names "Toronto-Dominion" and "Petro-Canada" are worth in excess of $3 billion each.

To learn about Canadian and global most valuable brands visit Interbrand at **www.interbrand.com.**

Similarly, the owners' equity figure on the balance sheet and the true market value of the equity need not be related. For financial managers, then, the accounting value of the equity is not an especially important concern; it is the market value that matters. Henceforth, whenever we speak of the value of an asset or the value of the firm, we will normally mean its *market value.* So, for example, when we say the goal of the financial manager is to increase the value of the stock, we mean the market value of the stock.

EXAMPLE 2.2   Market versus Book Values

The Kingston Corporation has fixed assets with a book value of $700 and an appraised market value of about $1,000. Net working capital is $400 on the books, but approximately $600 would be realized if all the current accounts were liquidated. Kingston has $500 in long-term debt, both book value and market value. What is the book value of the equity? What is the market value?

We can construct two simplified balance sheets, one in accounting (book value) terms and one in economic (market value) terms:

KINGSTON CORPORATION
Balance Sheets
Market Value versus Book Value

Assets	Book	Market	Liabilities and Shareholders' Equity	Book	Market
Net working capital	$ 400	$600	Long-term debt	$ 500	$ 500
Net fixed assets	700	1,000	Shareholders' equity	600	1,100
	$1,100	$1,600		$1,100	$1,600

In this example, shareholders' equity is actually worth almost twice as much as what is shown on the books. The distinction between book and market values is important precisely because book values can be so different from true economic value.

CONCEPT QUESTIONS

2.1a   What is the balance sheet identity?

2.1b   What is liquidity? Why is it important?

2.1c   What do we mean by financial leverage?

2.1d   Explain the difference between accounting value and market value. Which is more important to the financial manager? Why?

2.2 | THE INCOME STATEMENT

income statement
Financial statement summarizing a firm's performance over a period of time.

The **income statement** measures performance over some period of time, usually a quarter (3 months) or a year. The income statement equation is:

$$\text{Revenues} - \text{Expenses} = \text{Income} \qquad [2.2]$$

If you think of the balance sheet as a snapshot, then you can think of the income statement as a video recording covering the period between a before and an after picture. Table 2.2 gives a simplified income statement for Loonie Corporation.

The first thing reported on an income statement would usually be revenue and expenses from the firm's principal operations. Subsequent parts include, among other things, financing expenses such as interest paid. Taxes paid are reported separately. The last item is *net income* (the so-called bottom line). Net income is often expressed on a per-share basis and called *earnings per share (EPS).*

LOONIE CORPORATION 2008 Income Statement ($ in Millions)		
Net sales		$1,509
Cost of goods sold		750
Depreciation		65
Earnings before interest and taxes		$ 694
Interest paid		70
Taxable income		$ 624
Taxes		212
Net income		$ 412
Dividends	$103	
Addition to retained earnings	309	

TABLE 2.2

Income statement for Loonie Corporation

As indicated, Loonie paid cash dividends of $103. The difference between net income and cash dividends, $309, is the addition to retained earnings for the year. This amount is added to the cumulative retained earnings account on the balance sheet. If you look back at the two balance sheets for Loonie Corporation, you'll see that retained earnings did go up by this amount, $1,320 + 309 = $1,629.

Earnings and Dividends per Share   EXAMPLE 2.3

Suppose Loonie had 200 million shares outstanding at the end of 2008. Based on the income statement in Table 2.2, what was EPS? What were dividends per share?

From the income statement, Loonie had a net income of $412 million for the year. Total dividends were $103 million. Since 200 million shares were outstanding, we can calculate earnings per share and dividends per share as follows:

$$\text{Earnings per share} = \text{Net income/Total shares outstanding}$$
$$= \$412/200 = \$2.06 \text{ per share}$$
$$\text{Dividends per share} = \text{Total dividends/Total shares outstanding}$$
$$= \$103/200 = \$.515 \text{ per share}$$

When looking at an income statement, the financial manager needs to keep three things in mind: GAAP, cash versus noncash items, and time and costs.

GAAP and the Income Statement

An income statement prepared using GAAP will show revenue when it accrues. This is not necessarily when the cash comes in. The general rule (the recognition principle) is to recognize revenue when the earnings process is virtually complete and the value of an exchange of goods or services is known or can be reliably determined. In practice, this principle usually means that revenue is recognized at the time of sale, which need not be the same as the time of collection.

Expenses shown on the income statement are based on the matching principle. The basic idea here is to first determine revenues as described above and then match those revenues with the costs associated with producing them. So, if we manufacture a product and then sell it on credit, the revenue is recognized at the time of sale. The production and other costs associated with the sale of that product would likewise be recognized at that time. Once again, the actual cash outflows may have occurred at some very different times. Thus, as a result of the way revenues and expenses are reported, the figures shown on the income statement may not be at all representative of the actual cash inflows and outflows that occurred during a particular period.

Noncash Items

noncash items
Expenses charged against revenues that do not directly affect cash flow, such as depreciation.

A primary reason that accounting income differs from cash flow is that an income statement contains **noncash items.** The most important of these is *depreciation.* Suppose a firm purchases a fixed asset for $5,000 and pays in cash. Obviously, the firm has a $5,000 cash outflow at the time of purchase. However, instead of deducting the $5,000 as an expense, an accountant might depreciate the asset over a five-year period.

If the depreciation is straight-line and the asset is written down to zero over that period, then $5,000/5 = $1,000 would be deducted each year as an expense.[2] The important thing to recognize is that this $1,000 deduction isn't cash—it's an accounting number. The actual cash outflow occurred when the asset was purchased.

The depreciation deduction is simply another application of the matching principle in accounting. The revenues associated with an asset would generally occur over some length of time. So the accountant seeks to match the expense of purchasing the asset with the benefits produced from owning it.

As we will see, for the financial manager, the actual timing of cash inflows and outflows is critical in coming up with a reasonable estimate of market value, so we need to learn how to separate the cash flows from the noncash accounting entries. In reality, the difference between cash flow and accounting income can be pretty dramatic. For example, in 2005, COGECO Inc., a diversified communications company headquartered in Montreal, Quebec, reported a loss of $20 million. It sounds bad, but COGECO also reported a *positive* free cash flow of $45 million! In part, the difference was due to noncash accounting expenses.

Time and Costs

It is often useful to think of the future as having two distinct parts: the short run and the long run. These are not precise time periods. The distinction has to do with whether costs are fixed or variable. In the long run, all business costs are variable. Given sufficient time, assets can be sold, debts can be paid, and so on.

If our time horizon is relatively short, however, some costs are effectively fixed—they must be paid no matter what (property taxes, for example). Other costs such as wages to workers and payments to suppliers are still variable. As a result, even in the short run, the firm can vary its output level by varying expenditures in these areas.

The distinction between fixed and variable costs is important, at times, to the financial manager, but the way costs are reported on the income statement is not a good guide as to which costs are which. The reason is that, in practice, accountants tend to classify costs as either product costs or period costs.

---

[2]By "straight-line," we mean that the depreciation deduction is the same every year. By "written down to zero," we mean that the asset is assumed to have no value at the end of five years.

REALITY BYTES

Putting a Spin on Earnings

A goal of GAAP is to standardize the way companies report their financial situations, but the reality is that reported earnings are not spin-free. In fact, there are a variety of strategies that companies can use to inflate (or deflate) the earnings they report.

For example, "write-offs" can affect earnings. A write-off occurs when a company declares that an asset has become worthless, and any remaining book value of that asset is then taken as an expense, which reduces earnings. The size and timing of a write-off can be highly subjective and therefore easily manipulated. Inventory is a frequent target. The largest inventory write-off in history occurred in 2001 when Cisco Systems wrote off $2.25 billion worth in one shot. This dramatically reduced the company's earnings for the quarter and year. However, Cisco sold much of this "obsolete" inventory later, which meant that there was no cost on the income statement associated with that inventory when it was sold; the cost had already been charged. Effectively, Cisco reported these sales at a 100 percent profit margin.

An earnings management technique that has recently been in the news is called "cookie jar" accounting. In February

2006, Nortel Networks agreed to pay US $2.5 billion in cash and shares to settle its long-running accounting scandal. Specifically, Nortel was accused of manipulating its financial statements. It was alleged that Nortel used accounting manoeuvres to move earnings between quarters to meet analyst expectations, which led to an artificially inflated stock price. At its peak in 2000, Nortel stock was trading at $120, but it fell to $0.79 in 2002.

Another common earnings management tool concerns allowances for bad debts. When a company sells on credit, there is some probability that the borrower will not pay. Under GAAP, companies take an expense for projected uncollectible debts. If a company wants to increase earnings, it can simply understate its likely bad debts. Of course, the company can also overstate bad debts, which decreases earnings. Even though this sounds bad, it has a benefit: When the debts are paid in a later period, earnings will be increased.

These are just a few of the ways companies can spin earnings. The fact that earnings can be manipulated is the basis for a bit of financial wisdom that you would do well to remember: Earnings are an opinion; cash is a fact!

Product costs include such things as raw materials, direct labour expense, and manufacturing overhead. These are reported on the income statement as costs of goods sold, but they include both fixed and variable costs. Similarly, period costs are incurred during a particular time period and might be reported as selling, general, and administrative expenses. Once again, some of these period costs may be fixed and others may be variable. The company president's salary, for example, is a period cost and is probably fixed, at least in the short run.

The balance sheets and income statement we have been using thus far are hypothetical. Our nearby *Work the Web* box shows how to find actual balance sheets and income statements online for almost any company.

Earnings Management

The way that firms are required by GAAP to report financial results is intended to be objective and precise. In reality, there is plenty of wiggle room, and, as a result, companies have significant discretion over their reported earnings. For example, corporations frequently like to show investors that they have steadily growing earnings. To do this, they might take steps to over- or understate earnings at various times to smooth out dips and surges. Doing so falls under the heading of *earnings management*. Our *Reality Bytes* box above goes into more depth on this subject.

WORK THE WEB

Public companies are required to file regular reports, including annual and quarterly financial statements, with Canadian securities regulatory authorities. SEDAR (the System for Electronic Document Analysis and Retrieval) makes these reports available for free at **www.sedar.com.** We went to "Search Database" and then "Search for Public Company Documents." On the search form, we entered "Quebecor World," the communication company headquartered in Montreal, for the Company Name. We also selected "Annual Report" for Document Types, and January 1, 1997, the inception date of the SEDAR, for the starting Date of Filing. Here is a portion of what we got:

s e d a r ®

| NEW FILINGS | SEARCH DATABASE | COMPANY PROFILES | WEB LINKS | ABOUT SEDAR | SITE HELP | SEDAR RELEASE 8.0 |

Use of this site is subject to, and your continued use constitutes your
express agreement to be bound by, the
Terms of Use
Any unauthorized use of this site is strictly prohibited.
Link to IMPORTANT NOTICE OF CHANGES dated January 28, 2006

Privacy Statement

Company Search: Quebecor World
Industry Group: All
Document Selection: Annual Report

Sorted: By Issuer
Date From: January 1 1997
Date To: April 5 2007

Search results 1-21

Company Name	Date of Filing	Document Type	File Format	File Size
Quebecor World Inc.	Mar 30 2007	Annual report - English	PDF	12892 K
Quebecor World Inc.	Mar 24 2006	Annual report - English	PDF	2876 K
Quebecor World Inc.	Mar 31 2005	Annual report - English	PDF	3016 K

As of the date of this search, SEDAR had 21 (11 in English and 10 in French) of these reports for Quebecor World available for downloading. The annual report includes, among other things, the list of officers, financial statements for the previous fiscal year, and an explanation by the company for the financial results. Here is an exercise for you: Go back to the search form and look at the different types of documents available from SEDAR. Find the latest news release for Quebecor World. What is it about?

CONCEPT QUESTIONS

2.2a What is the income statement equation?

2.2b What are the three things to keep in mind when looking at an income statement?

2.2c Why is accounting income not the same as cash flow?

2.3 | CASH FLOW

At this point, we are ready to discuss perhaps one of the most important pieces of financial information that can be gleaned from financial statements: *cash flow.* By cash flow, we simply mean the difference between the number of dollars that came in and the number that went out. For example, if you were the owner of a business, you might be very interested in how much cash you actually took out of your business in a given year. How to determine this amount is one of the things we discuss next.

There is no standard financial statement that presents this information in the way that we wish. We will therefore discuss how to calculate cash flow for Loonie Corporation and point out how the result differs from that of standard financial statement calculations. Important note: there is a standard financial accounting statement called the *statement of cash flows,* but it is concerned with a somewhat different issue that should not be confused with what is discussed in this section.

From the balance sheet identity, we know that the value of a firm's assets is equal to the value of its liabilities plus the value of its equity. Similarly, the cash flow from the firm's assets must equal the sum of the cash flow to creditors and the cash flow to stockholders (or owners, if the business is not a corporation):

$$\begin{aligned} \text{Cash flow from assets} = {} & \text{Cash flow to creditors} \\ & + \text{Cash flow to stockholders} \end{aligned} \qquad \text{[2.3]}$$

This is the cash flow identity. What it reflects is the fact that a firm generates cash through its various activities, and that cash either is used to pay creditors or else is paid out to the owners of the firm. We discuss the various things that make up these cash flows next.

Cash Flow from Assets

Cash flow from assets involves three components: operating cash flow, capital spending, and change in net working capital. **Operating cash flow** refers to the cash flow that results from the firm's day-to-day activities of producing and selling. Expenses associated with the firm's financing of its assets are not included since they are not operating expenses.

In the normal course of events, some portion of the firm's cash flow is reinvested in the firm. *Capital spending* refers to the net spending on fixed assets (purchases of fixed assets less sales of fixed assets). Finally, *the change in net working capital* is the amount spent on net working capital. It is measured as the change in net working capital over the period being examined and represents the net increase in current assets over current liabilities. The three components of cash flow are examined in more detail below. In all our examples, all amounts are in millions of dollars.

Operating Cash Flow To calculate operating cash flow (OCF), we want to calculate revenues minus costs, but we don't want to include depreciation since it's not a cash outflow, and we don't want to include interest because it's a financing expense. We do want to include taxes, because taxes are, unfortunately, paid in cash.

If we look at Loonie Corporation's income statement (Table 2.2), we see that earnings before interest and taxes (EBIT) are $694. This is almost what we want, since it doesn't include interest paid. We need to make two adjustments. First, recall that depreciation is

cash flow from assets
The total of cash flow to creditors and cash flow to stockholders, consisting of the following: operating cash flow, capital spending, and changes in net working capital.

operating cash flow
Cash generated from a firm's normal business activities.

a noncash expense. To get cash flow, we first add back the $65 in depreciation since it wasn't a cash deduction. The other adjustment is to subtract the $212 in taxes, since these were paid in cash. The result is operating cash flow:

LOONIE CORPORATION 2008 Operating Cash Flow	
Earnings before interest and taxes	$694
+ Depreciation	65
− Taxes	212
Operating cash flow	$547

Loonie Corporation thus had a 2008 operating cash flow of $547.

Operating cash flow is an important number because it tells us, on a very basic level, whether or not a firm's cash inflows from its business operations are sufficient to cover its everyday cash outflows. For this reason, a negative operating cash flow is often a sign of trouble.

There is an unpleasant possibility for confusion when we speak of operating cash flow. In accounting practice, operating cash flow is often defined as net income plus depreciation. For Loonie Corporation, this would amount to $412 + 65 = $477. The accounting definition of operating cash flow differs from ours in one important way: Interest is deducted when net income is computed. Notice that the difference between the $547 operating cash flow we calculated and this $477 is $70, the amount of interest paid for the year. This definition of cash flow thus considers interest paid to be an operating expense. Our definition treats it properly as a financing expense. If there were no interest expense, the two definitions would be the same.

To finish our calculation of cash flow from assets for Loonie Corporation, we need to consider how much of the $547 operating cash flow was reinvested in the firm. We consider spending on fixed assets first.

Capital Spending   Net capital spending is just money spent on fixed assets less money received from the sale of fixed assets. At the end of 2007, net fixed assets for Loonie Corporation (Table 2.1) were $1,644. During the year, we wrote off (depreciated) $65 worth of fixed assets on the income statement. So, if we didn't purchase any new fixed assets, net fixed assets would have been $1,644 − 65 = $1,579 at year's end. The 2008 balance sheet shows $1,709 in net fixed assets, so we must have spent a total of $1,709 − 1,579 = $130 on fixed assets during the year:

Ending net fixed assets	$1,709
− Beginning net fixed assets	1,644
+ Depreciation	65
Net investment in fixed assets	$ 130

This $130 is our net capital spending for 2008.

Could net capital spending be negative? The answer is yes. This would happen if the firm sold off more assets than it purchased. The *net* here refers to purchases of fixed assets net of any sales of fixed assets.

Change in Net Working Capital In addition to investing in fixed assets, a firm will also invest in current assets. For example, going back to the balance sheet in Table 2.1, we see that at the end of 2008, Loonie had current assets of $1,403. At the end of 2007, current assets were $1,112, so, during the year, Loonie invested $1,403 − 1,112 = $291 in current assets.

As the firm changes its investment in current assets, its current liabilities will usually change as well. To determine the change in net working capital, the easiest approach is just to take the difference between the beginning and ending net working capital (NWC) figures. Net working capital at the end of 2008 was $1,403 − 389 = $1,014. Similarly, at the end of 2007, net working capital was $1,112 − 428 = $684. So, given these figures, we have:

Ending NWC	$1,014
− Beginning NWC	684
Change in NWC	$ 330

Net working capital thus increased by $330. Put another way, Loonie Corporation had a net investment of $330 in NWC for the year.

Conclusion Given the figures we've come up with, we're ready to calculate cash flow from assets. The total cash flow from assets is given by operating cash flow less the amounts invested in fixed assets and net working capital. So, for Loonie, we have:

LOONIE CORPORATION 2008 Cash Flow from Assets	
Operating cash flow	$547
− Net capital spending	130
− Change in NWC	330
Cash flow from assets	$ 87

From the cash flow identity above, this $87 cash flow from assets equals the sum of the firm's cash flow to creditors and its cash flow to stockholders. We consider these next.

It wouldn't be at all unusual for a growing corporation to have a negative cash flow. As we shall see below, a negative cash flow means that the firm raised more money by borrowing and selling stock than it paid out to creditors and stockholders that year.

A Note on "Free" Cash Flow Cash flow from assets sometimes goes by a different name, **free cash flow.** Of course, there is no such thing as "free" cash (we wish!). Instead, the name refers to cash that the firm is free to distribute to creditors and stockholders because it is not needed for working capital or fixed asset investments. We will stick with "cash flow from assets" as our label for this important concept because, in practice,

free cash flow
Another name for cash flow from assets.

there is some variation in exactly how free cash flow is computed; different users calculate it in different ways. Nonetheless, whenever you hear the phrase "free cash flow," you should understand that what is being discussed is cash flow from assets or something quite similar.

Cash Flow to Creditors and Stockholders

The cash flows to creditors and stockholders represent the net payments to creditors and owners during the year. They are calculated in a similar way. **Cash flow to creditors** is interest paid less net new borrowing; **cash flow to stockholders** is dividends paid less net new equity raised.

cash flow to creditors
A firm's interest payments to creditors less net new borrowings.

cash flow to stockholders
Dividends paid out by a firm less net new equity raised.

Cash Flow to Creditors   Looking at the income statement in Table 2.2, we see that Loonie paid $70 in interest to creditors. From the balance sheets in Table 2.1, long-term debt rose by $454 − 408 = $46. So, Loonie Corporation paid out $70 in interest, but it borrowed an additional $46. Net cash flow to creditors is thus:

LOONIE CORPORATION 2008 Cash Flow to Creditors	
Interest paid	$70
− Net new borrowing	46
Cash flow to creditors	$24

Cash flow to creditors is sometimes called *cash flow to bondholders;* we will use these terms interchangeably.

Cash Flow to Stockholders   From the income statement, dividends paid to stockholders amount to $103. To get net new equity raised, we need to look at the common stock and paid-in surplus account. This account tells us how much stock the company has sold. During the year, this account rose by $40, so $40 in net new equity was raised. Given this, we have:

LOONIE CORPORATION 2008 Cash Flow to Stockholders	
Dividends paid	$103
− Net new equity raised	40
Cash flow to stockholders	$ 63

The cash flow to stockholders for 2008 was thus $63.

Conclusion

The last thing that we need to do is to verify that the cash flow identity holds to be sure that we didn't make any mistakes. From above, cash flow from assets is $87. Cash flow to creditors and stockholders is $24 + 63 = $87, so everything checks out.

As our discussion indicates, it is essential that a firm keep an eye on its cash flow. The following serves as an excellent reminder of why doing so is a good idea, unless the firm's owners wish to end up in the poorhouse.

Quoth the Banker, "Watch Cash Flow"

Once upon a midnight dreary as I pondered weak and weary
Over many a quaint and curious volume of accounting lore,
Seeking gimmicks (without scruple) to squeeze through
      some new tax loophole,
Suddenly I heard a knock upon my door,
      Only this, and nothing more.

Then I felt a queasy tingling and I heard the cash a-jingling
As a fearsome banker entered whom I'd often seen before.
His face was money-green and in his eyes there could be seen
Dollar-signs that seemed to glitter as he reckoned up the score.
      "Cash flow," the banker said, and nothing more.

I had always thought it fine to show a jet black bottom line.
But the banker sounded a resounding, "No.
Your receivables are high, mounting upward toward the sky;
Write-offs loom. What matters is cash flow."
      He repeated, "Watch cash flow."

Then I tried to tell the story of our lovely inventory
Which, though large, is full of most delightful stuff.
But the banker saw its growth, and with a mighty oath
He waved his arms and shouted, "Stop! Enough!
      Pay the interest, and don't give me any guff!"

Next I looked for noncash items which could add ad infinitum
To replace the ever-outward flow of cash,
But to keep my statement black I'd held depreciation back,
And my banker said that I'd done something rash.
      He quivered, and his teeth began to gnash.

When I asked him for a loan, he responded, with a groan,
That the interest rate would be just prime plus eight,
And to guarantee my purity he'd insist on some security—
All my assets plus the scalp upon my pate.
      Only this, a standard rate.

Though my bottom line is black, I am flat upon my back,
My cash flows out and customers pay slow.
The growth of my receivables is almost unbelievable:
The result is certain—unremitting woe!
And I hear the banker utter an ominous low mutter,
      "Watch cash flow."

Herbert S. Bailey Jr.

Source: Reprinted from the January 13, 1975, issue of *Publishers Weekly,* published by R. R. Bowker, a Xerox company. Copyright © 1975 by the Xerox Corporation.

To which we can only add: "Amen."

An Example: Cash Flows for Dole Cola

This extended example covers the various cash flow calculations discussed in the chapter. It also illustrates a few variations that may arise.

Operating Cash Flow   During the year, Dole Cola, Inc., had sales and cost of goods sold of $600 and $300, respectively. Depreciation was $150 and interest paid was $30. Taxes were calculated at a straight 34 percent. Dividends were $30. (All figures are in millions of dollars.) What was operating cash flow for Dole? Why is this different from net income?

The easiest thing to do here is to go ahead and create an income statement. We can then pick up the numbers we need. Dole Cola's income statement is given below.

DOLE COLA 2008 Income Statement		
Net sales		$600
Cost of goods sold		300
Depreciation		150
Earnings before interest and taxes		$150
Interest paid		30
Taxable income		$120
Taxes		41
Net income		$ 79
Dividends	$30	
Addition to retained earnings	49	

Net income for Dole was thus $79. We now have all the numbers we need. Referring back to the Loonie Corporation example, we have:

DOLE COLA 2008 Operating Cash Flow	
Earnings before interest and taxes	$150
+ Depreciation	150
− Taxes	41
Operating cash flow	$259

As this example illustrates, operating cash flow is not the same as net income, because depreciation and interest are subtracted out when net income is calculated. If you recall our earlier discussion, we don't subtract these out in computing operating cash flow because depreciation is not a cash expense and interest paid is a financing expense, not an operating expense.

Net Capital Spending   Suppose beginning net fixed assets were $500 and ending net fixed assets were $750. What was the net capital spending for the year?

From the income statement for Dole, depreciation for the year was $150. Net fixed assets rose by $250. Dole thus spent $250 along with an additional $150, for a total of $400.

Change in NWC and Cash Flow from Assets   Suppose Dole Cola started the year with $2,130 in current assets and $1,620 in current liabilities. The corresponding ending figures were $2,260 and $1,710. What was the change in NWC during the year? What was cash flow from assets? How does this compare to net income?

Net working capital started out as $2,130 − 1,620 = $510 and ended up at $2,260 − 1,710 = $550. The change in NWC was thus $550 − 510 = $40. Putting together all the information for Dole Cola, we have

DOLE COLA 2008 Cash Flow from Assets	
Operating cash flow	$259
− Net capital spending	400
− Change in NWC	40
Cash flow from assets	−$181

Dole had a cash flow from assets of −$181. Net income was positive at $79. Is the fact that cash flow from assets was negative a cause for alarm? Not necessarily. The cash flow here is negative primarily because of a large investment in fixed assets. If these are good investments, then the resulting negative cash flow is not a worry.

Cash Flow to Creditors and Stockholders   We saw that Dole Cola had cash flow from assets of −$181. The fact that this is negative means that Dole raised more money in the form of new debt and equity than it paid out for the year. For example, suppose we know that Dole didn't sell any new equity for the year. What was cash flow to stockholders? To creditors?

Since it didn't raise any new equity, Dole's cash flow to stockholders is just equal to the cash dividend paid:

DOLE COLA 2008 Cash Flow to Stockholders	
Dividends paid	$30
− Net new equity	0
Cash flow to stockholders	$30

Now, from the cash flow identity, the total cash paid to creditors and stockholders was −$181. Cash flow to stock holders is $30, so cash flow to creditors must be equal to −$181 − 30 = −$211:

Cash flow to creditors + Cash flow to stockholders = −$181

Cash flow to creditors + $30   = −$181

Cash flow to creditors   = −$211

Since we know that cash flow to creditors is −$211 and interest paid is $30 (from the income statement), we can now determine net new borrowing. Dole must have borrowed $241 during the year to help finance the fixed asset expansion:

DOLE COLA 2008 Cash Flow to Creditors	
Interest paid	$ 30
− Net new borrowing	241
Cash flow to creditors	−$211

CONCEPT QUESTIONS

2.3a What is the cash flow identity? Explain what it says.

2.3b What are the components of operating cash flow?

2.3c Why is interest paid not a component of operating cash flow?

2.4 | TAXES

Nothing is certain but death and taxes, according to an old saying. While the first certainty is beyond the scope of this book, we will focus our attention on the second. Taxes are not only certain, but also important. As a matter of fact, taxes can be one of the largest cash outflows for both an individual and a firm. For example, for the fiscal year 2006, the Royal Bank of Canada's earnings before taxes were about $6.2 billion. Its tax bill, including all taxes paid worldwide, was a whopping $1.4 billion, or about 23 percent of its pretax earnings. The size of the tax bill is determined through the tax code, an often-amended set of rules. In this section, we examine personal and corporate tax rates. We use this knowledge to examine how different types of income are taxed at the personal and corporate level.

If the various rules of taxation seem a little bizarre or convoluted to you, keep in mind that the tax code is the result of political, not economic, forces. As a result, there is no reason why it has to make economic sense.

Personal Tax Rates

In Canada, individuals have to pay taxes on any employment income (salaries and wages), investment income (interest, dividends, and capital gains), and profits from sole proprietorships and partnerships. Taxes on all these incomes are paid to both federal and provincial governments. Table 2.3 shows federal and several provincial tax rates for individuals for 2007.

TABLE 2.3		Tax Rate (%)	Income Bracket $
Federal and provincial tax rates for individuals in 2007*	Federal	15.50	0 – 37,178
		22.00	37,179 – 74,357
		26.00	74,358 – 120,887
		29.00	120,888 and over
	British Columbia	5.70	0 – 34,397
		8.65	34,398 – 68,794
		11.10	68,795 – 78,984
		13.00	78,985 – 95,909
		14.70	95,910 and over
	Alberta	10.00	All income
	Ontario	6.05	0 – 35,488
		9.15	35,489 – 70,976
		11.16	70,977 and over
	Quebec	16.00	0 – 29,290
		20.00	29,291 – 58,595
		24.00	58,596 and over
	Nova Scotia	8.79	0 – 29,590
		14.95	29,591 – 59,180
		16.67	59,181 – 93,000
		17.50	93,001 and over

*Surtaxes imposed by the governments of Ontario and Nova Scotia are ignored.

Source: Canada Revenue Agency Web site (http://www.cra-arc.gc.ca/tax/individuals/faq/taxrates-e.html#federal). Reproduced with permission of the Minister of Public Works and Government Services Canada, 2006. Quebec rates: KPMG Web site (http://www.kpmg.ca/en/services/taxrates/personal.html)

As shown, the federal government and all the provinces except Alberta use a progressive tax system, in which higher income is taxed at a higher rate. Among all the provinces, Quebec has the highest tax rate, at 24 percent, which is applied to an income of $58,596 and over.

Average versus Marginal Tax Rates

In making financial decisions, it is frequently important to distinguish between average and marginal tax rates. Your **average tax rate** is your tax bill divided by your taxable income, in other words, the percentage of your income that goes to pay taxes. Your **marginal tax rate** is the extra tax you would pay if you earned one more dollar. The percentage tax rates shown in Table 2.3 are all marginal rates. Put another way, the tax rates in Table 2.3 apply to the part of income in the indicated range only, not all income.

The difference between average and marginal tax rates can best be illustrated with a simple example. Suppose you live in Ontario and have a taxable income of $100,000. What is your tax bill? From Table 2.3, you can figure your tax bill as:

average tax rate
Total taxes paid divided by total taxable income.

marginal tax rate
Amount of tax payable on the next dollar earned.

Federal taxes:		
.155	($37,178)	= $ 5,762.59
.22	($74,357 − 37,178)	= 8,179.38
.26	($100,000 − 74,357)	= 6,667.18
		$20,609.15
Provincial taxes:		
.0605	($35,488)	= $ 2,147.02
.0915	($70,976 − 35,488)	= 3,247.15
.1116	($100,000 − 70,976)	= 3,239.08
		$ 8,633.25

Your total tax is thus $29,242.40 = $20,609.15 + $8,633.25.[3]

In our example, what is the average tax rate? You had a taxable income of $100,000 and a tax bill of $29,242.40, so the average tax rate is $29,242.40/100,000 = 29.24%. What is the marginal tax rate? If you made one more dollar, the tax on that dollar would be:

Federal tax rate + Provincial tax rate = 26% + 11.16% = 37.16%

Thus, your marginal tax rate is 37.16 percent.

It will normally be the marginal tax rate that is relevant for financial decision making. This is because any new cash flows will be taxed at that marginal rate. Since financial decisions usually involve new cash flows or changes in existing ones, this rate will tell us the marginal effect on our tax bill.

Personal Taxes on Investment Income

In addition to salaries and wages, individuals can earn investment income such as interest, dividends, and capital gains. While interest is taxed at the same rates as ordinary income, dividends and capital gains receive preferential tax treatment. Therefore, we will discuss the calculation of taxes on dividends and capital gains in more detail in this section.

If you are interested in current taxation problems, visit the Canadian Tax Foundation Web site at www.ctf.ca.

Find the latest federal and provincial tax rates at the Canada Revenue Agency Web site at www.cra-arc.gc.ca.

---

[3]Your actual tax payable would be lower due to different tax credits available to an individual. For the sake of simplicity, we ignore them here.

EXAMPLE 2.4   **Deep in the Heart of Taxes**

Yi Wang is a resident of Alberta and has a taxable income of $85,000. What is her tax bill? What are her average and marginal tax rates?

Yi Wang needs to pay federal and provincial taxes. From Table 2.3, the federal tax rate applied to the first $37,178 is 15.5 percent; the rate applied to the next $37,179 is 22 percent; and the rate applied after that up to $120,887 is 26 percent. So Yi's federal taxes are .155 × $37,178 + .22 × 37,179 + .26 × (85,000 − 74,357) = $16,709.15. Alberta uses a *flat-rate* tax, so there is only one provincial tax rate for all income levels for its residents. Thus, Yi's provincial taxes are .10 × $85,000 = $8,500. Taken together, Yi Wang must pay $16,709.15 + 8,500 = $25,209.15 in taxes. The average tax rate is thus $25,209.15/85,000 = 29.66%. The marginal rate is 26% + 10% = 36 percent since Yi Wang's taxes would rise by 36 cents if she had another dollar in taxable income.

dividend tax credit
A tax credit on dividends earned on shares of Canadian companies by individuals.

Dividend Income   To encourage investment in Canadian companies and diminish double taxation, individuals receive a tax credit on dividends earned on shares of Canadian companies. It is called the **dividend tax credit**. Depending on the Canadian source of dividends, two types of dividend tax credits are used. The enhanced dividend tax credit is applied to "eligible dividends," which are paid by large corporations from taxable income that has not benefited from the small business deduction or any other special tax rate. The regular dividend tax credit is applied to all other Canadian dividends.

To calculate taxes on dividends, eligible Canadian dividends are grossed up by 45 percent and included in taxable income. Then a dividend tax credit is deducted from taxes payable. Because of this credit, dividends are taxed at a lower rate than ordinary income.

Capital Gains   When the selling price of an investment exceeds its purchase price, the difference is called the capital gain, and investors are required to pay tax on it. Similar to dividend income, capital gains are taxed at a lower rate. In fact, only half of the capital gain is taxed at the investor's marginal rate. As a result, the effective rate on capital gains is half of the marginal rate. Capital gains have a couple of additional advantages. First, capital losses can be used to reduce taxable capital gains. Second, capital gains taxes are paid only when an investment is sold. So the investment actually grows tax-free until the moment of its sale, which reduces the effective tax rate on capital gains even further.

You can find useful tax-related information at **www.taxtips.ca**.

Investors need to evaluate investments based on their after-tax cash flows. Different tax treatments of interest, dividends, and capital gains makes various investments more or less attractive depending on an individual's tax situation. As a summary, Table 2.4 shows the calculation of taxes on all three types of investment income for an Ontario resident in the top tax bracket.

Canadian Corporate Tax Rates

Like individuals, Canadian corporations have to pay income taxes to the federal and provincial governments. The corporate income tax rates in effect for 2007 are shown in Table 2.5.

As Table 2.5 shows, corporations in Canada are subject to different income tax rates depending on the size and type of business. For example, small businesses enjoy considerably lower income tax rates than large corporations, but savings vary across provinces.

Tax on Interest

Interest	$100.00
Federal tax at 29%	29.00
Provincial tax at 11.16%	11.16
Total tax	40.16

Tax on Dividends

Dividends	$100.00
Grossed up at 145%	145.00
Federal tax at 29%	42.05
Less dividend tax credit (18.9655% $\times$ $145)[*]	(27.50)
Federal tax payable	14.55
Provincial tax at 11.16%	16.18
Less dividend tax credit (6.7% $\times$ $145)[†]	(9.72)
Provincial tax payable	6.46
Total tax ($14.55 + $6.46)	21.01

Tax on Capital Gains

Capital gains	$100.00
Taxable capital gains (50% $\times$ $100)	50.00
Federal tax at 29%	14.50
Provincial tax at 11.16%	5.58
Total tax	20.08

TABLE 2.4

Taxes on $100 investment income for an Ontario resident in the top tax bracket (over $120,887) in 2007

[*]The federal dividend tax credit is 18.9655% of the taxable amount of eligible dividends.

[†]In 2007 the Ontario dividend tax credit is 6.7% on eligible dividends.

Source: Reproduced with permission of the Minister of Public Works and Government Services Canada, 2006. Quebec rates: KPMG website (http://www.kpmg.ca/en/services/taxrates/personal.html).

While a small corporation in Manitoba pays only 3 percent in provincial corporate income tax, its counterpart based in Quebec pays 8 percent.

Companies involved in manufacturing and processing goods in Canada are also taxed at various rates in different provinces and territories; for example, Yukon levies the lowest tax rate, at 2.5 percent. In contrast, two Maritime provinces, Nova Scotia and Prince Edward Island, do not offer any tax breaks to businesses engaged in manufacturing and processing (compared to the rate for general business) and impose the highest tax rate of 16 percent.

Corporate Taxation

Dividends As with individuals, Canadian corporations enjoy preferential tax treatment on dividend income and capital gains. Specifically, while individuals receive a dividend tax credit, Canadian corporations do not pay tax on dividends on shares from other Canadian corporations at all! Dividends received on shares from foreign companies, however, are taxed as ordinary income.

Capital Gains A capital gain arises when a corporation sells an asset at a price that is higher then its original cost. Only 50 percent of this capital gain is taxable. Moreover, capital losses may be applied against taxable capital gains to decrease or completely offset them. Note that corporations cannot claim a capital loss on assets that were depreciated.

TABLE 2.5	General Business	Manufacturing and Processing	Small Business (income up to $400,000[a])
Federal government	22.1[b]	22.1[b]	13.1[b]
British Columbia	12.0	12.0	4.5
Alberta	10.0	10.0	3.0
Saskatchewan	13.0[c]	10.0	4.5
Manitoba	14.0	14.0	3.0
Ontario	14.0	12.0	5.5
Quebec	9.9	9.9	8.0
New Brunswick	13.0	13.0	5.0
Nova Scotia	16.0	16.0	5.0
Prince Edward Island	16.0	16.0	4.3[d]
Newfoundland	14.0	5.0	5.0
Northwest Territories	11.5	11.5	4.0
Nunavut	12.0	12.0	4.0
Yukon	15.0	2.5	4.0

Corporate tax rates for 2007

[a]In Alberta, the small business rate applies to eligible small business income up to $430,000 in 2007. In Saskatchewan, the threshold rose to $450,000 (from $400,000) as of July 1, 2007.

[b]Includes federal surtax.

[c]Rate decreased from 14% as of July 1, 2007.

[d]Rate decreased from 5.4% as of April 1, 2007.

Source: Reprinted with permission of KPMG LLP (Canada).

Loss Carryover   Capital losses may be *carried back* three years or *carried forward* indefinitely to reduce capital gains in these years. Suppose Loonie Corporation had a net capital loss of $0.5 million in 2008 and net capital gains of $100,000 in each of the previous three years. Loonie could carry back a total of $300,000 to receive a tax refund. The remaining $200,000 portion of their 2008 net capital losses may be carried forward indefinitely to offset future capital gains.

carryover of losses
A tax provision allowing corporations with capital or operating losses to apply these losses to earlier or future years.

Net operating losses have a similar carryover provision. If a corporation had net operating losses in a particular year, these losses may be carried back for three years to receive a tax refund. Unlike capital losses, operating losses may be carried forward only for 20 years to decrease taxable income in those years.

There is one more thing to mention about the tax code as it affects corporations. As we noted in section 2.2, accounting depreciation is a noncash deduction. This deduction is called the Capital Cost Allowance (CCA) in Canada. The way that the CCA is computed for tax purposes is governed by tax law. We discuss it in detail in chapter 9.

CONCEPT QUESTIONS

2.4a   What is the difference between a marginal and an average tax rate?

2.4b   What is the dividend tax credit and what is its purpose?

2.4c   What does it mean to carryover a capital loss?

KEY EQUATIONS:

I. The balance sheet identity

$$\text{Assets} = \text{Liabilities} + \text{Shareholders' equity} \qquad [2.1]$$

II. The income statement equation

$$\text{Revenues} - \text{Expenses} = \text{Income} \qquad [2.2]$$

III. The cash flow identity

$$
\begin{aligned}
\text{Cash flow from assets} = &\ \text{Cash flow to creditors (bondholders)} \\
&+ \text{Cash flow to stockholders (owners)} \qquad [2.3]
\end{aligned}
$$

where

a. Cash flow from assets = Operating cash flow (OCF)
  − Net capital spending
  − Change in net working capital (NWC)

  (1) Operating cash flow = Earnings before interest and taxes (EBIT)
    + Depreciation − Taxes

  (2) Net capital spending = Ending net fixed assets − Beginning net fixed assests + Depreciation

  (3) Change in NWC = Ending NWC − Beginning NWC

b. Cash flow to creditors = Interest − Net new borrowing

c. Cash flow to stockholders = Dividends paid − Net new equity raised

SUMMARY AND CONCLUSIONS

This chapter has introduced you to some of the basics of financial statements, cash flow, and taxes. In it we saw that:

1. The book values on an accounting balance sheet can be very different from market values. The goal of financial management is to maximize the market value of the stock, not its book value.
2. Net income as it is computed on the income statement is not cash flow. A primary reason is that depreciation, a noncash expense, is deducted when net income is computed.
3. There is a cash flow identity, much like the balance sheet identity. It says that cash flow from assets equals cash flow to creditors and stockholders. The calculation of cash flow from financial statements isn't difficult. Care must be taken in handling noncash expenses, such as depreciation, and in not confusing operating costs with financing costs. Most of all, it is important not to confuse book values with market values and accounting income with cash flow.
4. Marginal and average tax rates can be different, and it is the marginal tax rate that is relevant for most financial decisions. Investment income such as interest, dividends, and capital gains are taxed differently in the hands of individuals and corporations.

CHAPTER REVIEW AND SELF-TEST PROBLEM

2.1 Cash Flow for Dominion Corporation. This problem will give you some practice working with financial statements and figuring cash flow. Based on the following information for Dominion Corporation, prepare an income statement for 2007 and balance sheets for 2006 and 2007. Next, following our Loonie Corporation examples in the chapter, calculate cash flow from assets for Dominion, cash flow to creditors, and cash flow to stockholders for 2007. Use a 34 percent tax rate throughout. You can check your answers below.

	2006	2007
Sales	$3,790	$3,990
Cost of goods sold	2,043	2,137
Depreciation	975	1,018
Interest	225	267
Dividends	200	225
Current assets	2,140	2,346
Net fixed assets	6,770	7,087
Current liabilities	994	1,126
Long-term debt	2,869	2,956

■ Answer to Chapter Review and Self-Test Problem

2.1 In preparing the balance sheets, remember that shareholders' equity is the residual. With this in mind, Dominion's balance sheets are as follows:

DOMINION CORPORATION Balance Sheets as of December 31, 2006 and 2007						
	2006	2007		2006	2007
Current assets	$2,140	$2,346	Current liabilities	$ 994	$1,126
Net fixed assets	6,770	7,087	Long-term debt	2,869	2,956
			Equity	5,047	5,351
Total assets	$8,910	$9,433	Total liabilities and shareholders' equity	$8,910	$9,433

The income statement is straightforward:

DOMINION CORPORATION 2007 Income Statement	
Sales	$3,990
Cost of goods sold	2,137
Depreciation	1,018
Earnings before interest and taxes	$ 835
Interest paid	267
Taxable income	$ 568
Taxes (34%)	193
Net income	$ 375
Dividends	$225
Addition to retained earnings	150

Notice that we've used a flat 34 percent tax rate. Also notice that the addition to retained earnings is just net income less cash dividends.

We can now pick up the figures we need to get operating cash flow:

DOMINION CORPORATION 2007 Operating Cash Flow	
Earnings before interest and taxes	$ 835
+ Depreciation	1,018
− Current taxes	193
Operating cash flow	$1,660

Next, we get the capital spending for the year by looking at the change in fixed assets, remembering to account for the depreciation:

Ending fixed assets	$7,087
− Beginning fixed assets	6,770
+ Depreciation	1,018
Net investment in fixed assets	$1,335

After calculating beginning and ending NWC, we take the difference to get the change in NWC:

Ending NWC	$1,220
− Beginning NWC	1,146
Change in NWC	$ 74

We now combine operating cash flow, net capital spending, and the change in net working capital to get the total cash flow from assets:

DOMINION CORPORATION 2007 Cash Flow from Assets	
Operating cash flow	$1,660
− Net capital spending	1,335
− Change in NWC	74
Cash flow from assets	$ 251

To get cash flow to creditors, notice that long-term borrowing increased by $87 during the year and that interest paid was $267, so:

DOMINION CORPORATION 2007 Cash Flow to Creditors	
Interest paid	$267
− Net new borrowing	87
Cash flow to creditors	$180

Finally, dividends paid were $225. To get net new equity, we have to do some extra calculating. Total equity was up by $5,351 − 5,047 = $304. Of this increase, $150 was from additions to retained earnings, so $154 in new equity was raised during the year. Cash flow to stockholders was thus:

DOMINION CORPORATION 2007 Cash Flow to Stockholders	
Dividends paid	$225
− Net new equity	154
Cash flow to stockholders	$ 71

As a check, notice that cash flow from assets ($251) does equal cash flow to creditors plus cash flow to stockholders ($180 + 71 = $251).

CRITICAL THINKING AND CONCEPTS REVIEW

2.1   **Liquidity.**   What does liquidity measure? Explain the trade-off a firm faces between high-liquidity and low-liquidity levels.

2.2   **Accounting and Cash Flows.**   Why is it that the revenue and cost figures shown on a standard income statement may not be representative of the actual cash inflows and outflows that occurred during a period?

2.3   **Book Values versus Market Values.**   In preparing a balance sheet, why do you think standard accounting practice focuses on historical cost rather than market value?

2.4   **Operating Cash Flow.**   In comparing accounting net income and operating cash flow, what two items do you find in net income that are not in operating cash flow? Explain what each is and why it is excluded in operating cash flow.

2.5   **Book Values versus Market Values.**   Under standard accounting rules, it is possible for a company's liabilities to exceed its assets. When this occurs, the owners' equity is negative. Can this happen with market values? Why or why not?

2.6   **Cash Flow from Assets.**   Suppose a company's cash flow from assets was negative for a particular period. Is this necessarily a good sign or a bad sign?

2.7   **Operating Cash Flow.**   Suppose a company's operating cash flow was negative for several years running. Is this necessarily a good sign or a bad sign?

2.8   **Net Working Capital and Capital Spending.**   Could a company's change in NWC be negative in a given year? (Hint: Yes.) Explain how this might come about. What about net capital spending?

2.9   **Cash Flow to Stockholders and Creditors.**   Could a company's cash flow to stockholders be negative in a given year? (Hint: Yes.) Explain how this might come about. What about cash flow to creditors?

2.10   **Firm Values.**   Look back at the L'Oréal example we discussed at the beginning of the chapter. Did stockholders in L'Oréal lose €1.8 billion as a result of the accounting changes? What is the basis for your conclusion?

Use the following information to answer the next two questions:

In June 2002, WorldCom, the telecommunications giant, surprised investors when it announced it had overstated net income in the prior two years by $3.8 billion.

At the centre of the controversy was Scott D. Sullivan, the former CFO. WorldCom had leased telephone lines from local companies with the expectation of reselling the use of the lines at a higher price. Under GAAP, these costs should have been reported as an expense on the income statement. Reportedly, however, Mr. Sullivan ordered that the costs be treated as money spent to purchase a fixed asset, so they were to be shown on the balance sheet as an asset and subsequently depreciated.

2.11 Corporate Ethics.   In the wake of this scandal, Mr. Sullivan was charged with fraud. Do you think this should be considered fraud? Why or why not? Why was this accounting method unethical?

2.12 Net Income and Cash Flows.   How did Mr. Sullivan's reclassifying of some costs as asset purchases affect net income at the time? In the future? How did this action affect cash flows? What does this tell you about the importance of examining cash flow relative to net income?

2.13 Average versus Marginal Tax Rates.   Which tax rate, average or marginal, is more relevant for financial decision making? Why?

2.14 Tax Rates.   Why do several provincial and territorial governments impose higher taxes on general business and lower tax rates on small businesses and businesses involved in manufacturing and processing goods in Canada?

QUESTIONS AND PROBLEMS

1. **Building a Balance Sheet.**   Brentwood Bat Factory, Inc., has current assets of $3,400, net fixed assets of $7,100, current liabilities of $1,900, and long-term debt of $5,200. What is the value of the shareholders' equity account for this firm? How much is net working capital?

2. **Building an Income Statement.**   Hoobstank, Inc., has sales of $565,000, costs of $240,000, depreciation expense of $74,000, interest expense of $41,000, and a tax rate of 35 percent. What is the net income for this firm?

3. **Dividends and Retained Earnings.**   Suppose the firm in Problem 2 paid out $45,000 in cash dividends. What is the addition to retained earnings?

4. **Per-Share Earnings and Dividends.**   Suppose the firm in Problem 3 had 30,000 shares of common stock outstanding. What is the earnings per share, or EPS, figure? What is the dividends per share figure?

5. **Market Values and Book Values.**   Klingon Widgets, Inc., purchased new cloaking machinery three years ago for $5 million. The machinery can be sold to the Romulans today for $4.6 million. Klingon's current balance sheet shows net fixed assets of $2,500,000, current liabilities of $875,000, and net working capital of $700,000. If all the current assets were liquidated today, the company would receive $1.6 million cash. What is the book value of Klingon's assets today? What is the market value?

6. **Personal Taxes.**   Andrew LaBelle, a resident of Quebec, had $80,000 in 2007 taxable income. Using the rates from Table 2.3 in the chapter, calculate Andrew's 2007 income taxes.

7. **Tax Rates.**   In Problem 6, what is the average tax rate? What is the marginal tax rate?

8. **Calculating OCF.**   White Trillium, Inc., has sales of $15,430, costs of $5,780, depreciation expense of $1,900, and interest expense of $1,450. If the tax rate is 35 percent, what is the operating cash flow, or OCF?

**Basic
(Questions 1–13)**

9. **Calculating Net Capital Spending.** Rotweiler Obedience School's December 31, 2006, balance sheet showed net fixed assets of $2.95 million, and the December 31, 2007, balance sheet showed net fixed assets of $3.36 million. The company's 2007 income statement showed a depreciation expense of $280,000. What was Rotweiler's net capital spending for 2007?

10. **Calculating Additions to NWC.** The December 31, 2006, balance sheet of Gretzky's Hockey Shop, Inc., showed current assets of $900 and current liabilities of $310. The December 31, 2007, balance sheet showed current assets of $920 and current liabilities of $305. What was the company's 2007 change in net working capital, or NWC?

11. **Cash Flow to Creditors.** The December 31, 2006, balance sheet of Rack 'N' Pinion, Inc., showed long-term debt of $1.7 million, and the December 31, 2007, balance sheet showed long-term debt of $1.9 million. The 2007 income statement showed an interest expense of $65,000. What was the firm's cash flow to creditors during 2007?

12. **Cash Flow to Stockholders.** The December 31, 2006, balance sheet of Rack 'N' Pinion, Inc., showed $180,000 in the common stock account and $3.7 million in the additional paid-in surplus account. The December 31, 2007, balance sheet showed $195,000 and $3.95 million in the same two accounts, respectively. If the company paid out $80,000 in cash dividends during 2007, what was the cash flow to stockholders for the year?

13. **Calculating Total Cash Flows.** Given the information for Rack 'N' Pinion, Inc., in Problems 11 and 12, suppose you also know that the firm's net capital spending for 2007 was $760,000, and that the firm reduced its net working capital investment by $135,000. What was the firm's 2007 operating cash flow, or OCF?

**Intermediate
(Questions 14–26)**

14. **Calculating Total Cash Flows.** Lakehead Co. shows the following information on its 2007 income statement: sales = $127,000; costs = $64,300; other expenses = $3,900; depreciation expense = $9,600; interest expense = $7,100; taxes = $15,210; dividends = $8,400. In addition, you're told that the firm issued $2,500 in new equity during 2007, and redeemed $3,800 in outstanding long-term debt.
    a.   What is the 2007 operating cash flow?
    b.   What is the 2007 cash flow to creditors?
    c.   What is the 2007 cash flow to stockholders?
    d.   If net fixed assets increased by $13,600 during the year, what was the addition to NWC?

15. **Using Income Statements.** Given the following information for Paula's Pizza Co., calculate the depreciation expense: sales = $34,000; costs = $23,000; addition to retained earnings = $2,100; dividends paid = $915; interest expense = $1,520; tax rate = 40 percent.

16. **Preparing a Balance Sheet.** Prepare a balance sheet for Prince Edward Island Potato Corp. as of December 31, 2007, based on the following information: cash = $234,000; patents and copyrights = $818,000; accounts payable = $627,000; accounts receivable = $241,000; tangible net fixed assets = $4,700,000; inventory = $498,000; notes payable = $176,000; accumulated retained earnings = $4,230,000; long-term debt = $913,000.

17. Residual Claims.   Chander, Inc., is obligated to pay its creditors $5,300 during the year.

    a.   What is the market value of the shareholders' equity if assets have a market value of equal $6,100?

    b.   What if assets equal $4,600?

18. Net Income and OCF.   During 2007, Belyk Paving Co. had sales of $3,100,000. Cost of goods sold, administrative and selling expenses, and depreciation expenses were $1,940,000, $475,000, and $530,000, respectively. In addition, the company had an interest expense of $210,000 and a tax rate of 35 percent. (Ignore any tax loss carryback or carryforward provisions.)

    a.   What is Belyk's net income for 2007?

    b.   What is its operating cash flow?

    c.   Explain your results in (a) and (b).

19. Accounting Values versus Cash Flows.   In Problem 18, suppose Belyk Paving Co. paid out $500,000 in cash dividends. Is this possible? If no new investments were made in net fixed assets or net working capital, and if no new stock was issued during the year, what do you know about the firm's long-term debt account?

20. Calculating Cash Flows.   Curling Manufacturing had the following operating results for 2007: sales = $15,370; cost of goods sold = $11,340; depreciation expense = $2,020; interest expense = $210; dividends paid = $380. At the beginning of the year, net fixed assets were $10,080, current assets were $2,520, and current liabilities were $1,890. At the end of the year, net fixed assets were $10,580, current assets were $3,910, and current liabilities were $2,270. The tax rate for 2007 was 35 percent.

    a.   What is net income for 2007?

    b.   What is the operating cash flow for 2007?

    c.   What is the cash flow from assets for 2007? Is this possible? Explain.

    d.   If no new debt was issued during the year, what is the cash flow to creditors? What is the cash flow to stockholders? Explain and interpret the positive and negative signs of your answers in (a) through (d).

21. Calculating Cash Flows.   Consider the following abbreviated financial statements for Chinook, Inc.:

CHINOOK, INC.					
Partial Balance Sheets as of December 31, 2006 and 2007					
	2006	2007		2006	2007
Assets			**Liabilities and Owners' Equity**		
Current assets	$1,710	$1,811	Current liabilities	$ 738	$1,084
Net fixed assets	7,920	8,280	Long-term debt	$4,320	5,040

CHINOOK, INC.	
2007 Income Statement	
Sales	$25,560
Costs	12,820
Depreciation	2,160
Interest paid	389

a. What is owners' equity for 2006 and 2007?

b. What is the change in net working capital for 2007?

c. In 2007, Chinook purchased $3,600 in new fixed assets. How much in fixed assets did Chinook sell? What is the cash flow from assets for the year? (The tax rate is 35 percent.)

d. During 2007, Chinook raised $1,080 in new long-term debt. How much long-term debt must Chinook have paid off during the year? What is the cash flow to creditors?

22. **Cash Flow Identity.**   Loyalist, Inc. reported the following financial statements for the last two years. Construct the cash flow identity for the company. Explain what each number means.

LOYALIST, INC.
Balance Sheet as of December 31, 2006

Assets		Liabilities	
Cash	$ 18,500	Accounts payable	$ 13,200
Accounts receivable	26,380	Notes payable	$ 20,150
Inventory	19,157	Current liabilities	$ 33,350
Current assets	$ 64,037		
		Long-term debt	$190,000
Net fixed assets	$478,370	Owners' equity	$319,057
		Total liabilities and	
Total assets	$542,407	owners' equity	$542,407

2007 Income Statement

Sales	$785,000
Cost of goods sold	380,590
Selling & administrative	173,240
Depreciation	75,800
EBIT	$155,370
Interest	26,800
EBT	$128,570
Taxes	44,999
Net income	$ 83,571
Dividends	$ 15,000
Addition to retained earnings	$ 68,571

LOYALIST, INC.
Balance Sheet as of December 31, 2007

Assets		Liabilities	
Cash	$ 19,870	Accounts payable	$ 14,600
Accounts receivable	29,305	Notes payable	22,870
Inventory	31,603	Current liabilities	$ 37,470
Current assets	$ 80,778		
		Long-term debt	$210,000
Net fixed assets	$564,320	Owners' equity	$397,628
		Total liabilities and	
Total assets	$645,098	owners' equity	$645,098

23. **Marginal versus Average Tax Rates.**   (Refer to Table 2.3.) Ping Chen and Tim Smith have the same $90,000 in taxable income, but Ping lives in British Columbia while Tim resides in Alberta.

a. What are their tax bills?

b. Suppose both Ping and Tim were asked to work overtime that would increase their taxable incomes by $1,000. How much in additional taxes will Ping and Tim pay? Are these amounts the same?

24. **Personal Taxes on Investment Income** (Refer to Tables 2.3 and 2.4.) Stephanie Bertolotti lives in Nova Scotia and earns $50,000 in wages. She also receives $200 in interest from a bank savings account, another $200 in eligible dividends from a Canadian corporation, and another $200 in capital gain from the sale of stocks. How much tax does Stephanie need to pay on each of her investment incomes? (Note that the provincial dividend tax credit for the residents of Nova Scotia is 7.7 percent.)

25. **Corporate Tax Rates.** (Refer to Table 2.5.) Corporation Goliath has $8,800,000 in taxable income, and Corporation David has $88,000 in taxable income. Both are manufacturing corporations and located in Ontario.

    a. What is the tax bill for each firm?

    b. Suppose both firms have identified a new project that will increase taxable income by $10,000. How much in additional taxes will each firm pay? Are these amounts the same?

26. **Carryover of Losses.** The taxable capital gain (loss) information for the Moose Head Corporation is given below. Show how Moose Head can minimize its taxes using the carryover of losses provision.

	2003	2004	2005	2006	2007	2008	2009	2010
Taxable capital gain (loss) in millions	$0.6	$0.4	$0.8	$0.2	($3.0)	$0.1	$0.4	$0.3

27. **Financial Statements and Cash Flow.** Mohawk Corporation had the following numbers in 2007 and 2008.

Challenge
(Question 27)

	2007	2008
Cash	$ 15,450	$ 16,200
Interest	24,000	25,000
Notes payable	21,500	19,000
Depreciation	60,700	60,700
Inventory	14,150	14,300
Cost of goods sold	320,860	340,930
Accounts receivable	22,163	24,350
Long-term debt	180,000	200,000
Selling and administrative expenses	130,560	125,000
Net fixed assets	500,000	510,000
Sales	800,000	850,000
Dividends	10,000	11,000
Accounts payable	12,500	13,000
Tax rate	30%	30%

    a. Prepare an income statement and balance sheet for Mohawk Corporation for 2007 and 2008.

    b. Construct the cash flow identity for Mohawk Corporation.

WHAT'S ON THE WEB?

2.1   **Change in Net Working Capital.**   Go to the Investor Relations area for
Biovail Corporation, a pharmaceutical company with headquarters in
Mississauga, Ontario, at **www.biovail.com**. Find the most recent annual
report and locate the balance sheets for the past two years. Use these balance
sheets to calculate the change in net working capital. How do you interpret
this number?

2.2   **Book Values versus Market Values.**   The home page for Loblaw Companies
Limited, Canada's largest food distributor, can be found at **www.loblaw.ca**.
In the "Investor Zone," locate the most recent annual report, which contains a
balance sheet for the company. What is the book value of equity for Loblaw?
The market value of a company is the number of shares of stock outstanding
times the price per share. This information can be found in Loblaw's annual
report. What is the market value of equity? Which number is more relevant for
shareholders?

2.3   **Net Working Capital.**   Enbridge Inc. is one of the world's largest energy
companies, with headquarters in Calgary, Alberta. Go to the company's home
page at **www.enbridge.com**, follow the link to the investor relations page,
and locate the annual reports. What was Enbridge's net working capital for the
most recent year? Does this number seem low to you, given Enbridge's current
liabilities? Does this indicate that Enbridge may be experiencing financial
problems? Why or why not?

2.4   **Cash Flows to Stockholders and Creditors.**   Shaw Communications Inc. is
a diversified Canadian communications company headquartered in Calgary,
Alberta. The company provides financial information for investors on its
Web site at **www.shaw.ca**. Follow the "Investor Relations" link and find the
most recent annual report. Using the consolidated statements of cash flows,
calculate the cash flow to stockholders and the cash flow to creditors.

2.5   **Personal Taxes and RRSP.**   Registered Retirement Savings Plans (RRSPs)
offer Canadians a tax-efficient way to save for retirement. RRSP contributions
are tax-deductible and grow tax-free until they are withdrawn. You can find
a Canadian Tax calculator at **www.taxtips.ca**. Follow the "Calculators" link
and select the Tax calculator. Enter your income for the current year, and
calculate your federal and provincial taxes, and average and marginal tax rates.
If you make a $1,000 RRSP contribution, what will be your new taxes and tax
rates? Why did they change? Enter the amount equal to your RRSP deduction
limit, which you can find on your last Notice of Assessment, as your RRSP
contribution. What will be your tax savings?

CASH FLOWS AND FINANCIAL STATEMENTS AT SUNSET CANOES, INC.

Sunset Canoes, Inc., is a small company that manufactures and sells canoes in Thunder Bay, Ontario. Tad Marks, the founder of the company, is in charge of the design and sale of the canoes, but his background is in canoeing, not business. As a result, the company's financial records are not maintained well.

The initial investment in Sunset Canoes was provided by Tad and his friends and family. Since the initial investment was relatively small, and the company has only made canoes for its own store, the investors haven't required detailed financial statements from Tad. However, thanks to word of mouth among avid canoers, sales have picked up recently, and Tad is considering a major expansion. His plans include opening another canoe store in Victoria, British Columbia, as well as supplying his canoes to other retailers.

Tad's expansion plans require a significant investment, which he plans to finance with a combination of additional funds from outside investors and money borrowed from banks. Naturally the new investors and creditors will require more organized and detailed financial statements than Tad has previously prepared. At the urging of his investors, Tad has hired financial analyst Paula Wolf to evaluate the performance of the company over the past year.

After rooting through old bank statements, sales receipts, tax returns, and other records, Paula has assembled the following information:

	2006	2007
Cost of goods sold	$118,034	$149,030
Cash	17,031	25,733
Depreciation	33,320	37,660
Interest expense	7,252	8,302
Selling & administrative expenses	23,212	30,296
Accounts payable	30,100	34,090
Fixed assets	147,000	187,600
Sales	231,546	282,240
Accounts receivable	12,068	15,654
Notes payable	13,720	14,980
Long-term debt	74,200	85,400
Inventory	25,396	34,851
New equity	0	14,000

Sunset Canoes currently pays out 30 percent of net income as dividends to Tad and the other original investors, and the company has a 20 percent tax rate. You are Paula's assistant, and she has asked you to prepare the following:

1. An income statement for 2006 and 2007.
2. A balance sheet for 2006 and 2007.
3. Operating cash flow for each year.
4. Cash flow from assets for 2007.
5. Cash flow to creditors for 2007.
6. Cash flow to stockholders for 2007.

QUESTIONS

1. How would you describe Sunset Canoes' cash flows for 2007? Write up a brief discussion.

2. In light of your discussion in the previous question, what do you think about Tad's expansion plans?

3

Working with Financial Statements

On April 17, 2007, shares of stock in TransCanada were trading for about $38. At that price, TransCanada had a price-earnings ratio of 17, meaning that investors were willing to pay $17 for every dollar in income earned by TransCanada. At the same time, investors were willing to pay a stunning $2,685 for each dollar earned by Nortel Networks, but only about $12 and $5 for each dollar earned by Canadian Imperial Bank of Commerce and Onex Corp., respectively. And there were stocks like NovaGold Resources, which, despite having no earnings (a loss actually), had a stock price of about $20 per share. Meanwhile, the average stock in the S&P/TSX Composite Index, which included 279 of the Canadian companies listed on the TSX, had a PE ratio of 16.8, so TransCanada was about average in this regard.

As we look at these numbers, an obvious question arises: Why were investors willing to pay so much more for a dollar of Nortel's earnings and so much less for a dollar earned by Onex? To understand the answer, we need to delve into subjects such as relative profitability and growth potential, and we also need to know how to compare financial and operating information across companies. And that is precisely what this chapter is about.

The PE ratio is just one example of a financial ratio. As we will see in this chapter, there are quite a number of such ratios, all designed to summarize specific aspects of a firm's financial position. In addition to discussing financial ratios and what they mean, we will have something to say about who uses this information and why.

The most important thing to carry away from this chapter is a good understanding of:

3.1 How to standardize financial statements for comparison purposes.

3.2 How to compute and, more important, interpret some common ratios.

3.3 How to analyze financial performance by using the Du Pont identity.

3.4 The relationship between growth and financing needs.

3.5 How to establish benchmarks for comparison purposes, and some of the problems in financial statement analysis.

In Chapter 2, we discussed some of the essential concepts of financial statements and cash flows. This chapter continues where our earlier discussion left off. Our goal here is to expand your understanding of the uses (and abuses) of financial statement information.

A good working knowledge of financial statements is desirable simply because such statements, and numbers derived from those statements, are the primary means of communicating financial information both within the firm and outside the firm. In short, much of the language of business finance is rooted in the ideas we discuss in this chapter.

Company financial information can be found in many places on the Web, including **ca.finance.yahoo .com** and **www.globeinvestor .com.**

In the best of all worlds, the financial manager has full market value information about all of the firm's assets. This will rarely (if ever) happen. So, the reason we rely on accounting figures for much of our financial information is that we are almost always unable to obtain all (or even part) of the market information that we want. The only meaningful yardstick for evaluating business decisions is whether or not they create economic value (see Chapter 1). However, in many important situations, it will not be possible to make this judgment directly because we can't see the market value effects.

We recognize that accounting numbers are often just pale reflections of economic reality, but they frequently are the best available information. For privately held corporations, not-for-profit businesses, and smaller firms, for example, very little direct market value information exists at all. The accountant's reporting function is crucial in these circumstances.

Clearly, one important goal of the accountant is to report financial information to the user in a form useful for decision making. Ironically, the information frequently does not come to the user in such a form. In other words, financial statements don't come with a user's guide. This chapter is a first step in filling this gap.

3.1 | STANDARDIZED FINANCIAL STATEMENTS

One obvious thing we might want to do with a company's financial statements is to compare them to those of other, similar companies. We would immediately have a problem, however. It's almost impossible to directly compare the financial statements for two companies because of differences in size.

For example, CIBC and Royal Bank of Canada are obviously serious rivals in the banking industry, but Royal Bank is almost twice as large (in terms of assets), so it is difficult to compare them directly. For that matter, it's difficult to even compare financial statements from different points in time for the same company if the company's size has changed. The size problem is compounded if we try to compare Royal Bank and, say, Citibank. Because Citibank's financial statements are denominated in U.S. dollars, then we have a size *and* a currency difference.

common-size statement
A standardized financial statement presenting all items in percentage terms. Balance sheet items are shown as a percentage of assets and income statement items as a percentage of sales.

To start making comparisons, one obvious thing we might try to do is to somehow standardize the financial statements. One very common and useful way of doing this is to work with percentages instead of total dollars. The resulting financial statements are called **common-size statements.** We consider these next.

Common-Size Balance Sheets

For easy reference, Maple Leaf Corporation's 2006 and 2007 balance sheets are provided in Table 3.1. Using these, we construct common-size balance sheets by expressing each

TABLE 3.1

MAPLE LEAF CORPORATION Balance Sheets as of December 31, 2006 and 2007 ($ in millions)		
	2006	2007
Assets		
Current assets		
Cash	$ 84	$ 98
Accounts receivable	165	188
Inventory	393	422
Total	$ 642	$ 708
Fixed assets		
Net plant and equipment	$2,731	$2,880
Total assets	$3,373	$3,588
Liabilities and Owners' Equity		
Current liabilities		
Accounts payable	$ 312	$ 344
Notes payable	231	196
Total	$ 543	$ 540
Long-term debt	$ 531	$ 457
Owners' equity		
Common stock and paid-in surplus	$ 500	$ 550
Retained earnings	1,799	2,041
Total	$2,299	$2,591
Total liabilities and owners' equity	$3,373	$3,588

item as a percentage of total assets. Maple Leaf's 2006 and 2007 common-size balance sheets are shown in Table 3.2.

Notice that some of the totals don't check exactly because of rounding errors. Also notice that the total change has to be zero since the beginning and ending numbers must add up to 100 percent.

In this form, financial statements are relatively easy to read and compare. For example, just looking at the two balance sheets for Maple Leaf, we see that current assets were 19.7 percent of total assets in 2007, up from 19.1 percent in 2006. Current liabilities declined from 16.0 percent to 15.1 percent of total liabilities and equity over that same time. Similarly, total equity rose from 68.1 percent of total liabilities and equity to 72.2 percent.

Overall, Maple Leaf's liquidity, as measured by current assets compared to current liabilities, increased over the year. Simultaneously, Maple Leaf's indebtedness diminished as a percentage of total assets. We might be tempted to conclude that the balance sheet has grown "stronger."

IBM's Web site has a good guide to reading financial statements. Select "Investor tools" at **www.ibm.com/investor**.

Common-Size Income Statements

A useful way of standardizing the income statement shown in Table 3.3 is to express each item as a percentage of total sales, as illustrated for Maple Leaf in Table 3.4.

This income statement tells us what happens to each dollar in sales. For Maple Leaf, interest expense eats up $.061 out of every sales dollar, and taxes take another $.081.

TABLE 3.2

MAPLE LEAF CORPORATION Common-Size Balance Sheets December 31, 2006 and 2007			
	2006	2007	Change
Assets			
Current assets			
Cash	2.5%	2.7%	+ .2%
Accounts receivable	4.9	5.2	+ .3
Inventory	11.7	11.8	+ .1
Total	19.1	19.7	+ .6
Fixed assets			
Net plant and equipment	80.9	80.3	− .6
Total assets	100.0%	100.0%	.0%
Liabilities and Owners' Equity			
Current liabilities			
Accounts payable	9.2%	9.6%	+ .4%
Notes payable	6.8	5.5	−1.3
Total	16.0	15.1	− .9
Long-term debt	15.7	12.7	−3.0
Owners' equity			
Common stock and paid-in surplus	14.8	15.3	+ .5
Retained earnings	53.3	56.9	+3.6
Total	68.1	72.2	+4.1
Total liabilities and owners' equity	100.0%	100.0%	.0%

TABLE 3.3

MAPLE LEAF CORPORATION 2007 Income Statement ($ in millions)		
Sales		$2,311
Cost of goods sold		1,344
Depreciation		276
Earnings before interest and taxes		$ 691
Interest paid		141
Taxable income		$ 550
Taxes (34%)		187
Net income		$ 363
Dividends	$121	
Addition to retained earnings	242	

When all is said and done, $.157 of each dollar flows through to the bottom line (net income), and that amount is split into $.105 retained in the business and $.052 paid out in dividends.

These percentages are very useful in comparisons. For example, a very relevant figure is the cost percentage. For Maple Leaf, $.582 of each $1.00 in sales goes to pay for goods sold. It would be interesting to compute the same percentage for Maple Leaf's main competitors to see how Maple Leaf stacks up in terms of cost control.

TABLE 3.4

MAPLE LEAF CORPORATION Common-Size Income Statement 2007		
Sales		100.0%
Cost of goods sold		58.2
Depreciation		11.9
Earnings before interest and taxes		29.9
Interest paid		6.1
Taxable income		23.8
Taxes (34%)		8.1
Net income		15.7%
Dividends	5.2%	
Addition to retained earnings	10.5	

CONCEPT QUESTIONS

3.1a Why is it often necessary to standardize financial statements?

3.1b Describe how common-size balance sheets and income statements are formed.

3.2 | RATIO ANALYSIS

Another way of avoiding the problems involved in comparing companies of different sizes is to calculate and compare **financial ratios.** Such ratios are ways of comparing and investigating the relationships between different pieces of financial information. We cover some of the more common ratios next, but there are many others that we don't touch on.

> **financial ratios**
> Relationships that are determined from a firm's financial information and used for comparison purposes.

One problem with ratios is that different people and different sources frequently don't compute them in exactly the same way, and this leads to much confusion. The specific definitions we use here may or may not be the same as ones you have seen or will see elsewhere. If you are ever using ratios as a tool for analysis, you should be careful to document how you calculate each one, and, if you are comparing your numbers to those of another source, be sure you know how their numbers are computed.

We will defer much of our discussion of how ratios are used and some problems that come up with using them until a bit later in the chapter. For now, for each of the ratios we discuss, several questions come to mind:

> Visit **sme.ic.gc.ca** and try an interactive on-line financial performance tool "Performance Plus," which lets you compare a company's financial data with Canadian industry averages.

1. How is it computed?
2. What is it intended to measure, and why might we be interested?
3. What is the unit of measurement?
4. What might a high or low value be telling us? How might such values be misleading?
5. How could this measure be improved?

Financial ratios are traditionally grouped into the following categories:

1. Short-term solvency, or liquidity, ratios.
2. Long-term solvency, or financial leverage, ratios.

3. Asset management, or turnover, ratios.
4. Profitability ratios.
5. Market value ratios.

We will consider each of these in turn. In calculating these numbers for Maple Leaf, we will use the ending balance sheet (2007) figures unless we explicitly say otherwise. Also notice that the various ratios are colour-keyed to indicate which numbers come from the **income statement** and which come from the **balance sheet.**

Short-Term Solvency, or Liquidity, Measures

As the name suggests, short-term solvency ratios as a group are intended to provide information about a firm's liquidity, and these ratios are sometimes called *liquidity measures*. The primary concern is the firm's ability to pay its bills over the short run without undue stress. Consequently, these ratios focus on current assets and current liabilities.

For obvious reasons, liquidity ratios are particularly interesting to short-term creditors. Since financial managers are constantly working with banks and other short-term lenders, an understanding of these ratios is essential.

One advantage of looking at current assets and liabilities is that their book values and market values are likely to be similar. Often (though not always), these assets and liabilities just don't live long enough for the two to get seriously out of step. On the other hand, like any type of near-cash, current assets and liabilities can and do change fairly rapidly, so today's amounts may not be a reliable guide to the future.

Current Ratio   One of the best-known and most widely used ratios is the *current ratio*. As you might guess, the current ratio is defined as:

$$\text{Current ratio} = \frac{\text{Current assets}}{\text{Current liabilities}} \qquad \text{[3.1]}$$

For Maple Leaf, the 2007 current ratio is:

$$\text{Current ratio} = \frac{\$708}{\$540} = 1.31 \text{ times}$$

Because current assets and liabilities are, in principle, converted to cash over the following 12 months, the current ratio is a measure of short-term liquidity. The unit of measurement is either dollars or times. So, we could say Maple Leaf has $1.31 in current assets for every $1 in current liabilities, or we could say Maple Leaf has its current liabilities covered 1.31 times over.

To a creditor, particularly a short-term creditor such as a supplier, the higher the current ratio, the better. To the firm, a high current ratio indicates liquidity, but it also may indicate an inefficient use of cash and other short-term assets. Absent some extraordinary circumstances, we would expect to see a current ratio of at least 1, because a current ratio of less than 1 would mean that net working capital (current assets less current liabilities) is negative. This would be unusual in a healthy firm, at least for most types of businesses.

The current ratio, like any ratio, is affected by various types of transactions. For example, suppose the firm borrows over the long term to raise money. The short-run effect would be an increase in cash from the issue proceeds and an increase in long-term debt. Current liabilities would not be affected, so the current ratio would rise.

Finally, note that an apparently low current ratio may not be a bad sign for a company with a large reserve of untapped borrowing power.

Current Events EXAMPLE 3.1

Suppose a firm were to pay off some of its suppliers and short-term creditors. What would happen to the current ratio? Suppose a firm buys some inventory. What happens in this case? What happens if a firm sells some merchandise?

The first case is a trick question. What happens is that the current ratio moves away from 1. If it is greater than 1 (the usual case), it will get bigger, but if it is less than 1, it will get smaller. To see this, suppose the firm has $4 in current assets and $2 in current liabilities for a current ratio of 2. If we use $1 in cash to reduce current liabilities, then the new current ratio is ($4 − 1)/($2 − 1) = 3. If we reverse the original situation to $2 in current assets and $4 in current liabilities, then the change will cause the current ratio to fall to 1/3 from 1/2.

The second case is not quite as tricky. Nothing happens to the current ratio because cash goes down while inventory goes up—total current assets are unaffected.

In the third case, the current ratio would usually rise because inventory is normally shown at cost and the sale would normally be at something greater than cost (the difference is the markup). The increase in either cash or receivables is therefore greater than the decrease in inventory. This increases current assets, and the current ratio rises.

Quick (or Acid-Test) Ratio Inventory is often the least liquid current asset. It's also the one for which the book values are least reliable as measures of market value since the quality of the inventory isn't considered. Some of the inventory may later turn out to be damaged, obsolete, or lost.

More to the point, relatively large inventories are often a sign of short-term trouble. The firm may have overestimated sales and overbought or overproduced as a result. In this case, the firm may have a substantial portion of its liquidity tied up in slow-moving inventory.

To further evaluate liquidity, the *quick,* or *acid-test, ratio* is computed just like the current ratio, except inventory is omitted:

$$\text{Quick ratio} = \frac{\text{Current assets} - \text{Inventory}}{\text{Current liabilities}} \qquad \textbf{[3.2]}$$

Notice that using cash to buy inventory does not affect the current ratio, but it reduces the quick ratio. Again, the idea is that inventory is relatively illiquid compared to cash.

For Maple Leaf, this ratio in 2007 was:

$$\text{Quick ratio} = \frac{\$708 - 422}{\$540} = .53 \text{ times}$$

The quick ratio here tells a somewhat different story than the current ratio, because inventory accounts for more than half of Maple Leaf's current assets. To exaggerate the point, if this inventory consisted of, say, unsold nuclear power plants, then this would be a cause for concern.

Cash Ratio A very short-term creditor might be interested in the *cash ratio:*

$$\text{Cash ratio} = \frac{\text{Cash}}{\text{Current liabilities}} \qquad \textbf{[3.3]}$$

You can verify that this works out to be .18 times for Maple Leaf.

Long-Term Solvency Measures

Long-term solvency ratios are intended to address the firm's long-run ability to meet its obligations, or, more generally, its financial leverage. These ratios are sometimes called *financial leverage ratios* or just *leverage ratios*. We consider three commonly used measures and some variations.

Total Debt Ratio   The *total debt ratio* takes into account all debts of all maturities to all creditors. It can be defined in several ways, the easiest of which is:

$$\text{Total debt ratio} = \frac{\text{Total assets} - \text{Total equity}}{\text{Total assets}}$$

[3.4]

$$= \frac{\$3,588 - 2,591}{\$3,588} = .28 \text{ times}$$

In this case, an analyst might say that Maple Leaf uses 28 percent debt.[1] Whether this is high or low or whether it even makes any difference depends on whether or not capital structure matters, a subject we discuss in Chapter 13.

Maple Leaf has $.28 in debt for every $1 in assets. Therefore, there is $.72 in equity ($1 − .28) for every $.28 in debt. With this in mind, we can define two useful variations on the total debt ratio, the *debt-equity ratio* and the *equity multiplier:*

The Business Development Bank of Canada has online ratio calculators. Go to **www.bdc.ca** and follow the "Business Tools" link and then "Ratio calculators."

$$\text{Debt-equity ratio} = \text{Total debt/Total equity}$$
$$= \$.28/\$.72 = .39 \text{ times}$$

[3.5]

$$\text{Equity multiplier} = \text{Total assets/Total equity}$$
$$= \$1/\$.72 = 1.39 \text{ times}$$

[3.6]

The fact that the equity multiplier is 1 plus the debt–equity ratio is not a coincidence:

$$\text{Equity multiplier} = \text{Total assets/Total equity} = \$1/\$.72 = 1.39 \text{ times}$$
$$= (\text{Total equity} + \text{Total debt})/\text{Total equity}$$
$$= 1 + \text{Debt-equity ratio} = 1.39 \text{ times}$$

The thing to notice here is that given any one of these three ratios, you can immediately calculate the other two, so they all say exactly the same thing.

Times Interest Earned   Another common measure of long-term solvency is the *times interest earned* (TIE) *ratio.* Once again, there are several possible (and common) definitions, but we'll stick with the most traditional:

$$\text{Times interest earned ratio} = \frac{\text{EBIT}}{\text{Interest}}$$

[3.7]

$$= \frac{\$691}{\$141} = 4.9 \text{ times}$$

As the name suggests, this ratio measures how well a company has its interest obligations covered, and it is often called the interest coverage ratio. For Maple Leaf, the interest bill is covered 4.9 times over.

Cash Coverage   A problem with the TIE ratio is that it is based on EBIT, which is not really a measure of cash available to pay interest. The reason is that depreciation, a

---

[1]Total equity here includes preferred stock (discussed in Chapter 7), if there is any. An equivalent numerator in this ratio would be (Current liabilities + Long-term debt).

non-cash expense, has been deducted out. Since interest is most definitely a cash outflow (to creditors), one way to define the *cash coverage ratio* is

$$\text{Cash coverage ratio} = \frac{\text{EBIT} + \text{Depreciation}}{\text{Interest}}$$

$$= \frac{\$691 + 276}{\$141} = \frac{\$967}{\$141} = 6.9 \text{ times}$$

[3.8]

The numerator here, EBIT plus depreciation, is often abbreviated EBDIT (earnings before depreciation, interest, and taxes). It is a basic measure of the firm's ability to generate cash from operations, and it is frequently used as a measure of cash flow available to meet financial obligations.

Asset Management, or Turnover, Measures

We next turn our attention to the efficiency with which Maple Leaf uses its assets. The measures in this section are sometimes called *asset utilization ratios.* The specific ratios we discuss can all be interpreted as measures of turnover. What they are intended to describe is how efficiently, or intensively, a firm uses its assets to generate sales. We first look at two important current assets: inventory and receivables.

Inventory Turnover and Days' Sales in Inventory   During the year, Maple Leaf had a cost of goods sold of $1,344. Inventory at the end of the year was $422. With these numbers, *inventory turnover* can be calculated as:

$$\text{Inventory turnover} = \frac{\text{Cost of goods sold}}{\text{Inventory}}$$

$$= \frac{\$1,344}{\$422} = 3.2 \text{ times}$$

[3.9]

In a sense, we sold off, or turned over, the entire inventory 3.2 times. As long as we are not running out of stock and thereby forgoing sales, the higher this ratio is, the more efficiently we are managing inventory.

If we know that we turned our inventory over 3.2 times during the year, then we can immediately figure out how long it took us to turn it over on average. The result is the average *days' sales in inventory:*

$$\text{Days' sales in inventory} = \frac{365 \text{ days}}{\text{Inventory turnover}}$$

$$= \frac{365}{3.2} = 114 \text{ days}$$

[3.10]

This tells us that, roughly speaking, inventory sits 114 days on average before it is sold. Alternatively, assuming we used the most recent inventory and cost figures, it will take about 114 days to work off our current inventory.

For example, we frequently hear things like "Majestic Motors has a 60 days' supply of cars." This means that, at current daily sales, it would take 60 days to deplete the available inventory. We could also say that Majestic has 60 days of sales in inventory.

Receivables Turnover and Days' Sales in Receivables   Our inventory measures give some indication of how fast we can sell products. We now look at how fast we collect on those sales. The *receivables turnover* is defined in the same way as inventory turnover:

$$\text{Receivables turnover} = \frac{\text{Sales}}{\text{Accounts receivable}}$$

$$= \frac{\$2{,}311}{\$188} = 12.3 \text{ times}$$

[3.11]

Loosely speaking, we collected our outstanding credit accounts and reloaned the money 12.3 times during the year.[2]

This ratio makes more sense if we convert it to days, so the *days'sales in receivables* is:

$$\text{Day's sales in receivables} = \frac{365 \text{ days}}{\text{Receivables turnovers}}$$

$$= \frac{365}{12.3} = 30 \text{ days}$$

[3.12]

Therefore, on average, we collect on our credit sales in 30 days. For obvious reasons, this ratio is very frequently called the *average collection period* (ACP).

Also note that if we are using the most recent figures, we can also say that we have 30 days' worth of sales currently uncollected. We will learn more about this subject when we study credit policy in Chapter17.

EXAMPLE 3.2   **Payables Turnover**

Here is a variation on the receivables collection period. How long, on average, does it take for Maple Leaf Corporation to *pay* its bills? To answer, we need to calculate the accounts payable turnover rate using cost of goods sold. We will assume that Maple Leaf purchases everything on credit.

The cost of goods sold is $1,344, and accounts payable are $344. The turnover is therefore $1,344/$344 = 3.9 times. So, payables turned over about every 365/3.9 = 94 days. On average, then, Maple Leaf takes 94 days to pay. As a potential creditor, we might take note of this fact.

Total Asset Turnover   Moving away from specific accounts like inventory or receivables, we can consider an important "big picture" ratio, the *total asset turnover* ratio. As the name suggests, total asset turnover is:

$$\text{Total asset turnover} = \frac{\text{Sales}}{\text{Total assets}}$$

$$= \frac{\$2{,}311}{\$3{,}588} = .64 \text{ times}$$

[3.13]

In other words, for every dollar in assets, we generated $.64 in sales.

A closely related ratio, the *capital intensity ratio,* is simply the reciprocal of (that is, 1 divided by) total asset turnover. It can be interpreted as the dollar investment in assets needed to generate $1 in sales. High values correspond to capital-intensive industries (such as public utilities). For Maple Leaf, total asset turnover is .64, so, if we flip this over, we get that capital intensity is $1/.64 = $1.56. That is, it takes Maple Leaf $1.56 in assets to create $1 in sales.

---

[2]Here we have implicitly assumed that all sales are credit sales. If they were not, then we would simply use total credit sales in these calculations, not total sales.

It might seem that a high total asset turnover ratio is always a good sign for a company, but it isn't necessarily. Consider a company with old assets. The assets would be almost fully depreciated and might be very outdated. In this case, the book value of assets is low, contributing to a higher asset turnover. Plus, the high turnover might also mean that the company will need to make major capital outlays in the near future. A low asset turnover might seem bad, but it could indicate the opposite: The company could have just purchased a lot of new equipment, which implies that the book value of assets is relatively high. These new assets could be more productive and efficient than those used by the company's competitors.

More Turnover **EXAMPLE 3.3**

Suppose you find that a particular company generates $.40 in sales for every dollar in total assets. How often does this company turn over its total assets?

The total asset turnover here is .40 times per year. It takes 1/.40 = 2.5 years to turn assets over completely.

Profitability Measures

The three measures we discuss in this section are probably the best known and most widely used of all financial ratios. In one form or another, they are intended to measure how efficiently the firm uses its assets and how efficiently the firm manages its operations. The focus in this group is on the bottom line—net income.

Profit Margin   Companies pay a great deal of attention to their *profit margin:*

$$\text{Profit margin} = \frac{\text{Net income}}{\text{Sales}}$$

$$= \frac{\$363}{\$2,311} = 15.7\%$$

[3.14]

This tells us that Maple Leaf, in an accounting sense, generates a little less than 16 cents in profit for every dollar in sales.

All other things being equal, a relatively high profit margin is obviously desirable. This situation corresponds to low expense ratios relative to sales. However, we hasten to add that other things are often not equal.

For example, lowering our sales price will usually increase unit volume, but will normally cause profit margins to shrink. Total profit (or, more importantly, operating cash flow) may go up or down, so the fact that margins are smaller isn't necessarily bad. After all, isn't it possible that, as the saying goes, "Our prices are so low that we lose money on everything we sell, but we make it up in volume!"?[3]

Two additional forms of profit margin are sometimes used. Gross profit margin measures the profitability of a company's sales after the costs of goods sold (COGS) have been subtracted:

$$\text{Gross profit margin} = \frac{\text{Sales} - \text{COGS}}{\text{Sales}}$$

---

[3]No, it's not; margins can be small, but they do need to be positive!

Operating profit margin measures profitability after all other expenses, except interest and taxes, have been deducted:

$$\text{Operating profit margin} = \frac{\text{EBIT}}{\text{Sales}}$$

Return on Assets   *Return on assets* (ROA) is a measure of profit per dollar of assets. It can be defined several ways, but the most common is:

$$\text{Return on assets} = \frac{\text{Net income}}{\text{Total assets}}$$

$$= \frac{\$363}{\$3,588} = 10.12\%$$

[3.15]

Return on Equity   *Return on equity* (ROE) is a measure of how the stockholders fared during the year. Since benefiting shareholders is our goal, ROE is, in an accounting sense, the true bottom-line measure of performance. ROE is usually measured as:

$$\text{Return on equity} = \frac{\text{Net income}}{\text{Total equity}}$$

$$= \frac{\$363}{\$2,591} = 14\%$$

[3.16]

Therefore, for every dollar in equity, Maple Leaf generated 14 cents in profit, but, again, this is only correct in accounting terms.

Because ROA and ROE are such commonly cited numbers, we stress that it is important to remember they are accounting rates of return. For this reason, these measures should properly be called *return on book assets* and *return on book equity*. In addition, ROE is sometimes called *return on net worth*. Whatever it's called, it would be inappropriate to compare the result to, for example, an interest rate observed in the financial markets.

The fact that ROE exceeds ROA reflects Maple Leaf's use of financial leverage. We will examine the relationship between these two measures in more detail below.

Market Value Measures

Our final group of measures is based, in part, on information not necessarily contained in financial statements—the market price per share of the stock. Obviously, these measures can be calculated directly only for publicly traded companies.

We assume that Maple Leaf has 33 million shares outstanding and the stock sold for $88 per share at the end of the year. If we recall that Maple Leaf's net income was $363 million, then we can calculate that its earnings per share were:

$$\text{EPS} = \frac{\text{Net income}}{\text{Shares outstanding}} = \frac{\$363}{33} = \$11$$

[3.17]

Price-Earnings Ratio   The first of our market value measures, the *price-earnings,* or PE, *ratio* (or multiple), is defined as:

$$\text{PE ratio} = \frac{\text{Price per share}}{\text{Earnings per share}}$$

$$= \frac{\$88}{\$11} = 8 \text{ times}$$

[3.18]

In the vernacular, we would say that Maple Leaf shares sell for eight times earnings, or we might say that Maple Leaf shares have, or "carry," a PE multiple of 8.

Since the PE ratio measures how much investors are willing to pay per dollar of current earnings, higher PEs are often taken to mean that the firm has significant prospects for future growth. Of course, if a firm had no or almost no earnings, its PE would probably be quite large; so, as always, care is needed in interpreting this ratio.

Market-to-Book Ratio   A second commonly quoted measure is the *market-to-book ratio:*

$$\text{Market-to-book ratio} = \frac{\text{Market value per share}}{\text{Book value per share}}$$

$$= \frac{\$88}{2,591/33} = \frac{\$88}{\$78.5} = 1.12 \text{ times} \qquad [3.19]$$

Notice that book value per share is total equity (not just common stock) divided by the number of shares outstanding.

Since book value per share is an accounting number, it reflects historical costs. In a loose sense, the market-to-book ratio therefore compares the market value of the firm's investments to their cost. A value less than 1 could mean that the firm has not been successful overall in creating value for its stockholders.

This completes our definition of some common ratios. We could tell you about more of them, but these are enough for now. We'll leave it here and go on to discuss some ways of using these ratios instead of just how to calculate them.

CONCEPT QUESTIONS

3.2a   What are the five groups of ratios? Give two or three examples of each kind.

3.2b   Turnover ratios all have one of two figures as numerators. What are these two figures? What do these ratios measure? How do you interpret the results?

3.2c   Profitability ratios all have the same figure in the numerator. What is it? What do these ratios measure? How do you interpret the results?

3.2d   Given the total debt ratio, what other two ratios can be computed? Explain how.

3.3 | THE DU PONT IDENTITY

As we mentioned in discussing ROA and ROE, the difference between these two profitability measures is a reflection of the use of debt financing, or financial leverage. We illustrate the relationship between these measures in this section by investigating a famous way of decomposing ROE into its component parts.

To begin, let's recall the definition of ROE:

$$\text{Return on equity} = \frac{\text{Net income}}{\text{Total equity}}$$

If we were so inclined, we could multiply this ratio by Assets/Assets without changing anything:

$$\text{Return on equity} = \frac{\text{Net income}}{\text{Total equity}} = \frac{\text{Net income}}{\text{Total equity}} \times \frac{\text{Assets}}{\text{Assets}}$$

$$= \frac{\text{Net income}}{\text{Assets}} \times \frac{\text{Assets}}{\text{Total equity}}$$

Notice that we have expressed the ROE as the product of two other ratios—ROA and the equity multiplier:

$$ROE = ROA \times Equity\ multiplier = ROA \times (1 + Debt\text{-}equity\ ratio)$$

Looking back at Maple Leaf, for example, we see that the debt-equity ratio was .39 and ROA was 10.12 percent. Our work here implies that Maple Leaf's ROE, as we previously calculated, is:

$$ROE = 10.12\% \times 1.39 = 14\%$$

We can further decompose ROE by multiplying the top and bottom by total sales:

$$ROE = \frac{Sales}{Sales} \times \frac{Net\ income}{Assets} \times \frac{Assets}{Total\ equity}$$

If we rearrange things a bit, ROE is:

$$ROE = \underbrace{\frac{Net\ income}{Sales} \times \frac{Sales}{Assets}}_{Return\ on\ assets} \times \frac{Assets}{Total\ equity}$$

[3.20]

$$= Profit\ margin \times Total\ asset\ turnover \times Equity\ multiplier$$

Du Pont identity
A way of breaking ROE into three parts: profit margin, total asset turnover, and financial leverage.

What we have now done is to partition ROA into its two component parts, profit margin and total asset turnover. This last expression is called the **Du Pont identity,** after the Du Pont Corporation, which popularized its use.

We can check this relationship for Maple Leaf by noting that the profit margin was 15.7 percent and the total asset turnover was .64. ROE should thus be:

$$
\begin{aligned}
ROE &= Profit\ margin \times Total\ asset\ turnover \times Equity\ multiplier \\
&= \quad .157 \quad\quad \times \quad\quad .64 \quad\quad \times \quad\quad 1.39 \\
&= \quad .14 \quad = \quad 14\%
\end{aligned}
$$

This 14 percent ROE is exactly what we had before.

The Du Pont identity tells us that ROE is affected by three things:

1. Operating efficiency (as measured by profit margin).
2. Asset use efficiency (as measured by total asset turnover).
3. Financial leverage (as measured by the equity multiplier).

Weakness in either operating or asset use efficiency (or both) will show up in a diminished return on assets, which will translate into a lower ROE.

Considering the Du Pont identity, it appears that a firm could leverage up its ROE by increasing its amount of debt. It turns out this will only happen if the firm's ROA exceeds the interest rate on the debt. More importantly, the use of debt financing has a number of other effects, and, as we discuss at some length in later chapters, the amount of leverage a firm uses is governed by its capital structure policy.

The decomposition of ROE we've discussed in this section is a convenient way of systematically approaching financial statement analysis. If ROE is unsatisfactory by some measure, then the Du Pont identity tells you where to start looking for the reasons.

An Expanded Du Pont Analysis

So far, we've seen how the Du Pont equation lets us break down ROE into its basic three components: profit margin, total asset turnover, and financial leverage. We now

TABLE 3.5

FINANCIAL STATEMENTS FOR MAGNA INTERNATIONAL For the year ended December 31, 2005 (US dollars in millions)					
Income Statement			**Balance Sheet**		
Sales	$22,811	Current assets		Current liabilities	
CoGS	19,831	Cash	$ 1,682	Accounts payable	$ 3,241
Gross profit	$ 2,980	Accounts receivable	3,533	Other	1,147
SG&A expense	1,198	Inventory	1,388	Total	$ 4,388
Other expenses	80	Total	$ 6,603		
Depreciation	711	Fixed assets	$ 5,718	Total long-term debt	$ 1,368
EBIT	$ 991			Total equity	$ 6,565
Interest	60	Total assets	$12,321	Total liabilities and equity	$12,321
EBT	931				
Taxes	292				
Net income	$ 639				

extend this analysis to take a closer look at how key parts of a firm's operations feed into ROE. To get going, we went to the SEDAR Web site (www.sedar.com) and found the 2005 annual report for Magna International, Inc., a supplier of automotive systems and components headquartered in Aurora, Ontario. In this report, we located the financial statements for the year ended December 31, 2005. What we found is summarized in Table 3.5.

Using the information in Table 3.5, Figure 3.1 shows how we can construct an expanded Du Pont analysis for Magna International and present that analysis in chart form. The advantage of the extended Du Pont chart is that it lets us examine several ratios at once, thereby getting a better overall picture of a company's performance and also allowing us to determine possible items to improve.

Looking at the left-hand side of our Du Pont chart in Figure 3.1, we see items related to profitability. As always, profit margin is calculated as net income divided by sales. But, as our chart emphasizes, net income depends on sales and a variety of costs, such as cost of goods sold (CoGS) and selling, general, and administrative expenses (SG&A expense). Magna International can increase its ROE by increasing sales and also by reducing one or more of these costs. In other words, if we want to improve profitability, our chart clearly shows us the areas on which we should focus.

Turning to the right-hand side of Figure 3.1, we have an analysis of the key factors underlying total asset turnover. Thus, for example, we see that reducing inventory holdings through more efficient management reduces current assets, which reduces total assets, which then improves total asset turnover.

CONCEPT QUESTIONS

3.3a Return on assets, or ROA, can be expressed as the product of two ratios. Which two?

3.3b Return on equity, or ROE, can be expressed as the product of three ratios. Which three?

FIGURE 3.1 Extended Du Pont Chart for Magna International

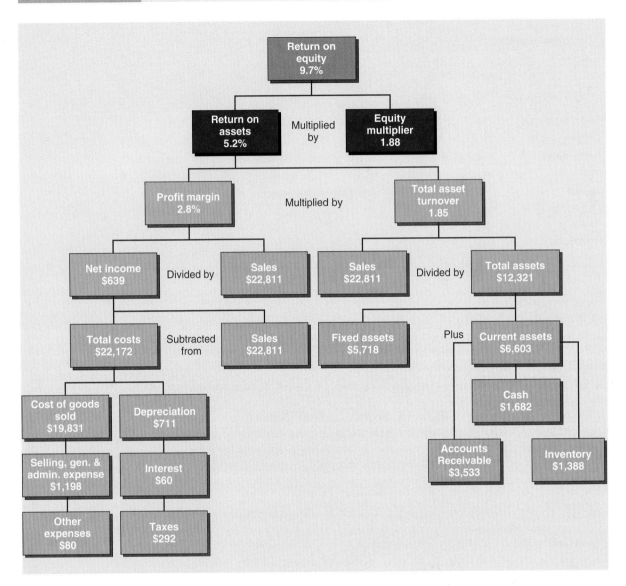

3.4 | INTERNAL AND SUSTAINABLE GROWTH

A firm's return on assets and return on equity are frequently used to calculate two additional numbers, both of which have to do with the ability to grow. We examine these next, and we introduce two basic ratios. Growth rates are discussed in our nearby Reality Bytes box.

Dividend Payout and Earnings Retention

As we have seen in various places, a net income gets divided into two pieces. The first piece is cash dividends paid to stockholders. Whatever is left over is the addition to retained earnings. For example, from Table 3.3, Maple Leaf's net income was $363, of which $121 was paid out in dividends. If we express dividends paid as a percentage of net income, the result is the *dividend payout ratio:*

$$
\begin{aligned}
\text{Dividend payout ratio} &= \text{Cash dividends/Net income} \\
&= \$121/\$363 \\
&= 33^{1}/_{3}\%
\end{aligned}
\qquad \text{[3.21]}
$$

What this tells us is that Maple Leaf pays out one-third of its net income in dividends.

Anything Maple Leaf does not pay out in the form of dividends must be retained in the firm, so we can define the *retention ratio* as:

$$
\begin{aligned}
\text{Retention ratio} &= \text{Addition to retained earnings/Net income} \\
&= \$242/\$363 \\
&= 66^{2}/_{3}\%
\end{aligned}
\qquad \text{[3.22]}
$$

So, Maple Leaf retains two-thirds of its net income. The retention ratio is also known as the *plow-back ratio* because it is, in effect, the portion of net income that is plowed back into the business.

Notice that net income must be either paid out or plowed back, so the dividend payout and plowback ratios have to add up to 1. Put differently, if you know one of these figures, you can figure the other one immediately.

Payout and Retention EXAMPLE 3.4

The Igloo Construction Corporation routinely pays out 40 percent of net income in the form of dividends. What is its plowback ratio? If net income was $800, how much did stockholders actually receive?

If the payout ratio is 40 percent, then the retention, or plowback, ratio must be 60 percent since the two have to add up to 100 percent. Dividends were 40 percent of $800, or $320.

ROA, ROE, and Growth

Investors and others are frequently interested in knowing how rapidly a firm's sales can grow. The important thing to recognize is that if sales are to grow, assets have to grow as well, at least over the long run. Further, if assets are to grow, then the firm must somehow obtain the money to pay for the needed acquisitions. In other words, growth has to be financed, and as a direct corollary, a firm's ability to grow depends on its financing policies.

A firm has two broad sources of financing: *internal* and *external.* Internal financing simply refers to what the firm earns and subsequently plows back into the business. External financing refers to funds raised by either borrowing money or selling stock.

The Internal Growth Rate Suppose a firm has a policy of financing growth using only internal financing. This means that the firm won't borrow any funds and won't sell any new stock. How rapidly can the firm grow? The answer is given by the **internal growth rate:**

$$
\text{Internal growth rate} = \frac{\text{ROA} \times b}{1 - \text{ROA} \times b}
\qquad \text{[3.23]}
$$

internal growth rate
The maximum possible growth rate for a firm that relies only on internal financing.

where ROA is, as usual, return on assets, and b is the retention, or plowback, ratio we just discussed.

REALITY BYTES

How Fast Is Too Fast?

Growth rates are an important tool for evaluating a company and, as we will see later, an important tool for valuing a company's stock. When thinking about (and calculating) growth rates, a little common sense goes a long way. For example, in the end of 2005 Canadian Tire had 14.9 million square feet of retail space. The company expected to increase its square footage by 1.5 million, which represented a 10 percent growth, over the next year. This doesn't sound too outrageous, but can Canadian Tire increase its square footage at 10 percent indefinitely?

We'll get into the calculation in our next chapter, but if you assume that Canadian Tire grows at 10 percent per year over the next 165 years, the company will have about 100.7 trillion square feet of property, which is more than the entire total land mass of Canada! In other words, if Canadian Tire keeps growing its retail space at 10 percent, the entire country will eventually be one big Canadian Tire store. Scary.

Rogers Communications is another example. The company had total revenues of about $7.5 billion in 2005. This represents an annual increase of 33 percent! How likely do you think it is that the company can continue this growth rate? If this growth continued, the company would have revenues of about $1.7 trillion in nineteen years, which exceeds the gross domestic product (GDP) of Canada. Obviously, Rogers Communications' growth rate will slow in the future.

What about growth in cash flow? As of the end of 2005, cash flow from operations for Teck Cominco, a diversified mining company headquartered in Vancouver, had grown, on average, at an annual rate of about 79 percent for the past five years. The company generated about $1.67 billion in operating cash flow for 2005. If the company's cash flow grew at the same rate for the next six years, it would generate almost $55 billion dollars per year, which is more than the total amount of Canadian currency in circulation.

As these examples show, growth rates can be deceiving. It is fairly easy for a small company to grow very fast. If a company has $100 dollars in sales, it only has to increase sales by another $100 to have a 100 percent increase in sales. If the company's sales are $10 billion, it has to increase sales by another $10 billion to achieve the same 100 percent increase. So, long-term growth rate estimates must be chosen very carefully. As a rule of thumb, for really long-term growth estimates, you should probably assume that a company will not grow much faster than the economy as a whole, which is about 1 to 3 percent (inflation-adjusted).

For example, for the Maple Leaf Corporation, we earlier calculated ROA as 10.12 percent. We also saw that the retention ratio is $66\frac{2}{3}$ percent, or $\frac{2}{3}$, so the internal growth rate is:

$$\text{Internal growth rate} = \frac{\text{ROA} \times b}{1 - \text{ROA} \times b}$$

$$= \frac{.1012 \times \frac{2}{3}}{1 - .1012 \times \frac{2}{3}}$$

$$= 7.23\%$$

Thus, if Maple Leaf relies solely on internally generated financing, it can grow at a maximum rate of 7.23 percent per year.

The Sustainable Growth Rate   If a firm only relies on internal financing, then, through time, its total debt ratio will decline. The reason is that assets will grow, but total debt will remain the same (or even fall if some is paid off). Frequently, firms have a particular total debt ratio or equity multiplier that they view as optimal (why this is so is the subject of Chapter 13).

With this in mind, we now consider how rapidly a firm can grow if (1) it wishes to maintain a particular total debt ratio and (2) it is unwilling to sell new stock. There are various reasons why a firm might wish to avoid selling stock, and equity sales by established firms are actually a relatively rare occurrence. Given these two assumptions, the maximum growth rate that can be achieved, called the **sustainable growth rate**, is:

$$\text{Sustainable growth rate} = \frac{\text{ROE} \times b}{1 - \text{ROE} \times b} \qquad \textbf{[3.24]}$$

Notice that this is the same as the internal growth rate, except that ROE is used instead of ROA.

Looking at Maple Leaf, we earlier calculated ROE as 14 percent, and we know that the retention ratio is $^2/_3$, so we can easily calculate sustainable growth as:

$$\text{Sustainable growth rate} = \frac{\text{ROE} \times b}{1 - \text{ROE} \times b}$$

$$= \frac{.14 \times {}^2/_3}{1 - .14 \times {}^2/_3}$$

$$= 10.29\%$$

If you compare this sustainable growth rate of 10.29 percent to the internal growth rate of 7.23 percent, you might wonder why it is larger. The reason is that, as the firm grows, it will have to borrow additional funds if it is to maintain a constant debt ratio. This new borrowing is an extra source of financing in addition to internally generated funds, so Maple Leaf can expand more rapidly.

Determinants of Growth   In our previous section, we saw that the return on equity, or ROE, could be decomposed into its various components using the Du Pont identity. Since ROE appears so prominently in the determination of the sustainable growth rate, the factors important in determining ROE are also important determinants of growth.

As we saw, ROE can be written as the product of three factors:

$$\text{ROE} = \text{Profit margin} \times \text{Total asset turnover} \times \text{Equity multiplier}$$

If we examine our expression for the sustainable growth rate, we see that anything that increases ROE will increase the sustainable growth rate by making the top bigger and the bottom smaller. Increasing the plowback ratio will have the same effect.

Putting it all together, what we have is that a firm's ability to sustain growth depends explicitly on the following four factors:

1. Profit margin. An increase in profit margin will increase the firm's ability to generate funds internally and thereby increase its sustainable growth.

2. Total asset turnover. An increase in the firm's total asset turnover increases the sales generated for each dollar in assets. This decreases the firm's need for new assets as sales grow and thereby increases the sustainable growth rate. Notice that increasing total asset turnover is the same thing as decreasing capital intensity.

3. Financial policy. An increase in the debt-equity ratio increases the firm's financial leverage. Since this makes additional debt financing available, it increases the sustainable growth rate.

4. Dividend policy. A decrease in the percentage of net income paid out as dividends will increase the retention ratio. This increases internally generated equity and thus increases internal and sustainable growth.

sustainable growth rate
The maximum possible growth rate for a firm that maintains a constant debt ratio and doesn't sell new stock.

The sustainable growth rate is a very useful number. What it illustrates is the explicit relationship between the firm's four major areas of concern: its operating efficiency as measured by profit margin, its asset use efficiency as measured by total asset turnover, its financial policy as measured by the debt-equity ratio, and its dividend policy as measured by the retention ratio. If sales are to grow at a rate higher than the sustainable growth rate, the firm must increase profit margins, increase total asset turnover, increase financial leverage, increase earnings retention, or sell new shares.

A Note on Sustainable Growth Rate Calculations   Very commonly, the sustainable growth rate is calculated using just the numerator in our expression, ROE × b. This causes some confusion, which we can clear up here. The issue has to do with how ROE is computed. Recall that ROE is calculated as net income divided by total equity. If total equity is taken from an ending balance sheet (as we have done consistently, and is commonly done in practice), then our formula is the right one. However, if total equity is from the beginning of the period, then the simpler formula is the correct one.

In principle, you'll get exactly the same sustainable growth rate regardless of which way you calculate it (as long as you match up the ROE calculation with the right formula). In reality, you may see some differences because of accounting-related complications. By the way, if you use the average of beginning and ending equity (as some advocate), yet another formula is needed. Also, all of our comments here apply to the internal growth rate as well.

CONCEPT QUESTIONS

3.4a   What does a firm's internal growth rate tell us?

3.4b   What does a firm's sustainable growth rate tell us?

3.4c   Why is the sustainable growth rate likely to be larger than the internal growth rate?

3.5 | USING FINANCIAL STATEMENT INFORMATION

Our last task in this chapter is to discuss in more detail some practical aspects of financial statement analysis. In particular, we will look at reasons for doing financial statement analysis, how to go about getting benchmark information, and some of the problems that come up in the process.

Why Evaluate Financial Statements?

As we have discussed, the primary reason for looking at accounting information is that we don't have, and can't reasonably expect to get, market value information. It is important to emphasize that, whenever we have market information, we will use it instead of accounting data. Also, if there is a conflict between accounting and market data, market data should be given precedence.

Financial statement analysis is essentially an application of "management by exception." In many cases, such analysis will boil down to comparing ratios for one business with some kind of average or representative ratios. Those ratios that seem to differ the most from the averages are tagged for further study.

Internal Uses Financial statement information has a variety of uses within a firm. Among the most important of these is performance evaluation. For example, managers are frequently evaluated and compensated on the basis of accounting measures of performance such as profit margin and return on equity. Also, firms with multiple divisions frequently compare the performance of those divisions using financial statement information.

Another important internal use of financial statement information involves planning for the future. Historical financial statement information is very useful for generating projections about the future and for checking the realism of assumptions made in those projections.

External Uses Financial statements are useful to parties outside the firm, including short-term and long-term creditors and potential investors. For example, we would find such information quite useful in deciding whether or not to grant credit to a new customer.

We would also use this information to evaluate suppliers, and suppliers would use our statements before deciding to extend credit to us. Large customers use this information to decide if we are likely to be around in the future. Credit-rating agencies rely on financial statements in assessing a firm's overall creditworthiness. The common theme here is that financial statements are a prime source of information about a firm's financial health.

We would also find such information useful in evaluating our main competitors. We might be thinking of launching a new product. A prime concern would be whether the competition would jump in shortly thereafter. In this case, we would be interested in our competitors' financial strength to see if they could afford the necessary development.

Finally, we might be thinking of acquiring another firm. Financial statement information would be essential in identifying potential targets and deciding what to offer.

Choosing a Benchmark

Given that we want to evaluate a division or a firm based on its financial statements, a basic problem immediately comes up. How do we choose a benchmark, or a standard of comparison? We describe some ways of getting started in this section.

Time-Trend Analysis One standard we could use is history. Suppose we found that the current ratio for a particular firm is 2.4 based on the most recent financial statement information. Looking back over the last 10 years, we might find that this ratio has declined fairly steadily over that period.

Based on this, we might wonder if the liquidity position of the firm has deteriorated. It could be, of course, that the firm has made changes that allow it to use its current assets more efficiently, that the nature of the firm's business has changed, or that business practices have changed. If we investigate, we might find any of these possible explanations. This is an example of what we mean by management by exception—a deteriorating time trend may not be bad, but it does merit investigation.

Peer Group Analysis The second means of establishing a benchmark is to identify firms similar in the sense that they compete in the same markets, have similar assets, and operate in similar ways. In other words, we need to identify a *peer group*. There are obvious problems with doing this since no two companies are identical. Ultimately, the choice of which companies to use as a basis for comparison is subjective.

North American Industry Classification System (NAICS)
North American code used to classify a firm by its type of business operations.

Learn more about NAICS at www.naics.com.

One common way of identifying potential peers is based on the **North American Industry Classification System** (NAICS, pronounced "nakes"). These are six-digit codes jointly established by Canada, Mexico and the United States as a uniform classification system for statistical reporting purposes. The NAICS was introduced in 1997 to replace the Standard Industrial Classification (SIC) system. Since then the NAICS was modified in 2002, and the next major revision is scheduled for 2007. Firms with the same NAICS code are assumed to be similar. While the first five digits are standardized in the international NAICS agreement, the sixth digit, where used, serves the needs of a specific country. Thus, six-digit Canadian codes may vary from their counterparts in the U.S. and Mexico.

The first two digits in a NAICS code specify one of 20 industry sectors. For example, firms engaged in finance and insurance have NAICS codes beginning with 52. Each additional digit narrows down the industry. So, companies with NAICS codes beginning with 522 are involved in lending funds raised from depositors or by issuing debt; those with codes beginning with 5221 are engaged in lending funds raised from deposits only; NAICS codes starting with 52211 are mostly chartered banks and trust companies; and, finally, NAICS code 522111 is assigned to establishments involved in personal and small-business commercial banking. Table 3.6 is a list of 20 two-digit codes (the first two digits of the six-digit NAICS codes) and the industries they represent.

However, NAICS codes are not perfect. For example, suppose you were examining financial statements for the Hudson's Bay Company (HBC), Canada's oldest general merchandise retailer. In a quick scan of the nearest financial database, you might find about ten businesses with this same NAICS code, but you might not be too comfortable with some of them. Sears Canada would seem to be a reasonable peer, but Otter Farm & Home Co-operative also carries the same industry code. Are HBC and Otter Farm & Home Co-operative really comparable?

TABLE **3.6**	Two-digit NAICS codes	
Code	**NAICS Sectors**	
11	Agriculture, Forestry, Fishing and Hunting	
21	Mining	
22	Utilities	
23	Construction	
31-33	Manufacturing	
42	Wholesale Trade	
44-45	Retail Trade	
48-49	Transportation and Warehousing	
51	Information	
52	Finance and Insurance	
53	Real Estate and Rental and Leasing	
54	Professional, Scientific, and Technical Services	
55	Management of Companies and Enterprises	
56	Administrative and Support and Waste Management and Remediation Services	
61	Education Services	
62	Health Care and Social Assistance	
71	Arts, Entertainment, and Recreation	
72	Accommodation and Food Services	
81	Other Services (except Public Administration)	
92	Public Administration	

WORK THE WEB

Financial ratios have become more available with the rise of the Web. One of the best sites is **today.reuters.com**. We went there and entered the ticker symbol "PCZ" (for Petro-Canada). Then we selected the "Ratios" link. Here is an abbreviated look at the results:

PETRO-CANADA (NYS)

LAST	CHANGE
40.78	▼ **-0.23 (-0.56%)** 4:00 PM ET

SECTOR: Energy | **INDUSTRY:** Oil & Gas - Integrated

Financial Strength

Financial Strength	Company	Industry	Sector	S&P 500
Quick Ratio (MRQ)	0.76	1.04	1.17	1.22
Current Ratio (MRQ)	0.95	1.39	1.55	1.77
LT Debt to Equity (MRQ)	0.30	0.13	0.34	0.64
Total Debt to Equity (MRQ)	0.30	0.15	0.37	0.81
Interest Coverage (TTM)	24.32	37.40	19.58	14.82

Most of the information is self-explanatory. The interest coverage ratio is the same as the times interest earned ratio discussed in the text. The abbreviation MRQ refers to results from the most recent quarterly financial statements, and TTM refers to results from the previous ("trailing") 12 months. Here's a question for you about Petro-Canada: What does it imply when the long-term debt-equity and total debt-equity ratios are the same? The site also provides a comparison to the industry, business sector, and S&P 500 average for the ratios. Other ratios are available on the site and some have five-year averages calculated. Have a look!

As this example illustrates, it is probably not appropriate to blindly use NAICS code-based averages. Instead, analysts often identify a set of primary competitors and then compute a set of averages based on just this group. Also, we may be more concerned with a group of the top firms in an industry, not the average firm. Such a group is called an *aspirant group,* because we aspire to be like them. In this case, a financial statement analysis reveals how far we have to go.

Canada's Business and Consumer Site includes business information for industry sectors. Go to **strategis.ic.gc.ca** and follow the "Business Information by Sector" link.

As we discussed in this chapter, ratios are an important tool for examining a company's performance. Gathering the necessary financial statements can be tedious and time-consuming. Fortunately, many sites on the Web provide this information for free. Our *Work the Web* box above shows how to get this information for Canadian companies traded on U.S. exchanges, along with some very useful benchmarking information. Be sure to look it over and then benchmark your favourite company.

REALITY BYTES

What's in a Ratio?

Abraham Briloff, a well-known financial commentator, famously remarked that "financial statements are like fine perfume; to be sniffed but not swallowed." As you have probably figured out by now, his point is that information gleaned from financial statements—and ratios and growth rates computed from that information—should be taken with a grain of salt.

For example, looking back at the beginning of the chapter, investors must really think that Nortel Networks will have extraordinary growth. After all, they are willing to pay $2,685 for every dollar the company earns, which means they must be expecting much greater earnings in the future. Of course, this PE ratio is too high to even be realistically evaluated. It was so high because Nortel's earnings for 2006 were very small. Indeed, earnings per share calculated based on net income for the preceding 12 months were only $0.01.

Another problem that can occur with ratio analysis is negative equity. Let's look at M8 Entertainment Inc., an independent film entertainment company traded on the TSX, for example. This company, with offices in Montreal and Los Angeles, reported a loss of about $14 million in the first half of 2006, and it had a book value of equity balance of negative $2.3 million. If you calculate the ROE of the company, you will find it is an enormous 609 percent, which does not make sense, given the company's losses. And the calculations for the market-to-book and PE ratios are both negative. How do you interpret a negative PE? We're not really sure either. Whenever a company has a negative book value of equity, it means the losses for the company have been so large that it has erased all equity. In this case, the ROE, PE ratio, and market-to-book ratio are not reported because they are meaningless.

Even if a company's book equity is positive, you still have to be careful. For example, consider Maytag, which had market-to-book ratio of about 30 at the end of 2004. Since this ratio measures the value created by the company for shareholders, this would seem to be a good sign. But a closer look shows that Maytag's book value of equity per share was $5.18 in 1999, but then dropped to $0.28 in 2000. This drop had to do with accounting for stock repurchases made by the company, not gains or losses, but it nonetheless dramatically increased the market-to-book ratio in that year and subsequent years as well.

Financial ratios are important tools used in evaluating companies of all types, but you cannot simply take a number as given. Instead, before doing any analysis, the first step is to ask whether the number actually makes sense.

Problems with Financial Statement Analysis

We close out our chapter on working with financial statements by discussing some additional problems that can arise in using financial statements. In one way or another, the basic problem with financial statement analysis is that there is no underlying theory to help us identify which items or ratios to look at and to guide us in establishing benchmarks.

As we discuss in other chapters, there are many cases where financial theory and economic logic provide guidance in making judgments about value and risk. Very little such help exists with financial statements. This is why we can't say which ratios matter the most and what a high or low value might be.

One particularly severe problem is that some firms are conglomerates, such as Canadian Tire Corporation, owning several lines of business: retail, gas stations, auto service, and financial services. The consolidated financial statements for such firms don't really fit any neat industry category. More generally, the kind of peer group analysis we have been describing is going to work best when the firms are strictly in the same line of business, the industry is competitive, and there is only one way of operating.

Another problem that is becoming increasingly common is that major competitors and natural peer group members in an industry may be scattered around the globe. The oil industry is an obvious example. The problem here is that financial statements from outside

Canada do not necessarily conform to GAAP (more precisely, different countries can have different GAAPs). The existence of different standards and procedures makes it very difficult to compare financial statements across national borders.

Even companies that are clearly in the same line of business may not be comparable. For example, utilities engaged in hydro-electric power generation are all classified in the same group (NAICS 221111). This group is often thought to be relatively homogeneous. However, utilities generally operate as regulated monopolies, so they don't compete with each other. Many have stockholders, and many are organized as cooperatives with no stockholders. Finally, profitability is strongly affected by regulatory environment, so utilities in different locations can be very similar but show very different profits.

Several other general problems crop up frequently. First, different firms use different accounting procedures—for inventory, for example. This makes it difficult to compare statements. Second, different firms end their fiscal years at different times. For firms in seasonal businesses (such as a retailer with a large Christmas season), this can lead to difficulties in comparing balance sheets because of fluctuations in accounts during the year. Finally, for any particular firm, unusual or transient events, such as a one-time profit from an asset sale, may affect financial performance. In comparing firms, such events can give misleading signals. Our nearby *Reality Bytes* box discusses some additional issues.

CONCEPT QUESTIONS

3.5a   What are some uses for financial statement analysis?

3.5b   What are NAICS codes and how might they be useful?

3.5c   Why do we say that financial statement analysis is management by exception?

3.5d   What are some of the problems that can come up with financial statement analysis?

KEY EQUATIONS:

I. Short-term solvency, or liquidity, ratios

$$\text{Current ratio} = \frac{\text{Current assets}}{\text{Current liabilities}} \qquad [3.1]$$

$$\text{Quick ratio} = \frac{\text{Current assets} - \text{Inventory}}{\text{Current liabilities}} \qquad [3.2]$$

$$\text{Cash ratio} = \frac{\text{Cash}}{\text{Current liabilities}} \qquad [3.3]$$

II. Long-term solvency, or financial leverage, ratios

$$\text{Total debt ratio} = \frac{\text{Total assets} - \text{Total equity}}{\text{Total assets}} \qquad [3.4]$$

$$\text{Debt-equity ratio} = \text{Total debt/Total equity} \qquad [3.5]$$

$$\text{Equity multiplier} = \text{Total assets/Total equity} \qquad [3.6]$$

$$\text{Times interest earned ratio} = \frac{\text{EBIT}}{\text{Interest}} \qquad [3.7]$$

$$\text{Cash coverage ratio} = \frac{\text{EBIT} + \text{Depreciation}}{\text{Interest}} \qquad [3.8]$$

III. Asset utilization, or turnover, ratios

$$\text{Inventory turnover} = \frac{\text{Cost of goods sold}}{\text{Inventory}} \qquad [3.9]$$

$$\text{Day's sales in inventory} = \frac{\text{365 days}}{\text{Inventory turnover}} \qquad [3.10]$$

$$\text{Receivables turnover} = \frac{\text{Sales}}{\text{Accounts receivable}} \qquad [3.11]$$

$$\text{Day's sales in receivables} = \frac{\text{365 days}}{\text{Receivables turnover}} \qquad [3.12]$$

$$\text{Total asset turnover} = \frac{\text{Sales}}{\text{Total assets}} \qquad [3.13]$$

IV. Profitability ratios

$$\text{Profit margin} = \frac{\text{Net income}}{\text{Sales}} \qquad [3.14]$$

Other forms of profit margin:

$$\text{Gross profit margin} = \frac{\text{Sales} - \text{COGS}}{\text{Sales}}$$

$$\text{Operating profit margin} = \frac{\text{EBIT}}{\text{Sales}}$$

$$\text{Return on assets (ROA)} = \frac{\text{Net income}}{\text{Total assets}} \qquad [3.15]$$

$$\text{Return on equity (ROE)} = \frac{\text{Net income}}{\text{Total equity}} \qquad [3.16]$$

V. Market value ratios

$$\text{Earnings per share (EPS)} = \frac{\text{Net income}}{\text{Shares outstanding}} \qquad [3.17]$$

$$\text{Price-earnings (PE) ratio} = \frac{\text{Price per share}}{\text{Earnings per share}} \qquad [3.18]$$

$$\text{Market-to-book ratio} = \frac{\text{Market value per share}}{\text{Book value per share}} \qquad [3.19]$$

VI. Du Pont identity

$$\text{ROE} = \text{Profit margin} \times \text{Total asset turnover} \times \text{Equity multiplier}$$

$$\text{ROE} = \frac{\text{Net income}}{\text{Sales}} \times \frac{\text{Sales}}{\text{Assets}} \times \frac{\text{Assets}}{\text{Total equity}} \qquad [3.20]$$

VII. Dividend payout and earnings retention

Dividend payout ratio = Cash dividends/Net income [3.21]

Retention ratio = Addition to retained earnings/Net income [3.22]

VIII. Internal growth rate

$$\text{Internal growth rate} = \frac{\text{ROA} \times b}{1 - \text{ROA} \times b}$$ [3.23]

where

b = **Plowback (retention) ratio**
= **Addition to retained earnings/Net income**
= **1 − Dividend payout ratio**

The internal growth rate is the maximum growth rate that can be achieved with no external financing of any kind.

IX. Sustainable growth rate

$$\text{Sustainable growth rate} = \frac{\text{ROE} \times b}{1 - \text{ROE} \times b}$$ [3.24]

The sustainable growth rate is the maximum growth rate that can be achieved with no external equity financing while maintaining a constant debt-equity ratio.

SUMMARY AND CONCLUSIONS

This chapter has discussed aspects of financial statement analysis, including

1. Standardized financial statements. We explained that differences in firm size make it difficult to compare financial statements, and we discussed how to form common-size statements to make comparisons easier.
2. Ratio analysis. Evaluating ratios of accounting numbers is another way of comparing financial statement information. We therefore defined and discussed a number of the most commonly reported and used financial ratios.
3. The Du Pont Identity. We discussed the famous Du Pont identity as a way of analyzing financial performance. We have seen how the Du Pont equation lets us break down ROE into its basic three components: profit margin, total asset turnover, and financial leverage.
4. Internal and sustainable growth. We defined the internal and sustainable growth rate, and we examined the connection between profitability, financial policy, and growth.
5. Using financial statements. We described how to establish benchmarks for comparison purposes and discussed some of the potential problems that can arise.

After you have studied this chapter, we hope that you will have some perspective on the uses and abuses of financial statements. You should also find that your vocabulary of business and financial terms has grown substantially.

www.mcgrawhill.ca/olc/ross

CHAPTER REVIEW AND SELF-TEST PROBLEMS

3.1 Common-Size Statements. Below are the most recent financial statements for Royal Roads Corp. Prepare a common-size income statement based on this information. How do you interpret the standardized net income? What percentage of sales goes to cost of goods sold?

ROYAL ROADS CORPORATION 2007 Income Statement ($ in millions)	
Sales	$3,756
Cost of goods sold	2,453
Depreciation	490
Earnings before interest and taxes	$ 813
Interest paid	613
Taxable income	$ 200
Taxes (34%)	68
Net income	$ 132
Dividends	$46
Addition to retained earnings	86

ROYAL ROADS CORPORATION
Balance Sheets as of December 31, 2006 and 2007
($ in millions)

Assets	2006	2007	Liabilities and Owners' Equity	2006	2007
Current assets			Current liabilities		
Cash	$ 120	$ 88	Accounts payable	$ 124	$ 144
Accounts receivable	224	192	Notes payable	1,412	1,039
Inventory	424	368	Total	$1,536	$1,183
Total	$ 768	$ 648	Long-term debt	$1,804	$2,077
Fixed assets			Owners' equity		
Net plant			Common stock		
and equipment	$5,228	$5,354	and paid-in surplus	$ 300	$ 300
			Retained earnings	2,356	2,442
Total assets	$5,996	$6,002	Total	$2,656	$2,742
			Total liabilities and owner's equity	$5,996	$6,002

3.2 Financial Ratios. Based on the balance sheets and income statement in the previous problem, calculate the following ratios for 2007:

Current ratio   _____

Quick ratio   _____

Cash ratio   _____

Inventory turnover   _____
Receivables turnover   _____
Days' sales in inventory   _____
Days' sales in receivables   _____
Total debt ratio   _____
Times interest earned ratio _____
Cash coverage ratio   _____

3.3 ROE and the Du Pont Identity. Calculate the 2007 ROE for the Royal Roads Corporation and then break down your answer into its component parts using the Du Pont identity.

3.4 Sustainable Growth. Based on the following information, what growth rate can Brock maintain if no external financing is used? What is the sustainable growth rate?

BROCK COMPANY Financial Statements					
Income Statement			**Balance Sheet**		
Sales	$2,750	Current assets	$ 600	Long-term debt	$ 200
Cost of sales	2,400	Net fixed assets	800	Equity	1,200
Tax (34%)	119	Total	$1,400	Total	$1,400
Net income	$ 231				
Dividends	$ 77				

■ Answers to Chapter Review and Self-Test Problems

3.1 We've calculated the common-size income statement below. Remember that we simply divide each item by total sales.

ROYAL ROADS CORPORATION 2007 Common-Size Income Statement		
Sales		100.0%
Cost of goods sold		65.3
Depreciation		13.0
Earnings before interest and taxes		21.6
Interest paid		16.3
Taxable income		5.3
Taxes (34%)		1.8
Net income		3.5%
Dividends	1.2%	
Addition to retained earnings	2.3	

Net income is 3.5 percent of sales. Since this is the percentage of each sales dollar that makes its way to the bottom line, the standardized net income is the firm's profit margin. Cost of goods sold is 65.3 percent of sales.

3.2 We've calculated the ratios below based on the ending figures. If you don't remember a definition, refer to the Key Equations.

Current ratio	$648/$1,183	= .55 times
Quick ratio	$280/$1,183	= .24 times
Cash ratio	$88/$1,183	= .07 times
Inventory turnover	$2,453/$368	= 6.7 times
Receivables turnover	$3,756/$192	= 19.6 times
Days' sales in inventory	365/6.7	= 54.5 days
Days' sales in receivables	365/19.6	= 18.6 days
Total debt ratio	$3,260/$6,002	= 54.3%
Times interest earned ratio	$813/$613	= 1.33 times
Cash coverage ratio	$1,303/$613	= 2.13 times

3.3 The return on equity is the ratio of net income to total equity. For Royal Roads, this is $132/$2,742 = 4.8%, which is not outstanding. Given the Du Pont identity, ROE can be written as:

ROE = Profit margin × Total asset turnover × Equity multiplier
 = $132/$3,756 × $3,756/$6,002 × $6,002/$2,742
 = 3.5% × .626 × 2.19
 = 4.8%

Notice that return on assets, ROA, is 3.5% × .626 = 2.2%.

3.4 Brock retains $b = (1 - .33) = \frac{2}{3} \approx .67$ of net income. Return on assets is $231/$1,400 = 16.5%. The internal growth rate is:

$$\frac{\text{ROA} \times b}{1 - \text{ROA} \times b} = \frac{.165 \times \frac{2}{3}}{1 - .165 \times \frac{2}{3}}$$
$$= 12.36\%$$

Return on equity for Brock is $231/$1,200 = 19.25%, so we can calculate the sustainable growth rate as:

$$\frac{\text{ROE} \times b}{1 - \text{ROE} \times b} = \frac{.1925 \times \frac{2}{3}}{1 - .1925 \times \frac{2}{3}}$$
$$= 14.72\%$$

CRITICAL THINKING AND CONCEPTS REVIEW

3.1 **Current Ratio.** What effect would the following actions have on a firm's current ratio? Assume that net working capital is positive.

a. Inventory is purchased.
b. A supplier is paid.
c. A short-term bank loan is repaid.
d. A long-term debt is paid off early.
e. A customer pays off a credit account.
f. Inventory is sold at cost.
g. Inventory is sold for a profit.

3.2   Current Ratio and Quick Ratio.   In recent years, Wild Rose Co. has greatly increased its current ratio. At the same time, the quick ratio has fallen. What has happened? Has the liquidity of the company improved?

3.3   Current Ratio.   Explain what it means for a firm to have a current ratio equal to .50. Would the firm be better off if the current ratio were 1.50? What if it were 15.0? Explain your answers.

3.4   Financial Ratios.   Fully explain the kind of information the following financial ratios provide about a firm:

   a.   Quick ratio

   b.   Cash ratio

   c.   Capital intensity ratio

   d.   Total asset turnover

   e.   Equity multiplier

   f.   Long-term debt ratio

   g.   Times interest earned ratio

   h.   Profit margin

   i.   Return on assets

   j.   Return on equity

   k.   Price-earnings ratio

3.5   Standardized Financial Statements.   What types of information do common-size financial statements reveal about the firm? What is the best use for these common-size statements?

3.6   Peer Group Analysis.   Explain what peer group analysis means. As a financial manager, how could you use the results of peer group analysis to evaluate the performance of your firm? How is a peer group different from an aspirant group?

3.7   Du Pont Identity.   Why is the Du Pont identity a valuable tool for analyzing the performance of a firm? Discuss the types of information it reveals as compared to ROE considered by itself.

3.8   Industry-Specific Ratios.   Specialized ratios are sometimes used in specific industries. For example, the so-called book-to-bill ratio is closely watched for semiconductor manufacturers. A ratio of .93 indicates that for every $100 worth of chips shipped over some period, only $93 worth of new orders were received. In November 2004, the North American semiconductor equipment industry's book-to-bill ratio was at parity, or 1.0, with orders of $1.35 billion and billings of $1.34 billion. The most recent peak in the book-to-bill ratio was in June 2004 when it reached 1.07. Orders for November 2004 declined 2 percent from October, but were up 46 percent from November 2003. Billings in November 2004 were down 6 percent from October but up 53 percent from November 2003. What is this ratio intended to measure? Why do you think it is so closely followed?

3.9   Industry-Specific Ratios.   So-called same-store sales are a very important measure for companies as diverse as Tim Hortons and Sears Canada. As the name suggests, examining same-store sales means comparing revenues from the same stores or restaurants at two different points in time. Why might companies focus on same-store sales rather than total sales?

3.10 Industry-Specific Ratios.   There are many ways of using standardized financial information beyond those discussed in this chapter. The usual goal is to put firms on an equal footing for comparison purposes. For example, for auto manufacturers, it is common to express sales, costs, and profits on a per-car basis. For each of the following industries, give an example of an actual company and discuss one or more potentially useful means of standardizing financial information:

a. Public utilities

b. Large retailers

c. Airlines

d. Online services

e. Hospitals

f. University textbook publishers

QUESTIONS AND PROBLEMS

**Basic
(Questions 1–25)**

1. **Calculating Liquidity Ratios.**   Lodgepole Pine, Inc., has net working capital of $1,100, current liabilities of $4,180, and inventory of $1,600. What is the current ratio? What is the quick ratio?

2. **Calculating Profitability Ratios.**   Nick's Bird Cages has sales of $43 million, total assets of $29 million, and total debt of $9.5 million. If the profit margin is 8 percent, what is net income? What is ROA? What is ROE?

3. **Calculating the Average Collection Period.**   Bonds Lumber Yard has a current accounts receivable balance of $527,381. Credit sales for the year just ended were $4,386,500. What is the receivables turnover? The days' sales in receivables? How long did it take on average for credit customers to pay off their accounts during the past year?

4. **Calculating Inventory Turnover.**   Windy Corporation has ending inventory of $865,371, and cost of goods sold for the year just ended was $4,378,650. What is the inventory turnover? The days' sales in inventory? How long on average did a unit of inventory sit on the shelf before it was sold?

5. **Calculating Leverage Ratios.**   Victoria Golf, Inc., has a total debt ratio of .55. What is its debt-equity ratio? What is its equity multiplier?

6. **Calculating Market Value Ratios.**   Niagara Cleaning, Inc., had additions to retained earnings for the year just ended of $380,000. The firm paid out $220,000 in cash dividends, and it has ending total equity of $5.5 million. If Niagara currently has 400,000 shares of common stock outstanding, what are earnings per share? Dividends per share? What is book value per share? If the stock currently sells for $32 per share, what is the market-to-book ratio? The price-earnings ratio?

7. **Du Pont Identity.**   If Ottawa Legal has an equity multiplier of 1.70, total asset turnover of 1.45, and a profit margin of 9 percent, what is its ROE?

8. **Du Pont Identity.**   Jiminy Cricket Removal has a profit margin of 11 percent, total asset turnover of 1.25, and ROE of 20.50 percent. What is this firm's debt-equity ratio?

9. **Calculating Average Payables Period.**   For the past year, Miguaska, Inc., had a cost of goods sold of $41,682. At the end of the year, the accounts payable balance was

$8,917. How long on average did it take the company to pay off its suppliers during the year? What might a large value for this ratio imply?

10. **Equity Multiplier and Return on Equity.** Sunny Beach Chair Company has a debt-equity ratio of .90. Return on assets is 7.9 percent, and total equity is $520,000. What is the equity multiplier? Return on equity? Net income?

11. **Internal Growth.** If Listen to Me, Inc., has a 12 percent ROA and a 25 percent payout ratio, what is its internal growth rate?

12. **Sustainable Growth.** If the Crash Davis Driving School has a 18.5 percent ROE and a 35 percent payout ratio, what is its sustainable growth rate?

13. **Sustainable Growth.** Based on the following information, calculate the sustainable growth rate for Maple Syrup Pies:

    Profit margin = 8.7%
    Capital intensity ratio = .60
    Debt-equity ratio = .40   1/600
    Net income = $40,000   1.40 Equity multiplier.
    Dividends = $9,000

    What is the ROE here?

14. **Sustainable Growth.** Assuming the following ratios are constant, what is the sustainable growth rate?

    Total asset turnover = 1.80
    Profit margin = 7.2%

    Equity multiplier = 2.15

    Payout ratio = 30%

Alberta Mining Company reports the following balance sheet information for 2006 and 2007. Use this information to work Problems 15 through 17.

ALBERTA MINING COMPANY					
Balance Sheets as of December 31, 2006 and 2007					
	2006	2007		2006	2007
Assets			**Liabilities and Owners' Equity**		
Current assets					
Cash	$ 19,250	$ 21,386	Current liabilities		
Accounts receivable	46,381	49,327	Accounts payable	$157,832	$141,368
Inventory	109,831	119,834	Notes payable	72,891	99,543
Total	$175,462	$190,547	Total	$230,723	$240,911
Fixed Assets			Long-term debt	$200,000	$250,000
Net plant and equipment	$612,832	$702,683	Owners' equity		
			Common stock and paid-in surplus	$175,000	$175,000
			Retained earnings	182,571	227,319
			Total	$357,571	$402,319
Total assets	$788,294	$893,230	Total liabilities and owners' equity	$788,294	$893,230

15. **Preparing Standardized Financial Statements.** Prepare the 2006 and 2007 common-size balance sheets for Alberta Mining.

16. **Calculating Financial Ratios.** Based on the balance sheets given for Alberta Mining, calculate the following financial ratios for each year:
    a. Current ratio
    b. Quick ratio
    c. Cash ratio
    d. Debt-equity ratio and equity multiplier
    e. Total debt ratio

17. **Du Pont Identity.** Suppose that the Alberta Mining Company had sales of $1,728,347 and net income of $148,320 for the year ending December 31, 2007. Calculate the Du Pont identity.

18. **Du Pont Identity.** The White Spruce Company has an ROA of 10 percent, a 7 percent profit margin, and an ROE of 18 percent. What is the company's total asset turnover? What is the equity multiplier?

19. **Return on Assets.** Gros Morne has a profit margin of 8 percent on sales of $23,000,000. If the firm has debt of $9,500,000 and total assets of $24,000,000, what is the firm's ROA?

20. **Calculating Internal Growth.** The most recent financial statements for Kayak Manufacturing Co. are shown below:

Income Statement		Balance Sheet			
Sales	$32,540	Current assets	$18,000	Debt	$28,200
Costs	10,680	Fixed assets	54,500	Equity	44,300
Taxable income	$21,860	Total	$72,500	Total	$72,500
Tax (35%)	7,651				
Net Income	$14,209				

Assets and costs are proportional to sales. Debt and equity are not. The company maintains a constant 40 percent dividend payout ratio. No external financing is possible. What is the internal growth rate?

21. **Calculating Sustainable Growth.** For Kayak Manufacturing in Problem 20, what is the sustainable growth rate?

22. **Total Asset Turnover.** Kaleb's Karate Supply had a profit margin of 10 percent, sales of $14 million, and total assets of $6 million. What was total asset turnover? If management set a goal of increasing total asset turnover to 2.75 times, what would the new sales figure need to be, assuming no increase in total assets?

23. **Return on Equity.** Taylor's Cleaning Service has a total debt ratio of .60, total debt of $165,000, and net income of $15,250. What is Taylor's return on equity?

24. **Market Value Ratios.** Lemon Lymon, Inc., has a current stock price of $65. For the past year the company had net income of $7,400,000, total equity of $32,450,000, and 3.6 million shares of stock outstanding. What is the earnings per share (EPS)? Price-earnings ratio? Book value per share? Market-to-book ratio?

25. Profit Margin. Donna's Donuts has total assets of $9,500,000 and a total asset turnover of 2.85 times. If the return on assets is 12 percent, what is Donna's profit margin?

26. Using the Du Pont Identity. Y3K, Inc., has sales of $8,750, total assets of $2,680, and a debt-equity ratio of .75. If its return on equity is 15 percent, what is its net income?

Intermediate
(Questions 26–43)

27. Ratios and Fixed Assets. The Hooya Company has a long-term debt ratio (i.e., the ratio of long-term debt to long-term debt plus equity) of 0.70 and a current ratio of 1.3. Current liabilities are $750, sales are $3,920, profit margin is 9 percent, and ROE is 18.5 percent. What is the amount of the firm's net fixed assets?

28. Profit Margin. In response to complaints about high prices, a grocery chain runs the following advertising campaign: "If you pay your child 50 cents to go buy $25 worth of groceries, then your child makes twice as much on the trip as we do." You've collected the following information from the grocery chain's financial statements:

	(millions)
Sales	$520.0
Net income	5.2
Total assets	110.0
Total debt	71.5

Evaluate the grocery chain's claim. What is the basis for the statement? Is this claim misleading? Why or why not?

29. Using the Du Pont Identity. The Concordia Company has net income of $147,650. There are currently 32.80 days' sales in receivables. Total assets are $980,000, total receivables are $138,600, and the debt-equity ratio is .80. What is Concordia's profit margin? Its total asset turnover? Its ROE?

30. Calculating the Cash Coverage Ratio. Delectable Turnip Inc.'s net income for the most recent year was $8,430. The tax rate was 34 percent. The firm paid $2,180 in total interest expense and deducted $2,683 in depreciation expense. What was Delectable Turnip's cash coverage ratio for the year?

31. Calculating the Times Interest Earned Ratio. For the most recent year, Wanda's Candles, Inc., had sales of $425,000, cost of goods sold of $104,000, depreciation expense of $51,000, and additions to retained earnings of $63,750. The firm currently has 20,000 shares of common stock outstanding, and the previous year's dividends per share were $1.80. Assuming a 34 percent income tax rate, what was the times interest earned ratio?

32. Return on Assets. A fire has destroyed a large percentage of the financial records of the Puffin Company. You have the task of piecing together information in order to release a financial report. You have found the return on equity to be 17 percent. Sales were $1,950,000, the total debt ratio was .60, and total debt was $750,000. What is the return on assets (ROA)?

33. **Ratios and Foreign Companies.**   King Albert Carpet PLC had a 2006 net loss of
    £14,537 on sales of £176,460 (both in thousands of pounds). What was the company's
    profit margin? Does the fact that these figures are quoted in a foreign currency make
    any difference? Why? In dollars, sales were $317,628. What was the net loss in dollars?

    Some recent financial statements for Blue Jay Golf, Inc., follow. Use this
    information to work Problems 34 through 37.

BLUE JAY GOLF, INC.				**BLUE JAY GOLF, INC.**		
Balance Sheets as of December 31, 2006 and 2007						
	2006	2007			2006	2007
Assets				**Liabilities and Owners' Equity**		
Current assets				Current liabilities		
Cash	$ 2,612	$ 2,783		Accounts payable	$ 1,975	$ 2,190
Accounts receivable	3,108	3,780		Notes payable	1,386	1,438
Inventory	9,840	10,970		Other	80	179
Total	$15,560	$17,533		Total	$ 3,441	$ 3,807
Fixed Assets				Long-term debt	12,510	13,840
Net plant and equipment	29,650	41,323		Owners' equity		
				Common stock and paid-in surplus	$25,000	$25,000
				Retained earnings	4,259	16,209
				Total	$29,259	$41,209
Total assets	$45,210	$58,856		Total	$45,210	$58,856

BLUE JAY GOLF, INC.		
2007 Income Statement		
Sales		$87,480
Cost of goods sold		56,820
Depreciation		3,217
Earnings before interest and taxes		$27,443
Interest paid		2,064
Taxable income		$25,379
Taxes (34%)		8,629
Net income		$16,750
Dividends	$ 4,800	
Addition to retained earnings	11,950	

34. **Calculating Financial Ratios.**   Find the following financial ratios for Blue Jay Golf
    (use year-end figures rather than average values where appropriate):

    Short-term solvency ratios

    a. Current ratio   _____

    b. Quick ratio   _____

    c. Cash ratio   _____

Asset utilization ratios

d. Total asset turnover   _____

e. Inventory turnover   _____

f. Receivables turnover   _____

Long-term solvency ratios

g. Total debt ratio   _____

h. Debt-equity ratio   _____

i. Equity multiplier   _____

j. Times interest earned ratio _____

k. Cash coverage ratio   _____

Profitability ratios

l. Profit margin   _____

m. Return on assets   _____

n. Return on equity   _____

35. **Du Pont Identity.**   Construct the Du Pont identity for Blue Jay Golf.

36. **Market Value Ratios.**   Blue Jay Golf has 10,000 shares of common stock outstanding, and the market price for a share of stock at the end of 2007 was $24. What is the price-earnings ratio? What are the dividends per share? What is the market-to-book ratio at the end of 2007?

37. **Interpreting Financial Ratios.**   After calculating the ratios for Blue Jay Golf, you have uncovered the following industry ratios for 2007:

	Lowest Quartile	Median	Highest Quartile
Current ratio	1.2	2.4	4.7
Total asset turnover	1.5	2.6	3.8
Debt-equity ratio	.25	.40	.60
Profit margin	8.4%	11.9%	16.3%

How is Blue Jay Golf performing based on these ratios?

38. **Growth and Profit Margin.**   Mackenzie Manufacturing wishes to maintain a growth rate of 7 percent a year, a debt-equity ratio of .60, and a dividend payout ratio of 35 percent. The ratio of total assets to sales is constant at 1.40. What profit margin must the firm achieve?

39. **Market Value Ratios.**   Nelson and St. Lawrence had the following numbers (in millions) for 2007. Calculate the earnings per share, market-to-book ratio, and price-earnings ratio for each company.

	Nelson	St. Lawrence
Net income	$216.38	$ 63.28
Shares outstanding	92.78	70.63
Stock price	50.12	22.16
Total equity	669.33	926.74

40. **Growth and Assets.**   A firm wishes to maintain an internal growth rate of 5 percent and a dividend payout ratio of 60 percent. The current profit margin is 9 percent and the firm uses no external financing sources. What must total asset turnover be?

41. **Sustainable Growth.**   Based on the following information, calculate the sustainable growth rate for Santana, Inc.:

> Profit margin = 7.5%
> Total asset turnover = 1.25
> Total debt ratio = .40
> Payout ratio = 30%

What is the ROA here?

42. **Sustainable Growth and Outside Financing.**   You've collected the following information about Fox, Inc.:

> Sales = $125,000
> Net income = $8,000
> Dividends = $3,400
> Total debt = $49,000
> Total equity = $33,000

What is the sustainable growth rate for Fox, Inc.? If it does grow at this rate, how much new borrowing will take place in the coming year, assuming a constant debt-equity ratio? What growth rate could be supported with no outside financing at all?

43. **Constraints on Growth.**   Bridal Gear, Inc., wishes to maintain a growth rate of 13 percent per year and a debt-equity ratio of .25. The profit margin is 7 percent, and total asset turnover is constant at 1.10. Is this growth rate possible? To answer, determine what the dividend payout ratio must be. How do you interpret the result?

**Challenge
(Questions 44–46)**

44. **Internal and Sustainable Growth Rates**   Best Buy reported the following numbers (in millions) for the years ending February 2004 and 2005. What are the internal and sustainable growth rates? What are the internal and sustainable growth rates using ROE × b (ROA × b) and the end of period equity (assets)? What are the growth rates if you use the beginning of period equity in this equation? Why aren't the growth rates the same? What is your best estimate of the internal and sustainable growth rates?

	2004	2005
Net income		$984.00
Dividends		99.08
Total assets	$8,652	10,294
Total equity	3,422	4,449

45. **Expanded Du Pont Identity.**   Canadian Tire Corp. reported the following income statement and balance sheet (in millions) for 2005. Construct the expanded Du Pont identity similar to Figure 3.1. What is the company's return on equity?

FINANCIAL STATEMENTS FOR CANADIAN TIRE				
For the year ended December 31, 2005				
(All numbers are in millions)				

Income Statement		Balance Sheet			
Sales	$7,775	Current assets		Current liabilities	
CoGS	6,978	Cash	$ 838	Accounts payable	$1,546
Depreciation	185	Accounts receivable	1,467	Other	275
EBIT	$ 612	Inventory	676		
Interest	92	Total	$2,981	Total	$1,821
EBT	$ 520	Fixed assets	$2,975	Total long-term debt	$1,624
Taxes	190			Total equity	$2,511
Net income	$ 330	Total assets	$5,956	Total liabilities and equity	$5,956

46. Financial Ratios. The McMaster Corporation has depreciation expenses of $300,000, fixed assets of $2,500,000, and equity of $5,400,000. Given the following ratios, fill in the missing entries.

Current ratio	3.2
Quick ratio	1.4
Cash ratio	1.2
Times interest earned ratio	6
Inventory turnover	1.92
Days' sales in receivables	20 days
Total asset turnover	1
Profit margin	0.08
Return on equity (ROE)	0.15

Income Statement		Balance Sheet			
Sales	$ ____	Current assets		Current liabilities	$ ____
CoGS	____	Cash	$ ____		
Depreciation	300,000	Accounts receivable	____		
EBIT	$ ____	Inventory	____		
Interest	____	Total	$ ____	Total	$ ____
EBT	$ ____	Fixed assets	$2,500,000	Total long-term debt	____
Taxes	____			Total equity	$5,400,000
Net income	$ ____	Total assets	$ ____	Total liabilities and equity	$ ____

WHAT'S ON THE WEB?

3.1 **Standardized Financial Statements.** Go to the "Investor Centre" link for Suncor Energy located at **www.suncor.ca**, and follow the "Financial Reports" link. You should find the annual reports with consolidated income statements and balance sheets at this link. Using this information, prepare the common-size income statements and balance sheets for the two most recent years.

3.2   **Ratio Analysis.**   You want to examine the financial ratios for TransCanada Corporation. Go to **today.reuters.com** and type in the ticker symbol for the company (TRP). Next, go to the "Ratios" link. You should find financial ratios for TransCanada and the industry, sector, and S&P 500 averages for each ratio.

   a.   What do TTM and MRQ mean?

   b.   How do TransCanada's recent profitability ratios compare to their values over the past five years? To the industry averages? To the sector averages? To the S&P 500 averages? Which is the better comparison group for TransCanada: the industry, sector, or S&P 500 averages? Why?

   c.   In what areas does TransCanada seem to outperform its competitors based on the financial ratios? Where does TransCanada seem to lag behind its competitors?

3.3   **Asset Utilization Ratios.**   Find the most recent financial statements for two companies headquartered in Quebec: Hart Stores, general merchandise retailer, at **www.hartstores.com** and Bombardier, aircraft and train manufacturer, at **www.bombardier.com**. Calculate the asset utilization ratio for these two companies. What does this ratio measure? Is the ratio similar for both companies? Why or why not?

3.4   **Du Pont Identity.**   You can find financial reports for Shaw Communications Inc. on the "Investor Relations" link at Shaw Communications' home page, **www.shaw.ca**. For the three most recent years, calculate the Du Pont identity for Shaw Communications. How has ROE changed over this period? How have changes in each component of the Du Pont identity affected ROE over this period?

MINI-CASE

RATIOS AND FINANCIAL PLANNING AT CANADIAN AIR, INC.

Chris Guthrie was recently hired by Canadian Air, Inc., to assist the company with its financial planning, and to evaluate the company's performance. Chris graduated from college five years ago with a finance degree. He has been employed in the finance department of a FP500 company since then.

Canadian Air was founded 10 years ago by friends Mark Sexton and Todd Story. The company has manufactured and sold light airplanes over this period, and the company's products have received high reviews for safety and reliability. The company has a niche market in that it sells primarily to individuals who own and fly their own airplanes. The company has two models, the Birdie, which sells for $53,000, and the Eagle, which sells for $78,000.

While the company manufactures aircraft, its operations are different from commercial aircraft companies. Canadian Air builds aircraft to order. By using prefabricated parts, the company is able to complete the manufacture of an airplane in only five weeks. The company also receives a deposit on each order, as well as another partial payment before the order is complete. In contrast, a commercial airplane may take one-and-one-half to two years to manufacture once the order is placed.

Mark and Todd have provided the following financial statements. Chris has gathered the industry ratios for the light airplane manufacturing industry.

Canadian Air, Inc.
2007 Income Statement

Sales	$12,870,000
Cost of goods sold	9,070,000
Other expenses	1,538,000
Depreciation	420,000
EBIT	$ 1,842,000
Interest	231,500
Taxable income	$ 1,610,500
Taxes (40%)	644,200
Net income	$ 966,300

Dividends	$289,890	
Add. to retained earnings	676,410	

Canadian Air, Inc.
2007 Balance Sheet

Assets		Liabilities & Equity	
Current assets		Current liabilities	
Cash	$ 234,000	Accounts payable	$ 497,000
Accounts receivable	421,000	Notes payable	1,006,000
Inventory	472,000	Total current liabilities	$1,503,000
Total current assets	$1,127,000		
Fixed assets		Long-term debt	$2,595,000
Net plant and equipment	$7,228,000	Shareholder equity	
		Common stock	$ 100,000
		Retained earnings	4,157,000
		Total equity	$4,257,000
Total assets	$8,355,000	Total liabilities & equity	$8,355,000

Light Airplane Industry Ratios			
	Lower Quartile	Median	Upper Quartile
Current ratio	0.50	1.43	1.89
Quick ratio	0.21	0.38	0.62
Cash ratio	0.08	0.21	0.39
Total asset turnover	0.68	0.85	1.38
Inventory turnover	4.89	6.15	10.89
Receivables turnover	6.27	9.82	14.11
Total debt ratio	0.44	0.52	0.61
Debt-equity ratio	0.79	1.08	1.56
Equity multiplier	1.79	2.08	2.56
Times interest earned	5.18	8.06	9.83
Cash coverage ratio	5.84	8.43	10.27
Profit margin	4.05%	6.98%	9.87%
Return on assets	6.05%	10.53%	13.21%
Return on equity	9.93%	16.54%	26.15%

QUESTIONS

1. Calculate the following ratios for Canadian Air: current ratio, quick ratio, cash ratio, total asset turnover, inventory turnover, receivables turnover, total debt ratio, debt-equity ratio, equity multiplier, times interest earned, cash coverage ratio, profit margin, return on assets, and return on equity.

2. Mark and Todd agree that a ratio analysis can provide a measure of the company's performance. They have chosen Boeing as an aspirant company. Would you choose Boeing as an aspirant company? Why or why not?

3. Compare the performance of Canadian Air to the industry. For each ratio, comment on why it might be viewed as positive or negative relative to the industry. Suppose you create an inventory ratio calculated by inventory divided by current liabilities. How do you think Canadian Air's ratio would compare to the industry average?

4. Calculate the internal growth rate and sustainable growth rate for Canadian Air. What do these numbers mean?

4

Introduction to Valuation: The Time Value of Money

On December 1, 2006, TD Waterhouse, Canada's largest discount broker and a subsidiary of the Toronto-Dominion Bank, was offering some Province of Quebec securities from its inventories for sale to the public. Each security represented the promise to repay the owner of one of these securities $1,000 on December 1, 2036, but investors would receive nothing until then. Investors were asked to pay $274.17 for each of these securities, so they would give up $274.17 on December 1, 2006, for the promise of a $1,000 payment 30 years later. Such a security, for which you pay some amount today in exchange for a promised lump sum to be received at a future date, is about the simplest possible type.

Is giving up $274.17 in exchange for $1,000 in 30 years a good deal? On the plus side, you get back $3.65 for every $1 you put up. That probably sounds good, but, on the downside, you have to wait 30 years to get it. What you need to know is how to analyze this trade-off; this chapter gives you the tools you need.

Specifically, our goal here is to introduce you to one of the most important principles in finance, the time value of money. What you will learn is how to determine the value today of some cash flow to be received later. This is a very basic business skill, and it underlies the analysis of many different types of investments and financing arrangements. In fact, almost all business activities, whether they originate in marketing, management, operations, or strategy, involve comparing outlays made today to benefits projected for the future. How to do this comparison is something everyone needs to understand; this chapter gets you started.

There are three essential things you should learn from this chapter:

4.1 How to determine the future value of an investment made today.

4.2 How to determine the present value of cash to be received at a future date.

4.3 How to find the return on an investment and the number of periods an investment needs to grow to a given amount.

One of the basic problems faced by the financial manager is how to determine the value today of cash flows expected in the future. For example, the jackpot in a PowerBall™ lottery drawing was $110 million. Does this mean the winning ticket was worth $110 million? The answer is no because the jackpot was actually going to pay out over a 20-year period at a rate of $5.5 million per year. How much was the ticket worth then? The answer depends on the time value of money, the subject of this chapter.

In the most general sense, the phrase *time value of money* refers to the fact that a dollar in hand today is worth more than a dollar promised at some time in the future. On a practical level, one reason for this is that you could earn interest while you waited; so, a dollar today would grow to more than a dollar later. The trade-off between money now and money later thus depends on, among other things, the rate you can earn by investing. Our goal in this chapter is to explicitly evaluate this trade-off between dollars today and dollars at some future time.

A thorough understanding of the material in this chapter is critical to understanding material in subsequent chapters, so you should study it with particular care. We will present a number of examples in this chapter. In many problems, your answer may differ from ours slightly. This can happen because of rounding and is not a cause for concern.

4.1 | FUTURE VALUE AND COMPOUNDING

future value (FV)
The amount an investment is worth after one or more periods.

The first thing we will study is future value. **Future value (FV)** refers to the amount of money an investment will grow to over some period of time at some given interest rate. Put another way, future value is the cash value of an investment at some time in the future. We start out by considering the simplest case, a single-period investment.

Investing for a Single Period

Suppose you were to invest $100 in a savings account that pays 10 percent interest per year. How much would you have in one year? You would have $110. This $110 is equal to your original *principal* of $100 plus $10 in interest that you earn. We say that $110 is the future value of $100 invested for one year at 10 percent, and we simply mean that $100 today is worth $110 in one year, given that 10 percent is the interest rate.

In general, if you invest for one period at an interest rate of r, your investment will grow to $(1 + r)$ per dollar invested. In our example, r is 10 percent, so your investment grows to $1 + .10 = 1.1$ dollars per dollar invested. You invested $100 in this case, so you ended up with $100 \times 1.10 = $110.

Investing for More Than One Period

Going back to our $100 investment, what will you have after two years, assuming the interest rate doesn't change? If you leave the entire $110 in the bank, you will earn $110 \times .10 = $11 in interest during the second year, so you will have a total of $110 + 11 = $121. This $121 is the future value of $100 in two years at 10 percent. Another way of looking at it is that one year from now you are effectively investing $110 at 10 percent for a year. This is a single-period problem, so you'll end up with $1.1 for every dollar invested, or $110 \times 1.1 = $121 total.

This $121 has four parts. The first part is the $100 original principal. The second part is the $10 in interest you earn in the first year, and the third part is another $10 you earn in the second year, for a total of $120. The last $1 you end up with (the fourth part) is interest you earn in the second year on the interest paid in the first year: $10 \times .10 = $1.

This process of leaving your money and any accumulated interest in an investment for more than one period, thereby reinvesting the interest, is called **compounding.** Compounding the interest means earning **interest on interest,** so we call the result **compound interest.** With **simple interest,** the interest is not reinvested, so interest is earned each period only on the original principal.

Interest on Interest   **EXAMPLE** **4.1**

Suppose you locate a two-year investment that pays 14 percent per year. If you invest $325, how much will you have at the end of the two years? How much of this is simple interest? How much is compound interest?

At the end of the first year, you will have $325 × (1 + .14) = $370.50. If you reinvest this entire amount, and thereby compound the interest, you will have $370.50 × 1.14 = $422.37 at the end of the second year. The total interest you earn is thus $422.37 − 325 = $97.37. Your $325 original principal earns $325 × .14 = $45.50 in interest each year, for a two-year total of $91 in simple interest. The remaining $97.37 − 91 = $6.37 results from compounding. You can check this by noting that the interest earned in the first year is $45.50. The interest on interest earned in the second year thus amounts to $45.50 × .14 = $6.37, as we calculated.

We now take a closer look at how we calculated the $121 future value. We multiplied $110 by 1.1 to get $121. The $110, however, was $100 also multiplied by 1.1. In other words:

$$\begin{aligned} \$121 &= \$110 \times 1.1 \\ &= (\$100 \times 1.1) \times 1.1 \\ &= \$100 \times (1.1 \times 1.1) \\ &= \$100 \times 1.1^2 \\ &= \$100 \times 1.21 \end{aligned}$$

At the risk of belabouring the obvious, let's ask: How much would our $100 grow to after three years? Once again, in two years, we'll be investing $121 for one period at 10 percent. We'll end up with $1.1 for every dollar we invest, or $121 × 1.1 = $133.1 total. This $133.1 is thus:

$$\begin{aligned} \$133.1 &= \$121 \times 1.1 \\ &= (\$110 \times 1.1) \times 1.1 \\ &= (\$100 \times 1.1) \times 1.1 \times 1.1 \\ &= \$100 \times (1.1 \times 1.1 \times 1.1) \\ &= \$100 \times 1.1^3 \\ &= \$100 \times 1.331 \end{aligned}$$

You're probably noticing a pattern to these calculations, so we can now go ahead and state the general result. As our examples suggest, the future value of $1 invested for t periods at a rate of r per period is:

$$\text{Future value} = \$1 \times (1 + r)^t \qquad \textbf{[4.1]}$$

The expression $(1 + r)^t$ is sometimes called the *future value interest factor* (or just *future value factor*) for $1 invested at r percent for t periods and can be abbreviated as FVIF(r,t).

In our example, what would your $100 be worth after five years? We can first compute the relevant future value factor as:

$$(1 + r)^t = (1 + .10)^5 = 1.1^5 = 1.6105$$

compounding
The process of accumulating interest in an investment over time to earn more interest.

interest on interest
Interest earned on the reinvestment of previous interest payments.

compound interest
Interest earned on both the initial principal and the interest reinvested from prior periods.

simple interest
Interest earned only on the original principal amount invested.

Year	Beginning Amount	Interest Earned	Ending Amount
1	$100.00	$10.00	$110.00
2	110.00	11.00	121.00
3	121.00	12.10	133.10
4	133.10	13.31	146.41
5	146.41	14.64	161.05
		Total interest $61.05	

Your $100 will thus grow to:

$$\$100 \times 1.6105 = \$161.05$$

The growth of your $100 each year is illustrated in Table 4.1. As shown, the interest earned in each year is equal to the beginning amount multiplied by the interest rate of 10 percent.

In Table 4.1, notice that the total interest you earn is $61.05. Over the five-year span of this investment, the simple interest is $100 × .10 = $10 per year, so you accumulate $50 this way. The other $11.05 is from compounding.

A brief introduction to key financial concepts is available at **www.teachmefinance .com.**

Figure 4.1 illustrates the growth of the compound interest in Table 4.1. Notice how the simple interest is constant each year, but the compound interest you earn gets bigger every year. The size of the compound interest keeps increasing because more and more interest builds up and there is thus more to compound.

Future values depend critically on the assumed interest rate, particularly for long-lived investments. Figure 4.2 illustrates this relationship by plotting the growth of $1 for different rates and lengths of time. Notice that the future value of $1 after 10 years is about

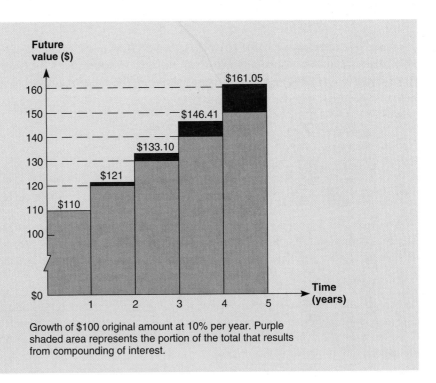

FIGURE 4.1

Future value, simple interest, and compound interest

Growth of $100 original amount at 10% per year. Purple shaded area represents the portion of the total that results from compounding of interest.

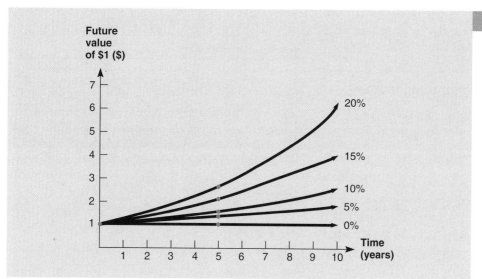

FIGURE 4.2

Future value of $1 for different periods and rates

$6.20 at a 20 percent rate, but it is only about $2.60 at 10 percent. In this case, doubling the interest rate more than doubles the future value.

To solve future value problems, we need to come up with the relevant future value factors. There are several different ways of doing this. In our example, we could have multiplied 1.1 by itself five times. This would work just fine, but it would get to be very tedious for, say, a 30-year investment.

Fortunately, there are several easier ways to get future value factors. Most calculators have a key labeled "y^x." You can usually just enter 1.1, press this key, enter 5, and press the "=" key to get the answer. This is an easy way to calculate future value factors because it's quick and accurate.

Alternatively, you can use a table that contains future value factors for some common interest rates and time periods. Table 4.2 contains some of these factors. Table A.1 in Appendix A at the end of the book contains a much larger set. To use the table, find the column that corresponds to 10 percent. Then look down the rows until you come to five periods. You should find the factor that we calculated, 1.6105.

Tables such as Table 4.2 are not as common as they once were because they predate inexpensive calculators and are only available for a relatively small number of rates. Interest rates are often quoted to three or four decimal places, so the tables needed to deal with these accurately would be quite large. As a result, the "real world" has moved away from using them. We will emphasize the use of a calculator in this chapter.

Number of	Interest Rates			
Periods	5%	10%	15%	20%
1	1.0500	1.1000	1.1500	1.2000
2	1.1025	1.2100	1.3225	1.4400
3	1.1576	1.3310	1.5209	1.7280
4	1.2155	1.4641	1.7490	2.0736
5	1.2763	1.6105	2.0114	2.4883

TABLE 4.2

Future value interest factors

These tables still serve a useful purpose. To make sure you are doing the calculations correctly, pick a factor from the table and then calculate it yourself to see that you get the same answer. There are plenty of numbers to choose from.

EXAMPLE 4.2   **Compound Interest**

You've located an investment that pays 12 percent. That rate sounds good to you, so you invest $400. How much will you have in three years? How much will you have in seven years? At the end of seven years, how much interest have you earned? How much of that interest results from compounding?

Based on our discussion, we can calculate the future value factor for 12 percent and three years as:

$$(1 + r)^t = 1.12^3 = 1.4049$$

Your $400 thus grows to:

$$\$400 \times 1.4049 = \$561.97$$

After seven years, you will have:

$$\$400 \times 1.12^7 = \$400 \times 2.2107 = \$884.27$$

Thus, you will more than double your money over seven years.

You invested $400, so the interest in the $884.27 future value is $884.27 − 400 = $484.27. At 12 percent, your $400 investment earns $400 × .12 = $48 in simple interest every year. Over seven years, the simple interest thus totals 7 × $48 = $336. The other $484.27 − 336 = $148.27 is from compounding.

Explore how compounding can affect your savings by using a compound interest calculator at www.citizensbank.ca.

The effect of compounding is not great over short time periods, but it really starts to add up as the horizon grows. To take an extreme case, suppose one of your more frugal ancestors had invested $5 for you at a 6 percent interest rate 200 years ago. How much would you have today? The future value factor is a substantial $1.06^{200} = 115,125.90$ (you won't find this one in a table), so you would have $5 × 115,125.90 = $575,629.50 today. Notice that the simple interest is just $5 × .06 = $.30 per year. After 200 years, this amounts to $60. The rest is from reinvesting. Such is the power of compound interest!

EXAMPLE 4.3   **How Much for Toronto?**

To further illustrate the effect of compounding for long horizons, consider the case of the "Toronto purchase." On September 23, 1787, Sir John Johnson, on behalf of His Majesty, purchased the lands north of Lake Ontario from the Mississauga Nation. The Crown paid 1,700 British pounds in goods, which is about 200,000 in present Canadian dollars. This sounds cheap, as an average house in Toronto costs more now. However, the First Nations people may have gotten the better end of the deal. To see why, suppose the Mississaugas had sold the goods and invested the $200,000 at 10 percent. How much would it be worth today?

Roughly 220 years have passed since the transaction. At 10 percent, $200,000 will grow by quite a bit over that time. How much? The future value factor is approximately:

$$(1 + r)^t = 1.1^{220} \approx 1,300,000,000$$

The future value is thus on the order of $200,000 × 1,300,000,000 = $0.26 × 10^{15}$, or about 0.26 quadrillion.

Well, $0.26 quadrillion is a lot of money. How much? If you had it, you could buy Ontario. All of it. Cash. With money left over to buy Quebec, British Columbia, and the rest of Canada, for that matter.

This example is something of an exaggeration, of course. In 1787, it would not have been easy to locate an investment that would pay 10 percent every year without fail for the next 220 years.

Calculator Hints   Using a Financial Calculator

Although there are the various ways of calculating future values we have described so far, many of you will decide that a financial calculator is the way to go. If you are planning on using one, you should read this extended hint; otherwise, skip it.

A financial calculator is simply an ordinary calculator with a few extra features. In particular, it knows some of the most commonly used financial formulas, so it can directly compute things like future values.

Financial calculators have the advantage that they handle a lot of the computation, but that is really all. In other words, you still have to understand the problem; the calculator just does some of the arithmetic. In fact, there is an old joke (somewhat modified) that goes like this: Anyone can make a mistake on a time value of money problem, but to really mess one up takes a financial calculator! We therefore have two goals for this section. First, we'll discuss how to compute future values. After that, we'll show you how to avoid the most common mistakes people make when they start using financial calculators.

How to Calculate Future Values with a Financial Calculator   Examining a typical financial calculator, you will find five keys of particular interest. They usually look like this:

For now, we need to focus on four of these. The keys labelled **PV** and **FV** are just what you would guess: present value and future value. The key labelled **N** refers to the *n*umber of periods, which is what we have been calling *t*. Finally, **I/Y** stands for the interest rate, which we have called *r*.*

If we have the financial calculator set up right (see our next section), then calculating a future value is very simple. Take a look back at our question involving the future value of $100 at 10 percent for five years. We have seen that the answer is $161.05. The exact keystrokes will differ depending on what type of calculator you use, but here is basically all you do:

1.   Enter −100. Press the **PV** key. (The negative sign is explained below.)
2.   Enter 10. Press the **I/Y** key. (Notice that we entered 10, not .10; see below.)
3.   Enter 5. Press the **N** key.

Now we have entered all of the relevant information. To solve for the future value, we need to ask the calculator what the FV is. Depending on your calculator, you either press the button labelled "CPT" (for compute) and then press **FV** , or else you just press **FV** . Either way, you should get 161.05. If you don't (and you probably won't if this is the first time you have used a financial calculator!), we will offer some help in our next section.

Before we explain the kinds of problems that you are likely to run into, we want to establish a standard format for showing you how to use a financial calculator. Using the example we just looked at, in the future we will illustrate such problems like this:

Enter   5   10   −100

N	I/Y	PMT	PV	FV

Solve for   161.05

---

*The reason financial calculators use N and I/Y is that the most common use for these calculators is determining loan payments. In this context, N is the number of payments and I/Y is the interest rate on the loan. But, as we will see, there are many other uses of financial calculators that don't involve loan payments and interest rates.

Here is an important tip: Appendix D in the back of the book contains some more detailed instructions for the most common types of financial calculators. See if yours is included, and, if it is, follow the instructions there if you need help. Of course, if all else fails, you can read the manual that came with the calculator.

How to Get the Wrong Answer Using a Financial Calculator   There are a couple of common (and frustrating) problems that cause a lot of trouble with financial calculators. In this section, we provide some important *dos* and *don'ts*. If you just can't seem to get a problem to work out, you should refer back to this section.

There are two categories we examine: three things you need to do only once and three things you need to do every time you work a problem. The things you need to do just once deal with the following calculator settings:

1. *Make sure your calculator is set to display a large number of decimal places.* Most financial calculators only display two decimal places; this causes problems because we frequently work with numbers—like interest rates—that are very small.

2. *Make sure your calculator is set to assume only one payment per period or per year.* Some financial calculators assume monthly payments (12 per year) unless you say otherwise.

3. *Make sure your calculator is in "end" mode.* This is usually the default, but you can accidentally change to "begin" mode.

If you don't know how to set these three things, see Appendix D or your calculator's operating manual.

There are also three things you need to do *every time you work a problem:*

1. *Before you start, completely clear out the calculator.* This is very important. Failure to do this is the number one reason for wrong answers; you simply must get in the habit of clearing the calculator every time you start a problem. How you do this depends on the calculator (see Appendix D), but you must do more than just clear the display. For example, on a Texas Instruments BA II Plus you must press **2nd** then **CLR TVM** for *clear time value of money.* There is a similar command on your calculator. Learn it!

   Note that turning the calculator off and back on won't do it. Most financial calculators remember everything you enter, even after you turn them off. In other words, they remember all your mistakes unless you explicitly clear them out. Also, if you are in the middle of a problem and make a mistake, *clear it out and start over.* Better to be safe than sorry.

2. *Put a negative sign on cash outflows.* Most financial calculators require you to put a negative sign on cash outflows and a positive sign on cash inflows. As a practical matter, this usually just means that you should enter the present value amount with a negative sign (because normally the present value represents the amount you give up today in exchange for cash inflows later). You enter a negative value on the BA II Plus by first entering a number and then pressing the **+/−** key. By the same token, when you solve for a present value, you shouldn't be surprised to see a negative sign.

3. *Enter the rate correctly.* Financial calculators assume that rates are quoted in percent, so if the rate is .08 (or 8 percent), you should enter 8, not .08.

If you follow these guidelines (especially the one about clearing out the calculator), you should have no problem using a financial calculator to work almost all of the problems in this and the next few chapters. We'll provide some additional examples and guidance where appropriate.

CONCEPT QUESTIONS

4.1a   What do we mean by the future value of an investment?

4.1b   What does it mean to compound interest? How does compound interest differ from simple interest?

4.1c   In general, what is the future value of $1 invested at r per period for t periods?

4.2 | PRESENT VALUE AND DISCOUNTING

When we discuss future value, we are thinking of questions such as the following: What will my $2,000 investment grow to if it earns a 6.5 percent return every year for the next six years? The answer to this question is what we call the future value of $2,000 invested at 6.5 percent for six years (verify that the answer is about $2,918).

There is another type of question that comes up even more often in financial management that is obviously related to future value. Suppose you need to have $10,000 in 10 years, and you can earn 6.5 percent on your money. How much do you have to invest today to reach your goal? You can verify that the answer is $5,327.26. How do we know this? Read on.

The Single-Period Case

We've seen that the future value of $1 invested for one year at 10 percent is $1.10. We now ask a slightly different question: How much do we have to invest today at 10 percent to get $1 in one year? In other words, we know the future value here is $1, but what is the **present value (PV)?** The answer isn't too hard to figure out. Whatever we invest today will be 1.1 times bigger at the end of the year. Since we need $1 at the end of the year:

present value (PV)
The current value of future cash flows discounted at the appropriate discount rate.

   Present value $\times$ 1.1 = $1

Or, solving for the present value:

   Present value = $1/1.1 = $.909

In this case, the present value is the answer to the following question: What amount, invested today, will grow to $1 in one year if the interest rate is 10 percent? Present value is thus just the reverse of future value. Instead of compounding the money forward into the future, we **discount** it back to the present.

discount
Calculate the present value of some future amount.

Single-Period PV   EXAMPLE 4.4

Suppose you need $400 to buy textbooks next year. You can earn 7 percent on your money. How much do you have to put up today?

   We need to know the PV of $400 in one year at 7 percent. Proceeding as above:

   Preset value $\times$ 1.07 = $400

We can now solve for the present value:

   Present value = $400 $\times$ (1/1.07) = $373.83

Thus, $373.83 is the present value. Again, this just means that investing this amount for one year at 7 percent will result in your having a future value of $400.

From our examples, the present value of $1 to be received in one period is generally given as:

$$PV = \$1 \times [1/(1 + r)] = \$1/(1 + r)$$

We next examine how to get the present value of an amount to be paid in two or more periods into the future.

Present Values for Multiple Periods

Suppose you need to have $1,000 in two years. If you can earn 7 percent, how much do you have to invest to make sure that you have the $1,000 when you need it? In other words, what is the present value of $1,000 in two years if the relevant rate is 7 percent?

Based on your knowledge of future values, you know that the amount invested must grow to $1,000 over the two years. In other words, it must be the case that:

$$\begin{aligned}\$1,000 &= PV \times 1.07 \times 1.07 \\ &= PV \times 1.07^2 \\ &= PV \times 1.1449\end{aligned}$$

Given this, we can solve for the present value:

$$\text{Present value} = \$1,000/1.1449 = \$873.44$$

Therefore, $873.44 is the amount you must invest in order to achieve your goal.

EXAMPLE 4.5 **Saving Up**

You would like to buy a new automobile. You have $50,000, but the car costs $68,500. If you can earn 9 percent, how much do you have to invest today to buy the car in two years? Do you have enough? Assume the price will stay the same.

What we need to know is the present value of $68,500 to be paid in two years, assuming a 9 percent rate. Based on our discussion, this is:

$$PV = \$68,500/1.09^2 = \$68,500/1.1881 = \$57,655.08$$

You're still about $7,655 short, even if you're willing to wait two years.

As you have probably recognized by now, calculating present values is quite similar to calculating future values, and the general result looks much the same. The present value of $1 to be received t periods into the future at a discount rate of r is:

$$PV = \$1 \times [1/(1 + r)^t] = \$1/(1 + r)^t \qquad [4.2]$$

discount rate
The rate used to calculate the present value of future cash flows.

The quantity in brackets, $1/(1 + r)^t$, goes by several different names. Since it's used to discount a future cash flow, it is often called a *discount factor*. With this name, it is not surprising that the rate used in the calculation is often called the **discount rate.** We will tend to call it this in talking about present values. The quantity in brackets is also called

Number of Periods	Interest Rates			
	5%	**10%**	**15%**	**20%**
1	.9524	.9091	.8696	.8333
2	.9070	.8264	.7561	.6944
3	.8638	.7513	.6575	.5787
4	.8227	.6830	.5718	.4823
5	.7835	.6209	.4972	.4019

TABLE 4.3

Present value interest factors

the *present value interest factor* (or just *present value factor*) for $1 at *r* percent for *t* periods and is sometimes abbreviated as PVIF(*r, t*). Finally, calculating the present value of a future cash flow to determine its worth today is commonly called **discounted cash flow (DCF) valuation.**

discounted cash flow (DCF) valuation
Valuation calculating the present value of a future cash flow to determine its value today.

To illustrate, suppose you need $1,000 in three years. You can earn 15 percent on your money. How much do you have to invest today? To find out, we have to determine the present value of $1,000 in three years at 15 percent. We do this by discounting $1,000 back three periods at 15 percent. With these numbers, the discount factor is:

$$1/(1 + .15)^3 = 1/1.5209 = .6575$$

The amount you must invest is thus:

$$\$1,000 \times .6575 = \$657.50$$

We say that $657.50 is the present, or discounted, value of $1,000 to be received in three years at 15 percent.

There are tables for present value factors just as there are tables for future value factors, and you use them in the same way (if you use them at all). Table 4.3 contains a small set of these factors. A much larger set can be found in Table A.2 in Appendix A.

In Table 4.3, the discount factor we just calculated, .6575, can be found by looking down the column labelled "15%" until you come to the third row. Of course, you could use a financial calculator, as we illustrate next.

Calculator Hints

You solve present value problems on a financial calculator just like you do future value problems. For the example we just examined (the present value of $1,000 to be received in three years at 15 percent), you would do the following:

Enter

3	15			1,000
N	I/Y	PMT	PV	FV

Solve for −657.50

Notice that the answer has a negative sign; as we discussed above, that's because it represents an outflow today in exchange for the $1,000 inflow later.

EXAMPLE 4.6   ## Deceptive Advertising

To attract customers, sometimes misleading advertising is used. For example, some businesses have been saying things like "Come try our product. If you do, we'll give you $100 just for coming by!" If you read the fine print, what you find out is that they will give you a savings certificate that will pay you $100 in 25 years or so. If the going interest rate on such certificates is 10 percent per year, how much are they really giving you today?

What you're actually getting is the present value of $100 to be paid in 25 years. If the discount rate is 10 percent per year, then the discount factor is:

$1/1.1^{25} = 1/10.8347 = .0923$

This tells you that a dollar in 25 years is worth a little more than nine cents today, assuming a 10 percent discount rate. Given this, the promotion is actually paying you about .0923 × $100 = $9.23. Maybe this is enough to draw customers, but it's not $100.

As the length of time until payment grows, present values decline. As Example 4.6 illustrates, present values tend to become small as the time horizon grows. If you look out far enough, they will always get close to zero. Also, for a given length of time, the higher the discount rate is, the lower is the present value. Put another way, present values and discount rates are inversely related. Increasing the discount rate decreases the PV and vice versa.

The relationship between time, discount rates, and present values is illustrated in Figure 4.3. Notice that by the time we get to 10 years, the present values are all substantially smaller than the future amounts.

CONCEPT QUESTIONS

4.2a   What do we mean by the present value of an investment?

4.2b   The process of discounting a future amount back to the present is the opposite of doing what?

4.2c   What do we mean by discounted cash flow, or DCF, valuation?

4.2d   In general, what is the present value of $1 to be received in t periods, assuming a discount rate of r per period?

FIGURE 4.3

Present value of $1 for different periods and rates.

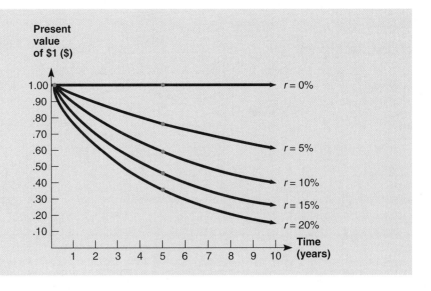

4.3 | MORE ON PRESENT AND FUTURE VALUES

If you look back at the expressions we came up with for present and future values, you will see there is a very simple relationship between the two. We explore this relationship and some related issues in this section.

Present versus Future Value

What we called the present value factor is just the reciprocal of (that is, 1 divided by) the future value factor:

Future value factor $= (1 + r)^t$

Present value factor $= 1 / (1 + r)^t$

For a downloadable, Windows-based financial calculator, go to **www.calculator.org**.

In fact, the easy way to calculate a present value factor on many calculators is to first calculate the future value factor and then press the **1/x** key to flip it over.

If we let FV_t stand for the future value after t periods, then the relationship between future value and present value can be written very simply as one of the following:

$$PV \times (1 + r)^t = FV_t$$
$$PV = FV_t/(1 + r)^t = FV_t \times [1/(1 + r)^t] \qquad \text{[4.3]}$$

This last result we will call the *basic present value equation.* We will use it throughout the text. There are a number of variations that come up, but this simple equation underlies many of the most important ideas in finance.

Evaluating Investments   **EXAMPLE 4.7**

To give you an idea of how we will be using present and future values, consider the following simple investment. Your company proposes to buy an asset for $335. This investment is very safe. You will sell off the asset in three years for $400. You know you could invest the $335 elsewhere at 10 percent with very little risk. What do you think of the proposed investment?

This is not a good investment. Why not? Because you can invest the $335 elsewhere at 10 percent. If you do, after three years it will grow to:

$$\$335 \times (1 + r)^t = \$335 \times 1.1^3$$
$$= \$335 \times 1.331$$
$$= \$445.89$$

Since the proposed investment only pays out $400, it is not as good as other alternatives we have. Another way of saying the same thing is to notice that the present value of $400 in three years at 10 percent is:

$$\$400 \times [1/(1 + r)^t] = \$400/1.1^3 = \$400/1.331 = \$300.53$$

This tells us that we only have to invest about $300 to get $400 in three years, not $335. We will return to this type of analysis later on.

Determining the Discount Rate

It will turn out that we will frequently need to determine what discount rate is implicit in an investment. We can do this by looking at the basic present value equation:

$$PV = FV_t/(1 + r)^t$$

There are only four parts to this equation: the present value (PV), the future value (FV$_t$), the discount rate (r), and the life of the investment (t). Given any three of these, we can always find the fourth.

EXAMPLE 4.8   **Finding *r* for a Single-Period Investment**

You are considering a one-year investment. If you put up $1,250, you will get back $1,350. What rate is this investment paying?

First, in this single-period case, the answer is fairly obvious. You are getting a total of $100 in addition to your $1,250. The implicit rate on this investment is thus $100/1,250 = 8 percent.

More formally, from the basic present value equation, the present value (the amount you must put up today) is $1,250. The future value (what the present value grows to) is $1,350. The time involved is one period, so we have:

$$\$1,250 = \$1,350/(1 + r)^t$$
$$1 + r = \$1,350/1,250 = 1.08$$
$$r = 8\%$$

In this simple case, of course, there was no need to go through this calculation, but, as we describe below, it gets a little harder when there is more than one period.

To illustrate what happens with multiple periods, let's say that we are offered an investment that costs us $100 and will double our money in eight years. To compare this to other investments, we would like to know what discount rate is implicit in these numbers. This discount rate is called the *rate of return,* or sometimes just *return,* on the investment. In this case, we have a present value of $100, a future value of $200 (double our money), and an eight-year life. To calculate the return, we can write the basic present value equation as:

$$PV = FV_t/(1 + r)^t$$
$$\$100 = \$200/(1 + r)^8$$

It could also be written as:

$$(1 + r)^8 = \$200/100 = 2$$

We now need to solve for r. There are three ways we could do it:

1. Use a financial calculator. (See below.)
2. Solve the equation for $1 + r$ by taking the eighth root of both sides. Since this is the same thing as raising both sides to the power of $^1/_8$, or .125, this is actually easy to do with the **y^x** key on a calculator. Just enter 2, then press **y^x** , enter .125, and press the **=** key. The eighth root should be about 1.09, which implies that r is 9 percent.
3. Use a future value table. The future value factor for eight years is equal to 2. If you look across the row corresponding to eight periods in Table A.1, you will see that a future value factor of 2 corresponds to the 9 percent column, again implying that the return here is 9 percent.

Actually, in this particular example, there is a useful "back of the envelope" means of solving for r—the Rule of 72. For reasonable rates of return, the time it takes to double your money is given approximately by $72/r\%$. In our example, this means that $72/r\% = 8$ years, implying that r is 9 percent, as we calculated. This rule is fairly accurate for discount rates in the 5 percent to 20 percent range.

The *Reality Bytes* box on the next page provides some examples of rates of return on collectibles. See if you can verify the numbers reported there.

Why does the Rule of 72 work? See www.moneychimp .com.

REALITY BYTES

How Much is a 10-Cent Canadian Coin Worth?

It used to be that trading in collectibles such as baseball cards, art, and old toys occurred mostly at auctions, swap meets, and collectible shops, all of which were limited to regional traffic. However, with the growing popularity of online auctions such as eBay, trading in collectibles has expanded to an international arena. The most visible form of collectible is probably the baseball card, but Furbies, Beanie Babies, and Pokémon cards have been extremely hot collectibles in the recent past. However, it's not just fad items that spark interest from collectors; virtually anything of sentimental value from days gone by is considered collectible, and, more and more, collectibles are being viewed as investments.

Collectibles typically provide no cash flows, except when sold, and condition and buyer sentiment are the major determinants of value. The rates of return have been amazing at times, but care is needed in interpreting them. For example, in August 2006, a 10-cent Canadian coin, minted from silver in 1875, was offered for sale on eBay. How much was the winning bid? How about the equivalent of 1,826.65 Canadian dollars? While this looks like an extraordinary jump in value to the untrained eye, check for yourself that the actual price appreciation of this coin was about 7.78 percent per year.

Another popular finance-related hobby is collecting paper money. Banknotes were first brought into Canada by British and French settlers. Created in 1867, the Dominion of Canada made the dollar its official currency in 1868. Some of the earliest issued banknotes are in high demand among collectors. For instance, a Bank of Ottawa $10 note issued in 1906 fetched the equivalent of 1,628.93 Canadian dollars on eBay in August 2006. The crisp uncirculated condition of the note contributed to its high price. This increase in value also seems like a very high return to the untrained eye, but, again, check for yourself to see that the return was only 5.22 percent per year.

Another collectible that has grown in popularity recently is older Namiki nibs. These lacquered fountain pens were manufactured during the 1920s and 1930s and have been called exquisite works of art. A particularly appealing pen, which was manufactured around 1930, sold for $39,600 during a 2004 auction. The same pen was priced at about $11,400 only three years earlier. This also seems like a very high return to the untrained eye, and indeed it is! Check for yourself that the return was about 51.45 percent per year.

Looking back at these investments, the Nakimi pen had the highest return recently. The problem is that to earn this return you had to purchase the pen when it was new and store it. Looking ahead, the corresponding problem is predicting what the future value of the next hot collectible will be. You will earn a positive return only if the market value of your asset rises above the purchase price at some point in the future. That, of course, is rarely assured. For example, Barbie dolls have in the past been a popular collectible; however, most collectors say the new Barbies, which today are mass-marketed at discount stores, will probably have little or no value as collectibles at any time in the future, so we don't recommend them for your retirement investing.

Double Your Fun   **EXAMPLE** **4.9**

You have been offered an investment that promises to double your money every 10 years. What is the approximate rate of return on the investment?

From the Rule of 72, the rate of return is given approximately by $72/r\% = 10$, so the rate is approximately $72/10 = 7.2\%$. Verify that the exact answer is 7.177 percent.

An increase in the tournament purse of the world-famous Rogers Cup offers another example on the growth rate. The Rogers Cup, which is effectively the Canadian Open tennis championship, has undergone several name changes since its start in 1881. Currently, it is the third oldest tennis tournament in the world, after Wimbledon and the U.S. Open. This tournament has consistently attracted the biggest names in the history of tennis. The world's number one player, Roger Federer, and a rising star, Ana Ivanovic, won the men's and women's singles, respectively, in 2006.

Originally tennis players competed only for a silver cup. The monetary reward of 10,000 Canadian dollars was first introduced in 1969, when amateurs and professionals were allowed to participate together. In 2006, the purse ballooned to 2.45 million U.S. dollars, the equivalent of 2.744 million Canadian dollars. What was the annual percentage increase in the prize money over this period?

In Canadian dollars, the future value is $2.744 million and the present value is $10,000. There are 37 years involved, so we need to solve for r in the following:

$$\$10,000 = \$2.744 \text{ million}/(1 + r)^{37}$$
$$(1 + r)^{37} = 274.4$$

Solving for r, we see that the tournament purse has grown at approximately 16.39 percent per year.

Calculator Hints

We can illustrate how to calculate unknown rates using a financial calculator using these numbers. For the Rogers Cup, you would do the following:

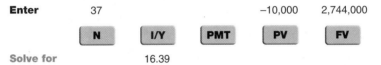

Enter   37   −10,000   2,744,000

| N | I/Y | PMT | PV | FV |

Solve for   16.39

As in our previous examples, notice the minus sign on the present value, representing the tournament purse in 1969.

EXAMPLE 4.10   **Saving for University**

You estimate that you will need about $80,000 to send your child to university in eight years. You have about $35,000 now. If you can earn 20 percent per year, will you make it? At what rate will you just reach your goal?

If you can earn 20 percent, the future value of your $35,000 in eight years will be:

$$FV = \$35,000 \times 1.20^8 = \$35,000 \times 4.2998 = \$150,493.59$$

So, you will make it easily. The minimum rate is the unknown r in the following:

$$FV = \$35,000 \times (1 + r)^8 = \$80,000$$
$$(1 + r)^8 = \$80,000/35,000 = 2.2857$$

Therefore, the future value factor is 2.2857. Looking at the row in Table A.1 that corresponds to eight periods, we see that our future value factor is roughly halfway between the ones shown for 10 percent (2.1436) and 12 percent (2.4760), so you will just reach your goal if you earn approximately 11 percent. To get the exact answer, we could use a financial calculator or we could solve for r:

$$(1 + r)^8 = \$80,000/35,000 = 2.2857$$
$$1 + r = 2.2857^{(1/8)} = 2.2857^{.125} = 1.1089$$
$$r = 10.89\%$$

Only 18,262.5 Days to Retirement EXAMPLE 4.11

You would like to retire in 50 years as a millionaire. If you have $10,000 today, what rate of return do you need to earn to achieve your goal?

The future value is $1,000,000. The present value is $10,000, and there are 50 years until retirement. We need to calculate the unknown discount rate in the following:

$$\$10{,}000 = \$1{,}000{,}000/(1 + r)^{50}$$
$$(1 + r)^{50} = 100$$

The future value factor is thus 100. You can verify that the implicit rate is about 9.65 percent.

Finding the Number of Periods

Suppose we were interested in purchasing an asset that costs $50,000. We currently have $25,000. If we can earn 12 percent on this $25,000, how long until we have the $50,000? Finding the answer involves solving for the last variable in the basic present value equation, the number of periods. You already know how to get an approximate answer to this particular problem. Notice that we need to double our money. From the Rule of 72, this will take about 72/12 = 6 years at 12 percent.

To come up with the exact answer, we can again manipulate the basic present value equation. The present value is $25,000, and the future value is $50,000. With a 12 percent discount rate, the basic equation takes one of the following forms:

$$\$25{,}000 = \$50{,}000/1.12^{t}$$
$$\$50{,}000/25{,}000 = 1.12^{t} = 2$$

We thus have a future value factor of 2 for a 12 percent rate. We now need to solve for t. If you look down the column in Table A.1 that corresponds to 12 percent, you will see that a future value factor of 1.9738 occurs at six periods. It will thus take about six years, as we calculated. To get the exact answer, we have to explicitly solve for t (or use a financial calculator). If you do this, you will find that the answer is 6.1163 years, so our approximation was quite close in this case.

Calculator Hints

If you do use a financial calculator, here are the relevant entries:

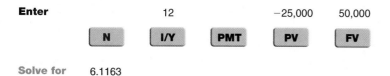

Enter		12		−25,000	50,000
	N	I/Y	PMT	PV	FV
Solve for	6.1163				

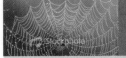

WORK THE WEB

How important is the time value of money? A recent search on one Web engine returned over 3.2 million hits! It is important to understand the calculations behind the time value of money, but the advent of financial calculators and spreadsheets has eliminated the need for tedious calculations. In fact, many Web sites offer time value of money calculators. The following is an example from Moneychimp's Web site, **www.moneychimp.com.** You need $50,000 in 20 years and will invest your money at 10.2 percent. How much do you need to deposit today? To use the calculator, you simply enter the values and hit "Calculate." The results look like this:

Inputs		
Future Value:	$	50,000.00
Years:		20
Discount Rate:		10.2 %
	Calculate	
Results		
Present Value:	$	7,167.01

Who said time value of money calculations are hard?

EXAMPLE 4.12   Waiting for Godot

You've been saving up to buy the Godot Company. The total cost will be $10 million. You currently have about $2.3 million. If you can earn 5 percent on your money, how long will you have to wait? At 16 percent, how long must you wait?

At 5 percent, you'll have to wait a long time. From the basic present value equation:

$2.3 = $10/1.05^t$
$1.05^t = 4.35$
$t = 30$ years

At 16 percent, things are a little better. Verify for yourself that it will take about 10 years.

This example finishes our introduction to basic time value of money concepts. As our *Work the Web* box (above) shows, online calculators are widely available to handle these calculations, but it is still important to know what is going on.

Spreadsheet strategies   Using a Spreadsheet for Time Value of Money Calculations

More and more, businesspeople from many different areas (and not just finance and accounting) rely on spreadsheets to do all the different types of calculations that come up in the real world. As a result, in this section, we will show you how to use a spreadsheet to handle the various time value of money problems we presented in this chapter. We will use Microsoft Excel™, but the commands are similar for other types of software. We assume you are already familiar with basic spreadsheet operations.

As we have seen, you can solve for any one of the following four potential unknowns: future value, present value, the discount rate, or the number of periods. With a spreadsheet, there is a separate formula for each. In Excel, these are as follows:

Learn more about using Excel for time value and other calculations at **www.studyfinance .com.**

To Find	Enter This Formula
Future value	= FV (rate,nper,pmt,pv)
Present value	= PV (rate,nper,pmt,fv)
Discount rate	= RATE (nper,pmt,pv,fv)
Number of periods	= NPER (rate,pmt,pv,fv)

In these formulas, pv and fv are present and future value, nper is the number of periods, and rate is the discount, or interest, rate.

There are two things that are a little tricky here. First, unlike a financial calculator, the spreadsheet requires that the rate be entered as a decimal. Second, as with most financial calculators, you have to put a negative sign on either the present value or the future value to solve for the rate or the number of periods. For the same reason, if you solve for a present value, the answer will have a negative sign unless you input a negative future value. The same is true when you compute a future value.

To illustrate how you might use these formulas, we will go back to an example in the chapter. If you invest $25,000 at 12 percent per year, how long until you have $50,000? You might set up a spreadsheet like this:

	A	B	C	D	E	F	G	H
1								
2	Using a spreadsheet for time value of money calculations							
3								
4	If we invest $25,000 at 12 percent, how long until we have $50,000? We need to solve for the							
5	unknown number of periods, so we use the formula NPER (rate, pmt, pv, fv).							
6								
7	Present value (pv):	$25,000						
8	Future value (fv):	$50,000						
9	Rate (rate):	.12						
10								
11	Periods:	6.116255						
12								
13	The formula entered in cell B11 is =NPER(B9,0,-B7,B8); notice that pmt is zero and that pv has a							
14	negative sign on it. Also notice that the rate is entered as a decimal, not a percentage.							

CONCEPT QUESTIONS

4.3a What is the basic present value equation?

4.3b What is the Rule of 72?

KEY EQUATIONS:

I. Symbols

PV = Present value, what future cash flows are worth today

FV_t = Future value, what cash flows are worth in the future at time t

r = Interest rate, rate of return, or discount rate per period—typically, but not always, one year

t = Number of periods—typically, but not always, the number of years

II. Future value of $1 invested at r percent per period for t periods

$$\text{Future value} = \$1 \times (1 + r)^t \tag{4.1}$$

The term $(1 + r)^t$ is called the *future value factor.*

III. Present value of $1 to be received in t periods at r percent per period

$$PV = \$1/(1 + r)^t \tag{4.2}$$

The term $1/(1 + r)^t$ is called the *present value factor.*

IV. The basic present value equation giving the relationship between present and future value is

$$PV \times (1 + r)^t = FV_t \tag{4.3}$$

$$PV = FV_t /(1 + r)^t = FV_t \times [1/(1 + r)^t]$$

SUMMARY AND CONCLUSIONS

This chapter has introduced you to the basic principles of present value and discounted cash flow valuation. In it, we explained a number of things about the time value of money, including:

1. For a given rate of return, the value at some point in the future of an investment made today can be determined by calculating the future value of that investment.

2. The current worth of a future cash flow can be determined for a given rate of return by calculating the present value of the cash flow involved.

3. The relationship between present value and future value for a given rate r and time t is given by the basic present value equation:

$$PV = FV_t /(1 + r)^t$$

As we have shown, it is possible to find any one of the four components (PV, FV_t, r, or t) given the other three.

The principles developed in this chapter will figure prominently in the chapters to come. The reason for this is that most investments, whether they involve real assets or financial assets, can be analyzed using the discounted cash flow, or DCF, approach. As a result, the DCF approach is broadly applicable and widely used in practice. Before going on, therefore, you might want to work through the problems below.

CHAPTER REVIEW AND SELF-TEST PROBLEMS

4.1 Calculating Future Values. Assume you deposit $1,000 today in an account that pays 8 percent interest. How much will you have in four years?

4.2 Calculating Present Values. Suppose you have just celebrated your 19th birthday. A rich uncle set up a trust fund for you that will pay you $100,000 when you turn 25. If the relevant discount rate is 11 percent, how much is this fund worth today?

4.3 Calculating Rates of Return. You've been offered an investment that will double your money in 12 years. What rate of return are you being offered? Check your answer using the Rule of 72.

4.4 Calculating the Number of Periods. You've been offered an investment that will pay you 7 percent per year. If you invest $10,000, how long until you have $20,000? How long until you have $30,000?

■ Answers to Chapter Review and Self-Test Problems

4.1 We need to calculate the future value of $1,000 at 8 percent for four years. The future value factor is:

$$1.08^4 = 1.3605$$

The future value is thus $1,000 × 1.3605 = $1,360.50.

4.2 We need the present value of $100,000 to be paid in six years at 11 percent. The discount factor is:

$$1/1.11^6 = 1/1.8704 = .5346$$

The present value is thus about $53,460.

4.3 Suppose you invest, say, $100. You will have $200 in 12 years with this investment. So, $100 is the amount you have today, the present value, and $200 is the amount you will have in 12 years, or the future value. From the basic present value equation, we have:

$$\$200 = \$100 \times (1 \times r)^{12}$$
$$2 = (1 \times r)^{12}$$

From here, we need to solve for r, the unknown rate. As shown in the chapter, there are several different ways to do this. We will take the 12th root of 2 (by raising 2 to the power of 1/12):

$$2^{(1/12)} = 1 + r$$
$$1.0595 = 1 + r$$
$$r = 5.95\%$$

Using the Rule of 72, we have $72/t = r\%$, or $72/12 = 6\%$, so our answer looks good (remember that the Rule of 72 is only an approximation).

4.4 The basic equation is:

$$\$20,000 = \$10,000 \times (1 + .07)^t$$
$$2 = (1 + .07)^t$$

If we solve for t, we get that $t = 10.24$ years. Using the Rule of 72, we get $72/7 = 10.29$ years, so, once again, our answer looks good. To get $30,000, verify for yourself that you will have to wait 16.24 years.

CRITICAL THINKING AND CONCEPTS REVIEW

4.1   **Compounding.**   What is compounding? What is discounting?

4.2   **Compounding and Periods.**   As you increase the length of time involved, what happens to future values? What happens to present values?

4.3   **Compounding and Interest Rates.**   What happens to a future value if you increase the rate r? What happens to a present value?

4.4   **Future Values.**   Suppose you deposit a large sum in an account that earns a low interest rate and simultaneously deposit a small sum in an account with a high interest rate. Which account will have the larger future value?

4.5   **Ethical Considerations.**   Take a look back at Example 4.6. Is it deceptive advertising? Is it unethical to advertise a future value like this without a disclaimer?

To answer the next four questions, refer to the Province of Quebec security offered by TD Waterhouse we discussed to open the chapter.

4.6   **Time Value of Money.**   Why would TD Waterhouse be willing to accept such a small amount today ($274.17) in exchange for the security that promises to repay almost four times that amount ($1,000) in the future?

4.7   **Time Value of Money.**   Would you be willing to pay $274.17 today in exchange for $1,000 in 30 years? What would be the key considerations in answering yes or no? Would your answer depend on who is making the promise to repay?

4.8   **Investment Comparison.**   Suppose that when TD Waterhouse offered the security for $274.17, the government of Canada had offered an essentially identical security. Do you think it would have had a higher or lower price? Why?

4.9   **Length of Investment.**   The Province of Quebec security is actively bought and sold by TD Waterhouse and other investment dealers. If you are given a price today, do you think the price would exceed the $274.17? Why? If you forecasted for the year 2012, do you think the price would be higher or lower than today's price? Why?

QUESTIONS AND PROBLEMS

**Basic
(Questions 1–15)**

1.   **Simple Interest versus Compound Interest.**   First City Bank pays 7 percent simple interest on its savings account balances, whereas Second City Bank pays 7 percent interest compounded annually. If you made a $6,000 deposit in each bank, how much more money would you earn from your Second City Bank account at the end of 10 years?

2.   **Calculating Future Values.**   For each of the following, compute the future value:

Present Value	Years	Interest Rate	Future Value
$ 3,150	3	18%	
7,810	10	6	
89,305	17	12	
227,382	22	5	

3. **Calculating Present Values.** For each of the following, compute the present value:

Present Value	Years	Interest Rate	Future Value
	9	4%	$ 15,451
	4	12	51,557
	16	22	886,073
	21	20	550,164

4. **Calculating Interest Rates.** Solve for the unknown interest rate in each of the following:

Present Value	Years	Interest Rate	Future Value
$ 221	5		$ 307
425	7		761
25,000	18		136,771
40,200	16		255,810

5. **Calculating the Number of Periods.** Solve for the unknown number of years in each of the following:

Present Value	Years	Interest Rate	Future Value
$ 250		6%	$ 1,105
1,941		5	3,860
21,320		14	387,120
32,500		29	198,212

6. **Calculating Interest Rates.** Assume the total cost of a college education will be $280,000 when your child enters college in 18 years. You presently have $39,000 to invest. What annual rate of interest must you earn on your investment to cover the cost of your child's college education?

7. **Calculating the Number of Periods.** At 7 percent interest, how long does it take to double your money? To quadruple it?

8. **Calculating Rates of Return.** In 2006, a Canadian silver dollar minted in 1948 was sold for the equivalent of $1,106.55 Canadian dollars on eBay. What was the rate of return on this investment?

9. **Calculating the Number of Periods.** You're trying to save to buy a new $140,000 Ferrari. You have $30,000 today that can be invested at your bank. The bank pays 4.2 percent annual interest on its accounts. How long will it be before you have enough to buy the car?

10. **Calculating Present Values.** Imprudential, Inc., has an unfunded pension liability of $800 million that must be paid in 20 years. To assess the value of the firm's stock, financial analysts want to discount this liability back to the present. If the relevant discount rate is 7 percent, what is the present value of this liability?

11. **Calculating Present Values.**   You have just received notification that you have won the $2 million first prize in the Centennial Lottery. However, the prize will be awarded on your 100th birthday (assuming you're around to collect), 80 years from now. What is the present value of your windfall if the appropriate discount rate is 13 percent?

12. **Calculating Future Values.**   Your coin collection contains 50 1952 silver dollars. If your grandparents purchased them for their face value when they were new, how much will your collection be worth when you retire in 2058, assuming they appreciate at a 5.3 percent annual rate?

13. **Calculating Interest Rates and Future Values.**   In 1895, the first U.S. Open Golf Championship was held. The winner's prize money was $150. In 2004, the winner's cheque was $1,125,000. What was the annual percentage increase in the winner's cheque over this period? If the winner's prize increases at the same rate, what will it be in 2040?

14. **Calculating Rates of Return.**   In 2006, a Canadian 10-cent coin minted in 1889 was sold for the equivalent of 1,179.57 Canadian dollars on eBay. What was the annual increase in the value of this coin?

15. **Calculating Rates of Return.**   Although appealing to more refined tastes, art as a collectible has not always performed so profitably. During 2003, Sotheby's sold the Edgar Degas bronze sculpture *Petite danseuse de quartorze ans* at auction for a price of $10,311,500. Unfortunately for the previous owner, he had purchased it in 1999 at a price of $12,377,500. What was his annual rate of return on this sculpture?

Intermediate (Questions 16–25)

16. **Calculating Rates of Return.**   Referring to the Province of Quebec security we discussed at the very beginning of the chapter:

   a.   Based on the $274.17 price, what rate was the Province of Quebec paying to borrow money?

   b.   Suppose that on December 1, 2010, this security's price will be $500. If an investor had purchased it for $274.17 four years earlier and sold it on this day, what annual rate of return would she have earned?

   c.   If an investor had purchased the security on December 1, 2010, and held it until it matured, what annual rate of return would she have earned?

17. **Calculating Present Values.**   Suppose you are still committed to owning a $140,000 Ferrari (see Question 9). If you believe your mutual fund can achieve a 10.75 percent annual rate of return, and you want to buy the car in 10 years on the day you turn 30, how much must you invest today?

18. **Calculating Future Values.**   You have just made your first $4,000 contribution to your registered retirement savings plan (RRSP). Assuming you earn a 12 percent rate of return and make no additional contributions, what will your account be worth when you retire in 45 years? What if you wait 10 years before contributing? (Does this suggest an investment strategy?)

19. **Calculating Future Values.**   You are scheduled to receive $13,000 in two years. When you receive it, you will invest it for six more years at 8 percent per year. How much will you have in eight years?

20. **Calculating the Number of Periods.**   You expect to receive $30,000 at graduation in two years. You plan on investing it at 9 percent until you have $140,000. How long will you wait from now? (Better than the situation in Question 9, but still no Ferrari.)

21. **Calculating Future Values.**   You have $9,000 to deposit. Regency Bank offers 12 percent per year compounded monthly (1 percent per month), while King Bank offers 12 percent but will only compound annually. How much will your investment be worth in 10 years at each bank?

22. **Calculating Interest Rates.**   An investment offers to triple your money in 24 months (don't believe it). What rate per six months are you being offered?

23. **Calculating the Number of Periods.**   You can earn .4 percent per month at your bank. If you deposit $1,300, how long must you wait until your account has grown to $2,500?

24. **Calculating Present Values.**   You need $50,000 in nine years. If you can earn .55 percent per month, how much will you have to deposit today?

25. **Calculating Present Values.**   You have decided that you want to be a millionaire when you retire in 45 years. If you can earn an 11 percent annual return, how much do you have to invest today? What if you can earn 5 percent?

26. **Calculating Future Values.**   You are saving money for the purchase of a cottage near a lake in Northern Ontario. Currently you have $10,000 in a bank savings account that pays 4 percent per year, and $40,000 in a stock mutual fund that expects to generate 10 percent per year for the next two years, and 7 percent per year afterwards. Your uncle has promised to give you $8,000 in three years that will be invested at 5 percent per year. How much money will you have in eight years?

**Challenge
(Questions 26–27)**

27. **Calculating Present Values.**   Ten years ago you invested in an emerging market mutual fund. This mutual fund had generated 25 percent per year for the first three years, then −15 percent per year for two years, followed by 8 percent per year during the last five years. Given that you have $35,000 at the end of this 10-year period, how much was your original investment?

WHAT'S ON THE WEB?

4.1   **Calculating Future Values.**   Go to **www.dinkytown.net** and find the "Savings Calculator" link among Canadian calculators. If you currently have $10,000 and invest this money at 9 percent, how much will you have in 30 years? Assume you will not make any additional contributions. How much will you have if you can earn 11 percent?

4.2   **Calculating the Number of Periods.**   Go to **www.dinkytown.net** and find the "Cool Million" link among Canadian calculators. You want to be a millionaire. You can earn 11.5 percent per year. Using your current age, at what age will you become a millionaire if you have $25,000 to invest, assuming you make no other deposits (ignore inflation)?

4.3   **Future Values and Taxes.**   Taxes can greatly affect the future value of your savings. The RRSP Planning Calculator at **www.morningstar.ca** adjusts your return for taxes. Enter your current age and zero for the marginal tax rate. Suppose you have $10,000 in both a non-registered savings account and a RRSP account. If your expected rate of return before retirement is 10 percent, how much will you have in each of your accounts at age 65? Now, determine your marginal tax rate based on your province of residence and expected income after graduation. How much will you have in each of your accounts? Why are the amounts different?

Discounted Cash Flow Valuation 5

After studying this chapter, you should have a good understanding of:

5.1 How to determine the future and present value of investments with multiple cash flows.

5.2 How to value level cash flows.

5.3 How interest rates are quoted (and misquoted).

5.4 Loan types and how loans are amortized or paid off.

In summer 2004, Canadian basketball player Steve Nash signed a lucrative contract with the Phoenix Suns paying him $65 million over five years. While the majority of Suns fans were excited about Nash coming to Phoenix, some thought he was overpaid and were concerned about his age: 30. Steve Nash did not disappoint. This energetic player from Victoria, British Columbia, became the first Canadian to win the Most Valuable Player (MVP) award, the NBA's highest individual recognition, and the second point guard in the history of the NBA to capture the award for two consecutive seasons. In May 2006, Nash was on *Time* magazine's list of the 100 most influential people in the world. Given Nash's recent accomplishments, his $65 million contract no longer looks like an overpayment. But was it so large in the first place, if we take into account that it was payable over several years? The total contract amount can be misleading. Although the exact financial terms of the contract were not disclosed, we can assume that it paid around $11 million in the first year, increased by $1 million each following year, and would reach $15 million in the fifth year. Since the payments were spread out over time, we must consider the time value of money, which means his contract was worth less than reported. How much did he really get? This chapter gives you the "tools of knowledge" to answer this question.

Because discounted cash flow valuation is so important, students who learn this material well will find that life is much easier down the road. Getting it straight now will save you a lot of headaches later.

In our previous chapter, we covered the basics of discounted cash flow valuation. However, so far, we have only dealt with single cash flows. In reality, most investments have multiple cash flows. For example, if Sears is thinking of opening a new department store, there will be a large cash outlay in the beginning and then cash inflows for many years. In this chapter, we begin to explore how to value such investments.

When you finish this chapter, you should have some very practical skills. For example, you will know how to calculate your own car payments or student loan payments. You will also be able to determine how long it will take to pay off a credit card if you make the minimum payment each month (a practice we do not recommend). We will show you how to compare interest rates to determine which are the highest and which are the lowest, and we will also show you how interest rates can be quoted in different, and at times deceptive, ways.

5.1 | FUTURE AND PRESENT VALUES OF MULTIPLE CASH FLOWS

Thus far, we have restricted our attention to either the future value of a lump-sum present amount or the present value of some single future cash flow. In this section, we begin to study ways to value multiple cash flows. We start with future value.

Future Value with Multiple Cash Flows

Suppose you deposit $100 today in an account paying 8 percent. In one year, you will deposit another $100. How much will you have in two years? This particular problem is relatively easy. At the end of the first year, you will have $108 plus the second $100 you deposit, for a total of $208. You leave this $208 on deposit at 8 percent for another year. At the end of this second year, the account is worth:

$208 × 1.08 = $224.64

Figure 5.1 is a *time line* that illustrates the process of calculating the future value of these two $100 deposits. Figures such as this one are very useful for solving complicated problems. Any time you are having trouble with a present or future value problem, drawing a time line will usually help you to see what is happening.

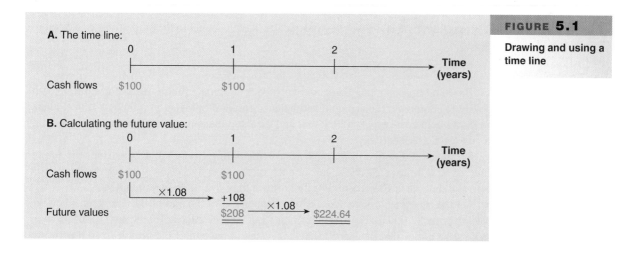

FIGURE 5.1

Drawing and using a time line

In the first part of Figure 5.1, we show the cash flows on the time line. The most important thing is that we write them down where they actually occur. Here, the first cash flow occurs today, which we label as Time 0. We therefore put $100 at Time 0 on the time line. The second $100 cash flow occurs one year from today, so we write it down at the point labelled as Time 1. In the second part of Figure 5.1, we calculate the future values one period at a time to come up with the final $224.64.

EXAMPLE 5.1   **Saving Up Revisited**

You think you will be able to deposit $4,000 at the end of each of the next three years in a bank account paying 8 percent interest. You currently have $7,000 in the account. How much will you have in three years? In four years?

At the end of the first year, you will have:

$7,000 × 1.08 + 4,000 = $11,560

At the end of the second year, you will have:

$11,560 × 1.08 + 4,000 = $16,484.80

Repeating this for the third year gives:

$16,484.80 × 1.08 + 4,000 = $21,803.58

Therefore, you will have $21,803.58 in three years. If you leave this on deposit for one more year (and don't add to it), at the end of the fourth year you'll have:

$21,803.58 × 1.08 = $23,547.87

When we calculated the future value of the two $100 deposits, we simply calculated the balance as of the beginning of each year and then rolled that amount forward to the next year. We could have done it another, quicker way. The first $100 is on deposit for two years at 8 percent, so its future value is:

$100 × 1.08^2 = $100 × 1.1664 = $116.64

The second $100 is on deposit for one year at 8 percent, and its future value is thus:

$100 × 1.08 = $108.00

The total future value, as we previously calculated, is equal to the sum of these two future values:

$116.64 + 108 = $224.64

Based on this example, there are two ways to calculate future values for multiple cash flows: (1) compound the accumulated balance forward one year at a time or (2) calculate the future value of each cash flow first and then add these up. Both give the same answer, so you can do it either way.

To illustrate the two different ways of calculating future values, consider the future value of $2,000 invested at the end of each of the next five years. The current balance is zero, and the rate is 10 percent. We first draw a time line as shown in Figure 5.2.

On the time line, notice that nothing happens until the end of the first year when we make the first $2,000 investment. This first $2,000 earns interest for the next four (not five) years. Also notice that the last $2,000 is invested at the end of the fifth year, so it earns no interest at all.

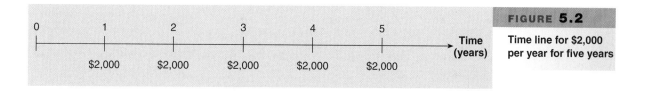

FIGURE **5.2**

Time line for $2,000 per year for five years

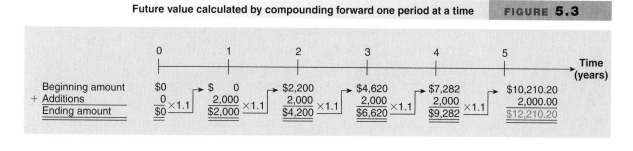

Future value calculated by compounding forward one period at a time

FIGURE **5.3**

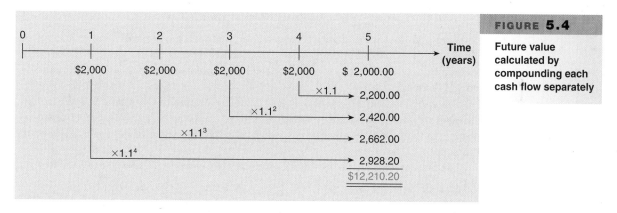

FIGURE **5.4**

Future value calculated by compounding each cash flow separately

Figure 5.3 illustrates the calculations involved if we compound the investment one period at a time. As illustrated, the future value is $12,210.20.

Figure 5.4 goes through the same calculations, but it uses the second technique. Naturally, the answer is the same.

Saving Up Once Again EXAMPLE 5.2

If you deposit $100 in one year, $200 in two years, and $300 in three years, how much will you have in three years? How much of this is interest? How much will you have in five years if you don't add additional amounts? Assume a 7 percent interest rate throughout.

We will calculate the future value of each amount in three years. Notice that the $100 earns interest for two years, and the $200 earns interest for one year. The final $300 earns no interest. The future values are thus:

$$\begin{array}{ll} \$100 \times 1.07^2 & = \$114.49 \\ \$200 \times 1.07 & = 214.00 \\ +\$300 & = \underline{\$300.00} \\ \text{Total future value} & = \underline{\underline{\$628.49}} \end{array}$$

(Continued)

The future value is thus $628.49. The total interest is:

$628.49 − (100 + 200 + 300) = $28.49

How much will you have in five years? We know that you will have $628.49 in three years. If you leave that in for two more years, it will grow to:

$628.49 × 1.07^2 = $628.49 × 1.1449 = $719.56

Notice that we could have calculated the future value of each amount separately. Once again, be careful about the lengths of time. As we previously calculated, the first $100 earns interest for only four years, the second deposit earns three years' interest, and the last earns two years' interest:

$$
\begin{array}{l}
\$100 \times 1.07^4 = \$100 \times 1.3108 = \$131.08 \\
\$200 \times 1.07^3 = \$200 \times 1.2250 = 245.01 \\
+\$300 \times 1.07^2 = \$300 \times 1.1449 = \underline{343.47} \\
\text{Total future value} = \underline{\underline{\$719.56}}
\end{array}
$$

Present Value with Multiple Cash Flows

It will turn out that we will very often need to determine the present value of a series of future cash flows. As with future values, there are two ways we can do it. We can either discount back one period at a time, or we can just calculate the present values individually and add them up.

Suppose you need $1,000 in one year and $2,000 more in two years. If you can earn 9 percent on your money, how much do you have to put up today to exactly cover these amounts in the future? In other words, what is the present value of the two cash flows at 9 percent?

The present value of $2,000 in two years at 9 percent is:

$2,000/$1.09^2$ = $1,683.36

The present value of $1,000 in one year is:

$1,000/1.09 = $917.43

Therefore, the total present value is:

$1,683.36 + 917.43 = $2,600.79

To see why $2,600.79 is the right answer, we can check to see that after the $2,000 is paid out in two years, there is no money left. If we invest $2,600.79 for one year at 9 percent, we will have:

$2,600.79 × 1.09 = $2,834.86

We take out $1,000, leaving $1,834.86. This amount earns 9 percent for another year, leaving us with:

$1,834.86 × 1.09 = $2,000

This is just as we planned. As this example illustrates, the present value of a series of future cash flows is simply the amount that you would need today in order to exactly duplicate those future cash flows (for a given discount rate).

An alternative way of calculating present values for multiple future cash flows is to discount back to the present, one period at a time. To illustrate, suppose we had an

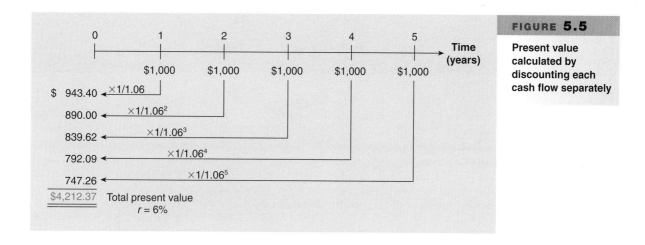

FIGURE 5.5

Present value calculated by discounting each cash flow separately

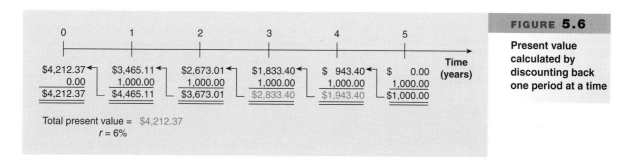

FIGURE 5.6

Present value calculated by discounting back one period at a time

investment that was going to pay $1,000 at the end of every year for the next five years. To find the present value, we could discount each $1,000 back to the present separately and then add the results up. Figure 5.5 illustrates this approach for a 6 percent discount rate. As shown, the answer is $4,212.37 (ignoring a small rounding error).

How Much Is It Worth?   **EXAMPLE 5.3**

You are offered an investment that will pay you $200 in one year, $400 the next year, $600 the next year, and $800 at the end of the next year. You can earn 12 percent on very similar investments. What is the most you should pay for this one?

We need to calculate the present value of these cash flows at 12 percent. Taking them one at a time gives:

$$
\begin{aligned}
\$200 \times 1/1.12^1 &= \$200/1.1200 = \$ \ \ 178.57 \\
\$400 \times 1/1.12^2 &= \$400/1.2544 = \ \ \ \ 318.88 \\
\$600 \times 1/1.12^3 &= \$600/1.4049 = \ \ \ \ 427.07 \\
+\$800 \times 1/1.12^4 &= \$800/1.5735 = \ \ \underline{\ \ \ \ 508.41} \\
&\text{Total present value} = \underline{\$1,432.93}
\end{aligned}
$$

If you can earn 12 percent on your money, then you can duplicate this investment's cash flows for $1,432.93, so this is the most you should be willing to pay.

REALITY BYTES

Jackpot!

If you, or someone you know, is a regular lottery player, you probably already understand that you are 20 times more likely to be killed by a lightning bolt than to win a big lottery jackpot. How bad are the odds? Nearby you will find a table comparing your chances of winning the Mega Millions Lottery to other events.

Big Game: Is It Worth the Gamble?	
Odds of winning Mega Millions jackpot	1:135,145,920*
Odds of being killed by a venomous spider	1:57,018,763
Odds of being killed by a dog bite	1:11,403,753
Odds of being killed by lightning	1:6,479,405
Odds of being killed by drowning	1:690,300
Odds of being killed falling from a bed or other furniture	1:388,411
Odds of being killed in a car crash	1:6,029

*Source: Virginia Lottery Web site. All other odds from the National Safety Council.

Sweepstakes may have different odds than lotteries, but the odds may not be much better. Probably the largest advertised grand prize ever was Pepsi's "Play for Billion," which, you guessed it, has a $1 billion (*billion!*) prize. Not bad for a day's work, but you still have to read the fine print. It turns out that the winner would be paid $5 million per year for the next 20 years, $10 million per year for years 21 to 39, and a lump sum $710 million in 40 years. From what you have learned, you know the value of the sweepstakes wasn't even close to $1 billion. In fact, at an interest rate of 10 percent, the present value is about $70.7 million.

Lottery jackpots are often paid out over 20 or more years, but the winner often can choose to take a lump sum cash payment instead. For some, the cash option is a lot better. In December 2004, a retired waitress in Massachusetts lost a lawsuit against the lottery in her state because they wouldn't pay out the winnings as a lump sum. She had won $5.6 million, which was to be paid out as $280,000 immediately and $280,000 per year for the next 19 years. However, since she was 94, she argued that she wouldn't be around to enjoy the money. When a lottery allows a cash option, a rule of thumb is that the cash option will be about one-half of the reported prize. Using this rule of thumb on the waitress's winnings, she would have received about $2.8 million in cash. So, what discount rate does this imply? Remembering that the first payment occurs immediately, we find the rate to be about 8.92 percent.

Some lotteries make your decision a little tougher. The Ontario Lottery will pay you either $2,000 a week for the rest of your life or $1.3 million now. Of course, there is the chance you might die in the near future, so the lottery guarantees that your heirs will collect the $2,000 weekly payments until the 20th anniversary of the first payment, or until you would have turned 91, whichever comes first. This payout scheme complicates your decision quite a bit. If you live for only the 20-year minimum, the break-even interest rate between the two options is about 5.13 percent per year, compounded weekly. If you expect to live longer than the 20-year minimum, you might be better off accepting $2,000 per week for life. Of course, if you manage to invest the $1.3 million lump sum at a rate of return of about 8 percent per year (compounded weekly), you can have your cake and eat it too since the investment will return $2,000 at the end of each week forever!

Alternatively, we could discount the last cash flow back one period and add it to the next-to-the-last cash flow:

$$\$1,000/1.06 + 1,000 = \$943.40 + 1,000 = \$1,943.40$$

We could then discount this amount back one period and add it to the Year 3 cash flow:

$$\$1,943.40/1.06 + 1,000 = \$1,833.40 + 1,000 = \$2,833.40$$

This process could be repeated as necessary. Figure 5.6 illustrates this approach and the remaining calculations.

As the *Reality Bytes* box above shows, calculating present values is a vital step in comparing alternative cash flows. We will have much more to say on this subject in subsequent chapters.

How Much Is It Worth? Part 2   EXAMPLE 5.4

You are offered an investment that will make three $5,000 payments. The first payment will occur four years from today. The second will occur in five years, and the third will follow in six years. If you can earn 11 percent, what is the most this investment is worth today? What is the future value of the cash flows?

We will answer the questions in reverse order to illustrate a point. The future value of the cash flows in six years is:

$$\$5,000 \times 1.11^2 + 5,000 \times 1.11 + 5,000 = \$6,160.50 + 5,550 + 5,000$$
$$= \$16,710.50$$

The present value must be:

$$\$16,710.50/1.11^6 = \$8,934.12$$

Let's check this. Taking them one at a time, the PVs of the cash flows are:

$$\$5,000 \times 1/1.11^6 = \$5,000/1.8704 = \$2,673.20$$
$$\$5,000 \times 1/1.11^5 = \$5,000/1.6851 = 2,967.26$$
$$+\$5,000 \times 1/1.11^4 = \$5,000/1.5181 = \underline{3,293.65}$$
$$\text{Total present value} = \underline{\$\,8,934.12}$$

This is as we previously calculated. The point we want to make is that we can calculate present and future values in any order and convert between them using whatever way seems most convenient. The answers will always be the same as long as we stick with the same discount rate and are careful to keep track of the right number of periods.

Calculator Hints   How to Calculate Present Values with Multiple Future Cash Flows Using a Financial Calculator

To calculate the present value of multiple cash flows with a financial calculator, we will simply discount the individual cash flows one at a time, using the same technique we used in our previous chapter, so this is not really new. There is a shortcut, however, that we can show you. We will use the numbers in Example 5.3 to illustrate.

To begin, of course, we first remember to clear out the calculator! Next, from Example 5.3, the first cash flow is $200 to be received in one year and the discount rate is 12 percent, so we do the following:

Enter

1	12			200
N	I/Y	PMT	PV	FV

Solve for   −178.57

Now you can write down this answer to save it, but that's inefficient. All calculators have a memory where you can store numbers. Why not just save it there? Doing so cuts way down on mistakes because you don't have to write down and/or rekey numbers, and it's much faster.

(continued)

Next we value the second cash flow. We need to change N to 2 and FV to 400. As long as we haven't changed anything else, we don't have to re-enter I/Y or clear out the calculator, so we have:

Enter   2   400

Solve for   −318.88

You save this number by adding it to the one you saved in our first calculation, and so on for the remaining two calculations.

As we will see in a later chapter, some financial calculators will let you enter all of the future cash flows at once, but we'll discuss that subject when we get to it.

A Note on Cash Flow Timing

In working present and future value problems, cash flow timing is critically important. In almost all such calculations, it is implicitly assumed that the cash flows occur at the *end* of each period. In fact, all the formulas we have discussed, all the numbers in a standard present value or future value table, and, very importantly, all the preset (or default) settings on a financial calculator or spreadsheet assume that cash flows occur at the end of each period. Unless you are very explicitly told otherwise, you should always assume that this is what is meant.

As a quick illustration of this point, suppose you are told that a three-year investment has a first-year cash flow of $100, a second-year cash flow of $200, and a third-year cash flow of $300. You are asked to draw a time line. Without further information, you should always assume that the time line looks like this:

On our time line, notice how the first cash flow occurs at the end of the first period, the second at the end of the second period, and the third at the end of the third period.

We will close out this section by answering the question we posed concerning Steve Nash's contract at the beginning of the chapter. Recall our assumption that the contract called for $11 million to be paid in the first year, increased by $1 million each following year, and reached $15 million at the end of the fifth year. If 12 percent is the appropriate interest rate, what kind of deal did the Canadian player get?

To answer, we can calculate the present value by discounting each year's salary back to the present as follows (notice we assumed the future salaries will be paid at the end of the year):

Year 1: $11,000,000 \times 1/1.12^1 = \$9,821,428.57$

Year 2: $12,000,000 \times 1/1.12^2 = \$9,566,326.53$

Year 3: $13,000,000 \times 1/1.12^3 = \$9,253,143.22$

Year 4: $14,000,000 \times 1/1.12^4 = \$8,897,253.10$

Year 5: $15,000,000 \times 1/1.12^5 = \$8,511,402.84$

If you add up the numbers, you will see that Nash's contract had a present value of about $46 million, considerably less than the $65 million value reported, but still pretty good.

Spreadsheet Strategies	How to Calculate Present Values with Multiple Future Cash Flows Using a Spreadsheet

Just as we did in our previous chapter, we can set up a basic spreadsheet to calculate the present values of the individual cash flows as follows. Notice that we have simply calculated the present values one at a time and added them up.

	A	B	C	D	E	F
1						
2			Using a spreadsheet to value multiple cash flows			
3						
4	What is the present value of $200 in one year, $400 the next year, $600 the next year, and $800 the					
5	last year if the discount rate is 12 percent?					
6						
7	Rate:	.12				
8						
9	Year	Cash flows	Present values	Formula used		
10	1	$200	$178.57	=PV($B$7,A10,0,-B10)		
11	2	$400	$318.88	=PV($B$7,A11,0,-B11)		
12	3	$600	$427.07	=PV($B$7,A12,0,-B12)		
13	4	$800	$508.41	=PV($B$7,A13,0,-B13)		
14						
15		Total PV:	$1,432.93	=SUM(C10:C13)		
16						
17	Notice the negative signs inserted in the PV formulas. These just make the present values have					
18	positive signs. Also, the discount rate in cell B7 is entered as $B$7 (an "absolute" reference) because					
19	it is used over and over. We could have just entered ".12" instead, but our approach is more flexible.					
20						
21						
22						

CONCEPT QUESTIONS

5.1a Describe how to calculate the future value of a series of cash flows.

5.1b Describe how to calculate the present value of a series of cash flows.

5.1c Unless we are explicitly told otherwise, what do we always assume about the timing of cash flows in present and future value problems?

5.2 | VALUING LEVEL CASH FLOWS: ANNUITIES AND PERPETUITIES

We will frequently encounter situations where we have multiple cash flows that are all the same amount. For example, a very common type of loan repayment plan calls for the borrower to repay the loan by making a series of equal payments for some length of time. Almost all consumer loans (such as car loans) and home mortgages feature equal payments, usually made each month.

annuity

A level stream of cash flows for a fixed period of time.

More generally, a series of constant, or level, cash flows that occur at the end of each period for some fixed number of periods is called an ordinary **annuity**; or, more correctly, the cash flows are said to be in ordinary annuity form. Annuities appear very frequently in financial arrangements, and there are some useful shortcuts for determining their values. We consider these next.

Present Value for Annuity Cash Flows

Suppose we were examining an asset that promised to pay $500 at the end of each of the next three years. The cash flows from this asset are in the form of a three-year, $500 ordinary annuity. If we wanted to earn 10 percent on our money, how much would we offer for this annuity?

From the previous section, we know that we can discount each of these $500 payments back to the present at 10 percent to determine the total present value:

$$
\begin{aligned}
\text{Present value} &= \$500/1.1^1 + 500/1.1^2 + 500/1.1^3 \\
&= \$500/1.10 + 500/1.21 + 500/1.331 \\
&= \$454.55 + 413.22 + 375.66 \\
&= \$1,243.43
\end{aligned}
$$

This approach works just fine. However, we will often encounter situations where the number of cash flows is quite large. For example, a typical home mortgage calls for monthly payments over 25 years, for a total of 300 payments. If we were trying to determine the present value of those payments, it would be useful to have a shortcut.

Since the cash flows on an annuity are all the same, we can come up with a very useful variation on the basic present value equation. It turns out that the present value of an annuity of C dollars per period for t periods when the rate of return, or interest rate, is r is given by:

$$
\begin{aligned}
\text{Annuity present value} &= C \times \left(\frac{1 - \text{Present value factor}}{r} \right) \\
&= C \times \left\{ \frac{1 - [1/(1 + r)^t]}{r} \right\}
\end{aligned}
$$

[5.1]

The term in parentheses on the first line is sometimes called the present value interest factor for annuities and abbreviated PVIFA(r, t).

The expression for the annuity present value may look a little complicated, but it isn't difficult to use. Notice that the term in square brackets on the second line, $1/(1 + r)^t$, is the same present value factor we've been calculating. In our example just above, the interest rate is 10 percent and there are three years involved. The usual present value factor is thus:

$$
\text{Present value factor} = 1/1.1^3 = 1/1.331 = .75131
$$

To calculate the annuity present value factor, we just plug this in:

$$
\begin{aligned}
\text{Annuity present value factor} &= (1 - \text{Present value factor})/r \\
&= (1 - .75131)/.10 \\
&= .248685/.10 = 2.48685
\end{aligned}
$$

Just as we calculated before, the present value of our $500 annuity is then:

$$
\text{Annuity present value} = \$500 \times 2.48685 = \$1,243.43
$$

Number of Periods	Interest Rates			
	5%	10%	15%	20%
1	.9524	.9091	.8696	.8333
2	1.8594	1.7355	1.6257	1.5278
3	2.7232	2.4869	2.2832	2.1065
4	3.5460	3.1699	2.8550	2.5887
5	4.3295	3.7908	3.3522	2.9906

TABLE 5.1

Annuity present value interest factors

How Much Can You Afford?   EXAMPLE 5.5

After carefully going over your budget, you have determined you can afford to pay $632 per month toward a new sports car. You call up your local bank and find out that the going rate is 1 percent per month for 48 months. How much can you borrow?

To determine how much you can borrow, we need to calculate the present value of $632 per month for 48 months at 1 percent per month. The loan payments are in ordinary annuity form, so the annuity present value factor is:

$$\text{Annuity PV factor} = (1 - \text{Present value factor})/r$$
$$= [1 - (1/1.01^{48})]/0.1$$
$$= (1 - .6203)/.01 = 37.9740$$

With this factor, we can calculate the present value of the 48 payments of $632 each as:

$$\text{Present value} = \$632 \times 37.9740 = \$24,000$$

Therefore, $24,000 is what you can afford to borrow and repay.

Annuity Tables   Just as there are tables for ordinary present value factors, there are tables for annuity factors as well. Table 5.1 contains a few such factors; Table A.3 in Appendix A contains a larger set. To find the annuity present value factor we just calculated, look for the row corresponding to three periods and then find the column for 10 percent. The number you see at that intersection should be 2.4869 (rounded to four decimal places), as we calculated. Once again, try calculating a few of these factors yourself and compare your answers to the ones in the table to make sure you know how to do it. If you are using a financial calculator, just enter $1 as the payment and calculate the present value; the result should be the annuity present value factor.

Calculator Hints   Annuity Present Values

To find annuity present values with a financial calculator, we need to use the **PMT** key (you were probably wondering what it was for). Compared to finding the present value of a single amount, there are two important differences. First, we enter the annuity cash flow using the **PMT** key, and, second, we don't enter anything for the future value, **FV**. So, for example, the problem we have been examining is a three-year, $500 annuity. If the discount rate is 10 percent, we need to do the following (after clearing out the calculator!):

Enter	3	10	500		
	N	**I/Y**	**PMT**	**PV**	**FV**
Solve for				−1,243.43	

As usual, we get a negative sign on the PV.

Spreadsheet Strategies   Annuity Present Values

Using a spreadsheet to work the same problem goes like this:

	A	B	C	D	E	F	G
1							
2		Using a spreadsheet to find annuity present values					
3							
4	What is the present value of $500 per year for 3 years if the discount rate is 10 percent?						
5	We need to solve for the unknown present value, so we use the formula PV(rate, nper, pmt, fv).						
6							
7	Payment amount per period:	$500					
8	Number of payments:	3					
9	Discount rate:	.1					
10							
11	Annuity present value:	$1,243.43					
12							
13	The formula entered in cell B11 is =PV(B9, B8, -B7, 0); notice that fv is zero and that pmt has a						
14	negative sign on it. Also notice that the discount rate is entered as a decimal, not a percentage.						
15							

Finding the Payment   Suppose you wish to start up a new business that specializes in the latest of health food trends, frozen yak milk. To produce and market your product, the Yakee Doodle Dandy, you need to borrow $100,000. Because it strikes you as unlikely that this particular fad will be long-lived, you propose to pay off the loan quickly by making five equal annual payments. If the interest rate is 18 percent, what will the payments be?

In this case, we know that the present value is $100,000. The interest rate is 18 percent, and there are five years to make payments. The payments are all equal, so we need to find the relevant annuity factor and solve for the unknown cash flow:

$$\text{Annuity present value} = \$100{,}000 = C \times (1 - \text{Present value factor})/r$$
$$\$100{,}000 = C \times (1 - 1/1.18^5)/.18$$
$$= C \times (1 - .4371)/.18$$
$$= C \times 3.1272$$
$$C = \$100{,}000/3.1272 = \$31{,}978$$

Therefore, you'll make five payments of just under $32,000 each.

Calculator Hints   Annuity Payments

Finding annuity payments is easy with a financial calculator. In our example just above, the PV is $100,000, the interest rate is 18 percent, and there are five years. We find the payment as follows:

Enter	5	18		100,000	
	N	I/Y	PMT	PV	FV
Solve for			−31,978		

Here we get a negative sign on the payment because the payment is an outflow for us.

Spreadsheet Strategies Annuity Payments

Using a spreadsheet to work the same problem goes like this:

	A	B	C	D	E	F	G
1							
2			Using a spreadsheet to find annuity payments				
3							
4	What is the annuity payment if the present value is $100,000, the interest rate is 18 percent, and						
5	there are 5 periods? We need to solve for the unknown payment in an annuity, so we use the						
6	formula PMT (rate, nper, pv, fv)						
7							
8	Annuity present value:	$100,000					
9	Number of payments:	5					
10	Discount rate:	.18					
11							
12	Annuity payment:	($31,977.78)					
13							
14	The formula entered in cell B12 is =PMT(B10, B9, -B8, 0); notice that fv is zero and that the payment						
15	has a negative sign because it is an outflow to us.						

Finding the Number of Payments   EXAMPLE 5.6

You ran a little short on your reading week trip, so you put $1,000 on your credit card. You can only afford to make the minimum payment of $20 per month. The interest rate on the credit card is 1.5 percent per month. How long will you need to pay off the $1,000?

What we have here is an annuity of $20 per month at 1.5 percent per month for some unknown length of time. The present value is $1,000 (the amount you owe today). We need to do a little algebra (or else use a financial calculator):

$$\$1,000 = \$20 \times (1 - \text{Present value factor})/0.015$$
$$(\$1,000/20) \times .015 = 1 - \text{Present value factor}$$
$$\text{Present value factor} = .25 = 1/(1 + r)^t$$
$$1.015^t = 1/.25 = 4$$

At this point, the problem boils down to asking the following question: How long does it take for your money to quadruple at 1.5 percent per month? Based on our previous chapter, the answer is about 93 months:

$$1.015^{93} = 3.99 \approx 4$$

It will take you about 93/12 = 7.75 years at this rate.

Calculator Hints   Finding the Number of Payments

To solve this one on a financial calculator, do the following:

Enter		1.5	−20	1,000	
	N	I/Y	PMT	PV	FV
Solve for	93.11				

(continued)

Notice that we put a negative sign on the payment you must make, and we have solved for the number of months. You still have to divide by 12 to get our answer. Also, some financial calculators won't report a fractional value for N; they automatically (without telling you) round up to the next whole period (not to the nearest value). With a spreadsheet, use the function = NPER(rate,pmt,pv,fv); be sure to put in a zero for fv and to enter −20 as the payment.

Finding the Rate   The last question we might want to ask concerns the interest rate implicit in an annuity. For example, an insurance company offers to pay you $1,000 per year for 10 years if you pay $6,710 up front. What rate is implicit in this 10-year annuity?

In this case, we know the present value ($6,710), we know the cash flows ($1,000 per year), and we know the life of the investment (10 years). What we don't know is the discount rate:

$$\$6,710 = \$1,000 \times (1 - \text{Present value factor})/r$$
$$\$6,710/1,000 = 6.71 = \{1 - [1/(1 + r)^{10}]\}/r$$

So, the annuity factor for 10 periods is equal to 6.71, and we need to solve this equation for the unknown value of r. Unfortunately, this is mathematically impossible to do directly. The only way to do it is to use a table or trial and error to find a value for r.

If you look across the row corresponding to 10 periods in Table A.3, you will see a factor of 6.7101 for 8 percent, so we see right away that the insurance company is offering just about 8 percent. Alternatively, we could just start trying different values until we got very close to the answer. Using this trial-and-error approach can be a little tedious, but, fortunately, machines are good at that sort of thing.[1]

To illustrate how to find the answer by trial and error, suppose a relative of yours wants to borrow $3,000. She offers to repay you $1,000 every year for four years. What interest rate are you being offered?

The cash flows here have the form of a four-year, $1,000 annuity. The present value is $3,000. We need to find the discount rate, r. Our goal in doing so is primarily to give you a feel for the relationship between annuity values and discount rates.

We need to start somewhere, and 10 percent is probably as good a place as any to begin. At 10 percent, the annuity factor is:

Annuity present value factor $= (1 - 1/1.10^4)/.10 = 3.1699$

The present value of the cash flows at 10 percent is thus:

Present value $= \$1,000 \times 3.1699 = \$3,169.90$

You can see that we're already in the right ballpark.

Is 10 percent too high or too low? Recall that present values and discount rates move in opposite directions: Increasing the discount rate lowers the PV and vice versa. Our present value here is too high, so the discount rate is too low. If we try 12 percent:

Present value $= \$1,000 \times (1 - 1/1.12^4)/.12 = \$3,037.35$

Now we're almost there. We are still a little low on the discount rate (because the PV is a little high), so we'll try 13 percent:

Present value $= \$1,000 \times (1 - 1/1.13^4)/.13 = \$2,974.47$

---

[1]Financial calculators rely on trial and error to find the answer. That's why they sometimes appear to be "thinking" before coming up with the answer. Actually, it is possible to directly solve for r if there are fewer than five periods, but it's usually not worth the trouble.

This is less than $3,000, so we now know that the answer is between 12 percent and 13 percent, and it looks to be about 12.5 percent. For practice, work at it for a while longer and see if you find that the answer is about 12.59 percent.

Calculator Hints   Finding the Rate

Alternatively, you could use a financial calculator to do the following:

Enter   4   1,000   −3,000

            [N]   [I/Y]   [PMT]   [PV]   [FV]

Solve for   12.59

Notice that we put a negative sign on the present value (why?). With a spreadsheet, use the function = RATE(nper,pmt,pv,fv); be sure to put in a zero for fv and to enter 1,000 as the payment and −3,000 as the pv.

Future Value for Annuities

On occasion, it's also handy to know a shortcut for calculating the future value of an annuity. As you might guess, there are future value factors for annuities as well as present value factors. In general, the future value factor for an annuity is given by:

$$\text{Annuity FV factor} = (\text{Future value factor} - 1)/r$$
$$= [(1 + r)^t - 1]/r \qquad \textbf{[5.2]}$$

To see how we use annuity future value factors, suppose you plan to contribute $2,000 every year into a retirement account paying 8 percent. If you retire in 30 years, how much will you have?

The number of years here, t, is 30, and the interest rate, r, is 8 percent, so we can calculate the annuity future value factor as:

$$\text{Annuity FV factor} = (\text{Future value factor} - 1)/r$$
$$= (1.08^{30} - 1)/.08$$
$$= (10.0627 - 1)/.08$$
$$= 113.2832$$

The future value of this 30-year, $2,000 annuity is thus:

$$\text{Annuity future value} = \$2,000 \times 113.2832$$
$$= \$226,566.4$$

Calculator Hints   Future Values of Annuities

Of course, you could solve this problem using a financial calculator by doing the following:

Enter   30   8   −2,000

            [N]   [I/Y]   [PMT]   [PV]   [FV]

Solve for   226,566.42

Notice that we put a negative sign on the payment (why?). With a spreadsheet, use the function = FV(rate,nper,pmt,pv); be sure to put in a zero for PV and to enter −2,000 as the payment.

A Note on Annuities Due

annuity due
An annuity for which the cash flows occur at the beginning of the period.

So far, we have only discussed ordinary annuities. These are the most important, but there is a variation that is fairly common. Remember that with an ordinary annuity, the cash flows occur at the end of each period. When you take out a loan with monthly payments, for example, the first loan payment normally occurs one month after you get the loan. However, when you lease an apartment, the first lease payment is usually due immediately. The second payment is due at the beginning of the second month, and so on. A lease is an example of an **annuity due.** An annuity due is an annuity for which the cash flows occur at the beginning of each period. Almost any type of arrangement in which we have to prepay the same amount each period is an annuity due.

There are several different ways to calculate the value of an annuity due. With a financial calculator, you simply switch it into "due" or "beginning" mode. It is very important to remember to switch it back when you are finished! Another way to calculate the present value of an annuity due can be illustrated with a time line. Suppose an annuity due has five payments of $400 each, and the relevant discount rate is 10 percent. The time line looks like this:

Notice how the cash flows here are the same as those for a *four*-year ordinary annuity, except that there is an extra $400 at Time 0. For practice, verify that the present value of a four-year $400 ordinary annuity at 10 percent is $1,267.95. If we add on the extra $400, we get $1,667.95, which is the present value of this annuity due.

There is an even easier way to calculate the present or future value of an annuity due. If we assume that cash flows occur at the end of each period when they really occur at the beginning, then we discount each one by one period too many. We could fix this by simply multiplying our answer by $(1 + r)$, where r is the discount rate. In fact, the relationship between the value of an annuity due and an ordinary annuity with the same number of payments is just:

$$\text{Annuity due value} = \text{Ordinary annuity value} \times (1 + r) \qquad \textbf{[5.3]}$$

This works for both present and future values, so calculating the value of an annuity due involves two steps: (1) calculate the present or future value as though it were an ordinary annuity and (2) multiply your answer by $(1 + r)$.

Perpetuities

perpetuity
An annuity in which the cash flows continue forever.

consol
A type of perpetuity.

We've seen that a series of level cash flows can be valued by treating those cash flows as an annuity. An important special case of an annuity arises when the level stream of cash flows continues forever. Such an asset is called a **perpetuity** since the cash flows are perpetual. Some perpetuities are also called **consols.** See Example 5.7 for an important example of a perpetuity.

Since a perpetuity has an infinite number of cash flows, we obviously can't compute its value by discounting each one. Fortunately, valuing a perpetuity turns out to be the easiest possible case. The present value of a perpetuity is simply:

$$\text{PV for a perpetuity} = C/r \qquad \textbf{[5.4]}$$

For example, an investment offers a perpetual cash flow of $500 every year. The return you require on such an investment is 8 percent. What is the value of this investment? The value of this perpetuity is:

$$\text{Perpetuity PV} = C/r = \$500/.08 = \$6,250$$

WORK THE WEB

As we discussed in our previous chapter, many Web sites have financial calculators. One of these sites is MoneyChimp, which is located at **www.moneychimp.com.** Suppose you retire with $1,000,000 and want to withdraw an equal amount each year for the next 30 years. If you can earn a 9 percent return, how much can you withdraw each year? Here is what MoneyChimp says:

Inputs		
Starting Principal:	$	1,000,000.00
Growth Rate:		9 %
Years to Pay Out:		30

Calculate

Results		
Annual Payout Amount:	$	89,299.40

According to the MoneyChimp calculator, the answer is $89,299.40. How important is it to understand what you are doing? Calculate this one for yourself, and you should get $97,336.35. Which one is right? You are, of course! What's going on is that MoneyChimp assumes (but tells you on a different page) that the annuity is in the form of an annuity due, not an ordinary annuity. Recall that with an annuity due the payments occur at the beginning of the period rather than at the end of the period. The moral of the story is clear: *Caveat calculator.*

This concludes our discussion of valuing investments with multiple cash flows. By now, you probably think that you'll just use online calculators to handle annuity problems. Before you do, see our *Work the Web* box above!

Preferred Stock   EXAMPLE 5.7

Preferred stock (or preference stock) is an important example of a perpetuity. When a corporation sells preferred stock, the buyer is promised a fixed cash dividend every period (usually every quarter) forever. This dividend must be paid before any dividend can be paid to regular stockholders, hence the term *preferred.*

Suppose the Alberta Co. wants to sell preferred stock at $100 per share. A very similar issue of preferred stock already outstanding has a price of $40 per share and offers a dividend of $1 every quarter. What dividend will Alberta have to offer if the preferred stock is going to sell?

The issue that is already out has a present value of $40 and a cash flow of $1 every quarter forever. Since this is a perpetuity:

Present value = $40 = $1 × (1/r)

$\qquad$ r = 2.5%

To be competitive, the new Alberta issue will also have to offer 2.5 percent *per quarter;* so, if the present value is to be $100, the dividend must be such that:

Present value = $100 = C × (1/.025)

$\qquad$ C = $2.5 (per quarter)

CONCEPT QUESTIONS

5.2a In general, what is the present value of an annuity of *C* dollars per period at a discount rate of *r* per period? The future value?

5.2b In general, what is the present value of a perpetuity?

5.3 | COMPARING RATES: THE EFFECT OF COMPOUNDING PERIODS

The last issue we need to discuss has to do with the way interest rates are quoted. This subject causes a fair amount of confusion because rates are quoted in many different ways. Sometimes the way a rate is quoted is the result of tradition, and sometimes it's the result of legislation. Unfortunately, at times, rates are quoted in deliberately deceptive ways to mislead borrowers and investors. We will discuss these topics in this section.

Effective Annual Rates and Compounding

If a rate is quoted as 10 percent compounded semiannually, then what this means is that the investment actually pays 5 percent every six months. A natural question then arises: Is 5 percent every six months the same thing as 10 percent per year? It's easy to see that it is not. If you invest $1 at 10 percent per year, you will have $1.10 at the end of the year. If you invest at 5 percent every six months, then you'll have the future value of $1 at 5 percent for two periods, or:

$$\$1 \times 1.05^2 = \$1.1025$$

This is $.0025 more. The reason is very simple. What has occurred is that your account was credited with $1 × .05 = 5 cents in interest after six months. In the following six months, you earned 5 percent on that nickel, for an extra 5 × .05 = .25 cent.

As our example illustrates, 10 percent compounded semiannually is actually equivalent to 10.25 percent per year. Put another way, we would be indifferent between 10 percent compounded semiannually and 10.25 percent compounded annually. Anytime we have compounding during the year, we need to be concerned about what the rate really is.

In our example, the 10 percent is called a **stated,** or **quoted, interest rate.** Other names are used as well. The 10.25 percent, which is actually the rate that you will earn, is called the **effective annual rate (EAR).** To compare different investments or interest rates, we will always need to convert to effective rates. Some general procedures for doing this are discussed next.

> **stated interest rate**
> The interest rate expressed in terms of the interest payment made each period. Also, *quoted interest rate.*

> **effective annual rate (EAR)**
> The interest rate expressed as if it were compounded once per year.

Calculating and Comparing Effective Annual Rates

To see why it is important to work only with effective rates, suppose you've shopped around and come up with the following three rates:

Bank A: 15 percent, compounded daily

Bank B: 15.5 percent, compounded quarterly

Bank C: 16 percent, compounded annually

Which of these is the best if you are thinking of opening a savings account? Which of these is best if they represent loan rates?

To begin, Bank C is offering 16 percent per year. Since there is no compounding during the year, this is the effective rate. Bank B is actually paying .155/4 = .03875, or 3.875 percent, per quarter. At this rate, an investment of $1 for four quarters would grow to:

$$\$1 \times 1.03845^4 = \$1.1642$$

The EAR, therefore, is 16.42 percent. For a saver, this is much better than the 16 percent rate Bank C is offering; for a borrower, it's worse.

Bank A is compounding every day. This may seem a little extreme, but it is very common to calculate interest daily. In this case, the daily interest rate is actually:

$$.15/365 = .000411$$

This is .0411 percent per day. At this rate, an investment of $1 for 365 periods would grow to:

$$\$1 \times 1.000411^{365} = \$1.1618$$

The EAR is 16.18 percent. This is not as good as Bank B's 16.42 percent for a saver, and not as good as Bank C's 16 percent for a borrower.

This example illustrates two things. First, the highest quoted rate is not necessarily the best. Second, compounding during the year can lead to a significant difference between the quoted rate and the effective rate. Remember that the effective rate is what you get or what you pay.

If you look at our examples, you see that we computed the EARs in three steps. We first divided the quoted rate by the number of times that the interest is compounded. We then added 1 to the result and raised it to the power of the number of times the interest is compounded. Finally, we subtracted the 1. If we let m be the number of times the interest is compounded during the year, these steps can be summarized simply as:

$$EAR = (1 + \text{Quoted rate}/m)^m - 1 \qquad [5.5]$$

For example, suppose you were offered 12 percent compounded monthly. In this case, the interest is compounded 12 times a year; so m is 12. You can calculate the effective rate as:

$$
\begin{aligned}
EAR &= (1 + \text{Quoted rate}/m)^m - 1 \\
&= (1 + .12/12)^{12} - 1 \\
&= 1.01^{12} - 1 \\
&= 1.126825 - 1 \\
&= 12.6825\%
\end{aligned}
$$

What's the EAR? EXAMPLE **5.8**

A bank is offering 12 percent compounded quarterly. If you put $100 in an account, how much will you have at the end of one year? What's the EAR? How much will you have at the end of two years?

The bank is effectively offering 12%/4 = 3% every quarter. If you invest $100 for four periods at 3 percent per period, the future value is:

$$
\begin{aligned}
\text{Future value} &= \$100 \times 1.03^4 \\
&= \$100 \times 1.1255 \\
&= \$112.55
\end{aligned}
$$

The EAR is 12.55 percent: $100 × (1 + .1255) = $112.55.

(continued)

We can determine what you would have at the end of two years in two different ways. One way is to recognize that two years is the same as eight quarters. At 3 percent per quarter, after eight quarters, you would have:

$$\$100 \times 1.03^8 = \$100 \times 1.2668 = \$126.68$$

Alternatively, we could determine the value after two years by using an EAR of 12.55 percent; so after two years you would have:

$$\$100 \times 1.1255^2 = \$100 \times 1.2688 = \$126.68$$

Thus, the two calculations produce the same answer. This illustrates an important point. Any time we do a present or future value calculation, the rate we use must be an actual or effective rate. In this case, the actual rate is 3 percent per quarter. The effective annual rate is 12.55 percent. It doesn't matter which one we use once we know the EAR.

EXAMPLE 5.9   **Quoting a Rate**

Now that you know how to convert a quoted rate to an EAR, consider going the other way. As a lender, you know you want to actually earn 18 percent on a particular loan. You want to quote a rate that features monthly compounding. What rate do you quote?

In this case, we know that the EAR is 18 percent, and we know that this is the result of monthly compounding. Let q stand for the quoted rate. We thus have:

$$EAR = (1 + \text{Quoted rate}/m)^m - 1$$
$$.18 = (1 + q/12)^{12} - 1$$
$$1.18 = (1 + q/12)^{12}$$

We need to solve this equation for the quoted rate. This calculation is the same as the ones we did to find an unknown interest rate in Chapter 4:

$$1.18^{(1/12)} = 1 + q/12$$
$$1.18^{.08333} = 1 + q/12$$
$$1.0139 = 1 + q/12$$
$$q = .0139 \times 12$$
$$= 16.68\%$$

Therefore, the rate you would quote is 16.68 percent, compounded monthly.

EARs and APRs

annual percentage rate (APR)
The interest rate charged per period multiplied by the number of periods per year.

Sometimes it's not altogether clear whether a rate is an effective annual rate or not. A case in point concerns what is called the **annual percentage rate (APR)** on a loan. Cost of borrowing disclosure regulations in Canada require that lenders disclose an APR on virtually all consumer loans. This rate must be displayed on a loan document in a prominent and unambiguous way.

Given that an APR must be calculated and displayed, an obvious question arises: Is an APR an effective annual rate? Put another way: If a bank quotes a car loan at 12 percent APR, is the consumer actually paying 12 percent interest? Surprisingly, the answer is no. There is some confusion over this point, which we discuss next.

The confusion over APRs arises because lenders are required by law to compute the APR in a particular way. By law, the APR is simply equal to the interest rate per period multiplied by the number of periods in a year. For example, if a bank is charging 1.2 percent per month on car loans, then the APR that must be reported is $1.2\% \times 12 = 14.4\%$. So, an APR is in fact a quoted, or stated, rate in the sense we've been discussing. For example, an

APR of 12 percent on a loan calling for monthly payments is really 1 percent per month. The EAR on such a loan is thus:

$$EAR = (1 + APR/12)^{12} - 1$$
$$= 1.01^{12} - 1 = 12.6825\%$$

What Rate Are You Paying? **EXAMPLE 5.10**

A typical credit card agreement quotes an interest rate of 18 percent APR. Monthly payments are required. What is the actual interest rate you pay on such a credit card?

Based on our discussion, an APR of 18 percent with monthly payments is really .18/12 = .015, or 1.5 percent, per month. The EAR is thus:

$$EAR = (1 + .18/12)^{12} - 1$$
$$= 1.015^{12} - 1$$
$$= 1.1956 - 1$$
$$= 19.56\%$$

This is the rate you actually pay.

The difference between an APR and an EAR probably won't be all that great (as long as the rates are relatively low), but it is somewhat ironic that disclosure regulations laws sometimes require lenders to be *un*truthful about the actual rate on a loan.

There can be a huge difference between the APR and EAR when interest rates are large. For example, consider "payday loans." Payday loans are short-term loans made to consumers, often for less than two weeks, and are offered by companies such as AmeriCash Advance and National Payday. The loans work like this: You write a cheque today that is postdated (i.e., the date on the cheque is in the future) and give it to the company. They give you some cash. When the cheque date arrives, you either go to the store and pay the cash amount of the cheque, or the company cashes it (or else automatically renews the loan).

For example, AmeriCash Advance allows you to write a cheque for $125 dated 15 days in the future, for which they give you $100 today. So what is the APR and EAR of this arrangement? First we need to find the interest rate, which we can find by the FV equation as:

$$FV = PV \times (1 + r)^1$$
$$\$125 = \$100 \times (1 + r)^1$$
$$1.25 = (1 + r)$$
$$r = .25 \text{ or } 25\%$$

That doesn't seem too bad until you remember this is the interest rate for *15 days!* The APR of the loan is:

$$APR = .25 \times 365/15$$
$$APR = 6.08333 \text{ or } 608.33\%$$

And the EAR for this loan is:

$$EAR = (1 + \text{Quoted rate}/m)^m - 1$$
$$EAR = (1 + .25)^{365/15} - 1$$
$$EAR = 227.1096 \text{ or } 22,710.96\%$$

Now that's an interest rate! Just to see what a difference a day (or three) makes, let's look at National Payday's terms. This company will allow you to write a postdated cheque for the same amount, but will give you 18 days to repay. Check for yourself that the APR of this arrangement is 506.94 percent and the EAR is 9,128.26 percent. Still not a loan we would like to take out!

EARs, APRs, Financial Calculators, and Spreadsheets

A financial calculator will convert a quoted rate (or an APR) to an EAR and back. Unfortunately, the specific procedures are too different from calculator to calculator for us to illustrate in general terms; you'll have to consult Appendix D or your calculator's operating manual. Typically, however, what we have called EAR is labelled "EFF" (for *effective*) on a calculator. More troublesome is the fact that what we have called a quoted rate (or an APR) is labelled "NOM" (for *nominal*). Unfortunately, the term *nominal rate* has come to have a different meaning that we will see in our next chapter. So, just remember that *nominal* in this context means quoted rate or APR.

With a spreadsheet, we can easily do these conversions. To convert a quoted rate (or an APR) to an effective rate in Excel, for example, use the formula EFFECT(nominal_rate,npery), where nominal_rate is the quoted rate or APR and npery is the number of compounding periods per year. Similarly, to convert an EAR to a quoted rate, use NOMINAL(effect_rate,npery), where effect_rate is the EAR.

CONCEPT QUESTIONS

5.3a If an interest rate is given as 12 percent, compounded daily, what do we call this rate?

5.3b What is an APR? What is an EAR? Are they the same thing?

5.3c In general, what is the relationship between a stated interest rate and an effective interest rate? Which is more relevant for financial decisions?

5.4 | LOAN TYPES AND LOAN AMORTIZATION

Whenever a lender extends a loan, some provision will be made for repayment of the principal (the original loan amount). A loan might be repaid in equal installments, for example, or it might be repaid in a single lump sum. Because the way that the principal and interest are paid is up to the parties involved, the number of possibilities is actually unlimited.

In this section, we describe a few forms of repayment that come up quite often; more complicated forms can usually be built up from these. The three basic types of loans are pure discount loans, interest-only loans, and amortized loans. Working with these loans is a very straightforward application of the present value principles that we have already developed.

Pure Discount Loans

The pure discount loan is the simplest form of loan. With such a loan, the borrower receives money today and repays a single lump sum at some time in the future. A one-year, 10 percent pure discount loan, for example, would require the borrower to repay $1.1 in one year for every dollar borrowed today.

Because a pure discount loan is so simple, we already know how to value one. Suppose a borrower was able to repay $25,000 in five years. If we, acting as the lender, wanted a 12 percent interest rate on the loan, how much would we be willing to lend? Put another way, what value would we assign today to that $25,000 to be repaid in five years? Based on our work in Chapter 4, we know that the answer is just the present value of $25,000 at 12 percent for five years:

Present value $= \$25,000/1.12^5$
$$= \$25,000/1.7623$$
$$= \$14,186$$

Pure discount loans are very common when the loan term is short, say, a year or less. In recent years, they have become increasingly common for much longer periods.

Treasury Bills   EXAMPLE **5.11**

When the Canadian government borrows money on a short-term basis (a year or less), it does so by selling what are called *Treasury bills,* or *T-bills* for short. A T-bill is a promise by the government to repay a fixed amount at some time in the future, for example, 3 months or 12 months.

Treasury bills are pure discount loans. If a T-bill promises to repay $10,000 in 12 months, and the market interest rate is 4 percent, how much will the bill sell for in the market?

Since the going rate is 4 percent, the T-bill will sell for the present value of $10,000 to be paid in one year at 4 percent, or:

Present value = $10,000/1.04 = $9,615.38

Interest-Only Loans

A second type of loan has a repayment plan that calls for the borrower to pay interest each period and to repay the entire principal (the original loan amount) at some point in the future. Such loans are called *interest-only loans.* Notice that if there is just one period, a pure discount loan and an interest-only loan are the same thing.

For example, with a three-year, 10 percent, interest-only loan of $1,000, the borrower would pay $1,000 $\times$ .10 = $100 in interest at the end of the first and second years. At the end of the third year, the borrower would return the $1,000 along with another $100 in interest for that year. Similarly, a 50-year interest-only loan would call for the borrower to pay interest every year for the next 50 years and then repay the principal. In the extreme, the borrower pays the interest every period forever and never repays any principal. As we discussed earlier in the chapter, the result is a perpetuity.

Most corporate bonds have the general form of an interest-only loan. Because we will be considering bonds in some detail in the next chapter, we will defer a further discussion of them for now.

Amortized Loans

With a pure discount or interest-only loan, the principal is repaid all at once. An alternative is an *amortized loan,* with which the lender may require the borrower to repay parts of the loan amount over time. The process of paying off a loan by making regular principal reductions is called *amortizing* the loan.

A simple way of amortizing a loan is to have the borrower pay the interest each period plus some fixed amount. This approach is common with medium-term business loans. For example, suppose a business takes out a $5,000, five-year loan at 9 percent. The loan agreement calls for the borrower to pay the interest on the loan balance each year and to reduce the loan balance each year by $1,000. Since the loan amount declines by $1,000 each year, it is fully paid in five years.

In the case we are considering, notice that the total payment will decline each year. The reason is that the loan balance goes down, resulting in a lower interest charge each year, while the $1,000 principal reduction is constant. For example, the interest in the first year will be $5,000 × .09 = $450. The total payment will be $1,000 + 450 = $1,450. In the second year, the loan balance is $4,000, so the interest is $4,000 × .09 = $360, and the total payment is $1,360. We can calculate the total payment in each of the remaining years by preparing a simple *amortization schedule* as follows:

Year	Beginning Balance	Total Payment	Interest Paid	Principal Paid	Ending Balance
1	$5,000	$1,450	$ 450	$1,000	$4,000
2	4,000	1,360	360	1,000	3,000
3	3,000	1,270	270	1,000	2,000
4	2,000	1,180	180	1,000	1,000
5	1,000	1,090	90	1,000	0
Totals		$6,350	$1,350	$5,000	

Notice that, in each year, the interest paid is just given by the beginning balance multiplied by the interest rate. Also notice that the beginning balance is given by the ending balance from the previous year.

Probably the most common way of amortizing a loan is to have the borrower make a single, fixed payment every period. Almost all consumer loans (such as car loans) and mortgages work this way. For example, suppose our five-year, 9 percent, $5,000 loan was amortized this way. How would the amortization schedule look?

We first need to determine the payment. From our discussion earlier in the chapter, we know that this loan's cash flows are in the form of an ordinary annuity. In this case, we can solve for the payment as follows:

$$\$5,000 = C \times (1 - 1/1.09^5)/.09$$
$$= C \times (1 - .6499)/.09$$

This gives us:

$$C = \$5,000/3.8897$$
$$= \$1,285.46$$

The borrower will therefore make five equal payments of $1,285.46. Will this pay off the loan? We will check by filling in an amortization schedule.

In our previous example, we knew the principal reduction each year. We then calculated the interest owed to get the total payment. In this example, we know the total payment. We will thus calculate the interest and then subtract it from the total payment to get the principal portion in each payment.

In the first year, the interest is $450, as we calculated before. Since the total payment is $1,285.46, the principal paid in the first year must be:

Principal paid = $1,285.46 − 450 = $835.46

The ending loan balance is thus:

Ending balance = $5,000 − 835.46 = $4,164.54

The interest in the second year is $4,164.54 × .09 = $374.81, and the loan balance declines by $1,285.46 − 374.81 = $910.65. We can summarize all of the relevant calculations in the following schedule:

Explore how to save and pay for your postsecondary education at www.canlearn.ca

Year	Beginning Balance	Total Payment	Interest Paid	Principal Paid	Ending Balance
1	$5,000.00	$1,285.46	$ 450.00	$ 835.46	$4,164.54
2	4,164.54	1,285.46	374.81	910.65	3,253.88
3	3,253.88	1,285.46	292.85	992.61	2,261.27
4	2,261.27	1,285.46	203.51	1,081.95	1,179.32
5	1,179.32	1,285.46	106.14	1,179.32	.00
Totals		$6,427.30	$1,427.31	$5,000.00	

693.75

Since the loan balance declines to zero, the five equal payments do pay off the loan. Notice that the interest paid declines each period. This isn't surprising since the loan balance is going down. Given that the total payment is fixed, the principal paid must be rising each period.

If you compare the two loan amortizations in this section, you will see that the total interest is greater for the equal total payment case, $1,427.31 versus $1,350. The reason for this is that the loan is repaid more slowly early on, so the interest is somewhat higher. This doesn't mean that one loan is better than the other; it simply means that one is effectively paid off faster than the other. For example, the principal reduction in the first year is $835.46 in the equal total payment case, compared to $1,000 in the first case. Spreadsheets are quite useful for preparing loan amortization schedules. See our *Spreadsheet Strategies* on the next page for an example.

Mortgages

Mortgages are loans used to purchase real estate. As a rule, the purchased real estate serves as collateral on these loans. Mortgages are commonly arranged as amortized loans,

mortgage
A loan collateralized with real estate.

How Much Are Your Payments? EXAMPLE 5.12

The Bank of British Columbia has offered you a $200,000 mortgage with a 25-year amortization period and a three-year quoted rate of 8 percent. How much will your monthly payments be?

First, we take into account the semiannual compounding of the quoted annual rate (APR):

$$EAR = (1 + \text{Quoted rate}/m)^m - 1$$
$$= (1 + 0.08/2)^2 - 1$$
$$= 8.16\%$$

Then we determine the effective monthly rate (EMR), because our mortgage payments are made monthly. In other words, we find what monthly rate compounded 12 times per year will give us the calculated EAR:

$$EAR = (1 + EMR)^{12} - 1$$
$$(1 + EAR) = (1 + EMR)^{12}$$
$$EMR = (EAR + 1)^{1/12} - 1$$
$$= (0.0816 + 1)^{1/12} - 1$$
$$= 0.006558197 = 0.6558197\%$$

•6806

6),500 = C × (1 + 1/(.08)₂

7.5625

Your mortgage requires 300 payments = 12 months × 25 years. Now we can use the annuity present value formula **[5.1]** to calculate the monthly payments:

$$\text{Annuity Present Value} = C \times [1 - 1/(1 + r)^t]/r$$
$$\$200,000 = C [1 - 1/1.006558197^{300}]/0.006558197$$
$$C = \$1,526.43$$

Spreadsheet Strategies Loan Amortization Using a Spreadsheet

Loan amortization is a very common spreadsheet application. To illustrate, we will set up the problem that we have just examined, a five-year, $5,000, 9 percent loan with constant payments. Our spreadsheet looks like this:

	A	B	C	D	E	F	G	H
1								
2				Using a spreadsheet to amortize a loan				
3								
4			Loan amount:	$5,000				
5			Interest rate:	.09				
6			Loan term:	5				
7			Loan payment:	**$1,285.46**				
8				Note: payment is calculated using PMT(rate,nper,-pv,fv).				
9		Amortization table:						
10								
11		Year	Beginning	Total	Interest	Principal	Ending	
12			Balance	Payment	Paid	Paid	Balance	
13		1	$5,000.00	$1,285.46	$450.00	$835.46	$4,164.54	
14		2	4,164.54	1,285.46	374.81	910.65	3,253.88	
15		3	3,253.88	1,285.46	292.85	992.61	2,261.27	
16		4	2,261.27	1,285.46	203.51	1,081.95	1,179.32	
17		5	1,179.32	1,285.46	106.14	1,179.32	.00	
18		Totals		$6,427.31	$1,427.31	$5,000.00		
19								
20		Formulas in the amortization table:						
21								
22		Year	Beginning	Total	Interest	Principal	Ending	
23			Balance	Payment	Paid	Paid	Balance	
24		1	=+D4	=$D$7	=+$D$5*C13	=+D13-E13	=+C13-F13	
25		2	=+G13	=$D$7	=+$D$5*C14	=+D14-E14	=+C14-F14	
26		3	=+G14	=$D$7	=+$D$5*C15	=+D15-E15	=+C15-F15	
27		4	=+G15	=$D$7	=+$D$5*C16	=+D16-E16	=+C16-F16	
28		5	=+G16	=$D$7	=+$D$5*C17	=+D17-E17	=+C17-F17	
29								
30		Note: totals in the amortization table are calculated using the SUM formula.						
31								

in which each payment includes both interest and principal. Usually mortgages are repaid by making monthly payments, while other payment frequencies, such as weekly and bi-weekly, are available as well. Because of their large size, mortgages have long maturities, up to 25–30 years.

Mortgages in Canada have two differences from typical loans. First, Canadian regulations require financial institutions to quote a mortgage rate assuming semiannual

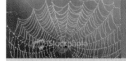

WORK THE WEB

Preparing a mortgage amortization table is one of the more tedious time value of money applications. Using a spreadsheet would make it relatively easy, but there are also Web sites available that will prepare an amortization table quickly and simply. One such site is Mortgage Intelligence. Their Web site **www.mortgageintelligence.ca** has a mortgage loan calculator. Go to "Handy Tools" and click on "Quick Calculator." Suppose you take a 25-year mortgage of $200,000 at 5.99 percent. What are your monthly payments? Using the calculator we get:

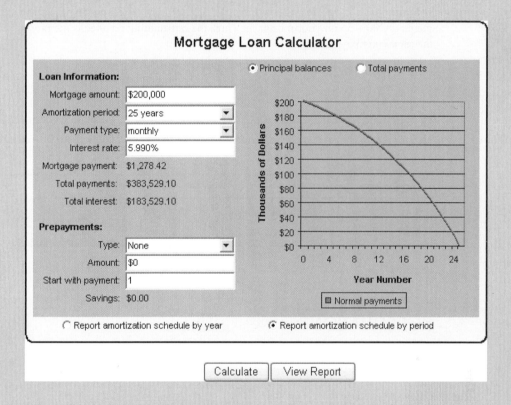

Try this example yourself and hit the "View Report" button. You will find that your first payment will consist of $292.32 in principal and $986.10 in interest. Over the life of the mortgage you will pay a total of $183,529.10 in interest.

Source: www.mortgageintelligence.ca.

compounding. Second, while an interest rate is used to determine payments over the whole amortization period, the interest rate is fixed for a period, called the term, which may be shorter than the amortization period. At the end of the term, which can be up to ten years, a new interest rate is negotiated for the remaining mortgage balance.

Quite likely, you will take out at least one mortgage in your lifetime; therefore, let us examine in detail how monthly payments are determined using the example below.

For Example 5.12, we can construct an amortization schedule for the first two payments:

Month	Beginning Balance	Total Payment	Interest Paid	Principal Paid	Ending Balance
1	$200,000.00	$1,526.43	$1,311.64	$214.79	$199,785.21
2	$199,785.21	$1,526.43	$1,310.23	$216.20	$199,569.01

Finally, how much will you still owe on your mortgage at the end of the 3-year term?

Since you have made 36 payments = 12 months × 3 years, you still owe 264 payments = 300 – 36 on your mortgage. Thus, the outstanding balance is the present value of the remaining payments:

Many Canadian banks provide mortgage calculators. Visit, for example, **www.tdcanadatrust.com/mortgages** and **www.rbcroyalbank.com/mortgages.**

$$\text{Annuity Present Value} = C \times [1 - 1/(1 + r)^t]/r$$
$$= \$1,526.43\,[1 - 1/1.00655820^{264}]/0.00655820$$
$$= \$191,310.87$$

We will close our discussion by noting again that several Web sites offer amortization schedules for mortgages in Canada. See our *Work the Web* box on page 151 for an example.

CONCEPT QUESTIONS

5.4a   What is a pure discount loan?

5.4b   What does it mean to amortize a loan?

KEY EQUATIONS:

I. Symbols

PV = Present value, what future cash flows are worth today

FV_t = Future value, what cash flows are worth in the future at time t

r = Interest rate, rate of return, or discount rate per period—typically, but not always, one year

t = Number of periods—typically, but not always, the number of years

C = Cash amount

II. Present value of C per period for t periods at r percent per period

$$PV = C \times \left\{ \frac{1 - [1/(1 + r)^t]}{r} \right\} \qquad [5.1]$$

The term $\left\{ \dfrac{1 - [1/(1 + r)^t]}{r} \right\}$ is called the *annuity present value factor.*

III. Future value of C invested per period for t periods at r percent per period

$$FV_t = C \times [(1 + r)^t - 1]/r \qquad [5.2]$$

The term $[(1 + r)^t - 1]/r$ is called the *annuity future value factor*

IV. Annuity Due Value

Annuity due value = Ordinary annuity value $\times$ (1 + r)   [5.3]

Annuity due has the same cash flow at the beginning of each period

V. Present Value of a perpetuity of C per period

$$PV = C/r \qquad [5.4]$$

A perpetuity has the same cash flow every period forever

VI. Effective Annual Rate

EAR = (1 + Quoted rate/m)^m − 1   [5.5]

Where m is the number of times the interest is compounded during the year

SUMMARY AND CONCLUSIONS

This chapter rounds out your understanding of fundamental concepts related to the time value of money and discounted cash flow valuation. Several important topics were covered, including:

1. There are two ways of calculating present and future values when there are multiple cash flows. Both approaches are straightforward extensions of our earlier analysis of single cash flows.

2. A series of constant cash flows that arrive or are paid at the end of each period is called an ordinary annuity, and we described some useful shortcuts for determining the present and future values of annuities.

3. Interest rates can be quoted in a variety of ways. For financial decisions, it is important that any rates being compared be first converted to effective rates. The relationship between a quoted rate, such as an annual percentage rate, or APR, and an effective annual rate, or EAR, is given by:

EAR = (1 + Quoted rate/m)^m − 1

where m is the number of times during the year the interest is compounded.

4. Many loans are annuities. The process of paying off a loan gradually is called amortizing the loan, and we discussed how amortization schedules are prepared and interpreted.

CHAPTER REVIEW AND SELF-TEST PROBLEMS

5.1 Present Values with Multiple Cash Flows. A first-round draft choice quarterback has been signed to a three-year, $10 million contract. The details include an immediate cash bonus of $1 million. The player is to receive $2 million in salary at the end of the first year, $3 million the next, and $4 million at the end of the last year. Assuming a 10 percent discount rate, is this package worth $10 million? How much is it worth?

5.2 Future Value with Multiple Cash Flows. You plan to make a series of deposits in an interest-bearing account. You will deposit $1,000 today, $2,000 in two years, and $8,000 in five years. If you withdraw $3,000 in three years and $5,000 in seven years, how much will you have after eight years if the interest rate is 9 percent? What is the present value of these cash flows?

5.3 Annuity Present Value. You are looking into an investment that will pay you $12,000 per year for the next 10 years. If you require a 15 percent return, what is the most you would pay for this investment?

5.4 APR versus EAR. The going rate on student loans is quoted as 9 percent APR. The terms of the loan call for monthly payments. What is the effective annual rate, or EAR, on such a student loan?

5.5 It's the Principal That Matters. Suppose you borrow $10,000. You are going to repay the loan by making equal annual payments for five years. The interest rate on the loan is 14 percent per year. Prepare an amortization schedule for the loan. How much interest will you pay over the life of the loan?

5.6 Just a Little Bit Each Month. You've recently finished your MBA at the Darnit School. Naturally, you must purchase a new car immediately. The car costs about $21,000. The bank quotes an interest rate of 15 percent APR for a 72-month loan with a 10 percent down payment. What will your monthly payment be? What is the effective interest rate on the loan?

■ Answers to Chapter Review and Self-Test Problems

5.1 Obviously, the package is not worth $10 million because the payments are spread out over three years. The bonus is paid today, so it's worth $1 million. The present values for the three subsequent salary payments are:

$$\$2/1.1 + 3/1.1^2 + 4/1.1^3 \qquad = \$2/1.1 + 3/1.21 + 4/1.331$$
$$= \$7.3028$$

The package is worth a total of $8.3028 million.

5.2 We will calculate the future value for each of the cash flows separately and then add up the results. Notice that we treat the withdrawals as negative cash flows:

$$\$1,000 \times 1.09^8 = \quad \$1,000 \times 1.9926 = \quad \$ \quad 1,992.60$$
$$\$2,000 \times 1.09^6 = \quad \$2,000 \times 1.6771 = \quad 3,354.20$$
$$-\$3,000 \times 1.09^5 = \quad -\$3,000 \times 1.5386 = \quad -4,615.87$$
$$\$8,000 \times 1.09^3 = \quad \$8,000 \times 1.2950 = \quad 10,360.23$$
$$-\$5,000 \times 1.09^1 = \quad -\$5,000 \times 1.0900 = \quad \underline{-5,450.00}$$
$$\text{Total future value} = \quad \$ \quad \underline{5,641.12}$$

This value includes a small rounding error.

To calculate the present value, we could discount each cash flow back to the present or we could discount back a single year at a time. However, since we already know that the future value in eight years is $5,641.12, the easy way to get the PV is just to discount this amount back eight years:

$$\text{Present value} = \$5,641.12/1.09^8$$
$$= \$5,641.12/1.9926$$
$$= \$2,831.03$$

We again ignore a small rounding error. For practice, you can verify that this is what you get if you discount each cash flow back separately.

5.3 The most you would be willing to pay is the present value of $12,000 per year for 10 years at a 15 percent discount rate. The cash flows here are in ordinary annuity form, so the relevant present value factor is:

$$\text{Annuity present value factor} = [1 - (1/1.15^{10})]/.15$$
$$= (1 - .2472)/.15$$
$$= 5.0188$$

The present value of the 10 cash flows is thus:

$$\text{Present value} = \$12,000 \times 5.0188$$
$$= \$60,225$$

This is the most you would pay.

5.4 A rate of 9 percent with monthly payments is actually $9\%/12 = .75\%$ per month. The EAR is thus:

$$\text{EAR} = (1 + .09/12)^{12} - 1 = 9.38\%$$

5.5 We first need to calculate the annual payment. With a present value of $10,000, an interest rate of 14 percent, and a term of five years, the payment can be determined from:

$$\$10,000 = \text{Payment} \times (1 - 1/1.14^5)/.14$$
$$= \text{Payment} \times 3.4331$$

Therefore, the payment is $10,000/3.4331 = $2,912.84 (actually, it's $2,912.8355; this will create some small rounding errors in the schedule below). We can now prepare the amortization schedule as follows:

Year	Beginning Balance	Total Payment	Interest Paid	Principal Paid	Ending Balance
1	$10,000.00	$ 2,912.84	$1,400.00	$ 1,512.84	$8,487.16
2	8,487.16	2,912.84	1,188.20	1,724.63	6,762.53
3	6,762.53	2,912.84	946.75	1,966.08	4,796.45
4	4,796.45	2,912.84	671.50	2,241.33	2,555.12
5	2,555.12	2,912.84	357.72	2,555.12	.00
Totals		$14,564.17	$4,564.17	$10,000.00	

5.6 The cash flows on the car loan are in annuity form, so we only need to find the payment. The interest rate is $15\%/12 = 1.25\%$ per month, and there are 72 months. The first thing we need is the annuity factor for 72 periods at 1.25 percent per period:

$$
\begin{aligned}
\text{Annuity present value factor} &= (1 - \text{Present value factor})/r \\
&= [1 - (1/1.0125^{72})]/.0125 \\
&= [1 - (1/2.4459)]/.0125 \\
&= (1 - .4088)/.0125 \\
&= 47.2925
\end{aligned}
$$

The present value is the amount we finance. With a 10 percent down payment, we will be borrowing 90 percent of $21,000, or $18,900.

So, to find the payment, we need to solve for C in the following:

$$
\begin{aligned}
\$18,900 &= C \times \text{Annuity present value factor} \\
&= C \times 47.2925
\end{aligned}
$$

Rearranging things a bit, we have:

$$
\begin{aligned}
C &= \$18,900 \times (1/47.2925) \\
&= \$18,900 \times .02115 \\
&= \$399.64
\end{aligned}
$$

Your payment is just under $400 per month.

The actual interest rate on this loan is 1.25 percent per month. Based on our work in the chapter, we can calculate the effective annual rate as:

$$
\text{EAR} = 1.0125^{12} - 1 = 16.08\%
$$

The effective rate is about one point higher than the quoted rate.

CRITICAL THINKING AND CONCEPTS REVIEW

5.1   Annuity Period.   As you increase the length of time involved, what happens to the present value of an annuity? What happens to the future value?

5.2   Interest Rates.   What happens to the future value of an annuity if you increase the rate r? What happens to the present value?

5.3   Annuity Present Values.   The Megabucks Lottery advertises a $10 million dollar grand prize. The winner receives $500,000 today and 19 annual payments of $500,000. A lump sum option of $5 million payable immediately is also available. Is this deceptive advertising?

5.4   Annuity Present Values.   Suppose you won the Megabucks Lottery in the previous question. What factors should you take into account in deciding whether you should take the annuity option or the lump sum option?

5.5   Present Value.   If you were an athlete negotiating a contract, would you want a big signing bonus payable immediately and smaller payments in the future, or vice versa? How about looking at it from the team's perspective?

5.6   Present Value.   Suppose two athletes sign 10-year contracts for $80 million. In one case, we're told that the $80 million will be paid in 10 equal installments. In the other case, we're told that the $80 million will be paid in 10 installments, but the installments will increase by 5 percent per year. Who got the better deal?

5.7   APR and EAR.   Should lending laws be changed to require lenders to report EARs instead of APRs? Why or why not?

5.8   Time Value.   On student loans, a common source of financial aid for university students, interest does not begin to accrue until graduation. Who receives larger benefits, a freshman or a senior? Explain.

5.9 **Time Value.** In words, how would you go about valuing the benefits of a student loan?

QUESTIONS AND PROBLEMS

1. **Present Value and Multiple Cash Flows.** St. John's Co. has identified an investment project with the following cash flows. If the discount rate is 10 percent, what is the present value of these cash flows? What is the present value at 18 percent? At 24 percent?

Basic
(Questions 1–28)

Year	Cash Flow
1	$ 900
2	600
3	1,100
4	1,480

2. **Present Value and Multiple Cash Flows.** Investment X offers to pay you $4,000 per year for 9 years, whereas Investment Y offers to pay you $6,000 per year for 5 years. Which of these cash flow streams has the higher present value if the discount rate is 5 percent? If the discount rate is 22 percent?

3. **Future Value and Multiple Cash Flows.** Wood Bison, Inc., has identified an investment project with the following cash flows. If the interest rate is 8 percent, what is the future value of these cash flows in Year 4? What is the future value at an interest rate of 11 percent? At 24 percent?

Year	Cash Flow
1	$ 600
2	800
3	1,200
4	2,000

4. **Calculating Annuity Present Value.** An investment offers $4,500 per year for 15 years, with the first payment occurring 1 year from now. If the required return is 10 percent, what is the value of the investment? What would the value be if the payments occurred for 40 years? For 75 years? Forever?

5. **Calculating Annuity Cash Flows.** If you put up $15,000 today in exchange for a 7.5 percent, 12-year annuity, what will the annual cash flow be?

6. **Calculating Annuity Values.** Your company will generate $60,000 in revenue each year for the next nine years from a new information database. The computer system needed to set up the database costs $325,000. If you can borrow the money to buy the computer system at 8.25 percent annual interest, can you afford the new system?

7. **Calculating Annuity Values.** If you deposit $3,000 at the end of each of the next 20 years into an account paying 8.5 percent interest, how much money will you have in the account in 20 years? How much will you have if you make deposits for 40 years?

8. **Calculating Annuity Values.** You want to have $40,000 in your savings account seven years from now, and you're prepared to make equal annual deposits into the account at the end of each year. If the account pays 5.25 percent interest, what amount must you deposit each year?

9. **Calculating Annuity Values.** Great Lakes Bank offers you a $30,000, seven-year term loan at 9 percent annual interest. What will your annual loan payment be?

10. **Calculating Perpetuity Values.** Eternal Life Insurance Co. is trying to sell you an investment policy that will pay you and your heirs $20,000 per year forever. If the required return on this investment is 8 percent, how much will you pay for the policy?

11. **Calculating Perpetuity Values.** In the previous problem, suppose the company told you the policy costs $270,000. At what interest rate would this be a fair deal?

12. **Calculating EAR.** Find the EAR in each of the following cases:

Stated Rate (APR)	Number of Times Compounded	Effective Rate (EAR)
8%	Quarterly	
10	Monthly	
14	Daily	
18	Semiannually	

13. **Calculating APR.** Find the APR, or stated rate, in each of the following cases:

Stated Rate (APR)	Number of Times Compounded	Effective Rate (EAR)
	Semiannually	12%
	Monthly	18
	Weekly	7
	Daily	11

14. **Calculating EAR.** Upper Canada Bank charges 13.1 percent compounded monthly on its business loans. Lower Canada Bank charges 13.4 percent compounded semiannually. As a potential borrower, which bank would you go to for a new loan?

15. **Calculating APR.** Buckeye Credit Corp. wants to earn an effective annual return on its consumer loans of 17 percent per year. The bank uses daily compounding on its loans. What interest rate is the bank required by law to report to potential borrowers? Explain why this rate is misleading to an uninformed borrower.

16. **Calculating Future Values.** What is the future value of $1,575 in 13 years assuming an interest rate of 10 percent compounded semiannually?

17. **Calculating Future Values.** Bucher Credit Bank is offering 3.9 percent compounded daily on its savings accounts. If you deposit $6,000 today, how much will you have in the account in five years? In 10 years? In 20 years?

18. **Calculating Present Values.** An investment will pay you $70,000 in six years. If the appropriate discount rate is 10 percent compounded daily, what is the present value?

19. **EAR versus APR.** Ricky Ripov's Pawn Shop charges an interest rate of 25 percent per month on loans to its customers. Like all lenders, Ricky must report an APR to consumers. What rate should the shop report? What is the effective annual rate?

20. **Calculating Loan Payments.** You want to buy a new sports coupe for $62,500, and the finance office at the dealership has quoted you an 8.2 percent APR loan for 60 months to buy the car. What will your monthly payments be? What is the effective annual rate on this loan?

21. Calculating Number of Periods. One of your customers is delinquent on his accounts payable balance. You've mutually agreed to a repayment schedule of $400 per month. You will charge 1.3 percent per month interest on the overdue balance. If the current balance is $12,815, how long will it take for the account to be paid off?

22. Calculating EAR. Friendly's Quick Loans, Inc., offers you "five for four, or I knock on your door." This means you get $4 today and repay $5 when you get your paycheck in one week (or else). What's the effective annual return Friendly's earns on this lending business? If you were brave enough to ask, what APR would Friendly's say you were paying?

23. Valuing Perpetuities. Maybepay Life Insurance Co. is selling a perpetual annuity contract that pays $3,000 monthly. The contract currently sells for $175,000. What is the monthly return on this investment vehicle? What is the APR? The effective annual return?

24. Calculating Annuity Future Values. You are to make monthly deposits of $250 into a retirement account that pays 11 percent interest compounded monthly. If your first deposit will be made one month from now, how large will your retirement account be in 30 years?

25. Calculating Annuity Future Values. In the previous problem, suppose you make $3,000 annual deposits into the same retirement account. How large will your account balance be in 30 years?

26. Calculating Annuity Present Values. Beginning three months from now, you want to be able to withdraw $2,000 each quarter from your bank account to cover college expenses over the next four years. If the account pays .75 percent interest per quarter, how much do you need to have in your bank account today to meet your expense needs over the next four years?

27. Discounted Cash Flow Analysis. If the appropriate discount rate for the following cash flows is 10 percent, what is the present value of the cash flows?

Year	Cash Flow
1	$700
2	900
3	400
4	800

28. Discounted Cash Flow Analysis. If the appropriate discount rate for the following cash flows is 7.83 percent per year, what is the present value of the cash flows?

Year	Cash Flow
1	$1,500
2	3,200
3	6,800
4	8,100

29. Simple Interest versus Compound Interest. First Simple Bank pays 9 percent simple interest on its investment accounts. If First Complex Bank pays interest on its accounts compounded annually, what rate should the bank set if it wants to match First Simple Bank over an investment horizon of 10 years?

**Intermediate
(Questions 29–59)**

www.mcgrawhill.ca/olc/ross

30. **Calculating Annuities Due.** You want to buy a new sports car from Muscle Motors for $56,000. The contract is in the form of a 60-month annuity due at a 8.15 percent APR. What will your monthly payment be?

31. **Calculating Interest Expense.** You receive a credit card application from Shady Banks Savings and Loan offering an introductory rate of 2.1 percent per year, compounded monthly for the first six months, increasing thereafter to 21 percent compounded monthly. Assuming you transfer the $6,000 balance from your existing credit card and make no subsequent payments, how much interest will you owe at the end of the first year?

32. **Calculating the Number of Periods.** You are saving to buy a $150,000 house. There are two competing banks in your area, both offering Guaranteed Investment Certificates (GICs) yielding 5 percent. How long will it take your initial $83,000 investment to reach the desired level at First Bank, which pays simple interest? How long at Second Bank, which compounds interest monthly?

33. **Calculating Future Values.** You have an investment that will pay you 1.19 percent per month. How much will you have per dollar invested in one year? In two years?

34. **Calculating Annuity Interest Rates.** Although you may know William Shakespeare from his classic literature, what is not well-known is that he was an astute investor. In 1604, when he was 40 and writing *King Lear,* Shakespeare grew worried about his eventual retirement. Afraid that he would become like King Lear in his retirement and need to beg hospitality from his children, he purchased grain "tithes," or shares in farm output, for 440 pounds. The tithes paid him 60 pounds per year for 31 years. Even though he died at the age of 52, his children received the remaining payments. What interest rate did the Bard of Avon receive on this investment?

35. **Comparing Cash Flow Streams.** You've just joined the investment banking firm of Dewey, Cheatum, and Howe. They've offered you two different salary arrangements. You can have $6,200 per month for the next two years, or you can have $4,900 per month for the next two years, along with a $30,000 signing bonus today. If the interest rate is 8 percent compounded monthly, which do you prefer?

36. **Calculating Present Value of Annuities.** Peter Lynchpin wants to sell you an investment contract that pays equal $18,000 amounts at the end of each of the next 20 years. If you require an effective annual return of 10 percent on this investment, how much will you pay for the contract today?

37. **Calculating Rates of Return.** You're trying to choose between two different investments, both of which have up-front costs of $50,000. Investment G returns $80,000 in six years. Investment H returns $140,000 in 13 years. Which of these investments has the higher return?

38. **Present Value and Interest Rates.** What is the relationship between the value of an annuity and the level of interest rates? Suppose you just bought a 10-year annuity of $6,000 per year at the current interest rate of 10 percent per year. What happens to the value of your investment if interest rates suddenly drop to 5 percent? What if interest rates suddenly rise to 15 percent?

39. **Calculating the Number of Payments.** You're prepared to make monthly payments of $140, beginning at the end of this month, into an account that pays 12 percent interest compounded monthly. How many payments will you have made when your account balance reaches $35,000?

40. **Calculating Annuity Present Values.** You want to borrow $60,000 from your local bank to buy a new sailboat. You can afford to make monthly payments of $1,300, but no more. Assuming monthly compounding, what is the highest rate you can afford on a 60-month APR loan?

41. Calculating Present Values. In the 1994 NBA draft, no one was surprised when the Milwaukee Bucks took Glenn "Big Dog" Robinson with the first pick. But Robinson wanted big bucks from the Bucks: a 13-year deal worth a total of $100 million. He had to settle for about $68 million over 10 years. His contract called for $2.9 million the first year, with annual raises of $870,000. So, how big a bite did Big Dog really take? Assume an 11 percent discount rate.

42. Calculating Present Values. In our previous question, we looked at the numbers for Big Dog's basketball contract. Now let's take a look at the terms for Shaquille "Shaq" O'Neal, the number one pick in 1992, who was drafted by the Orlando Magic. Shaquille signed a seven-year contract with estimated total payments of about $40 million. Although the precise terms were not disclosed, it was reported that Shaq would receive a salary of $3 million the first year, with raises of $900,000 each year thereafter. If the cash flows are discounted at the same 11 percent discount rate we used for Robinson, does the "Shaq Attack" result in the same kind of numbers? Did Robinson achieve his goal of being paid more than any other rookie in NBA history, including Shaq? Are the different contract lengths a factor? (Hint: Yes.)

43. EAR versus APR. You have just purchased a new warehouse. To finance the purchase, you've arranged for a 30-year mortgage loan for 80 percent of the $1,500,000 purchase price. The monthly payment on this loan will be $8,400. What is the APR on this loan? The EAR?

44. Annuity Values. You are planning your retirement in 10 years. You currently have $200,000 in a bond account and $400,000 in a stock account. You plan to add $10,000 per year at the end of each of the next 10 years to your bond account. The stock account will earn an 11.5 percent return and the bond account will earn a 7.5 percent return. When you retire, you plan to withdraw an equal amount for each of the next 25 years at the end of each year and have nothing left. Additionally, when you retire you will transfer your money to an account that earns 6.75 percent. How much can you withdraw each year?

45. Discount Interest Loans. This question illustrates what is known as *discount interest*. Imagine you are discussing a loan with a somewhat unscrupulous lender. You want to borrow $12,000 for one year. The interest rate is 11 percent. You and the lender agree that the interest on the loan will be .11 × $12,000 = $1,320. So the lender deducts this interest amount from the loan up front and gives you $10,680. In this case, we say that the discount is $1,320. What's wrong here?

46. Calculating Annuities Due. As discussed in the text, an ordinary annuity assumes equal payments at the end of each period over the life of the annuity. An *annuity due* is the same thing except the payments occur at the beginning of each period instead. Thus, a three-year annual annuity due would have periodic payment cash flows occurring at Years 0, 1, and 2, whereas a three-year annual ordinary annuity would have periodic payment cash flows occurring at Years 1, 2, and 3.

   a. At a 13 percent annual discount rate, find the present value of a four-year ordinary annuity contract of $900 payments.

   b. Find the present value of the same contract if it is an annuity due.

47. Annuity and Perpetuity Values. Mary is going to receive a 30-year annuity of $6,000. Nancy is going to receive a perpetuity of $6,000. If the appropriate interest rate is 8 percent, how much more is Nancy's cash flow worth?

48. Calculating Present Values. A 5-year annuity of ten $7,000 semiannual payments will begin nine years from now, with the first payment coming 9.5 years from now. If the discount rate is 12 percent compounded semiannually, what is the value of this annuity five years from now? What is the value three years from now? What is the current value of the annuity?

49. **Present Value and Multiple Cash Flows.**   What is the present value of $890 per year, at a discount rate of 9 percent, if the first payment is received 5 years from now and the last payment is received 20 years from now?

50. **Variable Interest Rates.**   A 10-year annuity pays $1,300 per month, and payments are made at the end of each month. If the interest rate is 11 percent compounded monthly for the first four years, and 8 percent compounded monthly thereafter, what is the present value of the annuity?

51. **Comparing Cash Flow Streams.**   You have your choice of two investment accounts. Investment A is a 10-year annuity that features end-of-month $1,600 payments and has an interest rate of 10 percent compounded monthly. Investment B is an 8 percent annually compounded lump-sum investment, also good for 10 years. How much money would you need to invest in B today for it to be worth as much as Investment A ten years from now?

52. **Calculating Present Value of a Perpetuity.**   Given an interest rate of 5.45 percent per year, what is the value at date $t = 9$ of a perpetual stream of $1,400 payments that begin at date $t = 15$?

53. **Calculating EAR.**   A local finance company quotes a 13 percent interest rate on one-year loans. So, if you borrow $20,000, the interest for the year will be $2,600. Because you must repay a total of $22,600 in one year, the finance company requires you to pay $22,600/12, or $1,833.33, per month over the next 12 months. Is this a 13 percent loan? What rate would legally have to be quoted? What is the effective annual rate?

54. **Calculating Future Values.**   If today is Year 0, what is the future value of the following cash flows five years from now? What is the future value 10 years from now? Assume a discount rate of 10.2 percent per year.

Year	Cash Flow
2	$25,000
3	45,000
5	65,000

55. **Amortization with Equal Payments.**   Prepare an amortization schedule for a three-year loan of $45,000. The interest rate is 11 percent per year, and the loan calls for equal annual payments. How much interest is paid in the third year? How much total interest is paid over the life of the loan?

56. **Amortization with Equal Principal Payments.**   Rework Problem 55 assuming that the loan agreement calls for a principal reduction of $15,000 every year instead of equal annual payments.

57. **Mortgage Payments.**   Your family is going to buy a condominium in Montreal. Therefore, you plan on taking out a 25-year mortgage for $120,000 at 7.95 percent APR. How much is your monthly payment?

58. **Mortgage Term.**   You are considering a purchase of a house in Toronto for $450,000. You will make a down payment of 25 percent of the value of the house and take out a mortgage for the remaining balance. A bank is offering you a

mortgage at 6.00 percent APR. If your current income allows payments of $2,100 per month, how long will it take you to repay the mortgage?

59. **Mortgage Payments.** You are about to purchase a new home for $150,000. You plan on making a down payment of 10 percent of the value of the house and taking out a mortgage for the remaining balance. A bank has offered you a traditional 25-year mortgage at 6.95 percent APR.

    a. How much is your monthly payment?

    b. Prepare an amortization schedule for the first four months.

    c. How much will you still owe on your mortgage after ten years?

60. **Future Values and Annuity.** You have decided to begin saving for your retirement, which will start in 35 years. You feel that beginning at the end of this year you will be able to save $2,000 per year for 10 years, and then $5,000 per year for the next 15 years. You are not planning on saving any money for the last 10 years before your retirement. Prior to your retirement you expect to earn 10 percent interest, compounded annually. After the retirement, you will be more conservative in your investments and only expect to earn 6 percent interest, compounded monthly. How much money can you withdraw in equal amounts at the beginning of each month during your retirement, so that you will have nothing left after 20 years?

Challenge (Questions 60–62)

61. **EAR and Annuities.** You are helping your friend plan for her retirement. Your friend's company has a new pension plan that will deposit $100 at the end of each month into her retirement fund (the first deposit will be made one month from today). She plans to retire exactly 25 years from today, and estimates that she will need $3,000 per month withdrawn at the beginning of each month for 20 years. If interest rates are 12 percent per year, compounded quarterly, how much must she deposit into her retirement fund at the end of each month (in equal amounts per month) over the next 25 years, in addition to the $100 deposited by the company, in order to meet her objective?

62. **Mortgage Payments.** You are about to buy a new condominium in downtown Vancouver for $300,000. You will make a down payment of 25 percent of the value of the condo and take out a mortgage for the remaining balance. The Bank of Vancouver has offered you a 30-year mortgage at 8.45 percent APR. You decide to repay your mortgage by making bi-weekly payments (i.e., 26 payments per year).

    a. How much is your bi-weekly payment?

    b. If you increase your bi-weekly payments by $200, when will you repay your mortgage?

    c. How much will you save in the total interest by increasing your bi-weekly payments?

WHAT'S ON THE WEB?

5.1   **Loan Payments.** Finding the time necessary until you pay off a loan is simple if you make equal payments each month. However, when paying off credit cards many individuals only make the minimum monthly payment, which is generally $10 or 2 percent to 3 percent of the balance, whichever is greater. You can find the cost of borrowing calculator at the Canada's Office of Consumer Affairs (OCA) Web site—**consumer.ic.gc.ca**. Choose "For Consumers" in the "OCA Resources" and then select "Calculators." You currently owe $10,000 on a credit card with a

17 percent interest rate compounded monthly and a minimum payment of $10 or 2 percent of your balance, whichever is greater. How soon will you pay off this debt if you make the minimum payment each month? How much total interest will you pay?

5.2   Annuity Payments.   The Bank of Canada has files listing historical interest rates on their Web site **www.bankofcanada.ca**. Select "Interest Rates" in the "Rates and Statistics" menu at the top of the home page. Click on "Selected Historical Interest Rates." You will find a listing for the Bank Rate. The file shows the monthly Bank Rates since January 1935. What is the highest rate over this period? The Bank of Canada charges the Bank Rate, which is the Bank's primarily tool for conducting its monetary policy, on one-day loans to financial institutions. Assume that you can borrow at the Bank Rate. If you had purchased a house for $150,000 when the Bank Rate was at its highest, what would your monthly payments have been on a 30-year mortgage? If you buy the house at the same price at the current Bank Rate, how much are your monthly payments on a 30-year mortgage?

5.3   Annuity Payments.   Visit ATB Financial, a full-service financial institution based in Edmonton, Alberta, at **www.atb.com**. Select "Retirement Calculators" in the "Calculators" menu on the top of the home page. Click on the "RSP" calculator. Suppose your retirement needs consist of $50,000 annual income for 15 years. Let us assume that the current value of your RSP is $10,000, and you expect these funds to grow at 9 percent before your retirement, and at 5 percent afterwards. If the inflation rate is 0 percent, and you have 45 years until the retirement, how much money will you have at the start of your retirement? How much money will you need based on your retirement needs? How much additional contribution do you need to make annually? How much additional contribution do you need to make weekly? Why do they differ?

5.4   Mortgage Amortization.   Fiscal Agents Financial Services Group has a large number of financial calculators on their Web site at **www.fiscalagents.com**. Follow the link for "Financial Tools." You will find a listing of financial work-sheets and calculators. Select "Mortgage Amortization Schedule Calculator" in the "Mortgage and Loan Calculators" box. This calculator will prepare an amortization table based on your inputs. For example, you want to buy a home for $200,000 on a 30-year mortgage with monthly payments at the rate currently quoted by the Royal Bank of Canada. What percentage of your first month's payment is principal? What percentage of your last month's payment is principal? What is the total interest paid on the loan?

5.5   Mortgage Amortization.   The loan mortgage calculator we discussed in our *Work the Web* box, at **www.mortgageintelligence.ca**, will not only prepare an amortization schedule based on your inputs, but will also determine the impact of any principal prepayments. Using mortgage information from the previous problem, what is the total interest paid on the loan if you prepay $100 each month. Why is it different from the interest paid in the other problem?

MINI-CASE

CANADIAN AIR'S LOAN

Mark Sexton and Todd Story, the co-owners of Canadian Air, Inc., were impressed by the work Chris Guthrie had done on financial planning (see Chapter 3). Using Chris's analysis, and looking at the demand for light aircraft, they have decided that their existing fabrication equipment needs replacement. Mark and Todd have identified suitable new equipment for sale, for about $20 million. Mark, Todd, and Chris are now ready to meet with Anita Vaughan, the loan officer for the Canadian National Bank. The purpose of meeting is to discuss the loan options available to the company to finance the new equipment.

Anita begins the meeting by discussing a 30-year loan. The loan would be repaid in equal monthly installments. Because of the previous relationship between Canadian Air and the bank, there would be no closing costs for the loan. Anita states that the APR of the loan would be 6.2 percent. Todd asks if a shorter loan is available. Anita says that the bank does have a 20-year loan available at the same APR.

Mark decides to ask Anita about a "smart loan" he discussed with a mortgage broker when he was refinancing his home loan. A smart loan works as follows: Every two weeks a payment is made that is exactly one-half of the traditional monthly loan payment. Anita informs him that the bank does have smart loans. The APR of the smart loan would be the same as the APR of the traditional loan. Mark nods his head. He then states this is the best loan option available to the company since it saves interest payments.

Anita agrees with Mark, but then suggests that a bullet loan, or balloon payment, would result in the greatest interest savings. At Todd's prompting she goes on to explain a bullet loan. The monthly payments of a bullet loan would be calculated using a 30-year traditional loan. In this case, there would be a 5-year bullet. This would mean that the company would make the payments for the traditional 30-year loan for the first five years, but immediately after the company makes the 60th payment, the bullet payment would be due. The bullet payment is the remaining principal of the loan. Chris then asks how the bullet payment is calculated. Anita tells him that the remaining principal can be calculated using an amortization table, but it is also the present value of the remaining 25 years of payments for the 30-year loan.

Todd has also heard of an interest-only loan and asks if this loan is available and what the terms would be. Anita says that the bank offers an interest-only loan with a term of 10 years and an APR of 3.5 percent. She goes on to further explain the terms. The company would be responsible for making interest payments each month on the amount borrowed. No principal payments are required. At the end of the 10-year term, the company would repay the $20 million. However, the company can make principal payments at any time. The principal payments would work just like those on a traditional loan. Principal payments would reduce the principal of the loan and reduce the interest due on the next payment.

Mark and Todd are satisfied with Anita's answers, but are still not sure of which loan they should choose. They have asked Chris to answer the following questions to help them choose the correct financing arrangement.

QUESTIONS

1. What are the monthly payments for a 30-year traditional loan? What are the payments for a 20-year traditional loan?

2. Prepare an amortization table for the first six months of the traditional 30-year loan. How much of the first payment goes toward principal?

3. How long would it take for Canadian Air to pay off the smart loan, assuming 30-year traditional loan payments? Why is this shorter than the time needed to pay off the traditional loan? How much interest would the company save?

4. Assume Canadian Air takes out a bullet loan under the terms described. What are the payments on the loan?

5. What are the payments for the interest-only loan?

6. Which loan is the best for the company? Are there any potential risks in this action?

6

Interest Rates and Bond Valuation

In its most basic form, a bond is a pretty simple thing. You loan a company (or government) some money, say $10,000, the company (or government) then pays you interest periodically, and finally repays the original loan amount of $10,000. But bonds can have different interest payments.

In June 2006, the Ontario government issued three types of Ontario Savings Bonds (OSB), or simply *Osbies.* The fixed rate bond paid the same interest rate of 4.10 percent until maturity. The variable-rate bond had a new rate every six months. Lastly, the step bond had an interest rate of 3.70 percent in the first year, 3.80 percent in the second year, 3.90 percent in the third year, 4.00 percent in the fourth year, and 4.25 percent in the last, fifth, year. How did investors react to these bonds? They purchased $1.374 billion worth!

This chapter takes what we have learned about the time value of money and shows how it can be used to value one of the most common of all financial assets, a bond. It then discusses bond features, bond types, and the operation of the bond market.

What we will see is that bond prices depend critically on interest rates, so we will go on to discuss some very fundamental issues regarding interest rates. Clearly, interest rates are important to everybody because they underlie what businesses of all types—small and large—must pay to borrow money.

After reading this chapter, you should understand:

6.1   Important bond features and bond valuation.

6.2   Bond indenture and its main provisions.

6.3   Bond ratings and what they mean.

6.4   Different types of bonds.

6.5   Bond markets and bond price reporting.

6.6   The impact of inflation on interest rates.

6.7   The term structure of interest rates and the determinants of bond yields.

Our goal in this chapter is to introduce you to bonds. We begin by showing how the techniques we developed in Chapters 4 and 5 can be applied to bond valuation. From there, we go on to discuss bond features and how bonds are bought and sold. One important thing we learn is that bond values depend, in large part, on interest rates. We therefore close out the chapter with an examination of interest rates and their behaviour.

6.1 | BONDS AND BOND VALUATION

When a corporation (or government) wishes to borrow money from the public on a long-term basis, it usually does so by issuing, or selling, debt securities that are generically called bonds. In this section, we describe the various features of corporate bonds and some of the terminology associated with bonds. We then discuss the cash flows associated with a bond and how bonds can be valued using our discounted cash flow procedure.

Bond Features and Prices

As we mentioned in our previous chapter, a bond is normally an interest-only loan, meaning that the borrower will pay the interest every period, but none of the principal will be repaid until the end of the loan. For example, suppose the Lucky Loonie Corporation wants to borrow $1,000 for 30 years. The interest rate on similar debt issued by similar corporations is 12 percent. Lucky Loonie will thus pay .12 × $1,000 = $120 in interest every year for 30 years. At the end of 30 years, Lucky Loonie will repay the $1,000. As this example suggests, a bond is a fairly simple financing arrangement. There is, however, a rich jargon associated with bonds, so we will use this example to define some of the more important terms.

In our example, the $120 regular interest payments that Lucky Loonie promises to make are called the bond's **coupons.** Because the coupon is constant and paid every year, the type of bond we are describing is sometimes called a *level coupon bond*. The amount that will be repaid at the end of the loan is called the bond's **face value** or **par value.** As in our example, this par value is usually $1,000 for corporate bonds, and a bond that sells for its par value is called a *par value bond*. Government of Canada and provincial bonds frequently have much larger face, or par, values. Finally, the annual coupon divided by the face value is called the **coupon rate** on the bond; in this case, because $120/1,000 = 12%, the bond has a 12 percent coupon rate.

The number of years until the face value is paid is called the bond's time to **maturity.** A corporate bond will frequently have a maturity of 30 years when it is originally issued, but this varies. Once the bond has been issued, the number of years to maturity declines as time goes by.

Bond Values and Yields

As time passes, interest rates change in the marketplace. The cash flows from a bond, however, stay the same. As a result, the value of the bond will fluctuate. When interest rates rise, the present value of the bond's remaining cash flows declines, and the bond is worth less. When interest rates fall, the bond is worth more.

To determine the value of a bond at a particular point in time, we need to know the number of periods remaining until maturity, the face value, the coupon, and the market interest rate for bonds with similar features. This interest rate required in the market on a bond is called the bond's **yield to maturity (YTM).** This rate is sometimes called the bond's

---

coupon
Stated interest payment made on a bond.

face value
The principal amount of a bond that is repaid at the end of the term. Also, *par value.*

coupon rate
The annual coupon divided by the face value of a bond.

maturity
Date on which the principal amount of a bond is paid.

yield to maturity (YTM)
The rate required in the market on a bond.

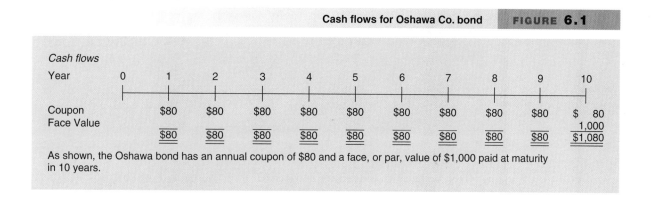

Cash flows for Oshawa Co. bond FIGURE **6.1**

As shown, the Oshawa bond has an annual coupon of $80 and a face, or par, value of $1,000 paid at maturity in 10 years.

yield for short. Given all this information, we can calculate the present value of the cash flows as an estimate of the bond's current market value.

For example, suppose the Oshawa Co. were to issue a bond with 10 years to maturity. The Oshawa bond has an annual coupon of $80. Similar bonds have a yield to maturity of 8 percent. Based on our preceding discussion, the Oshawa bond will pay $80 per year for the next 10 years in coupon interest. In 10 years, Oshawa will pay $1,000 to the owner of the bond. The cash flows from the bond are shown in Figure 6.1. What would this bond sell for?

As illustrated in Figure 6.1, the Oshawa bond's cash flows have an annuity component (the coupons) and a lump sum (the face value paid at maturity). We thus estimate the market value of the bond by calculating the present value of these two components separately and adding the results together. First, at the going rate of 8 percent, the present value of the $1,000 paid in 10 years is:

$$\text{Present value} = \$1,000/1.08^{10} = \$1,000/2.1589 = \$463.19$$

Second, the bond offers $80 per year for 10 years; the present value of this annuity stream is:

$$
\begin{aligned}
\text{Annuity present value} &= \$80 \times (1 - 1/1.08^{10})/.08 \\
&= \$80 \times (1 - 1/2.1589)/.08 \\
&= \$80 \times 6.7101 \\
&= \$536.81
\end{aligned}
$$

We can now add the values for the two parts together to get the bond's value:

$$\text{Total bond value} = \$463.19 + 536.81 = \$1,000$$

This bond sells for exactly its face value. This is not a coincidence. The going interest rate in the market is 8 percent. Considered as an interest-only loan, what interest rate does this bond have? With an $80 coupon, this bond pays exactly 8 percent interest only when it sells for $1,000.

To illustrate what happens as interest rates change, suppose that a year has gone by. The Oshawa bond now has nine years to maturity. If the interest rate in the market has risen to 10 percent, what will the bond be worth? To find out, we repeat the present value calculations with 9 years instead of 10, and a 10 percent yield instead of an 8 percent yield. First, the present value of the $1,000 paid in nine years at 10 percent is:

$$\text{Present value} = \$1,000/1.10^{9} = \$1,000/2.3579 = \$424.10$$

Second, the bond now offers $80 per year for nine years; the present value of this annuity stream at 10 percent is:

$$
\begin{aligned}
\text{Annuity present value} &= \$80 \times (1 - 1/1.10^9)/.10 \\
&= \$80 \times (1 - 1/2.3579)/.10 \\
&= \$80 \times 5.7590 \\
&= \$460.72
\end{aligned}
$$

We can now add the values for the two parts together to get the bond's value:

$$
\text{Total bond value} = \$424.10 + 460.72 = \$884.82
$$

Therefore, the bond should sell for about $885. In the vernacular, we say that this bond, with its 8 percent coupon, is priced to yield 10 percent at $885.

The Oshawa Co. bond now sells for less than its $1,000 face value. Why? The market interest rate is 10 percent. Considered as an interest-only loan of $1,000, this bond only pays 8 percent, its coupon rate. Because this bond pays less than the going rate, investors are only willing to lend something less than the $1,000 promised repayment. Because the bond sells for less than face value, it is said to be a *discount bond*.

The only way to get the interest rate up to 10 percent is to lower the price to less than $1,000 so that the purchaser, in effect, has a built-in gain. For the Oshawa bond, the price of $885 is $115 less than the face value, so an investor who purchased and kept the bond would get $80 per year and would have a $115 gain at maturity as well. This gain compensates the lender for the below-market coupon rate.

Another way to see why the bond is discounted by $115 is to note that the $80 coupon is $20 below the coupon on a newly issued par value bond, based on current market conditions. The bond would be worth $1,000 only if it had a coupon of $100 per year. In a sense, an investor who buys and keeps the bond gives up $20 per year for nine years. At 10 percent, this annuity stream is worth:

$$
\begin{aligned}
\text{Annuity present value} &= \$20 \times (1 - 1/1.10^9)/.10 \\
&= \$20 \times 5.7590 \\
&= \$115.18
\end{aligned}
$$

This is just the amount of the discount.

What would the Oshawa bond sell for if interest rates had dropped by 2 percent instead of rising by 2 percent? As you might guess, the bond would sell for more than $1,000. Such a bond is said to sell at a *premium* and is called a *premium bond*.

This case is just the opposite of that of a discount bond. The Oshawa bond now has a coupon rate of 8 percent when the market rate is only 6 percent. Investors are willing to pay a premium to get this extra coupon amount. In this case, the relevant discount rate is 6 percent, and there are nine years remaining. The present value of the $1,000 face amount is:

$$
\text{Present value} = \$1,000/1.06^9 = \$1,000/1.6895 = \$591.89
$$

The present value of the coupon stream is:

$$
\begin{aligned}
\text{Annuity present value} &= \$80 \times (1 - 1/1.06^9)/.06 \\
&= \$80 \times (1 - 1/1.6895)/.06 \\
&= \$80 \times 6.8017 \\
&= \$544.14
\end{aligned}
$$

We can now add the values for the two parts together to get the bond's value:

$$
\text{Total bond value} = \$591.89 + 544.14 = \$1,136.03
$$

The Education Centre "All About Bonds" at **www.qtrade.ca** has a lot of useful information about bonds.

Total bond value is therefore about $136 in excess of par value. Once again, we can verify this amount by noting that the coupon is now $20 too high, based on current market conditions. The present value of $20 per year for nine years at 6 percent is:

$$\text{Annuity present value} = \$20 \times (1 - 1/1.06^9)/.06$$
$$= \$20 \times 6.8017$$
$$= \$136.03$$

This is just as we calculated.

Based on our examples, we can now write the general expression for the value of a bond. If a bond has (1) a face value of F paid at maturity, (2) a coupon of C paid per period, (3) t periods to maturity, and (4) a yield of r per period, its value is:

$$\text{Bond value} = C \times [1 - 1/(1 + r)^t]/r + \qquad F/(1 + r)^t$$

| Bond value = | Present value of the coupons | + | Present value of the face amount | [6.1] |

Semiannual Coupons   EXAMPLE 6.1

In practice, bonds issued in Canada usually make coupon payments twice a year. So, if an ordinary bond has a coupon rate of 14 percent, then the owner will get a total of $140 per year, but this $140 will come in two payments of $70 each. Suppose we are examining such a bond. The yield to maturity is quoted at 16 percent.

Bond yields are quoted like APRs; the quoted rate is equal to the actual rate per period multiplied by the number of periods. In this case, with a 16 percent quoted yield and semiannual payments, the true yield is 8 percent per six months. The bond matures in seven years. What is the bond's price? What is the effective annual yield on this bond?

Based on our discussion, we know that the bond will sell at a discount because it has a coupon rate of 7 percent every six months when the market requires 8 percent every six months. So, if our answer exceeds $1,000, we know that we have made a mistake.

To get the exact price, we first calculate the present value of the bond's face value of $1,000 paid in seven years. This seven-year period has 14 periods of six months each. At 8 percent per period, the value is:

$$\text{Present value} = \$1,000/1.08^{14} = \$1,000/2.9372 = \$340.46$$

The coupons can be viewed as a 14-period annuity of $70 per period. At an 8 percent discount rate, the present value of such an annuity is:

$$\text{Annuity present value} = \$70 \times (1 - 1/1.08^{14})/.08$$
$$= \$70 \times (1 - .3405)/.08$$
$$= \$70 \times 8.2442$$
$$= \$577.10$$

The total present value gives us what the bond should sell for:

$$\text{Total present value} = \$340.46 + 577.10 = \$917.56$$

To calculate the effective yield on this bond, note that 8 percent every six months is equivalent to:

$$\text{Effective annual rate} = (1 + .08)^2 - 1 = 16.64\%$$

The effective yield, therefore, is 16.64 percent.

Different bond calculators are available at **www.investopedia .com/calculator**.

As we have illustrated in this section, bond prices and interest rates always move in opposite directions. When interest rates rise, a bond's value, like any other present value, will decline. Similarly, when interest rates fall, bond values rise. Even if we are considering a bond that is riskless in the sense that the borrower is certain to make all the payments, there is still risk in owning a bond. We discuss this next.

Interest Rate Risk

The risk that arises for bond owners from fluctuating interest rates is called *interest rate risk*. How much interest rate risk a bond has depends on how sensitive its price is to interest rate changes. This sensitivity directly depends on two things: the time to maturity and the coupon rate. As we will see momentarily, you should keep the following in mind when looking at a bond:

1. All other things being equal, the longer the time to maturity, the greater the interest rate risk.

2. All other things being equal, the lower the coupon rate, the greater the interest rate risk.

We illustrate the first of these two points in Figure 6.2. As shown, we compute and plot prices under different interest rate scenarios for 10 percent coupon bonds with maturities of 1 year and 30 years. Notice how the slope of the line connecting the prices is much steeper for the 30-year maturity than it is for the 1-year maturity bond. This steepness tells us that a relatively small change in interest rates will lead to a substantial change in the bond's value. In comparison, the one-year bond's price is relatively insensitive to interest rate changes.

Intuitively, we can see that the reason that longer-term bonds have greater interest rate sensitivity is that a large portion of a bond's value comes from the $1,000 face amount. The present value of this amount isn't greatly affected by a small change in interest rates if the amount is to be received in one year. Even a small change in the interest rate, however, once

---

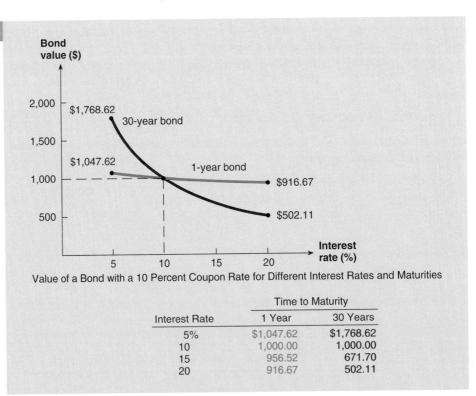

FIGURE 6.2

Interest rate risk and time to maturity

Value of a Bond with a 10 Percent Coupon Rate for Different Interest Rates and Maturities

	Time to Maturity	
Interest Rate	1 Year	30 Years
5%	$1,047.62	$1,768.62
10	1,000.00	1,000.00
15	956.52	671.70
20	916.67	502.11

it is compounded for 30 years, can have a significant effect on the present value. As a result, the present value of the face amount will be much more volatile with a longer-term bond.

The other thing to know about interest rate risk is that, like most things in finance and economics, it increases at a decreasing rate. In other words, if we compared a 10-year bond to a 1-year bond, we would see that the 10-year bond has much greater interest rate risk. However, if you were to compare a 20-year bond to a 30-year bond, you would find that the 30-year bond has somewhat greater interest rate risk because it has a longer maturity, but the difference in the risk would be fairly small.

The reason that bonds with lower coupons have greater interest rate risk is easy to understand. As we discussed earlier, the value of a bond depends on the present value of its coupons and the present value of the face amount. If two bonds with different coupon rates have the same maturity, then the value of the one with the lower coupon is proportionately more dependent on the face amount to be received at maturity. As a result, all other things being equal, its value will fluctuate more as interest rates change. Put another way, the bond with the higher coupon has a larger cash flow early in its life, so its value is less sensitive to changes in the discount rate.

Finding the Yield to Maturity: More Trial and Error

Frequently, we will know a bond's price, coupon rate, and maturity date, but not its yield to maturity. For example, suppose we are interested in a six-year, 8 percent coupon bond. A broker quotes a price of $955.14. What is the yield on this bond?

We've seen that the price of a bond can be written as the sum of its annuity and lump-sum components. Knowing that there is an $80 coupon for six years and a $1,000 face value, we can say that the price is:

$$\$955.14 = \$80 \times [1 - 1/(1 + r)^6]/r + 1{,}000/(1 + r)^6$$

where r is the unknown discount rate, or yield to maturity. We have one equation here and one unknown, but we cannot solve for r explicitly. The only way to find the answer is to use trial and error.

This problem is essentially identical to the one we examined in the last chapter when we tried to find the unknown interest rate on an annuity. However, finding the rate (or yield) on a bond is even more complicated because of the $1,000 face amount.

We can speed up the trial-and-error process by using what we know about bond prices and yields. In this case, the bond has an $80 coupon and is selling at a discount. We thus know that the yield is greater than 8 percent. If we compute the price at 10 percent:

> A bond yield calculator is available at **www.moneychimp .com**.

$$
\begin{aligned}
\text{Bond value} &= \$80 \times (1 - 1/1.10^6)/.10 + 1{,}000/1.10^6 \\
&= \$80 \times 4.3553 + 1{,}000/1.7716 \\
&= \$912.89
\end{aligned}
$$

At 10 percent, the value we calculate is lower than the actual price, so 10 percent is too high. The true yield must be somewhere between 8 and 10 percent. At this point, it's "plug and chug" to find the answer. You would probably want to try 9 percent next. If you did, you would see that this is in fact the bond's yield to maturity.

A bond's yield to maturity should not be confused with its **current yield,** which is simply a bond's annual coupon divided by its price. In the example we just worked, the bond's annual coupon was $80, and its price was $955.14. Given these numbers, we see that the current yield is $80/955.14 = 8.38$ percent, which is less than the yield to maturity of 9 percent. The reason the current yield is too low is that it only considers the coupon portion of your return; it doesn't consider the built-in gain from the price discount. For a premium bond, the reverse is true, meaning that current yield would be higher because it ignores the built-in loss.

Our discussion of bond valuation is summarized in Table 6.1.

> **current yield**
> A bond's annual coupon divided by its price.

TABLE 6.1	**I.** **Finding the value of a bond**
Summary of bond valuation	Bond value = $C \times [1 - 1/(1 + r)^t]/r + F/(1 + r)^t$

I.   **Finding the value of a bond**

Bond value = $C \times [1 - 1/(1 + r)^t]/r + F/(1 + r)^t$

where

C = Coupon paid each period

r = Rate per period

t = Number of periods

F = Bond's face value

II.   **Finding the yield on a bond**

Given a bond value, coupon, time to maturity, and face value, it is possible to find the implicit discount rate, or yield to maturity, by trial and error only. To do this, try different discount rates in the formula above until the calculated bond value equals the given bond value. Remember that increasing the rate *decreases* the bond value.

EXAMPLE 6.2   **Current Events**

A bond has a quoted price of $1,080.42. It has a face value of $1,000, a semiannual coupon of $30, and a maturity of five years. What is its current yield? What is its yield to maturity? Which is bigger? Why?

Notice that this bond makes semiannual payments of $30, so the annual payment is $60. The current yield is thus $60/1,080.42 = 5.55 percent. To calculate the yield to maturity, refer back to Example 6.1. Now, in this case, the bond pays $30 every six months and it has 10 six-month periods until maturity. So, we need to find r as follows:

$$\$1,080.42 = \$30 \times [1 - 1/(1 + r)^{10}]/r + 1,000/(1 + r)^{10}$$

After some trial and error, we find that r is equal to 2.1 percent. But, the tricky part is that this 2.1 percent is the yield *per six months*. We have to double it to get the yield to maturity, so the yield to maturity is 4.2 percent, which is less than the current yield. The reason is that the current yield ignores the built-in loss of the premium between now and maturity.

EXAMPLE 6.3   **Bond Yields**

You're looking at two bonds identical in every way except for their coupons and, of course, their prices. Both have 12 years to maturity. The first bond has a 10 percent coupon rate and sells for $935.08. The second has a 12 percent coupon rate. What do you think it would sell for?

Because the two bonds are very similar, they will be priced to yield about the same rate. We first need to calculate the yield on the 10 percent coupon bond. Proceeding as before, we know that the yield must be greater than 10 percent because the bond is selling at a discount. The bond has a fairly long maturity of 12 years. We've seen that long-term bond prices are relatively sensitive to interest rate changes, so the yield is probably close to 10 percent. A little trial and error reveals that the yield is actually 11 percent:

$$\begin{aligned}
\text{Bond value} &= \$100 \times (1 - 1/1.11^{12})/.11 + 1,000/1.11^{12} \\
&= \$100 \times 6.4924 + 1,000/3.4985 \\
&= \$649.24 + 285.84 \\
&= \$935.08
\end{aligned}$$

(Continued)

With an 11 percent yield, the second bond will sell at a premium because of its $120 coupon. Its value is:

Bond value = $120 × (1 − 1/1.11^{12})/.11 + 1,000/1.11^{12}
         = $120 × 6.4924 + 1,000/3.4985
         = $779.08 + 285.84
         = $1,064.92

Calculator Hints	How to Calculate Bond Prices and Yields Using a Financial Calculator

Many financial calculators have fairly sophisticated built-in bond valuation routines. However, these vary quite a lot in implementation, and not all financial calculators have them. As a result, we will illus-· trate a simple way to handle bond problems that will work on just about any financial calculator.

To begin, of course, we first remember to clear out the calculator! Next, for Example 6.3, we have two bonds to consider, both with 12 years to maturity. The first one sells for $935.08 and has a 10 percent coupon rate. To find its yield, we can do the following:

Notice that here we have entered both a future value of $1,000, representing the bond's face value, and a payment of 10 percent of $1,000, or $100, per year, representing the bond's annual coupon. Also notice that we have a negative sign on the bond's price, which we have entered as the present value.

For the second bond, we now know that the relevant yield is 11 percent. It has a 12 percent coupon and 12 years to maturity, so what's the price? To answer, we just enter the relevant values and solve for the present value of the bond's cash flows:

There is an important detail that comes up here. Suppose we have a bond with a price of $902.29, 10 years to maturity, and a coupon rate of 6 percent. As we mentioned earlier, most bonds actually make semiannual payments. Assuming that this is the case for the bond here, what's the bond's yield? To answer, we need to enter the relevant numbers like this:

Notice that we entered $30 as the payment because the bond actually makes payments of $30 every six months. Similarly, we entered 20 for N because there are actually 20 six-month periods. When we solve for the yield, we get 3.7 percent, but the tricky thing to remember is that this is the yield *per six months,* so we have to double it to get the right answer: 2 × 3.7 = 7.4 percent, which would be the bond's reported yield.

Spreadsheet Strategies | How to Calculate Bond Prices and Yields Using a Spreadsheet

Like financial calculators, most spreadsheets have fairly elaborate routines available for calculating bond values and yields; many of these routines involve details that we have not discussed. However, setting up a simple spreadsheet to calculate prices or yields is straightforward, as our next two spreadsheets show:

	A	B	C	D	E	F	G	H
1								
2		Using a spreadsheet to calculate bond yields						
3								
4	Suppose we have a bond with 22 years to maturity, a coupon rate of 8 percent, and a price of							
5	$960.17. If the bond makes semiannual payments, what is its yield to maturity?							
6								
7	Settlement date:	1/1/00						
8	Maturity date:	1/1/22						
9	Annual coupon rate:	.08						
10	Bond price (% of par):	96.017						
11	Face value (% of par):	100						
12	Coupons per year:	2						
13	Yield to maturity:	**.084**						
14								
15	The formula entered in cell B13 is =YIELD(B7,B8,B9,B10,B11,B12); notice that face value and bond							
16	price are entered as a percentage of face value.							
17								

	A	B	C	D	E	F	G	H
1								
2		Using a spreadsheet to calculate bond values						
3								
4	Suppose we have a bond with 22 years to maturity, a coupon rate of 8 percent, and a yield to							
5	maturity of 9 percent. If the bond makes semiannual payments, what is its price today?							
6								
7	Settlement date:	1/1/00						
8	Maturity date:	1/1/22						
9	Annual coupon rate:	.08						
10	Yield to maturity:	.09						
11	Face value (% of par):	100						
12	Coupons per year:	2						
13	Bond price (% of par):	**90.49**						
14								
15	The formula entered in cell B13 is =PRICE(B7,B8,B9,B10,B11,B12); notice that face value and bond							
16	price are entered as a percentage of face value.							
17								

In our spreadsheets, notice that we had to enter two dates, a settlement date and a maturity date. The settlement date is just the date you actually pay for the bond, and the maturity date is the day the bond actually matures. In most of our problems, we don't explicitly have these dates, so we have to make them up. For example, since our bond has 22 years to maturity, we just picked 1/1/2000 (January 1, 2000) as the settlement date and 1/1/2022 (January 1, 2022) as the maturity date. Any two dates would do as long as they were exactly 22 years apart, but these are particularly easy to work with. Finally, notice that we had to enter the coupon rate and yield to maturity in annual terms and then explicitly provide the number of coupon payments per year.

CONCEPT QUESTIONS

6.1a   What are the cash flows associated with a bond?

6.1b   What is the general expression for the value of a bond?

6.1c   Is it true that the only risk associated with owning a bond is that the issuer will not make all the payments? Explain.

6.2 | MORE ON BOND FEATURES

In this section, we continue our discussion of corporate debt by describing in some detail the basic terms and features that make up a typical long-term corporate bond. We discuss additional issues associated with long-term debt in subsequent sections.

Securities issued by corporations may be classified roughly as *equity securities* and *debt securities*. At the crudest level, a debt represents something that must be repaid; it is the result of borrowing money. When corporations borrow, they generally promise to make regularly scheduled interest payments and to repay the original amount borrowed (that is, the principal). The person or firm making the loan is called the *creditor,* or *lender.* The corporation borrowing the money is called the *debtor,* or *borrower.*

From a financial point of view, the main differences between debt and equity are the following:

1.   Debt is not an ownership interest in the firm. Creditors generally do not have voting power.

2.   The corporation's payment of interest on debt is considered a cost of doing business and is fully tax deductible. Dividends paid to stockholders are *not* tax deductible.

3.   Unpaid debt is a liability of the firm. If it is not paid, the creditors can legally claim the assets of the firm. This action can result in liquidation or reorganization, two of the possible consequences of bankruptcy. Thus, one of the costs of issuing debt is the possibility of financial failure. This possibility does not arise when equity is issued.

Information for bond investors can be found at **www.investinginbonds.com**.

Is It Debt or Equity?

Sometimes it is not clear if a particular security is debt or equity. For example, suppose a corporation issues a perpetual bond with interest payable solely from corporate income if and only if earned. Whether or not this is really a debt is hard to say and is primarily a legal and semantic issue. Courts and taxing authorities would have the final say.

Corporations are very adept at creating exotic, hybrid securities that have many features of equity but are treated as debt. Obviously, the distinction between debt and equity is very important for tax purposes. So, one reason that corporations try to create a debt security that is really equity is to obtain the tax benefits of debt and the bankruptcy benefits of equity.

As a general rule, equity represents an ownership interest, and it is a residual claim. This means that equity holders are paid after debt holders. As a result of this, the risks and benefits associated with owning debt and equity are different. To give just one example, note that the maximum reward for owning a debt security is ultimately fixed by the amount of the loan, whereas there is no upper limit to the potential reward from owning an equity interest.

Long-Term Debt: The Basics

Ultimately, all long-term debt securities are promises made by the issuing firm to pay principal when due and to make timely interest payments on the unpaid balance. Beyond this, there are a number of features that distinguish these securities from one another. We discuss some of these features next.

The maturity of a long-term debt instrument is the length of time the debt remains outstanding with some unpaid balance. Debt securities can be short term (with maturities of one year or less) or long term (with maturities of more than one year).[1] Short-term debt is sometimes referred to as *unfunded debt*.[2]

Debt securities are typically called *notes, debentures,* or *bonds.* Strictly speaking, a bond is a secured debt. However, in common usage, the word *bond* refers to all kinds of secured and unsecured debt. We will therefore continue to use the term generically to refer to long-term debt.

The two major forms of long-term debt are public issue and privately placed. We concentrate on public-issue bonds. Most of what we say about them holds true for private-issue, long-term debt as well. The main difference between public-issue and privately placed debt is that the latter is directly placed with a lender and not offered to the public. Because this is a private transaction, the specific terms are up to the parties involved.

There are many other dimensions to long-term debt, including such things as security, call features, sinking funds, ratings, and protective covenants. The following table illustrates these features for a bond issued by Shaw Communications Inc. on March 2, 2007. If some of the bond features look unfamiliar, have no fear. We will discuss them all presently.

Want detailed information on the amount and terms of the debt issued by a particular firm? Check out their prospectus by searching the System for Electronic Document Analysis and Retrieval (SEDAR) at **www.sedar.com.**

Features of a Shaw Communications Bond	
Term	**Explanation**
Amount of issue	$400 million	The company issued $400 million worth of bonds.
Date of issue	3/02/2007	The bonds were sold on 3/02/2007.
Maturity	3/02/2017	The bonds mature on 3/02/2017.
Face value	$1,000	The denomination of the bonds is $1,000.
Annual coupon	5.70	Each bondholder will receive $57.00 per bond per year (5.7% of face value).
Offer price	99.767	The offer price will be 99.767% of the $1,000 face value, or $997.67 per bond.
Coupon payment dates	3/02, 9/02	Coupons of $57.00/2 = $28.50 will be paid on these dates.
Form	Registered	The bonds are issued in registered form.
Security	Unsecured	The bonds are debentures.
Sinking fund	No	The bonds do not have a sinking fund.
Call provision	At any time	The bonds do not have a deferred call.
Call price	Principal or Canada Yield plus 0.44%	The bonds are redeemable at the company's option at the principal amount or "make-whole" call price, whichever is greater.
Rating	DBRS: BBB(low) Moody's: Ba1 S&P: BB+	The bonds are at the higher end of the speculative grade rating.

Source: www.sedar.com.

Many of these features will be detailed in the bond indenture, so we discuss this first.

---

[1]There is no universally agreed-upon distinction between short-term and long-term debt. In addition, people often refer to intermediate-term debt, which has a maturity of more than 1 year and less than 3 to 5, or even 10, years.

[2]The word *funding* is part of the jargon of finance. It generally refers to the long term. Thus, a firm planning to "fund" its debt requirements may be replacing short-term debt with long-term debt.

The Indenture

The **indenture** is the written agreement between the corporation (the borrower) and its creditors. It is sometimes referred to as the *deed of trust*.[3] Usually, a trustee (a bank, perhaps) is appointed by the corporation to represent the bondholders. The trust company must (1) make sure the terms of the indenture are obeyed, (2) manage the sinking fund (described in the following pages), and (3) represent the bondholders in default, that is, if the company defaults on its payments to them.

The bond indenture is a legal document. It can run several hundred pages and generally makes for very tedious reading. It is an important document, however, because it generally includes the following provisions:

1. The basic terms of the bonds.
2. The total amount of bonds issued.
3. A description of property used as security.
4. The repayment arrangements.
5. The call provisions.
6. Details of the protective covenants.

We discuss these features next.

Terms of a Bond   Corporate bonds usually have a face value (that is, a denomination) of $1,000. This is called the *principal value* and it is stated on the bond certificate. So, if a corporation wanted to borrow $1 million, 1,000 bonds would have to be sold. The par value (that is, initial accounting value) of a bond is almost always the same as the face value, and the terms are used interchangeably in practice.

Corporate bonds are usually in **registered form.** For example, the indenture might read as follows:

> Interest is payable semiannually on July 1 and January 1 of each year to the person in whose name the bond is registered at the close of business on June 15 or December 15, respectively.

This means that the company has a registrar who will record the ownership of each bond and record any changes in ownership. The company will pay the interest and principal by cheque mailed directly to the address of the owner of record. A corporate bond may be registered and have attached "coupons." To obtain an interest payment, the owner must separate a coupon from the bond certificate and send it to the company registrar (the paying agent).

Alternatively, the bond could be in **bearer form.** This means that the certificate is the basic evidence of ownership, and the corporation will "pay the bearer." Ownership is not otherwise recorded, and, as with a registered bond with attached coupons, the holder of the bond certificate detaches the coupons and sends them to the company to receive payment.

indenture
The written agreement between the corporation and the lender detailing the terms of the debt issue.

registered form
The form of bond issue in which the registrar of the company records ownership of each bond; payment is made directly to the owner of record.

bearer form
The form of bond issue in which the bond is issued without record of the owner's name; payment is made to whoever holds the bond.

---

[3]The term *loan agreement* or *loan contract* is usually used for privately placed debt and term loans.

There are two drawbacks to bearer bonds. First, they are difficult to recover if they are lost or stolen. Second, because the company does not know who owns its bonds, it cannot notify bondholders of important events. Bearer bonds have an advantage as well. Because the company does not need to record the bond's ownership, they are easy to trade. The anonymity of the ownership of bearer bonds also makes them popular among investors who try to hide their interest income from tax authorities. It is one of the reasons why international bonds are frequently issued in bearer form.

Security   Debt securities are classified according to the collateral and mortgages used to protect the bondholder.

Collateral is a general term that frequently means securities (for example, bonds and stocks) that are pledged as security for payment of debt. For example, collateral trust bonds often involve a pledge of common stock held by the corporation. However, the term *collateral* is commonly used to refer to any asset pledged on a debt.

Mortgage securities are secured by a mortgage on the real property of the borrower. The property involved is usually real estate, for example, land or buildings. The legal document that describes the mortgage is called a *mortgage trust indenture* or *trust deed.*

Sometimes mortgages are on specific property, for example, a railroad car. More often, blanket mortgages are used. A blanket mortgage pledges all the real property owned by the company.[4]

debenture
An unsecured debt, usually with a maturity of 10 years or more.

note
An unsecured debt, usually with a maturity under 10 years.

Bonds frequently represent unsecured obligations of the company. A **debenture** is an unsecured bond, one for which no specific pledge of property is made. The term **note** is generally used for such instruments if the maturity of the unsecured bond is less than 10 or so years when the bond is originally issued. Debenture holders only have a claim on property not otherwise pledged, in other words, the property that remains after mortgages and collateral trusts are taken into account.

The terminology that we use here and elsewhere in this chapter is standard in North America. Outside North America, these same terms can have different meanings. For example, bonds issued by the British government ("gilts") are called treasury "stock." Also, in the United Kingdom, a debenture is a *secured* obligation.

At the present time, almost all public bonds issued by industrial and financial companies are debentures. However, most utility and railroad bonds are secured by a pledge of assets.

Seniority   In general terms, *seniority* indicates preference in position over other lenders, and debts are sometimes labelled as *senior* or *junior* to indicate seniority. Some debt is *subordinated,* as in, for example, a subordinated debenture.

In the event of default, holders of subordinated debt must give preference to other specified creditors. Usually, this means that the subordinated lenders will be paid off only after the specified creditors have been compensated. However, debt cannot be subordinated to equity.

---

[4]Real property includes land and things "affixed thereto." It does not include cash or inventories.

Repayment Bonds can be repaid at maturity, at which time the bondholder will receive the stated, or face, value of the bond, or they may be repaid in part or in entirety before maturity. Early repayment in some form is more typical and is often handled through a sinking fund.

A **sinking fund** is an account managed by the bond trustee for the purpose of repaying the bonds. The company makes annual payments to the trustee, who then uses the funds to retire a portion of the debt. The trustee does this by either buying up some of the bonds in the market or calling in a fraction of the outstanding bonds. This second option is discussed in the next section.

There are many different kinds of sinking fund arrangements, and the details would be spelled out in the indenture. For example:

1. Some sinking funds start about 10 years after the initial issuance.
2. Some sinking funds establish equal payments over the life of the bond.
3. Some high-quality bond issues establish payments to the sinking fund that are not sufficient to redeem the entire issue. As a consequence, there is the possibility of a large "balloon payment" at maturity.

The Call Provision A **call provision** allows the company to repurchase, or "call," part or all of the bond issue at stated prices over a specific period. Corporate bonds are usually callable.

Generally, the call price is above the bond's stated value (that is, the par value). The difference between the call price and the stated value is the **call premium.** The amount of the call premium usually becomes smaller over time. One arrangement is to initially set the call premium equal to the annual coupon payment and then make it decline to zero as the call date moves closer to the time of maturity.

Call provisions are not usually operative during the first part of a bond's life. This makes the call provision less of a worry for bondholders in the bond's early years. For example, a company might be prohibited from calling its bonds for the first 10 years. This is a **deferred call provision.** During this period of prohibition, the bond is said to be **call protected.**

In just the last few years, use of a new type of call provision, a "make-whole" call, has become very widespread in the corporate bond market. With such a feature, bondholders receive exactly what the bonds are worth if they are called. When bondholders don't suffer a loss in the event of a call, they are "made whole."

To determine the make-whole call price, we calculate the present value of the remaining interest and principal payments at a rate specified in the indenture. For example, looking at our Shaw Communications issue, we see that the discount rate is "Canada Yield plus 0.44%." What this means is that we determine the discount rate by first finding a Government of Canada bond with the same maturity. We calculate the yield to maturity on the Government of Canada bond and then add on an additional 0.44 percent to get the discount rate we use.

Notice that, with a make-whole call provision, the call price is higher when interest rates are lower and vice versa (why?). Also notice that, as is common with a make-whole call, the Shaw Communications issue does not have a deferred call feature. Why might investors not be too concerned about the absence of this feature?

The "Bond" section at www.finpipe.com has many articles related to bonds.

sinking fund
An account managed by the bond trustee for early bond redemption.

call provision
An agreement giving the corporation the option to repurchase the bond at a specific price prior to maturity.

call premium
The amount by which the call price exceeds the par value of the bond.

deferred call provision
A call provision prohibiting the company from redeeming the bond prior to a certain date.

call protected bond
A bond that currently cannot be redeemed by the issuer.

protective covenant
A part of the indenture limiting certain actions that might be taken during the term of the loan, usually to protect the lender.

Protective Covenants   A **protective covenant** is that part of the indenture or loan agreement that limits certain actions a company might otherwise wish to take during the term of the loan. Protective covenants can be classified into two types: negative covenants and positive (or affirmative) covenants.

A *negative covenant* is a "thou shalt not" type of covenant. It limits or prohibits actions that the company might take. Here are some typical examples:

1. The firm must limit the amount of dividends it pays according to some formula.
2. The firm cannot pledge any assets to other lenders.
3. The firm cannot merge with another firm.
4. The firm cannot sell or lease any major assets without approval by the lender.
5. The firm cannot issue additional long-term debt.

A *positive covenant* is a "thou shalt" type of covenant. It specifies an action that the company agrees to take or a condition the company must abide by. Here are some examples:

1. The company must maintain its working capital at or above some specified minimum level.
2. The company must periodically furnish audited financial statements to the lender.
3. The firm must maintain any collateral or security in good condition.

This is only a partial list of covenants; a particular indenture may feature many different ones.

CONCEPT QUESTIONS

6.2a   What are the distinguishing features of debt as compared to equity?

6.2b   What is the indenture? What are protective covenants? Give some examples.

6.2c   What is a sinking fund?

6.3 | BOND RATINGS

Firms frequently pay to have their debt rated. The leading bond-rating firms in Canada are global debt rating agencies, Standard & Poor's (S&P) and Moody's, and Canadian debt rating agency, Dominion Bond Rating Service (DBRS), which is based in Toronto. The debt ratings are an assessment of the creditworthiness of the corporate issuer. The definitions of creditworthiness used by debt rating agencies are based on how likely the firm is to default and the protection creditors have in the event of a default.

It is important to recognize that bond ratings are concerned *only* with the possibility of default. Earlier, we discussed interest rate risk, which we defined as the risk of a change in the value of a bond resulting from a change in interest rates. Bond ratings do not address this issue. As a result, the price of a highly rated bond can still be quite volatile.

Bond ratings are constructed from information supplied by the corporation. The rating classes and some information concerning them are shown in the following table.

The highest rating a firm's debt can have is AAA or Aaa, and such debt is judged to be the best quality and to have the lowest degree of default risk. This rating is not awarded

	Investment-Quality Bond Ratings				Low-Quality, Speculative, and/or "Junk" Bond Ratings					
	High Grade		Medium Grade		Low Grade			Very Low Grade		
S&P	AAA	AA	A	BBB	BB	B	CCC	CC	C	D
DBRS	AAA	AA	A	BBB	BB	B	CCC	CC	C	D
Moody's	Aaa	Aa	A	Baa	Ba	B	Caa	Ca		C

S&P, DBRS	Moody's	
AAA	Aaa	Debt has the highest rating. Capacity to pay interest and principal is extremely strong.
AA	Aa	Debt has a very strong capacity to pay interest and repay principal. Together with the highest rating, this group comprises the high-grade bond class.
A	A	Debt rated A has a strong capacity to pay interest and repay principal, although it is somewhat more susceptible to the adverse effects of changes in circumstances and economic conditions than debt in higher-rated categories.
BBB	Baa	Debt is regarded as having an adequate capacity to pay interest and repay principal. However, adverse economic conditions or changing circumstances are more likely to lead to a weakened capacity to pay interest and repay principal for debt in this category than in higher-rated categories. These bonds are medium-grade obligations.
BB, B CCC CC C	Ba, B Caa Ca	Debt rated in these categories is regarded, on balance, as predominantly speculative with respect to capacity to pay interest and repay principal in accordance with the terms of the obligation. BB indicates the lowest degree of speculation, and C (or Ca for Moody's) the highest degree of speculation. Although such debt is likely to have some quality and protective characteristics, these are outweighed by large uncertainties or major risk exposures to adverse conditions. Some issues may be highly vulnerable to nonpayment.
D	C	Debt is in default.
NR		No rating has been requested, there is insufficient information, or the debt is not rated as a matter of policy.

At times, both S&P and Moody's use adjustments to these ratings called "notches." S&P uses plus and minus signs: A+ is the strongest A rating, and A− is the weakest. Moody's uses a 1, 2, or 3 designation, with 1 being the highest.

Sources: Standard & Poor's Ratings Definitions at *www.standardandpoors.com,* Long-Term Obligation Ratings at *www.moodys.ca,* Rating Scale: Bond and Long Term Debt at *www.dbrs.com.*

very often; AA or Aa ratings indicate very good quality debt and are much more common. The lowest rating is D (or C from Moody's), for debt that is in default.

Beginning in the 1980s, a growing part of corporate borrowing has taken the form of low-grade, or "junk," bonds. If these low-grade corporate bonds are rated at all, they are rated below investment grade by the major rating agencies. Investment-grade bonds are bonds rated at least BBB by S&P and DBRS, or Baa by Moody's. In October 2005, Metro, Inc., a leading Canadian food company, had the largest 10-year BBB-rated issue ($200 million) and the second largest 30-year BBB-rated issue ($400 million) in Canadian history. The record for the largest ever BBB-rated issue in Canada belongs to the $1.6-billion issue by Telus Corp. made in 2001.

Want to know what criteria are commonly used to rate corporate and provincial bonds? Go to **www.dbrs.com,** **www.standardandpoors.com,** and **www.moodys.com.**

Some bonds are called "crossover" bonds, because they have received a "split rating" by the rating agencies. For example, in October 2004 the University of Ontario Institute of Technology (UOIT) sold $220-million of 30-year debt that was rated BBB by DBRS and A2 by Moody's. Thus, DBRS rated the bonds as the lowest possible investment quality rating, while Moody's assigned a higher credit rating.

A bond's credit rating can change as the issuer's financial strength improves or deteriorates. For example, in November 2004 Bombardier Inc., the Montreal-based airplane and train maker, had its debt downgraded to junk status. Bonds that drop into junk territory are called "fallen angels." Why did this happen to Bombardier? A lot of reasons, but the rating agencies were particularly concerned about the bleak forecast for Bombardier's train division due to decreased orders from European customers and the fast decline of the market for its core 50-seat regional jet.

Why are credit ratings important? For companies, lower credit ratings lead to higher borrowing costs and a decline in credibility. For investors, lower credit ratings translate into increased risk associated with their investments. Defaults really do occur, and, when they do, investors can lose heavily. For example, in 2000 AmeriServe Food Distribution, Inc., which supplied restaurants such as Burger King with everything from burgers to giveaway toys, defaulted on $200 million in junk bonds. After the default, the bonds traded at just 18 cents on the dollar, leaving investors with a loss of more than $160 million.

CONCEPT QUESTIONS

6.3a What is a junk bond?

6.3b What does a bond rating say about the risk of fluctuations in a bond's value resulting from interest rate changes?

6.4 | SOME DIFFERENT TYPES OF BONDS

Thus far, we have considered only "plain vanilla" corporate bonds. In this section, we briefly look at bonds issued by governments and also at bonds with unusual features.

Government of Canada Bonds

The biggest borrower in Canada—by a wide margin—is the Government of Canada. In 2005, the total debt of the Canadian government was almost $500 billion. When the government wishes to borrow money for more than one year, it sells what are known as Government of Canada bonds (or simply Canada bonds) to the public. Currently, Government of Canada bonds have original maturities ranging from two to 30 years.

Most Government of Canada issues are just ordinary coupon bonds. Some older issues are callable, extendible or have other specific features. Before December 1993 the bonds were issued in both registered and bearer forms. Now they are issued in the registered form only. A relatively recent innovation is Government of Canada Real Return bonds. Such bonds have coupons and the principal that are adjusted according to the rate of inflation. Specifically, the principal of the real return bond increases in proportion to inflation. While the coupon rate stays the same, the actual coupon payments rise because of the higher principal. Other countries, including United States, Britain, Sweden, Australia, Israel, and France, have issued similar securities as well.

The most important characteristic of Government of Canada bonds, which is not shared by other debt issues, is the absence of the default risk. The Government of Canada has never defaulted on its debt, and (we hope) it will always come up with the money needed to make payments in the future.

Provinces, local governments, Crown corporations, and universities also borrow money by selling notes and bonds. Unlike Government of Canada bonds, they have varying degrees of default risk, and, in fact, they are rated much like corporate issues. They are also often callable.

Another distinguishing feature of Canada bonds is their high liquidity. Because of an active secondary market, it is very easy to buy and sell them. In contrast, lower-level governmental debt is frequently illiquid, and is primarily held until maturity.

Strip Bonds

A bond that pays no coupons at all must be offered at a price that is much lower than its stated value. These bonds have been called different names such as **strip bonds**, **zero coupon bonds** or simply *strips* or *zeroes*.[5] To create strip bonds, investment dealers separate coupons from a bond and then sell each coupon and the remaining principal individually.

strip bond/zero coupon bond
A bond that makes no coupon payments, and thus is initially priced at a deep discount.

Suppose the Eight-Inch Nails (EIN) Company issues a $1,000 face value, five-year strip bond. The initial price is set at $497. It is straightforward to verify that, at this price, the bond yields 15 percent to maturity. The total interest paid over the life of the bond is $1,000 - 497 = $503.

For tax purposes, the issuer of a strip bond deducts interest every year even though no interest is actually paid. Similarly, the owner must pay taxes on interest accrued every year, even though no interest is actually received.

Under current tax law, the implicit interest is determined by amortizing the loan. We do this by first calculating the bond's value at the beginning of each year. For example, after one year, the bond will have four years until maturity, so it will be worth $1,000/1.15^4 = 572; the value in two years will be $1,000/1.15^3 = 658; and so on. The implicit interest each year is simply the change in the bond's value for the year. The values and interest expenses for the EIN bond are listed in Table 6.2.

Another good bond market site is **money.cnn.com**.

Thus, EIN could deduct $75 in interest paid the first year and the owner of the bond would pay taxes on $75 of taxable income (even though no interest was actually received). This second tax feature makes taxable strip bonds less attractive to individuals. However, they are still a very attractive investment for tax-exempt investors with long-term dollar-denominated liabilities, such as pension funds and endowment funds because the future dollar value is known with relative certainty.

Floating-Rate Bonds

The conventional bonds we have talked about in this chapter have fixed-dollar obligations because the coupon rate is set as a fixed percentage of the par value. Similarly, the

Year	Beginning Value	Ending Value	Implicit Interest Expense
1	$497	$ 572	$ 75
2	572	658	86
3	658	756	98
4	756	870	114
5	870	1,000	130
Total			$503

TABLE 6.2

Interest expense for EIN's zeroes

---

[5]A bond issued with a very low coupon rate (as opposed to a zero coupon rate) is an original-issue discount (OID) bond.

principal is set equal to the par value. Under these circumstances, the coupon payment and principal are completely fixed.

With *floating-rate bonds (floaters),* the coupon payments are adjustable. The adjustments are tied to an interest rate index such as the Treasury bill rate or another short-term interest rate. For example, in May 2006 Calgary-based OPTI Canada Inc. sold US$450 million of floating-rate loans to U.S. institutional investors. The interest rate of the loans was LIBOR plus 1.75 percent. If you have never heard of the LIBOR rate, do not worry. We will discuss this major reference rate for international borrowing in Chapter 18.

The value of a floating-rate bond depends on exactly how the coupon payment adjustments are defined. In most cases, the coupon adjusts with a lag to some base rate. For example, suppose a coupon rate adjustment is made on June 1. The adjustment might be based on the simple average of Treasury bill yields during the previous three months. In addition, the majority of floaters have the following features:

1. The holder has the right to redeem the note at par on the coupon payment date after some specified amount of time. This is called a *put* provision, and it is discussed in the following section.

2. The coupon rate has a floor and a ceiling, meaning that the coupon is subject to a minimum and a maximum. In this case, the coupon rate is said to be "capped," and the upper and lower rates are sometimes called the *collar.*

Some bonds will have both fixed and floating rates during their lifetimes. For example, in March 2006, the Canadian Imperial Bank of Commerce raised $1.3 billion in 10-year notes. The notes promised a fixed 4.55 percent coupon rate for the first five years and a floating rate of the banker's acceptance rate plus one percent for the second five years.

Other Types of Bonds

Many bonds have unusual, or exotic, features. Unfortunately, there are far too many variations for us to cover in detail here. We therefore focus on only a few of the more common types.

Income bonds are similar to conventional bonds, except that coupon payments are dependent on company income. Specifically, coupons are paid to bondholders only if the firm's income is sufficient. This would appear to be an attractive feature, but income bonds are not very common.

A *convertible bond* can be swapped for a fixed number of shares of stock any time before maturity at the holder's option. Convertibles are relatively common, but the number has been decreasing in the last few years. A recent example of convertibles was US$30 million in convertible bonds issued by Taseko Mines Limited, headquartered in Vancouver, British Columbia, in August 2006. These bonds carried a coupon rate of 7.125 percent, had five years to maturity, and were convertible into shares of Taseko at a conversion price of US$3.350 (C$3.726), an approximate premium of 40 percent over the stock price at that time.

A *put bond,* or *retractable bond,* allows the *holder* to force the issuer to buy the bond back at a stated price. The put feature is therefore just the reverse of the call provision and is a relatively new development.

A given bond may have many unusual features. For example, two recent types of exotic bonds include CoCo bonds, which have a coupon payment, and NoNo bonds, which are zero coupon bonds. CoCo and NoNo bonds are contingent convertible, puttable, callable, subordinated bonds. The contingent convertible clause is similar to the normal conversion feature, except the contingency feature must be met. For example, a contingency feature may require that the company stock trade at 110 percent of the conversion price for 20 out of 30 days. Valuing a bond of this sort can be quite complex, and the yield to

REALITY BYTES

Exotic Bonds

Bonds come in many flavours. The unusual types are called "exotics" and can range from the fairly simple to the truly esoteric. Take the case of Countrywide Financial's convertible bonds. Holders of this issue almost never convert because the bond is usually worth more "alive" (unconverted) than "dead" (converted). But in October 2004, Countrywide's convertible bondholders were converting in droves. Why? A provision in the Countrywide bond allowed the bondholder to convert at the *average* stock price over the past 20 days. When the company announced poor earnings and lowered its future outlook, its stock dropped from $37.50 to $33.17. As a result, bond-holders could convert at the old prices and achieve a quick profit. This small provision was expected to cost Countrywide between $85 and $100 million.

Some bonds do not offer the traditional fixed income of ordinary debt instruments. For example, in September 2006 Royal Bank of Canada issued a five-year bond that would not pay any interest during the term of the bond. The amount payable upon maturity, however, will be equal to the sum of the principal plus 120 percent of the change in three global stock indexes. Thus, if the indexes perform well, an investor will enjoy a large payment at the time of maturity, but if the indexes do poorly, the investor will receive only the principal with no interest.

Other exotic bonds sport acronyms like EARNS, CATS, PETS, PINES, and CORTS. The acronym EARNS stands for Enhanced Accelerated Return Note Securities. Unlike ordinary debt instruments, EARNS do not pay interest during their lifetimes. A return, if any, is payable at maturity based on the return of a reference portfolio. For example, in July 2006, the National Bank of Canada issued $250 million of Oil Sands and Energy EARNS, whose reference portfolio included stocks of oil and energy companies. The EARNS promised an enhanced 150 percent of any positive return of the reference portfolio, while keeping at 100 percent the participation rate of any negative return. The EARNS represented unsecured and unsubordinated debt with the promised payment depending on the credit-worthiness of the National Bank of Canada.

CAT bonds are issued to cover insurance companies against natural catastrophes. The type of natural catastrophe is outlined in the bond. For example, about 30 percent of all CAT bonds protect against a North Atlantic hurricane. The way these issues are structured is that the borrowers can suspend payment temporarily (or even permanently) if they have significant hurricane-related losses. Unsurprisingly, the CAT bond market saw heavy trading in 2004 thanks to the three major hurricanes that hit Florida.

Perhaps the most unusual bond (and certainly the most ghoulish) is the "death bond." Companies such as Stone Street Financial purchase life insurance policies from individuals who are expected to die within the next 10 years. They then sell bonds that are paid off from the life insurance proceeds received when the policyholders die. The return on the bonds to investors depends on how long the policyholders live. A major risk is that if medical treatment advances quickly, it will raise the life expectancy of the policyholders, thereby decreasing the return to the bondholder.

maturity calculation is often meaningless. For example, in January 2005, a NoNo issued by Merrill Lynch was selling at a price of $1,023.29, with a yield to maturity of *negative* 1.05 percent. At the same time, a NoNo issued by Countrywide Financial was selling for $1,650.00, which implied a yield to maturity of *negative* 60.07 percent! The *Reality Bytes* box above provides some more examples of exotic bonds.

CONCEPT QUESTIONS

6.4a Why might an income bond be attractive to a corporation with volatile cash flows? Can you think of a reason why income bonds are not more popular?

6.4b What do you think would be the effect of a put feature on a bond's coupon? How about a convertibility feature? Why?

6.5 | BOND MARKETS

Bonds are bought and sold in enormous quantities every day. You may be surprised to learn that the trading volume in bonds on a typical day is many, many times larger than the trading volume in stocks (by trading volume, we simply mean the amount of money that changes hands). Here is a finance trivia question: What is the largest securities market in the world? Most people would guess the New York Stock Exchange. In fact, the largest securities market in the world in terms of trading volume is the U.S. Treasury market.

How Bonds Are Bought and Sold

As we mentioned all the way back in Chapter 1, most trading in bonds takes place over the counter, or OTC. Recall that this means that there is no particular place where buying and selling occur. Instead, dealers around the country (and around the world) stand ready to buy and sell. The various dealers are connected electronically.

One reason the bond markets are so big is that the number of bond issues far exceeds the number of stock issues. There are two reasons for this. First, a corporation would typically have only one common stock issue outstanding (there are exceptions to this that we discuss in our next chapter). However, a single large corporation could easily have a dozen or more note and bond issues outstanding. Beyond this, federal, provincial, and municipal borrowing is simply enormous. For example, even universities can issue bonds to pay for things such as new libraries, research centres, and lecture buildings.

Because the bond market is almost entirely OTC, it has historically had little or no *transparency*. A financial market is transparent if it is possible to easily observe its prices and trading volume. On the Toronto Stock Exchange, for example, it is possible to see the price and quantity for every single transaction. In contrast, in the bond market, it is usually not possible to observe either. Transactions are privately negotiated between parties, and there is little or no centralized reporting of transactions.

Although the total volume of trading in bonds far exceeds that in stocks, only a very small fraction of the total bond issues that exist actually trade on a given day. This fact, combined with the lack of transparency in the bond market, means that getting up-to-date prices on individual bonds is often difficult or impossible, particularly for smaller corporate or municipal issues. Instead, a variety of sources of estimated prices exist and are very commonly used. Bond markets are moving to the Web. See our *Work the Web* box opposite for more info.

Bond Price Reporting

To learn more about CanDeal, visit **www.candeal.ca.**

In July 2002, transparency in the Canadian debt market began to improve dramatically. CanDeal, Canada's online trading system for bond and money market securities, received regulatory approval from the Ontario Securities Commission (OSC) and the Investment Dealers Association of Canada (IDA). The introduction of CanDeal dramatically reduced the need to call different dealers to find out the prices for fixed income securities. CanDeal shows the best bid and ask prices for over 250 bonds, including all Treasury bills, Government of Canada bonds, and selected provincial and corporate bonds, but only for institutional investors. In August 2005, CanDeal formed a partnership with TradeWeb, the world's leading provider of online fixed-income markets, to give Canadian institutional investors electronic access to debt markets in the United States and Europe.

WORK THE WEB

Bond quotes have become more available with the rise of the Web. One site where you can find current prices on corporate bonds traded in the United States is **www.nasdbondinfo.com**. Many Canadian companies issue bonds in the U.S. corporate debt market. We went to the site and entered the ticker symbol "CNI" for the well-known Canadian National Railway company. We found a total of 13 bond issues outstanding. Below you will see the information we found about four of these issues.

Issue: CNI.GW CANADIAN NATIONAL RAILWAY CO 5.80 06/01/2016

In Portfolio	Rating Moody's/S&P/Fitch	Last Sale Date	Price	Yield	Most Recent Date	Price	Yield
☐	A3 / A- / N/A	08/31/2006	103.134	5.380936	08/31/2006	103.13	5.380936

Issue: CNI.GV CANADIAN NATIONAL RAILWAY CO 6.20 06/01/2036

In Portfolio	Rating Moody's/S&P/Fitch	Last Sale Date	Price	Yield	Most Recent Date	Price	Yield
☐	A3 / A- / N/A	08/28/2006	104.881	5.850978	08/28/2006	104.88	5.850978

Issue: CNI.GB CANADIAN NATIONAL RAILWAY COMPANY 7.625 05/15/2023

In Portfolio	Rating Moody's/S&P/Fitch	Last Sale Date	Price	Yield	Most Recent Date	Price	Yield
☐	A3 / A- / NR	07/19/2006	116.043	6.085969	07/19/2006	116.04	6.085969

Issue: CNI.GD CANADIAN NATIONAL RAILWAY COMPANY 6.80 07/15/2018

In Portfolio	Rating Moody's/S&P/Fitch	Last Sale Date	Price	Yield	Most Recent Date	Price	Yield
☐	A3 / A- / NR	08/22/2006	110.372	5.592976	08/22/2006	110.37	5.592976

Most of the information is self-explanatory. The price and yield columns show the price and yield to maturity of the most recent sales. Notice the last sale dates. Except the issue maturing in 2016, other issues had no bonds traded for several days (issues maturing in 2036 and 2018) or for more than one month (issue maturing in 2023). Another nice feature of this Web site is the "Descriptive Data" link, which gives you more information about the bond issue, such as call dates and coupon dates.

Individual investors can find information on federal, provincial, and corporate bonds, and different yields from the *National Post* (or similar financial newspaper). As we mentioned before, the Government of Canada debt market is the largest securities market in Canada. As with bond markets in general, it is an OTC market, so there is limited transparency. However, unlike the situation with bond markets in general, trading in Government of Canada issues, particularly those recently issued, is very heavy. Each day, representative prices for outstanding Government of Canada issues are reported.

Figure 6.3 shows a portion of the bond price and yield listings from Wednesday, July 19, 2006. Find the highlighted entry that begins with "Canada 10.500" under the "Federal" heading. This entry tells us that the bond is issued by the Government of Canada, and the bond's coupon rate is 10.5 percent. Government of Canada bonds all make semiannual payments and have a face value of $1,000, so this bond will pay $52.50 every six months until its maturity date. The next column shows that this bond matures on March 15, 2021.

FIGURE 6.3 Sample National Post bond prices and yields

Supplied by RBC Dominion Securities Inc. (5pm close, bid)

INDEXES

RBC Cap Index	Index Level	Total ret	Price ret	MTD tot.ret
Market	501.50	−0.31	−0.32	0.78
Short	400.50	−0.12	−0.13	0.56
Intermed	515.93	−0.30	−0.32	0.84
Long	675.33	−0.60	−0.61	1.07
Govts	495.30	−0.32	−0.33	0.79
Canadas	473.65	−0.28	−0.29	0.73
Provs	549.00	−0.40	−0.41	0.88
Munis	192.99	−0.36	−0.38	0.85
Corps	542.56	−0.26	−0.28	0.76

B O N D S   0 7 . 1 8 . 0 6

FEDERAL

	Coupon	Mat. date	Bid $	Yld%
Canada	4.500	Sep 01/07	100.16	4.34
Canada	2.750	Dec 01/07	97.96	4.30
Canada	12.750	Mar 01/08	113.07	4.29
Canada	3.750	Jun 01/08	99.08	4.26
Canada	10.000	Jun 01/08	110.23	4.24
Canada	6.000	Jun 01/08	103.09	4.26
Canada	4.250	Sep 01/08	99.90	4.30
Canada	4.250	Dec 01/08	99.87	4.31
Canada	11.000	Jun 01/09	117.87	4.30
Canada	5.000	Jun 01/09	103.16	4.30
Canada	4.250	Sep 01/09	99.75	4.34
Canada	10.750	Oct 01/09	118.92	4.34
Canada	9.500	Jun 01/10	118.13	4.35
Canada	5.500	Jun 01/10	104.01	4.36
Canada	4.000	Sep 01/10	98.67	4.36
Canada	9.000	Mar 01/11	119.15	4.37
Canada	6.000	Jun 01/11	106.93	4.40
Canada	8.500	Jun 01/11	117.79	4.39
Canada	3.750	Sep 01/11	97.03	4.40
Canada	5.250	Jun 01/12	104.22	4.42
Canada	5.250	Jun 01/13	104.74	4.44
Canada	10.250	Mar 15/14	137.13	4.47
Canada	5.000	Jun 01/14	103.47	4.47
Canada	11.250	Jun 01/15	149.06	4.48
Canada	4.500	Jun 01/15	100.06	4.49
Canada	4.000	Jun 01/16	95.92	4.52
Canada	10.500	Mar 15/21	162.83	4.57
Canada	9.750	Jun 01/22	155.44	4.57
Canada	9.250	Jun 01/23	152.64	4.55
Canada	8.000	Jun 01/23	139.74	4.59
Canada	9.000	Jun 01/25	155.15	4.60
Canada	8.000	Jun 01/27	145.42	4.59
Canada	5.750	Jun 01/29	116.42	4.58
Canada	5.750	Jun 01/33	118.42	4.55
Canada	5.000	Jun 01/37	107.83	4.53
CHT	4.750	Mar 15/07	100.24	4.37
CHT	5.100	Sep 15/07	100.72	4.45
CHT	4.400	Mar 15/08	99.95	4.43
CHT	3.700	Sep 15/08	98.53	4.42
CHT	4.100	Dec 15/08	99.25	4.43
CHT	3.550	Mar 15/09	97.79	4.45
CHT	4.650	Sep 15/09	100.54	4.46
CHT	3.750	Sep 15/10	97.57	4.48
CHT	3.550	Sep 15/10	96.51	4.48
CMHC	5.250	Dec 01/06	101.06	4.22
CMHC	5.300	Dec 03/07	101.35	4.27
EDC	5.500	Jun 01/12	104.87	4.54
EDC	5.000	Jun 09/09	101.41	4.41
EDC	5.100	Jun 02/14	103.12	4.62

PROVINCIAL

	Coupon	Mat. date	Bid $	Yld%
B C	6.000	Jun 09/08	102.85	4.41
B C	6.375	Aug 23/10	105.60	4.52
B C	5.750	Jan 09/12	105.60	4.58
B C	8.500	Aug 23/13	123.17	4.63
B C	6.150	Nov 19/27	115.41	4.97
B C	5.700	Jun 18/29	110.04	4.96
B C MF	5.500	Mar 24/08	101.64	4.44
B C MF	5.900	Jun 01/11	105.80	4.56
HydQue	6.500	Feb 15/11	107.76	4.60
HydQue	10.250	Jul 16/12	128.86	4.67
HydQue	11.000	Aug 15/20	159.07	5.07
HydQue	6.000	Aug 15/31	111.51	5.18
HydQue	6.500	Feb 15/35	119.73	5.15
HydQue	6.000	Feb 15/40	113.45	5.15
Manit	5.750	Dec 22/25	102.37	5.15
Manit	7.750	Dec 22/25	134.08	4.99
NewBr	5.700	Jun 02/08	102.27	4.42
NewBr	6.000	Dec 27/17	109.60	4.89
Newfld	6.150	Apr 17/28	113.77	5.09
NovaSc	6.600	Jun 01/27	119.85	5.05
Ontario	6.125	Sep 12/07	101.84	4.45
Ontario	5.700	Dec 01/08	102.79	4.44
Ontario	4.000	May 19/09	98.77	4.47
Ontario	6.200	Nov 19/09	105.23	4.49
Ontario	4.000	Nov 19/10	98.17	4.53
Ontario	6.100	Nov 19/10	106.14	4.52
Ontario	6.100	Dec 02/11	107.11	4.59
Ontario	5.375	Dec 02/12	104.07	4.63
Ontario	4.750	Jun 02/13	100.63	4.64
Ontario	5.000	Mar 08/14	101.78	4.72
Ontario	4.500	Mar 08/15	98.10	4.77
Ontario	4.400	Mar 08/16	96.74	4.83
Ontario	8.100	Sep 08/23	135.27	5.01
Ontario	7.600	Jun 02/27	132.59	5.05
Ontario	6.500	Mar 08/29	119.36	5.05
Ontario	5.850	Mar 08/33	111.35	5.07
Ontario	5.600	Jun 02/35	108.13	5.06
Ontario	4.700	Jun 02/37	94.43	5.06
OntHyd	5.600	Jun 02/08	102.09	4.42
OntHyd	6.500	Oct 01/07	102.32	4.48
Quebec	5.500	Jun 01/09	102.63	4.51
Quebec	6.250	Jun 01/10	106.47	4.60
Quebec	6.000	Oct 01/12	106.89	4.70
Quebec	5.250	Oct 01/13	102.85	4.78
Quebec	5.500	Dec 01/14	104.47	4.84
Quebec	5.000	Dec 01/15	100.67	4.91
Quebec	4.500	Dec 01/16	96.40	4.95
Quebec	9.375	Jan 16/23	147.22	5.10
Quebec	8.500	Jan 26/26	141.17	5.15
Quebec	6.000	Oct 01/29	111.30	5.16
Quebec	6.250	Jan 01/32	115.25	5.17
Quebec	5.750	Dec 01/36	108.93	5.16
Saskat	5.500	Jun 02/08		
Saskat	8.750	May 30/25		
Toronto	6.100	Aug 15/07		
Toronto	6.100	Dec 12/17		

CORPORATE

	Coupon	Mat. date
AGT Lt	8.800	Sep 22/25
BCE	6.750	Oct 30/07
Bell	6.550	May 01/29
BMO	6.903	Jun 30/10
BMO	6.647	Oct 31/10
BMO	4.690	Jan 31/11
BMO	6.685	Dec 31/11
BNS	3.470	Sep 02/08
BNS	4.515	Nov 19/08
BNS	3.930	Feb 18/10
BNS	7.310	Dec 31/10
CardTr2	3.869	Oct 15/10
CDP	4.200	Oct 14/08
CIBC	3.750	Sep 09/10
CIBC	4.550	Mar 28/11
Domtar	10.000	Apr 15/11
GE CAP	5.300	Jul 24/07
GE CAP	5.000	Apr 23/08
GE CAP	3.650	Jun 07/10
Genss	4.002	Mar 15/10
GldCrd	4.159	Oct 15/08
GrTAA	5.950	Dec 03/07
GrTAA	6.450	Dec 03/27
GTC Tr	6.200	Jun 01/07

Y I E L D S   &   R A T E S

Supplied by Reuters. Indicative late afternoon rates.

CANADIAN YIELDS

	Latest	Prev day	Week ago	4 wks ago
T-Bills				
1-month	4.02	4.01	4.05	4.09
3-month	4.16	4.15	4.19	4.27
6-month	4.28	4.24	4.28	4.40
1-year	4.40	4.35	4.39	4.48
Bonds				
2-year	4.25	4.21	4.23	4.34
5-year	4.34	4.29	4.30	4.39
7-year	4.41	4.36	4.37	4.44
10-year	4.49	4.44	4.43	4.49
30-year	4.55	4.50	4.49	4.52
Banker's acceptances (ask price)				
1-month	4.32	4.31	4.32	4.35
3-month	4.35	4.37	4.35	4.47
6-month	4.43	4.41	4.41	4.58

3-mth forward rate agreement

	Latest	Prev day	Week ago	4 wks ago
3-month	4.45	4.45	4.41	4.43
6-month	4.52	4.52	4.45	4.48
	4.52	4.52	4.47	4.49

U.S. YIELDS

T-Bills	Latest	Prev day	Week ago	4 wks ago
1-month	4.87	4.87	4.87	4.65
3-month	5.12	5.08	5.08	4.92
6-month	5.32	5.26	5.04	5.23
Bonds				
2-year	5.18	5.11	5.15	5.19
5-year	5.10	5.03	5.07	5.13
10-year	5.13	5.06	5.10	5.15
30-year	5.17	5.10	5.14	5.19

Commercial paper

	Latest	Prev day	Week ago	4 wks ago
1-month	5.22	5.21	5.21	5.13
3-month	5.29	5.29	5.29	5.01
6-month	5.35	5.36	5.35	5.27

3-mth forward rate agreement

	Latest	Prev day	Week ago	4 wks ago
3-month	5.62	5.56	5.62	5.60
6-month	5.61	5.53	5.59	5.61
9-month	5.58	5.49	5.56	5.57

INTERNATIONAL

Euro-deposit rates (bid)

	Latest	Prev day	Wk ago	4 wks ago
US$ 1-month	5.32	5.32	5.31	5.24
3-month	5.45	5.45	5.46	5.38
6-month	5.54	5.52	5.54	5.50

		Latest	Prev day	Wk ago	4 wks ago
C$	3-month	4.29	4.29	4.32	4.32
euro	3-month	3.07	3.07	3.05	2.97
¥	3-month	0.35	0.35	0.34	0.27
£	3-month	4.59	4.58	4.61	4.65

London interbank offer rate US$

	Latest	Prev day	Wk ago	4 wks ago
1-month	5.38	5.37	5.36	5.29
3-month	5.50	5.49	5.50	5.44
6-month	5.58	5.56	5.61	5.55

BANK RATES

Canada		U.S.	
Bank of Can.	4.50	Discount	6.25
O/N MM Fin Rate	4.21	Prime	8.25
Prime	6.00	Fed Funds	5.19
Call Loan Ave.	4.25		

Source: Reprinted by permission of the *National Post*, July 19, 2006, FP16.

The column marked "Bid $" gives the **bid price.** In general, in any OTC or dealer market, the bid price represents what a dealer is willing to pay for a security. The bid price on this Government of Canada bond is 162.83 percent of the face value, or 1628.30. Finally, the last number reported is the yield to maturity. Notice that this is a premium bond because it sells for more than its face value. Not surprisingly, its yield to maturity (4.57 percent) is less than its coupon rate (10.5 percent). If you examine the yields on the various issues in Figure 6.3, you will see that they vary by maturity. Why this occurs and what it might mean is one of the things we discuss in our next section.

bid price
The price a dealer is willing to pay for a security.

Canada Bonds Quotes   EXAMPLE 6.4

Locate the Government of Canada bond in Figure 6.3 with the largest coupon. What is its coupon payment? What is its bid price? Is it sold at a premium or a discount? Why?

Find the cheapest Government of Canada bond. What is its bid price? Why is it sold below its face value?

A Note on Bond Price Quotes   If you buy a bond between coupon payment dates, the price you pay is usually more than the price you are quoted. The reason is that standard convention in the bond market is to quote prices net of "accrued interest," meaning that accrued interest is deducted to arrive at the quoted price. This quoted price is called the **clean price.** The price you actually pay, however, includes the accrued interest. This price is the **dirty price,** also known as the "full" or "invoice" price.

An example is the easiest way to understand these issues. Suppose you buy a bond with a 12 percent annual coupon, payable semiannually. You actually pay $1,080 for this bond, so $1,080 is the dirty, or invoice, price. Further, on the day you buy it, the next coupon is due in four months, so you are between coupon dates. Notice that the next coupon will be $60.

The accrued interest on a bond is calculated by taking the fraction of the coupon period that has passed, in this case two months out of six, and multiplying this fraction by the next coupon, $60. So, the accrued interest in this example is $2/6 \times \$60 = \$20$. The bond's quoted price (i.e., its clean price) would be $\$1,080 - 20 = \$1,060$.

clean price
The price of a bond net of accrued interest; this is the price that is typically quoted.

dirty price
The price of a bond including accrued interest, also known as the *full* or *invoice price.* This is the price the buyer actually pays.

A Note on Treasury Bill Yields   The "Yields and Rates" section of Figure 6.3 shows yields on different securities, for example, Canadian and U.S. yields on T-bills, banker's acceptance, and commercial paper. These short-term securities do not carry interest, but are sold at a discount. Thus, if you buy them you will not collect any interest payments. Your return will come from the difference between the purchase price and the security's face value, which you will receive at maturity. To compare yields on securities of different maturities, their yields are annualized as:

$$r = \frac{\$1,000 - P}{P} \times \frac{365}{d} \qquad \textbf{[6.2]}$$

where

  r is the annualized yield,
  P is the discounted price of a security
  d is the number of days to maturity

You can learn how to determine bond and Treasury bill prices and yields at **www.fin.gc.ca/invest/ bondprice-e.html.**

Suppose a three-month (91 days), $1,000 T-bill is selling for $990. The annualized yield on this T-bill is:

$$r = \frac{\$1,000 - \$990}{\$990} \times \frac{365}{91}$$

$r = 4.05$ percent

EXAMPLE 6.5   ### Treasury Bill Yields

Find the latest Canadian yield on the 1-month T-bills in Figure 6.3. What is the current price of these T-bills?

The 1-month T-bills currently yield 4.02 percent. To calculate their price, we need to plug the yield and the days to maturity into formula 6.2:

$$0.0402 = \frac{\$1,000 - P}{P} \times \frac{365}{30}$$

$0.0033P = \$1,000 - P$

$1.0033P = \$1,000$

$P = \$996.71$

CONCEPT QUESTIONS

6.5a   Why do we say bond markets may have little or no transparency?

6.5b   What is a bond's bid price?

6.5c   What is the difference between a bond's clean price and dirty price?

6.6 | INFLATION AND INTEREST RATES

So far, we haven't considered the role of inflation in our various discussions of interest rates, yields, and returns. Because this is an important consideration, we consider the impact of inflation next.

Real versus Nominal Rates

In examining interest rates, or any other financial market rates such as discount rates, bond yields, rates of return, and required returns, it is often necessary to distinguish between **real rates** and **nominal rates**. Nominal rates are called "nominal" because they have not been adjusted for inflation. Real rates are rates that have been adjusted for inflation.

real rates
Interest rates or rates of return that have been adjusted for inflation.

To see the effect of inflation, suppose prices are currently rising by 5 percent per year. In other words, the rate of inflation is 5 percent. An investment is available that will be worth $115.50 in one year. It costs $100 today. Notice that with a present value of $100 and a future value in one year of $115.50, this investment has a 15.5 percent rate of return. In calculating this 15.5 percent return, we did not consider the effect of inflation, however, so this is the nominal return.

nominal rates
Interest rates or rates of return that have not been adjusted for inflation.

What is the impact of inflation here? To answer, suppose pizzas cost $5 apiece at the beginning of the year. With $100, we can buy 20 pizzas. Because the inflation rate is 5 percent, pizzas will cost 5 percent more, or $5.25, at the end of the year. If we take the investment, how many pizzas can we buy at the end of the year? Measured in pizzas, what is the rate of return on this investment?

Our $115.50 from the investment will buy us $115.50/5.25 = 22 pizzas. This is up from 20 pizzas, so our pizza rate of return is 10 percent. What this illustrates is that even though the nominal return on our investment is 15.5 percent, our buying power goes up by only 10 percent because of inflation. Put another way, we are really only 10 percent richer. In this case, we say that the real return is 10 percent.

Alternatively, we can say that with 5 percent inflation, each of the 115.50 nominal dollars we get is worth 5 percent less in real terms, so the real dollar value of our investment in a year is:

$115.50/1.05 = $110

What we have done is to *deflate* the $115.50 by 5 percent. Because we give up $100 in current buying power to get the equivalent of $110, our real return is again 10 percent. Now that we have removed the effect of future inflation, this $110 is said to be measured in current dollars.

The difference between nominal and real rates is important and bears repeating:

The nominal rate on an investment is the percentage change in the number of dollars you have.

The real rate on an investment is the percentage change in how much you can buy with your dollars, in other words, the percentage change in your buying power.

The Fisher Effect

Our discussion of real and nominal returns illustrates a relationship often called the **Fisher effect** (after the great economist Irving Fisher). Because investors are ultimately concerned with what they can buy with their money, they require compensation for inflation. Let R stand for the nominal rate and r stand for the real rate. The Fisher effect tells us that the relationship between nominal rates, real rates, and inflation can be written as:

$$1 + R = (1 + r) \times (1 + h) \qquad [6.3]$$

Fisher effect
The relationship between nominal returns, real returns, and inflation.

where h is the inflation rate.

In the preceding example, the nominal rate was 15.50 percent and the inflation rate was 5 percent. What was the real rate? We can determine it by plugging in these numbers:

$$1 + .1550 = (1 + r) \times (1 + .05)$$
$$1 + r = 1.1550/1.05 = 1.10$$
$$r = 10\%$$

This real rate is the same as we had before. If we take another look at the Fisher effect, we can rearrange things a little as follows:

$$1 + R = (1 + r) \times (1 + h)$$
$$R = r + h + r \times h \qquad [6.4]$$

What this tells us is that the nominal rate has three components. First, there is the real rate on the investment, r. Next, there is the compensation for the decrease in the value of the money originally invested because of inflation, h. The third component represents compensation for the fact that the dollars earned on the investment are also worth less because of the inflation.

You can find an inflation calculator and an investment calculator, which shows the effects of inflation on investments and savings, in "Rates and Statistics" at **www.bankofcanada.ca**.

This third component is usually small, so it is often dropped. The nominal rate is then approximately equal to the real rate plus the inflation rate:

$$R \approx r + h \qquad [6.5]$$

EXAMPLE 6.6

The Fisher Effect

If investors require a 10 percent real rate of return, and the inflation rate is 8 percent, what must the approximate nominal rate be? The exact nominal rate?

First of all, the nominal rate is approximately equal to the sum of the real rate and the inflation rate: 10% + 8% = 18%. From the Fisher effect, we have:

$$1 + R = (1 + r) \times (1 + h)$$
$$= 1.10 \times 1.08$$
$$= 1.1880$$

Therefore, the nominal rate will actually be closer to 19 percent.

It is important to note that financial rates, such as interest rates, discount rates, and rates of return, are almost always quoted in nominal terms. To remind you of this, we will henceforth use the symbol R instead of r in most of our discussions about such rates.

CONCEPT QUESTIONS

6.6a What is the difference between a nominal and a real return? Which is more important to a typical investor?

6.6b What is the Fisher effect?

6.7 | DETERMINANTS OF BOND YIELDS

We are now in a position to discuss the determinants of a bond's yield. As we will see, the yield on any particular bond is a reflection of a variety of factors, some common to all bonds and some specific to the issue under consideration.

The Term Structure of Interest Rates

term structure of interest rates
The relationship between nominal interest rates on default-free, pure discount securities and time to maturity; that is, the pure time value of money.

At any point in time, short-term and long-term interest rates will generally be different. Sometimes short-term rates are higher, sometimes lower. Figure 6.4 gives us a long-range perspective on this by showing almost a century of short- and long-term interest rates. As shown, over time, the difference between short- and long-term rates has ranged from essentially zero to up to several percentage points, both positive and negative.

The relationship between short-term and long-term interest rates is known as the **term structure of interest rates.** To be a little more precise, the term structure of interest rates tells us what *nominal* interest rates are on *default-free, pure discount* bonds of all maturities. These rates are, in essence, "pure" interest rates because they involve no risk of default

Canadian interest rates: 1920–2005   FIGURE **6.4**

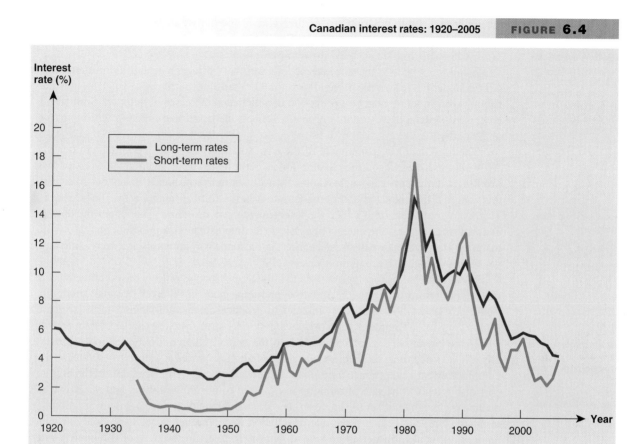

Source: Canadian interest rates 1920–2005. Used with permission of the Bank of Canada.

and a single, lump-sum future payment. In other words, the term structure tells us the pure time value of money for different lengths of time.

When long-term rates are higher than short-term rates, we say that the term structure is upward sloping, and when short-term rates are higher, we say it is downward sloping. The term structure can also be "humped." When this occurs, it is usually because rates increase at first, but then begin to decline as we look at longer and longer term rates. The most common shape of the term structure, particularly in modern times, is upward sloping, but the degree of steepness has varied quite a bit.

What determines the shape of the term structure? There are three basic components. The first two are the ones we discussed in our previous section: the real rate of interest and the rate of inflation. The real rate of interest is the compensation investors demand for forgoing the use of their money. You can think of it as the pure time value of money after adjusting for the effects of inflation.

The real rate of interest is the basic component underlying every interest rate, regardless of the time to maturity. When the real rate is high, all interest rates will tend to be higher, and vice versa. Thus, the real rate doesn't really determine the shape of the term structure; instead, it mostly influences the overall level of interest rates.

In contrast, the prospect of future inflation very strongly influences the shape of the term structure. Investors thinking about loaning money for various lengths of time

inflation premium
The portion of a nominal interest rate that represents compensation for expected future inflation.

recognize that future inflation erodes the value of the dollars that will be returned. As a result, investors demand compensation for this loss in the form of higher nominal rates. This extra compensation is called the **inflation premium**.

If investors believe that the rate of inflation will be higher in the future, then long-term nominal interest rates will tend to be higher than short-term rates. Thus, an upward-sloping term structure may be a reflection of anticipated increases in inflation. Similarly, a downward-sloping term structure probably reflects the belief that inflation will be falling in the future.

The third, and last, component of the term structure has to do with interest rate risk. As we discussed earlier in the chapter, longer-term bonds have much greater risk of loss resulting from changes in interest rates than do shorter-term bonds. Investors recognize this risk, and they demand extra compensation in the form of higher rates for bearing it. This extra compensation is called the **interest rate risk premium**. The longer the term to maturity, the greater is the interest rate risk, so the interest rate risk premium increases with maturity. However, as we discussed earlier, interest rate risk increases at a decreasing rate, so the interest rate risk premium does as well.[6]

interest rate risk premium
The compensation investors demand for bearing interest rate risk.

Putting the pieces together, we see that the term structure reflects the combined effect of the real rate of interest, the inflation premium, and the interest rate risk premium. Figure 6.5 shows how these can interact to produce an upward-sloping term structure (in the top part of Figure 6.5) or a downward-sloping term structure (in the bottom part).

In the top part of Figure 6.5, notice how the rate of inflation is expected to rise gradually. At the same time, the interest rate risk premium increases at a decreasing rate, so the combined effect is to produce a pronounced upward-sloping term structure. In the bottom part of Figure 6.5, the rate of inflation is expected to fall in the future, and the expected decline is enough to offset the interest rate risk premium and produce a downward-sloping term structure. Notice that if the rate of inflation was expected to decline by only a small amount, we could still get an upward-sloping term structure because of the interest rate risk premium.

Current interest rates are available at
**www.bankofcanada
.ca**
and
www.bankrate.ca.

We assumed in drawing Figure 6.5 that the real rate would remain the same. Actually, expected future real rates could be larger or smaller than the current real rate. Also, for simplicity, we used straight lines to show expected future inflation rates as rising or declining, but they do not necessarily have to look like this. They could, for example, rise and then fall, leading to a humped yield curve.

Bond Yields and the Yield Curve: Putting It All Together

Going back to Figure 6.3, recall that we saw that the yields on Treasury bills and bonds of different maturities are not the same. Each day, we can draw a plot of Treasury yields relative to maturity. This plot is called the **Canada Yield Curve** (or just the yield curve). Figure 6.6 shows the yield curve drawn from the yields in Figure 6.3.

Canada Yield Curve
A plot of the yields on Government of Canada bonds relative to maturity.

As you probably now suspect, the shape of the yield curve is a reflection of the term structure of interest rates. In fact, the Canada yield curve and the term structure of interest rates are almost the same thing. The only difference is that the term structure is based on pure discount bonds, whereas the yield curve is based on coupon bond yields. As a result,

---

[6]In days of old, the interest rate risk premium was called a "liquidity" premium. Today, the term *liquidity premium* has an altogether different meaning, which we explore in our next section. Also, the interest rate risk premium is sometimes called a maturity risk premium. Our terminology is consistent with the modern view of the term structure.

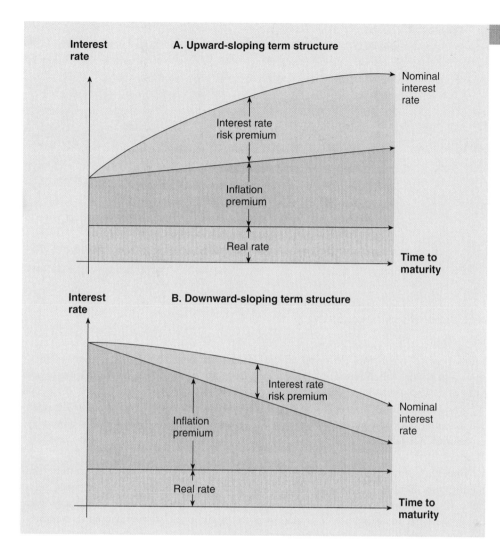

FIGURE 6.5

The term structure
of interest rates

Canada yields depend on the three components that underlie the term structure: the real rate, expected future inflation, and the interest rate risk premium.

Canada bonds have three important features that we need to remind you of: They are default-free, they are taxable, and they are highly liquid. This is not true of bonds in general, so we need to examine what additional factors come into play when we look at bonds issued by corporations or municipalities.

The first thing to consider is credit risk, that is, the possibility of default. Investors recognize that issuers other than the Government of Canada may or may not make all the promised payments on a bond, so they demand a higher yield as compensation for this risk. This extra compensation is called the **default risk premium**. Earlier in the chapter, we saw how bonds were rated based on their credit risk. What you will find if you start looking at bonds of different ratings is that lower-rated bonds have higher yields.

An important thing to recognize about a bond's yield is that it is calculated assuming that all the promised payments will be made. As a result, it is really a promised yield, and it may or may not be what you will earn. In particular, if the issuer defaults, your actual yield will be lower, probably much lower. This fact is particularly important when it comes

default risk premium
The portion of a nominal interest rate or bond yield that represents compensation for the possibility of default.

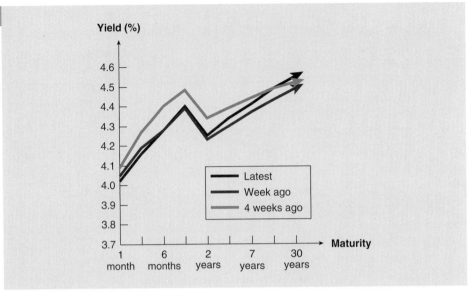

FIGURE 6.6

The Canada Yield Curve
Canada Yield Curve
July 18, 2006

Source: *National Post*, July 19, 2006, p. FP16.

to junk bonds. Thanks to a clever bit of marketing, such bonds are now commonly called high-yield bonds, which has a much nicer ring to it; but now you recognize that these are really high–*promised*-yield bonds.

Next, recall from Chapter 2 that dividends and capital gains are taxed at lower rates than the interest income generated by bonds. Investors demand the extra yield on a bond as compensation for the unfavourable tax treatment. This extra compensation is the **taxability premium**.

Finally, bonds have varying degrees of liquidity. As we discussed earlier, there are an enormous number of bond issues, most of which do not trade on a regular basis. As a result, if you wanted to sell quickly, you would probably not get as good a price as you could otherwise. Investors prefer liquid assets to illiquid ones, so they demand a **liquidity premium** on top of all the other premiums we have discussed. As a result, all else being the same, less liquid bonds will have higher yields than more liquid bonds.

taxability premium
The portion of a nominal interest rate or bond yield that represents compensation for unfavourable tax status.

liquidity premium
The portion of a nominal interest rate or bond yield that represents compensation for lack of liquidity.

Conclusion

If we combine all of the things we have discussed regarding bond yields, we find that bond yields represent the combined effect of no fewer than six things. The first is the real rate of interest. On top of the real rate are five premiums representing compensation for (1) expected future inflation, (2) interest rate risk, (3) default risk, (4) taxability, and (5) lack of liquidity. As a result, determining the appropriate yield on a bond requires careful analysis of each of these effects.

CONCEPT QUESTIONS

6.7a   What is the term structure of interest rates? What determines its shape?

6.7b   What is the Canada yield curve?

6.7c   What are the six components that make up a bond's yield?

KEY EQUATIONS:

I. Bond Value

If a bond has a face value of F paid at maturity, a coupon of C paid per period, t periods to maturity, and a yield of r per period, its value is:

Bond value = Present value + Present value
of the coupons   of the face amount

$$\textbf{Bond value} = C \times [1 - 1/(1+r)^t]/r + F/(1+r)^t \qquad [6.1]$$

II. T-Bill Yield

If a T-bill is trading at price P and has d days to maturity, its annualized yield r is:

$$r = \frac{\$1{,}000 - P}{P} \times \frac{365}{d} \qquad [6.2]$$

III. Fisher Effect

The relationship between nominal rates, R, real rates, r, and inflation, h, is:

$$1 + R = (1 + r) \times (1 + h) \qquad [6.3]$$

$$R = r + h + r \times h \qquad [6.4]$$

$$R \approx r + h \qquad [6.5]$$

SUMMARY AND CONCLUSIONS

This chapter has explored bonds and bond yields. We saw that:

1. Determining bond prices and yields is an application of basic discounted cash flow principles. Bond values move in the direction opposite that of interest rates, leading to potential gains or losses for bond investors.

2. Bonds have a variety of features spelled out in a document called the indenture.

3. Bonds are rated based on their default risk. Some bonds, such as Treasury bonds, have no risk of default, whereas so-called junk bonds have substantial default risk.

4. A wide variety of bonds exist, many of which contain exotic, or unusual, features.

5. Almost all bond trading is OTC, with little or no market transparency. As a result, bond price and volume information can be difficult to find.

6. Because of inflation, nominal rates are not equal to real rates, which reflect the percentage change in buying power.

7. Bond yields reflect the effect of six different things: the real rate and five premiums that investors demand as compensation for inflation, interest rate risk, default risk, taxability, and lack of liquidity.

In closing, we note that bonds are a vital source of financing to governments and corporations of all types. Bond prices and yields are a rich subject, and our one chapter, necessarily, touches on only the most important concepts and ideas. There is a great deal more we could say, but, instead, we will move on to stocks in our next chapter.

www.mcgrawhill.ca/olc/ross

CHAPTER REVIEW AND SELF-TEST PROBLEMS

6.1 Bond Values. A Mayflower Industries bond has a 10 percent coupon rate and a $1,000 face value. Interest is paid semiannually, and the bond has 20 years to maturity. If investors require a 12 percent yield, what is the bond's value? What is the effective annual yield on the bond?

6.2 Yields. A Canuck Corp. bond carries an 8 percent coupon, paid semiannually. The par value is $1,000, and the bond matures in six years. If the bond currently sells for $911.37, what is its yield to maturity? What is the effective annual yield?

■ Answers to Chapter Review and Self-Test Problems

6.1 Because the bond has a 10 percent coupon yield and investors require a 12 percent return, we know that the bond must sell at a discount. Notice that, because the bond pays interest semiannually, the coupons amount to $100/2 = $50 every six months. The required yield is 12%/2 = 6% every six months. Finally, the bond matures in 20 years, so there are a total of 40 six-month periods.

The bond's value is thus equal to the present value of $50 every six months for the next 40 six-month periods plus the present value of the $1,000 face amount:

$$\text{Bond value} = \$50 \times (1 - 1/1.06^{40})/.06 + 1{,}000/1.06^{40}$$
$$= \$50 \times 15.04630 + 1{,}000/10.2857$$
$$= \$849.54$$

Notice that we discounted the $1,000 back 40 periods at 6 percent per period, rather than 20 years at 12 percent. The reason is that the effective annual yield on the bond is $1.06^2 - 1 = 12.36\%$, not 12 percent. We thus could have used 12.36 percent per year for 20 years when we calculated the present value of the $1,000 face amount, and the answer would have been the same.

6.2 The present value of the bond's cash flows is its current price, $911.37. The coupon is $40 every six months for 12 periods. The face value is $1,000. So the bond's yield is the unknown discount rate in the following:

$$\$911.37 = \$40 \times [1 - 1/(1 + r)^{12}]/r + 1{,}000/(1 + r)^{12}$$

The bond sells at a discount. Because the coupon rate is 8 percent, the yield must be something in excess of that.

If we were to solve this by trial and error, we might try 12 percent (or 6 percent per six months):

$$\text{Bond value} = \$40 \times (1 - 1/1.06^{12})/.06 + 1{,}000/1.06^{12}$$
$$= \$832.32$$

This is less than the actual value, so our discount rate is too high. We now know that the yield is somewhere between 8 and 12 percent. With further trial and error (or a little machine assistance), the yield works out to be 10 percent, or 5 percent every six months.

By convention, the bond's yield to maturity would be quoted as $2 \times 5\% = 10\%$. The effective yield is thus $1.05^2 - 1 = 10.25\%$.

CRITICAL THINKING AND CONCEPTS REVIEW

6.1   **Treasury Bonds.**   Is it true that a Government of Canada security is risk-free?

6.2   **Interest Rate Risk.**   Which has greater interest rate risk, a 30-year Canada bond or a 30-year BB corporate bond?

6.3   **Treasury Pricing.**   With regard to bid and ask prices on a Canada bond, is it possible for the bid price to be higher? Why or why not?

6.4   **Yield to Maturity.**   Treasury bid and ask quotes are sometimes given in terms of yields, so there would be a bid yield and an ask yield. Which do you think would be larger? Explain.

6.5   **Call Provisions.**   A company is contemplating a long-term bond issue. It is debating whether or not to include a call provision. What are the benefits to the company from including a call provision? What are the costs? How do these answers change for a put provision?

6.6   **Coupon Rate.**   How does a bond issuer decide on the appropriate coupon rate to set on its bonds? Explain the difference between the coupon rate and the required return on a bond.

6.7   **Real and Nominal Returns.**   Are there any circumstances under which an investor might be more concerned about the nominal return on an investment than the real return?

6.8   **Bond Ratings.**   Companies pay rating agencies such as Dominion Bond Rating Service and S&P to rate their bonds, and the costs can be substantial. However, companies are not required to have their bonds rated in the first place; doing so is strictly voluntary. Why do you think they do it?

6.9   **Bond Ratings.**   Government of Canada bonds are not rated. Why? Often, junk bonds are not rated. Why?

6.10   **Crossover Bonds.**   Looking back at the crossover bonds we discussed in the chapter, why do you think split ratings such as these occur?

6.11   **Rating Agencies.**   Several years ago, a controversy erupted regarding bond-rating agencies when some agencies began to provide unsolicited bond ratings. Why do you think this is controversial?

6.12   **Bond Prices versus Yields.**

    a.   What is the relationship between the price of a bond and its YTM?

    b.   Explain why some bonds sell at a premium over par value while other bonds sell at a discount. What do you know about the relationship between the coupon rate and the YTM for premium bonds? What about for discount bonds? For bonds selling at par value?

    c.   What is the relationship between the current yield and YTM for premium bonds? For discount bonds? For bonds selling at par value?

QUESTIONS AND PROBLEMS

1.   **Interpreting Bond Yields.**   Is the yield to maturity on a bond the same thing as the required return? Is YTM the same thing as the coupon rate? Suppose today a 10 percent coupon bond sells at par. Two years from now, the required return on the same bond is 8 percent. What is the coupon rate on the bond now? The YTM?

Basic
(Questions 1–14)

2. **Interpreting Bond Yields.** Suppose you buy a 7 percent coupon, 20-year bond today when it's first issued. If interest rates suddenly rise to 15 percent, what happens to the value of your bond? Why?

3. **Bond Prices.** Liberty, Inc., has 9 percent coupon bonds on the market that have 7 years left to maturity. The bonds make annual payments. If the YTM on these bonds is 8 percent, what is the current bond price?

4. **Bond Yields.** The Timberlake-Jackson Wardrobe Co. has 8 percent coupon bonds on the market with nine years left to maturity. The bonds make annual payments. If the bond currently sells for $910.85, what is its YTM?

5. **Coupon Rates.** Athabasca Enterprises has bonds on the market making annual payments, with 14 years to maturity, and selling for $1,086. At this price, the bonds yield 6.8 percent. What must the coupon rate be on Athabasca's bonds?

6. **Bond Prices.** Pacific Dogwood Co. issued 11-year bonds one year ago at a coupon rate of 8.50 percent. The bonds make semiannual payments. If the YTM on these bonds is 7.90 percent, what is the current bond price?

7. **Bond Yields.** Plouf Co. issued 15-year bonds two years ago at a coupon rate of 7.8 percent. The bonds make semiannual payments. If these bonds currently sell for 92 percent of par value, what is the YTM?

8. **Coupon Rates.** Chesterfield Corporation has bonds on the market with 10.5 years to maturity, a YTM of 7.6 percent, and a current price of $1,080. The bonds make semiannual payments. What must the coupon rate be on Chesterfield's bonds?

9. **Calculating Real Rates of Return.** If Treasury bills are currently paying 6 percent and the inflation rate is 2.8 percent, what is the approximate real rate of interest? The exact real rate?

10. **Inflation and Nominal Returns.** Suppose the real rate is 3.9 percent and the inflation rate is 4.5 percent. What rate would you expect to see on a Treasury bill?

11. **Nominal and Real Returns.** An investment offers a 13 percent total return over the coming year. Lu Wang thinks the total real return on this investment will be only 10 percent. What does Lu believe the inflation rate will be over the next year?

12. **Nominal versus Real Returns.** Say you own an asset that had a total return last year of 12 percent. If the inflation rate last year was 3.5 percent, what was your real return?

13. **Using Treasury Quotes.** Locate the Treasury issue in Figure 6.3 maturing in June 2027. What is its coupon rate? What is its bid price? What is its yield?

14. **Using Treasury Quotes.** Locate the Treasury bond in Figure 6.3 maturing in June 2037. Is this a premium or a discount bond? What is its current yield? What is its yield to maturity?

**Intermediate
(Questions 15–31)**

15. **Bond Price Movements.** Bond X is a premium bond making annual payments. The bond pays an 8 percent coupon, has a YTM of 6 percent, and has 13 years to maturity. Bond Y is a discount bond making annual payments. This bond pays a 6 percent coupon, has a YTM of 8 percent, and also has 13 years to maturity. What are the prices of these bonds today? If interest rates remain unchanged, what do you expect the prices of these bonds to be in one year? In three years? In eight years? In 12 years? In 13 years? What's going on here? Illustrate your answers by graphing bond prices versus time to maturity.

16. Interest Rate Risk.   Both Bond Bill and Bond Ted have 7 percent coupons, make semiannual payments, and are priced at par value. Bond Bill has 3 years to maturity, whereas Bond Ted has 20 years to maturity. If interest rates suddenly rise by 2 percent, what is the percentage change in the price of Bond Bill? Of Bond Ted? If rates were to suddenly fall by 2 percent instead, what would the percentage change in the price of Bond Bill be then? Of Bond Ted? Illustrate your answers by graphing bond prices versus YTM. What does this problem tell you about the interest rate risk of longer-term bonds?

17. Interest Rate Risk.   Bond J is a 5 percent coupon bond. Bond S is a 11 percent coupon bond. Both bonds have eight years to maturity, make semiannual payments, and have a YTM of 7 percent. If interest rates suddenly rise by 2 percent, what is the percentage price change of these bonds? What if rates suddenly fall by 2 percent instead? What does this problem tell you about the interest rate risk of lower-coupon bonds?

18. Bond Yields.   White Birch Software has 8 percent coupon bonds on the market with 12 years to maturity. The bonds make semiannual payments and currently sell for 108 percent of par. What is the current yield on White Birch's bonds? The YTM? The effective annual yield?

19. Bond Yields.   Lumberjack Co. wants to issue new 20-year bonds for some much-needed expansion projects. The company currently has 9 percent coupon bonds on the market that sell for $1,073, make semiannual payments, and mature in 20 years. What coupon rate should the company set on its new bonds if it wants them to sell at par?

20. Accrued Interest.   You purchase a bond with an invoice price of $1,120. The bond has a coupon rate of 7.2 percent, and there are four months to the next coupon date. What is the clean price of the bond?

21. Accrued Interest.   You purchase a bond with coupon rate of 7.2 percent and a clean price of $865. If the next coupon payment is due in three months, what is the invoice price?

22. T-Bill Yields.   You purchase a 1-month T-bill with a face value of $1,000 for $995. What yield would be reported on this T-bill in a financial newspaper?

23. T-Bill Prices.   In the financial page of today's newspaper you see that 6-month T-bills yield 3.5 percent. What is the current price of these T-bills?

24. Using Bond Quotes.   Suppose the following bond quote for IOU Corporation appears in the financial page of today's newspaper. Assume the bond has a face value of $1,000, and the current date is April 15, 2008. What is the yield to maturity of the bond? What is the current yield?

	Coupon	Mat. date	Bid$	Yld%
IOU	7.375	Apr 15/18	769.355	??

25. Strip Bonds.   Suppose your company needs to raise $25 million and you want to issue 20-year bonds for this purpose. Assume the required return on your bond issue will be 7 percent, and you're evaluating two issue alternatives: a 7 percent annual coupon bond and a strip bond. Your company's tax rate is 35 percent.

   a.   How many of the coupon bonds would you need to issue to raise the $25 million? How many of the strips would you need to issue?

b. In 20 years, what will your company's repayment be if you issue the coupon bonds? What if you issue the strips?

c. Based on your answers in (*a*) and (*b*), why would you ever want to issue the strips? To answer, calculate the firm's after tax cash outflows for the first year under the two different scenarios.

26. **Finding the Maturity.**   You've just found a 10 percent coupon bond on the market that sells for par value. What is the maturity on this bond (Warning: Possible trick question)?

Use the following Canada bond quotes to answer questions 27 and 28. To calculate the number of years until maturity, assume that it is currently November 15, 2008.

	Coupon	Mat. date	Bid$	Yld%
Canada	??	Nov 15/16	109.94	5.83
Canada	7.375	Nov 15/22	119.56	??

27. **Bond Yields.**   In the table, find the Canada bond that matures in November 15, 2022. What is the yield to maturity for this bond?

28. **Coupon Rates.**   Find the Canada bond that matures in November 15, 2016. What is the coupon rate for this bond?

Use the following bond quotes to answer Questions 29–31. To calculate the number of years until maturity, assume that it is currently January 15, 2008.

	Coupon	Mat. date	Bid$	Yld%
Xenon Inc.	6.80	Jan 15/19	81.66	??
Kenny Corp	8.40	Jan 15/28	??	7.16
Williams Co.	??	Jan 15/20	108.65	8.41

29. **Bond Yields.**   What is the yield to maturity for the bond issued by Xenon Inc.?

30. **Bond Prices.**   What price would you expect to pay for the Kenny Corp. bond? What is the bond's current yield?

31. **Coupon Rates.**   What is the coupon rate for the Williams Co. bond?

Challenge
(Questions 32–33)

32. **Bond Prices.**   The Northern Lights Corporation has issued 30-year bonds. The bonds will pay nothing for the first 10 years, a 5 percent coupon rate for the next 10 years, and, finally, an 8 percent coupon rate for the last 10 years. The bonds have a face value of $50,000 and a YTM of 6 percent.

a. What is the current bond price if these bonds make semiannual payments?

b. What is the current bond price if these bonds make quarterly payments?

33. **Real Return bond.**   You are about to purchase a real return bond, issued by the Government of Canada. Suppose the bond will have a 4.5 percent coupon rate, make annual payments and mature in 5 years. To provide the fixed real return, the $1,000 principal value of the bond will be adjusted upward to match inflation. You expect the annual level of inflation to be 3 percent for the next five years. If the yield to maturity on this bond is 5 percent, what is the current bond price?

WHAT'S ON THE WEB?

6.1 **Bond Quotes.** You can find current bond prices at **www.nasdbondinfo.com**. You want to find the bond prices and yields for bonds issued by Royal Bank of Canada. Enter the ticker symbol "RY" to do a search. What is the shortest maturity bond issued by Royal Bank of Canada that is outstanding? What is the longest maturity bond? What is the credit rating for Royal Bank of Canada's bonds? Do all of the bonds have the same credit rating? Why do you think this is?

6.2 **Bond Yields.** You can find an online bond calculator at the Web site of Qtrade Investor, Canada's leading independent online brokerage, at **www.qtrade.ca**. Enter "Online Brokerage" and follow the "Education" link to find the "Bond Yield Calculator" in the "Bond Centre." What is the YTM for a bond that matures in August 2015 with a coupon rate of 9 percent and current price of 107.5? What about a bond with the same coupon and price that matures in August 2030? Why don't the bonds have the same YTM?

6.3 **Yield Curves.** The Bank of Canada has information regarding the latest bond yields at **www.bankofcanada.ca**. Follow the "Rates and Statistics" link and then click on "Interest Rates." You will find a link for Canadian Bonds. Graph the yield curve for Government of Canada bonds. What is the general shape of the yield curve? What does this imply about expected future inflation?

6.4 **Bond Rating.** You can find ratings of the bonds of your university or your province at **www.dbrs.com**. Follow the "Public Finance" link and then select "Universities." Find a bond issue of your or any other university. What rating has been assigned by the Dominion Bond Rating Service to this particular bond issue? Follow the "Public Finance" link and now select "Provinces." Find the rating of the long-term debt of the province where the university from the previous question is located. Is the province's debt rated higher, lower, or the same? How can you explain this?

FINANCING CANADIAN AIR'S EXPANSION PLANS WITH A BOND ISSUE

Mark Sexton and Todd Story, the owners of Canadian Air, have decided to expand their operations. They instructed their newly hired financial analyst, Chris Guthrie, to enlist an underwriter to help sell $20 million in new 10-year bonds to finance construction. Chris has entered into discussions with Danielle Ralston, an underwriter from the firm of Raines and Warren, about which bond features Canadian Air should consider and what coupon rate the issue will likely have.

Although Chris is aware of the bond features, he is uncertain as to the costs and benefits of some features, so he isn't clear on how each feature would affect the coupon rate of the bond issue. You are Danielle's assistant, and she has asked you to prepare a memo to Chris describing the effect of each of the following bond features on the coupon rate of the bond. She would also like you to list any advantages or disadvantages of each feature.

QUESTIONS

1. The security of the bond, that is, whether the bond has collateral.

2. The seniority of the bond.

3. The presence of a sinking fund.

4. A call provision with specified call dates and call prices.

5. A deferred call accompanying the above call provision.

6. A make-whole call provision.

7. Any positive covenants. Also, discuss several possible positive covenants Canadian Air might consider.

8. Any negative covenants. Also, discuss several possible negative covenants Canadian Air might consider.

9. A conversion feature (note that Canadian Air is not a publicly traded company).

10. A floating rate coupon.

7

Stock Valuation

When the Toronto Stock Exchange closed on April 25, 2007, the common stock of Canadian Pacific Railway was going for $71.95 per share. On that same day, stock of the Bank of Montreal closed at $71.88, while that of Gildan Activewear, a Montreal-based clothing company, closed at $70.60. Since the stock prices of these three companies were so similar, you might expect that they would be offering similar dividends to their stockholders, but you would be wrong. In fact, the Bank of Montreal's annual dividend was $2.60 per share, Canadian Pacific Railway's was $0.75, and Gildan Activewear was paying no dividend at all!

As we will see in this chapter, the dividends currently being paid are one of the primary factors we look at when we attempt to value common stocks. However, it is obvious from looking at Gildan Activewear that current dividends are not the end of the story, so this chapter explores dividends, stock values, and the connection between the two.

Going back to Chapter 1, we saw that the goal of financial management is to maximize stock prices, so an understanding of what determines share values is obviously a key concern. When a corporation has publicly held stock, its shares will often be bought and sold on one or more of the major stock exchanges, so we will examine how stock prices are reported in the financial press. We will also see that the shareholders in a corporation have certain rights, and that just how these rights are allocated can have a significant impact on corporate control and governance.

After taking stock in this chapter (pun completely intentional), you should know:

7.1 How stock prices depend on future dividends and dividend growth.

7.2 The different features of common and preferred stock.

7.3 How stock prices are reported in the financial press.

In our previous chapter, we introduced you to bonds and bond valuation. In this chapter, we turn to the other major source of financing for corporations, common and preferred stock. We first describe the cash flows associated with a share of stock and then go on to develop a very famous result, the dividend growth model. From there, we move on to examine various important features of common and preferred stock, focusing on shareholder rights. We close out the chapter with a discussion of how stock prices and other important information are reported in the financial press.

7.1 | COMMON STOCK VALUATION

A share of common stock is more difficult to value in practice than a bond, for at least three reasons. First, with common stock, not even the promised cash flows are known in advance. Second, the life of the investment is essentially forever, since common stock has no maturity. Third, there is no way to easily observe the rate of return that the market requires. Nonetheless, as we will see, there are cases in which we can come up with the present value of the future cash flows for a share of stock and thus determine its value.

Cash Flows

Imagine that you are considering buying a share of stock today. You plan to sell the stock in one year. You somehow know that the stock will be worth $70 at that time. You predict that the stock will also pay a $10 per share dividend at the end of the year. If you require a 25 percent return on your investment, what is the most you would pay for the stock? In other words, what is the present value of the $10 dividend along with the $70 ending value at 25 percent?

If you buy the stock today and sell it at the end of the year, you will have a total of $80 in cash. At 25 percent:

Present value = ($10 + 70)/1.25 = $64

Therefore, $64 is the value you would assign to the stock today.

More generally, let P_0 be the current price of the stock, and assign P_1 to be the price in one period. If D_1 is the cash dividend paid at the end of the period, then:

$$P_0 = (D_1 + P_1)/(1 + R) \qquad \text{[7.1]}$$

where R is the required return in the market on this investment.

Notice that we really haven't said much so far. If we wanted to determine the value of a share of stock today (P_0), we would first have to come up with the value in one year (P_1). This is even harder to do, so we've only made the problem more complicated.

What is the price in one period, P_1? We don't know, in general. Instead, suppose we somehow knew the price in two periods, P_2. Given a predicted dividend in two periods, D_2, the stock price in one period would be:

$$P_1 = (D_2 + P_2)/(1 + R)$$

If we were to substitute this expression for P_1 into our expression for P_0, we would have:

$$P_0 = \frac{D_1 + P_1}{1 + R} = \frac{D_1 + \dfrac{D_2 + P_2}{1 + R}}{1 + R}$$

$$= \frac{D_1}{(1 + R)^1} + \frac{D_2}{(1 + R)^2} + \frac{P_2}{(1 + R)^2}$$

Now we need to get a price in two periods. We don't know this either, so we can procrastinate again and write:

$$P_2 = (D_3 + P_3)/(1 + R)$$

If we substitute this back in for P_2, we have:

$$P_0 = \frac{D_1}{(1 + R)^1} + \frac{D_2}{(1 + R)^2} + \frac{P_2}{(1 + R)^2}$$

$$= \frac{D_1}{(1 + R)^1} + \frac{D_2}{(1 + R)^2} + \frac{\dfrac{D_3 + P_3}{1 + R}}{(1 + R)^2}$$

$$= \frac{D_1}{(1 + R)^1} + \frac{D_2}{(1 + R)^2} + \frac{D_3}{(1 + R)^3} + \frac{P_3}{(1 + R)^3}$$

You should start to notice that we can push the problem of coming up with the stock price off into the future forever. It is important to note that no matter what the stock price is, the present value is essentially zero if we push the sale of the stock far enough away. What we are eventually left with is the result that the current price of the stock can be written as the present value of the dividends beginning in one period and extending out forever:

$$P_0 = \frac{D_1}{(1 + R)^1} + \frac{D_2}{(1 + R)^2} + \frac{D_3}{(1 + R)^3} + \frac{D_4}{(1 + R)^4} + \frac{D_5}{(1 + R)^5} + \cdots \qquad \text{[7.2]}$$

We have illustrated here that the price of the stock today is equal to the present value of all of the future dividends. This is called the **dividend discount model**. How many future dividends are there? In principle, there can be an infinite number. This means that we still can't compute a value for the stock because we would have to forecast an infinite number of dividends and then discount them all. In the next section, we consider some special cases in which we can get around this problem.

dividend discount model
A model that determines the current price of a stock as the present value of all the future dividends.

Growth Stocks EXAMPLE 7.1

You might be wondering about shares of stock in companies such as Gildan Activewear, mentioned at the beginning of the chapter, that currently pay no dividends. Small, growing companies frequently plow back everything and thus pay no dividends. Are such shares worth nothing? It depends. When we say that the value of the stock is equal to the present value of the future dividends, we don't rule out the possibility that some number of those dividends are zero. They just can't *all* be zero.

Imagine a company that has a provision in its corporate charter that prohibits the paying of dividends now or ever. The corporation never borrows any money, never pays out any money to stockholders in any form whatsoever, and never sells any assets. Such a corporation couldn't really exist because the stockholders would not like it and they could always vote to amend the charter. If it did exist, however, what would the stock be worth?

The stock is worth absolutely nothing. Such a company is a financial "black hole." Money goes in, but nothing valuable ever comes out. Because nobody would ever get any return on this investment, the investment has no value. This example is a little absurd, but it illustrates that when we speak of companies that don't pay dividends, what we really mean is that they are not *currently* paying dividends.

Some Special Cases

There are a few very useful special circumstances under which we can come up with a value for the stock. What we have to do is make some simplifying assumptions about the pattern of future dividends. The two cases we consider are the following: (1) the dividend has a zero growth rate and (2) the dividend grows at a constant rate. We consider each of these separately.

Zero Growth   The case of zero growth is one we've already seen. A share of common stock in a company with a constant dividend is much like a share of preferred stock. From Chapter 5 (Example 5.7), we know that the dividend on a share of preferred stock has zero growth and thus is constant through time. For a zero growth share of common stock, this implies that:

$$D_1 = D_2 = D_3 = D = \text{constant}$$

So, the value of the stock is:

$$P_0 = \frac{D}{(1 + R)^1} + \frac{D}{(1 + R)^2} + \frac{D}{(1 + R)^3} + \frac{D}{(1 + R)^4} + \frac{D}{(1 + R)^5} + \cdots$$

Because the dividend is always the same, the stock can be viewed as an ordinary perpetuity with a cash flow equal to D every period. The per-share value is thus given by:

$$P_0 = D/R \qquad\qquad\qquad \text{[7.3]}$$

where R is the required return.

For example, suppose the Canadian Paradise Company has a policy of paying a $10 per share dividend every year. If this policy is to be continued indefinitely, what is the value of a share of stock if the required return is 20 percent? The stock in this case amounts to an ordinary perpetuity, so the stock is worth $10/.20 = $50 per share.

Constant Growth   Suppose we know that the dividend for some company always grows at a steady rate. Call this growth rate g. If we let D_0 be the dividend just paid, then the next dividend, D_1, is:

$$D_1 = D_0 \times (1 + g)$$

The dividend in two periods is:

$$
\begin{aligned}
D_2 &= D_1 \times (1 + g) \\
&= [D_0 \times (1 + g)] \times (1 + g) \\
&= D_0 \times (1 + g)^2
\end{aligned}
$$

We could repeat this process to come up with the dividend at any point in the future. In general, from our discussion of compound growth in Chapter 4, we know that the dividend t periods into the future, D_t, is given by:

$$D_t = D_0 \times (1 + g)^t$$

Students who are interested in equity valuation techniques should check out the Motley Fool at **www.fool.com/ School/IntroductionTo Valuation.htm.**

An asset with cash flows that grow at a constant rate forever is called a *growing perpetuity*. As we will see momentarily, there is a simple expression for determining the value of such an asset.

The assumption of steady dividend growth might strike you as peculiar. Why would the dividend grow at a constant rate? The reason is that, for many companies, steady growth in dividends is an explicit goal. This subject falls under the general heading of dividend policy, so we will defer further discussion of it to a later chapter.

Dividend Growth EXAMPLE 7.2

The Beaver Teeth Corporation has just paid a dividend of $3 per share. The dividend of this company grows at a steady rate of 8 percent per year. Based on this information, what will the dividend be in five years?

Here we have a $3 current amount that grows at 8 percent per year for five years. The future amount is thus:

$3 \times 1.08^5 = \$3 \times 1.4693 = \$4.41$

The dividend will therefore increase by $1.41 over the coming five years.

If the dividend grows at a steady rate, then we have replaced the problem of forecasting an infinite number of future dividends with the problem of coming up with a single growth rate, a considerable simplification. In this case, if we take D_0 to be the dividend just paid and g to be the constant growth rate, the value of a share of stock can be written as:

$$P_0 = \frac{D_1}{(1+R)^1} + \frac{D_2}{(1+R)^2} + \frac{D_3}{(1+R)^3} + \cdots$$
$$= \frac{D_0(1+g)^1}{(1+R)^1} + \frac{D_0(1+g)^2}{(1+R)^2} + \frac{D_0(1+g)^3}{(1+R)^3} + \cdots$$

As long as the growth rate, g, is less than the discount rate, R, the present value of this series of cash flows can be written very simply as:

$$P_0 = \frac{D_0 \times (1+g)}{R-g} = \frac{D_1}{R-g} \qquad [7.4]$$

This elegant result goes by a lot of different names. We will call it the **dividend growth model**. (It is a special case of the dividend discount model.) This formula is also often called the Gordon Model after Myron J. Gordon, the finance professor from the University of Toronto who developed it. By any name, it is very easy to use. To illustrate, suppose D_0 is $2.30, R is 13 percent, and g is 5 percent. The price per share in this case is:

$$P_0 = D_0 \times (1+g)/(R-g)$$
$$= \$2.30 \times 1.05/(.13 - .05)$$
$$= \$2.415/.08$$
$$= \$30.19$$

dividend growth model
A model that determines the current price of a stock as its dividend next period divided by the discounted rate less the dividend growth rate.

See the dividend growth model in action at **www.dividenddiscountmodel.com**.

We can actually use the dividend growth model to get the stock price at any point in time, not just today. In general, the price of the stock as of time t is:

$$P_t = \frac{D_t \times (1+g)}{(R-g)} = \frac{D_{t+1}}{R-g} \qquad [7.5]$$

In our example, suppose we are interested in the price of the stock in five years, P_5. We first need the dividend at Time 5, D_5. Because the dividend just paid is $2.30 and the growth rate is 5 percent per year, D_5 is:

$$D_5 = \$2.30 \times 1.05^5 = \$2.30 \times 1.2763 = \$2.935$$

From the dividend growth model, we get that the price of the stock in five years is:

$$P_5 = \frac{D_5 \times (1+g)}{R-g} = \frac{\$2.935 \times 1.05}{.13 - .05} = \frac{\$3.0822}{.08} = \$38.53$$

EXAMPLE 7.3

Gordon Growth Company

The next dividend for the Gordon Growth Company will be $4 per share. Investors require a 16 percent return on companies such as Gordon. Gordon's dividend increases by 6 percent every year. Based on the dividend growth model, what is the value of Gordon's stock today? What is the value in four years?

The only tricky thing here is that the next dividend, D_1, is given as $4, so we won't multiply this by $(1 + g)$. With this in mind, the price per share is given by:

$$P_0 = D_1/(R - g)$$
$$= \$4/(.16 - .06)$$
$$= \$4/.10$$
$$= \$40$$

Because we already have the dividend in one year, we know that the dividend in four years is equal to $D_1 \times (1 - g)^3 = \$4 \times 1.06^3 = \$4.764$. The price in four years is therefore:

$$P_4 = D_4 \times (1 + g)/(R - g)$$
$$= \$4.764 \times 1.06/(.16 - .06)$$
$$= \$5.05/.10$$
$$= \$50.50$$

Notice in this example that P_4 is equal to $P_0 \times (1 + g)^4$.

$$P_4 = \$50.50 = \$40 \times 1.06^4 = P_0 \times (1 + g)^4$$

To see why this is so, notice first that:

$$P_4 = D_5/(R - g)$$

However, D_5 is just equal to $D_1 \times (1 + g)^4$, so we can write P_4 as:

$$P_4 = D_1 \times (1 + g)^4/(R - g)$$
$$= [D_1/(R - g)] \times (1 + g)^4$$
$$= P_0 \times (1 + g)^4$$

This last example illustrates that the dividend growth model makes the implicit assumption that the stock price will grow at the same constant rate as the dividend. This really isn't too surprising. What it tells us is that if the cash flows on an investment grow at a constant rate through time, so does the value of that investment.

You might wonder what would happen with the dividend growth model if the growth rate, g, were greater than the discount rate, R. It looks like we would get a negative stock price because $R - g$ would be less than zero. This is not what would happen.

Instead, if the constant growth rate exceeds the discount rate, then the stock price is infinitely large. Why? If the growth rate is bigger than the discount rate, then the present value of the dividends keeps on getting bigger and bigger. Essentially, the same is true if the growth rate and the discount rate are equal. In both cases, the simplification that allows us to replace the infinite stream of dividends with the dividend growth model is "illegal," so the answers we get from the dividend growth model are nonsense unless the growth rate is less than the discount rate.

Finally, the expression we came up with for the constant growth case will work for any growing perpetuity, not just dividends on common stock. If C_1 is the next cash flow on a growing perpetuity, then the present value of the cash flows is given by:

$$\text{Present value} = C_1/(R - g) = C_0(1 + g)/(R - g)$$

Notice that this expression looks like the result for an ordinary perpetuity except that we have $R - g$ on the bottom instead of just R.

Nonconstant Growth   The last case we consider is nonconstant growth. The main reason to consider this case is to allow for "supernormal" growth rates over some finite length of time. As we discussed earlier, the growth rate cannot exceed the required return indefinitely, but it certainly could do so for some number of years. To avoid the problem of having to forecast and discount an infinite number of dividends, we will require that the dividends start growing at a constant rate sometime in the future.

For a simple example of nonconstant growth, consider the case of a company that is currently not paying dividends. You predict that, in five years, the company will pay a dividend for the first time. The dividend will be $.50 per share. You expect that this dividend will then grow at a rate of 10 percent per year indefinitely. The required return on companies such as this one is 20 percent. What is the price of the stock today?

To see what the stock is worth today, we first find out what it will be worth once dividends are paid. We can then calculate the present value of that future price to get today's price. The first dividend will be paid in five years, and the dividend will grow steadily from then on. Using the dividend growth model, we can say that the price in four years will be:

$$P_4 = D_4 \times (1 + g)/(R - g)$$
$$= D_5/(R - g)$$
$$= \$.50/(.20 - .10)$$
$$= \$5$$

If the stock will be worth $5 in four years, then we can get the current value by discounting this price back four years at 20 percent:

$$P_0 = \$5/1.20^4 = \$5/2.0736 = \$2.41$$

The stock is therefore worth $2.41 today.

The problem of nonconstant growth is only slightly more complicated if the dividends are not zero for the first several years. For example, suppose that you have come up with the following dividend forecasts for the next three years:

Year	Expected Dividend
1	$1.00
2	$2.00
3	$2.50

After the third year, the dividend will grow at a constant rate of 5 percent per year. The required return is 10 percent. What is the value of the stock today?

In dealing with nonconstant growth, a time line can be very helpful. Figure 7.1 illustrates one for this problem. The important thing to notice is when constant growth starts.

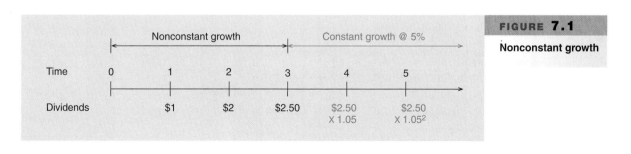

FIGURE 7.1

Nonconstant growth

As we've shown, for this problem, constant growth starts at Time 3. This means that we can use our constant growth model to determine the stock price at Time 3, P_3. By far the most common mistake in this situation is to incorrectly identify the start of the constant growth phase and, as a result, calculate the future stock price at the wrong time.

As always, the value of the stock is the present value of all the future dividends. To calculate this present value, we first have to compute the present value of the stock price three years down the road, just as we did before. We then have to add in the present value of the dividends that will be paid between now and then. So, the price in three years is:

$$P_3 = D_3 \times (1 + g)/(R - g)$$
$$= \$2.50 \times 1.05/(.10 - .05)$$
$$= \$52.50$$

We can now calculate the total value of the stock as the present value of the first three dividends plus the present value of the price at Time 3, P_3.

$$P_0 = \frac{D_1}{(1 + R)^1} + \frac{D_2}{(1 + R)^2} + \frac{D_3}{(1 + R)^3} + \frac{P_3}{(1 + R)^3}$$
$$= \frac{\$1}{1.10} + \frac{2}{1.10^2} + \frac{2.50}{1.10^3} + \frac{52.50}{1.10^3}$$
$$= \$.91 + 1.65 + 1.88 + 39.44$$
$$= \$43.88$$

The value of the stock today is thus $43.88.

EXAMPLE 7.4   **Supernormal Growth**

Chain Reaction, Inc., has been growing at a phenomenal rate of 30 percent per year because of its rapid expansion and explosive sales. You believe that this growth rate will last for three more years and that the rate will then drop to 10 percent per year. If the growth rate then remains at 10 percent indefinitely, what is the total value of the stock? Total dividends just paid were $5 million, and the required return is 20 percent.

Chain Reaction's situation is an example of supernormal growth. It is unlikely that a 30 percent growth rate can be sustained for any extended length of time. To value the equity in this company, we first need to calculate the total dividends over the supernormal growth period:

Year	Total Dividends (in millions)
1	$5.00 × 1.3 = $6.500
2	6.50 × 1.3 = 8.450
3	8.45 × 1.3 = 10.985

The price at Time 3 can be calculated as:

$$P_3 = D_3 \times (1 + g)/(R - g)$$

where g is the long-run growth rate. So we have:

$$P_3 = \$10.985 \times 1.10/(.20 - .10) = \$120.835$$

(continued)

To determine the value today, we need the present value of this amount plus the present value of the total dividends:

$$P_0 = \frac{D_1}{(1+R)^1} + \frac{D_2}{(1+R)^2} + \frac{D_3}{(1+R)^3} + \frac{P_3}{(1+R)^3}$$

$$= \frac{\$6.50}{1.20} + \frac{8.45}{1.20^2} + \frac{10.985}{1.20^3} + \frac{120.835}{1.20^3}$$

$$= \$5.42 + 5.87 + 6.36 + 69.93$$

$$= \$87.58$$

The total value of the stock today is thus $87.58 million. If there were, for example, 20 million shares, then the stock would be worth $87.58/20 = $4.38 per share.

Components of the Required Return

Thus far, we have taken the required return, or discount rate, *R,* as given. We will have quite a bit to say on this subject in Chapters 10 and 11. For now, we want to examine the implications of the dividend growth model for this required return. Earlier, we calculated P_0 as:

$$P_0 = D_1/(R - g)$$

If we rearrange this to solve for *R,* we get:

$$R - g = D_1/P_0$$
$$R = D_1/P_0 + g \qquad \textbf{[7.6]}$$

This tells us that the total return, *R,* has two components. The first of these, D_1/P_0, is called the **dividend yield.** Because this is calculated as the expected cash dividend divided by the current price, it is conceptually similar to the current yield on a bond.

dividend yield
A stock's expected cash dividend divided by its current price.

The second part of the total return is the growth rate, *g.* We know that the dividend growth rate is also the rate at which the stock price grows (see Example 7.3). Thus, this growth rate can be interpreted as the **capital gains yield,** that is, the rate at which the value of the investment grows.[1]

capital gains yield
The dividend growth rate, or the rate at which the value of an investment grows.

To illustrate the components of the required return, suppose we observe a stock selling for $20 per share. The next dividend will be $1 per share. You think that the dividend will grow by 10 percent per year more or less indefinitely. What return does this stock offer you if this is correct?

The dividend growth model calculates the total return as:

$$R = \text{Dividend yield} + \text{Capital gains yield}$$
$$R = D_1/P_0 + g$$

In this case, the total return works out to be:

$$R = \$1/20 + 10\%$$
$$= 5\% + 10\%$$
$$= 15\%$$

This stock, therefore, has a required return of 15 percent.

---

[1]Here and elsewhere, we use the term *capital gains* a little loosely. For the record, a capital gain (or loss) is, strictly speaking, something defined by the Canada Revenue Agency. For our purposes, it would be more accurate (but less common) to use the term *price appreciation* instead of *capital gain.*

We can verify this answer by calculating the price in one year, P_1, using 15 percent as the required return. Based on the dividend growth model, this price is:

$$P_1 = D_1 \times (1 + g)/(R - g)$$
$$= \$1 \times 1.10/(.15 - .10)$$
$$= \$1.10/.05$$
$$= \$22$$

Explore Value Line's investment research products and services at **www.valueline.com.**

Notice that this $22 is $20 × 1.1, so the stock price has grown by 10 percent, as it should. If you pay $20 for the stock today, you will get a $1 dividend at the end of the year, and you will have a $22 − 20 = $2 gain. Your dividend yield is thus $1/20 = 5%. Your capital gains yield is $2/20 = 10%, so your total return would be 5% + 10% = 15%.

To get a feel for actual numbers in this context, consider that, according to the March 16, 2007, issue of *The Value Line Investment Survey,* TransCanada's dividends were expected to grow by 4.0 percent over the next five or so years, compared to a historical growth rate of 7 percent over the preceding five years and 3.5 percent over the preceding 10 years. In 2007, the projected dividend for the coming year was given as $1.15. The stock price at that time was about $32 per share. What is the return investors require on TransCanada? Here, the dividend yield is about 3.6 percent and the capital gains yield is 4.0 percent, giving a total required return of 7.6 percent on TransCanada stock.

CONCEPT QUESTIONS

7.1a   What are the relevant cash flows for valuing a share of common stock?

7.1b   Does the value of a share of stock depend on how long you expect to keep it?

7.1c   What is the value of a share of stock when the dividend grows at a constant rate?

7.2 | SOME FEATURES OF COMMON AND PREFERRED STOCK

In discussing common stock features, we focus on shareholder rights and dividend payments. For preferred stock, we explain what "preferred" means, and we also debate whether preferred stock is really debt or equity.

Common Stock Features

common stock
Equity without priority for dividends or in bankruptcy.

The term **common stock** means different things to different people, but it is usually applied to stock that has no special preference either in paying dividends or in bankruptcy.

Shareholder Rights   The conceptual structure of the corporation assumes that shareholders elect directors who in turn hire management to carry out their directives. Shareholders, therefore, control the corporation through the right to elect the directors. Generally, only shareholders have this right.

Directors are elected each year at an annual meeting. Although there are exceptions (discussed in a moment), the general idea is "one share, one vote" (*not* one share*holder,* one vote). Corporate democracy is thus very different from our political democracy. In corporate democracy, the "golden rule" prevails absolutely.[2]

---

[2]The golden rule: Whoever has the gold makes the rules.

Directors are elected at an annual shareholders' meeting by a vote of the holders of a majority of shares who are present and entitled to vote. However, the exact mechanism for electing directors differs across companies. The most important difference is whether shares must be voted cumulatively or voted straight.

To illustrate the two different voting procedures, imagine that a corporation has two shareholders: Smith with 20 shares and Jones with 80 shares. Both want to be a director. However, Jones wants to prevent Smith from becoming a director. We assume that there are a total of four directors to be elected.

The effect of **cumulative voting** is to permit minority participation.[3] If cumulative voting is permitted, the total number of votes that each shareholder may cast is determined first. This is usually calculated as the number of shares (owned or controlled) multiplied by the number of directors to be elected.

With cumulative voting, the directors are elected all at once. In our example, this means that the top four vote getters will be the new directors. Individual shareholders can distribute votes however they wish.

Will Smith get a seat on the board? If we ignore the possibility of a five-way tie, then the answer is yes. Smith will cast $20 \times 4 = 80$ votes, and Jones will cast $80 \times 4 = 320$ votes. If Smith gives all his votes to himself, he is assured of a directorship. The reason is that Jones can't divide 320 votes among four candidates in such a way as to give all of them more than 80 votes, so Smith will finish fourth at worst.

In general, if there are N directors up for election, then $1/(N + 1)$ percent of the stock plus one share will guarantee you a seat. In our current example, this is $1/(4 + 1) = 20\%$ (plus one). So the more seats that are up for election at one time, the easier (and cheaper) it is to win one.

With **straight voting** the directors are elected one at a time. Each time, Smith can cast 20 votes and Jones can cast 80. As a consequence, Jones will elect all of the candidates. The only way to guarantee a seat is to own 50 percent plus one share. This also guarantees that you will win every seat, so it's really all or nothing.

cumulative voting
A procedure in which a shareholder may cast all votes for one member of the board of directors.

straight voting
A procedure in which a shareholder may cast all votes for each member of the board of directors.

Buying the Election | **EXAMPLE 7.5**

Stock in Acadia Corporation sells for $20 per share and features cumulative voting. There are 10,000 shares outstanding. If three directors are up for election, how much does it cost to ensure yourself a seat on the board?

The question here is how many shares of stock it will take to get a seat. The answer is 2,501, so the cost is $2,501 \times \$20 = \$50,020$. Why 2,501? Because there is no way the remaining 7,499 votes can be divided among three people to give all of them more than 2,501 votes. For example, suppose two people receive 2,502 votes and the first two seats. A third person can receive at most $10,000 - 2,502 - 2,502 - 2,501 = 2,495$, so the third seat is yours. Verify that we arrived at 2,501 using the formula described earlier.

As we've illustrated, straight voting can "freeze out" minority shareholders; that is the reason they often campaign for mandatory cumulative voting. However, in situations where cumulative voting is mandatory, devices have been worked out to minimize its impact.

---

[3]By minority participation, we mean participation by shareholders with relatively small amounts of stock.

One such device is to stagger the voting for the board of directors. With staggered elections, only a fraction of the directorships are up for election at a particular time. Thus, if only two directors are up for election at any one time, it will take $1/(2 + 1) = 33.33\%$ of the stock plus one share to guarantee a seat.

Overall, staggering has two basic effects:

1. Staggering makes it more difficult for a minority to elect a director when there is cumulative voting because there are fewer directors to be elected at one time.

2. Staggering makes takeover attempts less likely to be successful because it makes it more difficult to vote in a majority of new directors.

We should note that staggering may serve a beneficial purpose. It provides "institutional memory," that is, continuity on the board of directors. This may be important for corporations with significant long-range plans and projects.

proxy
A grant of authority by a shareholder allowing another individual to vote that shareholder's shares.

Proxy Voting   A **proxy** is the grant of authority by a shareholder to someone else to vote the shareholder's shares. For convenience, much of the voting in large public corporations is actually done by proxy.

As we have seen, with straight voting, each share of stock has one vote. The owner of 10,000 shares has 10,000 votes. Large companies have hundreds of thousands or even millions of shareholders. Shareholders can come to the annual meeting and vote in person, or they can transfer their right to vote to another party.

Obviously, management always tries to get as many proxies as possible transferred to it. However, if shareholders are not satisfied with management, an "outside" group of shareholders can try to obtain votes via proxy. They can vote by proxy in an attempt to replace management by electing enough directors. The resulting battle is called a *proxy fight*.

Classes of Stock   Some firms have different classes of common stock with unequal voting rights. In some cases, the superior class gives the holder more than one vote per share; in others, the superior class includes only a single vote per share, whereas the inferior shares have no voting rights.

Multiple-class shares are widely used in Canada, and many well-known companies, such as Bombardier, Canadian Tire, Magna International, and Rogers Communications, have more than one class of common shares. Rogers Communications, for example, has voting shares of common stock, with 50 votes per share each, and almost five times as many nonvoting shares outstanding. The president and CEO, Edward "Ted" S. Rogers, owns 91 percent of voting shares and, in fact, controls the company.

A primary reason for creating dual or multiple classes of stock has to do with control of the firm. If such stock exists, management of a firm can raise equity capital by issuing nonvoting or limited-voting stock while maintaining control. For example, the founder and chairman of Magna International Inc., Frank Stronach, controls the company with a minimum amount of equity by owning the majority of Class B shares. While there are almost 100 times as many Class A shares outstanding, Class B shares have 500 votes for each Class A share!

The subject of unequal voting rights is controversial in Canada, and the idea of one share, one vote has a strong following and a long history. Interestingly, shares with unequal voting rights are less common in the United States, but they are widespread in the United Kingdom and elsewhere around the world.

Other Rights The value of a share of common stock in a corporation is directly related to the general rights of shareholders. In addition to the right to vote for directors, shareholders usually have the following rights:

1. The right to share proportionally in dividends paid.
2. The right to share proportionally in assets remaining after liabilities have been paid in a liquidation.
3. The right to vote on stockholder matters of great importance, such as a merger.

Voting is usually done at the annual meeting or a special meeting.

In addition, shareholders sometimes have the right to share proportionally in any new stock sold. This is called the *preemptive right.*

Essentially, a preemptive right means that a company that wishes to sell stock must first offer it to the existing stockholders before offering it to the general public. The purpose is to give stockholders the opportunity to protect their proportionate ownership in the corporation.

Dividends A distinctive feature of corporations is that they have shares of stock on which they are authorized by law to pay dividends to their shareholders. **Dividends** paid to shareholders represent a return on the capital directly or indirectly contributed to the corporation by the shareholders. The payment of dividends is at the discretion of the board of directors.

Some important characteristics of dividends include the following:

1. Unless a dividend is declared by the board of directors of a corporation, it is not a liability of the corporation. A corporation cannot default on an undeclared dividend. As a consequence, corporations cannot become bankrupt because of nonpayment of dividends. The amount of the dividend and even whether it is paid are decisions based on the business judgment of the board of directors.
2. The payment of dividends by the corporation is not a business expense. Dividends are not deductible for corporate tax purposes. In short, dividends are paid out of the corporation's aftertax profits.
3. Dividends received by individual shareholders from Canadian companies are taxed at a lower rate than ordinary income because of the dividend tax credit explained in Chapter 2. Corporations that own stock in other corporations are permitted to exclude 100 percent of the dividend amounts they receive from taxable Canadian corporations.

Preferred Stock Features

Preferred stock differs from common stock because it has preference over common stock in the payment of dividends and in the distribution of corporation assets in the event of liquidation. *Preference* means only that the holders of the preferred shares must receive a dividend (in the case of an ongoing firm) before holders of common shares are entitled to anything.

Preferred stock is a form of equity from a legal and tax standpoint. It is important to note, however, that holders of preferred stock sometimes have no voting privileges.

Issue price Preferred shares have an issue price at which they are sold to the public, usually $25, $50, or $100 per share. The cash dividend is described in terms of dollars per share or a dividend yield on the share's issue price. For example, in January 2006, Sun Life

Margin notes:

You can find documents, such as annual reports, notice of meetings, prospectus, etc., filed by Canadian companies at **www.sedar.com.**

dividends
Payments by a corporation to shareholders, made in either cash or stock.

preferred stock
Stock with dividend priority over common stock, normally with a fixed dividend rate, sometimes without voting rights.

Financial sold preferred shares to the public at $25 per share with a dividend yield of 4.45 percent. This yield easily translates into an annual dividend of $1.1125 per share.

Cumulative and Noncumulative Dividends   A preferred dividend is *not* like interest on a bond. The board of directors may decide not to pay the dividends on preferred shares, and their decision may have nothing to do with the current net income of the corporation.

Dividends payable on preferred stock are either *cumulative* or *noncumulative; most* are cumulative. If preferred dividends are cumulative and are not paid in a particular year, they will be carried forward as an *arrearage.* Usually, both the accumulated (past) preferred dividends and the current preferred dividends must be paid before the common shareholders can receive anything.

Unpaid preferred dividends are *not* debts of the firm. Directors elected by the common shareholders can defer preferred dividends indefinitely. However, in such cases, common shareholders must also forgo dividends. In addition, holders of preferred shares are often granted voting and other rights if preferred dividends have not been paid for some time. For example, in November 2005, HSBC Bank Canada issued 7 million preferred shares that entitled the holders to receive a quarterly non-cumulative cash dividend of $0.3125 per share. If the bank fails to pay this dividend for a quarter, the preferred shareholders will receive one vote for each share in the election of directors. These voting rights will end as soon as HSBC Bank Canada resumes payment of the dividend. Because preferred stockholders receive no interest on the accumulated dividends, some have argued that firms have an incentive to delay paying preferred dividends, but, as we have seen, this may mean sharing control with preferred stockholders.

Is Preferred Stock Really Debt?   A good case can be made that preferred stock is really debt in disguise, a kind of equity bond. Preferred shareholders are only entitled to receive a stated dividend, and, if the corporation is liquidated, preferred shareholders are only entitled to the stated value of their preferred shares. Often, preferred stocks carry credit ratings much like those of bonds. Furthermore, preferred stock is sometimes convertible into common stock, and preferred stocks are often callable.

In addition, in recent years, many new issues of preferred stock have had obligatory sinking funds. The existence of such a sinking fund effectively creates a final maturity because it means that the entire issue will ultimately be retired. For these reasons, preferred stock seems to be a lot like debt. However, for tax purposes, preferred dividends are treated like common stock dividends.

CONCEPT QUESTIONS

7.2a   What rights do stockholders have?

7.2b   What is a proxy?

7.2c   Why is preferred stock called preferred?

7.3 | STOCK MARKET REPORTING

If you look through the pages of the *National Post* (or another financial newspaper), you will find information on a large number of stocks in several different markets. Figure 7.2

FIGURE 7.2

Sample stock
quotation from the
National Post

S & P / T S X 6 0

Figures supplied by Thomson Financial

Stock	Ticker	Close	Net ch	% ch	Vol 00s	Day high	Day low	% yield	P/E	52wk high	52wk low	Wk %ch	52wk %ch
ACE Aviatn B	ACE.B	30.98	-0.10	-0.3	10524	31.14	30.90	n.a.	7.7	40.01	25.98	-2.5	-4.6
AgnicoEag	AEM	40.57	-0.36	-0.9	6982	41.17	40.17	0.3	26.0	52.03	28.33	-6.9	+0.8
Agrium	AGU	46.65	-0.46	-1.0	5410	47.40	46.52	0.3	n.a.	48.22	22.32	-2.0	+64.6
Alcan	AL	66.25	+2.45	+3.8	24495	66.56	64.61	1.3	11.6	66.56	41.78	+6.3	+13.5
BCE	BCE	39.07	-0.29	-0.7	83422	39.30	39.03	3.7	18.4	40.31	25.32	+1.9	+27.2
BkMtl	BMO	71.88	+0.49	+0.7	9541	71.88	71.05	3.8	13.9	72.75	58.58	-1.2	+12.4
BkofNS	BNS	54.14	+0.14	+0.3	15627	54.23	53.90	3.1	14.4	54.73	41.55	+0.1	+16.7
Barrick	ABX	32.07	+0.19	+0.6	18310	32.29	31.78	0.8	20.0	39.69	29.68	-3.2	-6.1
Biovail	BVF	27.77	-0.30	-1.1	2443	28.16	27.70	6.0	19.2	31.00	16.25	+0.7	-2.6
Bombrdr B SV	BBD.B	4.60	+0.06	+1.3	37206	4.60	4.52	n.a.	34.4	4.87	2.90	+2.0	+13.6
Brkfld A LV	BAM.A	63.98	-0.03	nil	4988	64.50	63.65	1.3	19.6	68.41	42.59	-1.0	+40.5
Cameco	CCO	52.39	+0.26	+0.5	10364	53.00	52.06	0.4	49.0	54.99	35.35	-2.4	+12.4
CIBC	CM	98.98	+0.02	nil	4927	99.25	98.26	3.1	12.4	104.63	73.25	-0.7	+18.2
CN Rail	CNR	56.25	+0.57	+1.0	21458	56.43	55.68	1.5	14.3	57.35	44.43	-0.4	+6.4
CdnNatRes	CNQ	67.23	+0.63	+0.9	10802	67.65	65.72	0.5	14.3	69.37	45.49	+0.7	-3.2
CdnOilSnd	COS.UN	30.18	+1.19	+4.1	20820	30.47	28.80	4.0	16.9	38.75	24.32	+3.2	-13.4
CdnPacRail	CP	71.95	+1.41	+2.0	10149	73.48	71.25	1.3	13.9	73.48	51.05	+4.5	+18.0
CdnTireA NV	CTC.A	78.56	+1.16	+1.5	1729	79.18	77.50	0.9	18.1	79.83	61.25	-1.0	+22.5
CelesticaSV	CLS	7.25	-0.17	-2.3	6803	7.43	7.24	n.a.	n.a.	13.90	6.76	-3.2	-40.9
Cognos	CSN	47.03	+0.87	+1.9	2132	47.34	46.00	n.a.	32.7	53.38	28.44	-0.4	+8.3
Cott	BCB	18.48	-0.26	-1.4	1126	18.70	18.13	n.a.	n.a.	20.35	13.55	-3.2	+11.2
Enbridge	ENB	37.24	-0.17	-0.5	8861	37.74	37.13	3.3	20.6	41.48	31.75	+0.1	+12.0
EnCana	ECA	60.32	+0.22	+0.4	41233	61.32	59.55	1.5	10.7	62.52	48.28	-2.2	+4.7
FrdngCdnun	FDG.UN	26.90	+0.04	+0.1	5344	27.12	26.55	9.7	9.6	42.20	21.50	+0.4	-36.0
Goldcorp	G	28.29	+0.08	+0.3	26356	28.40	27.96	0.7	27.0	45.99	22.97	-5.7	-26.3
HuskyEnrg	HSE	85.01	+1.63	+2.0	4343	85.94	82.92	2.4	12.7	85.94	58.00	+2.4	+26.9
IPSCO	IPS	169.29	-0.68	-0.4	1348	170.60	166.72	0.5	11.9	179.35	90.00	-0.7	+46.8
ImpOil	IMO	43.39	+0.48	+1.1	4529	43.64	42.97	0.7	13.9	45.20	34.31	-2.4	+4.6
KinrossGld	K	15.18	-0.14	-0.9	35779	15.44	15.16	n.a.	29.0	17.00	9.92	-7.7	+12.6
Loblaw	L	50.25	+0.53	+1.1	3907	50.25	49.55	1.7	n.a.	57.83	44.92	+0.9	-10.9
Lundin	LUN	14.26	+0.06	+0.4	15473	14.29	14.05	n.a.	12.5	15.84	8.05	-5.3	+23.6
MDS	MDS	21.47	+0.30	+1.4	6669	21.59	21.11	0.5	n.a.	22.90	18.56	+0.1	-3.5
Magna A SV	MG.A	88.87	+0.82	+0.9	1086	88.93	87.86	1.0	16.4	96.00	76.69	+1.1	+1.6
Manulife	MFC	40.42	+0.32	+0.8	14403	40.44	40.05	2.0	16.0	41.49	33.83	-1.6	+9.3
NOVA Chem	NCX	37.40	+3.72	+11.0	14682	37.73	34.86	1.1	n.a.	38.90	29.50	+8.7	+9.3
NatlBK	NA	63.53	+0.43	+0.7	4522	63.55	63.01	3.4	11.8	66.80	55.89	-0.5	+2.4
Nexen	NXY	68.50	+0.62	+0.9	10152	69.02	67.80	0.3	29.9	75.20	50.82	-1.5	+4.4
Nortel	NT	27.00	-0.21	-0.8	8930	27.65	26.87	n.a.	n.a.	37.35	21.40	-1.1	-10.3
Novelis	NVL	49.78	-0.22	-0.4	7127	49.95	49.62	0.2	n.a.	51.81	20.60	-0.7	+83.4
PennWst un	PWT.UN	34.00	-0.05	-0.1	7213	34.21	33.95	12.0	10.2	47.77	31.60	-0.6	-24.4
PetroCan	PCA	49.59	+0.64	+1.3	29052	49.93	48.95	1.0	11.7	55.98	40.25	+6.1	-13.2
Potash	POT	208.45	-1.26	-0.6	1772	210.99	207.50	0.3	30.8	214.75	86.79	+0.7	+99.1
RschMotn	RIM	151.28	+3.28	+2.2	5083	152.50	148.90	n.a.	39.7	171.46	67.95	-0.3	+70.4
RogerCmBNV	RCI.B	43.16	-0.39	-0.9	20415	43.97	43.03	0.4	43.6	44.13	20.845	+2.8	+85.5
RoyalBK	RY	58.93	+0.03	+0.1	17588	59.07	58.51	3.1	15.0	59.95	43.52	-0.9	+25.5
ShawComB NV	SJR.B	44.50	+0.27	+0.6	2846	44.55	43.75	2.5	19.3	46.35	29.50	-2.8	+49.1
Shoppers	SC	51.15	+0.30	+0.6	5214	51.50	50.65	1.3	26.0	53.49	40.22	+0.9	+14.0
Sun Life Finl	SLF	53.53	+0.53	+1.0	10277	53.53	53.00	2.4	14.8	54.14	41.79	-0.1	+9.6
Suncor	SU	91.45	+1.41	+1.6	12722	91.91	89.49	0.3	14.1	99.13	71.18	-0.5	-6.5
TELUS	T	63.65	+0.41	+0.6	7093	63.65	63.05	2.4	19.5	65.60	43.52	+0.1	+34.9
TalismnEn	TLM	21.73	+0.25	+1.2	35072	21.93	21.35	0.7	16.3	22.32	16.12	-1.6	+0.3
TeckComB SV	TCK.B	87.20	+1.10	+1.3	12708	87.47	85.66	2.3	8.0	95.16	57.55	-0.4	+9.1
Thomson	TOC	48.30	+0.13	+0.3	6070	48.35	48.03	2.3	30.7	51.95	42.40	-0.4	+7.5
Tim Hortons	THI	35.98	-0.18	-0.5	3270	36.49	35.84	0.8	25.7	37.74	26.67	-1.3	+19.2
TD Bank	TD	68.37	+0.18	+0.3	14614	68.38	67.91	3.1	15.4	71.61	55.62	-1.6	+8.5
TransAlta	TA	26.95	-0.98	-3.5	17695	27.95	26.83	3.7	n.a.	28.23	22.25	+7.2	+16.2
TrnsCda	TRP	40.14	+0.96	+2.5	12258	40.14	39.23	3.4	18.7	41.35	30.77	+3.2	+19.4
WestonGeo	WN	76.50	+0.48	+0.6	739	76.62	75.64	1.9	n.a.	88.25	69.05	+0.6	-11.4
YamanaGld	YRI	16.21	+0.23	+1.4	19367	16.22	15.96	0.3	n.a.	17.86	8.65	-4.5	+35.3
YllwPgsun	YLO.UN	14.45	-0.01	-0.1	7739	14.49	14.38	7.5	17.0	16.50	11.55	+1.1	-9.4

Source: Sample stock quotation from the *National Post*, Thursday, April 26, 2007, page FP12. Data provided by Thomson Financial.

reproduces a small section of the stock page for the Toronto Stock Exchange (TSX) from Thursday, April 26, 2007. In Figure 7.2, locate the line for the Canadian Imperial Bank of Commerce (CIBC). With the column headings, the line reads:

Stock	Ticker	Close	Net ch	% ch	Vol 00s	Day high	Day low	% yield	P/E	52wk high	52wk low	Wk %ch	52wk %ch
CIBC	CM	98.98	+0.02	nil	4927	99.25	98.26	3.1	12.4	104.63	73.25	−0.7	+18.2

The first column shows the abbreviated company's name, CIBC. The "Ticker" column provides the ticker symbol, CM, used to uniquely identify shares of CIBC on the TSX. (By the way, CIBC is listed under the same ticker symbol on the NYSE as well, which is not necessarily the case for other Canadian firms listed on the U.S. stock markets.) "Close" is the closing price on the day (i.e., the last price at which a trade took place before the TSX closed for the day). The "Net ch" of +0.02 tells us that the closing price of $98.98 is $0.02 higher that it was the day before; so, we say that CIBC was up 0.02 for the day. In percentage terms this was a negligible increase, as shown in the "% ch" column.

WORK THE WEB

The Web is a great place to obtain the latest stock price information, and there are a slew of sites available to help you. Try pointing your Web browser to **ca.finance.yahoo.com**. Once there, you should see something like this on the page:

To look up a company, you must know its "ticker symbol" (or just ticker for short). You can click on the "Symbol Lookup" link and type in a company's name to find the ticker. For example, we typed in "THI," which is the ticker symbol for Tim Hortons, a quick service restaurant chain specializing in coffee, baked goods and lunches. Here is a portion of what we got:

There is a lot of information here and a lot of other links for you to explore, so have at it.

The column marked "Vol 00s" tells us how many shares traded during the day (in hundreds). For example, the 4927 for CIBC tells us that 492,700, or about 0.5 million shares, changed hands on this day alone. If the average price during the day was $99 or so, then the dollar volume of transactions was on the order of $99 × 0.5 million = $49.5 million worth for CIBC alone. This was actually a fairly routine day of trading in the CIBC shares and serves to illustrate how active the market can be for well-known companies.

The columns labelled "Day high" and "Day low" show the highest and lowest prices for the stock for the day. The CIBC stock was up to $99.25 and down to $98.26 during that day. The column marked "% yield" gives the dividend yield, which is 3.1 percent for CIBC. The next column, labelled "P/E," is the price-earnings ratio we discussed in Chapter 3. It is calculated as the closing price divided by annual earnings per share (based on the most recent four quarters). In the jargon of Bay Street, we might say that CIBC "sells for 12.4 times earnings."

Finally, two columns, marked "52wk high" and "52wk low," tell us the highest and lowest prices for the stock over the past 52 weeks. CIBC was trading as high as $104.63 and as low as $73.25 during that period. The last two numbers, −0.7 and +18.2, are the percentage changes for CIBC stock over the past 1 and 52 weeks, respectively.

Information on stock prices, along with a ton of other information, can be easily found on the Web for almost any public company. Our Work the Web box on the opposite page shows you how to get started.

You can get real-time stock quotes on the Web. See ca.finance.yahoo.com, finance.canada.com, or www.globeinvestor.com for details.

KEY EQUATIONS:

I. The general case

In general, the price today of a share of stock, P_0, is the present value of both its dividend and price in one period:

$$P_0 = (D_1 + P_1)/(1 + R) \qquad [7.1]$$

or the present value of all of its future dividends, $D_1, D_2, D_3...$:

$$P_0 = \frac{D_1}{(1 + R)^1} + \frac{D_2}{(1 + R)^2} + \frac{D_3}{(1 + R)^3} + \cdots \qquad [7.2]$$

where R is the required return.

II. Constant growth case

If the dividend is constant and equal D, then the price can be written as:

$$P_0 = D/R \qquad [7.3]$$

If the dividend grows at a steady rate, g, then the price can be written as:

$$P_0 = \frac{D_0 \times (1 + g)}{R - g} = \frac{D_1}{R - g} \qquad [7.4]$$

or

$$P_t = \frac{D_t \times (1 + g)}{R - g} = \frac{D_{t+1}}{R - g} \qquad [7.5]$$

This result is called the *dividend growth model*.

III. The required return, *R*, can be written as the sum of two things:

$$R = \frac{D_1}{P_0} + g \tag{7.6}$$

where D_1/P_0 is the *dividend yield* and *g* is the *capital gains yield* (which is the same thing as the growth rate in dividends for the steady growth case).

SUMMARY AND CONCLUSIONS

This chapter has covered the basics of stocks and stock valuation. The key points include:

1. The cash flows from owning a share of stock come in the form of future dividends. We saw that in certain special cases it is possible to calculate the present value of all the future dividends and thus come up with a value for the stock.

2. As the owner of shares of common stock in a corporation, you have various rights, including the right to vote to elect corporate directors. Voting in corporate elections can be either cumulative or straight. Most voting is actually done by proxy, and a proxy battle breaks out when competing sides try to gain enough votes to have their candidates for the board elected.

In addition to common stock, some corporations have issued preferred stock. The name stems from the fact that preferred stockholders must be paid first, before common stockholders can receive anything. Preferred stock has a fixed dividend.

3. Different stock price information is available in the financial press and on the Web.

This chapter completes Part 4 of our book. By now, you should have a good grasp of what we mean by present value. You should also be familiar with how to calculate present values, loan payments, and so on. In Part 5, we cover capital budgeting decisions. As you will see, the techniques you have learned in Chapters 4–7 form the basis for our approach to evaluating business investment decisions.

CHAPTER REVIEW AND SELF-TEST PROBLEMS

7.1 Dividend Growth and Stock Valuation.   The Elkhead Co. has just paid a cash dividend of $2 per share. Investors require a 16 percent return from investments such as this. If the dividend is expected to grow at a steady 8 percent per year, what is the current value of the stock? What will the stock be worth in five years?

7.2 Required Returns.   Suppose we observe a stock selling for $40 per share. The next dividend will be $1 per share, and you think the dividend will grow at 12 percent per year forever. What is the dividend yield in this case? The capital gains yield? The total required return?

■ Answers to Chapter Review and Self-Test Problems

7.1   The last dividend, D_0, was $2. The dividend is expected to grow steadily at 8 percent. The required return is 16 percent. Based on the dividend growth model, we can say that the current price is:

$$P_0 = D_1/(R - g) = D_0 \times (1 + g)/(R - g)$$
$$= \$2 \times 1.08/(.16 - .08)$$
$$= \$2.16/.08$$
$$= \$27$$

We could calculate the price in five years by calculating the dividend in five years and then using the growth model again. Alternatively, we could recognize that the stock price will increase by 8 percent per year and calculate the future price directly. We'll do both. First, the dividend in five years will be:

$$D_5 = D_0 \times (1 + g)^5$$
$$= \$2 \times 1.08^5$$
$$= \$2.9387$$

The price in five years would therefore be:

$$P_5 = D_5 \times (1 + g)/(R - g)$$
$$= \$2.9387 \times 1.08/.08$$
$$= \$3.1738/.08$$
$$= \$39.67$$

Once we understand the dividend model, however, it's easier to notice that:

$$P_5 = P_0 \times (1 + g)^5$$
$$= \$27 \times 1.08^5$$
$$= \$27 \times 1.4693$$
$$= \$39.67$$

Notice that both approaches yield the same price in five years.

7.2 The dividend yield is the next dividend, D_1, divided by the current price, P_0, or $\$1/40 = 2.5\%$. The capital gains yield is the same as the dividend growth rate, 12 percent. The total required return is the sum of the two, $2.5\% + 12\% = 14.5\%$.

CRITICAL THINKING AND CONCEPTS REVIEW

7.1 **Stock Valuation.**   Why does the value of a share of stock depend on dividends?

7.2 **Stock Valuation.**   A substantial percentage of the companies listed on the TSX and the TSX Venture Exchange don't pay dividends, but investors are nonetheless willing to buy shares in them. How is this possible, given your answer to the previous question?

7.3 **Dividend Policy.**   Referring to the previous questions, under what circumstances might a company choose not to pay dividends?

7.4 **Dividend Growth Model.**   Under what two assumptions can we use the dividend growth model presented in the chapter to determine the value of a share of stock? Comment on the reasonableness of these assumptions.

7.5 **Common versus Preferred Stock.**   Suppose a company has a preferred stock issue and a common stock issue. Both have just paid a $2 dividend. Which do you think will have a higher price, a share of the preferred or a share of the common?

7.6 **Dividend Growth Model.**   Based on the dividend growth model, what are the two components of the total return on a share of stock? Which do you think is typically larger?

7.7　Growth Rate.　In the context of the dividend growth model, is it true that the growth rate in dividends and the growth rate in the price of the stock are identical?

7.8　Voting Rights.　When it comes to voting in elections, what are the differences between political democracy and corporate democracy?

7.9　Corporate Ethics.　Is it unfair or unethical for corporations to create classes of stock with unequal voting rights?

7.10　Voting Rights.　Some companies, such as Google, have created classes of stock with little or no voting rights at all. Why would investors buy such stock?

7.11　Stock Valuation.　Evaluate the following statement: Managers should not focus on the current stock value because doing so will lead to an overemphasis on short-term profits at the expense of long-term profits.

QUESTIONS AND PROBLEMS

Basic
(Questions 1–13)

1.　**Stock Values.**　Money, Inc., just paid a dividend of $2.50 per share on its stock. The dividends are expected to grow at a constant rate of 5 percent per year, indefinitely. If investors require an 11 percent return on Money stock, what is the current price? What will the price be in three years? In 15 years?

2.　**Stock Values.**　The next dividend payment by the Bank of Labrador will be $1.80 per share. The dividends are anticipated to maintain a 6.5 percent growth rate, forever. If the Bank of Labrador stock currently sells for $47.00 per share, what is the required return?

3.　**Stock Values.**　For the company in the previous problem, what is the dividend yield? What is the expected capital gains yield?

4.　**Stock Values.**　Canadian Rockies Corporation will pay a $4.50 per share dividend next year. The company pledges to increase its dividend by 4 percent per year, indefinitely. If you require a 12 percent return on your investment, how much will you pay for the company's stock today?

5.　**Stock Valuation.**　Niagara Falls, Inc., is expected to maintain a constant 6 percent growth rate in its dividends, indefinitely. If the company has a dividend yield of 4.1 percent, what is the required return on the company's stock?

6.　**Stock Valuation.**　Suppose you know that a company's stock currently sells for $60 per share and the required return on the stock is 13 percent. You also know that the total return on the stock is evenly divided between capital gains yield and a dividend yield. If it's the company's policy to always maintain a constant growth rate in its dividends, what is the current dividend per share?

7.　**Stock Valuation.**　Moose Corp. pays a constant $15 dividend on its stock. The company will maintain this dividend for the next eight years and will then cease paying dividends forever. If the required return on this stock is 11 percent, what is the current share price?

8.　**Valuing Preferred Stock.**　Lacrosse, Inc., has an issue of preferred stock outstanding that pays a $7 dividend every year, in perpetuity. If this issue currently sells for $90.21 per share, what is the required return?

9.　**Voting Rights.**　After successfully completing your corporate finance class, you feel the next challenge ahead is to serve on the board of directors of Blubber Diet, Inc., Unfortunately you will be the only individual voting for you. If Blubber Diet has 250,000 shares outstanding and the stock currently sells for $45, how much will it cost you to buy a seat if the company uses straight voting? Assume that Blubber Diet uses cumulative voting and there are four seats in the current election; how much will it cost you to buy a seat now?

10. **Voting Rights.**   The Prairie Corporation has two million common shares outstanding. The firm has eight members on its board of directors, three of whom are up for election. How many shares are necessary to guarantee your election to the board if:

   a.   The voting procedure is cumulative?

   b.   The voting procedure is straight?

11. **Growth Rates.**   The stock price of York Co. is $70. Investors require a 12 percent rate of return on similar stocks. If the company plans to pay a dividend of $4.25 next year, what growth rate is expected for the company's stock price?

12. **Valuing Preferred Stock.**   E-Eyes.com has a new issue of preferred stock it calls 20/20 preferred. The stock will pay a $20 dividend per year, but the first dividend will not be paid until 20 years from today. If you require a 9 percent return on this stock, how much should you pay today?

13. **Stock Valuation.**   Eldorado Corp. will pay a dividend of $3.75 next year. The company has stated that it will maintain a constant growth rate of 5 percent a year forever. If you want a 15 percent rate of return, how much will you pay for the stock? What if you want a 10 percent rate of return? What does this tell you about the relationship between the required return and the stock price?

14. **Nonconstant Growth.**   Metallica Bearings, Inc., is a young start-up company. No dividends will be paid on the stock over the next six years, because the firm needs to plow back its earnings to fuel growth. The company will then pay a $7 per share dividend in year 7 and will increase the dividend by 5 percent per year thereafter. If the required return on this stock is 13 percent, what is the current share price?

Intermediate
(Questions 14–26)

15. **Nonconstant Dividends.**   Three Creeks, Inc., has an odd dividend policy. The company has just paid a dividend of $12 per share and has announced that it will increase the dividend by $5 per share for each of the next four years, and then never pay another dividend. If you require a 12 percent return on the company's stock, how much will you pay for a share today?

16. **Nonconstant Dividends.**   Toque Corporation is expected to pay the following dividends over the next four years: $9, $15, $17, and $3. Afterwards, the company pledges to maintain a constant 5 percent growth rate in dividends, forever. If the required return on the stock is 11 percent, what is the current share price?

17. **Supernormal Growth.**   Future Corp. is growing quickly. Dividends are expected to grow at a 20 percent rate for the next three years, with the growth rate falling off to a constant 6 percent thereafter. If the required return is 14 percent and the company just paid a $2.90 dividend, what is the current share price? Hint: Calculate the first four dividends.

18. **Negative Growth.**   Antiques R Us is a mature manufacturing firm. The company just paid a $9 dividend, but management expects to reduce the payout by 7 percent per year, indefinitely. If you require a 10 percent return on this stock, what will you pay for a share today?

19. **Finding the Dividend.**   Calgary Corporation stock currently sells for $84 per share. The market requires a 13 percent return on the firm's stock. If the company maintains a constant 6 percent growth rate in dividends, what was the most recent dividend per share paid on the stock?

20. **Using Stock Quotes.** You have found the following stock quote for Canadian Wheel, Inc., in the financial pages of today's newspaper. If the annual dividend is $1.37, what was the closing price for this stock? If the company currently has 269 million shares of stock outstanding, what was net income for the most recent four quarters?

Stock	Ticker	Close	Net ch	% ch	Vol 00s	Day high	Day low	% yield	P/E	52wk high	52wk low
Cnd Wheel	CWL	??	−0.27	−0.4	4634	63.73	61.37	2.2	38.0	72.46	34.14

21. **Capital Gains versus Income.** Consider four different stocks, all of which have a required return of 18 percent and a most recent dividend of $3.25 per share. Stocks W, X, and Y are expected to maintain constant growth rates in dividends for the foreseeable future of 10 percent, 0 percent, and −5 percent per year, respectively. Stock Z is a growth stock that will increase its dividend by 20 percent for the next two years and then maintain a constant 12 percent growth rate, thereafter. What is the dividend yield for each of these four stocks? What is the expected capital gains yield? Discuss the relationship among the various returns that you find for each of these stocks.

The following stock quotes appeared in the *National Post* on March 23, 2007. Use the information provided to answer Questions 22 to 26.

Stock	Ticker	Close	Net ch	% ch	Vol 00s	Day high	Day low	% yield	P/E	52wk high	52wk low
Loblaw	L	46.40	+1.02	−2.2	3332	47.50	46.25	1.8	n.a.	57.83	44.92
Magna A SV	MG.A	87.10	+0.10	+0.1	2008	87.51	86.73	1.0	15.5	96.00	76.69
Nexen	NXY	69.05	−0.62	−0.9	19629	71.20	68.85	0.3	30.2	75.20	50.82
Suncor	SU	83.88	+1.25	+1.5	12920	84.99	83.49	0.4	13.0	102.18	71.18
TELUS	T	57.40	−0.98	−1.7	12745	58.56	57.31	2.6	17.6	65.60	43.52

22. **Dividend Yield.** Find the quote for Loblaw Companies Ltd. (L). Assume that the dividend is constant. What was the highest dividend yield over the past year? What was the lowest dividend yield over the past year?

23. **Stock Valuation.** According to the March 16, 2007, issue of *The Value Line Investment Survey,* the growth rate in dividends for Suncor Energy, Inc. for the next five years is expected to be 7 percent. Suppose Suncor Energy meets this growth rate in dividends for the next five years and then the dividend growth rate falls to 5 percent indefinitely. Assume investors require an 11 percent return on Suncor Energy stock. Is the stock priced correctly? What factors could affect your answer?

24. **Stock Valuation.** According to the March 16, 2007, issue of *The Value Line Investment Survey,* the growth rate in dividends for Nexen Inc. for the previous ten years has been 6 percent. If investors feel this growth rate will continue, what is the required return for Nexen stock?

25. **Negative Growth.** According to the March 30, 2007, issue of *The Value Line Investment Survey,* the growth rate in dividends for Magna International for the next five years is expected to be −6.5 percent. If investors feel this negative growth rate will continue indefinitely, what is the required return for Magna International

stock? Does this number make sense? What are some of the potential reasons for the negative growth in dividends?

26. **Stock Valuation.** The March 30, 2007 issue of *The Value Line Investment Survey* projects a 17 percent dividend growth rate for TELUS Inc. What is the required return for the stock using the dividend growth model?

27. **Nonconstant Growth.** Erie Inc. has never paid a dividend, but the board of directors recently announced that the company would pay its first dividend of $3 per share exactly four years from now. This dividend is expected to grow by 10 percent for the following two years and then by 7 percent for one year. Afterwards, the company pledges to maintain a constant 3 percent growth rate in dividends. If you require a 15 percent return on the company's stock, how much will you pay for a share today?

Challenge (Questions 27–29)

28. **Growth Rates.** The Carleton Company has just paid a dividend of $2 per share, which is expected to grow at 8 percent per year for the next three years, and then at 4 percent per year forever. Investors require a return of 12 percent for the next three years, and then 9 percent per year forever. What is the current share price for Carleton stock?

29. **Growth Rates.** The Ontario Wine Corporation is experiencing rapid growth. Dividends are expected to grow at 25 percent per year for the next three years, and then at 15 percent per year, indefinitely. Ontario Wine just paid a dividend of $1.50 on its stock, which currently sells for $50 per share. What required return must investors be demanding on Ontario Wine stock?

WHAT'S ON THE WEB?

7.1 Dividend Growth Model. *The Value Line Investment Survey,* a weekly publication of Value Line, covers approximately 1,700 stocks in over 90 industries, including all the Canadian firms listed on the U.S. exchanges. Go to **www.valueline.com** and find free Value Line reports for the 30 companies that are members of the Dow Jones Industrial Average index. Locate the recent stock price and dividend per share for the Walt Disney company. Assume that its estimated dividend growth rate will continue forever, and use its return on shareholders equity as the required return. Use the dividend growth model to calculate the stock price for Disney. Is the computed stock price different from Walt Disney's actual recent price? How can you explain the difference?

7.2 Dividend Growth Model. According to the July 20, 2007, issue of *The Value Line Investment Survey,* the estimated dividend growth rate for Potash Corporation of Saskatchewan (POT) is 17 percent. Find the current stock price quote and dividend information at **ca.finance.yahoo.com.** If this dividend growth rate is correct, what is the required return for Potash Corp.? Does this number make sense to you?

7.3 Dividend Growth Model. Go to **www.dividenddiscountmodel.com** and enter BMO (for the Bank of Montreal) as the ticker symbol. You can enter a required return in the Discount Rate box and the site will calculate the stock price using the dividend growth model. If you want an 11 percent return, what price should you be willing to pay for the stock? At what required return does the current stock price make sense? You will need to enter different required returns until you arrive at the current stock price. Does this required return make sense? Using this market required return for Bank of Montreal, how does the price change if the required return increases by

1 percent? What does this tell you about the sensitivity of the dividend discount model to the inputs of the equation?

7.4 Stock Quotes.   What is the most expensive publicly traded stock in Canada? Go to **www.globeinvestor.com** and launch Filters. Type 100 for the Latest Closing Price in the "Price Performance Statistics" and click on "Get Results." How many stocks are traded above $100 per share? What is the most expensive stock? What are its current price and 52-week high and low? How many shares of this stock were traded today?

7.5 Supernormal Growth.   You are interested in buying stock in the Toronto-Dominion Bank (TD). According to *The Value Line Investment Survey* on February 2, 2007, the growth rate in dividends for Toronto-Dominion for the next five years is estimated to be 5.5 percent. You believe that this forecast is correct, but expect the growth rate to fall off to a constant 4 percent thereafter. Using the most recent dividend on **ca.finance.yahoo.com,** if you want a 10 percent return, how much should you be willing to pay for a share of stock?

8

Net Present Value and Other Investment Criteria

In June 2006, Canadian Tire corporation, a growing network of retail, petroleum, and financial services businesses, announced plans to build a $240 million warehouse in Coteau-du-Lac, Quebec. When fully operational, it will be the largest Canadian Tire distribution centre, will cover 1.5 million square feet, and will employ almost 1,000 full-time and part-time employees. As Canada's leading hard goods retailer, Canadian Tire was planning on using this warehouse for expansion into eastern Canada. Canadian Tire's decision, however, was not without risk. The company was facing stiff competition from Wal-Mart, which has almost 300 stores in Canada and keeps opening 15 to 20 new stores each year.

Canadian Tire's announcement offers an example of a capital budgeting decision. An expansion such as this one, with a $240 million price tag, is obviously a major undertaking, and the potential risks and rewards must be carefully weighed. In this chapter, we discuss the basic tools used in making such decisions.

This chapter introduces you to the practice of capital budgeting. Back in Chapter 1 we saw that increasing the value of the stock in a company is the goal of financial management. Thus, what we need to learn is how to tell whether a particular investment will achieve that or not. This chapter considers a variety of techniques that are actually used in practice. More important, it shows how many of these techniques can be misleading, and it explains why the net present value approach is the right one.

After studying this chapter, you should have a good understanding of:

8.1 The net present value criterion.

8.2 The payback rule and some of its shortcomings.

8.3 The internal rate of return criterion and its strengths and weaknesses.

8.4 The profitability index and its advantages and disadvantages.

8.5 The practice of capital budgeting in Canada.

In Chapter 1, we identified the three key areas of concern to the financial manager. The first of these was the following: What long-term investments should we make? We called this the *capital budgeting decision*. In this chapter, we begin to deal with the issues that arise in answering this question.

The process of allocating, or budgeting, capital is usually more involved than just deciding whether or not to buy a particular fixed asset. We will frequently face broader issues like whether or not we should launch a new product or enter a new market. Decisions such as these will determine the nature of a firm's operations and products for years to come, primarily because fixed asset investments are generally long-lived and not easily reversed once they are made.

For these reasons, the capital budgeting question is probably the most important issue in corporate finance. How a firm chooses to finance its operations (the capital structure question) and how a firm manages its short-term operating activities (the working capital question) are certainly issues of concern, but it is the fixed assets that define the business of the firm. Airlines, for example, are airlines because they operate airplanes, regardless of how they finance them.

Any firm possesses a huge number of possible investments. Each possible investment is an option available to the firm. Some options are valuable and some are not. The essence of successful financial management, of course, is learning to identify which are which. With this in mind, our goal in this chapter is to introduce you to the techniques used to analyze potential business ventures to decide which are worth undertaking.

We present and compare several different procedures used in practice. Our primary goal is to acquaint you with the advantages and disadvantages of the various approaches. As we shall see, the most important concept in this area is the idea of net present value. We consider this next.

8.1 | NET PRESENT VALUE

In Chapter 1, we argued that the goal of financial management is to create value for the stockholders. The financial manager must therefore examine a potential investment that is in light of its likely effect on the price of the firm's shares. In this section, we describe a widely used procedure for doing this, the net present value approach.

The Basic Idea

An investment is worth undertaking if it creates value for its owners. In the most general sense, we create value by identifying an investment that is worth more in the marketplace than it costs us to acquire. How can something be worth more than it costs? It's a case of the whole being worth more than the cost of the parts.

For example, suppose you buy a run-down house for $25,000 and spend another $25,000 on painters, plumbers, and so on to get it fixed up. Your total investment is $50,000. When the work is completed, you place the house back on the market and find that it's worth $60,000. The market value ($60,000) exceeds the cost ($50,000) by $10,000. What you have done here is to act as a manager and bring together some fixed assets (a house), some labour (plumbers, carpenters, and others), and some materials (carpeting, paint, and so on). The net result is that you have created $10,000 in value. Put another way, this $10,000 is the *value added* by management.

With our house example, it turned out *after the fact* that $10,000 in value was created. Things thus worked out very nicely. The real challenge, of course, would have been to somehow identify *ahead of time* whether or not investing the necessary $50,000 was a good idea in the first place. This is what capital budgeting is all about, namely, trying to determine whether a proposed investment or project will be worth more than it costs once it is in place.

For reasons that will be obvious in a moment, the difference between an investment's market value and its cost is called the **net present value** of the investment, abbreviated **NPV**. In other words, net present value is a measure of how much value is created or added today by undertaking an investment. Given our goal of creating value for the stockholders, the capital budgeting process can be viewed as a search for investments with positive net present values.

net present value (NPV)
The difference between an investment's market value and its cost.

With our run-down house, you can probably imagine how we would go about making the capital budgeting decision. We would first look at what comparable fixed-up properties were selling for in the market. We would then get estimates of the cost of buying a particular property, fixing it up, and bringing it to market. At this point, we have an estimated total cost and an estimated market value. If the difference is positive, then this investment is worth undertaking because it has a positive estimated net present value. There is risk, of course, because there is no guarantee that our estimates will turn out to be correct.

As our example illustrates, investment decisions are greatly simplified when there is a market for assets similar to the investment we are considering. Capital budgeting becomes much more difficult when we cannot observe the market price for at least roughly comparable investments. The reason is that we are then faced with the problem of estimating the value of an investment using only indirect market information. Unfortunately, this is precisely the situation the financial manager usually encounters. We examine this issue next.

Estimating Net Present Value

Imagine we are thinking of starting a business to produce and sell a new product, say, organic fertilizer. We can estimate the start-up costs with reasonable accuracy because we know what we will need to buy to begin production. Would this be a good investment? Based on our discussion, you know that the answer depends on whether or not the value of the new business exceeds the cost of starting it. In other words, does this investment have a positive NPV?

This problem is much more difficult than our "fixer-upper" house example, because entire fertilizer companies are not routinely bought and sold in the marketplace; so it is essentially impossible to observe the market value of a similar investment. As a result, we must somehow estimate this value by other means.

Based on our work in Chapters 4 and 5, you may be able to guess how we will go about estimating the value of our fertilizer business. We will first try to estimate the future cash flows we expect the new business to produce. We will then apply our basic discounted cash flow procedure to estimate the present value of those cash flows. Once we have this estimate, we then estimate NPV as the difference between the present value of the future cash flows and the cost of the investment. As we mentioned in Chapter 5, this procedure is often called **discounted cash flow**, or **DCF**, **valuation.**

discounted cash flow (DCF) valuation
The process of valuing an investment by discounting its future cash flows.

To see how we might go about estimating NPV, suppose we believe the cash revenues from our fertilizer business will be $20,000 per year, assuming everything goes as expected. Cash costs (including taxes) will be $14,000 per year. We will wind down the business in eight years. The plant, property, and equipment will be worth $2,000 as salvage at that time. The project costs $30,000 to launch. We use a 15 percent discount rate on new projects such as this one. Is this a good investment? If there are 1,000 shares of stock outstanding, what will be the effect on the price per share from taking the investment?

From a purely mechanical perspective, we need to calculate the present value of the future cash flows at 15 percent. The net cash inflow will be $20,000 cash income less $14,000 in costs per year for eight years. These cash flows are illustrated in Figure 8.1.

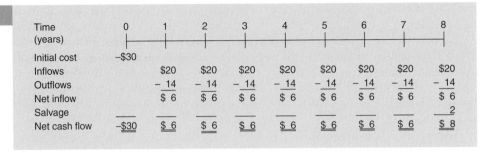

FIGURE 8.1

Project cash flows ($000)

As Figure 8.1 suggests, we effectively have an eight-year annuity of $20,000 − 14,000 = $6,000 per year along with a single lump-sum inflow of $2,000 in eight years. Calculating the present value of the future cash flows thus comes down to the same type of problem we considered in Chapter 5. The total present value is:

$$\text{Present value} = \$6,000 \times (1 - 1/1.15^8)/.15 + 2,000/1.15^8$$
$$= \$6,000 \times 4.4873 + 2,000/3.0590$$
$$= \$26,924 + 654$$
$$= \$27,578$$

When we compare this to the $30,000 estimated cost, the NPV is:

$$\text{NPV} = -\$30,000 + 27,578 = -\$2,422$$

Therefore, this is *not* a good investment. Based on our estimates, taking it would *decrease* the total value of the stock by $2,422. With 1,000 shares outstanding, our best estimate of the impact of taking this project is a loss of value of $2,422/1,000 = $2.422 per share.

Our fertilizer example illustrates how NPV estimates can be used to determine whether or not an investment is desirable. From our example, notice that if the NPV is negative, the effect on share value will be unfavourable. If the NPV were positive, the effect would be favourable. As a consequence, all we need to know about a particular proposal for the purpose of making an accept-reject decision is whether the NPV is positive or negative.

Given that the goal of financial management is to increase share value, our discussion in this section leads us to the *net present value rule:*

> An investment should be accepted if the net present value is positive and rejected if it is negative.

In the unlikely event that the net present value turned out to be exactly zero, we would be indifferent between taking the investment and not taking it.

Two comments about our example are in order. First and foremost, it is not the rather mechanical process of discounting the cash flows that is important. Once we have the cash flows and the appropriate discount rate, the required calculations are fairly straightforward. The task of coming up with the cash flows and the discount rate in the first place is much more challenging. We will have much more to say about this in our next chapter. For the remainder of this chapter, we take it as given that we have estimates of the cash revenues and costs and, where needed, an appropriate discount rate.

The second thing to keep in mind about our example is that the −$2,422 NPV is an estimate. Like any estimate, it can be high or low. The only way to find out the true NPV would be to place the investment up for sale and see what we could get for it. We generally won't be doing this, so it is important that our estimates be reliable. Once again, we will have more to say about this later. For the rest of this chapter, we will assume that the estimates are accurate.

Using the NPV Rule   EXAMPLE 8.1

Suppose we are asked to decide whether or not a new consumer product should be launched. Based on projected sales and costs, we expect that the cash flows over the five-year life of the project will be $2,000 in the first two years, $4,000 in the next two, and $5,000 in the last year. It will cost about $10,000 to begin production. We use a 10 percent discount rate to evaluate new products. What should we do here?

Given the cash flows and discount rate, we can calculate the total value of the product by discounting the cash flows back to the present:

$$\text{Present value} = \$2,000/1.1 + 2,000/1.1^2 + 4,000/1.1^3 + 4,000/1.1^4 + 5,000/1.1^5$$
$$= \$1,818 + 1,653 + 3,005 + 2,732 + 3,105$$
$$= \$12,313$$

Check out an NPV calculator at **www.investopedia.com/calculator**.

The present value of the expected cash flows is $12,313, but the cost of getting those cash flows is only $10,000, so the NPV is $12,313 − 10,000 = $2,313. This is positive; so, based on the net present value rule, we should take on the project.

Spreadsheet Strategies   Calculating NPVs with a Spreadsheet

Spreadsheets and financial calculators are commonly used to calculate NPVs. The procedures used by various financial calculators are too different for us to illustrate here, so we will focus on using a spreadsheet (financial calculators are covered in Appendix D). Examining the use of spreadsheets in this context also allows us to issue an important warning. Let's rework Example 8.1:

	A	B	C	D	E	F	G	H
1								
2		Using a spreadsheet to calculate net present values						
3								
4	From Example 8.1, the project's cost is $10,000. The cash flows are $2,000 per year for the first two							
5	years, $4,000 per year for the next two, and $5,000 in the last year. The discount rate is							
6	10 percent; what's the NPV?							
7								
8		Year	Cash flow					
9		0	−$10,000	Discount rate =		10%		
10		1	2,000					
11		2	2,000		NPV =	$2,102.72	(*wrong* answer)	
12		3	4,000		NPV =	$2,312.99	(*right* answer)	
13		4	4,000					
14		5	5,000					
15								
16	The formula entered in cell F11 is = NPV(F9,C9:C14). This gives the wrong answer because the							
17	NPV function actually calculates present values, not net present values.							
18								
19	The formula entered in cell F12 is = NPV(F9,C10:C14) + C9. This gives the right answer because the							
20	NPV function is used to calculate the present value of the cash flows and then the initial cost is							
21	subtracted to calculate the answer. Notice that we added cell C9 because it is already negative.							

As we have seen in this section, estimating NPV is one way of assessing the profitability of a proposed investment. It is certainly not the only way profitability is assessed, and we now turn to some alternatives. As we will see, when compared to NPV, each of the ways of assessing profitability that we examine is flawed in some key way; so, NPV is the preferred approach in principle, if not always in practice.

In our nearby *Spreadsheet Strategies* box, we rework Example 8.1. Notice that we have provided two answers. By comparing the answers to that found in Example 8.1, we see that the first answer is wrong even though we used the spreadsheet's NPV formula. What happened is that the "NPV" function in our spreadsheet is actually a PV function; unfortunately, one of the original spreadsheet programs many years ago got the definition wrong, and subsequent spreadsheets have copied it! Our second answer shows how to use the formula properly.

The example here illustrates the danger of blindly using calculators or computers without understanding what is going on; we shudder to think of how many capital budgeting decisions in the real world are based on incorrect use of this particular function. We will see another example of something that can go wrong with a spreadsheet later in the chapter.

CONCEPT QUESTIONS

8.1a   What is the net present value rule?

8.1b   If we say an investment has an NPV of $1,000, what exactly do we mean?

8.2 | THE PAYBACK RULE

It is very common in practice to talk of the payback on a proposed investment. Loosely, the *payback* is the length of time it takes to recover our initial investment, or "get our bait back." Because this idea is widely understood and used, we will examine it in some detail.

Defining the Rule

We can illustrate how to calculate a payback with an example. Figure 8.2 below shows the cash flows from a proposed investment. How many years do we have to wait until the accumulated cash flows from this investment equal or exceed the cost of the investment? As Figure 8.2 indicates, the initial investment is $50,000. After the first year, the firm has recovered $30,000, leaving $20,000 outstanding. The cash flow in the second year is exactly $20,000, so this investment "pays for itself" in exactly two years. Put another way, the **payback period** (or just payback) is two years. If we require a payback of, say, three years or less, then this investment is acceptable. This illustrates the *payback period rule:*

payback period
The amount of time required for an investment to generate cash flows sufficient to recover its initial cost.

> Based on the payback rule, an investment is acceptable if its calculated payback period is less than some prespecified number of years.

In our example, the payback works out to be exactly two years. This won't usually happen, of course. When the numbers don't work out exactly, it is customary to work with fractional years. For example, suppose the initial investment is $60,000, and the cash

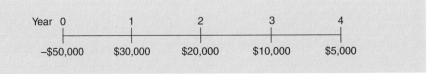

FIGURE 8.2

Net project cash flow

Year	0	1	2	3	4
	−$50,000	$30,000	$20,000	$10,000	$5,000

flows are $20,000 in the first year and $90,000 in the second. The cash flows over the first two years are $110,000, so the project obviously pays back sometime in the second year. After the first year, the project has paid back $20,000, leaving $40,000 to be recovered. To figure out the fractional year, note that this $40,000 is $40,000/90,000 = 4/9 of the second year's cash flow. Assuming that the $90,000 cash flow is paid uniformly throughout the year, the payback would thus be 1-4/9 years.

Calculating Payback   **EXAMPLE 8.2**

The projected cash flows from a proposed investment are:

Year	Cash Flow
1	$100
2	200
3	500

2.4

This project costs $500. What is the payback period for this investment?

The initial cost is $500. After the first two years, the cash flows total $300. After the third year, the total cash flow is $800, so the project pays back sometime between the end of Year 2 and the end of Year 3. Since the accumulated cash flows for the first two years are $300, we need to recover $200 in the third year. The third-year cash flow is $500, so we will have to wait $200/500 = .40 year to do this. The payback period is thus 2.4 years, or about two years and five months.

Now that we know how to calculate the payback period on an investment, using the payback period rule for making decisions is straightforward. A particular cutoff time is selected, say two years, and all investment projects that have payback periods of two years or less are accepted, and all of those that pay back in more than two years are rejected.

Table 8.1 illustrates cash flows for five different projects. The figures shown as the Year 0 cash flows are the cost of the investment. We examine these to indicate some peculiarities that can, in principle, arise with payback periods.

The payback for the first project, A, is easily calculated. The sum of the cash flows for the first two years is $70, leaving us with $100 − 70 = $30 to go. Since the cash flow in the third year is $50, the payback occurs sometime in that year. When we compare the $30 we need to the $50 that will be coming in, we get $30/50 = .60; so, payback will occur 60 percent of the way into the year. The payback period is thus 2.6 years.

Project B's payback is also easy to calculate: It *never* pays back because the cash flows never total up to the original investment. Project C has a payback of exactly four years because it supplies the $130 that B is missing in Year 4. Project D is a little strange. Because of the negative cash flow in Year 3, you can easily verify that it has two different payback periods, two years and four years. Which of these is correct? Both of them; the way the payback period is calculated doesn't guarantee a single answer. Finally, Project E

Year	A	B	C	D	E
0	−$100	−$200	−$200	−$200	−$ 50
1	30	40	40	100	100
2	40	20	20	100	− 50,000,000
3	50	10	10	− 200	
4	60		130	200	

TABLE 8.1

Expected cash flows for Projects A through E

is obviously unrealistic, but it does pay back in six months, thereby illustrating the point that a rapid payback does not guarantee a good investment.

Analyzing the Rule

When compared to the NPV rule, the payback period rule has some rather severe shortcomings. First, the payback period is calculated by simply adding up the future cash flows. There is no discounting involved, so the time value of money is completely ignored. The payback rule also fails to consider risk differences. The payback would be calculated the same way for both very risky and very safe projects.

Perhaps the biggest problem with the payback period rule is coming up with the right cutoff period, because we don't really have an objective basis for choosing a particular number. Put another way, there is no economic rationale for looking at payback in the first place, so we have no guide as to how to pick the cutoff. As a result, we end up using a number that is arbitrarily chosen.

Suppose we have somehow decided on an appropriate payback period, say two years or less. As we have seen, the payback period rule ignores the time value of money for the first two years. More seriously, cash flows after the second year are ignored entirely. To see this, consider the two investments, Long and Short, in Table 8.2. Both projects cost $250. Based on our discussion, the payback on Long is $2 + \$50/100 = 2.5$ years, and the payback on Short is $1 + \$150/200 = 1.75$ years. With a cutoff of two years, Short is acceptable and Long is not.

Is the payback period rule giving us the right decisions? Maybe not. Suppose again that we require a 15 percent return on this type of investment. We can calculate the NPV for these two investments as:

$$\text{NPV(Short)} = -\$250 + 100/1.15 + 200/1.15^2 = -\$11.81$$
$$\text{NPV(Long)} = -\$250 + 100 \times (1 - 1/1.15^4)/.15 = \$35.50$$

Now we have a problem. The NPV of the shorter-term investment is actually negative, meaning that taking it diminishes the value of the shareholders' equity. The opposite is true for the longer-term investment—it increases share value.

Our example illustrates two primary shortcomings of the payback period rule. First, by ignoring time value, we may be led to take investments (like Short) that actually are worth less than they cost. Second, by ignoring cash flows beyond the cutoff, we may be led to reject profitable long-term investments (like Long). More generally, using a payback period rule will tend to bias us towards shorter-term investments.

Redeeming Qualities of the Rule

Despite its shortcomings, the payback period rule is often used by large and sophisticated companies when they are making relatively minor decisions. There are several reasons for this. The primary reason is that many decisions simply do not warrant detailed analysis because the cost of the analysis would exceed the possible loss from a mistake. As a

TABLE 8.2	Year	Long	Short
Investment projected cash flows	0	−$250	−$250
	1	100	100
	2	100	200
	3	100	0
	4	100	0

practical matter, an investment that pays back rapidly and has benefits extending beyond the cutoff period probably has a positive NPV.

Small investment decisions are made by the hundreds every day in large organizations. Moreover, they are made at all levels. As a result, it would not be uncommon for a corporation to require, for example, a two-year payback on all investments of less than $10,000. Investments larger than this are subjected to greater scrutiny. The requirement of a two-year payback is not perfect for reasons we have seen, but it does exercise some control over expenditures and thus has the effect of limiting possible losses.

In addition to its simplicity, the payback rule has two other positive features. First, because it is biased towards short-term projects, it is biased towards liquidity. In other words, a payback rule tends to favour investments that free up cash for other uses more quickly. This could be very important for a small business; it would be less so for a large corporation. Second, the cash flows that are expected to occur later in a project's life are probably more uncertain. Arguably, a payback period rule adjusts for the extra riskiness of later cash flows, but it does so in a rather draconian fashion—by ignoring them altogether.

We should note here that some of the apparent simplicity of the payback rule is an illusion. The reason is that we still must come up with the cash flows first, and, as we discuss above, this is not at all easy to do. Thus, it would probably be more accurate to say that the *concept* of a payback period is both intuitive and easy to understand.

Summary of the Rule

To summarize, the payback period is a kind of "break-even" measure. Because time value is ignored, you can think of the payback period as the length of time it takes to break even in an accounting sense, but not in an economic sense. The biggest drawback to the payback period rule is that it doesn't ask the right question. The relevant issue is the impact an investment will have on the value of our stock, not how long it takes to recover the initial investment.

Nevertheless, because it is so simple, companies often use it as a screen for dealing with the myriad of minor investment decisions they have to make. There is certainly nothing wrong with this practice. Like any simple rule of thumb, there will be some errors in using it, but it wouldn't have survived all this time if it weren't useful. Now that you understand the rule, you can be on the alert for those circumstances under which it might lead to problems. To help you remember, the following table lists the pros and cons of the payback period rule.

Advantages and Disadvantages of the Payback Period Rule	
Advantages	**Disadvantages**
1. Easy to understand.	1. Ignores the time value of money.
2. Adjusts for uncertainty of later cash flows.	2. Requires an arbitrary cutoff point.
3. Biased towards liquidity.	3. Ignores cash flows beyond the cutoff date.
	4. Biased against long-term projects, such as research and development, and new projects.

CONCEPT QUESTIONS

8.2a In words, what is the payback period? The payback period rule?

8.2b Why do we say that the payback period is, in a sense, an accounting break-even measure?

8.3 | THE INTERNAL RATE OF RETURN

**internal rate of
return (IRR)**
The discount rate that
makes the NPV of an
investment zero.

We now come to the most important alternative to NPV, the **internal rate of return,** universally known as the **IRR**. As we will see, the IRR is closely related to NPV. With the IRR, we try to find a single rate of return that summarizes the merits of a project. Furthermore, we want this rate to be an "internal" rate in the sense that it only depends on the cash flows of a particular investment, not on rates offered elsewhere.

To illustrate the idea behind the IRR, consider a project that costs $100 today and pays $110 in one year. Suppose you were asked, "What is the return on this investment?" What would you say? It seems both natural and obvious to say that the return is 10 percent because, for every dollar we put in, we get $1.10 back. In fact, as we will see in a moment, 10 percent is the internal rate of return, or IRR, on this investment.

Is this project with its 10 percent IRR a good investment? Once again, it would seem apparent that this is a good investment only if our required return is less than 10 percent. This intuition is also correct and illustrates the *IRR rule:*

> Based on the IRR rule, an investment is acceptable if the IRR exceeds the required return. It should be rejected otherwise.

Imagine that we wanted to calculate the NPV for our simple investment. At a discount rate of *R,* the NPV is:

$$NPV = -\$100 + 110/(1 + R)$$

Now, suppose we didn't know the discount rate. This presents a problem, but we could still ask how high the discount rate would have to be before this project was unacceptable. We know that we are indifferent between taking and not taking this investment when its NPV is just equal to zero. In other words, this investment is *economically* a break-even proposition when the NPV is zero because value is neither created nor destroyed. To find the break-even discount rate, we set NPV equal to zero and solve for *R:*

$$NPV = 0 = -\$100 + 110/(1 + R)$$
$$\$100 = \$110/(1 + R)$$
$$1 + R = \$110/100 = 1.10$$
$$R = 10\%$$

This 10 percent is what we already have called the return on this investment. What we have now illustrated is that the internal rate of return on an investment (or just "return" for short) is the discount rate that makes the NPV equal to zero. This is an important observation, so it bears repeating:

> The IRR on an investment is the required return that results in a zero NPV when it is used as the discount rate.

The fact that the IRR is simply the discount rate that makes the NPV equal to zero is important because it tells us how to calculate the returns on more complicated investments. As we have seen, finding the IRR turns out to be relatively easy for a single-period investment. However, suppose you were now looking at an investment with the cash flows shown in Figure 8.3. As illustrated, this investment costs $100 and has a cash flow of $60 per year for two years, so it's only slightly more complicated than our single-period

FIGURE 8.3

Project cash flows

example. However, if you were asked for the return on this investment, what would you say? There doesn't seem to be any obvious answer (at least to us). However, based on what we now know, we can set the NPV equal to zero and solve for the discount rate:

$$NPV = 0 = -\$100 + 60/(1 + IRR) + 60/(1 + IRR)^2$$

Unfortunately, the only way to find the IRR in general is by trial and error, either by hand or by calculator. This is precisely the same problem that came up in Chapter 5 when we found the unknown rate for an annuity and in Chapter 6 when we found the yield to maturity on a bond. In fact, we now see that, in both of those cases, we were finding an IRR.

In this particular case, the cash flows form a two-period, $60 annuity. To find the unknown rate, we can try some different rates until we get the answer. If we were to start with a 0 percent rate, the NPV would obviously be $120 − 100 = $20. At a 10 percent discount rate, we would have:

$$NPV = -\$100 + 60/1.1 + 60/1.1^2 = \$4.13$$

Now, we're getting close. We can summarize these and some other possibilities as shown in Table 8.3. From our calculations, the NPV appears to be zero between 10 percent and 15 percent, so the IRR is somewhere in that range. With a little more effort, we can find that the IRR is about 13.1 percent. So, if our required return is less than 13.1 percent, we would take this investment. If our required return exceeds 13.1 percent, we would reject it.

By now, you have probably noticed that the IRR rule and the NPV rule appear to be quite similar. In fact, the IRR is sometimes simply called the *discounted cash flow,* or *DCF, return.* The easiest way to illustrate the relationship between NPV and IRR is to plot the numbers we calculated in Table 8.3. We put the different NPVs on the vertical axis, or *y*-axis, and the discount rates on the horizontal axis, or *x*-axis. If we had a very large number of points, the resulting picture would be a smooth curve called a **net present value profile**. Figure 8.4 illustrates the NPV profile for this project. Beginning with a 0 percent discount rate, we have $20 plotted directly on the *y*-axis. As the discount rate increases, the NPV declines smoothly. Where will the curve cut through the *x*-axis? This will occur where the NPV is just equal to zero, so it will happen right at the IRR of 13.1 percent.

In our example, the NPV rule and the IRR rule lead to identical accept-reject decisions. We will accept an investment using the IRR rule if the required return is less than 13.1 percent. As Figure 8.4 illustrates, however, the NPV is positive at any discount rate less than 13.1 percent, so we would accept the investment using the NPV rule as well. The two rules are equivalent in this case.

net present value profile
A graphical representation of the relationship between an investment's NPVs and various discount rates.

Discount Rate	NPV
0%	$20.00
5	11.56
10	4.13
15	− 2.46
20	− 8.33

TABLE 8.3

NPV at different discount rates

FIGURE **8.4**

An NPV profile

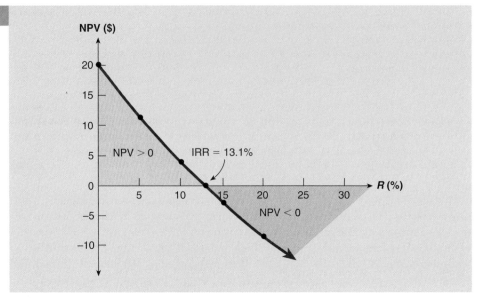

EXAMPLE **8.3** ### Calculating the IRR

A project has a total up-front cost of $435.44. The cash flows are $100 in the first year, $200 in the second year, and $300 in the third year. What's the IRR? If we require an 18 percent return, should we take this investment?

We'll describe the NPV profile and find the IRR by calculating some NPVs at different discount rates. You should check our answers for practice. Beginning with 0 percent, we have:

Discount Rate	NPV
0%	$164.56
5	100.36
10	46.15
15	.00
20	−39.61

The NPV is zero at 15 percent, so 15 percent is the IRR. If we require an 18 percent return, then we should not take the investment. The reason is that the NPV is negative at 18 percent (verify that it is − $24.47). The IRR rule tells us the same thing in this case. We shouldn't take this investment because its 15 percent return is below our required 18 percent return.

At this point, you may be wondering whether the IRR and NPV rules always lead to identical decisions. The answer is yes as long as two very important conditions are met. First, the project's cash flows must be *conventional*, meaning that the first cash flow (the initial investment) is negative and all the rest are positive. Second, the project must be *independent*, meaning that the decision to accept or reject this project does not affect the decision to accept or reject any other. The first of these conditions is typically met, but the second often is not. In any case, when one or both of these conditions are not met, problems can arise. We discuss some of these in a moment.

Spreadsheet Strategies Calculating IRRs with a Spreadsheet

Because IRRs are so tedious to calculate by hand, financial calculators and, especially, spreadsheets are generally used. The procedures used by various financial calculators are too different for us to illustrate here, so we will focus on using a spreadsheet (financial calculators are covered in Appendix D). As the following example illustrates, using a spreadsheet is very easy:

	A	B	C	D	E	F	G	H
1								
2	Using a spreadsheet to calculate internal rates of return							
3								
4	Suppose we have a four-year project that costs $500. The cash flows over the four-year life will be							
5	$100, $200, $300, and $400. What is the IRR?							
6								
7		Year	Cash flow					
8		0	−$500					
9		1	100		IRR =	27.3%		
10		2	200					
11		3	300					
12		4	400					
13								
14								
15	The formula entered in cell F9 is = IRR(C8:C12). Notice that the Year 0 cash flow has a negative sign,							
16	representing the initial cost of the project.							
17								

Problems with the IRR

The problems with the IRR come about when the cash flows are not conventional or when we are trying to compare two or more investments to see which is best. In the first case, surprisingly, the simple question "What's the return?" can become very difficult to answer. In the second case, the IRR can be a misleading guide.

Nonconventional Cash Flows Suppose we have a strip-mining project that requires a $60 investment. Our cash flow in the first year will be $155. In the second year, the mine is depleted, but we have to spend $100 to restore the terrain. As Figure 8.5 illustrates, both the first and third cash flows are negative.

To find the IRR on this project, we can calculate the NPV at various rates:

Discount Rate	NPV
0%	−$5.00
10	− 1.74
20	− .28
30	.06
40	− .31

The NPV appears to be behaving in a very peculiar fashion here. First, as the discount rate increases from 0 percent to 30 percent, the NPV starts out negative and becomes positive. This seems backward because the NPV is rising as the discount rate rises. It then starts getting smaller and becomes negative again. What's the IRR? To find out, we draw the NPV profile in Figure 8.6.

FIGURE 8.5

Project cash flows

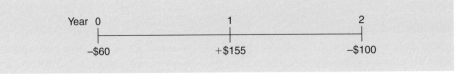

In Figure 8.6, notice that the NPV is zero when the discount rate is 25 percent, so this is the IRR. Or is it? The NPV is also zero at 33-1/3 percent. Which of these is correct? The answer is both or neither; more precisely, there is no unambiguously correct answer. This is the **multiple rates of return** problem. Many computer spreadsheet packages aren't aware of this problem and just report the first IRR that is found. Others report only the smallest positive IRR, even though this answer is no better than any other. For example, if you enter this problem in our spreadsheet above, it will simply report that the IRR is 25 percent.

multiple rates of return

The possibility that more than one discount rate makes the NPV of an investment zero.

In our current example, the IRR rule breaks down completely. Suppose our required return were 10 percent. Should we take this investment? Both IRRs are greater than 10 percent, so, by the IRR rule, maybe we should. However, as Figure 8.6 shows, the NPV is negative at any discount rate less than 25 percent, so this is not a good investment. When should we take it? Looking at Figure 8.6 one last time, we see that the NPV is positive only if our required return is between 25 percent and 33-1/3 percent.

The moral of the story is that when the cash flows aren't conventional, strange things can start to happen to the IRR. This is not anything to get upset about, however, because

FIGURE 8.6

NPV profile

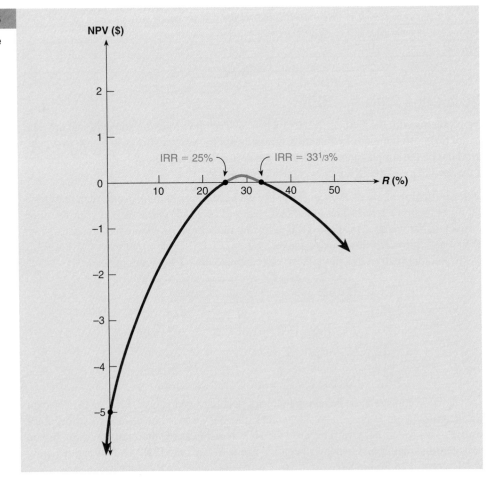

the NPV rule, as always, works just fine. This illustrates that, oddly enough, the obvious question "What's the rate of return?" may not always have a good answer.

What's the IRR?   **EXAMPLE 8.4**

You are looking at an investment that requires you to invest $51 today. You'll get $100 in one year, but you must pay out $50 in two years. What is the IRR on this investment?

You're on the alert now to the nonconventional cash flow problem, so you probably wouldn't be surprised to see more than one IRR. However, if you start looking for an IRR by trial and error, it will take you a long time. The reason is that there is no IRR. The NPV is negative at every discount rate, so we shouldn't take this investment under any circumstances. What's the return on this investment? Your guess is as good as ours.

Mutually Exclusive Investments   Even if there is a single IRR, another problem can arise concerning **mutually exclusive investment decisions**. If two investments, X and Y, are mutually exclusive, then taking one of them means that we cannot take the other. Two projects that are not mutually exclusive are said to be independent. For example, if we own one corner lot, then we can build a gas station or an apartment building, but not both. These are mutually exclusive alternatives.

mutually exclusive investment decisions
A situation where taking one investment prevents the taking of another.

Thus far, we have asked whether or not a given investment is worth undertaking. There is a related question, however, that comes up very often: Given two or more mutually exclusive investments, which one is the best? The answer is simple enough: The best one is the one with the largest NPV. Can we also say that the best one has the highest return? As we show, the answer is no.

To illustrate the problem with the IRR rule and mutually exclusive investments, consider the cash flows from the following two mutually exclusive investments:

Year	Investment A	Investment B
0	−$100	−$100
1	50	20
2	40	40
3	40	50
4	30	60

The IRR for A is 24 percent, and the IRR for B is 21 percent. Since these investments are mutually exclusive, we can only take one of them. Simple intuition suggests that Investment A is better because of its higher return. Unfortunately, simple intuition is not always correct.

To see why Investment A is not necessarily the better of the two investments, we've calculated the NPV of these investments for different required returns:

Discount Rate	NPV (A)	NPV (B)
0%	$60.00	$70.00
5	43.13	47.88
10	29.06	29.79
15	17.18	14.82
20	7.06	2.31
25	−1.63	−8.22

The IRR for A (24 percent) is larger than the IRR for B (21 percent). However, if you compare the NPVs, you'll see that which investment has the higher NPV depends on our required return. B has greater total cash flow, but it pays back more slowly than A. As a result, it has a higher NPV at lower discount rates.

In our example, the NPV and IRR rankings conflict for some discount rates. If our required return is 10 percent, for instance, then B has the higher NPV and is thus the better of the two, even though A has the higher return. If our required return is 15 percent, then there is no ranking conflict: A is better.

The conflict between the IRR and NPV for mutually exclusive investments can be illustrated by plotting their NPV profiles as we have done in Figure 8.7. In Figure 8.7, notice that the NPV profiles cross at 11.1 percent. Notice also that at any discount rate less than 11.1 percent, the NPV for B is higher. In this range, taking B benefits us more than taking A, even though A's IRR is higher. At any rate greater than 11.1 percent, Investment A has the greater NPV.

This example illustrates that whenever we have mutually exclusive projects, we shouldn't rank them based on their returns. More generally, anytime we are comparing investments to determine which is best, IRRs can be misleading. Instead, we need to look at the relative NPVs to avoid the possibility of choosing incorrectly. Remember, we're ultimately interested in creating value for the shareholders, so the option with the higher NPV is preferred, regardless of the relative returns.

If this seems counterintuitive, think of it this way. Suppose you have two investments. One has a 10 percent return and makes you $100 richer immediately. The other has a 20 percent return and makes you $50 richer immediately. Which one do you like better? We would rather have $100 than $50, regardless of the returns, so we like the first one better.

As we saw from Figure 8.7, the crossover rate for Investment A and Investment B is 11.1 percent. You might be wondering how we got this number. Actually, the calculation

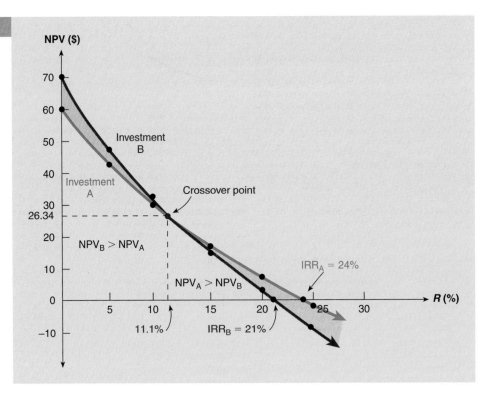

FIGURE 8.7

NPV profiles for mutually exclusive investments

is fairly easy. We begin by subtracting the cash flows of one project from the cash flows of the second project. In this case, we will subtract Investment B from Investment A. Doing so, we get:

Year	Investment A	Investment B	Cash Flow Difference (A – B)
0	−$100	−$100	$ 0
1	50	20	30
2	40	40	0
3	40	50	− 10
4	30	60	− 30

Now all we have to do is calculate the IRR for these differential cash flows, which works out to be 11.1 percent. Verify for yourself that if you subtract Investment A's cash flows from Investment B's cash flows the crossover rate is still 11.1 percent, so it doesn't matter which one you subtract from which.

Redeeming Qualities of the IRR

Despite its flaws, the IRR is very popular in practice, more so than even the NPV. It probably survives because it fills a need that the NPV does not. In analyzing investments, people in general, and financial analysts in particular, seem to prefer talking about rates of return rather than dollar values.

In a similar vein, the IRR also appears to provide a simple way of communicating information about a proposal. One manager might say to another, "Remodelling the clerical wing has a 20 percent return." This may somehow be simpler than saying, "At a 10 percent discount rate, the net present value is $4,000."

Finally, under certain circumstances, the IRR may have a practical advantage over the NPV. We can't estimate the NPV unless we know the appropriate discount rate, but we can still estimate the IRR. Suppose we didn't know the required return on an investment, but we found, for example, that it had a 40 percent return. We would probably be inclined to take it since it is very unlikely that the required return would be that high. The advantages and disadvantages of the IRR are summarized below.

Advantages and Disadvantages of the Internal Rate of Return	
Advantages	**Disadvantages**
1. Closely related to NPV, often leading to identical decisions.	1. May result in multiple answers with nonconventional cash flows.
2. Easy to understand and communicate.	2. May lead to incorrect decisions in comparisons of mutually exclusive investments.

CONCEPT QUESTIONS

8.3a Under what circumstances will the IRR and NPV rules lead to the same accept-reject decisions? When might they conflict?

8.3b Is it generally true that an advantage of the IRR rule over the NPV rule is that we don't need to know the required return to use the IRR rule?

8.4 | THE PROFITABILITY INDEX

profitability index (PI)
The present value of an investment's future cash flows divided by its initial cost. Also, *benefit-cost ratio*.

Another method used to evaluate projects involves the **profitability index (PI)**, or benefit-cost ratio. This index is defined as the present value of the future cash flows divided by the initial investment. So, if a project costs $200 and the present value of its future cash flows is $220, the profitability index value would be $220/200 = 1.10. Notice that the NPV for this investment is $20, so it is a desirable investment.

More generally, if a project has a positive NPV, then the present value of the future cash flows must be bigger than the initial investment. The profitability index would thus be bigger than 1.00 for a positive NPV investment and less than 1.00 for a negative NPV investment.

How do we interpret the profitability index? In our example, the PI was 1.10. This tells us that, per dollar invested, $1.10 in value or $.10 in NPV results. The profitability index thus measures "bang for the buck," that is, the value created per dollar invested. For this reason, it is often proposed as a measure of performance for government or other not-for-profit investments. Also, when capital is scarce, it may make sense to allocate it to those projects with the highest PIs.

The PI is obviously very similar to the NPV. However, consider an investment that costs $5 and has a $10 present value and an investment that costs $100 with a $150 present value. The first of these investments has an NPV of $5 and a PI of 2. The second has an NPV of $50 and a PI of 1.50. If these are mutually exclusive investments, then the second one is preferred, even though it has a lower PI. This ranking problem is very similar to the IRR ranking problem we saw in the previous section. In all, there seems to be little reason to rely on the PI instead of the NPV. Our discussion of the PI is summarized below.

Advantages and Disadvantages of the Profitability Index	
Advantages	**Disadvantages**
1. Closely related to NPV, generally leading to identical decisions.	1. May lead to incorrect decisions in comparisons of mutually exclusive investments.
2. Easy to understand and communicate.	
3. May be useful when available investment funds are limited.	

CONCEPT QUESTIONS

8.4a What does the profitability index measure?

8.4b How would you state the profitability index rule?

8.5 | THE PRACTICE OF CAPITAL BUDGETING

Given that NPV seems to be telling us directly what we want to know, you might be wondering why there are so many other procedures and why alternative procedures are commonly used. Recall that we are trying to make an investment decision and that we are frequently operating under considerable uncertainty about the future. We can only *estimate*

Average ranking of techniques (1 – most important)				
	Country		Firm Size	
Capital Budgeting Technique	Canada	United States	Large	Small
Net Present Value	1.98	2.00	1.5	2.2
Internal Rate of Return	2.22	1.73	1.7	2.2
Payback Period	2.42	2.59	3.0	2.3
Discounted Payback Period	3.05	3.34	3.1	3.3
Accounting Rate of Return	3.37	3.53	3.6	3.5
Modified Internal Rate of Return	3.78	3.97	4.0	3.7

TABLE 8.4

Capital budgeting techniques in practice

Source: J. D. Payne, W. C. Heath, and L. R. Gale, "Comparative Financial Practice in the US and Canada: Capital Budgeting and Risk Assessment Techniques," *Financial Practice and Education* 9 (Spring/Summer, 1999), pp. 16–24. Used with permission of Financial Management Association, University of South Florida, Tampa, FL 33620-5500, Phone: 813-974-2084.

the NPV of an investment in this case. The resulting estimate can be very "soft," meaning that the true NPV might be quite different.

Because the true NPV is unknown, the astute financial manager seeks clues to assess whether the estimated NPV is reliable. For this reason, firms would typically use multiple criteria for evaluating a proposal. For example, suppose we have an investment with a positive estimated NPV. Based on our experience with other projects, this one appears to have a short payback. In this case, the different indicators seem to agree that it's "all systems go." Put another way, the payback is consistent with the conclusion that the NPV is positive.

On the other hand, suppose we had a positive estimated NPV and a long payback. This could still be a good investment, but it looks like we need to be more careful in making the decision, since we are getting conflicting signals. If the estimated NPV is based on projections in which we have little confidence, then further analysis is probably in order. We will consider how to go about this analysis in more detail in the next chapter.

There have been a number of surveys conducted asking firms what types of investment criteria they actually use. Table 8.4 summarizes the results of a survey of managers at both large and small firms in Canada and the United States. A total of 155 managers responded, 65 from Canada and 90 from the U.S. Managers were asked to rank the importance of each of the capital budgeting techniques used in evaluating capital investment opportunities as one of the questions. Not surprisingly, NPV and IRR are the two most important techniques, particularly at larger firms. Canadian managers, however, seem to prefer NPV to IRR, while U.S. managers seem to prefer IRR to NPV. Their ranking of all other techniques is almost identical. After NPV and IRR, the payback criterion is the next most important technique. In fact, among smaller firms, payback is ranked just about as high as NPV and IRR. Accounting rates of return and other techniques are less important. For quick reference, all techniques discussed in this chapter are briefly summarized in Table 8.5.

CONCEPT QUESTIONS

8.5a What are the most commonly used capital budgeting procedures?

8.5b Since NPV is conceptually the best tool for capital budgeting, why do you think multiple measures are used in practice?

TABLE 8.5

Summary of investment criteria

I. Discounted cash flow criteria

 A. *Net present value (NPV)*. The NPV of an investment is the difference between its market value and its cost. The NPV rule is to take a project if its NPV is positive. NPV is frequently estimated by calculating the present value of the future cash flows (to estimate market value) and then subtracting the cost. NPV has no serious flaws; it is the preferred decision criterion.

 B. *Internal rate of return (IRR)*. The IRR is the discount rate that makes the estimated NPV of an investment equal to zero; it is sometimes called the *discounted cash flow (DCF) return*. The IRR rule is to take a project when its IRR exceeds the required return. IRR is closely related to NPV, and it leads to exactly the same decisions as NPV for conventional, independent projects. When project cash flows are not conventional, there may be no IRR or there may be more than one. More seriously, the IRR cannot be used to rank mutually exclusive projects; the project with the highest IRR is not necessarily the preferred investment.

 C. *Profitability index (PI)*. The PI, also called the *benefit-cost ratio*, is the ratio of present value to cost. The PI rule is to take an investment if the index exceeds 1. The PI measures the present value of an investment per dollar invested. It is quite similar to NPV, but, like IRR, it cannot be used to rank mutually exclusive projects. However, it is sometimes used to rank projects when a firm has more positive NPV investments than it can currently finance.

II. Payback criteria

 A. *Payback period*. The payback period is the length of time until the sum of an investment's cash flows equals its cost. The payback period rule is to take a project if its payback is *less* than some cutoff. The payback period is a flawed criterion primarily because it ignores risk, the time value of money, and cash flows beyond the cutoff point.

SUMMARY AND CONCLUSIONS

This chapter has covered the different criteria used to evaluate proposed investments. The four criteria, in the order in which we discussed them, are:

1. Net present value (NPV)

 NPV = Present value of future cash flows − Investment cost.

2. Payback period

 Payback period = Number of years that pass before the sum of an investment's cash flows equals the cost of the investment.

3. Internal rate of return (IRR)

 IRR = Discount rate that makes the net present value of an investment equal to zero.

4. Profitability index (PI)

$$PI = \frac{\text{Present value of future cash flows}}{\text{Investment cost}}$$

We illustrated how to calculate each of these and discussed the interpretation of the results. We also described the advantages and disadvantages of each of them. Ultimately, a good capital budgeting criterion must tell us two things. First, is a particular project a good investment? Second, if we have more than one good project, but we can only take one of them, which one should we take? The main point of this chapter is that only the NPV criterion can always provide the correct answer to both questions.

For this reason, NPV is one of the two or three most important concepts in finance, and we will refer to it many times in the chapters ahead. When we do, keep two things in mind: (1) NPV is always just the difference between the market value of an asset or project and its cost and (2) the financial manager acts in the shareholders' best interests by identifying and taking positive NPV projects.

Finally, we noted that NPVs can't normally be observed in the market; instead, they must be estimated. Because there is always the possibility of a poor estimate, financial managers use multiple criteria for examining projects. These other criteria provide additional information about whether a project truly has a positive NPV.

CHAPTER REVIEW AND SELF-TEST PROBLEMS

8.1 Investment Criteria.   This problem will give you some practice calculating NPVs and paybacks. A proposed overseas expansion has the following cash flows:

Year	Cash Flow
0	−$100
1	50
2	40
3	40
4	15

Calculate the payback and NPV at a required return of 15 percent.

8.2 Mutually Exclusive Investments.   Consider the following two mutually exclusive investments. Calculate the IRR for each. Under what circumstances will the IRR and NPV criteria rank the two projects differently?

Year	Investment A	Investment B
0	−$100	−$100
1	50	70
2	70	75
3	40	10

■ Answers to Chapter Review and Self-Test Problems

8.1   In the table below, we have listed the cash flows and their discounted values (at 15 percent).

Cash Flow		
Year	Undiscounted	Discounted (at 15%)
1	$ 50	$ 43.48
2	40	30.25
3	40	26.30
4	15	8.58
Total	$145	$108.6

Recall that the initial investment is $100. Examining the undiscounted cash flows, we see that the payback occurs between Years 2 and 3. The cash flows for the first two years are $90 total, so, going into the third year, we are short by $10. The total cash flow in Year 3 is $40, so the payback is 2 + $10/40 = 2.25 years.

Looking at the discounted cash flows, we see that the sum is $108.6, so the NPV is $8.6.

8.2   To calculate the IRR, we might try some guesses as in the following table:

Discount Rate	NPV(A)	NPV(B)
0%	$60.00	$55.00
10	33.36	33.13
20	13.43	16.20
30	−1.91	2.78
40	−13.99	−8.09

Several things are immediately apparent from our guesses. First, the IRR on A must be just a little less than 30 percent (why?). With some more effort, we find that it's 28.61 percent. For B, the IRR must be a little more than 30 percent (again, why?); it works out to be 32.37 percent. Also, notice that at 10 percent, the NPVs are very close, indicating that the NPV profiles cross in that vicinity. Verify that the NPVs are the same at 10.61 percent.

Now, the IRR for B is always higher. As we've seen, A has the larger NPV for any discount rate less than 10.61 percent, so the NPV and IRR rankings will conflict in that range. Remember, if there's a conflict, we will go with the higher NPV. Our decision rule is thus very simple: Take A if the required return is less than 10.61 percent, take B if the required return is between 10.61 percent and 32.37 percent (the IRR on B), and take neither if the required return is more than 32.37 percent.

CRITICAL THINKING AND CONCEPTS REVIEW

8.1   **Payback Period and Net Present Value.**   If a project with conventional cash flows has a payback period less than its life, can you definitively state the algebraic sign of the NPV? Why or why not?

8.2   **Net Present Value.**   Suppose a project has conventional cash flows and a positive NPV. What do you know about its payback? Its profitability index? Its IRR? Explain.

8.3   **Payback Period.**   Concerning payback:

a.   Describe how the payback period is calculated and describe the information this measure provides about a sequence of cash flows. What is the payback criterion decision rule?

b.   What are the problems associated with using the payback period as a means of evaluating cash flows?

c.   What are the advantages of using the payback period to evaluate cash flows? Are there any circumstances under which using payback might be appropriate? Explain.

8.4   **Net Present Value.**   Concerning NPV:

a.   Describe how NPV is calculated and describe the information this measure provides about a sequence of cash flows. What is the NPV criterion decision rule?

b.   Why is NPV considered to be a superior method of evaluating the cash flows from a project? Suppose the NPV for a project's cash flows is computed to be $2,500. What does this number represent with respect to the firm's shareholders?

8.5   **Internal Rate of Return.**   Concerning IRR:

a.   Describe how the IRR is calculated, and describe the information this measure provides about a sequence of cash flows. What is the IRR criterion decision rule?

b.   What is the relationship between IRR and NPV? Are there any situations in which you might prefer one method over the other? Explain.

c.   Despite its shortcomings in some situations, why do most financial managers use IRR along with NPV when evaluating projects? Can you think of a situation in which IRR might be a more appropriate measure to use than NPV? Explain.

8.6   **Profitability Index.**   Concerning the profitability index:

a.   Describe how the profitability index is calculated and describe the information this measure provides about a sequence of cash flows. What is the profitability index decision rule?

b.   What is the relationship between the profitability index and the NPV? Are there any situations in which you might prefer one method over the other? Explain.

8.7   **Payback and Internal Rate of Return.**   A project has perpetual cash flows of *C* per period, a cost of *I,* and a required return of *R*. What is the relationship between the project's payback and its IRR? What implications does your answer have for long-lived projects with relatively constant cash flows?

8.8   **International Investment Projects.**   In May 2006, Japanese auto maker Honda announced plans to build an engine plant in Alliston, Ontario. Honda apparently felt that it would be better able to compete and create value with Canadian-based facilities. Other companies, such as 3M and the Swiss pharmaceutical company Sandoz, have reached similar conclusions and taken similar actions. What are some of the reasons that foreign manufacturers of products as diverse as automobiles, tapes, and prescription drugs might arrive at this same conclusion?

8.9   Capital Budgeting Problems.   What are some of the difficulties that might come up in actual applications of the various criteria we discussed in this chapter? Which one would be the easiest to implement in actual applications? The most difficult?

8.10   Capital Budgeting in Not-for-Profit Entities.   Are the capital budgeting criteria we discussed applicable to not-for-profit corporations? How should such entities make capital budgeting decisions? What about the Canadian government? Should it evaluate spending proposals using these techniques?

8.11   Internal Rate of Return.   In a previous chapter, we discussed the yield to maturity (YTM) of a bond. In what ways are the IRR and the YTM similar? How are they different?

QUESTIONS AND PROBLEMS

**Basic
(Questions 1–21)**

1.   Calculating Payback.   What is the payback period for the following set of cash flows?

Year	Cash Flow
0	−$2,500
1	600
2	1,300
3	800
4	600

2.   Calculating Payback.   An investment project provides cash inflows of $830 per year for eight years. What is the project payback period if the initial cost is $3,400? What if the initial cost is $4,450? What if it is $6,800?

 3.   Calculating Payback.   Offshore Drilling Products, Inc., imposes a payback cutoff of three years for its international investment projects. If the company has the following two projects available, should it accept either of them?

Year	Cash Flow (A)	Cash Flow (B)
0	−$45,000	−$ 90,000
1	17,000	20,000
2	20,000	25,000
3	18,000	30,000
4	9,000	250,000

4.   Calculating NPV.   For the cash flows in the previous problem, suppose the firm uses the NPV decision rule. If the discount rate is 20 percent, should the company accept either of the projects?

 5.   Calculating IRR.   A firm evaluates all of its projects by applying the IRR rule. If the required return is 18 percent, should the firm accept the following project?

Year	Cash Flow
0	−$100,000
1	45,000
2	52,000
3	43,000

6. **Calculating NPV.** For the cash flows in the previous problem, suppose the firm uses the NPV decision rule. At a required return of 11 percent, should the firm accept this project? What if the required return was 23 percent?

7. **Calculating NPV and IRR.**   A project that provides annual cash flows of $1,200 for nine years costs $5,200 today. Is this a good project if the required return is 8 percent? What if it's 24 percent? At what discount rate would you be indifferent between accepting the project and rejecting it?

8. **Calculating IRR.** What is the IRR of the following set of cash flows?

Year	Cash Flow
0	−$28,000
1	12,500
2	18,700
3	11,800

9. **Calculating NPV.** For the cash flows in the previous problem, what is the NPV at a discount rate of zero percent? What if the discount rate is 10 percent? If it is 20 percent? If it is 30 percent?

10. **NPV versus IRR.** Wilbert & Sacha, LLC, has identified the following two mutually exclusive projects:

Year	Cash Flow (A)	Cash Flow (B)
0	−$30,000	−$30,000
1	16,000	6,000
2	13,000	11,000
3	8,000	12,000
4	5,000	19,000

a. What is the IRR for each of these projects? If you apply the IRR decision rule, which project should the company accept? Is this decision necessarily correct?

b. If the required return is 11 percent, what is the NPV for each of these projects? Which project will you choose if you apply the NPV decision rule?

c. Over what range of discount rates would you choose Project A? Project B? At what discount rate would you be indifferent between these two projects? Explain.

11. **NPV versus IRR.** Consider the following two mutually exclusive projects:

Year	Cash Flow (X)	Cash Flow (Y)
0	−$5,000	−$5,000
1	2,700	2,300
2	1,700	1,800
3	2,300	2,700

Sketch the NPV profiles for X and Y over a range of discount rates from zero to 25 percent. What is the crossover rate for these two projects?

12. Problems with IRR. Alberta Petroleum, Inc., is trying to evaluate a generation project with the following cash flows:

Year	Cash Flow
0	−$28,000,000
1	53,000,000
2	− 8,000,000

a. If the company requires a 10 percent return on its investments, should it accept this project? Why?

b. Compute the IRR for this project. How many IRRs are there? If you apply the IRR decision rule, should you accept the project or not? What's going on here?

 13. Calculating Profitability Index. What is the profitability index for the following set of cash flows if the relevant discount rate is 10 percent? What if the discount rate is 15 percent? If it is 22 percent?

Year	Cash Flow
0	−$15,000
1	9,000
2	6,000
3	4,500

14. Problems with Profitability Index. The Churchill Corporation is trying to choose between the following two mutually exclusive design projects:

Year	Cash Flow (I)	Cash Flow (II)
0	−$35,000	−$5,500
1	12,000	2,800
2	16,000	2,600
3	19,000	2,400

a. If the required return is 11 percent and Churchill applies the profitability index decision rule, which project should the firm accept?

b. If the company applies the NPV decision rule, which project should it take?

c. Explain why your answers in (a) and (b) are different.

15. Comparing Investment Criteria. Consider the following two mutually exclusive projects:

Year	Cash Flow (A)	Cash Flow (B)
0	−$252,000	−$24,000
1	18,000	14,400
2	36,000	12,600
3	38,400	11,400
4	510,000	9,800

Whichever project you choose, if any, you require a 15 percent return on your investment.

a. If you apply the payback criterion, which investment will you choose? Why?

b. If you apply the NPV criterion, which investment will you choose? Why?

c. If you apply the IRR criterion, which investment will you choose? Why?

d. If you apply the profitability index criterion, which investment will you choose? Why?

e. Based on your answers in (*a*) through (*d*), which project will you finally choose? Why?

16. **NPV and IRR.** Winnipeg Company is presented with the following two mutually exclusive projects. The required return for both projects is 15 percent.

Year	Project M	Project N
0	−$175,000	−$280,000
1	65,000	100,000
2	85,000	140,000
3	75,000	120,000
4	65,000	80,000

a. What is the IRR for each project?

b. What is the NPV for each project?

c. Which, if either, of the projects should the company accept?

17. **NPV and Profitability Index.** Yukon Manufacturing has the following two possible projects. The required return is 12 percent.

Year	Project Y	Project Z
0	−$45,000	−$65,000
1	18,000	26,000
2	17,000	24,000
3	16,000	22,000
4	15,000	22,000

a. What is the profitability index for each project?

b. What is the NPV for each project?

c. Which, if either, of the projects should the company accept?

18. **Crossover Point.** Makwa Enterprises has gathered projected cash flows for two projects. At what interest rate would Makwa be indifferent between the two projects? Which project is better if the required return is above this interest rate? Why?

Year	Project I	Project J
0	−$120,000	−$120,000
1	50,000	43,000
2	48,000	46,000
3	46,000	49,000
4	44,000	52,000

19. **Payback Period and IRR.** Suppose you have a project with a payback period exactly equal to the life of the project. What do you know about the IRR of the project? Suppose that the payback period is never. What do you know about the IRR of the project now?

20. **NPV and Discount Rates.** An investment has an installed cost of $513,250. The cash flows over the four-year life of the investment are projected to be $180,124, $195,467, $141,386, and $130,287. If the discount rate is zero, what is the NPV? If the discount rate is infinite, what is the NPV? At what discount rate is the NPV just equal to zero? Sketch the NPV profile for this investment based on these three points.

21. **NPV and Payback Period.** Kaleb Konstruction, Inc., has the following mutually exclusive projects available. The company has historically used a three-year cutoff for projects. The required return is 10 percent.

Year	Project F	Project G
0	−$150,000	−$240,000
1	80,000	60,000
2	60,000	70,000
3	75,000	90,000
4	60,000	140,000
5	50,000	120,000

a. Calculate the payback period for both projects.
b. Calculate the NPV for both projects.
c. Which project, if any, should the company accept?

Intermediate
(Questions 22–26)

22. **Crossover and NPV.** Burns Auto has the following two mutually exclusive projects available.

Year	Project R	Project S
0	−$40,000	−$58,000
1	20,000	24,000
2	15,000	24,000
3	15,000	18,000
4	8,000	12,000
5	8,000	12,000

What is the crossover rate for these two projects? What is the NPV of each project at the crossover rate?

23. **Calculating IRR.** A project has the following cash flows:

Year	Cash Flow
0	$64,000
1	− 30,000
2	− 48,000

What is the IRR for this project? If the required return is 12 percent, should the firm accept the project? What is the NPV of this project? What is the NPV of the project if the required return is 0 percent? 24 percent? What is going on here? Sketch the NPV profile to help you with your answer.

24. **Multiple IRRs.**   This problem is useful for testing the ability of financial calculators and computer software. Consider the following cash flows. When should we take this project? (Hint: search for IRRs between 20 percent and 70 percent.)

Year	Cash Flow
0	–$ 504
1	2,862
2	– 6,070
3	5,700
4	– 2,000

25. **NPV and the Profitability Index.**   If we define the NPV index as the ratio of NPV to cost, what is the relationship between this index and the profitability index?

26. **Cash Flow Intuition.**   A project has an initial cost of I, has a required return of R, and pays C annually for N years.

  a.   Find C in terms of I and N such that the project has a payback period just equal to its life.

  b.   Find C in terms of I, N, and R such that this is a profitable project according to the NPV decision rule.

  c.   Find C in terms of I, N, and R such that the project has a benefit-cost ratio of 2.

27. **NPV and IRR.**   The Rockies Adventure company is considering a project with an initial cash outflow of $50,000. A cash flow at the end of the first year will be $3,000, and the cash flows are projected to grow at an annual rate of 6 percent forever. The company's required rate of return is 9 percent.

  Challenge
  (Questions 27–28)

  a.   What is the project NPV?

  b.   What is the project IRR?

  c.   At what growth rate in its cash flows would the company be indifferent between accepting the project and rejecting it?

28. **NPV.**   The Victoria company is considering the installation of new, energy-efficient lighting in its headquarters tower in Montreal at the cost of $10,000. This new lighting will save 1,200 kilowatt-hours (kwh) of electricity each month. The cost of electricity is rising steadily, starting today. Next month the cost of one kwh will be $0.07, and the cost is expected to rise at the same rate each month forever. The Victoria's required return is 12 percent per year, compounded monthly. What is the minimum monthly kwh percentage rate increase that would make the installation of the new lighting worthwhile?

647,264

WHAT'S ON THE WEB?

8.1 Net Present Value.   You have a project that has an initial cash outflow of –$20,000 and cash inflows of $6,000, $5,000, $4,000, and $3,000, respectively, for the next four years. Go to **www.datadynamica.com** and follow the "On-line IRR NPV Calculator" link. Enter the cash flows. If the required return is 12 percent, what is the NPV of the project? The IRR?

8.2 Internal Rate of Return.   Using the online calculator from the previous problem, find the IRR for a project with cash flows of –$500, $1,200, and –$400. What is going on here?

Making Capital Investment Decisions

In September 2006, CanJet Airlines, the Halifax-based discount air carrier, suddenly halted all regularly scheduled flights, blaming fierce competition, rising airport fees, and high fuel prices. This decision brought to an end CanJet's plan of becoming a national carrier, and was not the first project abandoned by this four-year-old airline. Earlier, in 2004, when larger competitor WestJet Airlines moved its eastern hub from Hamilton to Toronto, CanJet increased the number of its flights from the Hamilton International airport. The next year, however, it ceased operations from Hamilton. In 2005, CanJet started seasonal flights to Vancouver, only to discontinue them soon after.

In November 2006, after cancelling its scheduled service, CanJet Airlines began charter flights to popular sun spot destinations. The charter business carries less risk than regularly scheduled flights, but usually offers lower profit margins. Time will show whether this was a good decision.

Naturally, CanJet Airlines had not planned to abandon its earlier projects, but it happened. For example, as the short life and quick death of its flights to Vancouver shows, projects don't always go the way companies think they will. This chapter explores how this can happen, and what companies can do to analyze and possibly avoid these situations.

In broader terms, this chapter follows up on our previous one by delving more deeply into capital budgeting. We have two main tasks. First, recall that in the last chapter, we saw that cash flow estimates are the critical input into a net present value analysis, but we didn't say very much about where these cash flows come from; so, we will now examine this question in some detail. Our second goal is to learn how to critically examine NPV estimates and, in particular, how to evaluate the sensitivity of NPV estimates to assumptions made about the uncertain future.

After studying this chapter, you should have a good understanding of:

9.1 How to determine relevant cash flows for a proposed investment.

9.2 Different types of incremental cash flows.

9.3 How to prepare pro forma financial statements and estimate project cash flows.

9.4 The impact of net working capital and depreciation on project cash flow.

9.5 Forecasting risk and sources of value in a new project.

9.6 How to use scenario and sensitivity analyses.

9.7 Different managerial options and capital rationing.

So far, we've covered various parts of the capital budgeting decision. Our task in this chapter is to start bringing these pieces together. In particular, we will show you how to "spread the numbers" for a proposed investment or project and, based on those numbers, make an initial assessment about whether or not the project should be undertaken.

In the discussion that follows, we focus on the process of setting up a discounted cash flow analysis. From the last chapter, we know that the projected future cash flows are the key element in such an evaluation. Accordingly, we emphasize working with financial and accounting information to come up with these figures.

In evaluating a proposed investment, we pay special attention to deciding what information is relevant to the decision at hand and what information is not. As we shall see, it is easy to overlook important pieces of the capital budgeting puzzle. We also describe how to go about evaluating the results of our discounted cash flow analysis.

9.1 | PROJECT CASH FLOWS: A FIRST LOOK

The effect of taking a project is to change the firm's overall cash flows today and in the future. To evaluate a proposed investment, we must consider these changes in the firm's cash flows and then decide whether or not they add value to the firm. The first (and most important) step, therefore, is to decide which cash flows are relevant and which are not.

Relevant Cash Flows

What is a relevant cash flow for a project? The general principle is simple enough: A relevant cash flow for a project is a change in the firm's overall future cash flow that comes about as a direct consequence of the decision to take that project. Because the relevant cash flows are defined in terms of changes in, or increments to, the firm's existing cash flow, they are called the **incremental cash flows** associated with the project.

The concept of incremental cash flow is central to our analysis, so we will state a general definition and refer back to it as needed:

> The incremental cash flows for project evaluation consist of *any and all* changes in the firm's future cash flows that are a direct consequence of taking the project.

incremental cash flows
The difference between a firm's future cash flows with a project and those without the project.

This definition of incremental cash flows has an obvious and important corollary: Any cash flow that exists regardless of whether or *not* a project is undertaken is *not* relevant.

The Stand-Alone Principle

In practice, it would be very cumbersome to actually calculate the future total cash flows to the firm with and without a project, especially for a large firm. Fortunately, it is not really necessary to do so. Once we identify the effect of undertaking the proposed project on the firm's cash flows, we need only focus on the project's resulting incremental cash flows. This is called the **stand-alone principle**.

What the stand-alone principle says is that, once we have determined the incremental cash flows from undertaking a project, we can view that project as a kind of "minifirm" with its own future revenues and costs, its own assets, and, of course, its own cash flows. We will then be primarily interested in comparing the cash flows from this minifirm to the cost of acquiring it. An important consequence of this approach is that we will be evaluating the proposed project purely on its own merits, in isolation from any other activities or projects.

stand-alone principle
The assumption that evaluation of a project may be based solely on that project's incremental cash flows.

CONCEPT QUESTIONS

9.1a   What are the relevant incremental cash flows for project evaluation?

9.1b   What is the stand-alone principle?

9.2 | INCREMENTAL CASH FLOWS

We are concerned here only with those cash flows that are incremental and that result from a project. Looking back at our general definition, it seems easy enough to decide whether a cash flow is incremental or not. Even so, there are a few situations where mistakes are easy to make. In this section, we describe some of these common pitfalls and how to avoid them.

Sunk Costs

sunk cost
A cost that has already been incurred and cannot be recouped and therefore should not be considered in an investment decision.

A **sunk cost**, by definition, is a cost we have already paid or have already incurred the liability to pay. Such a cost cannot be changed by the decision today to accept or reject a project. Put another way, the firm will have to pay this cost no matter what. Based on our general definition of incremental cash flow, such a cost is clearly not relevant to the decision at hand. So, we will always be careful to exclude sunk costs from our analysis.

That a sunk cost is not relevant seems obvious given our discussion. Nonetheless, it's easy to fall prey to the sunk cost fallacy. For example, suppose Canadian Syrup Company hires a financial consultant to help evaluate whether or not a line of maple syrup should be launched. When the consultant turns in the report, Canadian Syrup objects to the analysis because the consultant did not include the hefty consulting fee as a cost of the maple syrup project.

Who is correct? By now, we know that the consulting fee is a sunk cost, because the consulting fee must be paid whether or not the maple syrup line is actually launched (this is an attractive feature of the consulting business).

Opportunity Costs

opportunity cost
The most valuable alternative that is given up if a particular investment is undertaken.

When we think of costs, we normally think of out-of-pocket costs, namely, those that require us to actually spend some amount of cash. An **opportunity cost** is slightly different; it requires us to give up a benefit. A common situation arises where a firm already owns some of the assets a proposed project will be using. For example, we might be thinking of converting an old rustic cotton mill we bought years ago for $100,000 into "upmarket" condominiums.

If we undertake this project, there will be no direct cash outflow associated with buying the old mill since we already own it. For purposes of evaluating the condo project, should we then treat the mill as "free"? The answer is no. The mill is a valuable resource used by the project. If we didn't use it here, we could do something else with it. Like what? The obvious answer is that, at a minimum, we could sell it. Using the mill for the condo complex thus has an opportunity cost: We give up the valuable opportunity to do something else with it.[1]

---

[1]Economists sometimes use the acronym *TANSTAAFL,* which is short for "There ain't no such thing as a free lunch," to describe the fact that only very rarely is something truly free.

There is another issue here. Once we agree that the use of the mill has an opportunity cost, how much should the condo project be charged? Given that we paid $100,000, it might seem that we should charge this amount to the condo project. Is this correct? The answer is no, and the reason is based on our discussion concerning sunk costs.

The fact that we paid $100,000 some years ago is irrelevant. That cost is sunk. At a minimum, the opportunity cost that we charge the project is what the mill would sell for today (net of any selling costs), because this is the amount that we give up by using it instead of selling it.

Side Effects

Remember that the incremental cash flows for a project include all the changes in the *firm's* future cash flows. It would not be unusual for a project to have side, or spillover, effects, both good and bad. For example, if Bombardier introduces a new line of corporate jets, some of the sales might come at the expense of its other corporate jets. This is called **erosion**, and the same general problem could occur for any multiline consumer product producer or seller.[2] In this case, the cash flows from the new line should be adjusted downward to reflect lost profits on other lines.

In accounting for erosion, it is important to recognize that any sales lost as a result of our launching a new product might be lost anyway because of future competition. Erosion is only relevant when the sales would not otherwise be lost.

erosion
The cash flows of a new project that come at the expense of a firm's existing projects.

Net Working Capital

Normally, a project will require that the firm invest in net working capital in addition to long-term assets. For example, a project will generally need some amount of cash on hand to pay any expenses that arise. In addition, a project will need an initial investment in inventories and accounts receivable (to cover credit sales). Some of this financing will be in the form of amounts owed to suppliers (accounts payable), but the firm will have to supply the balance. This balance represents the investment in net working capital.

It's easy to overlook an important feature of net working capital in capital budgeting. As a project winds down, inventories are sold, receivables are collected, bills are paid, and cash balances can be drawn down. These activities free up the net working capital originally invested. So, the firm's investment in project net working capital closely resembles a loan. The firm supplies working capital at the beginning and recovers it towards the end.

Financing Costs

In analyzing a proposed investment, we will not include interest paid or any other financing costs such as dividends or principal repaid, because we are interested in the cash flow generated by the assets of the project. As we mentioned in Chapter 2, interest paid, for example, is a component of cash flow to creditors, not cash flow from assets.

More generally, our goal in project evaluation is to compare the cash flow from a project to the cost of acquiring that project in order to estimate NPV. The particular mixture of debt and equity a firm actually chooses to use in financing a project is a managerial variable and primarily determines how project cash flow is divided between owners and creditors. This is not to say that financing arrangements are unimportant. They are just something to be analyzed separately. We will cover this in Chapter 13.

---

[2]More colourfully, erosion is sometimes called *piracy* or *cannibalism*.

Other Issues

There are some other things to watch out for. First, we are only interested in measuring cash flow. Moreover, we are interested in measuring it when it actually occurs, not when it accrues in an accounting sense. Second, we are always interested in *aftertax* cash flow since taxes are definitely a cash outflow. In fact, whenever we write "incremental cash flows," we mean aftertax incremental cash flows. Remember, however, that aftertax cash flow and accounting profit, or net income, are entirely different things.

CONCEPT QUESTIONS

9.2a   What is a sunk cost? An opportunity cost?

9.2b   Explain what erosion is and why it is relevant.

9.2c   Explain why interest paid is not a relevant cash flow for project evaluation.

9.3 | PRO FORMA FINANCIAL STATEMENTS AND PROJECT CASH FLOWS

The first thing we need when we begin evaluating a proposed investment is a set of pro forma, or projected, financial statements. Given these, we can develop the projected cash flows from the project. Once we have the cash flows, we can estimate the value of the project using the techniques we described in the previous chapter.

Getting Started: Pro Forma Financial Statements

pro forma financial statements
Financial statements projecting future years' operations.

Pro forma financial statements are a convenient and easily understood means of summarizing much of the relevant information for a project. To prepare these statements, we will need estimates of quantities such as unit sales, the selling price per unit, the variable cost per unit, and total fixed costs. We will also need to know the total investment required, including any investment in net working capital.

To illustrate, suppose we think we can sell 50,000 cans of bear attractant per year at a price of $4.00 per can. It costs us about $2.50 per can to make the attractant, and a new product such as this one typically has only a three-year life (perhaps because the customer base dwindles rapidly). We require a 20 percent return on new products.

Fixed costs for the project, including such things as rent on the production facility, will run $12,000 per year. Further, we will need to invest a total of $90,000 in manufacturing equipment. For simplicity, we will assume that this $90,000 will be depreciated straight-line to zero over the three-year life of the project.[3] Furthermore, the cost of removing the equipment will roughly equal its actual value in three years, so it will be essentially worthless on a market value basis as well. Finally, the project will require an initial $20,000 investment in net working capital. As usual, the tax rate is 34 percent.

In Table 9.1, we organize these initial projections by first preparing the pro forma income statement for each of the three years. Once again, notice that we have *not* deducted any interest expense. This will always be so. As we described earlier, interest paid is a financing expense, not a component of operating cash flow.

We can also prepare a series of abbreviated balance sheets that show the capital requirements for the project as we've done in Table 9.2. Here we have net working capital

---

[3]We introduce real-life complications of depreciation in the next section.

		TABLE **9.1**
Sales (50,000 units at $4.00/unit)	$200,000	**Projected income statement, bear attractant project, years 1–3**
Variable costs ($2.50/unit)	125,000	
Gross profit	$ 75,000	
Fixed costs	12,000	
Depreciation ($90,000/3)	30,000	
EBIT	$ 33,000	
Taxes (34%)	11,220	
Net income	$ 21,780	

	Year				TABLE **9.2**
	0	**1**	**2**	**3**	**Projected capital requirements, bear attractant project**
Net working capital	$ 20,000	$20,000	$20,000	$ 0	
Net fixed assets	90,000	60,000	30,000	0	
Total investment	$110,000	$80,000	$50,000	$ 0	

of $20,000 in each year except the last one, when it will be recovered. Fixed assets are $90,000 at the start of the project's life (Year 0), and they decline by the $30,000 in depreciation each year, ending up at zero. Notice that the total investment given here for future years is the total book, or accounting, value, not market value.

At this point, we need to start converting this accounting information into cash flows. We consider how to do this next.

Project Cash Flows

To develop the cash flows from a project, we need to recall (from Chapter 2) that cash flow from assets has three components: operating cash flow, capital spending, and additions to net working capital. To evaluate a project, or minifirm, we need to arrive at estimates for each of these.

Once we have estimates of the components of cash flow, we will calculate cash flow for our minifirm just as we did in Chapter 2 for an entire firm:

Project cash flow = Project operating cash flow
                    − Project change in net working capital   **[9.1]**
                    − Project capital spending

We consider these components next.

Project Operating Cash Flow   To determine the operating cash flow associated with a project, we first need to recall the definition of operating cash flow:

Operating cash flow = Earnings before interest and taxes
                      + Depreciation   **[9.2]**
                      − Taxes

To illustrate the calculation of operating cash flow, we will use the projected information from the shark attractant project. For ease of reference, Table 9.3 repeats the income statement.

Sales	$200,000
Variable costs	125,000
Fixed costs	12,000
Depreciation	30,000
EBIT	$ 33,000
Taxes (34%)	11,220
Net income	$ 21,780

EBIT	$33,000
Depreciation	+ 30,000
Taxes	− 11,220
Operating cash flow	$51,780

		Year		
	0	**1**	**2**	**3**
Operating cash flow		$51,780	$51,780	$51,780
Change in NWC	−$ 20,000			+ 20,000
Capital spending	− 90,000			
Total project cash flow	−$110,000	$51,780	$51,780	$71,780

Given the income statement in Table 9.3, calculating the operating cash flow is very straightforward. As we see in Table 9.4, projected operating cash flow for the bear attractant project is $51,780.

Project Net Working Capital and Capital Spending   We next need to take care of the fixed asset and net working capital requirements. Based on our balance sheets above, the firm must spend $90,000 up front for fixed assets and invest an additional $20,000 in net working capital. The immediate outflow is thus $110,000. At the end of the project's life, the fixed assets will be worthless (the salvage value will be zero), but the firm will recover the $20,000 that was tied up in working capital. This will lead to a $20,000 cash *inflow* in the last year.

On a purely mechanical level, notice that whenever we have an investment in net working capital, that same investment has to be recovered; in other words, the same number needs to appear at some time in the future with the opposite sign.

Projected Total Cash Flow and Value

Given the information we've accumulated, we can finish the preliminary cash flow analysis as illustrated in Table 9.5.

Now that we have cash flow projections, we are ready to apply the various criteria we discussed in the last chapter. First, the NPV at the 20 percent required return is:

$$\text{NPV} = -\$110,000 + 51,780/1.2 + 51,780/1.2^2 + 71,780/1.2^3$$
$$= \$10,648$$

So, based on these projections, the project creates over $10,000 in value and should be accepted. Also, the return on this investment obviously exceeds 20 percent (since the NPV is positive at 20 percent). After some trial and error, we find that the IRR works out to be about 25.8 percent.

In addition, if required, we could go ahead and calculate the payback and the Profitability Index, or PI. Inspection of the cash flows shows that the payback on this project is just a little over two years (verify that it's about 2.1 years).

From the last chapter, we know that the PI is the present value of the future cash flows divided by the initial investment. The present value of future cash flows is $51,780/1.2 + 51,780/1.2^2 + 51,780/1.2^3 = \$120,648$. Thus the PI is $\$120,648/110,000 = 1.10$. The PI tells us that the project creates $1.10 in value per each invested dollar.

The Tax Shield Approach

A useful variation on our basic definition of operating cash flow (OCF) is the *tax shield* approach. The tax shield definition of OCF is:

$$\text{OCF} = (\text{Sales} - \text{Costs}) \times (1 - T_c) + \text{Depreciation} \times T_c \qquad \text{[9.3]}$$

where T_c is the corporate tax rate. Assuming that $T_c = 34\%$, the OCF works out to be:

$$
\begin{aligned}
\text{OCF} &= (\$200,000 - 137,000) \times .66 + 30,000 \times .34 \\
&= \$41,580 + 10,200 \\
&= \$51,780
\end{aligned}
$$

This is just as we had before.

This approach views OCF as having two components. The first part is what the project's cash flow would be if there were no depreciation expense. In this case, this would-have-been cash flow is $41,580.

The second part of OCF in this approach is the depreciation deduction multiplied by the tax rate. This is called the **depreciation tax shield**. We know that depreciation is a noncash expense. The only cash flow effect of deducting depreciation is to reduce our taxes, a benefit to us. At the current 34 percent corporate tax rate, every dollar in depreciation expense saves us 34 cents in taxes. So, in our example, the $30,000 depreciation deduction saves us $30,000 \times .34 = \$10,200$ in taxes.

The tax shield approach will always give the same answer as our basic approach, so you might wonder why we bother. The answer is that it is sometimes a little simpler to use, particularly for projects that involve cost-cutting.

depreciation tax shield
The tax saving that results from the depreciation deduction, calculated as depreciation multiplied by the corporate tax rate.

CONCEPT QUESTIONS

9.3a What is the definition of project operating cash flow? How does this differ from net income?

9.3b In the bear attractant project, why did we add back the firm's net working capital investment in the final year?

9.3c What is the "depreciation tax shield"?

9.4 | MORE ON PROJECT CASH FLOW

In this section, we take a closer look at some aspects of project cash flow. In particular, we discuss project net working capital in more detail. We then examine current tax laws regarding depreciation.

A Closer Look at Net Working Capital

In calculating operating cash flow, we did not explicitly consider the fact that some of our sales might be on credit. Also, we may not have actually paid some of the costs shown. In either case, the cash flow has not yet occurred. We show here that these possibilities are not a problem as long as we don't forget to include additions to net working capital in our analysis. This discussion thus emphasizes the importance and the effect of doing so.

Suppose during a particular year of a project we have the following simplified income statement:

Sales	$500
Costs	310
Net income	$190

We assume that depreciation and taxes are zero. No fixed assets are purchased during the year. Also, to illustrate a point, we assume that the only components of net working capital are accounts receivable and payable. The beginning and ending amounts for these accounts are:

	Beginning of Year	End of Year	Change
Accounts receivable	$880	$910	+$30
Accounts payable	550	605	+ 55
Net working capital	$330	$305	−$25

Based on this information, what is total cash flow for the year? We can first just mechanically apply what we have been discussing to come up with the answer. Operating cash flow in this particular case is the same as EBIT and Net Income since there are no taxes or depreciation and thus equals $190. Also, notice that net working capital actually *declined* by $25, so the change in net working capital is negative. This just means that $25 was freed up during the year. There was no capital spending, so the total cash flow for the year is:

$$\text{Total cash flow} = \text{Operating cash flow} - \text{Change in NWC} - \text{Capital spending}$$
$$= \$190 - (-25) - 0$$
$$= \$215$$

Now, we know that this $215 total cash flow has to be "dollars in" less "dollars out" for the year. We could therefore ask a different question: What were cash revenues for the year? Also, what were cash costs?

To determine cash revenues, we need to look more closely at net working capital. During the year, we had sales of $500. However, accounts receivable rose by $30 over the same time period. What does this mean? The $30 increase tells us that sales exceeded collections by $30. In other words, we haven't yet received the cash from $30 of the $500 in sales. As a result, our cash inflow is $500 − 30 = $470. In general, cash income is sales minus the increase in accounts receivable.

Cash outflows can be similarly determined. We show costs of $310 on the income statement, but accounts payable increased by $55 during the year. This means that we have not yet paid $55 of the $310, so cash costs for the period are just $310 − 55 = $255. In other words, in this case, cash costs equal costs less the increase in accounts payable.

Putting this information together, cash inflows less cash outflows is $470 − 255 = $215, just as we had before. Notice that:

$$
\begin{aligned}
\text{Cash flow} &= \text{Cash inflow} - \text{Cash outflow} \\
&= (\$500 - 30) - (310 - 55) \\
&= (\$500 - 310) - (30 - 55) \\
&= \text{Operating cash flow} - \text{Change in NWC} \\
&= \$190 - (-25) \\
&= \$215
\end{aligned}
$$

More generally, this example illustrates that including net working capital changes in our calculations has the effect of adjusting for the discrepancy between accounting sales and costs and actual cash receipts and payments.

Cash Collections and Costs EXAMPLE 9.1

For the year just completed, the Combat Wombat Telestat Co. (CWT) reports sales of $998 and costs of $734. You have collected the following beginning and ending balance sheet information:

	Beginning	Ending
Accounts receivable	$100	$110
Inventory	100	80
Accounts payable	100	70
Net working capital	$100	$120

Based on these figures, what are cash inflows? Cash outflows? What happened to each account? What is net cash flow?

Sales were $998, but receivables rose by $10. So cash collections were $10 less than sales, or $988. Costs were $734, but inventories fell by $20. This means that we didn't replace $20 worth of inventory, so costs are actually overstated by this amount. Also, payables fell by $30. This means that, on a net basis, we actually paid our suppliers $30 more than we received from them, resulting in a $30 understatement of costs. Adjusting for these events, cash costs are $734 − 20 + 30 = $744. Net cash flow is $988 − 744 = $244.

Finally, notice that net working capital increased by $20 overall. We can check our answer by noting that the original accounting sales less costs of $998 − 734 is $264. In addition, CWT spent $20 on net working capital, so the net result is a cash flow of $264 − 20 = $244, as we calculated.

Capital Cost Allowance

As we note elsewhere, accounting depreciation is a noncash deduction. As a result, depreciation has cash flow consequences only because it affects the tax bill. The way that depreciation is computed for tax purposes is thus the relevant method for capital investment decisions. Not surprisingly, the procedures are governed by tax law. The *Income Tax Act* of Canada enables companies to deduct the decline in the value of assets that occurs through their use for income tax purposes. This deduction is called the **Capital Cost Allowance (CCA)**.

capital cost allowance (CCA)
The deduction allowed for income tax purposes in respect to the decline in the value of assets that occurs through their use.

Calculating the CCA is relatively mechanical. While there are a number of *if*s, *and*s, and *but*s involved, the basic idea is that every asset falls into a particular class. All assets of the same class are then depreciated as if they were a single asset. Each class has an assigned CCA rate, based, as a rule, on the expected economic life (how long we expect the asset to be in service) of the assets in that class. For example, buildings have a CCA rate of 4 percent, whereas computer software has a CCA rate of 100 percent. In some cases the government uses the allowable CCA rate as a tool to encourage investment in certain areas. For instance, in the 2005 budget the government created Class 43.2 with an accelerated CCA rate of 50 percent to encourage increased use of renewable energy sources.

For most of the asset classes, the CCA follows the declining balance method. Under this method a specified rate is applied to the remaining balance, and, as a result, both the remaining balance and the CCA decline each successive year. For some assets, such as leasehold improvements, patents, and licenses, the CCA follows the straight-line depreciation method. Several typical asset classes and associated CCA rates are described in Table 9.6. Remember that land cannot be depreciated.

undepreciated capital cost (UCC)
The asset class's balance of the capital cost available for CCA.

To illustrate how the CCA is calculated, we consider a car costing $20,000. Looking at Table 9.6, we see that automobiles fall in class 10, with a 30 percent CCA rate. We compute the CCA each year by multiplying the car's book value for tax purposes, called the **undepreciated capital cost (UCC)**, by its CCA rate of 30 percent. Note that for the first year, we have to follow the Canada Revenue Agency's **half-year rule**. According to this rule, only half of the car's purchase cost is used to calculate CCA in the first year of its use. In other words, this rule assumes that assets are put in use in the middle of the year in which they are purchased. The CCA in the first year is thus $.5 \times \$20,000 \times .3 = \$3,000$. For the first six years, all calculations are summarized in Table 9.7.

half-year rule
Only one-half of the purchase cost of an asset is eligible for CCA in the first year of use.

Notice that the UCC will never decline to zero, because each CCA is a fraction of the ending UCC. This means that as long as we own the asset, it will continue to generate CCA tax shields. We will discuss what happens when the asset is sold in the next section.

TABLE 9.6 Some Capital Cost Allowance Classes		
Class	**Rate**	**Typical Assets**
1	4%	Buildings
8	20	Furniture, equipment
9	25	Aircraft
10	30	Automobiles, electronic equipment
12	100	Computer software
13	Straight-line	Leasehold improvements
14	Straight-line	Patents, licenses, and franchises
43	30	Manufacturing equipment
43.2	50	Renewable energy generation equipment

TABLE 9.7 Capital Cost Allowance for a car			
Year	**Beginning UCC**	**CCA**	**Ending UCC**
1	$20,000	$3,000*	$ 17,000
2	17,000	5,100	11,900
3	11,900	3,570	8,330
4	8,330	2,499	5,831
5	5,831	1,749	4,082
6	4,082	1,225	2,857

*Half-year rule

Sale of Assets

When we sell an asset, the UCC in its asset class is decreased by the sale price of the asset or its original cost, whichever is less. This amount is called the **adjusted cost of disposal**. Suppose we wanted to sell the car after six years. Based on historical averages, it will be worth, say, 25 percent of the purchase price, or $.25 \times \$20,000 = \$5,000$. Because the sale price of $5,000 is less than the car's original cost, the adjusted cost of disposal is $5,000, and the UCC in class 10 is decreased by $5,000. Tax implications of the sale of the car will depend on whether we still have assets left in that class (the asset class continues) or not (the asset class is terminated).

adjusted cost of disposal
The amount subtracted from the asset class's UCC when an asset is sold; equal to the sale price of the asset or its original cost, whichever is less.

Asset Class is Terminated   Suppose you sold the car for $5,000, and your company does not have any other assets remaining in CCA Class 10. In this case, your company would have to pay taxes at the ordinary income tax rate on the difference between the adjusted cost of disposal of $5,000 and the UCC of $2,857. This difference is called a **recapture**, and it is treated as income for tax purposes. For a corporation in the 34 percent bracket, the tax liability is $.34 \times (\$5,000 - \$2,857) = \$728.62$.

The reason that taxes must be paid in this situation is that the difference in the adjusted cost of disposal and the UCC is "excess" CCA, and it must be "recaptured" when the asset is sold. What this means is that, as it turns out, we overdepreciated the asset by $5,000 - \$2,857 = \$2,143$. Since we deducted $2,143 too much in depreciation, we paid $728.62 too little in taxes, and we simply have to make up the difference.

Notice that this is *not* a tax on a capital gain. As a general (albeit rough) rule, a capital gain only occurs if the sale price exceeds the original cost. However, what is and what is not a capital gain is ultimately up to taxing authorities, and the specific rules can be very complex. We will ignore capital gains taxes for the most part.

If the UCC exceeds the adjusted cost of disposal, then the difference is called a **terminal loss**. This loss is deductible from taxable income and, therefore, results in a tax saving. For example, if we sell the car after five years for $2,000, the UCC exceeds the adjusted cost of disposal by $857. In this case, a tax saving of $.34 \times \$857 = \$291.38$ is realized.

Finally, if the UCC is equal to the adjusted cost of disposal, we do not have a recapture or a terminal loss.

recapture
The taxable amount created when an asset is sold; equal to the excess of the adjusted cost of disposal over the asset class's UCC.

terminal loss
The tax deductible amount created when an asset class is terminated; equal to the excess of the asset class's UCC over the adjusted cost of disposal.

Asset Class Continues   When your company has other assets remaining in Class 10, the sale of the car will not trigger immediate tax implications. The difference between the adjusted cost of disposal and the UCC, however, will affect the size of CCA in future years. If we sold the car for $5,000, the $5,000 removed from the asset class would be $2,143 more than the UCC of the car after six years. To make up for this overdepreciation, the future CCA will be lower. In contrast, if we sold the car for $2,000, the $2,000 deducted from the asset class would be $857 less than the UCC of the car. Thus, the future CCA will be higher, as $857 is depreciated over the following years.

CCA Calculations   EXAMPLE 9.2

The Staple Supply Co. has just purchased a new computerized information system with an installed cost of $160,000. The computer falls under CCA Class 10. What are the yearly capital cost allowances? Based on historical experience, we think that the system will be worth only $10,000 when we get rid of it in four years. What are the tax consequences of the sale if the company has several other computers still in use in four years? Assume a 34 percent tax rate. Now suppose the company does not have any computers left in four years. What is the total aftertax cash flow from the sale?

(continued)

The yearly capital cost allowances are presented below:

Year	Beginning UCC	CCA	Ending UCC
1	$ 160,000	$24,000*	$136,000
2	136,000	40,800	95,200
3	95,200	28,560	66,640
4	66,640	19,992	46,648

*Half-year rule

Class 10 asks for the use of a CCA rate of 30 percent. Therefore, the yearly capital cost allowances are calculated by multiplying the beginning UCC for each year, except Year 1, by .30. For Year 1, under the half-year rule, only half of the purchase price of the computerized information system is used to determine the CCA: .5 × $160,000 × .3 = $24,000.

After four years, the ending UCC is $46,648, but the computerized information system is sold for $10,000. Thus, the UCC of the Class 10 assets is decreased by $10,000, and the future CCA will be higher as the asset class continues. This sale does not trigger any tax consequences in Year 4.

If the sale of the computerized information system terminates Class 10 assets, we will have a terminal loss, which is equal to the excess of the asset class's UCC over the adjusted cost of disposal: $46,648 − $10,000 = $36,648. This loss, of course, is like depreciation because it isn't a cash expense. What really happens? Two things. First: We get $10,000 from the buyer. Second: Given the 34 percent tax rate, we save .34 × $36,648 = $12,460 in taxes. So, the total aftertax cash flow from the sale is a $22,460 cash inflow.

An Example: The Majestic Mulch and Compost Company (MMCC)

At this point, we want to go through a somewhat more involved capital budgeting analysis. Keep in mind as you read that the basic approach here is exactly the same as that in the bear attractant example above. We have only added some more "real-world" detail (and a lot more numbers).

MMCC is investigating the feasibility of a new line of power mulching tools aimed at the growing number of home composters. Based on exploratory conversations with buyers for large garden shops, it projects unit sales as follows:

Year	Unit Sales
1	3,000
2	5,000
3	6,000
4	6,500
5	6,000
6	5,000
7	4,000
8	3,000

The new power mulcher will be priced to sell at $120 per unit to start. When the competition catches up after three years, however, MMCC anticipates that the price will drop to $110.

The power mulcher project will require $20,000 in net working capital at the start. Subsequently, total net working capital at the end of each year will be about 15 percent of sales for that year. The variable cost per unit is $60, and total fixed costs are $25,000 per year.

It will cost about $800,000 to buy the equipment necessary to begin production. This investment is primarily in industrial equipment and thus falls in Class 8 with a CCA rate of 20 percent. The equipment will actually be worth about 20 percent of its cost in eight years, or $.20 \times \$800,000 = \$160,000$. The relevant tax rate is 40 percent, and the required return is 15 percent. Based on this information, should MMCC proceed?

Operating Cash Flows There is a lot of information here that we need to organize. The first thing we can do is calculate projected sales. Sales in the first year are projected at 3,000 units at $120 apiece, or $360,000 total. The remaining figures are shown in Table 9.8.

Next, we compute the CCA on the $800,000 investment in Table 9.9. Note that under the half-year rule, only half of the purchase price of the equipment is used to calculate the CCA in Year 1. With this information, we can prepare the pro forma income statements, as shown in Table 9.10. From here, computing the operating cash flows is straightforward. The results are illustrated in the first part of Table 9.12 (on page 275).

Changes in NWC Now that we have the operating cash flows, we need to determine the changes in NWC. By assumption, net working capital requirements change as sales change. In each year, we will generally either add to or recover some of our project net working capital. Recalling that NWC starts out at $20,000 and then rises to 15 percent of sales, we can calculate the amount of NWC for each year as illustrated in Table 9.11.

As illustrated, during the first year, net working capital grows from $20,000 to $.15 \times \$360,000 = \$54,000$. The increase in net working capital for the year is thus $54,000 - 20,000 = \$34,000$. The remaining figures are calculated the same way.

Year	Unit Price	Unit Sales	Revenues
1	$120	3,000	$360,000
2	120	5,000	600,000
3	120	6,000	720,000
4	110	6,500	715,000
5	110	6,000	660,000
6	110	5,000	550,000
7	110	4,000	440,000
8	110	3,000	330,000

TABLE 9.8

Projected revenues, power mulcher project

Year	Beginning UCC	CCA	Ending UCC
1	$800,000	$ 80,000*	$720,000
2	720,000	144,000	576,000
3	576,000	115,200	460,800
4	460,800	92,160	368,640
5	368,640	73,728	294,912
6	294,912	58,982	235,930
7	235,930	47,186	188,744
8	188,744	37,749	150,995

TABLE 9.9

Annual CCA, power mulcher project (CCA Class 8, 20% rate)

*Half-year rule

TABLE 9.10	Pro forma income statements, power mulcher project

	Year							
	1	2	3	4	5	6	7	8
Unit price	$ 120	$ 120	$ 120	$ 110	$ 110	$ 110	$ 110	$ 110
Unit sales	3,000	5,000	6,000	6,500	6,000	5,000	4,000	3,000
Revenues	$360,000	$600,000	$720,000	$715,000	$660,000	$550,000	$440,000	$330,000
Variable costs	180,000	300,000	360,000	390,000	360,000	300,000	240,000	180,000
Fixed costs	25,000	25,000	25,000	25,000	25,000	25,000	25,000	25,000
CCA	80,000	144,000	115,200	92,160	73,728	58,982	47,186	37,749
EBIT	$ 75,000	$131,000	$219,800	$207,840	$201,272	$166,018	$127,814	$ 87,251
Taxes (40%)	30,000	52,400	87,920	83,136	80,509	66,407	51,126	34,901
Net Income	$ 45,000	$ 78,600	$131,880	$124,704	$120,763	$ 99,611	$ 76,688	$ 52,351

TABLE 9.11	Year	Revenues	Net Working Capital	Cash Flow
Changes in net working capital, power mulcher project	0		$ 20,000	−$20,000
	1	$360,000	54,000	− 34,000
	2	600,000	90,000	− 36,000
	3	720,000	108,000	− 18,000
	4	715,000	107,250	750
	5	660,000	99,000	8,250
	6	550,000	82,500	16,500
	7	440,000	66,000	16,500
	8	330,000	49,500	16,500

Remember that an increase in net working capital is a cash outflow, so we use a negative sign in this table to indicate an additional investment that the firm makes in net working capital. A positive sign represents net working capital returning to the firm. Thus, for example, $16,500 in NWC flows back to the firm in Year 6. Over the project's life, net working capital builds to a peak of $108,000 and declines from there as sales begin to drop off.

We show the result for changes in net working capital in the second part of Table 9.12. Notice that at the end of the project's life there is $49,500 in net working capital still to be recovered. Therefore, in the last year, the project returns $16,500 of NWC during the year and then returns the remaining $49,500 at the end of the year, for a total of $66,000.

Capital Spending   Finally, we have to account for the long-term capital invested in the project. In this case, we invest $800,000 at Year 0. By assumption, this equipment will be worth $160,000 at the end of the project. It will have an undepreciated capital cost of $150,995 at that time, as shown in Table 9.9. Thus, the adjusted cost of disposal exceeds the UCC by $160,000 − $150,995 = $9,005. As we discussed above, this difference is treated as income in Year 8 if MMCC does not have any assets left in Class 8. We assume the asset class continues, so there is no extra tax payment. The initial investment and salvage value are shown in the third part of Table 9.12.

Total Cash Flow and Value   We now have all the cash flow pieces, and we put them together in Table 9.13. In addition to the total project cash flows, we have calculated the

TABLE 9.12 Projected cash flows, power mulcher project

					Year				
	0	1	2	3	4	5	6	7	8
I. Operating Cash Flow									
EBIT		$ 75,000	$131,000	$219,800	$ 207,840	$201,272	$166,018	$127,814	$ 87,251
CCA		80,000	144,000	115,200	92,160	73,728	58,982	47,186	37,749
Taxes (40%)		− 30,000	− 52,400	− 87,920	− 83,136	− 80,509	− 66,407	− 51,126	− 34,901
Operating cash flow		$125,000	$222,600	$247,080	$ 216,864	$194,491	$158,593	$123,874	$ 90,099
II. Net Working Capital									
Initial NWC	−$ 20,000								
Increases in NWC		−$ 34,000	−$ 36,000	−$ 18,000	$ 750	$ 8,250	$ 16,500	$ 16,500	$ 16,500
NWC recovery									49,500
Changes in NWC	−$ 20,000	−$ 34,000	−$ 36,000	−$ 18,000	$ 750	$ 8,250	$ 16,500	$ 16,500	$ 66,000
III. Capital Spending									
Initial outlay	−$800,000								
Aftertax salvage									$160,000
Capital spending	−$800,000								$160,000

TABLE 9.13 Projected total cash flows, power mulcher project

					Year				
	0	1	2	3	4	5	6	7	8
Operating cash flow		$125,000	$ 222,600	$247,080	$216,864	$194,491	$158,593	$123,874	$ 90,099
Changes in NWC	−$ 20,000	− 34,000	− 36,000	− 18,000	750	8,250	16,500	16,500	66,000
Capital Spending	− 800,000								160,000
Total project cash flow	−$820,000	$ 91,000	$ 186,600	$229,080	$217,614	$202,741	$175,093	$140,374	$316,099
Cumulative cash flow	−$820,000	−$729,000	−$ 542,400	−$313,320	−$ 95,706	$107,035	$282,128	$422,503	$738,602
Discounted cash flow @ 15%	−$820,000	79,130	141,096	150,624	124,422	100,798	75,698	52,772	103,333

Net present value (15%) = $7,873
Internal rate of return = 15.26%
Payback = 4.47 years

cumulative cash flows and the discounted cash flows. At this point, it's essentially "plug-and-chug" to calculate the net present value, internal rate of return, and payback.

If we sum the discounted flows and the initial investment, the net present value (at 15 percent) works out to be $7,873. This is positive, so, based on these preliminary projections, the power mulcher project is acceptable. The internal, or DCF, rate of return is slightly greater than 15 percent since the NPV is positive. It works out to be 15.26 percent, again indicating that the project is acceptable.

Looking at the cumulative cash flows, we see that the project paid back sometime in the fifth year, since the cumulative cash flow is positive after five years. The fractional year works out to be $95,706/202,741 = .47$, so the payback is 4.47 years. We can't say whether or not this is good since we don't have a benchmark for MMCC. This is the usual problem with payback periods.

Present Value of CCA Tax Shield

Our example of the power mulcher project shows that a capital budgeting analysis involves considerable number crunching, even for a project that is expected to last eight years. Imagine you have to perform a similar analysis for a project that will last 30 years. It would be a very time-consuming task, if you used only a calculator. Even if you used a computer spreadsheet, it would be a challenge to set up the analysis. The good news is that the tax shield approach discussed earlier can considerably speed up the process by using the present value of the CCA tax shield formula, which we will discuss next. Recall the two components of the tax shield definition of OCF:

$$OCF = (Sales - Costs) \times (1 - T_c) + Depreciation \times T_c$$

Rather than estimating OCF for each year and then finding the present value of the total cash flows, we can find the present value of each part and then add the present values. A main advantage of this approach is that we can find the present value of the second component, the depreciation tax shield, with just one formula. It is called the present value of the CCA tax shield:

$$PV \text{ of CCA tax shield} = \frac{CdT_c}{d + k} \times \frac{1 + 0.5k}{1 + k} - \frac{SdT_c}{d + k} \times \frac{1}{(1 + k)^n} \qquad [9.4]$$

where

C = Cost of the asset that is added to the asset class
d = CCA rate for the asset class
T_c = Corporate tax rate
k = Discount rate
S = Salvage value of the asset
n = Number of years until the asset will be sold

Note that the present value of the CCA tax shield equation consists of two parts:

$\dfrac{CdT_c}{d + k} \times \dfrac{1 + 0.5k}{1 + k}$ calculates the present value of the CCA tax shield, assuming that the CCA tax shield continues in perpetuity.

$\dfrac{SdT_c}{d + k} \times \dfrac{1}{(1 + k)^n}$ calculates the present value of lost CCA tax shield due to salvage value.

For our power mulcher project, the present value of the CCA tax shield works out to be:

PV of CCA tax shield $= \dfrac{CdT_c}{d+k} \times \dfrac{1+0.5k}{1+k} - \dfrac{SdT_c}{d+k} \times \dfrac{1}{(1+k)^n}$

$$= \dfrac{\$800{,}000 \times .20 \times .40}{.20 + .15} \times \dfrac{1 + 0.5 \times .15}{1 + .15} - \dfrac{\$160{,}000 \times .20 \times .40}{.20 + .15}$$

$$\times \dfrac{1}{(1 + .15)^8}$$

$$= \$158{,}976$$

Keep in mind that the present value of the CCA tax shield equation provides a final answer only if the CCA asset class continues after the sale of the asset. If the CCA asset class is terminated, in addition to this equation, we have to find the UCC at the end of the project and calculate the present value of any tax liability or tax savings resulting from the sale of the asset.

To find the present value of the first component of the tax shield definition of OCF, we calculate (Sales − Costs) × $(1 - T_c)$ for each year and find their present values as seen on the first two parts of Table 9.14. Their total present value is $645,099, as shown in the third part of Table 9.14.

Changes in net working capital and capital spending are computed in the same manner. The first part of Table 9.14 shows the annual numbers for net working capital and capital spending, which are similar to the numbers in Table 9.12. The third part of Table 9.14 displays their total present values.

When we add the total of the present value of the four sources of cash flow, we find the NPV of the project. It works out to be $7,200, which is slightly less than what we found earlier in Table 9.13. Which number is accurate? As a matter of fact, the tax shield approach that uses the present value of the CCA tax shield equation produces a more accurate estimation of the NPV. It takes into account the change in the future CCA when the adjusted cost of disposal and the UCC are not equal to each other. Recall that in our power mulcher project the adjusted cost of disposal exceeds the UCC by $9,005. Because we overdepreciated the assets by $9,005, the future CCA will be lower as the asset class continues. The present value of the CCA tax shield equation takes this into account and so gives a more accurate estimation of NPV.

Conclusion

This completes our preliminary DCF analysis. Where do we go from here? If we have a great deal of confidence in our projections, then there is no further analysis to be done. We should begin production and marketing immediately. It is unlikely that this will be the case. It is important to remember that the result of our analysis is an estimate of NPV, and we will usually have less than complete confidence in our projections. This means we have more work to do. In particular, we will almost surely want to spend some time evaluating the quality of our estimates. We will take up this subject in the next several sections.

CONCEPT QUESTIONS

9.4a Why is it important to consider changes in net working capital in developing cash flows? What is the effect of doing so?

9.4b How is depreciation calculated under current tax law? What is the assumption behind the half-year rule?

TABLE 9.14 Tax shield approach, power mulcher project

	Year								
	0	1	2	3	4	5	6	7	8
I. Projected Cash Flows									
(Sales − Costs)(1 − T_c)		$93,000	$165,000	$201,000	$180,000	$165,000	$135,000	$105,000	$75,000
Changes in NWC	−$ 20,000	− 34,000	− 36,000	− 18,000	750	8,250	16,500	16,500	66,000
Capital Spending	− 800,000								160,000
II. Discounted Cash Flows @ 15%									
PV of (Sales − Costs)(1 − T_c)		$80,870	$124,764	$132,161	$102,916	$ 82,034	$ 58,364	$ 39,473	$ 24,518
PV of changes in NWC	−$ 20,000	− 29,565	− 27,221	− 11,835	429	4,102	7,133	6,203	21,576
PV of capital spending	− 800,000								52,304
III. Total Discounted Cash Flows									

Total PV of	$645,099
(Sales − Costs)(1 − T_c)	
Total PV of changes in NWC	− 49,179
Total PV of capital spending	− 747,696
Total PV of CCA tax shield	158,976
NPV (15%)	$ 7,200

9.5 | EVALUATING NPV ESTIMATES

As we discussed in Chapter 8, an investment has a positive net present value if its market value exceeds its cost. Such an investment is desirable because it creates value for its owner. The primary problem in identifying such opportunities is that most of the time we can't actually observe the relevant market value. Instead, we estimate it. Having done so, it is only natural to wonder whether or not our estimates are at least close to the true values. We consider this question next.

The Basic Problem

Suppose we are working on a preliminary DCF analysis along the lines we described in previous sections. We carefully identify the relevant cash flows, avoiding such things as sunk costs, and we remember to consider working capital requirements. We add back any depreciation; we account for possible erosion; and we pay attention to opportunity costs. Finally, we double-check our calculations, and, when all is said and done, the bottom line is that the estimated NPV is positive.

Now what? Do we stop here and move on to the next proposal? Probably not. The fact that the estimated NPV is positive is definitely a good sign, but, more than anything, this tells us that we need to take a closer look.

If you think about it, there are two circumstances under which a discounted cash flow analysis could lead us to conclude that a project has a positive NPV. The first possibility is that the project really does have a positive NPV. That's the good news. The bad news is the second possibility: A project may appear to have a positive NPV because our estimate is inaccurate.

Notice that we could also err in the opposite way. If we conclude that a project has a negative NPV when the true NPV is positive, then we lose a valuable opportunity.

Forecasting Risk

The key inputs into a DCF analysis are projected future cash flows. If these projections are seriously in error, then we have a classic GIGO, or garbage-in, garbage-out, system. In this case, no matter how carefully we arrange the numbers and manipulate them, the resulting answer can still be grossly misleading. This is the danger in using a relatively sophisticated technique like DCF. It is sometimes easy to get caught up in number crunching and forget the underlying nuts-and-bolts economic reality.

The possibility that we will make a bad decision because of errors in the projected cash flows is called **forecasting risk** (or *estimation risk*). Because of forecasting risk, there is the danger that we will think a project has a positive NPV when it really does not. How is this possible? It occurs if we are overly optimistic about the future, and, as a result, our projected cash flows don't realistically reflect the possible future cash flows. Our *Reality Bytes* box on the next page shows what can happen in such cases.

So far, we have not explicitly considered what to do about the possibility of errors in our forecasts, so our goal is to develop some tools that will be useful in identifying areas where potential errors exist and where they might be especially damaging. In one form or another, we will be trying to assess the economic "reasonableness" of our estimates. We will also be wondering how much damage will be done by errors in those estimates.

forecasting risk
The possibility that errors in projected cash flows will lead to incorrect decisions. Also, *estimation risk*.

REALITY BYTES

When Things Go Wrong . . .

If you think about it, the decision by a company to acquire another company is a capital budgeting decision. One important difference, however, is that an acquisition may be more expensive than a typical project, and possibly *much* more expensive. Of course, as with any other project, acquisitions can fail. When they do, the losses can be huge.

In December 1999, for example, Air Canada acquired Canadian Airlines for $92 million and became the tenth largest airline in the world. In the past, these companies had battled fiercely for market share, losing millions of dollars. The acquisition was expected to solve their financial troubles by creating a single dominant carrier in Canada.

This undertaking, however, imposed many challenges, such as the integration of the two companies, restructuring Canadian Airlines' $3.5 billion debt, and cutting jobs. As a result, Air Canada's problems started almost immediately. For instance, the merging of flight schedules created mass confusion at airports, delayed departures, and resulted in lost luggage. Thousands of disgruntled passengers could not reach Air Canada operators over busy phone lines. Air Canada also complained that Canadian Airlines was in a worse financial situation than it had initially realized. To decrease its operating costs, Air Canada began cutting thousands of jobs. Nevertheless, the losses were mounting, and Air Canada began losing about $1 million a day. By October 2001, Air Canada had laid off 12,500 employees and was asking the government for a $4 billion bailout. The government, however, refused to bail out the airline that controlled 80 percent of the domestic market.

Competition from emerging discount carrier WestJet and the decline in air travel following the September 11, 2001, terrorist attacks and the SARS outbreak made things worse for Air Canada. By April 2003, the company had lost more than $1.6 billion and was not generating enough cash to pay its debt. To keep running, Air Canada filed for bankruptcy protection.

One of the largest acquisitions in U.S. history was America Online's (AOL) purchase of Time Warner in 2001. AOL purchased Time Warner under the assumption that AOL was part of the "new economy" and primed for fast growth. Time Warner was the "old" communications company, owning cable stations and a music label, among other things. But things didn't work as well as planned. Infighting among employees from the two companies hurt production and morale. In 2002, accounting irregularities were uncovered at AOL, and, as a result of the acquisition costs, the company was saddled with massive debt. To make matters worse, AOL began to lose customers and money. Although AOL was the acquirer, and once dominant partner, things got so bad at AOL that the company changed its name back to Time Warner. To cap things off, in 2002, Time Warner wrote off a stunning $54 billion in assets associated with the acquisition, which was at the time the largest such write-off in history.

Sources of Value

The first line of defense against forecasting risk is simply to ask: What is it about this investment that leads to a positive NPV? We should be able to point to something specific as the source of value. For example, if the proposal under consideration involved a new product, then we might ask questions such as the following: Are we certain that our new product is significantly better than that of the competition? Can we truly manufacture at lower cost, or distribute more effectively, or identify undeveloped market niches, or gain control of a market?

These are just a few of the potential sources of value. There are many others. A key factor to keep in mind is the degree of competition in the market. It is a basic principle of economics that positive NPV investments will be rare in a highly competitive environment. Therefore, proposals that appear to show significant value in the face of stiff competition are particularly troublesome, and the likely reaction of the competition to any innovations must be closely examined.

The point to remember is that positive NPV investments are probably not all that common, and the number of positive NPV projects is almost certainly limited for any given firm. If we can't articulate some sound economic basis for thinking ahead of time that we have found something special, then the conclusion that our project has a positive NPV should be viewed with some suspicion.

CONCEPT QUESTIONS

9.5a What is forecasting risk? Why is it a concern for the financial manager?
9.5b What are some potential sources of value in a new project?

9.6 | SCENARIO AND OTHER WHAT-IF ANALYSES

Our basic approach to evaluating cash flow and NPV estimates involves asking what-if questions. Accordingly, we discuss some organized ways of going about a what-if analysis. Our goal in doing so is to assess the degree of forecasting risk and to identify those components most critical to the success or failure of an investment.

Getting Started

We are investigating a new project. Naturally, the first thing we do is estimate NPV based on our projected cash flows. We will call this the *base case*. Now, however, we recognize the possibility of error in those cash flow projections. After completing the base case, we thus wish to investigate the impact of different assumptions about the future on our estimates.

One way to organize this investigation is to put an upper and lower bound on the various components of the project. For example, suppose we forecast sales at 100 units per year. We know this estimate may be high or low, but we are relatively certain it is not off by more than 10 units in either direction. We would thus pick a lower bound of 90 and an upper bound of 110. We go on to assign such bounds to any other cash flow components we are unsure about.

When we pick these upper and lower bounds, we are not ruling out the possibility that the actual values could be outside this range. What we are saying, loosely speaking, is that it is unlikely that the true average (as opposed to our estimated average) of the possible values is outside this range.

An example is useful to illustrate the idea here. The project under consideration costs $200,000, has a five-year life, and has no salvage value. Depreciation is straight-line to zero. The required return is 12 percent, and the tax rate is 34 percent. In addition, we have compiled the following information:

	Base Case	Lower Bound	Upper Bound
Unit sales	6,000	5,500	6,500
Price per unit	$ 80	$ 75	$ 85
Variable costs per unit	$ 60	$ 58	$ 62
Fixed costs per year	$50,000	$45,000	$55,000

With this information, we can calculate the base-case NPV by first calculating net income:

Sales	$480,000
Variable costs	360,000
Fixed costs	50,000
Depreciation	40,000
EBIT	$ 30,000
Taxes (34%)	10,200
Net income	$ 19,800

Operating cash flow is thus $30,000 + 40,000 − 10,200 = $59,800 per year. At 12 percent, the five-year annuity factor is 3.6048, so the base-case NPV is:

$$\text{Base-case NPV} = -\$200,000 + 59,800 \times 3.6048$$
$$= \$15,567$$

Thus, the project looks good so far.

Scenario Analysis

scenario analysis
The determination of
what happens to NPV
estimates when we ask
what-if questions.

The basic form of what-if analysis is called **scenario analysis**. What we do is investigate the changes in our NPV estimates that result from asking questions like, What if unit sales realistically should be projected at 5,500 units instead of 6,000?

Once we start looking at alternative scenarios, we might find that most of the plausible ones result in positive NPVs. In this case, we have some confidence in proceeding with the project. If a substantial percentage of the scenarios look bad, then the degree of forecasting risk is high and further investigation is in order.

There are a number of possible scenarios we could consider. A good place to start is with the worst-case scenario. This will tell us the minimum NPV of the project. If this is positive, we will be in good shape. While we are at it, we will go ahead and determine the other extreme, the best case. This puts an upper bound on our NPV.

To get the worst case, we assign the least favourable value to each item. This means *low* values for items such as units sold and price per unit and *high* values for costs. We do the reverse for the best case. For our project, these values would be:

	Worst Case	Best Case
Unit sales	5,500	6,500
Price per unit	$75	$85
Variable costs per unit	$62	$58
Fixed costs	$55,000	$45,000

With this information, we can calculate the net income and cash flows under each scenario (check these for yourself):

Scenario	Net Income	Cash Flow	Net Present Value	IRR
Base case	$19,800	$59,800	$ 15,567	15.1%
Worst case*	− 15,510	24,490	− 111,719	−14.4
Best case	59,730	99,730	159,504	40.9

*We assume a tax credit is created in our worst-case scenario.

What we learn is that under the worst scenario, the cash flow is still positive at $24,490. That's good news. The bad news is that the return is −14.4 percent in this case, and the NPV is −$111,719. Since the project costs $200,000, we stand to lose a little more than half of the original investment under the worst possible scenario. The best case offers an attractive 41 percent return.

The terms *best case* and *worst case* are very commonly used, and we will stick with them, but we should note that they are somewhat misleading. The absolutely best thing that could happen would be something absurdly unlikely, such as launching a new diet soda and subsequently learning that our (patented) formulation also just happens to cure the common cold. Similarly, the true worst case would involve some incredibly remote possibility of total disaster. We're not claiming that these things don't happen; once in a while they do. Some products, such as personal computers, succeed beyond the wildest of expectations, and some, such as asbestos, turn out to be absolute catastrophes. Instead, our point is that in assessing the reasonableness of an NPV estimate, we need to stick to cases that are reasonably likely to occur.

Instead of *best* and *worst,* then, it is probably more accurate to say *optimistic* and *pessimistic.* In broad terms, if we were thinking about a reasonable range for, say, unit sales, then what we call the best case would correspond to something near the upper end of that range. The worst case would simply correspond to the lower end.

As we have mentioned, there are an unlimited number of different scenarios that we could examine. At a minimum, we might want to investigate two intermediate cases by going halfway between the base amounts and the extreme amounts. This would give us five scenarios in all, including the base case.

Beyond this point, it is hard to know when to stop. As we generate more and more possibilities, we run the risk of "paralysis of analysis." The difficulty is that no matter how many scenarios we run, all we can learn are possibilities, some good and some bad. Beyond that, we don't get any guidance as to what to do. Scenario analysis is thus useful in telling us what can happen and in helping us gauge the potential for disaster, but it does not tell us whether or not to take on the project.

Sensitivity Analysis

Sensitivity analysis is a variation on scenario analysis that is useful in pinpointing the areas where forecasting risk is especially severe. The basic idea with a sensitivity analysis is to freeze all of the variables except one and then see how sensitive our estimate of NPV is to changes in that one variable. If our NPV estimate turns out to be very sensitive to relatively small changes in the projected value of some component of project cash flow, then the forecasting risk associated with that variable is high.

sensitivity analysis
Investigation of what happens to NPV when only one variable is changed.

To illustrate how sensitivity analysis works, we go back to our base case for every item except unit sales. We can then calculate cash flow and NPV using the largest and smallest unit sales figures.

Scenario	Unit Sales	Cash Flow	Net Present Value	IRR
Base case	6,000	$59,800	$15,567	15.1%
Worst case	5,500	53,200	− 8,226	10.3
Best case	6,500	66,400	39,357	19.7

The results of our sensitivity analysis for unit sales can be illustrated graphically as in Figure 9.1. Here we place NPV on the vertical axis and unit sales on the horizontal axis. When we plot the combinations of unit sales versus NPV, we see that all possible

You can find a cash flow sensitivity analysis worksheet at **http://www.toolkit .com/tools.**

FIGURE **9.1**

**Sensitivity analysis
for unit sales**

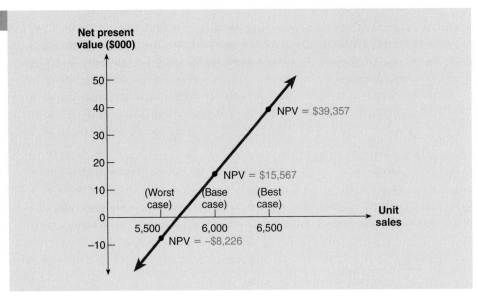

FIGURE **9.1**

**Sensitivity analysis
for unit sales**

combinations fall on a straight line. The steeper the resulting line is, the greater is the sensitivity of the estimated NPV to the projected value of the variable being investigated.

By way of comparison, we now freeze everything except fixed costs and repeat the analysis:

Scenario	Fixed Costs	Cash Flow	Net Present Value	IRR
Base case	$50,000	$59,800	$15,567	15.1%
Worst case	55,000	56,500	3,670	12.7
Best case	45,000	63,100	27,461	17.4

What we see here is that, given our ranges, the estimated NPV of this project is more sensitive to projected unit sales than it is to projected fixed costs. In fact, under the worst case for fixed costs, the NPV is still positive.

As we have illustrated, sensitivity analysis is useful in pinpointing those variables that deserve the most attention. If we find that our estimated NPV is especially sensitive to a variable that is difficult to forecast (such as unit sales), then the degree of forecasting risk is high. We might decide that further market research would be a good idea in this case.

Because sensitivity analysis is a form of scenario analysis, it suffers from the same drawbacks. Sensitivity analysis is useful for pointing out where forecasting errors will do the most damage, but it does not tell us what to do about possible errors.

CONCEPT QUESTIONS

9.6a   What are scenario and sensitivity analyses?

9.6b   What are the drawbacks to what-if analyses?

9.7 | ADDITIONAL CONSIDERATIONS IN CAPITAL BUDGETING

Our final task for this chapter is a brief discussion of two additional considerations in capital budgeting: managerial options and capital rationing. Both of these can be very important in practice, but, as we will see, explicitly dealing with either of them is difficult.

Managerial Options and Capital Budgeting

In our capital budgeting analysis thus far, we have more or less ignored the possibility of future managerial actions. Implicitly, we have assumed that once a project is launched, its basic features cannot be changed. For this reason, we say that our analysis is *static* (as opposed to dynamic).

In reality, depending on what actually happens in the future, there will always be ways to modify a project. We will call these opportunities **managerial options**. Because they involve real (as opposed to financial) assets, such options are often called "real" options. There are a great number of these options. The way a product is priced, manufactured, advertised, and produced can all be changed, and these are just a few of the possibilities. We discuss some of the most important managerial options in the next few sections.

managerial options
Opportunities that managers can exploit if certain things happen in the future. Also known as "real" options.

Contingency Planning   The various what-if procedures in this chapter have another use. We can also view them as primitive ways of exploring the dynamics of a project and investigating managerial options. What we think about in this case are some of the possible futures that could come about and what actions we might take if they do.

For example, we might find that a project fails to break even when sales drop below 10,000 units. This is a fact that is interesting to know, but the more important thing is to then go on and ask, What actions are we going to take if this actually occurs? This is called **contingency planning**, and it amounts to an investigation of some of the managerial options implicit in a project.

contingency planning
Taking into account the managerial options implicit in a project.

There is no limit to the number of possible futures, or contingencies, that we could investigate. However, there are some broad classes, and we consider these next.

The option to expand   One particularly important option we have not explicitly addressed is the option to expand. If we truly find a positive NPV project, then there is an obvious consideration. Can we expand the project or repeat it to get an even larger NPV? Our static analysis implicitly assumes that the scale of the project is fixed.

For example, if the sales demand for a particular product were to greatly exceed expectations, we might investigate increasing production. If this were not feasible for some reason, then we could always increase cash flow by raising the price. Either way, the potential cash flow is higher than we have indicated because we have implicitly assumed that no expansion or price increase is possible. Overall, because we ignore the option to expand in our analysis, we *underestimate* NPV (all other things being equal).

The option to abandon   At the other extreme, the option to scale back or even abandon a project is also quite valuable. For example, if a project does not even cover its own expenses, we might be better off if we just abandoned it. Our DCF analysis implicitly assumes that we would keep operating even in this case.

In reality, if sales demand were significantly below expectations, we might be able to sell off some capacity or put it to another use. Maybe the product or service could be redesigned or otherwise improved. Regardless of the specifics, we once again *under-estimate* NPV if we assume that the project must last for some fixed number of years, no matter what happens in the future.

The option to wait   Implicitly, we have treated proposed investments as if they were "go or no-go" decisions. Actually, there is a third possibility. The project can be postponed, perhaps in hope of more favourable conditions. We call this the option to wait.

For example, suppose an investment costs $120 and has a perpetual cash flow of $10 per year. If the discount rate is 10 percent, then the NPV is $10/.10 − 120 = −$20, so the project should not be undertaken now. However, this does not mean that we should forget about the project forever, because in the next period, the appropriate discount rate could be different. If it fell to, say, 5 percent, then the NPV would be $10/.05 − 120 = $80, and we would take the project.

More generally, as long as there is some possible future scenario under which a project has a positive NPV, then the option to wait is valuable.

To illustrate some of these ideas, consider the case of Euro Disney. The deal to open Euro Disney occurred in 1987, and the park opened its doors outside of Paris in 1992. Disney's management thought Europeans would go goofy over the new park, but trouble soon began. The number of visitors never met expectations, in part because the company priced tickets too high. Disney also decided not to serve alcohol in a country that was accustomed to wine with meals. French labour inspectors fought Disney's strict dress codes, and so on.

After several years of operations, the park began serving wine in its restaurants, lowered ticket prices, and made other adjustments. In other words, management exercised its option to reformulate the product. The park began to make a small profit. Then, the company exercised the option to expand by adding a "second gate," which was another theme park next to Euro Disney named Walt Disney Studios. The second gate was intended to encourage visitors to extend their stays. But the new park flopped. The reasons included high ticket prices, attractions geared toward Hollywood rather than European filmmaking, labour strikes in Paris, and a summer heat wave.

By the summer of 2003, Euro Disney was close to bankruptcy again. Executives discussed a variety of options. These options ranged from letting the company go broke (the option to abandon) to pulling the Disney name from the park. In 2005 the company finally agreed to a restructuring with the help of the French government.

The whole idea of managerial options was summed up aptly by Jay Rasulo, the overseer of Disney's theme parks, when he said: "One thing we know for sure is that you never get it 100 percent right the first time. We open every one of our parks with the notion that we're going to add content."

Strategic Options   Companies sometimes undertake new projects just to explore possibilities and evaluate potential future business strategies. This is a little like testing the water by sticking a toe in before diving. Such projects are difficult to analyze using conventional DCF methods because most of the benefits come in the form of **strategic options**, that is, options for future, related business moves. Projects that create such options may be very valuable, but that value is difficult to measure. Research and development, for example, is an important and valuable activity for many firms precisely because it creates options for new products and procedures.

strategic options
Options for future, related business products or strategies.

To give another example, a large manufacturer might decide to open a retail outlet as a pilot study. The primary goal is to gain some market insight. Because of the high start-up costs, this one operation won't break even. However, based on the sales experience from the pilot, we can then evaluate whether or not to open more outlets, to change the product mix, to enter new markets, and so on. The information gained and the resulting options for actions are all valuable, but coming up with a reliable dollar figure is probably not feasible.

Conclusion We have seen that incorporating options into capital budgeting analysis is not easy. What can we do about them in practice? The answer is that we can only keep them in the back of our minds as we work with the projected cash flows. We will tend to underestimate NPV by ignoring options. The damage might be small for a highly structured, very specific proposal, but it might be great for an exploratory one.

Capital Rationing

Capital rationing is said to exist when we have profitable (positive NPV) investments available but we can't get the needed funds to undertake them. For example, as division managers for a large corporation, we might identify $5 million in excellent projects, but find that, for whatever reason, we can spend only $2 million. Now what? Unfortunately, for reasons we will discuss, there may be no truly satisfactory answer.

capital rationing
The situation that exists if a firm has positive NPV projects but cannot obtain the necessary financing.

Soft Rationing The situation we have just described is **soft rationing**. This occurs when, for example, different units in a business are allocated some fixed amount of money each year for capital spending. Such an allocation is primarily a means of controlling and keeping track of overall spending. The important thing about soft rationing is that the corporation as a whole isn't short of capital; more can be raised on ordinary terms if management so desires.

soft rationing
The situation that occurs when units in a business are allocated a certain amount of financing for capital budgeting.

If we face soft rationing, the first thing to do is try and get a larger allocation. Failing that, then one common suggestion is to generate as large a net present value as possible within the existing budget. This amounts to choosing those projects with the largest benefit-cost ratio (profitability index).

Strictly speaking, this is the correct thing to do only if the soft rationing is a one-time event; that is, it won't exist next year. If the soft rationing is a chronic problem, then something is amiss. The reason goes all the way back to Chapter 1. Ongoing soft rationing means we are constantly bypassing positive NPV investments. This contradicts our goal of the firm. If we are not trying to maximize value, then the question of which projects to take becomes ambiguous because we no longer have an objective goal in the first place.

Hard Rationing With **hard rationing**, a business cannot raise capital for a project under any circumstances. For large, healthy corporations, this situation probably does not occur very often. This is fortunate because with hard rationing, our DCF analysis breaks down, and the best course of action is ambiguous.

hard rationing
The situation that occurs when a business cannot raise financing for a project under any circumstances.

The reason DCF analysis breaks down has to do with the required return. Suppose we say that our required return is 20 percent. Implicitly, we are saying that we will take a project with a return that exceeds this. However, if we face hard rationing, then we are not going to take a new project no matter what the return on that project is, so the whole concept of a required return is ambiguous. About the only interpretation we can give this situation is that the required return is so large that no project has a positive NPV in the first place.

Hard rationing can occur when a company experiences financial distress, meaning that bankruptcy is a possibility. Also, a firm may not be able to raise capital without violating a pre-existing contractual agreement. We discuss these situations in greater detail in Chapter 13.

CONCEPT QUESTIONS

9.7a Why do we say that our standard discounted cash flow analysis is static?

9.7b What are managerial options in capital budgeting? Give some examples.

9.7c What is capital rationing? What types are there? What problems does capital rationing create for discounted cash flow analysis?

KEY EQUATIONS:

I. Project Cash Flows

$$
\begin{aligned}
\textbf{Project cash flow} = &\ \textbf{Project operating cash flow} \\
&- \textbf{Project change in net working capital} \\
&- \textbf{Project capital spending}
\end{aligned}
\tag{9.1}
$$

$$
\begin{aligned}
\textbf{Operating cash flow} = &\ \textbf{Earnings before interest and taxes} \\
&+ \textbf{Depreciation} \\
&- \textbf{Taxes}
\end{aligned}
\tag{9.2}
$$

II. The Tax Shield Approach

$$
\textbf{Operating cash flow} = (\textbf{Sales} - \textbf{Costs}) \times (1 - T_c) + \textbf{Depreciation} \times T_c
$$
where T_c = the corporate tax rate. $\tag{9.3}$

$$
\textbf{PV of CCA tax shield} = \frac{CdT_c}{d + k} \times \frac{1 + 0.5k}{1 + k} - \frac{SdT_c}{d + k} \times \frac{1}{(1 + k)^n}
\tag{9.4}
$$
where

C = Cost of the asset that is added to the asset class

d = CCA rate for the asset class

T_c = Corporate tax rate

k = Discount rate

S = Salvage value of the asset

n = Number of years until the asset will be sold

SUMMARY AND CONCLUSIONS

This chapter has described how to go about putting together a discounted cash flow analysis and evaluating the results. In it, we covered:

1. The identification of relevant project cash flows.

2. Handling different cash flows, including sunk costs, opportunity costs, financing costs, net working capital, and erosion.

3. Preparing and using pro forma, or projected, financial statements. We showed how pro forma financial statement information is useful in coming up with projected cash flows.

4. The role of net working capital and depreciation in project cash flows. We saw that including the change in net working capital was important because it adjusted for the

discrepancy between accounting revenues and costs and cash revenues and costs. We also went over the calculation of capital cost allowance under current tax law.

5. The origin of forecasting risk and the first line of defence against it.

6. The use of scenario and sensitivity analysis. These tools are widely used to evaluate the impact of assumptions made about future cash flows and NPV estimates.

7. Additional issues in capital budgeting. We examined the managerial options implicit in many capital budgeting situations. We also discussed the capital rationing problem.

The discounted cash flow analysis we've covered here is a standard tool in the business world. It is a very powerful tool, so care should be taken in its use. The most important thing is to get the cash flows identified in a way that makes economic sense. This chapter gives you a good start on learning to do this.

CHAPTER REVIEW AND SELF-TEST PROBLEMS

9.1 Calculating Operating Cash Flow. Mater Pasta, Inc., has projected a sales volume of $1,432 for the second year of a proposed expansion project. Costs normally run 70 percent of sales, or about $1,002 in this case. The depreciation will be $80, and the tax rate is 40 percent. What is the operating cash flow?

9.2 Scenario Analysis. A project under consideration costs $500,000, has a five-year life, and has no salvage value. Depreciation is straight-line to zero. The required return is 15 percent, and the tax rate is 34 percent. Sales are projected at 400 units per year. Price per unit is $3,000, variable cost per unit is $1,900, and fixed costs are $250,000 per year. No net working capital is required.

Suppose you think the unit sales, price, variable cost, and fixed cost projections are accurate to within 5 percent. What are the upper and lower bounds for these projections? What is the base-case NPV? What are the best- and worst-case scenario NPVs?

■ Answers to Chapter Review and Self-Test Problems

9.1 First, we can calculate the project's EBIT, its tax bill, and its net income.

$$\text{EBIT} = \$1,432 - 1,002 - 80 = \$350$$
$$\text{Taxes} = \$350 \times .40 = \$140$$
$$\text{Net income} = \$350 - 140 = \$210$$

With these numbers, operating cash flow is:

$$\text{OCF} = \text{EBIT} + \text{Depreciation} - \text{Taxes}$$
$$= \$350 + 80 - 140$$
$$= \$290$$

9.2 We can summarize the relevant information as follows:

	Base Case	Lower Bound	Upper Bound
Unit sales	400	380	420
Price per unit	$ 3,000	$ 2,850	$ 3,150
Variable costs per unit	$ 1,900	$ 1,805	$ 1,995
Fixed costs	$250,000	$237,500	$262,500

The depreciation is $100,000 per year, and the tax rate is 34 percent, so we can calculate the cash flows under each scenario. Remember that we assign high costs and low prices and volume under the worst case and just the opposite for the best case.

Scenario	Unit Sales	Price	Variable Costs	Fixed Costs	Cash Flow
Base case	400	$3,000	$1,900	$250,000	$159,400
Best case	420	3,150	1,805	237,500	250,084
Worst case	380	2,850	1,995	262,500	75,184

At 15 percent, the five-year annuity factor is 3.35216, so the NPVs are:

$$
\begin{aligned}
\text{Base-case NPV} &= -\$500,000 + 159,400 \times 3.35216 \\
&= \$34,334
\end{aligned}
$$

$$
\begin{aligned}
\text{Best-case NPV} &= -\$500,000 + 250,084 \times 3.35216 \\
&= \$338,320
\end{aligned}
$$

$$
\begin{aligned}
\text{Worst-case NPV} &= -\$500,000 + 75,184 \times 3.35216 \\
&= -\$247,972
\end{aligned}
$$

CRITICAL THINKING AND CONCEPTS REVIEW

9.1 **Opportunity Cost.** In the context of capital budgeting, what is an opportunity cost?

9.2 **CCA.** Suppose a firm has a terminal loss on the sale of an asset. Taking only taxes into consideration, would the firm prefer that this asset class be terminated or continued? Why?

9.3 **Net Working Capital.** In our capital budgeting examples, we assumed that a firm would recover all of the working capital it invested in a project. Is this a reasonable assumption? When might it not be valid?

9.4 **Stand-Alone Principle.** Suppose a financial manager is quoted as saying, "Our firm uses the stand-alone principle. Because we treat projects like minifirms in our evaluation process, we include financing costs because they are relevant at the firm level." Critically evaluate this statement.

9.5 **Cash Flow and Depreciation.** "When evaluating projects, we're only concerned with the relevant incremental aftertax cash flows. Therefore, because depreciation is a noncash expense, we should ignore its effects when evaluating projects." Critically evaluate this statement.

9.6 **Capital Budgeting Considerations.** A major textbook publisher has an existing finance textbook. The publisher is debating whether or not to produce an "essentialized" version, meaning a shorter (and lower-priced) book. What are some of the considerations that should come into play?

To answer the next three questions, refer to the following example. In 2003, Porsche unveiled its new sports-utility vehicle (SUV), the Cayenne. With a price tag of over $40,000, the Cayenne goes from zero to 62 mph in 9.7 seconds. Porsche's decision to enter the SUV market was in response to the runaway success of other high-priced SUVs such as the Mercedes-Benz M-class. Vehicles in this class had generated years of very high profits. The Cayenne certainly spiced up the market, and Porsche subsequently introduced the Cayenne Turbo, which goes from zero to 62 mph in 5.6 seconds and has a top speed of 165 mph. The price tag for the Cayenne Turbo? Almost $100,000!

Some analysts questioned Porsche's entry into the luxury SUV market. The analysts were concerned not only that Porsche was a late entry into the market, but also that the introduction of the Cayenne would damage Porsche's reputation as a maker of high-performance automobiles.

9.7 Erosion. In evaluating the Cayenne, would you consider the possible damage to Porsche's reputation?

9.8 Capital Budgeting. Porsche was one of the last manufacturers to enter the sports-utility vehicle market. Why would one company decide to proceed with a product when other companies, at least initially, decide not to enter the market?

9.9 Capital Budgeting. In evaluating the Cayenne, what do you think Porsche needs to assume regarding the substantial profit margins that exist in this market? Is it likely they will be maintained as the market becomes more competitive, or will Porsche be able to maintain the profit margin because of its image and the performance of the Cayenne?

9.10 Sensitivity Analysis and Scenario Analysis. What is the essential difference between sensitivity analysis and scenario analysis?

9.11 Marginal Cash Flows. A co-worker claims that looking at all this marginal this and incremental that is just a bunch of nonsense, and states, "Listen, if our average revenue doesn't exceed our average cost, then we will have a negative cash flow, and we will go broke!" How do you respond?

9.12 Capital Rationing. Going all the way back to Chapter 1, recall that we saw that partnerships and proprietorships can face difficulties when it comes to raising capital. In the context of this chapter, the implication is that small businesses will generally face what problem?

9.13 Forecasting Risk. What is forecasting risk? In general, would the degree of forecasting risk be greater for a new product or a cost-cutting proposal? Why?

9.14 Options and NPV. What is the option to abandon? The option to expand? Explain why we tend to underestimate NPV when we ignore these options.

QUESTIONS AND PROBLEMS

1. Relevant Cash Flows. Kenny, Inc., is looking at setting up a new manufacturing plant in South Park. The company bought some land six years ago for $7 million in anticipation of using it as a warehouse and distribution site, but the company has since decided to rent facilities elsewhere. The land would net $8.1 million if it were sold today. The company now wants to build its new manufacturing plant on this land; the plant will cost $15 million to build, and the site requires $750,000 worth of grading before it is suitable for construction. What is the proper cash flow amount to use as the initial investment in fixed assets when evaluating this project? Why?

Basic (Questions 1–20)

2. Relevant Cash Flows. Winnebagel Corp. currently sells 19,000 motor homes per year at $50,000 each, and 6,000 luxury motor coaches per year at $90,000 each. The company wants to introduce a new portable camper to fill out its product line; it hopes to sell 14,000 of these campers per year at $16,000 each. An independent consultant has determined that if Winnebagel introduces the new campers, it should boost the sales of its existing motor homes by 2,500 units per year, and reduce the sales of its motor coaches by 900 units per year. What is the amount to use as the annual sales figure when evaluating this project? Why?

3. **Calculating Projected Net Income.**   A proposed new investment has projected sales of $950,000. Variable costs are 60 percent of sales, and fixed costs are $210,000; depreciation is $102,000. Prepare a pro forma income statement assuming a tax rate of 35 percent. What is the projected net income?

4. **Calculating OCF.**   Consider the following income statement:

Sales	$687,500
Costs	343,860
Depreciation	110,000
EBIT	?
Taxes (35%)	?
Net income	?

Fill in the missing numbers and then calculate the OCF. What is the CCA tax shield?

5. **CCA and UCC.**   A piece of newly purchased industrial equipment costs $975,000. It falls in CCA Class 8, with a rate of 20 percent for tax purposes. Calculate the annual capital cost allowances (CCA) and end-of-the-year book values (UCC) for this equipment for the first five years.

6. **CCA and UCC.**   Trinity Corp. purchased a private jet for $200,000 for the use of its senior managers. The jet falls in CCA Class 9, with a 25 percent rate. Calculate the annual capital cost allowances (CCA) and end-of-the-year book values (UCC) for this equipment for the first seven years.

7. **CCA and Aftertax Cash Flow.**   Consider an asset that costs $580,000 and falls in CCA Class 10, with a 30 percent rate. The asset is to be used in a six-year project; at the end of the project, the asset can be sold for $105,000. The relevant tax rate is 35 percent. What is the aftertax cash flow from the sale if the asset class is terminated? What is the aftertax cash flow from the sale if the asset class continues?

8. **CCA and Aftertax Cash Flow.**   An asset used in a four-year project falls in CCA Class 8 for tax purposes. The asset has an acquisition cost of $7,100,000 and will be sold for $1,500,000 at the end of the project. The tax rate is 34 percent. What is the aftertax cash flow from the sale if the asset class is terminated? What is the aftertax cash flow from the sale if the asset class continues?

9. **Calculating Project OCF.**   Herrera Music Company is considering the sale of a new sound board used in recording studios. The new board would sell for $25,000, and the company expects to sell 1,800 per year. If the company sells the new board, it would lose sales of 150 sound boards per year of the model it currently sells. The old board retails for $22,000. Variable costs are 55 percent of sales, depreciation on the equipment to produce the new board will be $1,500,000 per year, and fixed costs are $890,000 per year. If the tax rate is 38 percent, what is the annual OCF for the project?

10. **Calculating Project OCF.**   Nipissing, Inc., is considering a new three-year expansion project that requires an initial fixed asset investment of $2.4 million. The fixed asset falls in CCA Class 8 with a 20 percent rate for tax purposes. When the project is

completed, the fixed asset will be worthless, and Nipissing will have other assets remaining in that CCA class. The project is estimated to generate $2,550,000 in annual sales, with costs of $1,180,000. If the tax rate is 35 percent, what is the OCF for each year of this project?

11. **Calculating Project NPV.** In the previous problem, suppose the required return on the project is 14 percent. What is the project's NPV?

12. **Calculating Project NPV.** In the previous problem, suppose the project requires an initial investment in net working capital of $250,000 and the fixed asset will have a market value of $300,000 at the end of the project. What is the new NPV?

13. **NPV and CCA.** In the previous problem, suppose the fixed asset actually falls into CCA Class 10, with a 30 percent rate. All the other facts are the same. What is the new NPV?

14. **Project Evaluation.** Kolby's Korndogs is looking at a new sausage system with an installed cost of $490,000. The system will be depreciated at a 20 percent CCA rate. At the end of the project's five-year life, the sausage system can be sold for $40,000, and Kolby's Korndogs will have other assets remaining in that asset class. The sausage system will save the firm $146,000 per year in pretax operating costs, and the system requires an initial investment in net working capital of $35,000. If the tax rate is 34 percent and the discount rate is 8 percent, what is the NPV of this project?

15. **Project Evaluation.** Your firm is contemplating the purchase of a new $850,000 computer-based order entry system. The system falls in CCA Class 10 with a 30 percent rate for tax purposes. At the end of the project's five-year life, the system will be worth $180,000, and your firm will have other assets remaining in that asset class. You will save $310,000 before taxes per year in order processing costs, and you will be able to reduce working capital by $75,000 at the beginning of the project. Working capital will revert back to normal at the end of the project. If the tax rate is 35 percent, what is the IRR for this project?

16. **Project Evaluation.** In the previous problem, suppose your required return on the project is 20 percent and your pretax cost savings are $340,000 per year. Will you accept the project? What if the pretax cost savings are only $280,000 per year?

17. **Scenario Analysis.** Crankshaft Transmissions, Inc., has the following estimates for its new gear assembly project: price = $1,320 per unit; variable costs = $270 per unit; fixed costs = $6 million; quantity = 75,000 units. Suppose the company believes all of its estimates are accurate only to within ±15 percent. What values should the company use for the four variables given here when it performs its best-case scenario analysis? What about the worst-case scenario?

18. **Sensitivity Analysis.** For the company in the previous problem, suppose management is most concerned about the impact of its price estimate on the project's profitability. How could you address this concern for Crankshaft Transmissions? Describe how you would calculate your answer. What values would you use for the other forecast variables?

19. **Sensitivity Analysis.** We are evaluating a project that costs $1,390,000, has a six-year life, and has no salvage value. Assume that depreciation is straight-line to zero over the life of the project. Sales are projected at 110,000 units per year. Price per unit is $36, variable cost per unit is $22, and fixed costs are $975,000 per year. The tax rate is 35 percent, and we require a 15 percent return on this project.

a.   Calculate the base-case cash flow and NPV. What is the sensitivity of NPV to changes in the sales figure? Explain what your answer tells you about a 500-unit decrease in projected sales.

   b.   What is the sensitivity of OCF to changes in the variable cost figure? Explain what your answer tells you about a $1 decrease in estimated variable costs.

20. Scenario Analysis.   In the previous problem, suppose the projections given for price, quantity, variable costs, and fixed costs are all accurate to within ±10 percent. Calculate the best-case and worst-case NPV figures.

**Intermediate
(Questions 21–25)**

21. Calculating Project Cash Flows and NPV.   Pappy's Potato has come up with a new product, the Potato Pet (they are freeze-dried to last longer). Pappy's paid $120,000 for a marketing survey to determine the viability of the product. It is felt that Potato Pet will generate sales of $430,000 per year. The fixed costs associated with this will be $165,000 per year, and variable costs will amount to 20 percent of sales. The equipment necessary for production of the Potato Pets will cost $520,000, will have no salvage value, and will be depreciated in a straight-line manner to zero over the four years of the product life (as with all fads, it is felt the sales will end quickly). This is the only initial cost for the production. Pappy's is in a 40 percent tax bracket and has a required return of 13 percent. Calculate the payback period, NPV, and IRR.

22. Project Analysis.   Elrond's Machine Shop is considering a four-year project to improve its production efficiency. Buying a new machine press for $480,000 is estimated to result in $205,000 in annual pretax cost savings. The press falls in CCA Class 43, with a 30 percent rate, and it will have a salvage value of $55,000 at the end of the project. Elrond will have other assets left in that asset class when the project is completed. The press also requires an initial investment in spare parts inventory of $21,000, along with an additional $3,000 in inventory for each succeeding year of the project. If the shop's tax rate is 34 percent and its discount rate is 15 percent, should Elrond buy and install the machine press?

23. Project Analysis.   Jeans Paradise, Inc., is considering a purchase of new equipment that will cost $600,000. This equipment will produce 40,000 pairs of white jeans per year for ten years. The white jeans will be sold at a price of $50 for the first five years and $40 afterwards. Variable costs remain at $10 per pair of jeans during the ten-year period. The equipment will be depreciated at a CCA rate of 30 percent, and the company always expects to have several pieces of equipment in that CCA Class. After ten years, the equipment will be sold for $80,000. A $40,000 initial investment in net working capital is required, which will be recovered at the end of the project. A $10,000 study, just completed by the company's consultants, suggests that if Jeans Paradise starts selling white jeans, the before-tax operating revenue from the existing sale of its black jeans will decline by $9,000 per year. Jeans Paradise is in a 40 percent tax bracket and has a required return of 16 percent. Should Jeans Paradise start producing the white jeans?

24. Sensitivity Analysis.   Consider a three-year project with the following information: initial fixed asset investment = $625,000; straight-line depreciation to zero over the five-year life; zero salvage value; price = $29; variable costs = $18; fixed costs = $185,000; quantity sold = 100,000 units; tax rate = 34 percent. How sensitive is OCF to changes in quantity sold?

25. Sensitivity Analysis.   You are considering a new product launch. The project will cost $950,000, have a four-year life, and have no salvage value; depreciation is straight-line to zero. Sales are projected at 180 units per year; price per unit will be

$18,500, variable cost per unit will be $14,000, and fixed costs will be $185,000 per year. The required return on the project is 15 percent, and the relevant tax rate is 35 percent.

a. Based on your experience, you think the unit sales, variable cost, and fixed cost projections given here are probably accurate to within ±10 percent. What are the upper and lower bounds for these projections? What is the base-case NPV? What are the best-case and worst-case scenarios?

b. Evaluate the sensitivity of your base-case NPV to changes in fixed costs.

26. **Project Analysis.** McGilla Golf has decided to sell a new line of golf clubs. The clubs will sell for $650 per set and have a variable cost of $340 per set. The company has spent $150,000 for a marketing study that determined the company will sell 60,000 sets per year for seven years. The marketing study also determined that the company will lose sales of 10,000 sets of its high-priced clubs. The high-priced clubs sell at $1,100 and have variable costs of $550. The company will also increase sales of its cheap clubs by 15,000 sets. The cheap clubs sell for $300 and have variable costs of $100 per set. The fixed costs each year will be $9,000,000. The company has also spent $1,000,000 on research and development for the new clubs. The plant and equipment required will cost $18,400,000, will be depreciated at a CCA rate of 30 percent (Class 43), and will have a salvage value of $3,000,000. McGilla Golf will have other assets left in that asset class when the project is finished. The new clubs will also require an increase in net working capital of $1,100,000 that will be returned at the end of the project. The tax rate is 40 percent, and the cost of capital is 14 percent. Calculate the payback period, the NPV, and the IRR.

27. **Scenario Analysis.** In the previous problem, you feel that the values are accurate to within only ±10 percent. What are the best-case and worst-case NPVs? (Hint: The price and variable costs for the two existing sets of clubs are known with certainty; only the sales gained or lost are uncertain.)

Challenge
(Questions 26–27)

MINI-CASE

CONFEDERATION ELECTRONICS

Confederation Electronics is a mid-sized electronics manufacturer located in Markham, Ontario. The company president is Shelly Couts, who inherited the company. The company originally repaired radios and other household appliances when it was founded over 70 years ago. Over the years, the company has expanded, and it is now a reputable manufacturer of various specialty electronic items. Jay McCanless, a recent MBA graduate, has been hired by the company in its finance department.

One of the major revenue-producing items manufactured by Confederation Electronics is a Personal Digital Assistant (PDA). Confederation Electronics currently has one PDA model on the market and sales have been excellent. The PDA is a unique item in that it comes in a variety of tropical colours and is pre-programmed to play Jimmy Buffet music. However, as with any electronic item, technology changes rapidly, and the current PDA has limited features in comparison with newer models. Confederation Electronics spent $750,000 to develop a prototype for a new PDA that has all the features of the existing one, but adds new features such as cell phone capability. The company has spent a further $200,000 for a market-

ing study to determine the expected sales figures for the new PDA.

Confederation Electronics can manufacture the new PDA for $86 each in variable costs. Fixed costs for the operation are estimated to run $3 million per year. The estimated sales volume is 70,000, 80,000, 100,000, 85,000, and 75,000 per each year for the next five years, respectively. The unit price of the new PDA will be $250. The necessary equipment can be purchased for $15 million and falls in CCA Class 43, with a 30 percent rate. When the project is completed, Confederation Electronics will have other assets remaining in that CCA asset class. It is believed the value of the equipment in five years will be $3 million.

Net working capital for the PDAs will be 20 percent of sales and will occur with the timing of the cash flows for the year (i.e., there is no initial outlay for NWC). Changes in NWC will thus first occur in Year 1 with the first year's sales. Confederation Electronics has a 35 percent corporate tax rate and a 12 percent required return.

Shelly has asked Jay to prepare a report that answers the following questions:

QUESTIONS

1. What is the payback period of the project?

2. What is the profitability index of the project?

3. What is the IRR of the project?

4. What is the NPV of the project?

5. How sensitive is the NPV to changes in the price of the new PDA?

6. How sensitive is the NPV to changes in the quantity sold?

7. Should Confederation Electronics produce the new PDA?

8. Suppose Confederation Electronics loses sales on other models because of the introduction of the new model. How would this affect your analysis?

10 Some Lessons from Capital Market History

With the total return of the S&P/TSX Composite index over 17 percent in 2006, the Canadian stock market performance was well above average. It was an even better year for investors in the stock of Blue Pearl Mining, which gained a whopping 1,310 percent, and investors in Theratechnologies, a biopharmaceutical company, had to be shocked by the 564 percent gain of that stock. Of course, not all stocks increased in value during the year. Stock in Point North Energy, an oil and gas exploration company, fell 97 percent, and stock in WEX Pharmaceuticals, a neuro-bioscience company, dropped 83 percent. These examples show that there were tremendous potential profits to be made during 2006, but there was also the risk of losing money, and lots of it. So what should you, as a stock market investor, expect when you invest your own money? In this chapter, we study over seven decades of market history to find out.

This chapter and the next take us into new territory: the relation between risk and return. As you will see, this chapter has a lot of very practical information for anyone thinking of investing in financial assets such as stocks and bonds. For example, suppose you were to start investing in stocks today. Do you think your money would grow at an average rate of 5 percent per year? Or 10 percent? Or 20 percent? This chapter gives you an idea of what to expect (the answer may surprise you). The chapter also shows how risky certain investments can be, and it gives you the tools to think about risk in an objective way.

After studying this chapter, you should have a good understanding of:

10.1 How to calculate the return on an investment.

10.2 The historical record of capital market returns.

10.3 The historical returns on various important types of investments.

10.4 The historical risks on various important types of investments.

10.5 The difference between the arithmetic and geometric average returns.

10.6 The capital market efficiency and its three forms.

Thus far, we haven't had much to say about what determines the required return on an investment. In one sense, the answer is very simple: The required return depends on the risk of the investment. The greater the risk, the greater is the required return.

Having said this, we are left with a somewhat more difficult problem. How can we measure the amount of risk present in an investment? Put another way, what does it mean to say that one investment is riskier than another? Obviously, we need to define what we mean by risk if we are going to answer these questions. This is our task in the next two chapters.

From the last several chapters, we know that one of the responsibilities of the financial manager is to assess the value of proposed investments. In doing this, it is important that we first look at what financial investments have to offer. At a minimum, the return we require from a proposed nonfinancial investment must be at least as large as what we can get from buying financial assets of similar risk.

Our goal in this chapter is to provide a perspective on what capital market history can tell us about risk and return. The most important thing to get out of this chapter is a feel for the numbers. What is a high return? What is a low one? More generally, what returns should we expect from financial assets and what are the risks from such investments? This perspective is essential for understanding how to analyze and value risky investment projects.

We start our discussion of risk and return by describing the historical experience of investors in Canadian financial markets. In 1957, for example, the stock market lost 21 percent of its value. The next year, however, the stock market gained 31 percent. In more recent memory, the market lost about 11 percent of its value on October 19, 1987, alone. Just two days later, the market went up by 9 percent. What lessons, if any, can financial managers learn from such shifts in the stock market? We will explore the last half century (and then some) of market history to find out.

Not everyone agrees on the value of studying history. On the one hand, there is philosopher George Santayana's famous comment "Those who do not remember the past are condemned to repeat it." On the other hand, there is industrialist Henry Ford's equally famous comment "History is more or less bunk." Nonetheless, perhaps everyone would agree with the following observation from Mark Twain: "October. This is one of the peculiarly dangerous months to speculate in stocks in. The others are July, January, September, April, November, May, March, June, December, August, and February."

There are two central lessons that emerge from our study of market history. First: There is a reward for bearing risk. Second: The greater the potential reward, the greater the risk. To understand these facts about market returns, we devote much of this chapter to reporting the statistics and numbers that make up the modern capital market history of Canada. In the next chapter, these facts provide the foundation for our study of how financial markets put a price on risk.

The number of Web sites devoted to financial markets and instruments is astounding, and increasing daily. Be sure to check out the textbook's Online Learning Centre (OLC) for links to finance-related sites! www.mcgrawhill.ca/olc/ross

10.1 | RETURNS

We wish to discuss historical returns on different types of financial assets. The first thing we need to do, then, is to briefly discuss how to calculate the return from investing.

Dollar Returns

If you buy an asset of any sort, your gain (or loss) from that investment is called your *return on investment*. This return will usually have two components. First: You may receive some cash directly while you own the investment. This is called the income component of your

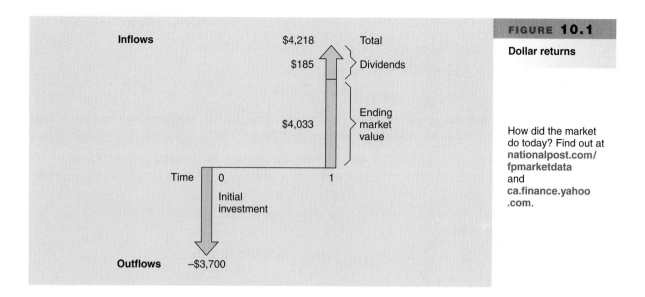

FIGURE **10.1**

Dollar returns

How did the market do today? Find out at **nationalpost.com/ fpmarketdata** and **ca.finance.yahoo .com**.

return. Second: The value of the asset you purchase will often change. In this case, you have a capital gain or capital loss on your investment.[1]

To illustrate, suppose the Video Concept Company has several thousand shares of stock outstanding. You purchased some of these shares of stock in the company at the beginning of the year. It is now year-end, and you want to determine how well you have done on your investment.

First, over the year, a company may pay cash dividends to its shareholders. As a stock-holder in Video Concept Company, you are a part owner of the company. If the company is profitable, it may choose to distribute some of its profits to shareholders (we discuss the details of dividend policy in Chapter 14). So, as the owner of some stock, you will receive some cash. This cash is the income component from owning the stock.

In addition to the dividend, the other part of your return is the capital gain or capi-tal loss on the stock. This part arises from changes in the value of your investment. For example, consider the cash flows illustrated in Figure 10.1. At the beginning of the year, the stock is selling for $37 per share. If you buy 100 shares, you have a total outlay of $3,700. Suppose, over the year, the stock pays a dividend of $1.85 per share. By the end of the year, then, you will have received income of:

Dividend = $1.85 × 100 = $185

Also, the value of the stock rises to $40.33 per share by the end of the year. Your 100 shares are worth $4,033, so you have a capital gain of:

Capital gain = ($40.33 − 37) × 100 = $333

On the other hand, if the price had dropped to, say, $34.78, you would have had a capital loss of:

Capital loss = ($34.78 − 37) × 100 = −$222

Notice that a capital loss is the same thing as a negative capital gain.

---

[1]As we mentioned in an earlier chapter, strictly speaking, what is and what is not a capital gain (or loss) is determined by the Canada Revenue Agency. We thus use the terms loosely.

The total dollar return on your investment is the sum of the dividend and the capital gain:

Total dollar return = Dividend income + Capital gain (or loss)   [10.1]

In our first example, the total dollar return is thus given by:

Total dollar return = $185 + 333 = $518

Notice that, if you sold the stock at the end of the year, the total amount of cash you would have would be your initial investment plus the total return. In the preceding example, then:

$$\begin{aligned} \text{Total cash if stock is sold} &= \text{Initial investment} + \text{Total return} \\ &= \$3,700 + 518 \\ &= \$4,218 \end{aligned}$$ [10.2]

As a check, notice that this is the same as the proceeds from the sale of the stock plus the dividends:

$$\begin{aligned} \text{Proceeds from stock sale} + \text{Dividends} &= \$40.33 \times 100 + 185 \\ &= \$4,033 + 185 \\ &= \$4,218 \end{aligned}$$

Suppose you hold on to your Video Concept stock and don't sell it at the end of the year. Should you still consider the capital gain as part of your return? Isn't this only a "paper" gain and not really a return if you don't sell the stock?

The answer to the first question is a strong yes, and the answer to the second is an equally strong no. The capital gain is every bit as much a part of your return as the dividend, and you should certainly count it as part of your return. That you actually decided to keep the stock and not sell (you don't "realize" the gain) is irrelevant because you could have converted it to cash if you had wanted to. Whether you choose to do so or not is up to you.

After all, if you insisted on converting your gain to cash, you could always sell the stock at year-end and immediately reinvest by buying the stock back. There is no net difference between doing this and just not selling (assuming, of course, that there are no tax consequences from selling the stock). Again, the point is that whether you actually cash out and buy sodas (or whatever) or reinvest by not selling doesn't affect the return you earn.

Percentage Returns

It is usually more convenient to summarize information about returns in percentage terms, rather than dollar terms, because that way your return doesn't depend on how much you actually invest. The question we want to answer is this: How much do we get for each dollar we invest?

To answer this question, let P_t be the price of the stock at the beginning of the year and let D_{t+1} be the dividend paid on the stock during the year. Consider the cash flows in Figure 10.2. These are the same as those in Figure 10.1, except that we have now expressed everything on a per-share basis.

In our example, the price at the beginning of the year was $37 per share and the dividend paid during the year on each share was $1.85. As we discussed in Chapter 7, expressing the dividend as a percentage of the beginning stock price results in the dividend yield:

$$\begin{aligned} \text{Dividend yield} &= D_{t+1}/P_t \\ &= \$1.85/37 = .05 = 5\% \end{aligned}$$ [10.3]

This says that, for each dollar we invest, we get five cents in dividends.

Go to
**www.smartmoney
.com/marketmap**
for a cool Java applet
that shows today's
returns by market
sector.

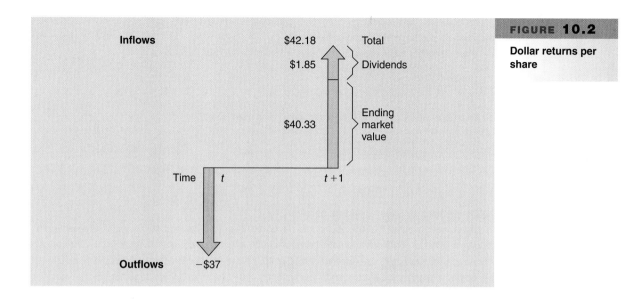

FIGURE 10.2

Dollar returns per share

The second component of our percentage return is the capital gains yield. Recall (from Chapter 7) that this is calculated as the change in the price during the year (the capital gain) divided by the beginning price:

$$\text{Capital gains yield} = (P_{t+1} - P_t)/P_t \qquad \qquad \textbf{[10.4]}$$
$$= (\$40.33 - 37)/37$$
$$= \$3.33/37$$
$$= 9\%$$

So, per dollar invested, we get nine cents in capital gains.

Putting it together, per dollar invested, we get 5 cents in dividends and 9 cents in capital gains; so, we get a total of 14 cents. Our percentage return is 14 cents on the dollar, or 14 percent.

To check this, notice that we invested $3,700 and ended up with $4,218. By what percentage did our $3,700 increase? As we saw, we picked up $4,218 − 3,700 = $518. This is a $518/3,700 = 14% increase.

To give a more concrete example, stock in the Bank of Nova Scotia (BNS) began 2006 at $46.14 a share. BNS paid a dividend of $1.56 per share during 2006, and the stock price at the end of the year was $52.10. What was the return on BNS for the year? For practice, see if you agree that the answer is 16.30 percent. Of course, negative returns occur as well. For example, in 2006 NOVA Chemicals' stock price at the beginning of the year was $38.81 per share, and a dividend of $0.40 was paid. The stock ended the year at $32.50 per share. Verify that the loss was 15.23 percent for the year.

Calculating Returns   EXAMPLE 10.1

Suppose you buy some stock for $25 per share. At the end of the year, the price is $35 per share. During the year, you get a $2 dividend per share. This is the situation illustrated in Figure 10.3. What is

(continued)

the dividend yield? The capital gains yield? The percentage return? If your total investment was $1,000, how much do you have at the end of the year?

Your $2 dividend per share works out to a dividend yield of:

Dividend yield $= D_{t+1}/P_t$
$$= \$2/25 = .08 = 8\%$$

The per-share capital gain is $10, so the capital gains yield is:

Capital gains yield $= (P_{t+1} - P_t)/P_t$
$$= (\$35 - 25)/25$$
$$= \$10/25$$
$$= 40\%$$

The total percentage return is thus 48 percent.

If you had invested $1,000, you would have had $1,480 at the end of the year, representing a 48 percent increase. To check this, note that your $1,000 would have bought you $1,000/25 = 40 shares. Your 40 shares would then have paid you a total of 40 × $2 = $80 in cash dividends. Your $10 per share gain would have given you a total capital gain of $10 × 40 = $400. Add these together, and you get the $480 increase.

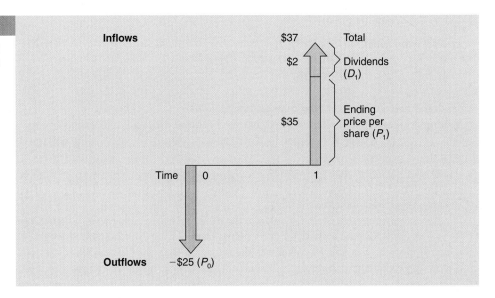

FIGURE 10.3

Cash flow—an investment example

CONCEPT QUESTIONS

10.1a   What are the two parts of total return?

10.1b   Why are unrealized capital gains or losses included in the calculation of returns?

10.1c   What is the difference between a dollar return and a percentage return? Why are percentage returns more convenient?

10.2 | THE HISTORICAL RECORD

Capital market history can tell us what to expect in the way of returns from risky assets. In this section, we present year-to-year historical rates of return on five important types of financial investments.[2] The returns can be interpreted as what you would have earned if you had held portfolios of the following:

For more on market history, visit **www.globalfindata .com** where you can download free sample data.

1. Canadian large-company stocks. This large-company stock portfolio is based on the S&P/TSX Composite index, which consists of the largest Canadian companies (in terms of total market value of outstanding stock).

2. U.S. large-company stocks. This large-company stock portfolio is based on the Standard & Poor's 500 index, which contains 500 of the largest companies in the United States.

3. Canadian small-company stocks. This is a portfolio composed of stock of smaller companies, again measured by the market value of outstanding stock, that are included in the BMO Small Cap Index.

4. Long-term Government of Canada bonds. This is a portfolio of Government of Canada bonds with over 10 years to maturity.

5. Government of Canada Treasury bills. This is a portfolio of Treasury bills (T-bills for short) with a three-month maturity.

These returns are not adjusted for inflation or taxes; thus, they are nominal, pretax returns.

In addition to the year-to-year returns on these financial instruments, the year-to-year percentage change in the consumer price index (CPI) is also computed. This is a commonly used measure of inflation, so we can calculate real returns using this as the inflation rate.

A First Look

Before looking closely at the different portfolio returns, we take a look at the big picture. Figure 10.4 shows what happened to $1 invested in these different portfolios at the beginning of 1934. The growth in value for each of the different portfolios over the 73-year period ending in 2006 is given separately (the small-cap stocks are omitted). Notice that to get everything on a single graph, some modification in scaling is used. As is commonly done with financial series, the vertical axis is scaled such that equal distances measure equal percentage (as opposed to dollar) changes in values.

Go to **www.bigcharts.com** to see both intraday and long-term charts.

Looking at Figure 10.4, we see that the U.S. large-company, or "large-cap" (short for large-capitalization), investment did the best overall. Every dollar invested grew to $2,436.38 over the 73 years. The Canadian large-company stock portfolio also did well; a dollar invested in it grew to $1,484.70.

At the other end, the T-bill portfolio grew to only $31.28. This is even less impressive when we consider the inflation over this period. As illustrated, the increase in the price level was such that $15.32 is needed just to replace the original $1.

Given the historical record, why would anybody buy anything other than large-company stocks? If you look closely at Figure 10.4, you will probably see the answer. The T-bill portfolio and the long-term government bond portfolio grew more slowly than did the stock portfolios, but they also grew much more steadily. The stocks ended up on top, but, as you can see,

---

[2]The returns were obtained from Global Financial Data and BMO Capital Markets.

| FIGURE **10.4** | A $1 investment in different types of portfolios: 1934–2006 (Year-end 1933 = $1) |

Source: Used with permission of Global Financial Data.

they grew quite erratically at times. For example, the Canadian large-company stocks had a smaller return than the long-term government bonds in 30 out of 73 years.

A Closer Look

To illustrate the variability of the different investments, Figures 10.5 through 10.8 plot the year-to-year percentage returns in the form of vertical bars drawn from the horizontal axis. The height of the bar tells us the return for the particular year. For example, looking at the long-term government bonds (Figure 10.7), we see that the largest historical return (44.93 percent) occurred in 1982. This was a good year for bonds. In comparing these charts, notice the differences in the vertical axis scales. With these differences in mind, you can see how predictably the Treasury bills (Figure 10.7) behaved compared to the small stocks (Figure 10.6).

The returns shown in these bar graphs are sometimes very large. Looking at the graphs, we see, for example, that the largest single-year return was an impressive 52.26 percent for

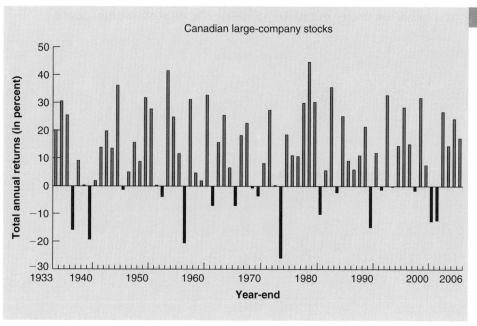

Source: Used with permission of Global Financial Data.

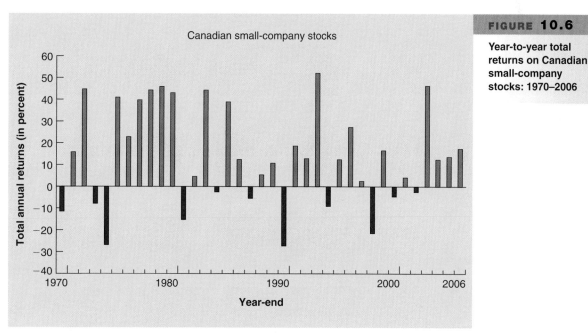

Source: Used with permission of BMO Capital Markets.

the small-cap stocks in 1993. In the same year, the Canadian large-company stocks "only" returned 32.55 percent. In contrast, the largest Treasury bill return was 19.23 percent in 1981. For future reference, the actual year-to-year returns for the Canadian large-company stocks, U.S. large-company stocks, Canadian small-company stocks, long-term government bonds, Treasury bills, and the CPI are shown in Table 10.1.

FIGURE 10.7   **Year-to-year total returns on long-term government bonds and T-bills: 1934–2006**

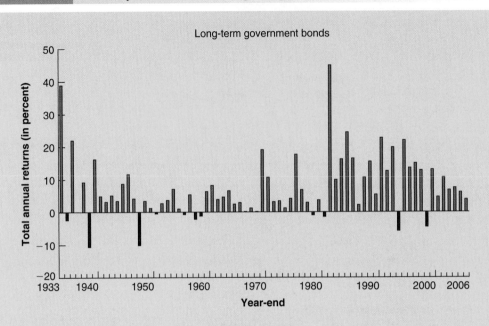

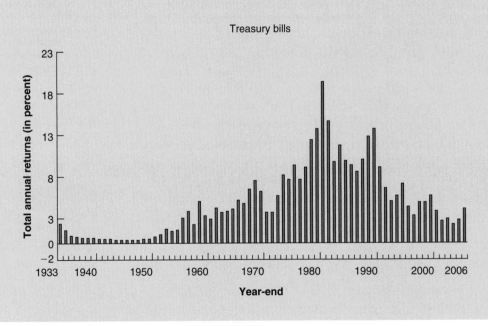

Source: Used with permission of Global Financial Data.

Year	Canadian Large Company Stocks	U.S. Large Company Stocks	Canadian Small Company Stocks	Long-Term Government Bonds	3-month Treasury Bills	Consumer Price Index
1934	20.14	−2.34		38.92	2.32	1.18
1935	30.51	47.22		−2.29	1.59	2.33
1936	25.54	32.8		21.91	0.85	1.14
1937	−15.79	−35.26		0.00	0.72	4.49
1938	9.13	33.2		9.27	0.60	−2.15
1939	0.17	−0.91		−10.66	0.70	2.20
1940	−19.21	−10.08		16.29	0.71	5.38
1941	1.92	−11.77		4.83	0.58	6.12
1942	13.92	21.07		3.10	0.54	2.88
1943	19.65	25.76		5.11	0.48	1.87
1944	13.43	19.69		3.38	0.39	−1.83
1945	35.99	36.46		8.79	0.36	1.87
1946	−1.46	−8.18		11.72	0.39	5.50
1947	5.01	5.24		4.20	0.41	14.78
1948	15.60	5.1		−10.04	0.41	9.09
1949	8.66	18.06		3.51	0.49	0.69
1950	31.68	30.58		1.13	0.55	6.21
1951	27.69	24.55		−0.52	0.80	10.39
1952	0.19	18.5		2.66	1.08	−1.18
1953	−3.75	−1.1		3.77	1.70	0.00
1954	41.45	52.4		7.15	1.45	0.00
1955	24.72	31.43		1.03	1.63	0.60
1956	11.52	6.63		−0.79	2.96	2.96
1957	−20.58	−10.85		5.40	3.83	1.72
1958	31.25	43.34		−2.05	2.28	2.82
1959	4.59	11.90		−1.13	4.92	1.10
1960	1.78	0.48		6.43	3.25	1.63
1961	32.75	26.81		8.23	2.85	0.00
1962	−7.09	−8.78		3.89	4.13	1.60
1963	15.60	22.69		4.58	3.62	2.11
1964	25.43	16.36		6.51	3.81	2.06
1965	6.68	12.36		2.43	4.06	3.03
1966	−7.07	−10.10		3.02	5.11	3.43
1967	18.09	23.94		0.14	4.74	3.79
1968	22.45	11		1.18	6.45	4.11
1969	−0.81	−8.47		0.15	7.43	4.82
1970	−3.57	3.94	−11.69	19.19	6.16	1.26
1971	8.01	14.3	15.83	10.61	3.62	4.96
1972	27.38	18.99	44.71	3.16	3.62	5.12
1973	0.27	−14.69	−7.82	3.39	5.61	9.36
1974	−25.93	−26.47	−26.88	1.24	8.11	12.33
1975	18.48	37.23	40.99	4.03	7.65	9.45
1976	11.02	23.93	22.77	17.72	9.24	5.85
1977	10.71	−7.16	39.93	6.76	7.58	9.47
1978	29.72	6.57	44.41	2.91	9.03	8.41
1979	44.77	18.61	46.04	−1.01	12.33	9.76
1980	30.13	32.5	42.86	3.55	13.57	11.11

TABLE 10.1

Year-to-year total returns: 1934–2006

(continued)

TABLE 10.1

(continued)

Year	Canadian Large Company Stocks	U.S. Large Company Stocks	Canadian Small Company Stocks	Long-Term Government Bonds	3-month Treasury Bills	Consumer Price Index
1981	−10.25	−4.92	−15.10	−1.35	19.23	12.18
1982	5.54	21.55	4.55	44.93	14.52	9.24
1983	35.49	22.56	44.30	10.02	9.72	4.60
1984	−2.39	6.27	−2.33	16.27	11.64	3.69
1985	25.07	31.73	38.98	24.40	9.85	4.38
1986	8.95	18.67	12.33	16.47	9.35	4.19
1987	5.88	5.25	−5.47	2.25	8.46	4.15
1988	11.08	16.61	5.46	10.57	9.91	3.99
1989	21.37	31.69	10.66	15.60	12.73	5.23
1990	−14.80	−3.10	−27.32	5.30	13.59	4.97
1991	12.02	30.46	18.51	22.62	9.08	3.79
1992	−1.43	7.62	13.01	12.49	6.56	2.13
1993	32.55	10.08	52.26	19.76	4.95	1.69
1994	−0.18	1.32	−9.21	−5.81	5.68	0.20
1995	14.53	37.58	12.55	22.06	7.11	1.75
1996	28.35	22.96	27.49	13.60	4.29	2.20
1997	14.98	33.36	2.60	14.89	3.25	0.75
1998	−1.58	28.58	−21.46	12.91	4.83	1.02
1999	31.71	21.04	16.42	−4.51	4.79	2.58
2000	7.41	−9.10	−4.29	13.03	5.61	3.23
2001	−12.57	−11.89	4.12	4.72	3.81	0.70
2002	−12.44	−22.10	−2.50	10.60	2.57	3.88
2003	26.72	28.68	46.30	6.82	2.90	1.99
2004	14.48	10.88	12.62	7.59	2.24	2.12
2005	24.13	4.91	13.75	6.14	2.77	2.15
2006	17.26	15.79	17.59	3.97	4.12	1.64

Sources: Used with permission of Global Financial Data.

FIGURE 10.8

Year-to-year inflation: 1934–2006

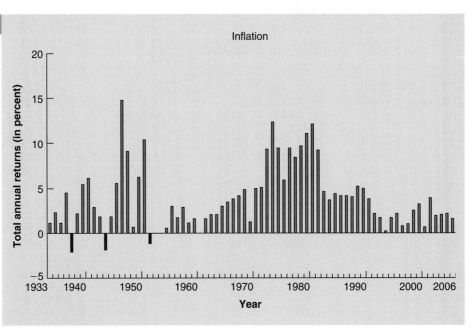

Source: Used with permission of Global Financial Data.

10.3 | AVERAGE RETURNS: THE FIRST LESSON

As you've probably begun to notice, the history of capital market returns is too complicated to be of much use in its undigested form. We need to begin summarizing all these numbers. Accordingly, we discuss how to go about condensing the detailed data. We start out by calculating average returns.

Calculating Average Returns

The obvious way to calculate the average returns on the different investments in Table 10.1 is simply to add up the yearly returns and divide by 73. The result is the historical average of the individual values.

For example, if you add up the returns for the large Canadian stocks for the 73 years, you will get about 852.6. The average annual return is thus 852.6/73 = 11.7%. You interpret this 11.7 percent just like any other average. If you picked a year at random from the 73-year history and you had to guess what the return in that year was, the best guess would be 11.7 percent.

Average Returns: The Historical Record

Table 10.2 shows the average returns for the investments we have discussed. As shown, in a typical year, the small stocks increased in value by 14.0 percent. Notice also how much larger the stock returns are than the bond returns.

These averages are, of course, nominal since we haven't worried about inflation. Notice that the average inflation rate was 3.9 percent per year over this 73-year span. The nominal return on Treasury bills was 4.9 percent per year. The average real return on Treasury bills was thus approximately 1 percent per year; so, the real return on T-bills has been quite low historically.

Investment	Average Return
Canadian large stocks	11.7%
U.S. large stocks	12.8
Canadian small stocks*	14.0
Long-term government bonds	7.4
Treasury bills	4.9
Inflation	3.9

TABLE 10.2

Average annual returns: 1934–2006

*Average return on small stocks is based on data from 1970 to 2006.
Sources: Used with permission of Global Financial Data.

TABLE **10.3**		

Investment	Average Return	Risk Premium
Canadian large stocks	11.7%	6.8%
U.S. large stocks	12.8	7.9
Canadian small stocks*	14.0	9.1
Long-term government bonds	7.4	2.5
Treasury bills	4.9	0.0

Average annual returns and risk premiums: 1934–2006

*Average return on small stocks is based on data from 1970 to 2006.

Sources: Used with permission of Global Financial Data.

At the other extreme, small stocks had an average real return of about $14.0\% - 3.9\% = 10.1\%$, which is relatively large. If you remember the Rule of 72 (Chapter 4), then you recall that a quick back-of-the-envelope calculation tells us that 10.1 percent real growth doubles your buying power about every seven years. Notice also that the real value of the Canadian large stock portfolio increased by 7.8 percent in a typical year.

Risk Premiums

Now that we have computed some average returns, it seems logical to see how they compare with each other. Based on our discussion above, one such comparison involves government-issued securities. These are free of much of the variability we see in, for example, the stock market.

The government borrows money by issuing bonds. These bonds come in different forms. The ones we will focus on are the Treasury bills. These have the shortest time to maturity of the different government bonds. Because the government can always raise taxes to pay its bills, this debt is virtually free of any default risk over its short life. Thus, we will call the rate of return on such debt the *risk-free return,* and we will use it as a kind of benchmark.

A particularly interesting comparison involves the virtually risk-free return on T-bills and the very risky return on common stocks. The difference between these two returns can be interpreted as a measure of the *excess return* on the average risky asset (assuming the stock of a large Canadian corporation has about average risk compared to all risky assets).

We call this the "excess" return since it is the additional return we earn by moving from a relatively risk-free investment to a risky one. Because it can be interpreted as a reward for bearing risk, we will call it a **risk premium**.

risk premium
The excess return required from an investment in a risky asset over that required from a risk-free investment.

From Table 10.2, we can calculate the risk premiums for the different investments. We report only the nominal risk premium in Table 10.3 because there is only a slight difference between the historical nominal and real risk premiums.

The risk premium on T-bills is shown as zero in the table because we have assumed that they are riskless.

The First Lesson

Looking at Table 10.3, we see that the average risk premium earned by a typical Canadian large-company stock is $11.7\% - 4.9\% = 6.8\%$. This is a significant reward. The fact that it exists historically is an important observation, and it is the basis for our first lesson: Risky assets, on average, earn a risk premium. Put another way: There is a reward for bearing risk.

Why is this so? Why, for example, is the risk premium for small stocks larger than the risk premium for large stocks? More generally, what determines the relative sizes of the risk premiums for the different assets? The answers to these questions are at the heart of modern finance, and the next chapter is devoted to them. For now, part of the answer can be found by looking at the historical variability of the returns of these different investments. So, to get started, we now turn our attention to measuring variability in returns.

CONCEPT QUESTIONS

10.3a   What do we mean by excess return and risk premium?

10.3b   What was the real (as opposed to nominal) risk premium on the common stock portfolio?

10.3c   What was the nominal risk premium on long-term government bonds? The real risk premium?

10.3d   What is the first lesson from capital market history?

10.4 | THE VARIABILITY OF RETURNS: THE SECOND LESSON

We have already seen that the year-to-year returns on common stocks tend to be more volatile than the returns on, say, long-term government bonds. We now discuss measuring this variability so we can begin examining the subject of risk.

Frequency Distributions and Variability

To get started, we can draw a *frequency distribution* for the Canadian large-company stock returns like the one in Figure 10.9. What we have done here is to count up the number of times the annual return on the large stock portfolio falls within each 10 percent range. For example, in Figure 10.9, the height of 13 in the range 20 percent to 30 percent means that 13 of the 73 annual returns were in that range. Notice also that the returns are very concentrated between −10 and 40 percent.

What we need to do now is to actually measure the spread in returns. We know, for example, that the return on small stocks in a typical year was 14.0 percent. We now want to know how far the actual return deviates from this average in a typical year. In other words, we need a measure of how volatile the return is. The **variance** and its square root, the **standard deviation**, are the most commonly used measures of volatility. We describe how to calculate them next.

variance
The average squared difference between the actual return and the average return.

standard deviation
The positive square root of the variance.

The Historical Variance and Standard Deviation

The variance essentially measures the average squared difference between the actual returns and the average return. The bigger this number is, the more the actual returns tend to differ from the average return. Also, the larger the variance or standard deviation is, the more spread out the returns will be.

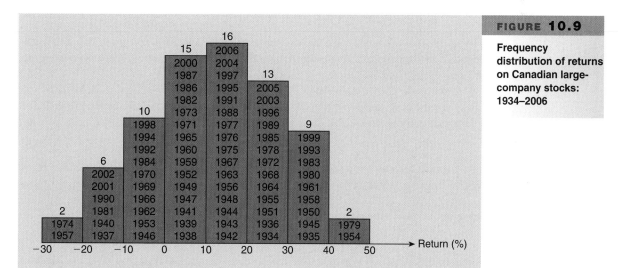

FIGURE 10.9

Frequency distribution of returns on Canadian large-company stocks: 1934–2006

Source: Used with permission of Global Financial Data.

The way we will calculate the variance and standard deviation depends on the specific situation. In this chapter, we are looking at historical returns; so, the procedure we describe here is the correct one for calculating the *historical* variance and standard deviation. If we were examining projected future returns, then the procedure would be different. We describe this procedure in the next chapter.

To illustrate how we calculate the historical variance, suppose a particular investment had returns of 10 percent, 12 percent, 3 percent, and −9 percent over the last four years. The average return is $(.10 + .12 + .03 - .09)/4 = 4\%$. Notice that the return is never actually equal to 4 percent. Instead, the first return deviates from the average by $.10 - .04 = .06$, the second return deviates from the average by $.12 - .04 = .08$, and so on. To compute the variance, we square each of these deviations, add up the squares, and divide the result by the number of returns less 1, or 3 in this case. This information is summarized in the following table.

For an easy-to-read review of basic stats, check out www.robertniles.com/stats.

Year	(1) Actual Return	(2) Average Return	(3) Deviation (1) − (2)	(4) Squared Deviation
1	.10	.04	.06	.0036
2	.12	.04	.08	.0064
3	.03	.04	−.01	.0001
4	−.09	.04	−.13	.0169
Totals	.16		.00	.0270

In the first column, we write down the four actual returns. In the third column, we calculate the difference between the actual returns and the average by subtracting out 4 percent. Finally, in the fourth column, we square the numbers in Column 3 to get the squared deviations from the average.

The variance can now be calculated by dividing .0270, the sum of the squared deviations, by the number of returns less 1. Let $Var(R)$ or σ^2 (read this as "sigma squared") stand for the variance of the return:

$$Var(R) = \sigma^2 = .027/(4 - 1) = .009$$

The standard deviation is the square root of the variance. So, if $SD(R)$ or σ stands for the standard deviation of the return:

$$SD(R) = \sigma = \sqrt{.009} = .09487$$

The square root of the variance is used because the variance is measured in "squared" percentages and thus is hard to interpret. The standard deviation is an ordinary percentage, so the answer here could be written as 9.487 percent.

In the table above, notice that the sum of the deviations is equal to zero. This will always be the case, and it provides a good way to check your work. In general, if we have T historical returns, where T is some number, we can write the historical variance as:

$$Var(R) = \frac{1}{T - 1} [(R_1 - \overline{R})^2 + \cdots + (R_T - \overline{R})^2] \qquad \textbf{[10.5]}$$

This formula tells us to do just what we did above: Take each of the T individual returns $(R_1, R_2, \ldots)$ and subtract the average return, $\overline{R}$; square the results, and add up all these squares; and finally, divide this total by the number of returns less $1(T - 1)$. The standard deviation is always the square root of $Var(R)$:

$$SD(R) = \sigma = \sqrt{Var(R)} \qquad \textbf{[10.6]}$$

Standard deviations are a widely used measure of volatility. Our nearby *Work the Web* box gives a real-world example.

WORK THE WEB

Standard deviations are widely reported for mutual funds. For example, the Investors Dividend Fund is Canada's largest mutual fund, with almost $14 billion in assets. How volatile is it? To find out, we went to **www.globefund.com**, typed the fund's name "Investors Dividend," and selected the series A units. Here is a portion of what we found:

Source: Reprinted with permission from *The Globe and Mail.*

The standard deviation for the Investors Dividend Fund, reported as a "3-year risk," is 5.40 percent. When you consider that the average stock has a standard deviation of about 50 percent, this seems like a very low number. The reason for the low standard deviation has to do with the power of diversification, a topic we discuss in the next chapter. In addition, only 81 percent of the fund assets are invested in stocks, while the rest is invested in less volatile bonds and cash. The fund has had positive returns over different time periods. For example, over the last three years, investors in the Investors Dividend Fund earned a respectable 12.10 percent return per year, which is higher than the group average of 10.68 percent, but still lower than the market index return of 16.65 percent. Also on the last row, you will see the beta coefficient, which is another measure of risk. The "beta" for the Investors Dividend Fund is 0.49. We will have more to say about this number—lots more—in the next chapter.

The Historical Record

Figure 10.10 summarizes much of our discussion of capital market history so far. It displays average returns, standard deviations, and frequency distributions of annual returns on a common scale. In Figure 10.10, notice, for example, that the standard deviation for the small-stock portfolio (22.5 percent per year) is more than 5 times that of the T-bill portfolio's standard deviation (4.1 percent per year). We will return to these figures shortly.

Normal Distribution

For many different random events in nature, a particular frequency distribution, the **normal distribution** (or *bell curve*), is useful for describing the probability of ending up in a given range. For example, the idea behind "grading on a curve" comes from the fact that exam scores often resemble a bell curve.

normal distribution
A symmetric, bell-shaped frequency distribution that is completely defined by its average and standard deviation.

EXAMPLE 10.2

Calculating the Variance and Standard Deviation

Suppose the Supertech Company and the Hyperdrive Company have experienced the following returns in the last four years:

Year	Supertech Returns	Hyperdrive Returns
2004	−.20	.05
2005	.50	.09
2006	.30	−.12
2007	.10	.20

What are the average returns? The variances? The standard deviations? Which investment was more volatile?

To calculate the average returns, we add up the returns and divide by 4. The results are:

Supertech average return $= \bar{R} = .70/4 = .175$
Hyperdrive average return $= \bar{R} = .22/4 = .055$

To calculate the variance for Supertech, we can summarize the relevant calculations as follows:

Year	(1) Actual Return	(2) Average Return	(3) Deviation (1) − (2)	(4) Squared Deviation
2004	−.20	.175	−.375	.140625
2005	.50	.175	.325	.105625
2006	.30	.175	.125	.015625
2007	.10	.175	−.075	.005625
Totals	.70		.000	.267500

Since there are four years of returns, we calculate the variances by dividing .2675 by $(4 − 1) = 3$:

	Supertech	Hyperdrive
Variance (σ^2)	.2675/3 = .0892	.0529/3 = .0176
Standard deviation (σ)	$\sqrt{.0892} = .2987$	$\sqrt{.0176} = .1327$

For practice, verify that you get the same answer as we do for Hyperdrive. Notice that the standard deviation for Supertech, 29.87 percent, is a little more than twice Hyperdrive's 13.27 percent; Supertech was thus the more volatile investment.

Figure 10.11 illustrates a normal distribution and its distinctive bell shape. As you can see, this distribution has a much cleaner appearance than the actual return distributions illustrated in Figure 10.10. Even so, like the normal distribution, the actual distributions do appear to be at least roughly mound shaped and symmetric. When this is true, the normal distribution is often a very good approximation.

Also, keep in mind that the distributions in Figure 10.10 are based on only 73 yearly observations, while Figure 10.11 is, in principle, based on an infinite number. So, if we had been able to observe returns for, say, 1,000 years, we might have filled in a lot of the irregularities and ended up with a much smoother picture. For our purposes, it is enough to observe that the returns are at least roughly normally distributed.

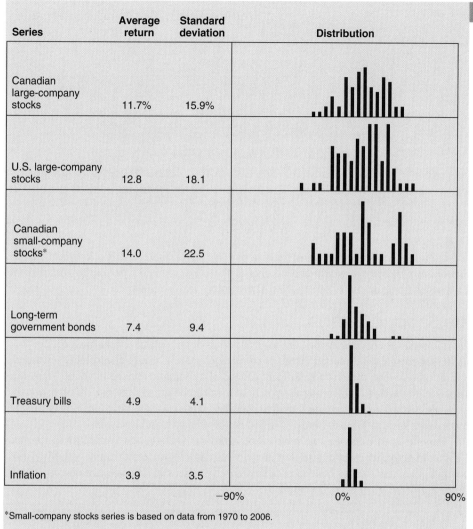

FIGURE 10.10

Historical returns, standard deviations, and frequency distributions: 1934–2006

Series	Average return	Standard deviation	Distribution
Canadian large-company stocks	11.7%	15.9%	
U.S. large-company stocks	12.8	18.1	
Canadian small-company stocks*	14.0	22.5	
Long-term government bonds	7.4	9.4	
Treasury bills	4.9	4.1	
Inflation	3.9	3.5	

*Small-company stocks series is based on data from 1970 to 2006.

*Sources: Used with permission of Global Financial Data.

The usefulness of the normal distribution stems from the fact that it is completely described by the average and the standard deviation. If you have these two numbers, then there is nothing else to know. For example, with a normal distribution, the probability that we end up within one standard deviation of the average is about two-thirds. The probability that we end up within two standard deviations is about 95 percent. Finally, the probability of being more than three standard deviations away from the average is less than 1 percent. These ranges and the probabilities are illustrated in Figure 10.11.

To see why this is useful, recall from Figure 10.10 that the standard deviation of returns on the Canadian large-company stocks is 15.9 percent. The average return is 11.7 percent. So, assuming that the frequency distribution is at least approximately normal, the probability that the return in a given year is in the range of −4.2 percent to 27.6 percent (11.7 percent plus or minus one standard deviation, 15.9 percent) is about two-thirds. This range is illustrated in Figure 10.11. In other words, there is about one chance in three that the return will be *outside* this range. This literally tells you that, if you buy stocks in large companies, you should expect to be outside this range in one year out of every three. This reinforces our

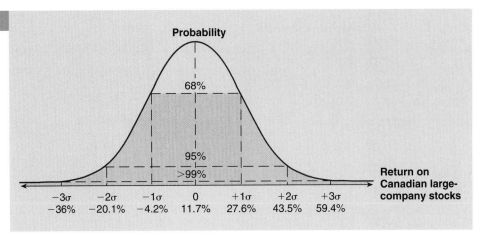

FIGURE 10.11

The normal distribution.
Illustrated returns are based on the historical return and standard deviation for a portfolio of Canadian large-company stocks.

earlier observations about stock market volatility. However, there is only a 5 percent chance (approximately) that we would end up outside the range of -20.1 percent to 43.5 percent (11.7 percent plus or minus $2 \times 15.9\%$). These points are also illustrated in Figure 10.11.

The Second Lesson

Our observations concerning the year-to-year variability in returns are the basis for our second lesson from capital market history. On average, bearing risk is handsomely rewarded, but, in a given year, there is a significant chance of a dramatic change in value. Thus, our second lesson is this: The greater the potential reward, the greater the risk. In other words, as an old proverb says: nothing ventured, nothing gained. If you put your money in safe investments such as Treasury bills, you will not be able to reap large gains.

Thus far in this chapter, we have emphasized the year-to-year variability in returns. We should note that even day-to-day movements can exhibit considerable volatility. For example, Canadian stocks have experienced large declines in value in just one day many times, as illustrated in the following table:

Top 10 One-Day Percentage Decreases in the S&P/TSX Index from 1976 to 2006			
October 19, 1987	−11.1%	October 27, 1997	−6.2%
October 25, 2000	−8.1	August 27, 1998	−6.0
October 26, 1987	−7.6	April 14, 2000	−5.5
October 20, 1987	−6.9	March 27, 1980	−5.3
February 16, 2001	−6.4	September 25, 1981	−4.4

Source: Global Financial Data.

This table also highlights the importance of looking at returns in terms of percentages rather than dollar amounts or index points. For example, on February 16, 2001, the S&P/TSX index plummeted 574 points, or 6.4 percent. It was the second worst day for Canadian stocks in terms of points since 1976. In terms of percentage points, however, it was only the fifth-largest decrease. This is precisely why we relied on percentage returns when we examined market history in this chapter.[3]

---

[3]By the way, as you may have noticed, what's kind of weird is that five of the 10 worst days in the history of the S&P/TSX since 1976 occurred in October, including the top four. We have no clue as to why. Furthermore, looking back at the Mark Twain quote near the beginning of the chapter, how do you suppose he knew? Sounds like a case for *CSI: Bay Street*.

Using Capital Market History

Based on the discussion in this section, you should begin to have an idea of the risks and rewards from investing. For example, in 2006, Treasury bills were paying about 4 percent. Suppose we had an investment that we thought had about the same risk as a portfolio of Canadian large-firm common stocks. At a minimum, what return would this investment have to offer for us to be interested?

From Table 10.3, the risk premium on Canadian large-company stocks has been 6.8 percent historically, so a reasonable estimate of our required return would be this premium plus the T-bill rate, 6.8% + 4% = 10.8%. If we were thinking of starting a new business, then the risks of doing so might resemble those of investing in small-company stocks. In this case, the risk premium is 9.1 percent, so we might require more like 13.1 percent from such an investment at a minimum.

We will discuss the relationship between risk and required return in more detail in the next chapter. For now, you should notice that a projected internal rate of return, or IRR, on a risky investment in the 10 percent to 20 percent range isn't particularly outstanding. It depends on how much risk there is. This, too, is an important lesson from capital market history.

The discussion in this section shows that there is much to be learned from capital market history. As the accompanying *Reality Bytes* box describes, capital market history also provides some odd coincidences.

Investing in Growth Stocks   EXAMPLE 10.3

The term *growth stock* is frequently a euphemism for small-company stock. Are such investments suitable for "widows and orphans"? Before answering, you should consider their historical volatility. For example, from the historical record, what is the approximate probability that you will actually lose 9 percent or more of your money in a single year if you buy a portfolio of such companies?

Looking back at Figure 10.10, we see that the average return on small stocks is 14.0 percent and the standard deviation is 22.5 percent. Assuming that the returns are approximately normal, there is about a one-third probability that you will experience a return outside the range of −8.5 percent to 36.5 percent (14.0% ± 22.5%).

Because the normal distribution is symmetric, the odds of being above or below this range are equal. There is thus a one-sixth chance (half of one-third) that you will lose more than 8.5 percent. So, you should expect this to happen once in every six years, on average. Such investments can thus be *very* volatile, and they are not well suitable for those who cannot afford the risk.

CONCEPT QUESTIONS

10.4a   In words, how do we calculate a variance? A standard deviation?

10.4b   With a normal distribution, what is the probability of ending up more than one standard deviation below the average?

10.4c   Assuming that long-term government bonds have an approximately normal distribution, what is the approximate probability of earning 16.8 percent or more in a given year? With T-bills, approximately what is this probability?

10.4d   What is the second lesson from capital market history?

REALITY BYTES

The Super Guide to Investing

Every year, in late January or early February, more than 3 million Canadians and almost 90 million Americans watch television for a prediction of how well the stock market is going to do in the upcoming year. So you missed it this year? Maybe not. The stock market predictor we're talking about is the Super Bowl!

The Super Bowl indicator has become one of the more famous (or infamous) indicators of stock market performance. Here's how it works. In the 1960s, the original National Football League (NFL) and the upstart American Football League (AFL) were fighting for dominance. The Super Bowl indicator says that if a team from the original AFL wins the Super Bowl, the market posts a negative return for the year, and, if a team from the original NFL wins, the market will post a gain for the year. So, how has the Super Bowl predictor performed? While originally proposed for the prediction of the U.S. stock market, the Super Bowl indicator did a decent job in foreseeing the performance of both the U.S. and Canadian markets. Out of 40 Super Bowls, it was correct 30 times for the Canadian stock market and 32 times for the U.S. stock market—an 80 percent accuracy rate. The indicator was especially impressive for the first 31 Super Bowls, when it made 28 correct predictions for the U.S. market!

The Miami Dolphins, an AFL team, are perhaps the best market predictor. When Miami won the Super Bowl in 1973, the U.S. stock market proceeded to drop by 14.7 percent, while the Canadian market barely edged into positive territory. The next year, the Dolphins beat the Minnesota Vikings, and both the S&P 500 and the S&P/TSX lost more than 25 percent, one of the worst one-year performances in U.S. and Canadian stock market histories. When the Dolphins lost the Super Bowl in 1972, 1983, and 1985, both markets posted double-digit gains each year.

So you are ready to bet the farm on the Super Bowl indicator? Maybe that's not a good idea. Since 1998, the performance of the Super Bowl indicator has been quite shaky. Out of nine tries, it made four wrong predictions for the Canadian market and five for the U.S. market. Given the recent dismal performance of the Super Bowl predictor, maybe it is time to replace it with another indicator? Actually, one possible indicator with deep Canadian roots has made perfect predictions of the Canadian stock market in this millennium. This stock market predictor is the Stanley Cup! Starting from the 2000 Stanley Cup, if the winning team was from the Western conference, the market had a loss for the year, and, if the winning team was from the Eastern conference, the market had a gain for the year. Has the Stanley Cup indicator continued making correct predictions after 2006?

So you want more predictors? How about the hemline indicator, also known as the "bull markets and bare knees" indicator? Through much of the nineteenth century, long skirts dominated women's fashion, and the stock market experienced many bear markets. In the 1920s, flappers revealed their knees and the stock market boomed. Even the stock market crash of October 1987 was predicted by hemlines. During the 1980s, miniskirts flourished, but by October 1987 a fashion shift had women wearing longer skirts.

These are only three examples of what are known as "technical" trading rules. There are lots of others. How seriously should you take them? That's up to you, but our advice is to keep in mind that life is full of odd coincidences. Just because a bizarre stock market predictor seems to have worked well in the past doesn't mean that it's going to work in the future.

10.5 | MORE ON AVERAGE RETURNS

Thus far in this chapter, we have looked closely at simple average returns. But there is another way of computing an average return. The fact that average returns are calculated two different ways leads to some confusion, so our goal in this section is to explain the two approaches and also the circumstances under which each is appropriate.

Arithmetic versus Geometric Averages

Let's start with a simple example. Suppose you buy a particular stock for $100. Unfortunately, the first year you own it, it falls to $50. The second year you own it, it rises back to $100, leaving you where you started (no dividends were paid).

What was your average return on this investment? Common sense seems to say that your average return must be exactly zero since you started with $100 and ended with $100. But if we calculate the returns year-by-year, we see that you lost 50 percent the first year (you lost half of your money). The second year, you made 100 percent (you doubled your money). Your average return over the two years was thus $(-50\% + 100\%)/2 = 25\%$!

So which is correct, 0 percent or 25 percent? The answer is that both are correct: They just answer different questions. The 0 percent is called the **geometric average return**. The 25 percent is called the **arithmetic average return**. The geometric average return answers the question *"What was your average compound return per year over a particular period?"* The arithmetic average return answers the question *"What was your return in an average year over a particular period?"*

Notice that, in previous sections, the average returns we calculated were all arithmetic averages, so we already know how to calculate them. What we need to do now is (1) learn how to calculate geometric averages and (2) learn the circumstances under which one average is more meaningful than the other.

geometric average return

The average compound return earned per year over a multiyear period.

arithmetic average return

The return earned in an average year over a multiyear period.

Calculating Geometric Average Returns

First, to illustrate how we calculate a geometric average return, suppose a particular investment had annual returns of 10 percent, 12 percent, 3 percent, and -9 percent over the last four years. The geometric average return over this four-year period is calculated as $(1.10 \times 1.12 \times 1.03 \times .91)^{1/4} - 1 = 3.66\%$. In contrast, the average arithmetic return we have been calculating is $(.10 + .12 + .03 - .09)/4 = 4.0\%$.

In general, if we have T years of returns, the geometric average return over these T years is calculated using this formula:

$$\text{Geometric average return} = [(1 + R_1) \times (1 + R_2) \times \cdots \times (1 + R_T)]^{1/T} - 1 \quad \textbf{[10.7]}$$

This formula tells us that four steps are required:

1. Take each of the T annual returns $R_1, R_2, \ldots, R_T$ and add a one to each (after converting them to decimals!).
2. Multiply all the numbers from step 1 together.
3. Take the result from step 2 and raise it to the power of $1/T$.
4. Finally, subtract one from the result of step 3. The result is the geometric average return.

Calculating the Geometric Average Return | EXAMPLE **10.4**

Calculate the geometric average return for large-company Canadian stocks for the first five years in Table 10.1, 1934–1938.

First, convert percentages to decimal returns, add one, and then calculate their product:

Large-Company Stocks Returns	Product
20.14	1.2014
30.51	×1.3051
25.54	×1.2554
−15.79	×0.8421
9.13	×1.0913
	1.8089

(continued)

Notice that the number 1.8089 is what our investment is worth after five years if we started with a one dollar investment. The geometric average return is then calculated as

Geometric average return $1.8089^{1/5} - 1 = 0.1259$, or 12.59%

Thus the geometric average return is about 12.59 percent in this example. Here is a tip: If you are using a financial calculator, you can put $1 in as the present value, $1.8089 as the future value, and 5 as the number of periods. Then, solve for the unknown rate. You should get the same answer we did.

One thing you may have noticed in our examples thus far is that the geometric average returns seem to be smaller. It turns out that this will always be true (as long as the returns are not all identical, in which case the two "averages" would be the same). To illustrate, Table 10.4 shows the arithmetic averages and standard deviations from Figure 10.10, along with the geometric average returns.

As shown in Table 10.4, the geometric averages are all smaller, but the magnitude of the difference varies quite a bit. The reason is that the difference is greater for more volatile investments. In fact, there is useful approximation for calculating the geometric average return. Assuming all the numbers are expressed in decimals (as opposed to percentages), the geometric average return is approximately equal to the arithmetic average return minus half the variance. For example, looking at the Canadian large-company stocks, the arithmetic average is .117 and the standard deviation is .159, implying that the variance is .025281. The approximate geometric average is thus $.117 - .025281/2 = .1044$, which is quite close to the actual value.

EXAMPLE 10.5   **More Geometric Averages**

Take a look back at Figure 10.4. There, we showed the value of a $1 investment after 73 years. Use the value for the Canadian large-company stock investment to check the geometric average in Table 10.4.

In Figure 10.4, the large-company investment grew to $1,484.70 over 73 years. The geometric average return is thus

Geometric average return $= 1,484.70^{1/73} - 1 = .1052$, or 10.5%

TABLE 10.4		**Average Return**		**Standard Deviation**
Geometric versus Arithmetic Average Returns: 1934–2006	**Series**	**Geometric**	**Arithmetic**	
	Canadian large-company stocks	10.5%	11.7%	15.9%
	U.S. large-company stocks	11.3	12.8	18.1
	Canadian small-company stocks	11.7	14.0	22.5
	Long-term government bonds	7.0	7.4	9.4
	Treasury bills	4.8	4.9	4.1
	Inflation	3.8	3.9	3.5

Source: Used with permission of Global Financial Data.

Arithmetic Average Return or Geometric Average Return?

When we look at historical returns, the difference between the geometric and arithmetic average returns isn't too hard to understand. To put it another way, the geometric average tells you what you actually earned per year on average, compounded annually. The arithmetic average tells you what you earned in a typical year. You should use whichever one answers the question you want answered.

A somewhat trickier question concerns which average return to use when forecasting future wealth levels, and there's a lot of confusion on this point among analysts and financial planners. First, let's get one thing straight: If you *know* the true arithmetic average return, then this is what you should use in your forecast. So, for example, if you know the arithmetic return is 10 percent, then your best guess of the value of a $1,000 investment in 10 years is the future value of $1,000 at 10 percent for 10 years, or $2,593.74.

The problem we face, however, is that we usually only have *estimates* of the arithmetic and geometric returns, and estimates have errors. In this case, the arithmetic average return is probably too high for longer periods and the geometric average is probably too low for shorter periods. So, you should regard long-run projected wealth levels calculated using arithmetic averages as optimistic. Short-run projected wealth levels calculated using geometric averages are probably pessimistic.

As a practical matter, if you are using averages calculated over a long period of time (such as the 73 years we use) to forecast up to a decade or so into the future, then you should use the arithmetic average. If you are forecasting a few decades into the future (such as you might do for retirement planning), then you should just split the difference between the arithmetic and geometric average returns. Finally, if for some reason you are doing very long forecasts covering many decades, use the geometric average.

This concludes our discussion of geometric versus arithmetic averages. One last note: In the future, when we say "average return," we mean arithmetic unless we explicitly say otherwise.

CONCEPT QUESTIONS

10.5a If you wanted to forecast what the stock market is going to do over the next year, should you use an arithmetic or geometric average?

10.5b If you wanted to forecast what the stock market is going to do over the next century, should you use an arithmetic or geometric average?

10.6 | CAPITAL MARKET EFFICIENCY

Capital market history suggests that the market values of stocks and bonds can fluctuate widely from year to year. Why does this occur? At least part of the answer is that prices change because new information arrives, and investors reassess asset values based on that information.

The behaviour of market prices has been extensively studied. A question that has received particular attention is whether prices adjust quickly and correctly when new information arrives. A market is said to be *efficient* if this is the case. To be more precise,

efficient capital market
Market in which security prices reflect available information.

in an **efficient capital market**, current market prices fully reflect available information. By this we simply mean that, based on available information, there is no reason to believe that the current price is too low or too high.

The concept of market efficiency is a rich one, and much has been written about it. A full discussion of the subject goes beyond the scope of our study of business finance. However, because the concept figures so prominently in studies of market history, we briefly describe the key points here.

Price Behaviour in an Efficient Market

To illustrate how prices behave in an efficient market, suppose the F-Stop Camera Corporation (FCC) has, through years of secret research and development, developed a camera with an autofocus system double the speed of those now available. FCC's capital budgeting analysis suggests that launching the new camera is a highly profitable move; in other words, the NPV appears to be positive and substantial. The key assumption thus far is that FCC has not released any information about the new system, so the fact of its existence is "inside" information only.

Now consider a share of stock in FCC. In an efficient market, its price reflects what is known about FCC's current operations and profitability, and it reflects market opinion about FCC's potential for future growth and profits. The value of the new autofocusing system is not reflected, however, because the market is unaware of its existence.

If the market agrees with FCC's assessment of the value of the new project, FCC's stock price will rise when the decision to launch is made public. For example, assume the announcement is made in a press release on Wednesday morning. In an efficient market, the price of shares in FCC will adjust quickly to this new information. Investors should not be able to buy the stock on Wednesday afternoon and make a profit on Thursday. This would imply that it took the stock market a full day to realize the implication of the FCC press release. If the market is efficient, the price of shares of FCC stock on Wednesday afternoon will already reflect the information contained in the Wednesday morning press release.

Figure 10.12 presents three possible stock price adjustments for FCC. In the figure, Day 0 represents the announcement day. As illustrated, before the announcement, FCC's stock sells for $140 per share. The NPV per share of the new system is, say, $40, so the new price will be $180 once the value of the new project is fully reflected.

The solid line in Figure 10.12 represents the path taken by the stock price in an efficient market. In this case, the price adjusts immediately to the new information and no further changes in the price of the stock take place. The broken line in Figure 10.12 depicts a delayed reaction. Here, it takes the market eight days or so to fully absorb the information. Finally, the dotted line illustrates an overreaction and subsequent adjustment to the correct price.

The broken line and the dotted line in Figure 10.12 illustrate paths that the stock price might take in an inefficient market. If, for example, stock prices don't adjust immediately to new information (the broken line), then buying stock immediately following the release of new information and then selling it several days later would be a positive NPV activity because the price is too low for several days after the announcement.

The Efficient Markets Hypothesis

efficient markets hypothesis (EMH)
The hypothesis that actual capital markets, such as the TSX, are efficient.

The **efficient markets hypothesis (EMH)** asserts that well-organized capital markets, such as the TSX and the NYSE, are efficient markets, at least as a practical matter. In other words, an advocate of the EMH might argue that while inefficiencies may exist, they are relatively small and not common.

Reaction of stock price to new information in efficient and inefficient markets   FIGURE **10.12**

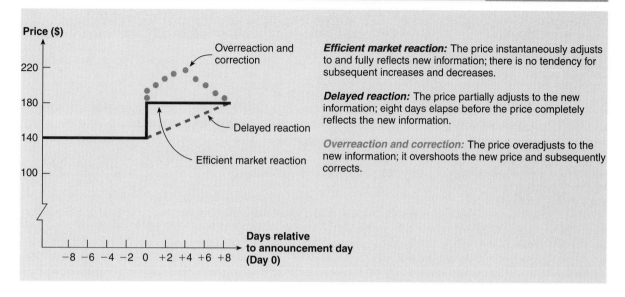

Efficient market reaction: The price instantaneously adjusts to and fully reflects new information; there is no tendency for subsequent increases and decreases.

Delayed reaction: The price partially adjusts to the new information; eight days elapse before the price completely reflects the new information.

Overreaction and correction: The price overadjusts to the new information; it overshoots the new price and subsequently corrects.

If a market is efficient, then there is a very important implication for market participants: All investments in an efficient market are *zero* NPV investments. The reason is not complicated. If prices are neither too low nor too high, then the difference between the market value of an investment and its cost is zero; hence, the NPV is zero. As a result, in an efficient market, investors get exactly what they pay for when they buy securities, and firms receive exactly what their stocks and bonds are worth when they sell them.

What makes a market efficient is competition among investors. Many individuals spend their entire lives trying to find mispriced stocks. For any given stock, they study what has happened in the past to the stock's price and its dividends. They learn, to the extent possible, what a company's earnings have been, how much it owes to creditors, what taxes it pays, what businesses it is in, what new investments are planned, how sensitive it is to changes in the economy, and so on.

Not only is there a great deal to know about any particular company, there is a powerful incentive for knowing it, namely, the profit motive. If you know more about some company than other investors in the marketplace, you can profit from that knowledge by investing in the company's stock if you have good news and by selling it if you have bad news.

The logical consequence of all this information being gathered and analyzed is that mispriced stocks will become fewer and fewer. In other words, because of competition among investors, the market will become increasingly efficient. A kind of equilibrium comes into being where there is just enough mispricing around for those who are best at identifying it to make a living at it. For most other investors, the activity of information gathering and analysis will not pay.[4] Having said this, the accompanying *Reality Bytes* box indicates just how hard it is for *anybody* to "beat the market."

Look under the "Contents" link at **www.investorhome .com** for more info on the EMH.

---

[4]The idea behind the EMH can be illustrated by the following short story: A student was walking down the hall with her finance professor when they both saw a $20 bill on the ground. As the student bent down to pick it up, the professor shook her head slowly and, with a look of disappointment on her face, said patiently to the student, "Don't bother. If it were really there, someone else would have picked it up already." The moral of the story reflects the logic of the efficient markets hypothesis: If you think you have found a pattern in stock prices or a simple device for picking winners, you probably have not.

REALITY BYTES

Can the Pros Beat the Market?

2006 was a great year for investors in the Sentry Select Precious Metals Growth mutual fund, which gained almost 72 percent for the year. And thanks to a good performance in October, the Sceptre Equity Growth outperformed the BMO Small Cap Index for the seventh year in a row. But the question remains: Can professional investors consistently beat the market?

One thing we know for sure is that past performance is no predictor of future returns. For example, in 2001 the Altamira Science and Technology had been the best performing mutual fund in the Science and Technology group for the previous five years, with an average annual return above 40 percent. But the next five years weren't as kind to the investors in this fund. The average annual return for 2002 to 2006 dropped to negative 7.2 percent, which was one of the worst five-year performances in the group. Following the old saying "What goes up, must come down," other funds have had similar stories. In 1993, the Front Street Small Cap Canadian had the highest return of 159.3 percent among all mutual funds in Canada, only to lose 15.3 percent the following year. Similarly,

AIM Global Technology gained 200.3 percent in 1999, but lost 27.9 percent in 2000, followed by two more years of double-digit losses.

Can mutual fund managers collectively beat the market? Consider 2005, when the S&P/TSX gained 24.1 percent. Canadian equity funds averaged 21.2 percent for the year, so mutual fund managers underperformed the market. Only 56 out of 248 mutual funds in the Pure Canadian Equity group beat the market. What about 2004? The result was similar. Canadian equity mutual funds gained on average 14.2 percent, while the S&P/TSX increased 14.5 percent. In fact, over the years, the track record of the pros is relatively clear: More often than not, they underperform.

The inability of the pros to consistently beat the market doesn't prove that markets are efficient. The evidence does, however, lend some credence to the semistrong form version of market efficiency. Plus, it adds to a growing body of evidence that tends to support a basic premise: While it may be possible to outperform the market for relatively short periods of time, it is very difficult to do so consistently over the long haul.

Some Common Misconceptions about the EMH

No idea in finance has attracted as much attention as that of efficient markets, and not all of the attention has been flattering. Rather than rehash the arguments here, we will be content to observe that some markets are more efficient than others. For example, financial markets on the whole are probably much more efficient than real asset markets.

Having said this, it is the case that much of the criticism of the EMH is misguided because it is based on a misunderstanding of what the hypothesis says and what it doesn't say. For example, when the notion of market efficiency was first publicized and debated in the popular financial press, it was often characterized by words to the effect that "throwing darts at the financial page will produce a portfolio that can be expected to do as well as any managed by professional security analysts."

Confusion over statements of this sort has often led to a failure to understand the implications of market efficiency. For example, sometimes it is wrongly argued that market efficiency means that it doesn't matter how you invest your money because the efficiency of the market will protect you from making a mistake. However, a random dart thrower might wind up with all of the darts sticking into one or two high-risk stocks that deal in genetic engineering. Would you really want all of your money in two such stocks?

What efficiency does imply is that the price a firm will obtain when it sells a share of its stock is a "fair" price in the sense that it reflects the value of that stock given the information available about the firm. Shareholders do not have to worry that they are paying too much for a stock with a low dividend or some other sort of characteristic because the market has already incorporated that characteristic into the price. We sometimes say the information has been "priced out."

The concept of efficient markets can be explained further by replying to a frequent objection. It is sometimes argued that the market cannot be efficient because stock prices fluctuate from day to day. If the prices are right, the argument goes, then why do they change so much and so often? From our discussion above, we can see that these price movements are in no way inconsistent with efficiency. Investors are bombarded with new information every day. The fact that prices fluctuate is, at least in part, a reflection of that information flow. In fact, the absence of price movements in a world that changes as rapidly as ours would suggest inefficiency.

The Forms of Market Efficiency

It is common to distinguish between three forms of market efficiency. Depending on the degree of efficiency, we say that markets are either *weak form efficient, semistrong form efficient,* or *strong form efficient.* The difference between these forms relates to what information is reflected in prices.

We start with the extreme case. If the market is strong form efficient, then *all* information of *every* kind is reflected in stock prices. In such a market, there is no such thing as inside information. Therefore, in our FCC example above, we apparently were assuming that the market was not strong form efficient.

Casual observation, particularly in recent years, suggests that inside information does exist and it can be valuable to possess. Whether it is lawful or ethical to use that information is another issue. In any event, we conclude that private information about a particular stock may exist that is not currently reflected in the price of the stock. For example, prior knowledge of a takeover attempt could be very valuable.

The second form of efficiency, semistrong efficiency, is the most controversial. If a market is semistrong form efficient, then all *public* information is reflected in the stock price. The reason this form is controversial is that it implies that security analysts who try to identify mispriced stocks using, for example, financial statement information are wasting their time because that information is already reflected in the current price.

The third form of efficiency, weak form efficiency, suggests that, at a minimum, the current price of a stock reflects its own past prices. In other words, studying past prices in an attempt to identify mispriced securities is futile if the market is weak form efficient. While this form of efficiency might seem rather mild, it implies that searching for patterns in historical prices that are useful in identifying mispriced stocks will not work (this practice, known as "technical" analysis, is quite common).

What does capital market history say about market efficiency? Here again, there is great controversy. At the risk of going out on a limb, the evidence does seem to tell us three things. First: Prices do appear to respond very rapidly to new information, and the response is at least not grossly different from what we would expect in an efficient market. Second: The future of market prices, particularly in the short run, is very difficult to predict based on publicly available information. Third: If mispriced stocks do exist, then there is no obvious means of identifying them. Put another way: Simpleminded schemes based on public information will probably not be successful.

CONCEPT QUESTIONS

10.6a What is an efficient market?

10.6b What are the forms of market efficiency?

KEY EQUATIONS:

I. Dollar Returns

Total dollar return = Dividend income + Capital gain (or loss)   [10.1]

Total cash if stock is sold = Initial investment + Total return   [10.2]

II. Percentage Returns

Dividend yield $= D_{t+1}/P_t$ [10.3]

where

P_t = the price of the stock at the beginning of the year

D_{t+1} = the dividend paid on the stock during the year

Capital gains yield $= (P_{t+1} - P_t)/P_t$ [10.4]

where

P_{t+1} = the price of the stock at the end of the year

III. Variability of Returns

Variance of returns, Var(R) or σ^2:

$$\mathbf{Var}(\pmb{R}) = \frac{1}{T-1}[(\pmb{R}_1 - \overline{\pmb{R}})^2 + \cdots + (\pmb{R}_T - \overline{\pmb{R}})^2]$$ [10.5]

where

T = the number of periods

R_t = the return in period T

Standard deviation of returns, SD(R) or σ:

$$\mathbf{SD}(\pmb{R}) = \pmb{\sigma} = \sqrt{\pmb{Var(R)}} = \sqrt{\frac{1}{T-1}[(\pmb{R}_1 - \overline{\pmb{R}})^2 + \cdots + (\pmb{R}_T - \overline{\pmb{R}})^2]}$$ [10.6]

IV. Geometric Average Returns

Geometric average return $= [(1 + R_1)^2 \times (1 + R_2)^2 \times \cdots \times (1 + R_T)]^{1/T} - 1$
    [10.7]

SUMMARY AND CONCLUSIONS

This chapter has explored the subject of capital market history. Such history is useful because it tells us what to expect in the way of returns from risky assets. We summed up our study of market history with two key lessons:

1. Risky assets, on average, earn a risk premium. There is a reward for bearing risk.

2. The greater the potential reward from a risky investment, the greater is the risk.

These lessons have significant implications for the financial manager. We will be considering these implications in the chapters ahead.

We also discussed the concept of market efficiency. In an efficient market, prices adjust quickly and correctly to new information. Consequently, asset prices in efficient markets are rarely too high or too low. How efficient capital markets (such as the TSX) really are is a matter of debate, but, at a minimum, they are probably much more efficient than most real asset markets(e.g., real estate).

CHAPTER REVIEW AND SELF-TEST PROBLEMS

10.1 Recent Return History. Use Table 10.1 to calculate the average return over the years 2001–2005 for Canadian large-company stocks, long-term government bonds, and Treasury bills.

10.2 More Recent Return History. Calculate the standard deviations using information from Problem 10.1. Which of the investments was the most volatile over this period?

■ Answers to Chapter Review and Self-Test Problems

10.1 We calculate the averages as follows:

	Actual Returns and Averages		
Year	Large Company Stocks	Long-Term Government Bonds	3-month Treasury Bills
2001	−0.1257	0.0472	0.0381
2002	−0.1244	0.1060	0.0257
2003	0.2672	0.0682	0.0290
2004	0.1448	0.0759	0.0224
2005	0.2413	0.0614	0.0277
Average:	0.0806	0.0717	0.0286

10.2 We first need to calculate the deviations from the average returns. Using the averages from Problem 10.1, we get:

	Deviations from Average Returns		
Year	Large Company Stocks	Long-Term Government Bonds	3-month Treasury Bills
2001	−0.2064	−0.0245	0.0095
2002	−0.2050	0.0342	−0.0029
2003	0.1866	−0.0036	0.0004
2004	0.0642	0.0042	−0.0062
2005	0.1606	−0.0103	−0.0009
Total:	0.0000	0.0000	0.0000

We square these deviations and calculate the variances and standard deviations:

	Squared Deviations from Average Returns		
Year	Large Company Stocks	Long-Term Government Bonds	3-month Treasury Bills
2001	0.042586	0.000601	0.000091
2002	0.042035	0.001170	0.000008
2003	0.034823	0.000013	0.000000
2004	0.004116	0.000018	0.000038
2005	0.025800	0.000106	0.000001
Variance:	0.037340	0.000477	0.000035
Standard deviation:	0.193235	0.021843	0.005881

To calculate the variances we added up the squared deviations and divided by 4, the number of returns less 1. Notice that the stocks had substantially greater volatility with a larger average return. Once again, such investments are risky, particularly over short periods of time.

CRITICAL THINKING AND CONCEPTS REVIEW

10.1   **Investment Selection.**   Given that Blue Pearl Mining was up by 1,310 percent for 2006, why didn't all investors hold Blue Pearl Mining?

10.2   **Investment Selection.**   Given that Point North Energy was down by 97 percent for 2006, why did some investors hold the stock? Why didn't they sell out before the price declined so sharply?

10.3   **Risk and Return.**   We have seen that over long periods of time, stock investments have tended to substantially outperform bond investments. However, it is not at all uncommon to observe investors with long horizons holding entirely bonds. Are such investors irrational?

10.4   **Market Efficiency Implications.**   Explain why a characteristic of an efficient market is that investments in that market have zero NPVs.

10.5   **Efficient Markets Hypothesis.**   A stock market analyst is able to identify mispriced stocks by comparing the average price for the last 10 days to the average price for the last 60 days. If this is true, what do you know about the market?

10.6   **Semistrong Efficiency.**   If a market is semistrong form efficient, is it also weak form efficient? Explain.

10.7   **Efficient Markets Hypothesis.**   What are the implications of the efficient markets hypothesis for investors who buy and sell stocks in an attempt to "beat the market"?

10.8   **Stocks versus Gambling.**   Critically evaluate the following statement: Playing the stock market is like gambling. Such speculative investing has no social value, other than the pleasure people get from this form of gambling.

10.9   **Efficient Markets Hypothesis.**   There are several celebrated investors and stock pickers frequently mentioned in the financial press who have recorded huge returns on their investments over the past two decades. Is the success of these particular investors an invalidation of the EMH? Explain.

10.10   **Efficient Markets Hypothesis.**   For each of the following scenarios, discuss whether profit opportunities exist from trading in the stock of the firm under the conditions that (1) the market is not weak form efficient, (2) the market is weak form but not semistrong form efficient, (3) the market is semistrong form but not strong form efficient, and (4) the market is strong form efficient.

  a.   The stock price has risen steadily each day for the past 30 days.

  b.   The financial statements for a company were released three days ago, and you believe you've uncovered some anomalies in the company's inventory and cost control reporting techniques that are causing the firm's true liquidity strength to be understated.

  c.   You observe that the senior management of a company has been buying a lot of the company's stock on the open market over the past week.

QUESTIONS AND PROBLEMS

Basic
(Questions 1–18)

1.   **Calculating Returns.**   Suppose a stock had an initial price of $83 per share, paid a dividend of $1.40 per share during the year, and had an ending share price of $91. Compute the percentage total return.

2.   **Calculating Yields.**   In Problem 1, what was the dividend yield? The capital gains yield?

3.   **Calculating Returns.**   Rework Problems 1 and 2 assuming the ending share price is $76.

4. **Calculating Returns.** Suppose you bought a 9 percent coupon bond one year ago for $1,120. The bond sells for $1,074 today.

   a. Assuming a $1,000 face value, what was your total dollar return on this investment over the past year?

   b. What was your total nominal rate of return on this investment over the past year?

   c. If the inflation rate last year was 3 percent, what was your total real rate of return on this investment?

5. **Nominal versus Real Returns.** What was the arithmetic average annual return on Canadian large-company stock from 1934 through 2006:

   a. In nominal terms?

   b. In real terms?

6. **Real Returns.** What is the historical real return on long-term government bonds from 1934 to 2006? On small-company stocks?

7. **Calculating Returns and Variability.** Using the following returns, calculate the average returns, the variances, and the standard deviations for X and Y.

	Returns	
Year	X	Y
1	11%	36%
2	6	−7
3	−8	21
4	28	−12
5	13	43

8. **Risk Premiums.** Refer to Table 10.1 in the text and look at the period from 1969 through 1974.

   a. Calculate the arithmetic average returns for Canadian large-company stocks and T-bills over this time period.

   b. Calculate the standard deviation of the returns for Canadian large-company stocks and T-bills over this time period.

   c. Calculate the observed risk premium in each year for the Canadian large-company stocks versus the T-bills. What was the arithmetic average risk premium over this period? What was the standard deviation of the risk premium over this period?

   d. Is it possible for the risk premium to be negative before an investment is undertaken? Can the risk premium be negative after the fact? Explain.

9. **Calculating Returns and Variability.** You've observed the following returns on Mary Ann Data Corporation's stock over the past five years: −16 percent, 21 percent, 4 percent, 16 percent, and 19 percent.

   a. What was the arithmetic average return on Mary Ann's stock over this five-year period?

   b. What was the variance of Mary Ann's returns over this period? The standard deviation?

10. **Calculating Real Returns and Risk Premiums.** For Problem 9, suppose the average inflation rate over this period was 4.2 percent and the average T-bill rate over the period was 5.1 percent.

    a. What was the average real return on Mary Ann's stock?

    b. What was the average nominal risk premium on Mary Ann's stock?

11. **Calculating Real Rates.** Given the information in Problem 10, what was the average real risk-free rate over this time period? What was the average real risk premium?

12. **Effects of Inflation.** Look at Table 10.1 and Figure 10.7 in the text. When were T-bill rates at their highest over the period from 1934 through 2006? Why do you think they were so high during this period? What relationship underlies your answer?

13. **Calculating Returns.** You purchased a zero-coupon bond one year ago for $152.37. The market interest rate is now 10 percent. If the bond had 20 years to maturity when you originally purchased it, what was your total return for the past year?

14. **Calculating Returns.** You bought a share of 5 percent preferred stock for $84.12 last year. The market price for your stock is now $80.27. What is your total return for last year?

15. **Calculating Returns.** You bought a stock three months ago for $38.65 per share. The stock paid no dividends. The current share price is $42.02. What is the APR of your investment? The EAR?

 16. **Calculating Real Returns.** Refer to Table 10.1. What was the average real return for Treasury bills from 1934 through 1938?

17. **Return Distributions.** Refer back to Figure 10.10. What range of returns would you expect to see 68 percent of the time for long-term government bonds? What about 95 percent of the time?

18. **Return Distributions.** Refer back to Figure 10.10. What range of returns would you expect to see 68 percent of the time for small-company stocks? What about 95 percent of the time?

Intermediate (Questions 19–25)

19. **Calculating Returns and Variability.** You find a certain stock that had returns of 8 percent, −13 percent, −7 percent, and 29 percent for four of the last five years. If the average return of the stock over this period was 11 percent, what was the stock's return for the missing year? What is the standard deviation of the stock's returns?

20. **Arithmetic and Geometric Returns.** A stock has had returns of 29 percent, 14 percent, 23 percent, −8 percent, 9 percent, and −14 percent over the last six years. What are the arithmetic and geometric returns for the stock?

 21. **Arithmetic and Geometric Returns.** A stock has had the following year-end prices and dividends:

Year	Price	Dividend
1	$43.12	—
2	49.07	$0.55
3	51.19	0.60
4	47.24	0.63
5	56.09	0.72
6	67.21	0.81

What are the arithmetic and geometric returns for the stock?

22. **Calculating Returns.** Refer to Table 10.1 in the text and look at the period from 1971 through 1977.

    a. Calculate the average return for Treasury bills and the average annual inflation rate (consumer price index) for this period.

    b. Calculate the standard deviation of Treasury bill returns and inflation over this time period.

   c.   Calculate the real return for each year. What is the average real return for
         Treasury bills?

   d.   Many people consider Treasury bills to be risk-free. What does this tell you
         about the potential risks of Treasury bills?

23. Calculating Investment Returns.   You bought one of Lakeland Manufacturing
      Co.'s 8 percent coupon bonds one year ago for $1,028.50. These bonds make
      annual payments and mature six years from now. Suppose you decide to sell your
      bonds today, when the required return on the bonds is 7 percent. If the inflation
      rate was 4.8 percent over the past year, what would be your total real return on
      investment?

24. Using Return Distributions.   Suppose the returns on long-term government bonds
      are normally distributed. Based on the historical record, what is the approximate
      probability that your return on these bonds will be less than −2 percent in a given
      year? What range of returns would you expect to see 95 percent of the time?
      What range would you expect to see 99 percent of the time?

25. Using Return Distributions.   Suppose the returns on T-bills are normally distributed.
      Based on the historical record, what is the approximate probability that your return
      on T-bills will be more than 13.1 percent in a given year? What range of returns
      would you expect to see 68 percent of the time? What about 99 percent of the time?

26. Using Return Distributions.   Assuming that the returns from holding small-
      company stocks are normally distributed, what is the approximate probability that
      your money will double in value in a single year? What about triple in value?

**Challenge
(Questions 26–28)**

27. Distributions.   In the previous problem, what is the probability that the return is less
      than −100 percent (think)? What are the implications for the distribution of returns?

28. Using Return Distributions.   Suppose the returns on Canadian large stocks are
      normally distributed. Based on the historical records, what is the approximate
      probability that you will have a positive return in a given year?

WHAT'S ON THE WEB?

10.1   Historical Interest Rates.   Go to the Bank of Canada Web site at
         www.bankofcanada.ca and select "Interest Rates" in the "Rates and Statistics"
         menu at the top of the home page. By clicking on "Selected Historical Interest
         Rates," you will find a list of links for different historical interest rates. Follow the
         "All Corporates, long-term" link in the "Other Bonds: Average Weighted Yield"
         category and you will find the monthly yields of Canadian long-term corporate
         bonds. Calculate the average annual corporate bond yield for 2004 and 2005.
         Compare this number to the long-term government bond returns and Treasury bill
         returns found in Table 10.1. How does the corporate bond yield compare to these
         numbers? Do you expect this relationship to always hold? Why or why not?

10.2   Market Efficiency.   What are the best performing stocks over the past year?
         Go to **www.globeinvestor.com** and launch Filters. In the "Price Performance
         Statistics" category type 200 for the minimum value of "1 Year % Change" and
         click on "Get Results." How many stocks have increased more than 200 percent
         over the past year? Now go back and type −90 for the maximum value of
         "1 Year % Change." How many stocks have dropped more than 90 percent in
         value over the past year? What does this say about market efficiency?

Risk and Return

11

In November 2006, Onex Corp., Power Financial Corp., and Canadian Natural Resources Ltd. joined a host of other companies in announcing operating results. All three companies reported considerable increases in their third quarter earnings compared to the same period a year ago. As you might expect, news such as this tends to move stock prices.

The earnings of Onex, Canada's largest buyout corporation, rose to $0.24 per share from $0.09 a year earlier. The company's stock went up by 2.4 percent on this news. Also, Power Financial, which controls Canada's biggest mutual fund company and third-largest life insurer, reported a doubling of its earnings over the previous year. But investors didn't jump at the news: The stock price hardly moved at all on that day. Finally, Canadian Natural Resources, the country's second largest oil exporter, reported a sevenfold increase in its earnings, easily topping analyst estimates. Did investors cheer? Not exactly: the stock price fell by 5 percent.

These announcements would seem to be essentially the same, but only one was viewed as good news, after which the stock price rose, while one was seen as neutral, as the stock price remained the same, and one was viewed as bad news, after which the stock price fell.

So when is good news really good news? The answer is fundamental to understanding risk and return, and—the good news is—this chapter explores it in some detail.

This chapter continues the discussion we began in the previous chapter. We've seen pretty clearly that some investments have greater risks than others. We now begin to drill down a bit to investigate one of the most fundamental problems in finance: Just what is risk?

In our last chapter, we learned some important lessons from capital market history. Most importantly, there is a reward, on average, for bearing risk. We called this reward a *risk premium.* The second lesson is that this risk premium is larger for riskier investments. This chapter explores the economic and managerial implications of this basic idea.

Thus far, we have concentrated mainly on the return behaviour of a few large portfolios. We need to expand our consideration to include individual assets. Specifically, we have two tasks to accomplish. First, we have to define risk and then discuss how to measure it. We then must quantify the relationship between an asset's risk and its required return.

When we examine the risks associated with individual assets, we find there are two types of risk: systematic and unsystematic. This distinction is crucial because, as we will see, systematic risk affects almost all assets in the economy, at least to some degree, while unsystematic risk affects at most a small number of assets. We then develop the principle of diversification, which shows that highly diversified portfolios will tend to have almost no unsystematic risk.

The principle of diversification has an important implication: To a diversified investor, only systematic risk matters. It follows that in deciding whether or not to buy a particular individual asset, a diversified investor will only be concerned with that asset's systematic risk. This is a key observation, and it allows us to say a great deal about the risks and returns on individual assets. In particular, it is the basis for a famous relationship between risk and return called the *security market line,* or SML. To develop the SML, we introduce the equally famous "beta" coefficient, one of the centrepieces of modern finance. Beta and the SML are key concepts because they supply us with at least part of the answer to the question of how to go about determining the required return on an investment.

11.1 | EXPECTED RETURNS AND VARIANCES

In our previous chapter, we discussed how to calculate average returns and variances using historical data. We now begin to discuss how to analyze returns and variances when the information we have concerns future possible returns and their probabilities.

Expected Return

We start with a straightforward case. Consider a single period of time, say, a year. We have two stocks, L and U, which have the following characteristics: Stock L is expected to have a return of 25 percent in the coming year. Stock U is expected to have a return of 20 percent for the same period.

In a situation like this, if all investors agreed on the expected returns, why would anyone want to hold Stock U? After all, why invest in one stock when the expectation is that another will do better? Clearly, the answer must depend on the risk level of the two investments. The return on Stock L, although it is *expected* to be 25 percent, could actually turn out to be higher or lower.

For example, suppose the economy booms. In this case, we think Stock L will have a 70 percent return. If the economy enters a recession, we think the return will be -20 percent. In this case, we say that there are two *states of the economy,* which means that these are the only two possible situations. This setup is oversimplified, of course, but it allows us to illustrate some key ideas without a lot of computation.

Suppose we think a boom and a recession are equally likely to happen, for a 50-50 chance of each. Table 11.1 illustrates the basic information we have described and some additional information about Stock U. Notice that Stock U earns 30 percent if there is a recession and 10 percent if there is a boom.

State of Economy	Probability of State of Economy	Security Returns If State Occurs	
		Stock L	Stock U
Recession	.5	−20%	30%
Boom	.5	70	10
	1.0		

Obviously, if you buy one of these stocks, say Stock U, what you earn in any particular year depends on what the economy does during that year. However, suppose the probabilities stay the same through time. If you hold U for a number of years, you'll earn 30 percent about half the time and 10 percent the other half. In this case, we say that your **expected return** on Stock U, $E(R_U)$, is 20 percent:

expected return
Return on a risky asset
expected in the future.

$$E(R_U) = .50 \times 30\% + .50 \times 10\% = 20\%$$

In other words, you should expect to earn 20 percent from this stock, on average.

For Stock L, the probabilities are the same, but the possible returns are different. Here we lose 20 percent half the time, and we gain 70 percent the other half. The expected return on L, $E(R_L)$, is thus 25 percent:

$$E(R_L) = .50 \times -20\% + .50 \times 70\% = 25\%$$

Table 11.2 illustrates these calculations.

In our previous chapter, we defined the risk premium as the difference between the return on a risky investment and that on a risk-free investment, and we calculated the historical risk premiums on some different investments. Using our projected returns, we can calculate the *projected,* or *expected, risk premium* as the difference between the expected return on a risky investment and the certain return on a risk-free investment.

For example, suppose risk-free investments are currently offering 8 percent. We will say that the risk-free rate, which we label as R_f, is 8 percent. Given this, what is the projected risk premium on Stock U? On Stock L? Since the expected return on Stock U, $E(R_U)$, is 20 percent, the projected risk premium is:

$$\begin{aligned} \text{Risk premium} &= \text{Expected return} - \text{Risk-free rate} \\ &= E(R_U) - R_f \\ &= 20\% - 8\% \\ &= 12\% \end{aligned} \qquad [11.1]$$

Similarly, the risk premium on Stock L is $25\% - 8\% = 17\%$.

(1) State of Economy	(2) Probability of State of Economy	Stock L		Stock U	
		(3) Rate of Return If State Occurs	(4) Product (2)×(3)	(5) Rate of Return If State Occurs	(6) Product (2)×(5)
Recession	.5	−.20	−.10	.30	.15
Boom	.5	.70	.35	.10	.05
	1.0		$E(R_L) = .25$		$E(R_U) = .2$

In general, the expected return on a security or other asset is simply equal to the sum of the possible returns multiplied by their probabilities. So, if we had 100 possible returns, we would multiply each one by its probability and then add the results up. The result would be the expected return. The risk premium would then be the difference between this expected return and the risk-free rate.

Unequal Probabilities **EXAMPLE 11.1**

Look again at Tables 11.1 and 11.2. Suppose you thought a boom would occur only 20 percent of the time instead of 50 percent. What are the expected returns on Stocks U and L in this case? If the risk-free rate is 10 percent, what are the risk premiums?

The first thing to notice is that a recession must occur 80 percent of the time $(1 - .20 = .80)$ since there are only two possibilities. With this in mind, we see that Stock U has a 30 percent return in 80 percent of the years and a 10 percent return in 20 percent of the years. To calculate the expected return, we again just multiply the possibilities by the probabilities and add up the results:

$E(R_U) = .80 \times 30\% + .20 \times 10\% = 26\%$

Table 11.3 summarizes the calculations for both stocks. Notice that the expected return on L is −2 percent.

The risk premium for Stock U is $26\% - 10\% = 16\%$ in this case. The risk premium for Stock L is negative: $-2\% - 10\% = -12\%$. This is a little odd, but, for reasons we discuss later, it is not impossible.

Calculating the Variance

To calculate the variances of the returns on our two stocks, we first determine the squared deviations from the expected return. We then multiply each possible squared deviation by its probability. We add these up, and the result is the variance. The standard deviation, as always, is the square root of the variance.

To illustrate, Stock U above has an expected return of $E(R_U) = 20\%$. In a given year, it will actually return either 30 percent or 10 percent. The possible deviations are thus $30\% - 20\% = 10\%$ and $10\% - 20\% = -10\%$. In this case, the variance is:

$$\text{Variance} = \sigma_U^2 = .50 \times (10\%)^2 + .50 \times (-10\%)^2 = .01$$

The standard deviation is the square root of this:

$$\text{Standard deviation} = \sigma_U = \sqrt{.01} = .10 = 10\%$$

(1) State of Economy	(2) Probability of State of Economy	Stock L (3) Rate of Return If State Occurs	(4) Product (2)×(3)	Stock U (5) Rate of Return If State Occurs	(6) Product (2)×(5)
Recession	.8	−.20	−.16	.30	.24
Boom	.2	.70	.14	.10	.02
	1.0		$E(R_L) = -.02$		$E(R_U) = .26$

TABLE 11.3

Calculation of expected return

	TABLE 11.4
Calculation of variance	

(1) State of Economy	(2) Probability of State of Economy	(3) Return Deviation from Expected Return	(4) Squared Return Deviation from Expected Return	(5) Product (2)×(4)
Stock L				
Recession	.5	$-.20 - .25 = -.45$	$-.45^2 = .2025$	.10125
Boom	.5	$.70 - .25 = .45$	$.45^2 = .2025$	.10125
	1.0			$\sigma_L^2 = .2025$
Stock U				
Recession	.5	$.30 - .20 = .10$	$.10^2 = .01$	.00500
Boom	.5	$.10 - .20 = -.10$	$-.10^2 = .01$	.00500
	1.0			$\sigma_U^2 = .0100$

Table 11.4 summarizes these calculations for both stocks. Notice that Stock L has a much larger variance.

When we put the expected return and variability information for our two stocks together, we have:

	Stock L	Stock U
Expected return, $E(R)$	25%	20%
Variance, σ^2	.2025	.0100
Standard deviation, σ	45%	10%

EXAMPLE 11.2   **More Unequal Probabilities**

Going back to Example 11.1, what are the variances on the two stocks once we have unequal probabilities? The standard deviations?

We can summarize the needed calculations as follows:

(1) State of Economy	(2) Probability of State of Economy	(3) Return Deviation from Expected Return	(4) Squared Return Deviation from Expected Return	(5) Product (2)×(4)
Stock L				
Recession	.80	$-.20 - (-.02) = -.18$	.0324	.02592
Boom	.20	$.70 - (-.02) = .72$	.5184	.10368
				$\sigma_L^2 = .12960$
Stock U				
Recession	.80	$.30 - .26 = .04$	.0016	.00128
Boom	.20	$.10 - .26 = -.16$	.0256	.00512
				$\sigma_U^2 = .00640$

Based on these calculations, the standard deviation for L is $\sigma_L = \sqrt{.1296} = .36$, or 36%. The standard deviation for U is much smaller; $\sigma_U = \sqrt{.0064} = .08$, or 8%.

Stock L has a higher expected return, but U has less risk. You could get a 70 percent return on your investment in L, but you could also lose 20 percent. Notice that an investment in U will always pay at least 10 percent.

Which of these two stocks should you buy? We can't really say; it depends on your personal preferences. We can be reasonably sure, however, that some investors would prefer L to U and some would prefer U to L.

You've probably noticed that the way we calculated expected returns and variances here is somewhat different from the way we did it in the last chapter. The reason is that, in Chapter 10, we were examining actual historical returns, so we estimated the average return and the variance based on some actual events. Here, we have projected *future* returns and their associated probabilities, so this is the information with which we must work.

CONCEPT QUESTIONS

11.1a How do we calculate the expected return on a security?

11.1b In words, how do we calculate the variance of the expected return?

11.2 | PORTFOLIOS

Thus far in this chapter, we have concentrated on individual assets considered separately. However, most investors actually hold a **portfolio** of assets. All we mean by this is that investors tend to own more than just a single stock, bond, or other asset. Given that this is so, portfolio return and portfolio risk are of obvious relevance. Accordingly, we now discuss portfolio expected returns and variances.

portfolio
Group of assets such as stocks and bonds held by an investor.

Portfolio Weights

There are many equivalent ways of describing a portfolio. The most convenient approach is to list the percentages of the total portfolio's value that are invested in each portfolio asset. We call these percentages the **portfolio weight**.

For example, if we have $50 in one asset and $150 in another, then our total portfolio is worth $200. The percentage of our portfolio in the first asset is $50/200 = .25. The percentage of our portfolio in the second asset is $150/200, or .75. Our portfolio weights are thus .25 and .75. Notice that the weights have to add up to 1.00 since all of our money is invested somewhere.[1]

portfolio weight
Percentage of a portfolio's total value in a particular asset.

Portfolio Expected Returns

Let's go back to Stocks L and U. You put half your money in each. The portfolio weights are obviously .50 and .50. What is the pattern of returns on this portfolio? The expected return?

---

[1] Some of it could be in cash, of course, but we would then just consider the cash to be one of the portfolio assets.

	(1) State of Economy	(2) Probability of State of Economy	(3) Portfolio Return If State Occurs	(4) Product (2)×(3)
TABLE 11.5 Expected return on an equally weighted portfolio of Stock L and Stock U	Recession	.50	$.50 \times -20\% + .50 \times 30\% = 5\%$	.025
	Boom	.50	$.50 \times 70\% + .50 \times 10\% = 40\%$	.200
		1.00		$E(R_P) = .225$

To answer these questions, suppose the economy actually enters a recession. In this case, half your money (the half in L) loses 20 percent. The other half (the half in U) gains 30 percent. Your portfolio return, R_P, in a recession will thus be:

$$R_P = .50 \times -20\% + .50 \times 30\% = 5\%$$

Table 11.5 summarizes the remaining calculations. Notice that when a boom occurs, your portfolio will return 40 percent:

$$R_P = .50 \times 70\% + .50 \times 10\% = 40\%$$

As indicated in Table 11.5, the expected return on your portfolio, $E(R_P)$, is 22.5 percent.

We can save ourselves some work by calculating the expected return more directly. Given these portfolio weights, we could have reasoned that we expect half of our money to earn 25 percent (the half in L) and half of our money to earn 20 percent (the half in U). Our portfolio expected return is thus:

$$\begin{aligned} E(R_P) &= .50 \times E(R_L) + .50 \times E(R_U) \\ &= .50 \times 25\% + .50 \times 20\% \\ &= 22.5\% \end{aligned}$$

This is the same portfolio expected return we had before.

This method of calculating the expected return on a portfolio works no matter how many assets there are in the portfolio. Suppose we had n assets in our portfolio, where n is any number. If we let x_i stand for the percentage of our money in Asset i, then the expected return is:

$$E(R_P) = x_1 \times E(R_1) + x_2 \times E(R_2) + \cdots + x_n \times E(R_n) \qquad \text{[11.2]}$$

This says that the expected return on a portfolio is a straightforward combination of the expected returns on the assets in that portfolio. This seems somewhat obvious, but, as we will examine next, the obvious approach is not always the right one.

EXAMPLE 11.3 **Portfolio Expected Return**

Suppose we have the following projections on three stocks:

State of Economy	Probability of State	Returns		
		Stock A	**Stock B**	**Stock C**
Boom	.40	10%	15%	20%
Bust	.60	8	4	0

(continued)

We want to calculate portfolio expected returns in two cases. First: What would be the expected return on a portfolio with equal amounts invested in each of the three stocks? Second: What would be the expected return if half of the portfolio were in A, with the remainder equally divided between B and C?

From our earlier discussions, the expected returns on the individual stocks are (check these for practice):

$E(R_A) = 8.8\%$
$E(R_B) = 8.4\%$
$E(R_C) = 8.0\%$

If a portfolio has equal investments in each asset, the portfolio weights are all the same. Such a portfolio is said to be *equally weighted*. Since there are three stocks in this case, the weights are all equal to $1/3$. The portfolio expected return is thus:

$E(R_P) = 1/3 \times 8.8\% + 1/3 \times 8.4\% + 1/3 \times 8.0\% = 8.4\%$

In the second case, verify that the portfolio expected return is 8.5 percent.

Portfolio Variance

From our discussion above, the expected return on a portfolio that contains equal investments in Stocks U and L is 22.5 percent. What is the standard deviation of return on this portfolio? Simple intuition might suggest that half of the money has a standard deviation of 45 percent and the other half has a standard deviation of 10 percent, so the portfolio's standard deviation might be calculated as:

$\sigma_P = .50 \times 45\% + .50 \times 10\% = 27.5\%$

Unfortunately, this approach is completely incorrect!

Let's see what the standard deviation really is. Table 11.6 summarizes the relevant calculations. As we see, the portfolio's variance is about .031, and its standard deviation is less than we thought—it's only 17.5 percent. What is illustrated here is that the variance on a portfolio is not generally a simple combination of the variances of the assets in the portfolio.

We can illustrate this point a little more dramatically by considering a slightly different set of portfolio weights. Suppose we put $2/11$ (about 18 percent) in L and the other $9/11$ (about 82 percent) in U. If a recession occurs, this portfolio will have a return of:

$R_P = 2/11 \times -20\% + 9/11 \times 30\% = 20.91\%$

If a boom occurs, this portfolio will have a return of:

$R_P = 2/11 \times 70\% + 9/11 \times 10\% = 20.91\%$

TABLE 11.6

Variance on an equally weighted portfolio of Stock L and Stock U

(1) State of Economy	(2) Probability of State of Economy	(3) Portfolio Return If State Occurs	(4) Squared Deviation from Expected Return	(5) Product (2)×(4)
Recession	.50	5%	$(.05 - .225)^2 = .030625$	.0153125
Boom	.50	40	$(.40 - .225)^2 = .030625$	.0153125
	1.00			$\sigma_P^2 = .0306025$
				$\sigma_P = \sqrt{.030625} = 17.5\%$

Notice that the return is the same no matter what happens. No further calculations are needed: This portfolio has a zero variance. Apparently, combining assets into portfolios can substantially alter the risks faced by the investor. This is a crucial observation, and we will begin to explore its implications in the next section.

EXAMPLE 11.4

Portfolio Variance and Standard Deviation

In Example 11.3, what are the standard deviations on the two portfolios? To answer, we first have to calculate the portfolio returns in the two states. We will work with the second portfolio, which has 50 percent in Stock A and 25 percent in each of Stocks B and C. The relevant calculations can be summarized as follows:

State of Economy	Probability of State	Returns			
		Stock A	Stock B	Stock C	Portfolio
Boom	.40	10%	15%	20%	13.75%
Bust	.60	8	4	0	5.00

The portfolio return when the economy booms is calculated as:

$$.50 \times 10\% + .25 \times 15\% + .25 \times 20\% = 13.75\%$$

The return when the economy goes bust is calculated the same way. The expected return on the portfolio is .085 percent. The variance is thus:

$$\sigma^2 = .40 \times (.1375 - .085)^2 + .60 \times (.05 - .085)^2$$
$$= .0018375$$

The standard deviation is thus about 4.3 percent. For our equally weighted portfolio, verify that the standard deviation is about 5.4 percent.

CONCEPT QUESTIONS

11.2a What is a portfolio weight?

11.2b How do we calculate the expected return on a portfolio?

11.2c Is there a simple relationship between the standard deviation on a portfolio and the standard deviations of the assets in the portfolio?

11.3 | ANNOUNCEMENTS, SURPRISES, AND EXPECTED RETURNS

Now that we know how to construct portfolios and evaluate their returns, we begin to describe more carefully the risks and returns associated with individual securities. Thus far, we have measured volatility by looking at the difference between the actual return on an asset or portfolio, R, and the expected return, $E(R)$. We now look at why such deviations exist.

Expected and Unexpected Returns

To begin, for concreteness, we consider the return on the stock of a company called Flyers. What will determine this stock's return in, say, the coming year?

The return on any stock traded in a financial market is composed of two parts. First, the normal, or expected, return from the stock is the part of the return that shareholders in the market predict or expect. This return depends on the information shareholders have that bears on the stock, and it is based on the market's understanding today of the important factors that will influence the stock in the coming year.

The second part of the return on the stock is the uncertain, or risky, part. This is the portion that comes from unexpected information revealed within the year. A list of all possible sources of such information would be endless, but here are a few examples:

News about research on Flyers.
Government figures released on gross domestic product (GDP).
The results from the latest arms control talks.
The news that Flyers's sales figures are higher than expected.
A sudden, unexpected drop in interest rates.

Want the latest financial news? Visit **www.bloomberg.com**.

Based on this discussion, one way to express the return on Flyers stock in the coming year would be:

$$\text{Total return} = \text{Expected return} + \text{Unexpected return}$$
$$R = E(R) + U \qquad [11.3]$$

where R stands for the actual total return in the year, $E(R)$ stands for the expected part of the return, and U stands for the unexpected part of the return. What this says is that the actual return, R, differs from the expected return, $E(R)$, because of surprises that occur during the year. In any given year, the unexpected return will be positive or negative, but, through time, the average value of U will be zero. This simply means that, on average, the actual return equals the expected return.

Announcements and News

We need to be careful when we talk about the effect of news items on the return. For example, suppose Flyers's business is such that the company prospers when GDP grows at a relatively high rate and suffers when GDP is relatively stagnant. In this case, in deciding what return to expect this year from owning stock in Flyers, shareholders either implicitly or explicitly must think about what GDP is likely to be for the year.

When the government actually announces GDP figures for the year, what will happen to the value of Flyers stock? Obviously, the answer depends on what figure is released. More to the point, however, the impact depends on how much of that figure is *new* information.

At the beginning of the year, market participants will have some idea or forecast of what the yearly GDP will be. To the extent that shareholders have predicted GDP, that prediction will already be factored into the expected part of the return on the stock, $E(R)$. On the other hand, if the announced GDP is a surprise, then the effect will be part of U, the unanticipated portion of the return.

As an example, suppose shareholders in the market had forecast that the GDP increase this year would be .5 percent. If the actual announcement this year is exactly .5 percent, the same as the forecast, then the shareholders don't really learn anything, and the announcement isn't news. There will be no impact on the stock price as a result. This is like receiving confirmation of something that you suspected all along; it doesn't reveal anything new.

A common way of saying that an announcement isn't news is to say that the market has already "discounted" the announcement. The use of the word *discount* here is different from the use of the term in computing present values, but the spirit is the same. When we discount a dollar in the future, we say it is worth less to us because of the time value of money. When we say that we discount an announcement, or a news item, we mean that it has less of an impact on the market because the market already knew much of it.

For example, going back to Flyers, suppose the government announces that the actual GDP increase during the year has been 1.5 percent. Now shareholders have learned something, namely, that the increase is one percentage point higher than they had forecast. This difference between the actual result and the forecast, one percentage point in this example, is sometimes called the *innovation* or the *surprise*.

An announcement, then, can be broken into two parts, the anticipated, or expected, part and the surprise, or innovation:

$$\text{Announcement} = \text{Expected part} + \text{Surprise} \qquad \text{[11.4]}$$

The expected part of any announcement is the part of the information that the market uses to form the expectation, $E(R)$, of the return on the stock. The surprise is the news that influences the unanticipated return on the stock, U.

www.baystreet.ca and www.stockhouse.ca are great sites for stock info.

To take another example, if shareholders knew in January that the president of the firm was going to resign, the official announcement in February would be fully expected and would be discounted by the market. Because the announcement was expected before February, its influence on the stock would have taken place before February. The announcement itself will contain no surprise, and the stock's price shouldn't change at all when it is actually made.

The fact that only the unexpected, or surprise, part of an announcement matters explains why two companies can make similar announcements but experience different stock price reactions. For example, to open the chapter, we compared Onex, Power Financial, and Canadian Natural Resources. In Onex's case, the company's good quarterly performance was rewarded with a stock price increase. In the case of Power Financial, earnings were increased by a one-time gain coming from a sale. Excluding the gain, net income was actually slightly below analyst estimates. In the case of Canadian Natural Resources, the news was announced on a day when investors turned sour on the future of stocks in general (keep this in mind as you read the next section).

Our discussion of market efficiency in the previous chapter bears on this discussion. We are assuming that relevant information known today is already reflected in the expected return. This is identical to saying that the current price reflects relevant publicly available information. We are thus implicitly assuming that markets are at least reasonably efficient in the semistrong form sense.

Henceforth, when we speak of news, we will mean the surprise part of an announcement and not the portion that the market has expected and therefore already discounted.

CONCEPT QUESTIONS

11.3a What are the two basic parts of a return?

11.3b Under what conditions will an announcement have no effect on common stock prices?

11.4 | RISK: SYSTEMATIC AND UNSYSTEMATIC

The unanticipated part of the return, that portion resulting from surprises, is the true risk of any investment. After all, if we always receive exactly what we expect, then the investment is perfectly predictable and so, by definition, risk-free. In other words, the risk of owning an asset comes from surprises—unanticipated events.

There are important differences, though, among various sources of risk. Look back at our previous list of news stories. Some of these stories are directed specifically at Flyers, and some are more general. Which of the news items are of specific importance to Flyers?

Announcements about interest rates or GDP are clearly important for nearly all companies, whereas the news about Flyers's president, its research, or its sales is of specific interest to Flyers. We will distinguish between these two types of events, because, as we shall see, they have very different implications.

Systematic and Unsystematic Risk

The first type of surprise, the one that affects a large number of assets, we will label **systematic risk**. Because systematic risks have marketwide effects, they are sometimes called *market risks.*

The second type of surprise we will call **unsystematic risk**. An unsystematic risk is one that affects a single asset or a small group of assets. Because these risks are unique to individual companies or assets, they are sometimes called *unique* or *asset-specific risks.* We will use these terms interchangeably.

As we have seen, uncertainties about general economic conditions, such as GDP, interest rates, or inflation, are examples of systematic risks. These conditions affect nearly all companies to some degree. An unanticipated increase, or surprise, in inflation, for example, affects wages and the costs of the supplies that companies buy; it affects the value of the assets that companies own; and it affects the prices at which companies sell their products. Forces such as these, to which all companies are susceptible, are the essence of systematic risk.

In contrast, the announcement of an oil strike by a company will primarily affect that company and, perhaps, a few others (such as primary competitors and suppliers). It is unlikely to have much of an effect on the world oil market, however, or on the affairs of companies not in the oil business, so this is an unsystematic event.

systematic risk
A risk that influences a large number of assets. Also *market risk.*

unsystematic risk
A risk that affects at most a small number of assets. Also *unique* or *asset-specific risk.*

Systematic and Unsystematic Components of Return

The distinction between a systematic risk and an unsystematic risk is never really as exact as we make it out to be. Even the most narrow and peculiar bit of news about a company ripples through the economy. This is true because every enterprise, no matter how tiny, is a part of the economy. It's like the tale of a kingdom that was lost because one horse lost a shoe. This is mostly hairsplitting, however. Some risks are clearly much more general than others. We'll see some evidence on this point in just a moment.

The distinction between the types of risk allows us to break down the surprise portion, U, of the return on Flyers's stock into two parts. From before, we had the actual return broken down into its expected and surprise components:

$$R = E(R) + U$$

We now recognize that the total surprise for Flyers, U, has a systematic and an unsystematic component, so:

$$R = E(R) + \text{Systematic portion} + \text{Unsystematic portion} \qquad \textbf{[11.5]}$$

Because it is traditional, we will use the Greek letter epsilon, ϵ, to stand for the unsystematic portion. Since systematic risks are often called market risks, we will use the letter m

to stand for the systematic part of the surprise. With these symbols, we can rewrite the total return:

$$R = E(R) + U$$
$$= E(R) + m + \epsilon$$

The important thing about the way we have broken down the total surprise, U, is that the unsystematic portion, ϵ, is more or less unique to Flyers. For this reason, it is unrelated to the unsystematic portion of return on most other assets. To see why this is important, we need to return to the subject of portfolio risk.

CONCEPT QUESTIONS

11.4a   What are the two basic types of risk?

11.4b   What is the distinction between the two types of risk?

11.5 | DIVERSIFICATION AND PORTFOLIO RISK

We've seen earlier that portfolio risks can, in principle, be quite different from the risks of the assets that make up the portfolio. We now look more closely at the riskiness of an individual asset versus the risk of a portfolio of many different assets. We will once again examine some market history to get an idea of what happens with actual investments in the capital markets.

The Effect of Diversification: Another Lesson from Market History

In our previous chapter, we saw that the standard deviation of the annual return on a portfolio of several hundred large common stocks has historically been 16 percent per year for the Toronto Stock Exchange and about 18 percent per year for the New York Stock Exchange (see Table 10.4, for example). Does this mean that the standard deviation of the annual return on a typical stock is about 16 or 18 percent? As you might suspect by now, the answer is *no*. This is an extremely important observation.

For more on risk and diversification, visit **www.investopedia.com/university**.

To examine the relationship between portfolio size and portfolio risk, Table 11.7 illustrates typical average annual standard deviations for portfolios that contain different numbers of randomly selected NYSE securities.

In Column 2 of Table 11.7, we see that the standard deviation for a "portfolio" of one security is about 49 percent. What this means is that, if you randomly selected a single NYSE stock and put all your money into it, your standard deviation of return would typically be a substantial 49 percent per year. If you were to randomly select two stocks and invest half your money in each, your standard deviation would be about 37 percent on average, and so on.

The important thing to notice in Table 11.7 is that the standard deviation declines as the number of securities is increased. By the time we have 100 randomly chosen stocks, the portfolio's standard deviation has declined by about 60 percent, from 49 percent to about 20 percent. With 500 securities, the standard deviation is 19.27 percent, similar to the 18.1 percent we saw in our previous chapter for the U.S. large company stock portfolio. The small difference exists because the portfolio securities and time periods examined are not identical.

(1) Number of Stocks in Portfolio	(2) Average Standard Deviation of Annual Portfolio Returns	(3) Ratio of Portfolio Standard Deviation to Standard Deviation of a Single Stock
1	49.24%	1.00
2	37.36	.76
4	29.69	.60
6	26.64	.54
8	24.98	.51
10	23.93	.49
20	21.68	.44
30	20.87	.42
40	20.46	.42
50	20.20	.41
100	19.69	.40
200	19.42	.39
300	19.34	.39
400	19.29	.39
500	19.27	.39
1,000	19.21	.39

TABLE 11.7

Standard deviations of annual portfolio returns

Sources: These figures are from Table 1 in Meir Statman, "How Many Stocks Make a Diversified Portfolio?" *Journal of Financial and Quantitative Analysis* 22 (September 1987), pp. 353–64. They were derived from E. J. Elton and M. J. Gruber, "Risk Reduction and Portfolio Size: An Analytic Solution," *Journal of Business* 50 (October 1977), pp. 415–37.

The Principle of Diversification

Figure 11.1 illustrates the point we've been discussing. What we have plotted is the standard deviation of return versus the number of stocks in the portfolio. Notice in Figure 11.1 that the benefit in terms of risk reduction from adding securities drops off as we add more and more. By the time we have 10 securities, most of the effect is already realized, and by the time we get to 30 or so, there is very little remaining benefit.

Figure 11.1 illustrates two key points. First: Some of the riskiness associated with individual assets can be eliminated by forming portfolios. The process of spreading an investment across assets (and thereby forming a portfolio) is called *diversification*. The well-known proverb "don't put all your eggs in one basket" gives a good illustration of diversification. If you put your eggs in several baskets, you will not break them all, if you drop a basket. Thus, the **principle of diversification** tells us that spreading an investment across many assets will eliminate some of the risk. The green shaded area in Figure 11.1, labeled "diversifiable risk," is the part that can be eliminated by diversification.

The second point is equally important: There is a minimum level of risk that cannot be eliminated simply by diversifying. This minimum level is labelled "nondiversifiable risk" in Figure 11.1. Taken together, these two points are another important lesson from capital market history: Diversification reduces risk, but only up to a point. Put another way: Some risk is diversifiable and some is not.

principle of diversification
Spreading an investment across a number of assets will eliminate some, but not all, of the risk.

Diversification and Unsystematic Risk

From our discussion of portfolio risk, we know that some of the risk associated with individual assets can be diversified away and some cannot. We are left with an obvious question: Why is this so? It turns out that the answer hinges on the distinction we made earlier between systematic and unsystematic risk.

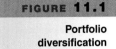

FIGURE 11.1

Portfolio diversification

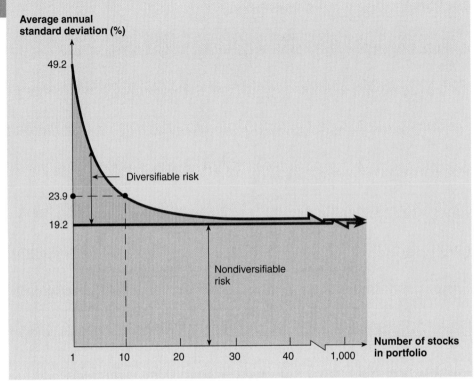

By definition, an unsystematic risk is one that is particular to a single asset or, at most, a small group. For example, if the asset under consideration is stock in a single company, the discovery of positive NPV projects such as successful new products and innovative cost savings will tend to increase the value of the stock. Unanticipated lawsuits, industrial accidents, strikes, and similar events will tend to decrease future cash flows and thereby reduce share values.

Here is the important observation: If we only held a single stock, then the value of our investment would fluctuate because of company-specific events. If we hold a large portfolio, on the other hand, some of the stocks in the portfolio will go up in value because of positive company-specific events and some will go down in value because of negative events. The net effect on the overall value of the portfolio will be relatively small, however, as these effects will tend to cancel each other out.

Now we see why some of the variability associated with individual assets is eliminated by diversification. When we combine assets into portfolios, the unique, or unsystematic, events—both positive and negative—tend to "wash out" once we have more than just a few assets.

This is an important point that bears restating:

> Unsystematic risk is essentially eliminated by diversification, so a relatively large portfolio has almost no unsystematic risk.

In fact, the terms *diversifiable risk* and *unsystematic risk* are often used interchangeably.

Diversification and Systematic Risk

We've seen that unsystematic risk can be eliminated by diversifying. What about systematic risk? Can it also be eliminated by diversification? The answer is no because, by definition, a systematic risk affects almost all assets to some degree. As a result, no matter how many assets we put into a portfolio, the systematic risk doesn't go away. Thus, for obvious reasons, the terms *systematic risk* and *nondiversifiable risk* are used interchangeably.

Because we have introduced so many different terms, it is useful to summarize our discussion before moving on. What we have seen is that the total risk of an investment, as measured by the standard deviation of its return, can be written as:

$$\text{Total risk} = \text{Systematic risk} + \text{Unsystematic risk} \qquad \textbf{[11.6]}$$

Systematic risk is also called *nondiversifiable risk* or *market risk.* Unsystematic risk is also called *diversifiable risk, unique risk,* or *asset-specific risk.* For a well-diversified portfolio, the unsystematic risk is negligible. For such a portfolio, essentially all of the risk is systematic.

CONCEPT QUESTIONS

11.5a What happens to the standard deviation of return for a portfolio if we increase the number of securities in the portfolio?

11.5b What is the principle of diversification?

11.5c Why is some risk diversifiable?

11.5d Why can't systematic risk be diversified away?

11.6 | SYSTEMATIC RISK AND BETA

The question that we now begin to address is this: What determines the size of the risk premium on a risky asset? Put another way: Why do some assets have a larger risk premium than other assets? The answer to these questions, as we discuss next, is also based on the distinction between systematic and unsystematic risk.

The Systematic Risk Principle

Thus far, we've seen that the total risk associated with an asset can be decomposed into two components: systematic and unsystematic risk. We have also seen that unsystematic risk can be essentially eliminated by diversification. The systematic risk present in an asset, on the other hand, cannot be eliminated by diversification.

Based on our study of capital market history, we know that there is a reward, on average, for bearing risk. However, we now need to be more precise about what we mean by risk. The **systematic risk principle** states that the reward for bearing risk depends only on the systematic risk of an investment. The underlying rationale for this principle is straightforward: Since unsystematic risk can be eliminated at virtually no cost (by diversifying), there is no reward for bearing it. Put another way: The market does not reward risks that are borne unnecessarily.

The systematic risk principle has a remarkable and very important implication:

systematic risk principle
The expected return on a risky asset depends only on that asset's systematic risk.

> The expected return on an asset depends only on that asset's systematic risk.

There is an obvious corollary to this principle: No matter how much total risk an asset has, only the systematic portion is relevant in determining the expected return (and the risk premium) on that asset.

TABLE 11.8	Company	Beta Coefficient (β_i)
Beta coefficients for selected Canadian companies	TransCanada	0.55
	Royal Bank of Canada	0.70
	BCE Inc.	0.80
	Canadian Pacific Railway	0.90
	Magna International	1.00
	Biovail	1.15
	Bombardier	1.30
	Research in Motion	1.40
	Nortel Networks	1.65

Source: The Value Line Investment Survey, various issues, 2006.

Measuring Systematic Risk

beta coefficient
Amount of systematic risk present in a particular risky asset relative to that in an average risky asset.

Since systematic risk is the crucial determinant of an asset's expected return, we need some way of measuring the level of systematic risk for different investments. The specific measure we will use is called the **beta coefficient**, for which we will use the Greek symbol β. A beta coefficient, or beta for short, tells us how much systematic risk a particular asset has relative to an average asset. By definition, an average asset has a beta of 1.0 relative to itself. An asset with a beta of .50, therefore, has half as much systematic risk as an average asset; an asset with a beta of 2.0 has twice as much.

Table 11.8 contains the estimated beta coefficients for the stocks of some well-known companies. (This particular source rounds numbers to the nearest .05.) The range of betas in Table 11.8 is typical for stocks of large Canadian corporations. Betas outside this range occur, but they are less common.

The important thing to remember is that the expected return, and thus the risk premium, on an asset depends only on its systematic risk. Since assets with larger betas have greater systematic risks, they will have greater expected returns. Thus, from Table 11.8, an investor who buys stock in TransCanada with a beta of 0.55, should expect to earn less, on average, than an investor who buys stock in Research In Motion with a beta of about 1.40. See our *Work the Web* box opposite to learn how to find betas online.

Note that the beta coefficient for Nortel Networks is 2.52 in the *Work the Web* box, but it is only 1.65 in Table 11.8. In fact, various sources of financial information frequently

---

EXAMPLE 11.5   Total Risk versus Beta

Consider the following information on two securities. Which has greater total risk? Which has greater systematic risk? Greater unsystematic risk? Which asset will have a higher risk premium?

	Standard Deviation	Beta
Security A	40%	.50
Security B	20	1.50

From our discussion in this section, Security A has greater total risk, but it has substantially less systematic risk. Since total risk is the sum of systematic and unsystematic risk, Security A must have greater unsystematic risk. Finally, from the systematic risk principle, Security B will have a higher risk premium and a greater expected return, despite the fact that it has less total risk.

WORK THE WEB

Suppose you want to find the beta for a company like Nortel Networks. One way is to go to the Web. We went to **ca.finance.yahoo.com**, entered the ticker symbol NT for Nortel Networks, and followed the "Key Statistics" link. Here is part of what we found:

FINANCIAL HIGHLIGHTS

Fiscal Year

Fiscal Year Ends:	31-Dec
Most Recent Quarter (mrq):	30-Jun-06

Profitability

Profit Margin (ttm):	-21.04%
Operating Margin (ttm):	-1.78%

Management Effectiveness

Return on Assets (ttm):	-0.70%
Return on Equity (ttm):	-94.00%

Income Statement

Revenue (ttm):	10.64B
Revenue Per Share (ttm):	2.453
Revenue Growth (lfy)³:	4.80%
Gross Profit (ttm)²:	4.31B
EBITDA (ttm):	86.00M
Net Income Avl to Common (ttm):	-2.25B
Diluted EPS (ttm):	-0.516
Earnings Growth (lfy)³:	N/A

Balance Sheet

Total Cash (mrq):	1.90B
Total Cash Per Share (mrq):	0.439
Total Debt (mrq)²:	3.77B
Total Debt/Equity (mrq):	3.247
Current Ratio (mrq):	1.252
Book Value Per Share (mrq):	0.268

TRADING INFORMATION

Stock Price History

Beta:	2.52
52-Week Change:	-33.54%
52-Week Change (relative to S&P500):	14.16%
52-Week High ():	3.43
52-Week Low ():	N/A
50-Day Moving Average:	2.2492
200-Day Moving Average:	2.2634

Share Statistics

Average Volume (3 month):	19,120,900
Average Volume (10 day):	15,000,700
Shares Outstanding:	4.34B
Float:	4.33B
% Held by Insiders:	0.05%
% Held by Institutions:	36.20%
Shares Short (as of 10-Oct-06):	22.36M
Daily Volume (as of 10-Oct-06):	N/A
Short Ratio (as of 10-Oct-06):	1.1
Short % of Float (as of 10-Oct-06):	0.50%
Shares Short (prior month):	39.74M

The reported beta for Nortel Networks is 2.52, which means that Nortel has about two-and-one-half times the systematic risk of a typical stock. You would expect that the company is very risky, and looking at the other numbers, we agree. Nortel's revenue is $10.64 billion, an impressive number, but net income is *negative* $2.25 billion. That's not good! Digging deeper, we see that all Nortel's profitability measures have negative values, among which ROE is an astounding negative 94 percent. In all, Nortel Networks appears to be a good candidate for a high beta.

show different betas for the same companies. To learn more about discrepancies in "real-world" betas, see the *Reality Bytes* box on the next page.

Portfolio Betas

Earlier, we saw that the riskiness of a portfolio has no simple relationship to the risks of the assets in the portfolio. A portfolio beta, however, can be calculated just like a portfolio expected return.

Betas are easy to find on the Web. Try **www.theglobeandmail .com** and **ca.finance. yahoo.com.**

REALITY BYTES

Beta, Beta, Who's Got the Beta?

Based on what we've studied so far, you can see that beta is a pretty important topic. You might wonder then, are all published betas created equal? Read on for a partial answer to this question.

We did some checking on betas and found some interesting results. *The Value Line Investment Survey* is one of the best-known sources for information on publicly traded companies. However, with the explosion of online investing, there has been a corresponding increase in the amount of investment information available online. We decided to compare the betas presented by Value Line to those reported by Yahoo! Finance (ca.finance.yahoo.com) and Globeandmail.com (www.theglobeandmail.com). What we found leads to an important note of caution.

Consider Research in Motion, producer of the famous BlackBerry device. Its beta reported by Yahoo! Finance was 3.63, which was much larger than Value Line's beta of 1.40. In contrast, both of the online betas for Shaw Communications, 0.98 and 0.38, were below the Value Line beta of 1.20.

Technology companies were not the only ones that showed a divergence in betas from different sources. For example, the reported beta for Toronto-based Agnico-Eagle Mines ranged from 0.26 on Yahoo! Finance to 1.85 on Globeandmail.com, while Value Line's beta of 0.75 was between the two.

We also found some unusual, and even hard to believe, estimates for beta. Globeandmail.com had a very low beta of 0.04 for Calgary-headquartered TransAlta Corporation, while Value Line reported 0.55. Even more remarkable was the beta estimate for Evolution Petroleum, a U.S. energy corporation. Whereas Value Line did not report a beta for this company, Yahoo! Finance estimated the beta at −6.19 (notice the minus sign!). It is possible for a company to have a negative beta, but it is unlikely for it to be of such magnitude.

There are a few lessons to be learned from all of this. First, not all betas are created equal. Some are computed using weekly returns and some using daily returns. Some are computed using 60 months of stock returns; some consider more or fewer months. Some betas are computed by comparing the stock to the S&P/TSX index, while others use alternative indices. Finally, some reporting firms (including Value Line) make adjustments to raw betas to reflect information other than just the fluctuation in stock prices.

The second lesson is perhaps more subtle and comes from the beta of Evolution Petroleum. We are interested in knowing what the betas of the stocks will be in the future, but betas have to be estimated using historical data. Any time we use the past to predict the future, there is the danger of a poor estimate. As we will see later in the chapter (and the next one), it is very unlikely that Evolution Petroleum has a beta of −6.19. Instead, the estimate is almost certainly a poor one. The moral of the story is that, as with any financial tool, beta is not a black box that should be taken without question.

For example, looking again at Table 11.8, suppose you put half of your money in BCE and half in Bombardier. What would the beta of this combination be? Since BCE has a beta of .80 and Bombardier has a beta of 1.30, the portfolio's beta, β_P, would be:

$$\beta_P = .50 \times \beta_{BCE} + .50 \times \beta_{Bombardier}$$
$$= .50 \times .80 + .50 \times 1.30$$
$$= 1.05$$

In general, if we had n assets in a portfolio, we would multiply each asset's beta β_i by its portfolio weight x_i and then add the results up to get the portfolio's beta:

$$\beta_P = x_1 \times \beta_1 + x_2 \times \beta_2 + \ldots + x_n \times \beta_n \qquad \text{[11.7]}$$

Portfolio Betas   **EXAMPLE 11.6**

Suppose we had the following investments:

Security	Amount Invested	Expected Return	Beta
Stock A	$1,000	8%	.80
Stock B	2,000	12	.95
Stock C	3,000	15	1.10
Stock D	4,000	18	1.40

What is the expected return on this portfolio? What is the beta of this portfolio? Does this portfolio have more or less systematic risk than an average asset?

To answer, we first have to calculate the portfolio weights. Notice that the total amount invested is $10,000. Of this, $1,000/10,000=10% is invested in Stock A. Similarly, 20 percent is invested in Stock B, 30 percent is invested in Stock C, and 40 percent is invested in Stock D. The expected return, $E(R_P)$, is thus:

$$E(R_P) = .10 \times E(R_A) + .20 \times E(R_B) + .30 \times E(R_C) + .40 \times E(R_D)$$
$$= .10 \times 8\% + .20 \times 12\% + .30 \times 15\% + .40 \times 18\%$$
$$= 14.9\%$$

Similarly, the portfolio beta, β_R is:

$$\beta_P = .10 \times \beta_A + .20 \times \beta_B + .30 \times \beta_C + .40 \times \beta_D$$
$$= .10 \times .80 + .20 \times .95 + .30 \times 1.10 + .40 \times 1.40$$
$$= 1.16$$

This portfolio thus has an expected return of 14.9 percent and a beta of 1.16. Since the beta is larger than 1.0, this portfolio has greater systematic risk than an average asset.

CONCEPT QUESTIONS

11.6a   What is the systematic risk principle?

11.6b   What does a beta coefficient measure?

11.6c   How do you calculate a portfolio beta?

11.6d   True or false: The expected return on a risky asset depends on that asset's total risk. Explain.

11.7 | THE SECURITY MARKET LINE

We're now in a position to see how risk is rewarded in the marketplace. To begin, suppose that Asset A has an expected return of $E(R_A) = 20\%$ and a beta of $\beta_A = 1.6$. Furthermore, the risk-free rate is $R_f = 8\%$. Notice that a risk-free asset, by definition, has no systematic risk (or unsystematic risk), so a risk-free asset has a beta of 0.

Beta and the Risk Premium

Consider a portfolio made up of Asset A and a risk-free asset. We can calculate some different possible portfolio expected returns and betas by varying the percentages invested in these two assets. For example, if 25 percent of the portfolio is invested in Asset A, then the expected return is:

$$E(R_P) = .25 \times E(R_A) + (1 - .25) \times R_f$$
$$= .25 \times 20\% + .75 \times 8\%$$
$$= 11.0\%$$

Similarly, the beta on the portfolio, β_P, would be:

$$\beta_P = .25 \times \beta_A + (1 - .25) \times 0$$
$$= .25 \times 1.6$$
$$= .40$$

Notice that, since the weights have to add up to 1, the percentage invested in the risk-free asset is equal to 1 minus the percentage invested in Asset A.

One thing that you might wonder about is whether it is possible for the percentage invested in Asset A to exceed 100 percent. The answer is yes. The way this can happen is for the investor to borrow at the risk-free rate. For example, suppose an investor has $100 and borrows an additional $50 at 8 percent, the risk-free rate. The total investment in Asset A would be $150, or 150 percent of the investor's wealth. The expected return in this case would be:

$$E(R_P) = 1.50 \times E(R_A) + (1 - 1.50) \times R_f$$
$$= 1.50 \times 20\% - .50 \times 8\%$$
$$= 26.0\%$$

The beta on the portfolio would be:

$$\beta_P = 1.50 \times \beta_A + (1 - 1.50) \times 0$$
$$= 1.50 \times 1.6$$
$$= 2.4$$

We can calculate some other possibilities as follows:

Percentage of Portfolio in Asset A	Portfolio Expected Return	Portfolio Beta
0%	8%	.0
25	11	.4
50	14	.8
75	17	1.2
100	20	1.6
125	23	2.0
150	26	2.4

In Figure 11.2A, these portfolio expected returns are plotted against the portfolio betas. Notice that all the combinations fall on a straight line.

The Reward-to-Risk Ratio   What is the slope of the straight line in Figure 11.2A? As always, the slope of a straight line is equal to "the rise over the run." In this case, as we move out of the risk-free asset into Asset A, the beta increases from 0 to 1.6 (a "run" of 1.6). At the

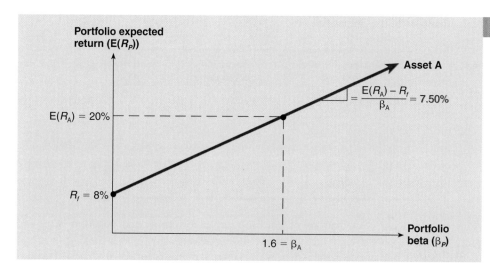

FIGURE 11.2A

Portfolio expected returns and betas for Asset A

same time, the expected return goes from 8 percent to 20 percent, a "rise" of 12 percent. The slope of the line is thus $12\%/1.6 = 7.50\%$.

Notice that the slope of our line is just the risk premium on Asset A, $E(R_A) - R_f$, divided by Asset A's beta, β_A. This slope is called the *reward-to-risk ratio*:

$$
\text{Reward-to-risk ratio} = \frac{E(R_A) - R_f}{\beta_A}
$$

$$
= \frac{20\% - 8\%}{1.6} = 7.50\%
$$

[11.8]

Thus, Asset A offers a *reward-to-risk ratio* of 7.50 percent.[2] In other words, Asset A has a risk premium of 7.50 percent per "unit" of systematic risk.

The Basic Argument Now suppose we consider a second asset, Asset B. This asset has a beta of 1.2 and an expected return of 16 percent. Which investment is better, Asset A or Asset B? You might think that, once again, we really cannot say. Some investors might prefer A; some investors might prefer B. Actually, however, we can say: A is better because, as we shall demonstrate, B offers inadequate compensation for its level of systematic risk, at least relative to A.

To begin, we calculate different combinations of expected returns and betas for portfolios of Asset B and a risk-free asset just as we did for Asset A. For example, if we put 25 percent in Asset B and the remaining 75 percent in the risk-free asset, the portfolio's expected return would be:

$$
\begin{aligned}
E(R_P) &= .25 \times E(R_B) + (1 - .25) \times R_f \\
&= .25 \times 16\% + .75 \times 8\% \\
&= 10.0\%
\end{aligned}
$$

Similarly, the beta on the portfolio, β_P, would be:

$$
\begin{aligned}
\beta_P &= .25 \times \beta_B + (1 - .25) \times 0 \\
&= .25 \times 1.2 \\
&= .30
\end{aligned}
$$

---

[2]This ratio is sometimes called the *Treynor index,* after one of its originators.

Some other possibilities are as follows:

Percentage of Portfolio in Asset B	Portfolio Expected Return	Portfolio Beta
0%	8%	.0
25	10	.3
50	12	.6
75	14	.9
100	16	1.2
125	18	1.5
150	20	1.8

When we plot these combinations of portfolio expected returns and portfolio betas in Figure 11.2B, we get a straight line just as we did for Asset A.

The key thing to notice is that when we compare the results for Assets A and B, as in Figure 11.2C, the line describing the combinations of expected returns and betas for Asset A is higher than the one for Asset B. What this tells us is that for any given level of systematic risk (as measured by β), some combination of Asset A and the risk-free asset always offers a larger return. This is why we were able to state that Asset A is a better investment than Asset B.

Another way of seeing that A offers a superior return for its level of risk is to note that the slope of our line, which is the reward-to-risk ratio for Asset B, is:

$$\text{Reward-to-Risk Ratio} = \frac{E(R_B) - R_f}{\beta_B}$$
$$= \frac{16\% - 8\%}{1.2} = 6.67\%$$

Thus, Asset B has a reward-to-risk ratio of 6.67 percent, which is less than the 7.5 percent offered by Asset A.

The Fundamental Result The situation we have described for Assets A and B cannot persist in a well-organized, active market, because investors would be attracted to Asset A

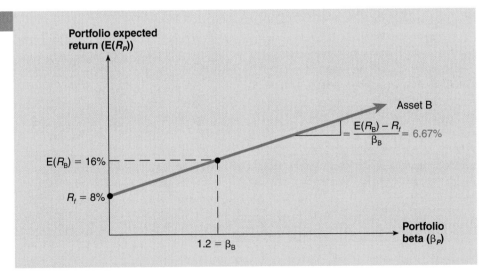

FIGURE 11.2B

Portfolio expected returns and betas for Asset B

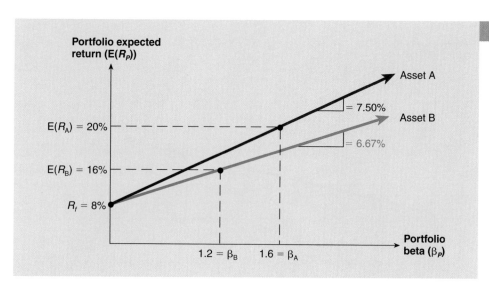

FIGURE 11.2C

Portfolio expected returns and betas for both assets

and away from Asset B. As a result, Asset A's price would rise and Asset B's price would fall. Since prices and returns move in opposite directions, the result would be that Asset A's expected return would decline and B's would rise.

This buying and selling would continue until the two assets plotted on exactly the same line, which means they would offer the same reward for bearing risk. In other words, in an active, competitive market, we must have that:

$$\frac{E(R_A) - R_f}{\beta_A} = \frac{E(R_B) - R_f}{\beta_B}$$

This is the fundamental relationship between risk and return.

Our basic argument can be extended to more than just two assets. In fact, no matter how many assets we had, we would always reach the same conclusion:

> The reward-to-risk ratio must be the same for all the assets in the market.

This result is really not so surprising. What it says, for example, is that, if one asset has twice as much systematic risk as another asset, its risk premium will simply be twice as large.

Since all of the assets in the market must have the same reward-to-risk ratio, they all must plot on the same line. This argument is illustrated in Figure 11.3. As shown, Assets A and B plot directly on the line and thus have the same reward-to-risk ratio. If an asset plotted above the line, such as C in Figure 11.3, its price would rise, and its expected return would fall until it plotted exactly on the line. Similarly, if an asset plotted below the line, such as D in Figure 11.3, its expected return would rise until it too plotted directly on the line.

The arguments we have presented apply to active, competitive, well-functioning markets. The financial markets, such as the TSX, NYSE, and Nasdaq best meet these criteria. Other markets, such as real asset markets, may or may not. For this reason, these concepts are most useful in examining financial markets. We will thus focus on such markets here. However, as we discuss in the last section, the information about risk and return gleaned from financial markets is crucial in evaluating the investments that a corporation makes in real assets.

FIGURE 11.3

Expected returns and systematic risk

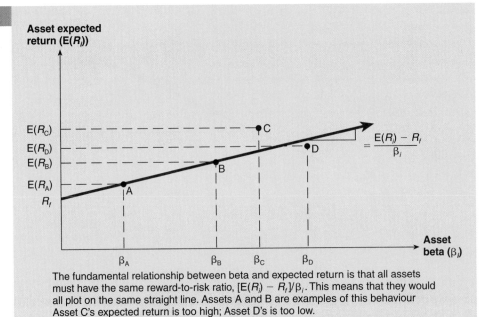

The fundamental relationship between beta and expected return is that all assets must have the same reward-to-risk ratio, $[E(R_i) - R_f]/\beta_i$. This means that they would all plot on the same straight line. Assets A and B are examples of this behaviour Asset C's expected return is too high; Asset D's is too low.

EXAMPLE 11.7 | **Buy Low, Sell High**

An asset is said to be *overvalued* if its price is too high given its expected return and risk. Suppose you observe the following situation:

Security	Expected Return	Beta
Fama Co.	14%	1.3
French Co.	10	.8

The risk-free rate is currently 6 percent. Is one of the two securities above overvalued relative to the other?

To answer, we compute the reward-to-risk ratio for both. For Fama, this ratio is $(14\% - 6\%)/1.3 = 6.15\%$. For French, this ratio is 5 percent. What we conclude is that French offers an insufficient expected return for its level of risk, at least relative to Fama. Since its expected return is too low, its price is too high. In other words, French is overvalued relative to Fama, and we would expect to see its price fall relative to Fama's. Notice that we could also say Fama is *undervalued* relative to French.

The Security Market Line

The line that results when we plot expected returns and beta coefficients is obviously of some importance, so it's time we gave it a name. This line, which we use to describe the relationship between systematic risk and expected return in financial markets, is usually called the **security market line**, or **SML**. After NPV, the SML is arguably the most important concept in modern finance.

Market Portfolios   It will be very useful to know the equation of the SML. There are many different ways we could write it, but one way is particularly common. Suppose we consider a portfolio made up of all of the assets in the market. We'll call such a portfolio a market portfolio, and express the expected return on this market portfolio as $E(R_M)$.

Since all the assets in the market must plot on the SML, so must a market portfolio made up of those assets. To determine where it plots on the SML, we need to know the beta of the market portfolio, β_M. Since this portfolio is representative of all of the assets in the market, it must have average systematic risk. In other words, it has a beta of 1.0. We could therefore write the slope of the SML as:

$$\text{SML slope} = \frac{E(R_M) - R_f}{\beta_M} = \frac{E(R_M) - R_f}{1} = E(R_M) - R_f$$

The term $E(R_M) - R_f$ is often called the **market risk premium** since it is the risk premium on a market portfolio.

The Capital Asset Pricing Model   To finish up, if we let $E(R_i)$ and β_i stand for the expected return and beta, respectively, on any asset in the market, then we know that asset must plot on the SML. As a result, we know that its reward-to-risk ratio is the same as that of the overall market:

$$\frac{E(R_i) - R_f}{\beta_i} = E(R_M) - R_f$$

If we rearrange this, then we can write the equation for the SML as:

$$E(R_i) = R_f + [E(R_M) - R_f] \times \beta_i \qquad \text{[11.9]}$$

This result is identical to the famous **capital asset pricing model (CAPM)**.

What the CAPM shows is that the expected return for a particular asset depends on three things:

1.   *The pure time value of money.* As measured by the risk-free rate, R_f, this is the reward for merely waiting for your money, without taking any risk.
2.   *The reward for bearing systematic risk.* As measured by the market risk premium, $[E(R_M) - R_f]$, this component is the reward the market offers for bearing an average amount of systematic risk in addition to waiting.
3.   *The amount of systematic risk.* As measured by β_i, this is the amount of systematic risk present in a particular asset, relative to an average asset.

By the way, the CAPM works for portfolios of assets just as it does for individual assets. In an earlier section, we saw how to calculate a portfolio's β. To find the expected return on a portfolio, we simply use this β in the CAPM equation.

Figure 11.4 summarizes our discussion of the SML and the CAPM. As before, we plot expected return against beta. Now we recognize that, based on the CAPM, the slope of the SML is equal to the market risk premium, $[E(R_M) - R_f]$.

security market line (SML)
Positively sloped straight line displaying the relationship between expected return and beta.

market risk premium
Slope of the SML, the difference between the expected return on a market portfolio and the risk-free rate.

capital asset pricing model (CAPM)
Equation of the SML showing the relationship between the expected return and the beta.

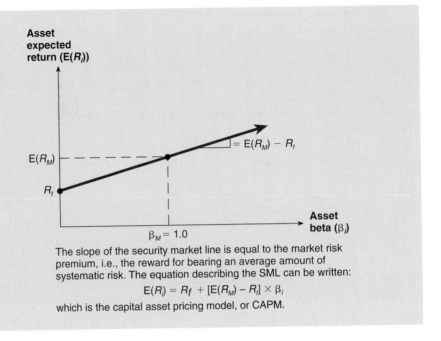

FIGURE 11.4

The security market
line, or SML

**Asset
expected
return ($E(R_i)$)**

$E(R_M)$

R_f

$= E(R_M) - R_f$

$\beta_M = 1.0$

**Asset
beta (β_i)**

The slope of the security market line is equal to the market risk
premium, i.e., the reward for bearing an average amount of
systematic risk. The equation describing the SML can be written:

$$E(R_i) = R_f + [E(R_M) - R_f] \times \beta_i$$

which is the capital asset pricing model, or CAPM.

This concludes our presentation of concepts related to the risk-return trade-off. For future reference, Table 11.9 summarizes the various concepts in the order in which we discussed them.

EXAMPLE 11.8   Risk and Return

Suppose the risk-free rate is 4 percent, the market risk premium is 8.6 percent, and a particular stock has a beta of 1.3. Based on the CAPM, what is the expected return on this stock? What would the expected return be if the beta were to double?

   With a beta of 1.3, the risk premium for the stock would be 1.3 × 8.6%, or 11.18 percent. The risk-free rate is 4 percent, so the expected return is 15.18 percent. If the beta doubled to 2.6, the risk premium would double to 22.36 percent, so the expected return would be 26.36 percent.

CONCEPT QUESTIONS

11.7a   What is the fundamental relationship between risk and return in well-functioning markets?

11.7b   What is the security market line? Why must all assets plot directly on it in a well-functioning market?

11.7c   What is the capital asset pricing model, or CAPM? What does it tell us about the required return on a risky investment?

11.8 | THE SML AND THE COST OF CAPITAL: A PREVIEW

Our goal in studying risk and return is twofold. First, risk is an extremely important consideration in almost all business decisions, so we want to discuss just what risk is and how

TABLE 11.9	**Summary of risk and return concepts**

I. Total return

The *total return* on an investment has two components: the expected return and the unexpected return. The unexpected return comes about because of unanticipated events. The risk from investing stems from the possibility of an unanticipated event.

II. Total risk

The *total risk* of an investment is measured by the variance or, more commonly, the standard deviation of its return.

III. Systematic and unsystematic risks

Systematic risks (also called *market risks*) are unanticipated events that affect almost all assets to some degree because the effects are economywide. *Unsystematic risks* are unanticipated events that affect single assets or small groups of assets. Unsystematic risks are also called *unique* or *asset-specific risks*.

IV. The effect of diversification

Some, but not all, of the risk associated with a risky investment can be eliminated by diversification. The reason is that unsystematic risks, which are unique to individual assets, tend to wash out in a large portfolio, but systematic risks, which affect all of the assets in a portfolio to some extent, do not.

V. The systematic risk principle and beta

Because unsystematic risk can be freely eliminated by diversification, the *systematic risk principle* states that the reward for bearing risk depends only on the level of systematic risk. The level of systematic risk in a particular asset, relative to the average, is given by the beta of that asset.

VI. The reward-to-risk ratio and the security market line

The *reward-to-risk ratio* for Asset i is the ratio of its risk premium, $E(R_i) - R_f$, to its beta, β_i:

$$\frac{E(R_i) - R_f}{\beta_i}$$

In a well-functioning market, this ratio is the same for every asset. As a result, when asset expected returns are plotted against asset betas, all assets plot on the same straight line, called the *security market line* (SML).

VII. The capital asset pricing model

From the SML, the expected return on Asset i can be written:

$$E(R_i) = R_f + [E(R_M) - R_f] \times \beta_i$$

This is the *capital asset pricing model* (CAPM). The expected return on a risky asset thus has three components. The first is the pure time value of money, R_f; the second is the market risk premium, $[E(R_M) - R_f]$; and the third is the beta for that asset, β_i.

it is rewarded in the market. Our second purpose is to learn what determines the appropriate discount rate for future cash flows. We briefly discuss this second subject now; we discuss it in more detail in Chapter 12.

The Basic Idea

The security market line tells us the reward for bearing risk in financial markets. At an absolute minimum, any new investment our firm undertakes must offer an expected return that is no worse than what the financial markets offer for the same risk. The reason for this is simply that our shareholders can always invest for themselves in the financial markets.

The only way we benefit our shareholders is by finding investments with expected returns that are superior to what the financial markets offer for the same risk. Such an investment will have a positive NPV. So, if we ask, What is the appropriate discount rate? the answer is that we should use the expected return offered in financial markets on investments with the same systematic risk.

In other words, to determine whether or not an investment has a positive NPV, we essentially compare the expected return on that new investment to what the financial market offers on an investment with the same beta. This is why the SML is so important; it tells us the "going rate" for bearing risk in the economy.

The Cost of Capital

cost of capital
The minimum required return on a new investment.

The appropriate discount rate on a new project is the minimum expected rate of return an investment must offer to be attractive. This minimum required return is often called the **cost of capital** associated with the investment. It is called this because the required return is what the firm must earn on its capital investment in a project just to break even. It can thus be interpreted as the opportunity cost associated with the firm's capital investment.

Notice that when we say an investment is attractive if its expected return exceeds what is offered in financial markets for investments of the same risk, we are effectively using the internal rate of return, or IRR, criterion that we developed and discussed in Chapter 8. The only difference is that now we have a much better idea of what determines the required return on an investment. This understanding will be critical when we discuss cost of capital and capital structure in Part Seven of our book.

CONCEPT QUESTIONS

11.8a   If an investment has a positive NPV, would it plot above or below the SML? Why?

11.8b   What is meant by the term *cost of capital*?

KEY EQUATIONS:

I. Symbols

$E(R_i)$ = the expected return on asset i
$E(R_P)$ = the expected return on a portfolio
R_f = the risk-free rate
n   = the number of assets in a portfolio
x_i = the portfolio weight of asset i
β_i = the beta of asset i
β_P = the beta of a portfolio

II. Risk Premium

$$\text{Risk premium} = \text{Expected return} - \text{Risk-free rate}$$
$$= E(R_i) - R_f \qquad [11.1]$$

III. Expected Return on a Portfolio

$$E(R_P) = x_1 \times E(R_1) + x_2 \times E(R_2) + \ldots + x_n \times E(R_n) \qquad [11.2]$$

IV. Total Return and Total Risk

$$\text{Total return} = \text{Expected return} + \text{Unexpected return}$$
$$R = E(R) + U \qquad [11.3]$$

$$\text{Announcement} = \text{Expected part} + \text{Surprise} \qquad [11.4]$$

$$R = E(R) + \text{Systematic portion} + \text{Unsystematic portion} \qquad [11.5]$$

Total risk = **Systematic risk + Unsystematic risk** [11.6]

V. Beta Coefficient

Beta coefficient measures the level of systematic risk in a particular asset.
Portfolio beta:

$$\beta_P = x_1 \times \beta_1 + x_2 \times \beta_2 + \cdots + x_n \times \beta_n \tag{11.7}$$

VI. The Reward-to-risk ratio

$$\text{Reward-to-risk ratio} = \frac{E(R_i) - R_f}{\beta_i} \tag{11.8}$$

VII. The Capital Asset Pricing Model (CAPM)

$$E(R_i) = R_f + [E(R_M) - R_f] \times \beta_i \tag{11.9}$$

SUMMARY AND CONCLUSIONS

This chapter has covered the essentials of risk. Along the way, we have introduced a number of definitions and concepts. The most important of these is the security market line, or SML. The SML is important because it tells us the reward offered in financial markets for bearing risk. Once we know this, we have a benchmark against which we compare the returns expected from real asset investments to determine if they are desirable.

Because we have covered quite a bit of ground, it's useful to summarize the basic economic logic underlying the SML as follows:

1. Based on capital market history, there is a reward for bearing risk. This reward is the risk premium on an asset.

2. The total risk associated with an asset has two parts: systematic risk and unsystematic risk. Unsystematic risk can be freely eliminated by diversification (this is the principle of diversification), so only systematic risk is rewarded. As a result, the risk premium on an asset is determined by its systematic risk. This is the systematic risk principle.

3. An asset's systematic risk, relative to the average, can be measured by its beta coefficient, β_i. The risk premium on an asset is then given by its beta coefficient multiplied by the market risk premium, $[E(R_M) - R_f] \times \beta_i$.

4. The expected return on an asset, $E(R_i)$, is equal to the risk-free rate, R_f, plus the risk premium:

$$E(R_i) = R_f + [E(R_M) - R_f] \times \beta_i$$

This is the equation of the SML, and it is often called the *capital asset pricing model,* or CAPM.

This chapter completes our discussion of risk and return and concludes Part Six of our book. Now that we have a better understanding of what determines a firm's cost of capital for an investment, the next several chapters examine more closely how firms raise the long-term capital needed for investment.

www.mcgrawhill.ca/olc/ross

CHAPTER REVIEW AND SELF-TEST PROBLEMS

11.1   Expected Return and Standard Deviation. This problem will give you some practice calculating measures of prospective portfolio performance. There are two assets and three states of the economy:

(1) State of Economy	(2) Probability of State of Economy	(3) Stock A Rate of Return If State Occurs	(4) Stock B Rate of Return If State Occurs
Recession	.10	−.20	.30
Normal	.60	.10	.20
Boom	.30	.70	.50

What are the expected returns and standard deviations for these two stocks?

11.2   Portfolio Risk and Return. In the previous problem, suppose you have $20,000 total. If you put $6,000 in Stock A and the remainder in Stock B, what will be the expected return and standard deviation on your portfolio?

11.3   Risk and Return. Suppose you observe the following situation:

Security	Beta	Expected Return
Cooley, Inc.	1.6	19%
Moyer Co.	1.2	16

If the risk-free rate is 8 percent, are these securities correctly priced? What would the risk-free rate have to be if they are correctly priced?

11.4   CAPM. Suppose the risk-free rate is 8 percent. The expected return on the market is 14 percent. If a particular stock has a beta of .60, what is its expected return based on the CAPM? If another stock has an expected return of 20 percent, what must its beta be?

■ Answers to Chapter Review and Self-Test Problems

**11.1   **The expected returns are just the possible returns multiplied by the associated probabilities:

$$E(R_A) = .10 \times -.20 + .60 \times .10 + .30 \times .70 = 25\%$$
$$E(R_B) = .10 \times .30 + .60 \times .20 + .30 \times .50 = 30\%$$

The variances are given by the sums of the squared deviations from the expected returns multiplied by their probabilities:

$$\sigma_A^2 = .10 \times (-.20 - .25)^2 + .60 \times (.10 - .25)^2 + .30 \times (.70 - .25)^2$$
$$= .10 \times -.45^2 + .60 \times -.15^2 + .30 \times .45^2$$
$$= .10 \times .2025 + .60 \times .0225 + .30 \times .2025$$
$$= .0945$$

$$\sigma_B^2 = .10 \times (.30 - .30)^2 + .60 \times (.20 - .30)^2 + .30 \times (.50 - .30)^2$$
$$= .10 \times .00^2 + .60 \times -.10^2 + .30 \times .20^2$$
$$= .10 \times .00 + .60 \times .01 + .30 \times .04$$
$$= .0180$$

The standard deviations are thus:

$$\sigma_A = \sqrt{.0945} = 30.74\%$$
$$\sigma_B = \sqrt{.0180} = 13.42\%$$

11.2 The portfolio weights are $\$6{,}000/20{,}000 = .30$ and $\$14{,}000/20{,}000 = .70$. The expected return is thus:

$$E(R_P) = .30 \times E(R_A) + .70 \times E(R_B)$$
$$= .30 \times 25\% + .70 \times 30\%$$
$$= 28.50\%$$

Alternatively, we could calculate the portfolio's return in each of the states:

(1) State of Economy	(2) Probability of State of Economy	(3) Portfolio Return If State Occurs
Recession	.10	$.30 \times -.20 + .70 \times .30 = .15$
Normal	.60	$.30 \times .10 + .70 \times .20 = .17$
Boom	.30	$.30 \times .70 + .70 \times .50 = .56$

The portfolio's expected return is:

$$E(R_P) = .10 \times .15 + .60 \times .17 + .30 \times .56 = 28.50\%$$

This is the same as we had before.

The portfolio's variance is:

$$\sigma_P^2 = .10 \times (.15 - .285)^2 + .60 \times (.17 - .285)^2 + .30 \times (.56 - .285)^2$$
$$= .03245$$

So the standard deviation is $\sqrt{.03245} = 18.01\%$

11.3 If we compute the reward-to-risk ratios, we get $(19\% - 8\%)/1.6 = 6.875\%$ for Cooley versus 6.67% for Moyer. Relative to that of Cooley, Moyer's expected return is too low, so its price is too high.

If they are correctly priced, then they must offer the same reward-to-risk ratio. The risk-free rate would have to be such that:

$$(19\% - R_f)/1.6 = (16\% - R_f)/1.2$$

With a little algebra, we find that the risk-free rate must be 7 percent:

$$(19\% - R_f) = (16\% - R_f)(1.6/1.2)$$
$$19\% - 16\% \times {}^4/_3 = R_f - R_f \times {}^4/_3$$
$$R_f = 7\%$$

11.4 Since the expected return on the market is 14 percent, the market risk premium is
14% − 8% = 6% (the risk-free rate is 8 percent). The first stock has a beta of .60,
so its expected return is 8% + .60 × 6% = 11.6%.

For the second stock, notice that the risk premium is 20% − 8% = 12%.
Since this is twice as large as the market risk premium, the beta must be exactly
equal to 2. We can verify this using the CAPM:

$$E(R_i) = R_f + [E(R_M) − R_f] \times \beta_i$$
$$20\% = 8\% + (14\% − 8\%) \times \beta_i$$
$$\beta_i = 12\%/6\% = 2.0$$

CRITICAL THINKING AND CONCEPTS REVIEW

11.1 **Diversifiable and Nondiversifiable Risks.** In broad terms, why is some
risk diversifiable? Why are some risks nondiversifiable? Does it follow that an
investor can control the level of unsystematic risk in a portfolio, but not the level
of systematic risk?

11.2 **Information and Market Returns.** Suppose the government announces that,
based on a just-completed survey, the growth rate in the economy is likely
to be 2 percent in the coming year, as compared to 5 percent for the year just
completed. Will security prices increase, decrease, or stay the same following this
announcement? Does it make any difference whether or not the 2 percent figure
was anticipated by the market? Explain.

11.3 **Systematic versus Unsystematic Risk.** Classify the following events as
mostly systematic or mostly unsystematic. Is the distinction clear in every case?

a. Short-term interest rates increase unexpectedly.

b. The interest rate a company pays on its short-term debt borrowing is
increased by its bank.

c. Oil prices unexpectedly decline.

d. An oil tanker ruptures, creating a large oil spill.

e. A manufacturer loses a multimillion-dollar product liability suit.

f. A Supreme Court of Canada decision substantially broadens producer
liability for injuries suffered by product users.

11.4 **Systematic versus Unsystematic Risk.** Indicate whether the following events
might cause stocks in general to change price, and whether they might cause Big
Widget Corp.'s stock to change price.

a. The government announces that inflation unexpectedly jumped by 2 percent
last month.

b. Big Widget's quarterly earnings report, just issued, generally fell in line with
analysts' expectations.

c. The government reports that economic growth last year was at 3 percent,
which generally agreed with most economists' forecasts.

d. The directors of Big Widget die in a plane crash.

e. Parliament approves changes to the tax code that will increase the top marginal
corporate tax rate. The legislation had been debated for the previous six months.

11.5 Expected Portfolio Returns. If a portfolio has a positive investment in every asset, can the expected return on the portfolio be greater than that on every asset in the portfolio? Can it be less than that on every asset in the portfolio? If you answer yes to one or both of these questions, give an example to support your answer.

11.6 Diversification. True or false: The most important characteristic in determining the expected return of a well-diversified portfolio is the variances of the individual assets in the portfolio. Explain.

11.7 Portfolio Risk. If a portfolio has a positive investment in every asset, can the standard deviation on the portfolio be less than that on every asset in the portfolio? What about the portfolio beta?

11.8 Beta and CAPM. Is it possible that a risky asset could have a beta of zero? Explain. Based on the CAPM, what is the expected return on such an asset? Is it possible that a risky asset could have a negative beta? What does the CAPM predict about the expected return on such an asset? Can you give an explanation for your answer?

11.9 Corporate Downsizing. In recent years, it has been common for companies to experience significant stock price changes in reaction to announcements of massive layoffs. Critics charge that such events encourage companies to fire longtime employees and that Bay Street is cheering them on. Do you agree or disagree?

11.10 Earnings and Stock Returns. As indicated by a number of examples in this chapter, earnings announcements by companies are closely followed by, and frequently result in, share price revisions. Two issues should come to mind. First: Earnings announcements concern past periods. If the market values stocks based on expectations of the future, why are numbers summarizing past performance relevant? Second: These announcements concern accounting earnings. Going back to Chapter 2, such earnings may have little to do with cash flow, so again, why are they relevant?

QUESTIONS AND PROBLEMS

**Basic
(Questions 1–26)**

1. **Determining Portfolio Weights.** What are the portfolio weights for a portfolio that has 75 shares of Stock A that sell for $69 per share and 50 shares of Stock B that sell for $52 per share?

2. **Portfolio Expected Return.** You own a portfolio that has $900 invested in Stock A and $1,700 invested in Stock B. If the expected returns on these stocks are 10 percent and 16 percent, respectively, what is the expected return on the portfolio?

3. **Portfolio Expected Return.** You own a portfolio that is 30 percent invested in Stock X, 45 percent in Stock Y, and 25 percent in Stock Z. The expected returns on these three stocks are 10 percent, 14 percent, and 16 percent, respectively. What is the expected return on the portfolio?

4. **Portfolio Expected Return.** You have $10,000 to invest in a stock portfolio. Your choices are Stock X with an expected return of 15 percent and Stock Y with an expected return of 9 percent. If your goal is to create a portfolio with an expected return of 13.30 percent, how much money will you invest in Stock X? In Stock Y?

5. Calculating Expected Return. Based on the following information, calculate the expected return.

State of Economy	Probability of State of Economy	Rate of Return If State Occurs
Recession	.20	−.08
Boom	.80	.21

6. Calculating Expected Return. Based on the following information, calculate the expected return.

State of Economy	Probability of State of Economy	Rate of Return If State Occurs
Recession	.25	−.09
Normal	.60	.13
Boom	.15	.30

$.25(.09 - .06)^2 +$

$.06$

7. Calculating Returns and Standard Deviations. Based on the following information, calculate the expected return and standard deviation for the two stocks.

State of Economy	Probability of State of Economy	Rate of Return If State Occurs	
		Stock A	Stock B
Recession	.15	.02	−.20
Normal	.55	.08	.13
Boom	.30	.13	.33

8. Calculating Expected Returns. A portfolio is invested 35 percent in Stock G, 50 percent in Stock J, and 15 percent in Stock K. The expected returns on these stocks are 9 percent, 13 percent, and 19 percent, respectively. What is the portfolio's expected return? How do you interpret your answer?

9. Returns and Standard Deviations. Consider the following information:

State of Economy	Probability of State of Economy	Rate of Return If State Occurs		
		Stock A	Stock B	Stock C
Boom	.30	.08	.02	.33
Bust	.70	.14	.24	−.06

a. What is the expected return on an equally weighted portfolio of these three stocks?

b. What is the variance of a portfolio invested 20 percent each in A and B and 60 percent in C?

10. Returns and Standard Deviations.   Consider the following information:

State of Economy	Probability of State of Economy	Rate of Return If State Occurs		
		Stock A	Stock B	Stock C
Boom	.20	.30	.45	.33
Good	.40	.12	.10	.15
Poor	.30	.01	−.15	−.05
Bust	.10	−.20	−.30	−.09

   a.   Your portfolio is invested 40 percent each in A and C and 20 percent in B. What is the expected return of the portfolio?

   b.   What is the variance of this portfolio? The standard deviation?

11. Calculating Portfolio Betas.   You own a stock portfolio invested 20 percent in Stock Q, 20 percent in Stock R, 10 percent in Stock S, and 50 percent in Stock T. The betas for these four stocks are .73, .86, 1.25, and 1.84, respectively. What is the portfolio beta?

12. Calculating Portfolio Betas.   You own a portfolio equally invested in a risk-free asset and two stocks. If one of the stocks has a beta of 1.9 and the total portfolio is equally as risky as the market, what must the beta be for the other stock in your portfolio?

13. Using CAPM.   A stock has a beta of 1.2, the expected return on the market is 13 percent, and the risk-free rate is 5 percent. What must the expected return on this stock be?

14. Using CAPM.   A stock has an expected return of 15 percent, the risk-free rate is 4.5 percent, and the market risk premium is 8.5 percent. What must the beta of this stock be?

15. Using CAPM.   A stock has an expected return of 15 percent, its beta is 1.15, and the risk-free rate is 5.5 percent. What must the expected return on the market be?

16. Using CAPM.   A stock has an expected return of 11.80 percent and a beta of .85, and the expected return on the market is 12.80 percent. What must the risk-free rate be?

17. Using CAPM.   A stock has a beta of 1.3 and an expected return of 15 percent. A risk-free asset currently earns 5.5 percent.

   a.   What is the expected return on a portfolio that is equally invested in the two assets?

   b.   If a portfolio of the two assets has a beta of .8, what are the portfolio weights?

   c.   If a portfolio of the two assets has an expected return of 12 percent, what is its beta?

   d.   If a portfolio of the two assets has a beta of 2.60, what are the portfolio weights? How do you interpret the weights for the two assets in this case? Explain.

18. Using the SML.   Asset W has an expected return of 16 percent and a beta of 1.3. If the risk-free rate is 5 percent, complete the following table for portfolios of Asset W and a risk-free asset. Illustrate the relationship between portfolio expected return and portfolio beta by plotting the expected returns against the betas. What is the slope of the line that results?

Percentage of Portfolio in Asset W	Portfolio Expected Return	Portfolio Beta
0%		
25		
50		
75		
100		
125		
150		

19. **Reward-to-Risk Ratios.** Stock Y has a beta of 1.50 and an expected return of 17 percent. Stock Z has a beta of .80 and an expected return of 10.5 percent. If the risk-free rate is 5.5 percent and the market risk premium is 7.5 percent, are these stocks correctly priced?

20. **Reward-to-Risk Ratios.** In the previous problem, what would the risk-free rate have to be for the two stocks to be correctly priced relative to each other?

21. **Portfolio Returns.** Using information from Table 10.2 on capital market history, determine the return on a portfolio that was equally invested in Canadian large-company stocks and long-term government bonds. What was the return on a portfolio that was equally invested in small stocks and Treasury bills?

22. **Portfolio Expected Return.** You have $250,000 to invest in a stock portfolio. Your choices are Stock H with an expected return of 17 percent and Stock L with an expected return of 10 percent. If your goal is to create a portfolio with an expected return of 13 percent, how much money will you invest in Stock H? In Stock L?

23. **Returns and Deviations.** Consider the following information:

State of Economy	Probability of State of Economy	Stock A Rate of Return	Stock B Rate of Return	Stock C Rate of Return
Boom	.30	.02	.03	.26
Bust	.70	.14	.18	−.02

a. What is the expected return on an equally weighted portfolio of these three stocks?

b. What is the standard deviation of a portfolio invested 25 percent in A and B and 50 percent in C?

24. **Returns and Deviations.** Consider the following information:

State of Economy	Probability of State of Economy	Stock A Rate of Return	Stock B Rate of Return	Stock C Rate of Return
Boom	.10	.18	.35	.20
Good	.60	.11	.15	.11
Poor	.20	.06	−.05	.02
Bust	.10	.01	−.40	−.08

a. Your portfolio is invested 30 percent each in B and C and 40 percent in A. What is the portfolio's expected return?

b. What is the variance of this portfolio? The standard deviation?

25. **Calculating Portfolio Weights.** Stock J has a beta of 1.2 and an expected return of 17 percent, while Stock K has a beta of .75 and an expected return of 9 percent. You want a portfolio with the same risk as the market. How much will you invest in each stock? What is the expected return of your portfolio?

26. **Calculating Portfolio Weights and Expected Return.** You have a portfolio with the following:

Stock	Number of Shares	Price	Expected Return
W	600	$41	12%
X	800	27	16
Y	500	65	14
Z	700	49	15

What is the expected return of your portfolio?

27. **Analyzing a Portfolio.** You have $100,000 to invest in either Stock D, Stock F, or a risk-free asset. You must invest all of your money. Your goal is to create a portfolio that has an expected return of 12.75 percent. If D has an expected return of 17 percent, F has an expected return of 10 percent, and the risk-free rate is 6 percent, and if you invest $50,000 in Stock D, how much will you invest in Stock F?

28. **Portfolio Returns and Deviations.** Consider the following information on a portfolio of three stocks:

State of Economy	Probability of State of Economy	Stock A Rate of Return	Stock B Rate of Return	Stock C Rate of Return
Boom	.15	.05	.25	.60
Normal	.70	.09	.12	.20
Bust	.15	.12	−.13	−.40

a. If your portfolio is invested 30 percent each in A and B and 40 percent in C, what is the portfolio's expected return? The variance? The standard deviation?

b. If the expected T-bill rate is 4.25 percent, what is the expected risk premium on the portfolio?

29. **CAPM.** Using the CAPM, show that the ratio of the risk premiums on two assets is equal to the ratio of their betas.

30. **Analyzing a Portfolio.** You want to create a portfolio equally as risky as the market, and you have $500,000 to invest. Given this information, fill in the rest of the following table:

Asset	Investment	Beta
Stock A	$130,000	.90
Stock B	150,000	1.15
Stock C		1.50
Risk-free asset		

31. **Analyzing a Portfolio.** You have $100,000 to invest in a portfolio containing Stock X, Stock Y, and a risk-free asset. You must invest all of your money. Your goal is

Intermediate
(Questions 27–30)

Challenge
(Questions 31–32)

to create a portfolio that has an expected return of 16 percent and that has only 85 percent of the risk of the overall market. If X has an expected return of 22 percent and a beta of 1.4, Y has an expected return of 17 percent and a beta of 1.3, and the risk-free rate is 6 percent, how much money will you invest in Stock Y? How do you interpret your answer?

32. **Systematic versus Unsystematic Risk.**   Consider the following information on Stocks I and II:

State of Economy	Probability of State of Economy	Rate of Return If State Occurs	
		Stock I	Stock II
Recession	.20	.02	−.20
Normal	.60	.32	.12
Irrational exuberance	.20	.18	.40

The market risk premium is 12 percent, and the risk-free rate is 4 percent. Which stock has the most systematic risk? Which one has the most unsystematic risk? Which stock is "riskier"? Explain.

WHAT'S ON THE WEB

11.1   **Expected Return.**   You want to find the expected return for Encana using the CAPM. First, you need the market risk premium. Go to **www.bankofcanada.ca**, find the "Rates and Statistics" link, and the "Interest Rates" link. Find the current interest rate for three-month Treasury bills. Use the average Canadian large-company stock return in Table 10.3 to calculate the market risk premium. Next, go to **ca.finance.yahoo.com**, enter the ticker symbol ECA for Encana and follow the "Key Statistics" link. In the Trading Information section you will find the beta for Encana. What is the expected return for IPSCO using CAPM? What assumptions did you make to arrive at this number?

11.2   **Portfolio Beta.**   You have decided to invest in an equally weighted portfolio consisting of the Bank of Nova Scotia, Alcan, BCE, and Canadian Pacific Railway and need to find the beta of your portfolio. Go to **www.theglobeandmail.com** and follow the "Lookup" link in the "Stock Profile" section to find the ticker symbols for each of these companies. Next, go back to **www.theglobeandmail.com**, enter one of the ticker symbols and get a stock profile. Find the beta for this company in the "Price and per Share Statistics" section. You will then need to find the beta for each of the companies. What is the beta for your portfolio?

11.3   **Beta.**   Which stock has the highest and lowest betas? Go to **finance.yahoo.com** and locate the Stock Screener. Enter 3 as the minimum value. How many stocks have a beta greater than 3? What about 4? Which stock has the highest beta? Go back to the screener and enter 3 as the maximum value. How many stocks have a beta in this range? Which stock has the lowest beta?

11.4   **Mutual Fund Beta.**   Betas are widely reported for mutual funds. Go to **www. globefund.com** and enter "TD Precious Metals" for the fund name. Locate the beta for this mutual fund. Next, go back to **www.globefund.com,** enter "TD Canadian Equity" and find its beta. Which fund has the highest beta? Do these betas measure the same systematic risk? Why or why not?

MINI-CASE

A PENSION PLAN AT CANADIAN AIR

You recently graduated from college, and your job search led you to Canadian Air. Since you felt the company's business was headed skyward, you accepted their job offer. As you are finishing your employment paperwork, Chris Guthrie, who works in the Finance Department, stops by to inform you about the company's pension plan.

Different types of pension plans are offered by many companies. A pension plan is tax deferred, which means that any deposits you make into the plan are deducted from your current income, so no current taxes are paid on the money. For example, assume your salary will be $30,000 per year. If you contribute $1,500 to the pension plan, you will pay taxes only on $28,500 in income. No taxes will be due on any capital gains or plan income while you are invested in the plan, but you will pay taxes when you withdraw the money at retirement. You can contribute up to five percent of your salary to the plan. As is common, Canadian Air also has a five percent match program. This means that the company will match your contribution dollar-for-dollar up to five percent of your salary, but you must contribute to get the match.

Canadian Air's pension plan has several options for investments, most of which are mutual funds. As you know, a mutual fund is a portfolio of assets. When you purchase shares in a mutual fund, you are actually purchasing partial ownership of the fund's assets, similar to purchasing shares of stock in a company. The return of the fund is the weighted average of the return of the assets owned by the fund, minus any expenses. The largest expense is typically the management fee paid to the fund manager who makes all of the investment decisions for the fund. Canadian Air uses Arias Financial Services as its pension plan administrator.

Chris Guthrie then explains that the retirement investment options offered for employees are as follows:

1. *Company stock.* One option is stock in Canadian Air. The company is currently privately held. The price you would pay for the stock is based on an annual appraisal, less a 20 percent discount. When you interviewed with the owners, Mark Sexton and Todd Story, they informed you that the company stock was expected to be publicly sold in three to five years. If you needed to sell the stock before it became publicly traded, the company would buy it back at the then-current appraised value.

2. *Arias S&P/TSX Index Fund.* This mutual fund tracks the S&P/TSX. Stocks in the fund are weighted exactly the same as they are in the S&P/TSX. This means that the fund's return is approximately the return of the S&P/TSX, minus expenses. With an index fund, the manager is not required to research stocks and make investment decisions, so fund expenses are usually low. The Arias S&P/TSX Index Fund charges expenses of 0.20 percent of assets per year.

3. *Arias Small-Cap Fund.* This fund primarily invests in small capitalization stocks. As such, the returns of the fund are more volatile. The fund can also invest 10 percent of its assets in companies based outside Canada. This fund charges 1.70 percent of assets in expenses per year.

4. *Arias Large-Company Stock Fund.* This fund invests primarily in large capitalization stocks of companies based in Canada. The fund is managed by Melissa Arias and has outperformed the market in six of the last eight years. The fund charges 1.50 percent in expenses.

5. *Arias Bond Fund.* This fund invests in long-term corporate bonds issued by Canadian companies. The fund is restricted to investments in bonds with an investment grade credit rating. This fund charges 1.40 percent in expenses.

6. *Arias Money Market Fund.* This fund invests in short-term, high credit quality debt instruments, which include Treasury bills. As such, the return on money market funds is only slightly higher than the return on Treasury bills. Because of the credit quality and short-term nature of the investments, there is only a very slight risk of negative return. The fund charges 0.60 percent in expenses.

QUESTIONS

1. What advantages/disadvantages do the mutual funds offer compared to company stock for your retirement investing?

2. Notice that, for every dollar you invest, Canadian Air also invests a dollar. What return on your investment does this represent? What does your answer suggest about matching programs?

3. Assume you decide you should invest at least part of your money in large capitalization stocks of companies based in Canada. What are the advantages and disadvantages of choosing the Arias Large-Company Stock Fund compared to the Arias S&P/TSX Index Fund?

4. The returns of the Arias Small-Cap Fund are the most volatile of all the mutual funds offered in the pension plan. Why would you ever want to invest in this fund? When you examine the expenses of the mutual funds, you will notice that this fund also has the highest expenses. Will this affect your decision to invest in this fund?

5. You are considering an asset allocation that will consist of 10 percent in the money market account, 40 percent in the Small-Stock Fund, which has a beta of 1.40, and 50 percent in the S&P/TSX Index Fund, which has a beta of 1.0. What is the beta of your portfolio?

6. A measure of risk-adjusted performance that is often used in practice is the Sharpe ratio. The Sharpe ratio is calculated as the risk premium of an asset divided by its standard deviation.

a. The standard deviations and returns for the funds over the past 10 years are listed below. Assuming a risk-free rate of 4 percent, calculate the Sharpe ratio for each of these. In broad terms, what do you suppose the Sharpe ratio is intended to measure?

b. Assume that the expected return and standard deviation of the company stock will be the same as the expected returns and standard deviation for small-company stocks given in Figure 10.10. Calculate the Sharpe ratio for the company stock.

c. Is our assumption about the risk and return on the company's stock reasonable? Why or why not?

	10-year Annual Return	Standard Deviation
Arias S&P/TSX Index Fund	11.48%	15.82%
Arias Small-Cap Fund	16.68	19.64
Arias Large-Company Stock Fund	11.85	16.01
Arias Bond Fund	9.67	10.83

12

Cost of Capital

In the third quarter of 2006, the rail equipment division of Montreal-based Bombardier was booking large orders. These included a $3.5 billion contract with French National Railways to supply 372 trains for the Paris network, a $425 million contract with Transport for London to supply 152 electric multiple-unit cars for the London network, and a $1.65 billion contract for Rapid Rail System in South Africa. Each contract represented a major undertaking in terms of time and money for the train manufacturer. So how do companies like Bombardier decide which projects to invest in and which to reject? The answer is that many companies rely heavily on the weighted average cost of capital (WACC): the return a company must earn to satisfy all its investors, including stockholders, bondholders, and preferred stockholders.

Regulatory agencies also use the WACC heavily in order to determine the "fair return" in some regulated industries. For example, the Canadian Transportation Agency approved a 7.75 percent pre-tax WACC for Canadian National Railway for 2005. In this chapter we learn how to compute a firm's cost of capital and find out what it means to the firm and its investors. We will also learn when to use the firm's cost of capital and, perhaps more important, when not to use it.

From our chapters on capital budgeting, we know that the discount rate, or required return, on an investment is a critical input. Thus far, however, we haven't discussed how to come up with that particular number, so it's time now to do so. This chapter brings together many of our earlier discussions dealing with stocks and bonds, capital budgeting, and risk and return. Our goal is to illustrate how firms go about determining the required return on a proposed investment.

After studying this chapter, you should have a good understanding of:

12.1 The primary determinant of the cost of capital.

12.2 How to determine a firm's cost of equity capital.

12.3 How to determine a firm's cost of debt and preferred stock.

12.4 How to determine a firm's weighted average cost of capital.

12.5 Some of the pitfalls associated with a firm's weighted average cost of capital and what to do about them.

12.6 How to calculate a firm's weighted average cost of capital using online sources.

uppose you have just become the president of a large company and the first decision you face is whether to go ahead with a plan to renovate the company's warehouse distribution system. The plan will cost the company $50 million, and it is expected to save $12 million per year after taxes over the next six years.

This is a familiar problem in capital budgeting. To address it, you would determine the relevant cash flows, discount them, and, if the net present value is positive, take on the project; if the NPV is negative, you would scrap it. So far, so good; but what should you use as the discount rate?

From our discussion of risk and return, you know that the correct discount rate depends on the riskiness of the warehouse distribution system. In particular, the new project will have a positive NPV only if its return exceeds what the financial markets offer on investments of similar risk. We called this minimum required return the *cost of capital* associated with the project.[1]

Thus, to make the right decision as president, you must examine what the capital markets have to offer and use this information to arrive at an estimate of the project's cost of capital. Our primary purpose in this chapter is to describe how to go about doing this. There are a variety of approaches to this task, and a number of conceptual and practical issues arise.

One of the most important concepts we develop is that of the *weighted average cost of capital* (WACC). This is the cost of capital for the firm as a whole, and it can be interpreted as the required return on the overall firm. In discussing the WACC, we will recognize the fact that a firm will normally raise capital in a variety of forms and that these different forms of capital may have different costs associated with them.

We also recognize in this chapter that taxes are an important consideration in determining the required return on an investment, because we are always interested in valuing the aftertax cash flows from a project. We will therefore discuss how to incorporate taxes explicitly into our estimates of the cost of capital.

12.1 | THE COST OF CAPITAL: SOME PRELIMINARIES

In Chapter 11, we developed the security market line, or SML, and used it to explore the relationship between the expected return on a security and its systematic risk. We concentrated on how the risky returns from buying securities looked from the viewpoint of, for example, a shareholder in the firm. This helped us understand more about the alternatives available to an investor in the capital markets.

In this chapter, we turn things around a bit and look more closely at the other side of the problem, which is how these returns and securities look from the viewpoint of the companies that issue the securities. The important fact to note is that the return an investor in a security receives is the cost of that security to the company that issued it.

Required Return versus Cost of Capital

When we say that the required return on an investment is, say, 10 percent, we usually mean that the investment will have a positive NPV only if its return exceeds 10 percent. Another way of interpreting the required return is to observe that the firm must earn 10 percent on the investment just to compensate its investors for the use of the capital needed to finance the project. This is why we could also say that 10 percent is the cost of capital associated with the investment.

To illustrate the point further, imagine we are evaluating a risk-free project. In this case, how to determine the required return is obvious: We look at the capital markets and observe the current rate offered by risk-free investments, and we use this rate to discount the project's cash flows. Thus, the cost of capital for a risk-free investment is the risk-free rate.

---

[1]The term *cost of money* is also used.

If this project is risky, then, assuming that all the other information is unchanged, the required return is obviously higher. In other words, the cost of capital for this project, if it is risky, is greater than the risk-free rate, and the appropriate discount rate would exceed the risk-free rate.

We will henceforth use the terms *required return, appropriate discount rate,* and *cost of capital* more or less interchangeably because, as the discussion in this section suggests, they all mean essentially the same thing. The key fact to grasp is that the cost of capital associated with an investment depends on the risk of that investment. In other words, it's the **use** of the money, not the source, that matters. This is one of the most important lessons in corporate finance, so it bears repeating:

> The cost of capital depends primarily on the use of the funds, not the source.

It is a common error to forget this crucial point and fall into the trap of thinking that the cost of capital for an investment depends primarily on how and where the capital is raised.

Financial Policy and Cost of Capital

We know that the particular mixture of debt and equity a firm chooses to employ—its capital structure—is a managerial variable. In this chapter, we will take the firm's financial policy as given. In particular, we will assume that the firm has a fixed debt-equity ratio that it maintains. This ratio reflects the firm's *target* capital structure. How a firm might choose that ratio is the subject of a later chapter.

From our discussion above, we know that a firm's overall cost of capital will reflect the required return on the firm's assets as a whole. Given that a firm uses both debt and equity capital, this overall cost of capital will be a mixture of the returns needed to compensate its creditors and its stockholders. In other words, a firm's cost of capital will reflect both its cost of debt capital and its cost of equity capital. We discuss these costs separately in the sections below.

CONCEPT QUESTIONS

12.1a What is the primary determinant of the cost of capital for an investment?

12.1b What is the relationship between the required return on an investment and the cost of capital associated with that investment?

12.2 | THE COST OF EQUITY

We begin with the most difficult question on the subject of cost of capital: What is the firm's overall **cost of equity**? The reason this is a difficult question is that there is no way of directly observing the return that the firm's equity investors require on their investment. Instead, we must somehow estimate it. This section discusses two approaches to determining the cost of equity: the dividend growth model approach and the security market line, or SML, approach.

cost of equity
The return that equity investors require on their investment in the firm.

The Dividend Growth Model Approach

The easiest way to estimate the cost of equity capital is to use the dividend growth model we developed in Chapter 7. Recall that, under the assumption that the firm's dividend will grow at a constant rate g, the price per share of the stock, P_0, can be written as:

$$P_0 = \frac{D_0 \times (1 + g)}{R_E - g} = \frac{D_1}{R_E - g}$$

where D_0 is the dividend just paid and D_1 is the next period's projected dividend. Notice that we have used the symbol R_E (the E stands for *equity*) for the required return on the stock.

As we discussed in Chapter 7, we can rearrange this to solve for R_E as follows:

$$R_E = D_1/P_0 + g \qquad\qquad\qquad [12.1]$$

Since R_E is the return that the shareholders require on the stock, it can be interpreted as the firm's cost of equity capital.

Implementing the Approach   To estimate R_E using the dividend growth model approach, we obviously need three pieces of information: P_0, D_0, and g. Of these, for a publicly traded, dividend-paying company, the first two can be observed directly, so they are easily obtained.[2] Only the third component, the expected growth rate in dividends, must be estimated.

To illustrate how we estimate R_E, suppose Great Northern Utilities, a large public utility, paid a dividend of $4 per share last year. The stock currently sells for $60 per share. You estimate that the dividend will grow steadily at 6 percent per year into the indefinite future. What is the cost of equity capital for Great Northern Utilities?

Using the dividend growth model, we calculate that the expected dividend for the coming year, D_1, is:

$$\begin{aligned}
D_1 &= D_0 \times (1 + g) \\
&= \$4 \times 1.06 \\
&= \$4.24
\end{aligned}$$

Given this, the cost of equity, R_E, is:

$$\begin{aligned}
R_E &= D_1/P_0 + g \\
&= \$4.24/60 + .06 \\
&= 13.07\%
\end{aligned}$$

The cost of equity is thus 13.07%.

Estimating g   To use the dividend growth model, we must come up with an estimate for g, the growth rate. There are essentially two ways of doing this: (1) use historical growth rates or (2) use analysts' forecasts of future growth rates. Analysts' forecasts are available from a variety of sources. Naturally, different sources will have different estimates, so one approach might be to obtain multiple estimates and then average them.

Alternatively, we might observe dividends for the previous, say, five years, calculate the year-to-year growth rates, and average them. For example, suppose we observe the following for some company:

Year	Dividend
2003	$1.10
2004	1.20
2005	1.35
2006	1.40
2007	1.55

Aggregate growth estimates can be found at www.zacks.com/research/earnings.

---

[2]Notice that if we have D_0 and g, we can simply calculate D_1 by multiplying D_0 by $(1 + g)$.

We can calculate the percentage change in the dividend for each year as follows:

Year	Dividend	Dollar Change	Percentage Change
2003	$1.10	—	—
2004	1.20	$.10	9.09%
2005	1.35	.15	12.50
2006	1.40	.05	3.70
2007	1.55	.15	10.71

Notice that we calculated the change in the dividend on a year-to-year basis and then expressed the change as a percentage. Thus, in 2004, for example, the dividend rose from $1.10 to $1.20, for an increase of $.10. This represents a $.10/1.10 = 9.09% increase.

If we average the four growth rates, the result is (9.09 + 12.50 + 3.70 + 10.71)/4 = 9%, so we could use this as an estimate for the expected growth rate, g. Notice that this 9 percent growth rate we have calculated is a simple, or arithmetic average. Going back to Chapter 10, we also could calculate a geometric growth rate. Here, the dividend grows from $1.10 to $1.55 over a four-year period. What's the compound, or geometric growth rate? See if you don't agree that it's 8.95 percent; you can view this as a simple time value of money problem where $1.10 is the present value and $1.55 is the future value.

As usual, the geometric average (8.95 percent) is lower than the arithmetic average (9.09 percent), but the difference here is not likely to be of any practical significance. In general, if the dividend has grown at a relatively steady rate, as we assume when we use this approach, then it can't make much difference which way we calculate the average dividend growth rate.

Advantages and Disadvantages of the Approach The primary advantage of the dividend growth model approach is its simplicity. It is both easy to understand and easy to use. However, there are a number of associated practical problems and disadvantages.

First and foremost, the dividend growth model is obviously only applicable to companies that pay dividends. This means that the approach is useless in many cases. Furthermore, even for companies that do pay dividends, the key underlying assumption is that the dividend grows at a constant rate. As our example above illustrates, this will never be *exactly* the case. More generally, the model is really only applicable to cases in which reasonably steady growth is likely to occur.

A second problem is that the estimated cost of equity is very sensitive to the estimated growth rate. For a given stock price, an upward revision of g by just one percentage point, for example, increases the estimated cost of equity by at least a full percentage point. Since D_1 will probably be revised upward as well, the increase will actually be somewhat larger than that.

Finally, this approach really does not explicitly consider risk. Unlike the SML approach (which we consider next), this one has no direct adjustment for the riskiness of the investment. For example, there is no allowance for the degree of certainty or uncertainty surrounding the estimated growth rate in dividends. As a result, it is difficult to say whether or not the estimated return is commensurate with the level of risk.[3]

---

[3]There is an implicit adjustment for risk because the current stock price is used. All other things being equal, the higher the risk, the lower is the stock price. Further, the lower the stock price, the greater is the cost of equity, again assuming that all the other information is the same.

The SML Approach

In Chapter 11, we discussed the security market line, or SML. Our primary conclusion was that the required or expected return on a risky investment depends on three things:

1. The risk-free rate, R_f
2. The market risk premium, $E(R_M) - R_f$
3. The systematic risk of the asset relative to average, which we called its beta coefficient, β

Using the SML, we can write the expected return on the company's equity, $E(R_E)$, as:

$$E(R_E) = R_f + \beta_E \times [E(R_M) - R_f]$$

where β_E is the estimated beta for the equity. To make the SML approach consistent with the dividend growth model, we will drop the Es denoting expectations and henceforth write the required return from the SML, R_E, as:

$$R_E = R_f + \beta_E \times (R_M - R_f) \qquad [12.2]$$

Implementing the Approach   To use the SML approach, we need a risk-free rate, R_f, an estimate of the market risk premium, $R_M - R_f$, and an estimate of the relevant beta, β_E. In Chapter 10 (Table 10.3), we saw that one estimate of the market risk premium (based on large-cap Canadian common stocks) is 6.8 percent. Government of Canada Treasury bills are paying about 4 percent as this is being written, so we will use this as our risk-free rate. Beta coefficients for publicly traded companies are widely available.

To find T-bill rates, look under the "FP Market Data" link at www.nationalpost.com.

To illustrate, in Chapter 11, we saw that BCE had an estimated beta of .80 (Table 11.8). We could thus estimate BCE's cost of equity as:

$$\begin{aligned} R_{BCE} &= R_f + \beta_{BCE} \times (R_M - R_f) \\ &= 4\% + .80 \times 6.8\% \\ &= 9.44\% \end{aligned}$$

Thus, using the SML approach, BCE's cost of equity is about 9 percent.

Advantages and Disadvantages of the Approach   The SML approach has two primary advantages. First: It explicitly adjusts for risk. Second: It is applicable to companies other than just those with steady dividend growth. Thus, it may be useful in a wider variety of circumstances.

There are drawbacks, of course. The SML approach requires that two things be estimated, the market risk premium and the beta coefficient. To the extent that our estimates are poor, the resulting cost of equity will be inaccurate. For example, our estimate of the market risk premium, 6.8 percent, is based on about 73 years of returns on a particular portfolio of stocks. Using different time periods or different stocks could result in very different estimates.

Finally, as with the dividend growth model, we essentially rely on the past to predict the future when we use the SML approach. Economic conditions can change very quickly, so, as always, the past may not be a good guide to the future. In the best of all worlds, both approaches (dividend growth model and SML) are applicable and result in similar answers. If this happens, we might have some confidence in our estimates. We might also wish to compare the results to those for other, similar companies as a reality check.

The Cost of Equity **EXAMPLE 12.1**

Suppose stock in Alpha Air Freight has a beta of 1.2. The market risk premium is 8 percent, and the risk-free rate is 6 percent. Alpha's last dividend was $2 per share, and the dividend is expected to grow at 8 percent indefinitely. The stock currently sells for $30. What is Alpha's cost of equity capital?

We can start off by using the SML. Doing this, we find that the expected return on the common stock of Alpha Air Freight is:

$$R_E = R_f + \beta_E \times (R_M - R_f)$$
$$= 6\% + 1.2 \times 8\%$$
$$= 15.6\%$$

This suggests that 15.6 percent is Alpha's cost of equity. We next use the dividend growth model. The projected dividend is $D_0 \times (1 + g) = \$2 \times 1.08 = \$2.16$, so the expected return using this approach is:

$$R_E = D_1/P_0 + g$$
$$= \$2.16/30 + .08$$
$$= 15.2\%$$

Our two estimates are reasonably close, so we might just average them to find that Alpha's cost of equity is approximately 15.4 percent.

CONCEPT QUESTIONS

12.2a What do we mean when we say that a corporation's cost of equity capital is 16 percent?

12.2b What are two approaches to estimating the cost of equity capital?

12.3 | THE COSTS OF DEBT AND PREFERRED STOCK

In addition to ordinary equity, firms use debt and, to a lesser extent, preferred stock to finance their investments. As we discuss next, determining the costs of capital associated with these sources of financing is much easier than determining the cost of equity.

The Cost of Debt

The **cost of debt** is the return that the firm's creditors demand on new borrowing. In principle, we could determine the beta for the firm's debt and then use the SML to estimate the required return on debt just as we estimate the required return on equity. This isn't really necessary, however.

Unlike a firm's cost of equity, its cost of debt can normally be observed either directly or indirectly, because the cost of debt is simply the interest rate the firm must pay on new borrowing, and we can observe interest rates in the financial markets. For example, if the firm already has bonds outstanding, then the yield to maturity on those bonds is the market-required rate on the firm's debt.

Alternatively, if we knew that the firm's bonds were rated, say, AA, then we could simply find out what the interest rate on newly issued AA-rated bonds was. Either way, there is no need to actually estimate a beta for the debt since we can directly observe the rate we want to know.

There is one thing to be careful about, though. The coupon rate on the firm's outstanding debt is irrelevant here. That just tells us roughly what the firm's cost of debt was back

cost of debt
The return that lenders require on the firm's debt.

when the bonds were issued, not what the cost of debt is today.[4] This is why we have to look at the yield on the debt in today's marketplace. For consistency with our other notation, we will use the symbol R_D for the cost of debt.

EXAMPLE 12.2   **The Cost of Debt**

Suppose the Canadian Wire Company issued a 30-year, 7 percent bond eight years ago. The bond is currently selling for 96 percent of its face value, or $960. What is Canadian Wire's cost of debt?

Going back to Chapter 6, we need to calculate the yield to maturity on this bond. Since the bond is selling at a discount, the yield is apparently greater than 7 percent, but not much greater, because the discount is fairly small. You can verify that the yield to maturity is about 7.37 percent, assuming annual coupons. Canadian Wire's cost of debt, R_D, is thus 7.37 percent.

The Cost of Preferred Stock

Determining the *cost of preferred stock* is quite straightforward. As we discussed in Chapters 6 and 7, preferred stock has a fixed dividend paid every period forever, so a share of preferred stock is essentially a perpetuity. The cost of preferred stock, R_P, is thus:

$$R_P = D/P_0 \qquad\qquad\qquad [12.3]$$

where D is the fixed dividend and P_0 is the current price per share of the preferred stock. Notice that the cost of preferred stock is simply equal to the dividend yield on the preferred stock. Alternatively, preferred stocks are rated in much the same way as bonds, so the cost of preferred stock can be estimated by observing the required returns on other, similarly rated shares of preferred stock.

EXAMPLE 12.3   **Sun Life Financial's Cost of Preferred Stock**

In December 2006, Sun Life Financial had several issues of preferred stock that traded on the TSX. One issue paid $1.48 annually per share and sold for $25.89 per share. The other paid $1.50 per share annually and sold for $25.91 per share. What was Sun Life Financial's cost of preferred stock?

Using the first issue, the cost of preferred stock was:

$$R_P = D/P_0$$
$$= \$1.48/25.89$$
$$= 5.72\%$$

Using the second issue, the cost was:

$$R_P = D/P_0$$
$$= \$1.50/25.91$$
$$= 5.79\%$$

So, Sun Life Financial's cost of preferred stock appears to have been in the 5.7 to 5.8 percent range.

CONCEPT QUESTIONS

12.3a   How can the cost of debt be calculated?

12.3b   How can the cost of preferred stock be calculated?

12.3c   Why is the coupon rate a bad estimate of a firm's cost of debt?

---

[4]The firm's cost of debt based on its historic borrowing is sometimes called the *embedded debt cost*.

12.4 | THE WEIGHTED AVERAGE COST OF CAPITAL

Now that we have the costs associated with the main sources of capital the firm employs, we need to worry about the specific mix. As we mentioned above, we will take this mix, which is the firm's capital structure, as given for now. Also, we will focus mostly on debt and ordinary equity in this discussion.

The Capital Structure Weights

We will use the symbol E (for *equity*) to stand for the *market* value of the firm's equity. We calculate this by taking the number of shares outstanding and multiplying it by the price per share. Similarly, we will use the symbol D (for *debt*) to stand for the *market* value of the firm's debt. For long-term debt, we calculate this by multiplying the market price of a single bond by the number of bonds outstanding.

If there are multiple bond issues (as there normally would be), we repeat this calculation for each and then add up the results. If there is debt that is not publicly traded (because it is held by a life insurance company, for example), we must observe the yield on similar, publicly traded debt and then estimate the market value of the privately held debt using this yield as the discount rate. For short-term debt, the book (accounting) values and market values should be somewhat similar, so we might use the book values as estimates of the market values.

Finally, we will use the symbol V (for *value*) to stand for the combined market value of the debt and equity:

$$V = E + D \qquad\qquad [12.4]$$

If we divide both sides by V, we can calculate the percentages of the total capital represented by the debt and equity:

$$100\% = E/V + D/V \qquad\qquad [12.5]$$

These percentages can be interpreted just like portfolio weights, and they are often called the *capital structure weights.*

For example, if the total market value of a company's stock were calculated as $200 million and the total market value of the company's debt were calculated as $50 million, then the combined value would be $250 million. Of this total, $E/V = \$200/250 = 80\%$, so 80 percent of the firm's financing would be equity and the remaining 20 percent would be debt.

We emphasize here that the correct way to proceed is to use the *market* values of the debt and equity. Under certain circumstances, such as when considering a privately owned company, it may not be possible to get reliable estimates of these quantities. In this case, we might go ahead and use the accounting values for debt and equity. While this would probably be better than nothing, we would have to take the answer with a grain of salt.

Taxes and the Weighted Average Cost of Capital

There is one final issue we need to discuss. Recall that we are always concerned with after-tax cash flows. If we are determining the discount rate appropriate to those cash flows, then the discount rate also needs to be expressed on an aftertax basis.

As we discussed previously in various places in this book (and as we will discuss later), the interest paid by a corporation is deductible for tax purposes. Payments to stockholders, such as dividends, are not. What this means, effectively, is that the government pays some of the interest. Thus, in determining an aftertax discount rate, we need to distinguish between the pretax and the aftertax cost of debt.

To illustrate, suppose a firm borrows $1 million at 9 percent interest. The corporate tax rate is 34 percent. What is the aftertax interest rate on this loan? The total interest bill will be $90,000 per year. This amount is tax deductible, however, so the $90,000 interest reduces our tax bill by $.34 \times \$90,000 = \$30,600$. The aftertax interest bill is thus $\$90,000 - 30,600 = \$59,400$. The aftertax interest rate is thus $\$59,400/1$ million $= 5.94\%$.

Notice that, in general, the aftertax interest rate is simply equal to the pretax rate multiplied by 1 minus the tax rate. Thus, if we use the symbol T_C to stand for the corporate tax rate, then the aftertax rate that we use for the cost of debt can be written as $R_D \times (1 - T_C)$. For example, using the numbers above, we find that the aftertax interest rate is $9\% \times (1 - .34) = 5.94\%$.

Collecting together the various topics we have discussed in this chapter, we now have the capital structure weights along with the cost of equity and the aftertax cost of debt. To calculate the firm's overall cost of capital, we multiply the capital structure weights by the associated costs and add up the pieces. The result of this is the **weighted average cost of capital**, or **WACC**.

weighted average cost of capital (WACC)
The weighted average of the cost of equity and the aftertax cost of debt.

$$\text{WACC} = (E/V) \times R_E + (D/V) \times R_D \times (1 - T_C) \qquad [12.6]$$

This WACC has a very straightforward interpretation. It is the overall return the firm must earn on its existing assets to maintain the value of its stock. This is an important point, so it bears repeating:

> The WACC is the overall return the firm must earn on its existing assets to maintain the value of the stock.

The WACC is also the required return on any investments by the firm that have essentially the same risks as existing operations. So, if we were evaluating the cash flows from a proposed expansion of our existing operations, this is the discount rate we would use.

If a firm uses preferred stock in its capital structure, then our expression for the WACC needs a simple extension. If we define P/V as the percentage of the firm's financing that comes from preferred stock, then the WACC is simply:

$$\text{WACC} = (E/V) \times R_E + (P/V) \times R_P + (D/V) \times R_D \times (1 - T_C) \qquad [12.7]$$

where R_P is the cost of preferred stock.

The WACC is increasingly being used by corporations to evaluate financial performance. The *Reality Bytes* box opposite provides some details on how this is being done.

EXAMPLE 12.4   **Calculating the WACC**

The B. B. Lean Co. has 1.4 million shares of stock outstanding. The stock currently sells for $20 per share. The firm's debt is publicly traded and was recently quoted at 93 percent of face value. It has a total face value of $5 million, and it is currently priced to yield 11 percent. The risk-free rate is 8 percent, and the market risk premium is 7 percent. You've estimated that Lean has a beta of .74. If the corporate tax rate is 34 percent, what is the WACC of Lean Co.?

We can first determine the cost of equity and the cost of debt. From the SML, the cost of equity is $8\% + .74 \times 7\% = 13.18\%$. The total value of the equity is 1.4 million $\times$ $20 = $28 million. The pretax cost of debt is the current yield to maturity on the outstanding debt, 11 percent. The debt sells for 93 percent of its face value, so its current market value is $.93 \times \$5$ million $= \$4.65$ million. The total market value of the equity and debt together is $28 + 4.65 = $32.65 million.

From here, we can calculate the WACC easily enough. The percentage of equity used by Lean to finance its operations is $28/32.65 = 85.76\%$. Since the weights have to add up to 1.0, the percentage of debt is $1.0 - .8576 = 14.24\%$. The WACC is thus:

$$
\begin{aligned}
\text{WACC} &= (E/V) \times R_E + (D/V) \times R_D \times (1 - T_C) \\
&= .8576 \times 13.18\% + .1424 \times 11\% \times (1 - .34) \\
&= 12.34\%
\end{aligned}
$$

B. B. Lean thus has an overall weighted average cost of capital of 12.34 percent.

REALITY BYTES

EVA: An Old Idea Moves into the Modern Age

You might not think of Alcan, Domtar, and Loblaw as having much in common. However, all three have linked their fortunes to a way of managing and measuring corporate performance that depends critically on the cost of capital. It goes by many names, but consulting firm Stern Stewart & Co., a well-known advocate, calls its particular flavour "economic value added," or EVA. Ottawa-based Corporate Renaissance Group calculates its version of EVA and calls it "economic value created," or EVC. Whatever the name, EVA and its cousins have become an important tool for corporate management since the mid-1990s.

Briefly stated, EVA is a method of measuring financial performance. One way to compute EVA is first to calculate the return on invested capital and its overall cost (i.e., WACC). Then you identify how much capital is tied up in your business. Next, you calculate the difference between the return on invested capital and its overall cost, and multiply this difference by the amount of capital. The result is the amount, in dollars, you provide to your investors beyond what is required by the cost of capital. A positive value means that you earned more than your cost of capital, thereby creating value, and vice versa (this is just a quick overview; for more detail visit www.eva.com). In an equation form, EVA can be written as:

EVA = (Return on capital − Cost of capital) × Capital

Corporate Renaissance Group calculates EVA for Canadian companies. In 2002, 44 percent of 453 companies traded on the TSX increased value for their shareholders, while 56 percent of these companies destroyed value. Over the years, several companies have shown consistently strong performances. For example, in 2002, Leon's Furniture, Cognos, and Sceptre Investment Counsel had finished in the top 20 percent of their industries in each of the previous eight years. In contrast, some companies have been perennial poor performers, for example, Canlan Ice Sports and Napier Environmental

Technologies were in the bottom 20 percent of their industries in each of the previous eight years. Some of the names among the consistent value destroyers may surprise you. For example, Ballard Power Systems had been decreasing shareholder value for seven years. While Ballard's stock had an impressive run in the 1990s, the company could not generate returns above its cost of capital. Investors' expectations about the growth of the fuel cell market and Ballard's potential to dominate this market drove Ballard's stock to a high of about $165 in 2000. These expectations have not become reality yet, and, as a result, Ballard's stock was trading at under $7 in December 2006.

One thing the EVA ranking of Canadian companies has done is to show the changing face of the economy. For instance, while the majority of the top value creators came from the oil and gas sector in 2002, the best creators were technology companies. Aastra Technologies was the best value creator among the companies, with more than $200 million in assets, and Cryptologic was the best among the companies with less than $200 million in assets. Consider that Aastra Technologies has only been publicly traded since 1999, and Cryptologic since 1996. This highlights the impact of technology companies on the economy.

As we all know, what goes up can come crashing down. For example, Bioscrypt was historically a strong performer. In 2000, this Ontario-based technology company ranked in the top 20 percent of its industry for four of the previous eight years. The company, however, dropped to the bottom 20 percent in 2002.

While EVA and its variants are sound in principle, they still have shortcomings. For one thing, they are typically computed using asset book values instead of market values. For another, they sometimes are based on accounting measures of income when cash flow would be a better choice. Nonetheless, potential problems aside, the concept of EVA focuses management attention on creating wealth for investors. That, in itself, makes EVA a worthwhile tool.

Solving the Warehouse Problem and Similar Capital Budgeting Problems

Now we can use the WACC to solve the warehouse problem we posed at the beginning of the chapter. However, before we rush to discount the cash flows at the WACC to estimate NPV, we need to first make sure we are doing the right thing.

Going back to first principles, we need to find an alternative in the financial markets that is comparable to the warehouse renovation. To be comparable, an alternative must be

TABLE 12.1

Summary of capital cost calculations

I. The cost of equity, R_E

A. Dividend growth model approach (from Chapter 7):

$$R_E = D_1/P_0 + g$$

where D_1 is the expected dividend in one period, g is the dividend growth rate, and P_0 is the current stock price.

B. SML approach (from Chapter 11):

$$R_E = R_f + \beta_E \times (R_M - R_f)$$

where R_f is the risk-free rate, R_M is the expected return on the overall market, and β_E is the systematic risk of the equity.

II. The cost of debt, R_D

A. For a firm with publicly held debt, the cost of debt can be measured as the yield to maturity on the outstanding debt. The coupon rate is irrelevant. Yield to maturity is covered in Chapter 6.

B. If the firm has no publicly traded debt, then the cost of debt can be measured as the yield to maturity on similarly rated bonds (bond ratings are discussed in Chapter 6).

III. The weighted average cost of capital, WACC

A. The firm's WACC is the overall required return on the firm as a whole. It is the appropriate discount rate to use for cash flows similar in risk to the overall firm.

B. The WACC is calculated as:

$$WACC = (E/V) \times R_E + (D/V) \times R_D \times (1 - T_C)$$

where T_C is the corporate tax rate, E is the *market* value of the firm's equity, D is the *market* value of the firm's debt, and $V = E + D$. Note that E/V is the percentage of the firm's financing (in market value terms) that is equity, and D/V is the percentage that is debt.

of the same risk as the warehouse project. Projects that have the same risk are said to be in the same risk class.

The WACC for a firm reflects the risk and the target capital structure of the firm's existing assets as a whole. As a result, strictly speaking, the firm's WACC is the appropriate discount rate only if the proposed investment is a replica of the firm's existing operating activities.

In broader terms, whether or not we can use the firm's WACC to value the warehouse project depends on whether the warehouse project is in the same risk class as the firm. We will assume that this project is an integral part of the overall business of the firm. In such cases, it is natural to think that the cost savings will be as risky as the general cash flows of the firm, and the project will thus be in the same risk class as the overall firm. More generally, projects like the warehouse renovation that are intimately related to the firm's existing operations are often viewed as being in the same risk class as the overall firm.

We can now see what the president should do. Suppose the firm has a target debt-equity ratio of 1/3. It implies that E/V is .75 and D/V is .25. Further suppose the cost of debt is 10 percent, and the cost of equity is 20 percent. Assuming a 34 percent tax rate, the WACC will then be:

$$\begin{aligned}
WACC &= (E/V) \times R_E + (D/V) \times R_D \times (1 - T_C) \\
&= .75 \times 20\% + .25 \times 10\% \times (1 - .34) \\
&= 16.65\%
\end{aligned}$$

Recall that the warehouse project had a cost of $50 million and expected aftertax cash flows (the cost savings) of $12 million per year for six years. The NPV is thus:

$$NPV = -\$50 + \frac{12}{(1 + WACC)^1} + \cdots + \frac{12}{(1 + WACC)^6}$$

Since the cash flows are in the form of an ordinary annuity, we can calculate this NPV using 16.65 percent (the WACC) as the discount rate as follows:

$$\text{NPV} = -\$50 + 12 \times \frac{1 - [1/(1 + .1665)^6]}{.1665}$$
$$= -\$50 + 12 \times 3.6222$$
$$= -\$6.53 \text{ million}$$

Should the firm take on the warehouse renovation? The project has a negative NPV using the firm's WACC. This means that the financial markets offer superior projects in the same risk class (namely, the firm itself). The answer is clear: The project should be rejected. Our discussion of the WACC is summarized in Table 12.1 (opposite).

CONCEPT QUESTIONS

12.4a How is the WACC calculated?

12.4b Why do we multiply the cost of debt by $(1 - T_C)$ when we compute the WACC?

12.4c Under what conditions is it correct to use the WACC to determine NPV?

12.5 | DIVISIONAL AND PROJECT COSTS OF CAPITAL

As we have seen, using the WACC as the discount rate for future cash flows is only appropriate when the proposed investment is similar to the firm's existing activities. This is not as restrictive as it sounds. If we were in the pizza business, for example, and we were thinking of opening a new location, then the WACC would be the discount rate to use. The same would be true of a retailer thinking of a new store, a manufacturer thinking of expanding production, or a consumer products company thinking of expanding its markets.

Nonetheless, despite the usefulness of the WACC as a benchmark, there will clearly be situations where the cash flows under consideration have risks distinctly different from those of the overall firm. We consider how to cope with this problem next.

The SML and the WACC

When we are evaluating investments with risks that are substantially different from those of the overall firm, the use of the WACC will potentially lead to poor decisions. Figure 12.1 illustrates why.

In Figure 12.1, we have plotted an SML corresponding to a risk-free rate of 7 percent and a market risk premium of 8 percent. To keep things simple, we consider an all-equity company with a beta of 1. As we have indicated, the WACC and the cost of equity are exactly equal to 15 percent for this company since there is no debt.

Suppose our firm uses its WACC to evaluate all investments. This means that any investment with a return of greater than 15 percent will be accepted and any investment with a return of less than 15 percent will be rejected. We know from our study of risk and return, however, that a desirable investment is one that plots above the SML. As Figure 12.1 illustrates, using the WACC for all types of projects can result in the firm's incorrectly accepting relatively risky projects and incorrectly rejecting relatively safe ones.

$.15 + .0025 \times .66$

12.9%

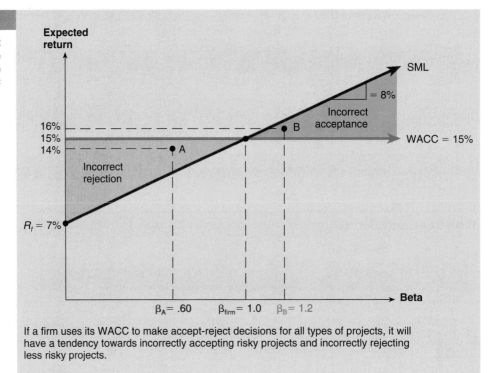

If a firm uses its WACC to make accept-reject decisions for all types of projects, it will have a tendency towards incorrectly accepting risky projects and incorrectly rejecting less risky projects.

For example, consider Point A. This project has a beta of $\beta_A = .60$ compared to the firm's beta of 1.0. It has an expected return of 14 percent. Is this a desirable investment? The answer is yes, because its required return is only:

$$\text{Required return} = R_f + \beta_A \times (R_M - R_f)$$
$$= 7\% + .60 \times 8\%$$
$$= 11.8\%$$

However, if we use the WACC as a cutoff, then this project will be rejected because its return is less than 15 percent. This example illustrates that a firm that uses its WACC as a cutoff will tend to reject profitable projects with risks less than those of the overall firm.

At the other extreme, consider Point B. This project has a beta of $\beta_B = 1.2$. It offers a 16 percent return, which exceeds the firm's cost of capital. This is not a good investment, however, because, given its level of systematic risk, its return is inadequate. Nonetheless, if we use the WACC to evaluate it, it will appear to be attractive. So the second error that will arise if we use the WACC as a cutoff is that we will tend to make unprofitable investments with risks greater than those of the overall firm. As a consequence, through time, a firm that uses its WACC to evaluate all projects will have a tendency to both accept unprofitable investments and become increasingly risky.

Divisional Cost of Capital

The same type of problem with the WACC can arise in a corporation with more than one line of business. Imagine, for example, a corporation that has two divisions, a regulated telephone company and an electronics manufacturing operation. The first of these (the phone operation) has relatively low risk; the second has relatively high risk.

In this case, the firm's overall cost of capital is really a mixture of two different costs of capital, one for each division. If the two divisions were competing for resources, and the firm used a single WACC as a cutoff, which division would tend to be awarded greater funds for investment?

The answer is that the riskier division would tend to have greater returns (ignoring the greater risk), so it would tend to be the "winner." The less glamorous operation might have great profit potential that would end up being ignored. Large corporations in Canada and the United States are aware of this problem, and many work to develop separate divisional costs of capital.

The Pure Play Approach

We've seen that using the firm's WACC inappropriately can lead to problems. How can we come up with the appropriate discount rates in such circumstances? Because we cannot observe the returns on these investments, there generally is no direct way of coming up with a beta, for example. Instead, what we must do is examine other investments outside the firm that are in the same risk class as the one we are considering and use the market-required returns on these investments as the discount rate. In other words, we will try to determine what the cost of capital is for such investments by trying to locate some similar investments in the marketplace.

For example, going back to our telephone division, suppose we want to come up with a discount rate to use for that division. What we can do is identify several other phone companies that have publicly traded securities. We might find that a typical phone company has a beta of .80, AA-rated debt, and a capital structure that is about 50 percent debt and 50 percent equity. Using this information, we could develop a WACC for a typical phone company and use this as our discount rate.

Alternatively, if we were thinking of entering a new line of business, we would try to develop the appropriate cost of capital by looking at the market-required returns on companies already in that business. In the language of Bay Street, a company that focuses only on a single line of business is called a *pure play*. For example, if you wanted to bet on the price of crude oil by purchasing common stocks, you would try to identify companies that dealt exclusively with this product since they would be the most affected by changes in the price of crude oil. Such companies would be called *pure plays* on the price of crude oil.

What we try to do here is to find companies that focus as exclusively as possible on the type of project in which we are interested. Our approach, therefore, is called the **pure play approach** to estimating the required return on an investment. To illustrate, suppose Tim Hortons decides to enter the wireless communications business with a line of machines called CoffeeBerry. The risks involved are quite different from those in the fast-food business. As a result, Tim Hortons would need to look at companies already in the wireless communications business to compute a cost of capital for the new division. An obvious "pure play" candidate would be Research In Motion, which is predominately in this line of business. Rogers Communications, on the other hand, would not be as good a choice, because it has several different product lines.

In Chapter 3, we discussed the subject of identifying similar companies for comparison purposes. The same problems we described there come up here. The most obvious one is that we may not be able to find any suitable companies. In this case, how to objectively determine a discount rate becomes a very difficult question. Even so, the important thing is to be aware of the issue so that we at least reduce the possibility of the kinds of mistakes that can arise when the WACC is used as a cutoff on all investments.

pure play approach
Use of a WACC that is unique to a particular project, based on companies in similar lines of business.

The Subjective Approach

Because of the difficulties that exist in objectively establishing discount rates for individual projects, firms often adopt an approach that involves making subjective adjustments to the overall WACC. To illustrate, suppose a firm has an overall WACC of 14 percent. It places all proposed projects into four categories as follows:

Category	Examples	Adjustment Factor	Discount Rate
High risk	New products	+6%	20%
Moderate risk	Cost savings, expansion of existing lines	+0	14
Low risk	Replacement of existing equipment	−4	10
Mandatory	Pollution control equipment	n/a	n/a

n/a = Not applicable.

The effect of this crude partitioning is to assume that all projects either fall into one of three risk classes or else are mandatory. In this last case, the cost of capital is irrelevant since the project must be taken. Of course, the firm's WACC may change through time as economic conditions change. As this happens, the discount rates for the different types of projects will also change.

Within each risk class, some projects will presumably have more risk than others, and the danger of incorrect decisions will still exist. Figure 12.2 illustrates this point. Comparing Figures 12.1 and 12.2, we see that similar problems exist, but the magnitude of the potential error is less with the subjective approach. For example, the project labelled "A" would be accepted if the WACC were used, but it is rejected once it is classified as a high-risk investment. What this illustrates is that some risk adjustment, even if it is subjective, is probably better than no risk adjustment.

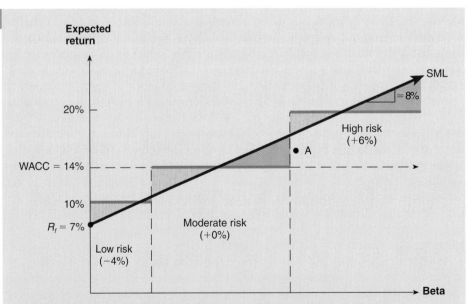

FIGURE 12.2

The security market line, SML, and the subjective approach

With the subjective approach, the firm places projects into one of several risk classes. The discount rate used to value the project is then determined by adding (for high risk) or subtracting (for low risk) an adjustment factor to or from the firm's WACC. This results in fewer incorrect decisions than if the firm simply used the WACC to make the decisions.

It would be better, in principle, to objectively determine the required return for each project separately. However, as a practical matter, it may not be possible to go much beyond subjective adjustments because either the necessary information is unavailable or else the cost and effort required are simply not worthwhile.

CONCEPT QUESTIONS

12.5a What are the likely consequences if a firm uses its WACC to evaluate all proposed investments?

12.5b What is the pure play approach to determining the appropriate discount rate? When might it be used?

12.6 | CALCULATING THE WACC FOR TRANSCANADA

In this section, we illustrate how to calculate the WACC for TransCanada, a well-known natural gas company headquartered in Calgary, Alberta. Our goal is to take you through, on a step-by-step basis, the process of finding and using the information needed using online sources. As you will see, there is a fair amount of detail involved, but the necessary information is, for the most part, readily available.

TransCanada's Cost of Equity

Our first stop is the stock price for TransCanada, available in the Today's Markets section at www.theglobeandmail.com (ticker: "TRP"). As of December 12, 2006, here's what the screen looked like:

Price and per Share Statistics

Stock Price	39.90	Market Capitalization(mil)	19,614	Common Shares Outstanding(mil)	488
52-Week High	40.34			1-Yr Change Earnings*	11.1
52-Week Low	30.77	Indicated Annual Dividend	1.28	1-Yr Change Cash Flow*	
1-Yr % Change Price	9.0	Dividend Yield	3.2	1-Yr Change Sales*	21.4
3-Yr % Change Price	42.8	Price/EPS*	16.9	EPS*	2.38
5-Yr % Change Price	106.5	Price/Cash Flow per share	10.01	Cash Flow/Share	4.01
200-Day Average Volume(000)	1,027,935.0	Price/Sales per share	3.19	Sales/Share	12.60
Beta	.30	Price/Book value per share	2.72	Book Value/Share	14.79

*TTM (Trailing 12 Months) **MRQ(Most Recent Quarter)

Annual Results

	3-Yr. Growth %	Dec 2005 (12 Months C$)	Dec 2004 (12 Months C$)	Dec 2003 (12 Months C$)	Dec 2002 (12 Months C$)
Total Revenue(mil)	9.1	6,879	5,973	5,582	5,300
Sales/Share	4.93	12.6	11.4	11.1	10.9
Profit(mil)	17.4	1,209	1,032	851	747
EPS	16.87	2.49	2.13	1.76	1.56
Cash Flow/Share	1.65	4.0	3.5	3.8	3.8
Book Value/Share	7.25	14.79	13.54	12.61	11.99
Return on Common Equity	n/a	17.56	16.31	14.38	13.37
Debt to Equity	n/a	1.55	1.68	1.83	1.83

According to this screen, TransCanada has 488 million shares of stock outstanding. The book value per share is $14.79, but the stock sells for $39.90. Total equity is therefore about $7.218 billion on a book value basis, but it is closer to $19.471 billion on a market value basis.

The SML Approach To estimate TransCanada's cost of equity, we will assume a market risk premium of 6.8 percent, similar to what we calculated in Chapter 10. TransCanada's beta on www.theglobeandmail.com is 0.30, which is considerably lower than the beta of the average stock. To check this number, we went to ca.finance.yahoo.com. The beta estimate we found there was 0.44, so we will average these two numbers and use 0.37 as our estimate for beta. According to the FP Market Data section of www.nationalpost.com, T-bills were paying about 4.17 percent. Using the SML to estimate the cost of equity, we find:

$$R_E = 0.0417 + 0.37(0.068) = 0.0669 \text{ or } 6.69\%$$

The Dividend Growth Model Approach   TransCanada has a long history of dividend payments, so calculating the future growth rate for the dividend growth model is not problematic. We went to the company's Web site at www.transcanada.com and found dividend information in the Investor Centre menu. To estimate the growth rate, we compute the percentage changes in the dividend for each year since 2000 and average them:

Year	Dividend	Dollar Change	Percentage Change
2000	$ .80	—	—
2001	.90	$.10	12.50%
2002	1.00	.10	11.11
2003	1.08	.08	8.00
2004	1.16	.08	7.41
2005	1.22	.06	5.17
2006	1.28	.06	4.92
Average			8.18

The average of the six growth rates is 8.18%, so we can use it as an estimate for the expected growth rate. Note, however, that the growth rate has been steadily declining and dropped to 4.92% in 2006. Therefore, the expected growth rate of 8.18 percent may be too optimistic. To get a second opinion, under the analysts' estimates link at ca.finance.yahoo.com, we found the following:

Growth Est	TRP.TO	Industry	Sector	S&P 500
Current Qtr.	4.2%	N/A	N/A	15.9%
Next Qtr.	8.7%	N/A	N/A	6.6%
This Year	6.3%	N/A	N/A	15.5%
Next Year	8.6%	N/A	N/A	9.2%
Past 5 Years (per annum)	N/A	N/A	N/A	N/A
Next 5 Years (per annum)	6.0%	N/A	N/A	N/A
Price/Earnings (avg. for comparison categories)	18.8	N/A	N/A	16.19
PEG Ratio (avg. for comparison categories)	3.13	N/A	N/A	N/A

Analysts estimate the growth in earnings per share for the company will be 6.0 percent for the next five years. For now, we will use this growth rate in the dividend growth model to estimate the cost of equity. The estimated cost of equity using the dividend growth model is thus:

$$R_E = \left(\frac{\$1.28(1 + .06)}{\$39.90} \right) + .06 = .094 \text{ or } 9.4\%$$

Determining the Best Estimate   Notice that the estimates for the cost of equity (6.69% and 9.4%) are not close. Remember that each method of estimating the cost of equity relies on different assumptions, so different estimates should not surprise us. If the estimates are different, there are two simple solutions. First, we could ignore one of the estimates. We would look at each estimate to see if one of them seemed too high or too low to be reasonable. Second, we could average the two estimates. Averaging the two estimates for TransCanada's cost of equity gives us a cost of equity of 8.04 percent. Since this seems like a reasonable number, we will use it in calculating the cost of capital.

TransCanada's Cost of Debt

To find information about TransCanada's debt, we went to www.sedar.com and found the 2005 annual report, which provides detailed information about outstanding bonds, and the latest quarterly report, which lists bonds issued in 2006. TransCanada has a large number of bonds outstanding with maturity dates ranging from 2007 to 2036 denominated in Canadian and U.S. dollars. The total book value of TransCanada's debt is about $10.577 billion. If you remember our previous discussion on bonds, the bond market is not as liquid as the stock market, and much less transparent.

It would be very difficult for us to find the market value for all of TransCanada's bonds. The good news is that the market values and book values of debt are usually similar. This is why companies frequently use the book values for debt in WACC calculations.

To estimate the cost of debt, we have to find its yield to maturity. Therefore, we went to www.nasdbondinfo.com. We should note here that finding the yield to maturity for all of a company's outstanding bond issues on a single day is unusual. Only two issues of TransCanada's bonds were traded on December 12, 2006, which had yields to maturity of 5.71 percent and 5.84 percent. Averaging these two yields to maturity gives us a cost of debt of 5.78 percent.

TransCanada's Cost of Preferred Stock

From TransCanada's annual report we find that the company has three issues of preferred stock. To calculate the cost of preferred stock, we have to combine these issues by computing a weighted average. The book values and fixed dividends of the preferred stock are obtained from the 2005 annual report. We calculate the dividend yield on each issue by dividing the fixed dividend by the market price per share of the preferred stock.

To calculate the weighted average cost of preferred stock, we take the percentage of the total preferred shares represented by each issue and multiply by the dividend yield on the issue. We then add them together to get the overall weighted average preferred stock cost. We use both book values and market values here for comparison. The results of the calculations are as follows:

Preferred Series	Dividend Yield	Book Value (in millions)	Percentage of Total	Market Value (in millions)	Percentage of Total	Book Values	Market Values
8.25%	7.83%	536	0.58	$ 564.9	0.56	4.54%	4.38%
Series U	5.08	195	0.21	220.4	0.22	1.07	1.12
Series Y	5.03	194	0.21	222.6	0.22	1.06	1.11
Total		925	1.00	$1,007.9	1.00	6.67	6.61

As these calculations show, TransCanada's cost of preferred stock is 6.67 percent on a book value basis and 6.61 percent on a market value basis. Thus, for TransCanada, whether the market values or book values are used makes no difference. We will use the cost of preferred stock of 6.61 percent, calculated on a market value basis, in our WACC computations.

TransCanada's WACC

We now have the various pieces necessary to calculate TransCanada's WACC. First, we need to calculate the capital structure weights. On a book value basis, TransCanada's equity,

WORK THE WEB

So how does our estimate of the WACC for TransCanada compare to others? One place to find estimates for WACC is **www.valuepro.net**. We went there and found the following information for TransCanada.

Online Valuation for TRP - 12 / 15 / 2006

Intrinsic Stock Value   44.05   [Recalculate]   [Value Another Stock]

Excess Return Period (yrs)	10	Depreciation Rate (% of Rev)	16.61
Revenues ($mil)	6594.1	Investment Rate (% of Rev)	12.31
Growth Rate (%)	7.5	Working Capital (% of Rev)	-7.49
Net Oper. Profit Margin (%)	22.21	Short-Term Assets ($mil)	1346.8
Tax Rate (%)	35.758	Short-Term Liab. ($mil)	2764
Stock Price ($)	34.0200	Equity Risk Premium (%)	3
Shares Outstanding (mil)	487.2	Company Beta	0.5775
10-Yr Treasury Yield (%)	5	Value Debt Out. ($mil)	9096.2
Bond Spread Treasury (%)	1.5	Value Pref. Stock Out. ($mil)	461.0
Preferred Stock Yield (%)	7.5	Company WACC (%)	5.86

As you can see, ValuePro estimates the WACC for TransCanada as 5.86 percent, which is close to our estimate of 6.56 percent. The methods used by this site are not identical to ours, but they are similar in the most important regards. Visit the site to learn more, if you are so inclined.

Source: ValuPro, Online Valuation for TRP. Used with permission of Gary Gray.

debt, and preferred stock are worth $7.218 billion, $10.577 billion, and $0.925 billion, respectively. The total value is $18.72 billion, so the equity, debt, and preferred stock percentages are $7.218 billion/18.72 billion = .39, $10.577 billion/18.72 billion = .56, and $0.925 billion/18.72 billion = .05. Using an average tax rate of 34 percent for TransCanada during 2005, its WACC is:

$$\text{WACC} = E/V \times R_E + P/V \times R_P + D/V \times R_D \times (1 - T_C)$$
$$= .39 \times 8.04\% + .05 \times 6.61\% + 0.56 \times 5.78\% \times (1 - .34)$$
$$= 5.60\%$$

Thus, using book value capital structure weights, we get about 5.60 percent for TransCanada's WACC.

If we use market value weights, however, the WACC will be higher. To see why, notice that on a market value basis, TransCanada's equity and preferred stock are worth $19.471 billion and $1.008 billion, respectively. The capital structure weights are therefore

$19.471 billion/31.056 billion = .63 for equity, $10.577 billion/31.056 billion = .34 for debt, and $1.008 billion/31.056 billion = .03 for preferred stock. Thus, the equity percentage is much higher if we use market value weights. With these weights, Trans-Canada's WACC is:

$$WACC = .63 \times 8.04\% + .03 \times 6.61\% + 0.34 \times 5.78\% \times (1 - .34)$$
$$= 6.56\%$$

Thus, using market value weights, we get 6.56 percent for TransCanada's WACC, which is one percentage point higher than the 5.60 percent WACC we got using book value weights.

As this example illustrates, using book values can lead to trouble, particularly if equity book values are used. Going back to Chapter 3, recall that we discussed the market-to-book ratio (the ratio of market value per share to book value per share). This ratio is usually substantially bigger than 1. For TransCanada, for example, verify that it's about 2.7; so book values significantly overstate the percentage of TransCanada's financing that comes from debt. In addition, if we were computing a WACC for a company that did not have publicly traded stock, we would try to come up with a suitable market-to-book ratio by looking at publicly traded companies, and we would then use this ratio to adjust the book value of the company under consideration. As we have seen, failure to do so can lead to significant underestimation of the WACC. See our nearby *Work the Web* box for more on the WACC.

CONCEPT QUESTIONS

12.6a What are the possible solutions if the dividend growth model and SML approaches produce different estimates for the cost of equity?

12.6b What are the likely consequences of using book value rather than market value capital structure weights to calculate the WACC?

KEY EQUATIONS:

I. The cost of equity, R_E

A. Dividend growth model approach:

$$R_E = D_1/P_0 + g \tag{12.1}$$

where

D_1 = the expected dividend in one period

g = the dividend growth rate

P_0 = the current stock price

B. SML approach:

$$R_E = R_f + \beta_E \times (R_M - R_f) \tag{12.2}$$

where

R_f = the risk-free rate

R_M = the expected return on the overall market

β_E = the systematic risk of the equity

II. The capital structure weights

$$V = E + D \qquad\qquad\qquad [12.4]$$

$$100\% = E/V + D/V \qquad\qquad\qquad [12.5]$$

where

V = the combined market value of the debt and equity

D = the market value of the debt

E = the market value of the equity

III. The weighted average cost of capital, WACC

$$\textbf{WACC} = (E/V) \times R_E + (D/V) \times R_D \times (1 - T_C) \qquad\qquad [12.6]$$

where

T_C = the corporate tax rate

R_D = the cost of debt

$$\textbf{WACC} = (E/V) \times R_E + (P/V) \times R_P + (D/V) \times R_D \times (1 - T_C) \qquad [12.7]$$

where

P = the market value of the preferred stock

R_P = the cost of preferred stock

SUMMARY AND CONCLUSIONS

This chapter has discussed cost of capital. The main points are:

1. The cost of capital associated with an investment depends on the risk of that investment, not on how and where the capital is raised.

2. The cost of equity is not directly observable. Two approaches to estimate the cost of equity are the dividend growth model approach and the security market line, or SML, approach. While the dividend growth model approach is simple, it is only applicable to companies that pay dividends, and it does not explicitly consider risk. In contrast, the SML approach is applicable to any company for which the value of beta coefficient can be determined, and it explicitly adjusts for risk.

3. The cost of debt can be observed because it is simply the interest rate that the firm would pay on new borrowing. This interest rate is equal to the yield to maturity on the firm's existing debt or the debt issued by other firms of similar risk. The cost of preferred stock is equal to its dividend yield, and it is observable in the financial markets as well.

4. The weighted average cost of capital, or WACC, is the required rate of return on the overall firm. It is also the discount rate appropriate for cash flows that are similar in risk to the overall firm. We described how the WACC can be calculated, and we illustrated how it can be used in certain types of analysis.

5. When the risk of an investment is substantially different from the risk of the overall firm, it is inappropriate to use the WACC as the discount rate. To handle such cases, we described some alternative approaches to developing discount rates, such as the pure play approach and the subjective approach.

6. A number of online sources have the information needed to calculate the WACC for public companies. As an example, we showed how to calculate the WACC for TransCanada.

CHAPTER REVIEW AND SELF-TEST PROBLEMS

12.1 Calculating the Cost of Equity. Suppose stock in Queen Corporation has a beta of .90. The market risk premium is 7 percent, and the risk-free rate is 8 percent. Queen's last dividend was $1.80 per share, and the dividend is expected to grow at 7 percent indefinitely. The stock currently sells for $25. What is Queen's cost of equity capital?

12.2 Calculating the WACC. In addition to the information in the previous problem, suppose Queen has a target debt-equity ratio of 50 percent. Its cost of debt is 8 percent, before taxes. If the tax rate is 34 percent, what is the WACC?

■ Answers to Chapter Review and Self-Test Problems

12.1 We start off with the SML approach. Based on the information given, the expected return on Queen's common stock is:

$$R_E = R_f + \beta_E \times (R_M - R_f)$$
$$= 8\% + .9 \times 7\%$$
$$= 14.3\%$$

We now use the dividend growth model. The projected dividend is $D_0 \times (1 + g) = \$1.80 \times 1.07 = \$1.926$, so the expected return using this approach is:

$$R_E = D_1/P_0 + g$$
$$= \$1.926/25 + .07$$
$$= 14.704\%$$

Since these two estimates, 14.3 percent and 14.7 percent, are fairly close, we will average them. Queen's cost of equity is approximately 14.5 percent.

12.2 Since the target debt-equity ratio is .50, Queen uses $.50 in debt for every $1.00 in equity. In other words, Queen's target capital structure is $1/3$ debt and $2/3$ equity. The WACC is thus:

$$\text{WACC} = (E/V) \times R_E + (D/V) \times R_D \times (1 - T_C)$$
$$= 2/3 \times 14.5\% + 1/3 \times 8\% \times (1 - .34)$$
$$= 11.427\%$$

CRITICAL THINKING AND CONCEPTS REVIEW

12.1 WACC. On the most basic level, if a firm's WACC is 12 percent, what does this mean?

12.2 Book Values versus Market Values. In calculating the WACC, if you had to use book values for either debt or equity, which would you choose? Why?

12.3 Project Risk. If you can borrow all the money you need for a project at 6 percent, doesn't it follow that 6 percent is your cost of capital for the project?

12.4 WACC and Taxes. Why do we use an aftertax figure for cost of debt but not for cost of equity?

12.5 Cost of Equity Estimation. What are the advantages of using the dividend growth model for determining the cost of equity capital? What are the disadvantages? What specific piece of information do you need to find the cost of equity using this model? What are some of the ways in which you could get an estimate of this number?

12.6   Cost of Equity Estimation.   What are the advantages of using the SML approach to finding the cost of equity capital? What are the disadvantages? What are the specific pieces of information needed to use this method? Are all of these variables observable, or do they need to be estimated? What are some of the ways in which you could get these estimates?

12.7   Cost of Debt Estimation.   How do you determine the appropriate cost of debt for a company? Does it make a difference if the company's debt is privately placed as opposed to being publicly traded? How would you estimate the cost of debt for a firm whose only debt issues are privately held by institutional investors?

12.8   Cost of Capital.   Suppose Tom O'Bedlam, president of Bedlam Products, Inc., has hired you to determine the firm's cost of debt and cost of equity capital.

  a.   The stock currently sells for $50 per share, and the dividend per share will probably be about $5. Tom argues, "It will cost us $5 per share to use the stockholders' money this year, so the cost of equity is equal to 10 percent ($5/50)." What's wrong with this conclusion?

  b.   Based on the most recent financial statements, Bedlam Products' total liabilities are $8 million. Total interest expense for the coming year will be about $1 million. Tom therefore reasons, "We owe $8 million, and we will pay $1 million interest. Therefore, our cost of debt is obviously $1 million/ 8 million = 12.5%." What's wrong with this conclusion?

  c.   Based on his own analysis, Tom is recommending that the company increase its use of equity financing, because "debt costs 12.5 percent, but equity only costs 10 percent; thus equity is cheaper." Ignoring all the other issues, what do you think about the conclusion that the cost of equity is less than the cost of debt?

12.9   Company Risk versus Project Risk.   Both Dow Chemical Company, a large natural gas user, and Superior Oil, a major natural gas producer, are thinking of investing in natural gas wells near Edmonton. Both are all-equity–financed companies. Dow and Superior are looking at identical projects. They've analyzed their respective investments, which would involve a negative cash flow now and positive expected cash flows in the future. These cash flows would be the same for both firms. No debt would be used to finance the projects. Both companies estimate that their project would have a net present value of $1 million at an 18 percent discount rate and a −$1.1 million NPV at a 22 percent discount rate. Dow has a beta of 1.25, whereas Superior has a beta of .75. The expected risk premium on the market is 8 percent, and risk-free bonds are yielding 12 percent. Should either company proceed? Should both? Explain.

12.10   Divisional Cost of Capital.   Under what circumstances would it be appropriate for a firm to use different costs of capital for its different operating divisions? If the overall firm WACC were used as a cutoff for all divisions, would the riskier divisions or the more conservative divisions tend to get most of the investment projects? Why? If you were to try to estimate the appropriate cost of capital for different divisions, what problems might you encounter? What are two techniques you could use to develop a rough estimate for each division's cost of capital?

QUESTIONS AND PROBLEMS

Basic
(Questions 1–23)

1.   Calculating Cost of Equity.   The Troxel Co. just issued a dividend of $2.30 per share on its common stock. The company is expected to maintain a constant

6 percent growth rate in its dividends indefinitely. If the stock sells for $42 a share, what is the company's cost of equity?

2. **Calculating Cost of Equity.** Aurora Corporation's common stock has a beta of 1.15. If the risk-free rate is 5 percent and the expected return on the market is 12 percent, what is Aurora's cost of equity capital?

3. **Calculating Cost of Equity.** Stock in CDB Industries has a beta of 1.15. The market risk premium is 8 percent, and T-bills are currently yielding 4 percent. CDB's most recent dividend was $1.80 per share, and dividends are expected to grow at a 5 percent annual rate indefinitely. If the stock sells for $34 per share, what is your best estimate of CDB's cost of equity?

4. **Calculating Cost of Equity.** Suppose Ishtiryak Ltd. just issued a dividend of $1.38 per share on its common stock. The company paid dividends of $1.02, $1.08, $1.16, and $1.30 per share in the last four years. If the stock currently sells for $39, what is your best estimate of the company's cost of equity capital using arithmetic and geometric growth rates?

5. **Calculating Cost of Preferred Stock.** Big Show Bank has an issue of preferred stock with a $7.50 stated dividend that just sold for $93 per share. What is the bank's cost of preferred stock?

6. **Calculating Cost of Debt.** ICU Window, Inc., is trying to determine its cost of debt. The firm has a debt issue outstanding with seven years to maturity that is quoted at 106 percent of face value. The issue makes semiannual payments and has an embedded cost of 7.6 percent annually. What is ICU's pretax cost of debt? If the tax rate is 38 percent, what is the aftertax cost of debt?

7. **Calculating Cost of Debt.** Jason's Oil issued a 30-year, 8 percent semiannual bond 8 years ago. The bond currently sells for 94 percent of its face value. The company's tax rate is 35 percent.

   a. What is the pretax cost of debt?

   b. What is the aftertax cost of debt?

   c. Which is more relevant, the pretax or the aftertax cost of debt? Why?

8. **Calculating Cost of Debt.** For the firm in Problem 7, suppose the book value of the debt issue is $30 million. In addition, the company has a second debt issue, a zero coupon bond with 20 years left to maturity; the book value of this issue is $90 million, and it sells for 21.5 percent of par. What is the total book value of debt? The total market value? What is the aftertax cost of debt now?

9. **Calculating WACC.** Lawrence Corporation has a target capital structure of 50 percent common stock, 5 percent preferred stock, and 45 percent debt. Its cost of equity is 14 percent, the cost of preferred stock is 6 percent, and the cost of debt is 7.5 percent. The relevant tax rate is 35 percent.

   a. What is Lawrence's WACC?

   b. The company president has approached you about Lawrence's capital structure. He wants to know why the company doesn't use more preferred stock financing, since it costs less than debt. What would you tell the president?

10. **Taxes and WACC.** Elliston Manufacturing has a target debt-equity ratio of .6. Its cost of equity is 15 percent, and its cost of debt is 9 percent. If the tax rate is 35 percent, what is Elliston's WACC?

11. **Finding the Target Capital Structure.** Fama's Llamas has a WACC of 11.50 percent. The company's cost of equity is 15 percent, and its cost of debt is 8 percent. The tax rate is 35 percent. What is Fama's target debt-equity ratio?

12. **Book Value versus Market Value.** Rooster, Inc., has 10 million shares of common stock outstanding. The current share price is $49, and the book value per share is $5. Rooster also has two bond issues outstanding. The first bond issue has a face value of $75 million, has a 7.5 percent coupon, and sells for 102 percent of par. The second issue has a face value of $40 million, has a 7 percent coupon, and sells for 104 percent of par. The first issue matures in 10 years, the second in 6 years.

   a. What are Rooster's capital structure weights on a book value basis?

   b. What are Rooster's capital structure weights on a market value basis?

   c. Which are more relevant, the book or market value weights? Why?

13. **Calculating the WACC.** In Problem 12, suppose the most recent dividend was $2.60 and the dividend growth rate is 7 percent. Assume that the overall cost of debt is the weighted average of that implied by the two outstanding debt issues. Both bonds make semiannual payments. The tax rate is 35 percent. What is the company's WACC?

14. **WACC.** Starship, Inc., has a target debt-equity ratio of .80. Its WACC is 10.50 percent, and the tax rate is 35 percent.

   a. If Starship's cost of equity is 14 percent, what is its pretax cost of debt?

   b. If the aftertax cost of debt is 6.5 percent, what is the cost of equity?

15. **Finding the WACC.** Given the following information for Fairview Co., find the WACC. Assume the company's tax rate is 35 percent.

Debt:	7,000 8 percent coupon bonds outstanding, $1,000 par value, 20 years to maturity, selling for 104 percent of par; the bonds make semiannual payments.
Common stock:	120,000 shares outstanding, selling for $82 per share; beta is 1.20.
Preferred stock:	10,000 shares of 5.25 percent preferred stock outstanding, currently selling for $80 per share.
Market:	7 percent market risk premium and 4.5 percent risk-free rate.

16. **Finding the WACC.** Humber Mining Corporation has eight million shares of common stock outstanding, 400,000 shares of 5 percent preferred stock outstanding, and 150,000 6.5 percent semiannual bonds outstanding, par value $1,000 each. The common stock currently sells for $57 per share and has a beta of 1.25, the preferred stock currently sells for $78 per share, and the bonds have 15 years to maturity and sell for 94 percent of par. The market risk premium is 8 percent, T-bills are yielding 5.5 percent, and Humber Mining's tax rate is 34 percent.

   a. What is the firm's market value capital structure?

   b. If Humber Mining is evaluating a new investment project that has the same risk as the firm's typical project, what rate should the firm use to discount the project's cash flows?

17. **SML and WACC.** An all-equity firm is considering the following projects:

Project	Beta	Expected Return
W	.60	11%
X	.90	12
Y	1.20	14
Z	1.80	19

The T-bill rate is 6 percent, and the expected return on the market is 13 percent.

a. Which projects have a higher expected return than the firm's 13 percent cost of capital?

b. Which projects should be accepted?

c. Which projects will be incorrectly accepted or rejected if the firm's overall cost of capital were used as a cutoff?

18. **Calculating the WACC.** You are given the following information concerning Canadore Enterprises:

Debt:	4,000 8 percent coupon bonds outstanding, with 20 years to maturity, and a quoted price of 114. These bonds pay interest semiannually.
Common stock:	150,000 shares of common stock selling for $50 per share. The stock has a beta of 1.05 and will pay a dividend of $3.25 next year. The dividend is expected to grow by 5 percent per year indefinitely.
Preferred stock:	8,000 shares of 5.2 percent preferred stock selling at $96 per share.
Market:	A 12 percent expected return, a 4.5 percent risk-free rate, and a 35 percent tax rate.

Calculate the WACC for Canadore Enterprises.

19. **Calculating the WACC.** In the previous problem, suppose that Canadore Enterprises feels that it should have a capital structure of 25 percent debt, 5 percent preferred stock, and 70 percent equity. Assuming that the cost of each form of financing remains the same, what is Canadore's new cost of capital?

20. **Calculating Capital Structure Weights.** Vanier Industrial Machines issued 80,000 zero coupon bonds four years ago. The bonds originally had 30 years to maturity with a 7.4 percent yield to maturity. Interest rates have recently decreased, and the bonds now have a 6.5 percent yield to maturity. If Vanier has a $30 million market value of equity, what weight should it use for debt when calculating the cost of capital?

21. **Calculating the Cost of Equity.** Over the past five years, a stock has paid dividends of $1.20, $1.34, $1.48, $1.53, and $1.62. The most recent stock price is $51. What is your best estimate of the cost of equity for this company using arithmetic and geometric growth rates?

22. **Calculating the WACC.** Your company has four million shares of common stock outstanding with a par value of $1 and a current market price of $39. The market risk premium is 7.5 percent, and Treasury bills are yielding 4.8 percent. There are also 75,000 bonds outstanding with a 9 percent semiannual coupon, 18 years to maturity, and a current price of 110. If the stock has a beta of 1.05, what is the WACC for your company? The tax rate is 35 percent.

23. **Calculating the WACC.** Gnomes R Us is considering a new project. The company has a debt-equity ratio of .70. The company's cost of equity is 10.90 percent, and the aftertax cost of debt is 6.25 percent. The firm feels that the project is riskier than the company as a whole and that it should use an adjustment factor of +3 percent. What is the WACC it should use for the project?

24. **WACC and NPV.** Maslyn, Inc., is considering a project that will result in initial aftertax cash savings of $5 million at the end of the first year, and these savings will grow at a rate of 4 percent per year indefinitely. The firm has a target debt-equity ratio of .6, a cost of equity of 15 percent, and an aftertax cost of debt of 8 percent. The cost-saving proposal is somewhat riskier than the usual project the firm undertakes; management uses the subjective approach and applies an adjustment

**Intermediate
(Questions 24–27)**

factor of +2 percent to the cost of capital for such risky projects. Under what circumstances should Maslyn take on the project?

25. **WACC and NPV.** Cusic Cordwood Co. has a project available that will provide aftertax cash flows of $320,000 for the next six years. The project has more risk than the company, so the president has told you to use an adjustment factor of +2 percent in your calculations. The company uses 65 percent equity and 35 percent debt in its capital structure. The cost of equity is 11.8 percent, and the aftertax cost of debt is 7.2 percent. What is the most Cusic can afford to pay for the new project?

26. **Calculating the Cost of Debt.** Ying Import has several bond issues outstanding, each making semiannual interest payments. The bonds are listed in the table below. If the corporate tax rate is 34 percent, what is the aftertax cost of Ying's debt?

Bond	Coupon Rate	Price Quote	Maturity	Face Value
1	6.00%	102	5 years	$20,000,000
2	7.60	110	8 years	40,000,000
3	7.20	99	15½ years	45,000,000
4	8.90	112	25 years	60,000,000

27. **Calculating the Cost of Equity.** Seneca Industries stock has a beta of 1.15. The company just paid a dividend of $.60, and the dividends are expected to grow at 5 percent. The expected return of the market is 11.5 percent, and Treasury bills are yielding 5.5 percent. The most recent stock price for Seneca is $54.

   a. Calculate the cost of equity using the dividend growth model.

   b. Calculate the cost of equity using the SML method.

   c. Why do you think your estimates in (a) and (b) are so different?

Challenge
(Question 28)

28. **Project Evaluation.** This is a comprehensive project evaluation problem bringing together much of what you have learned in this and previous chapters. Suppose you have been hired as a financial consultant to Defense Electronics, Inc. (DEI), a large, publicly traded firm that is the market share leader in radar detection systems (RDSs). The company is looking at setting up a manufacturing plant overseas to produce a new line of RDSs. This will be a five-year project. The company bought some land three years ago for $6 million in anticipation of using it as a toxic dump site for waste chemicals, but it built a piping system to safely discard the chemicals instead. If the land were sold today, the net proceeds would be $7.4 million after taxes. The company wants to build its new manufacturing plant on this land; the plant will cost $8.8 million to build. The following market data on DEI's securities are current:

Debt: 15,000 8 percent coupon bonds outstanding, 20 years to maturity, selling for 96 percent of par; the bonds have a $1,000 par value each and make semiannual payments.

Common stock: 300,000 shares outstanding, selling for $68 per share; the beta is 1.25.

Preferred stock: 20,000 shares of 6 percent preferred stock outstanding, selling for $78 per share.

Market: 7.5 percent expected market risk premium; 5.20 percent risk-free rate.

DEI's tax rate is 34 percent. The project requires $825,000 in initial net working capital investment to get operational, which will be recovered at the end of the project.

   a. Calculate the project's Time 0 cash flow, taking into account all side effects.

b. The new RDS project is somewhat riskier than a typical project for DEI, primarily because the plant is being located overseas. Management has told you to use an adjustment factor of $+2$ percent to account for this increased riskiness. Calculate the appropriate discount rate to use when evaluating DEI's project.

c. The manufacturing plant falls in CCA Class 43 with a 30 percent rate for tax purposes. At the end of the project (i.e., the end of Year 5), the plant can be scrapped for $1.75 million. What is the aftertax cash flow from the sale of the manufacturing plant, if DEI will not have any assets remaining in that CCA class?

d. The company will incur $1,050,000 in annual fixed costs. The plan is to manufacture 11,000 RDSs per year and sell them at $10,000 per machine; the variable production costs are $9,200 per RDS. What are the operating cash flows, OCF, for each year of this project?

e. Finally, DEI's president wants you to throw all your calculations, all your assumptions, and everything else into a report for the chief financial officer; all he wants to know is what the RDS project's internal rate of return, IRR, and net present value, NPV, are. What will you report?

WHAT'S ON THE WEB?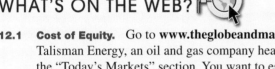

12.1 **Cost of Equity.** Go to **www.theglobeandmail.com** and look up the beta for Talisman Energy, an oil and gas company headquartered in Calgary, Alberta, in the "Today's Markets" section. You want to estimate the cost of equity for the company. Find the current Treasury bill rate in the FP Market Data section at **www.nationalpost.com**. Using the historical market risk premium, what is the estimated cost of equity for Talisman Energy using the SML approach? Now find the analyst's growth rate estimates for the next five years for the company at **ca.finance.yahoo.com**. Using this growth rate in the dividend growth model, what is the estimated cost of equity? Now find the dividends paid by the company over the past five years and calculate the arithmetic and geometric growth rate in dividends. Using these growth rates, what is the estimated cost of equity? Looking at these four estimates, what cost of equity would you use for the company?

12.2 **Cost of Debt.** Go to **www.nasdbondinfo.com** and look up the outstanding bonds for TELUS, a telecommunications company based in British Columbia. Record the most recent price and YTM of each bond issue. Now go to **www.sedar.com** and find the most recent quarterly or annual report filed by the company and find the book value of each bond issue. Assuming TELUS's tax rate is 38 percent, what is the cost of debt using book value weights? What is the cost of debt using market value weights? Which of these numbers is more relevant?

12.3 **Cost of Preferred.** Go to **ca.finance.yahoo.com** and look up the outstanding preferred share issues for Power Financial Corporation. Record the most recent price and dividend yield for each preferred issue. Now go to **www.sedar.com** and find the most recent annual report filed by the company and find the number of shares outstanding for each preferred shares issue. What is the weighted average cost of preferred stock?

www.mcgrawhill.ca/olc/ross

MINI-CASE

COST OF CAPITAL FOR HUBBARD COMPUTER, INC.

You have recently been hired by Hubbard Computer, Inc. (HCI), in its relatively new treasury management department. HCI was founded in Markham, Ontario, eight years ago by Bob Hubbard. The company operates 74 stores across Canada and plans to open its first five stores in the United States next year. HCI is privately owned by Bob and his family, and had sales of $97 million last year.

HCI primarily sells to in-store customers who come to the store and talk with a sales representative. The sales representative helps the customer decide on the computer and peripherals that suit the customer's computing needs. After the order is taken, the customer pays for the order immediately, and the computer is made to fill the order. Delivery of the computer averages 15 days, and is guaranteed in 30 days.

HCI's growth to date has been financed by its profits. When the company had enough capital, it would open a new store. Other than scouting locations, relatively little formal analysis has been used in its capital budgeting process. Bob has just read about capital budgeting techniques and has come to you for help. For starters, the company has never attempted to determine its cost of capital, and Bob would like you to perform the analysis. Since the company is privately owned, it is difficult to determine the cost of equity for the company. Bob wants you to use the pure play approach to estimate the cost of capital for HCI, and has chosen Dell as a representative company. The following steps will allow you to calculate this estimate.

1. Most U.S. publicly traded corporations are required to submit quarterly (10Q) and annual reports (10K) to the SEC, detailing the financial operations of the company over the past quarter or year, respectively. These corporate filings are available on the SEC Web site at www.sec.gov. Go to the SEC Web site, follow the "Search for Company Filings" link, the "Companies & Other Files" link, enter "Dell Computer," and search for SEC filings made by Dell. Find the most recent 10Q or 10K and download the form. Look on the balance sheet to find the book value of debt and the book value of equity. If you look further down the report, you should find a section titled "Long-term Debt and Interest Rate Risk Management" that will provide a breakdown of Dell's long-term debt.

2. To estimate the cost of equity for Dell, go to finance.yahoo.com and enter the ticker symbol DELL. Follow the various links to answer the following questions: What is the most recent stock price listed for Dell? What is the market value of equity, or market capitalization? How many shares of stock does Dell have outstanding? What is the most recent annual dividend? Can you use the dividend growth model in this case? What is the beta for Dell? Now go back to finance.yahoo.com and follow the "Bonds" link. What is the yield on 3-month U.S. Treasury bills? Using the historical market risk premium, what is the cost of equity for Dell using the SML approach?

3. You now need to calculate the cost of debt for Dell. Go to www.nasdbondinfo.com, enter Dell as the company and find the yield to maturity

for each of Dell's bonds. What is the weighted average cost of debt for Dell using the book value weights and the market value weights? Does it make a difference in this case if you use book value weights or market value weights?

4.   You now have all the information you need to calculate the weighted average cost of capital for Dell. Do this by using book value weights and market value weights. Assume Dell has a 35 percent marginal tax rate. Which cost of capital number is more relevant?

5.   You used Dell as a pure play company to estimate the cost of capital for HCl. Are there any potential problems with this approach in this situation?

Leverage and Capital Structure

13

This chapter provides you with the basics on some of the most important issues in finance, including:

13.1 The relationship between the WACC and the value of the firm.

13.2 The effect of financial leverage.

13.3 The choice of capital structure with no taxes.

13.4 The impact of corporate taxes on the capital structure decision.

13.5 Two types of bankruptcy costs.

13.6 The static theory of capital structure.

13.7 Variation of observed capital structures.

13.8 The essentials of the bankruptcy process.

What do Canadian National Railway (CN), Neptune Technologies & Bioressources (Neptune), and BCE have in common? In 2006 all three companies made decisions about how much debt to carry relative to equity. CN filed papers to issue US$1.5 billion of debt over the next two years. Among other things, the company planned to use the proceeds to buy back shares. It essentially meant that the company was going to swap debt for equity. In contrast, Neptune, the Laval-based biotechnology company, eliminated $5.6 million of debt and issued about 4.7 million common shares. BCE issued neither debt nor equity, choosing instead to use the proceeds from the sale of its assets to buy back shares, rather than reduce its debt. Moody's, a debt rating agency, looked unkindly on this action and downgraded BCE's debt. Why did CN intend to swap debt for equity, while Neptune decided to swap equity for debt? Why did BCE decide to reduce equity rather than debt? Why was BCE penalized for it with a lower debt rating? We will explore these questions and other issues in this chapter.

A firm's choice of how much debt it should have relative to equity is known as a capital structure decision. Such a choice has many implications for a firm and is far from being a settled issue in either theory or practice. In this chapter, we discuss the basic ideas underlying capital structures and how firms choose them.

A firm's capital structure is really just a reflection of its borrowing policy. Should we borrow a lot of money, or just a little? At first glance, it probably seems that debt is something to be avoided. After all, the more debt a firm has, the greater the risk of bankruptcy. What we learn is that debt is really a double-edged sword, and, properly used, debt can be enormously beneficial to the firm.

Striking the right balance is what the capital structure issue is all about.

Thus far, we have taken the firm's capital structure as given. Debt-equity ratios don't just drop on firms from the sky, of course, so now it's time to wonder where they do come from. Going back to Chapter 1, we call decisions about a firm's debt-equity ratio *capital structure decisions.*[1]

For the most part, a firm can choose any capital structure that it wants. If management so desired, a firm could issue some bonds and use the proceeds to buy back some stock, thereby increasing the debt-equity ratio. Alternatively, it could issue stock and use the money to pay off some debt, thereby reducing the debt-equity ratio. Activities such as these that alter the firm's existing capital structure are called capital *restructurings.* In general, such restructurings take place whenever the firm substitutes one capital structure for another while leaving the firm's assets unchanged.

Since the assets of a firm are not directly affected by a capital restructuring, we can examine the firm's capital structure decision separately from its other activities. This means that a firm can consider capital restructuring decisions in isolation from its investment decisions. In this chapter, then, we will ignore investment decisions and focus on the long-term financing, or capital structure, question.

What we will see in this chapter is that capital structure decisions can have important implications for the value of the firm and its cost of capital. We will also find that important elements of the capital structure decision are easy to identify, but precise measures of these elements are generally not obtainable. As a result, we are only able to give an incomplete answer to the question of what the best capital structure might be for a particular firm at a particular time.

13.1 | THE CAPITAL STRUCTURE QUESTION

How should a firm go about choosing its debt-equity ratio? Here, as always, we assume that the guiding principle is to choose the course of action that maximizes the value of a share of stock. However, when it comes to capital structure decisions, this is essentially the same thing as maximizing the value of the whole firm, and, for convenience, we will tend to frame our discussion in terms of firm value.

In Chapter 12, we discussed the concept of the firm's weighted average cost of capital, or WACC. You may recall that the WACC tells us that the firm's overall cost of capital is a weighted average of the costs of the various components of the firm's capital structure. When we described the WACC, we took the firm's capital structure as given. Thus, one important issue that we will want to explore in this chapter is what happens to the cost of capital when we vary the amount of debt financing, or the debt-equity ratio.

A primary reason for studying the WACC is that the value of the firm is maximized when the WACC is minimized. To see this, recall that the WACC is the discount rate appropriate for the firm's overall cash flows. Since values and discount rates move in opposite directions, minimizing the WACC will maximize the value of the firm's cash flows.

Thus, we will want to choose the firm's capital structure so that the WACC is minimized. For this reason, we will say that one capital structure is better than another if it results in a lower weighted average cost of capital. Further, we say that a particular debt-equity ratio represents the *optimal capital structure* if it results in the lowest possible WACC. This optimal capital structure is sometimes called the firm's *target* capital structure as well.

---

[1]It is conventional to refer to decisions regarding debt and equity as *capital structure decisions.* However, the term *financial structure* would be more accurate, and we use the terms interchangeably.

13.2 | THE EFFECT OF FINANCIAL LEVERAGE

In this section, we examine the impact of financial leverage on the payoffs to stockholders. As you may recall, financial leverage refers to the extent to which a firm relies on debt. The more debt financing a firm uses in its capital structure, the more financial leverage it employs.

As we describe, financial leverage can dramatically alter the payoffs to shareholders in the firm. Remarkably, however, financial leverage may not affect the overall cost of capital. If this is true, then a firm's capital structure is irrelevant because changes in capital structure won't affect the value of the firm. We will return to this issue a little later.

The Impact of Financial Leverage

We start by illustrating how financial leverage works. For now, we ignore the impact of taxes. Also, for ease of presentation, we describe the impact of leverage in terms of its effects on earnings per share, EPS, and return on equity, ROE. These are, of course, accounting numbers and, as such, are not our primary concern. Using cash flows instead of these accounting numbers would lead to precisely the same conclusions, but a little more work would be needed. We discuss the impact of leverage on market values in a subsequent section.

Financial Leverage, EPS, and ROE: An Example   The Trans Am Corporation currently has no debt in its capital structure. The CFO, Ms. Morris, is considering a restructuring that would involve issuing debt and using the proceeds to buy back some of the outstanding equity. Table 13.1 presents both the current and proposed capital structures. As shown, the firm's assets have a market value of $8 million, and there are 400,000 shares outstanding. Because Trans Am is an all-equity firm, the price per share is $20.

The proposed debt issue would raise $4 million; the interest rate would be 10 percent. Since the stock sells for $20 per share, the $4 million in new debt would be used to purchase $4 million/20 = 200,000 shares, leaving 200,000 outstanding. After the restructuring, Trans Am would have a capital structure that was 50 percent debt, so the debt-equity ratio would be 1. Notice that, for now, we assume that the stock price will remain at $20.

TABLE **13.1** **Current and proposed capital structures for the Trans Am Corporation**		Current	Proposed
	Assets	$8,000,000	$8,000,000
	Debt	$ 0	$4,000,000
	Equity	$8,000,000	$4,000,000
	Debt-equity ratio	0	1
	Share price	$ 20	$ 20
	Shares outstanding	400,000	200,000
	Interest rate	10%	10%

Current Capital Structure: No Debt			
	Recession	**Expected**	**Expansion**
EBIT	$500,000	$1,000,000	$1,500,000
Interest	0	0	0
Net income	$500,000	$1,000,000	$1,500,000
ROE	6.25%	12.50%	18.75%
EPS	$ 1.25	$ 2.50	$ 3.75

Proposed Capital Structure: Debt = $4 million			
	Recession	**Expected**	**Expansion**
EBIT	$500,000	$1,000,000	$1,500,000
Interest	400,000	400,000	400,000
Net income	$100,000	$ 600,000	$1,100,000
ROE	2.50%	15.00%	27.50%
EPS	$ .50	$ 3.00	$ 5.50

TABLE 13.2

Capital structure
scenarios for
the Trans Am
Corporation

To investigate the impact of the proposed restructuring, Ms. Morris has prepared Table 13.2, which compares the firm's current capital structure to the proposed capital structure under three scenarios. The scenarios reflect different assumptions about the firm's EBIT. Under the expected scenario, the EBIT is $1 million. In the recession scenario, EBIT falls to $500,000. In the expansion scenario, it rises to $1.5 million.

To illustrate some of the calculations in Table 13.2, consider the expansion case. EBIT is $1.5 million. With no debt (the current capital structure) and no taxes, net income is also $1.5 million. In this case, there are 400,000 shares worth $8 million total. EPS is therefore $1.5million/400,000 = $3.75 per share. Also, since accounting return on equity, ROE, is net income divided by total equity, ROE is $1.5million/8 million = 18.75%.[2]

With $4 million in debt (the proposed capital structure), things are somewhat different. Since the interest rate is 10 percent, the interest bill is $400,000. With EBIT of $1.5 million, interest of $400,000, and no taxes, net income is $1.1 million. Now there are only 200,000 shares worth $4 million total. EPS is therefore $1.1 million/200,000 = $5.5 per share versus the $3.75 per share that we calculated above. Furthermore, ROE is $1.1 million/ 4 million = 27.5%. This is well above the 18.75 percent we calculated for the current capital structure.

EPS versus EBIT   The impact of leverage is evident in Table 13.2 when the effect of the restructuring on EPS and ROE is examined. In particular, the variability in both EPS and ROE is much larger under the proposed capital structure. This illustrates how financial leverage acts to magnify gains and losses to shareholders.

In Figure 13.1, we take a closer look at the effect of the proposed restructuring. This figure plots earnings per share, EPS, against earnings before interest and taxes, EBIT, for the current and proposed capital structures. The blue line, labelled "No debt," represents the case of no leverage. This line begins at the origin, indicating that EPS would be zero if EBIT were zero. From there, every $400,000 increase in EBIT increases EPS by $1 (because there are 400,000 shares outstanding).

---

[2]ROE is discussed in some detail in Chapter 3.

FIGURE 13.1

Financial leverage:
EPS and EBIT
for the Trans Am
Corporation

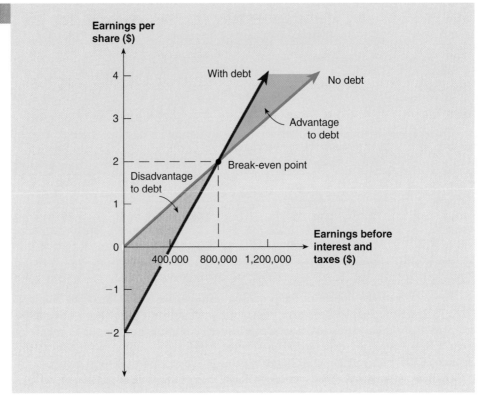

The red line represents the proposed capital structure. Here, EPS is negative if EBIT is zero. This follows because $400,000 of interest must be paid regardless of the firm's profits. Since there are 200,000 shares in this case, the EPS is −$2 per share as shown. Similarly, if EBIT were $400,000, EPS would be exactly zero.

The important thing to notice in Figure 13.1 is that the slope of the red line is steeper. In fact, for every $400,000 increase in EBIT, EPS rises by $2, so the line is twice as steep. This tells us that EPS is twice as sensitive to changes in EBIT because of the financial leverage employed.

Another observation to make in Figure 13.1 is that the lines intersect. At that point, EPS is exactly the same for both capital structures. To find this point, note that EPS is equal to EBIT/400,000 in the no-debt case. In the with-debt case, EPS is (EBIT − $400,000)/200,000. If we set these equal to each other, EBIT is:

$$\text{EBIT}/400,000 = (\text{EBIT} − \$400,000)/200,000$$
$$\text{EBIT} = 2 \times (\text{EBIT} − \$400,000)$$
$$\text{EBIT} = \$800,000$$

When EBIT is $800,000, EPS is $2 per share under either capital structure. This is labelled as the break-even point in Figure 13.1; we could also call it the indifference point. If EBIT is above this level, leverage is beneficial; if it is below this point, it is not.

There is another, more intuitive, way of seeing why the break-even point is $800,000. Notice that, if the firm has no debt and its EBIT is $800,000, its net income is also $800,000. In this case, the ROE is $800,000/8,000,000 = 10%. This is precisely the same as the interest rate on the debt, so the firm earns a return that is just sufficient to pay the interest.

> **Break-Even EBIT** **EXAMPLE 13.1**
>
> The MPD Corporation has decided in favour of a capital restructuring. Currently, MPD uses no-debt financing. Following the restructuring, however, debt will be $1 million. The interest rate on the debt will be 9 percent. MPD currently has 200,000 shares outstanding, and the price per share is $20. If the restructuring is expected to increase EPS, what is the minimum level for EBIT that MPD's management must be expecting? Ignore taxes in answering.
>
> To answer, we calculate the break-even EBIT. At any EBIT above this, the increased financial leverage will increase EPS, so this will tell us the minimum level for EBIT. Under the old capital structure, EPS is simply EBIT/200,000. Under the new capital structure, the interest expense will be $1 million × .09 = $90,000. Furthermore, with the $1 million proceeds, MPD will repurchase $1 million/20 = 50,000 shares of stock, leaving 150,000 outstanding. EPS is thus (EBIT − $90,000)/150,000.
>
> Now that we know how to calculate EPS under both scenarios, we set the two expressions for EPS equal to each other and solve for the break-even EBIT:
>
> $$EBIT/200,000 = (EBIT - \$90,000)/150,000$$
> $$EBIT = (4/3) \times (EBIT - \$90,000)$$
> $$EBIT = \$360,000$$
>
> Verify that, in either case, EPS is $1.80 when EBIT is $360,000. Management at MPD is apparently of the opinion that EPS will exceed $1.80.

Corporate Borrowing and Homemade Leverage

Based on Tables 13.1 and 13.2 and Figure 13.1, Ms. Morris draws the following conclusions:

1. The effect of financial leverage depends on the company's EBIT. When EBIT is relatively high, leverage is beneficial.

2. Under the expected scenario, leverage increases the returns to shareholders, as measured by both ROE and EPS.

3. Shareholders are exposed to more risk under the proposed capital structure since the EPS and ROE are much more sensitive to changes in EBIT in this case.

4. Because of the impact that financial leverage has on both the expected return to stockholders and the riskiness of the stock, capital structure is an important consideration.

The first three of these conclusions are clearly correct. Does the last conclusion necessarily follow? Surprisingly, the answer is no. As we discuss next, the reason is that shareholders can adjust the amount of financial leverage by borrowing and lending on their own. This use of personal borrowing to alter the degree of financial leverage is called **homemade leverage**.

We will now illustrate that it actually makes no difference whether or not Trans Am adopts the proposed capital structure, because any stockholder who prefers the proposed capital structure can simply create it using homemade leverage. To begin, the first part of Table 13.3 shows what will happen to an investor who buys $2,000 worth of Trans Am stock if the proposed capital structure is adopted. This investor purchases 100 shares of stock. From Table 13.2, EPS will either be $.50, $3, or $5.50, so the total earnings for 100 shares will either be $50, $300, or $550 under the proposed capital structure.

homemade leverage
The use of personal borrowing to change the overall amount of financial leverage to which the individual is exposed.

TABLE 13.3			
Proposed capital structure versus original capital structure with homemade leverage			

Proposed Capital Structure

	Recession	Expected	Expansion
EPS	$ .50	$ 3.00	$ 5.50
Earnings for 100 shares	50.00	300.00	550.00
Net cost = 100 shares at $20 = $2,000			

Original Capital Structure and Homemade Leverage

	Recession	Expected	Expansion
EPS	$ 1.25	$ 2.50	$ 3.75
Earnings for 200 shares	250.00	500.00	750.00
Less: Interest on $2,000 at 10%	200.00	200.00	200.00
Net earnings	$ 50.00	$300.00	$550.00
Net cost = 200 shares at $20 − Amount borrowed = $4,000 − 2,000 = $2,000			

Now, suppose Trans Am does not adopt the proposed capital structure. In this case, EPS will be $1.25, $2.50, or $3.75. The second part of Table 13.3 demonstrates how a stockholder who prefers the payoffs under the proposed structure can create them using personal borrowing. To do this, the stockholder borrows $2,000 at 10 percent on his or her own. Our investor uses this amount, along with the original $2,000, to buy 200 shares of stock. As shown, the net payoffs are exactly the same as those for the proposed capital structure.

How did we know to borrow $2,000 to create the right payoffs? We are trying to replicate Trans Am's proposed capital structure at the personal level. The proposed capital structure results in a debt-equity ratio of 1. To replicate this capital structure at the personal level, the stockholder must borrow enough to create this same debt-equity ratio. Since the stockholder has $2,000 in equity invested, borrowing another $2,000 will create a personal debt-equity ratio of 1.

This example demonstrates that investors can always increase financial leverage themselves to create a different pattern of payoffs. It thus makes no difference whether or not Trans Am chooses the proposed capital structure.

EXAMPLE 13.2 **Unlevering the Stock**

In our Trans Am example, suppose management adopted the proposed capital structure. Further, suppose that an investor who owned 100 shares preferred the original capital structure. Show how this investor could "unlever" the stock to recreate the original payoffs.

To create leverage, investors borrow on their own. To undo leverage, investors must loan out money. For Trans Am, the corporation borrowed an amount equal to half its value. The investor can unlever the stock by simply loaning out money in the same proportion. In this case, the investor sells 50 shares for $1,000 total and then loans out the $1,000 at 10 percent. The payoffs are calculated in the table below.

	Recession	Expected	Expansion
EPS (proposed structure)	$ .50	$ 3.00	$ 5.50
Earnings for 50 shares	25.00	150.00	275.00
Plus: Interest on $1,000 @ 10%	100.00	100.00	100.00
Total payoff	$125.00	$250.00	$375.00

These are precisely the payoffs the investor would have experienced under the original capital structure.

13.3 | CAPITAL STRUCTURE AND THE COST OF EQUITY CAPITAL

We have seen that there is nothing special about corporate borrowing because investors can borrow or lend on their own. As a result, whichever capital structure Trans Am chooses, the stock price will be the same. Trans Am's capital structure is thus irrelevant, at least in the simple world we have examined.

Our Trans Am example is based on a famous argument advanced by two Nobel laureates, Franco Modigliani and Merton Miller, whom we will henceforth call M&M. What we illustrated for the Trans Am Corporation is a special case of **M&M Proposition I**. M&M Proposition I states that it is completely irrelevant how a firm chooses to arrange its finances.

> **M&M Proposition I**
> The value of the firm is independent of its capital structure.

M&M Proposition I: The Pie Model

One way to illustrate M&M Proposition I is to imagine two firms that are identical on the left-hand side of the balance sheet. Their assets and operations are exactly the same. The right-hand sides are different because the two firms finance their operations differently. In this case, we can view the capital structure question in terms of a "pie" model. Why we choose this name is apparent in Figure 13.2. Figure 13.2 gives two possible ways of cutting up this pie between the equity slice, *E,* and the debt slice, *D:* 40%-60% and 60%-40%. However, the size of the pie in Figure 13.2 is the same for both firms because the value of the assets is the same. This is precisely what M&M Proposition I states: The size of the pie doesn't depend on how it is sliced. In other words, the value of the firm levered (V_L) is equal to the value of the firm unlevered (V_U):

> To learn more about Nobel laureates in Economics, go to **nobelprize.org/nobel_prizes/economics/laureates.**

$$V_L = V_U \qquad [13.1]$$

The Cost of Equity and Financial Leverage: M&M Proposition II

Although changing the capital structure of the firm may not change the firm's *total* value, it does cause important changes in the firm's debt and equity. We now examine what happens

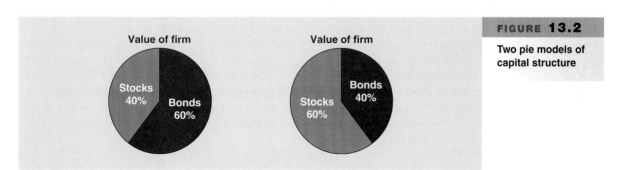

FIGURE 13.2

Two pie models of capital structure

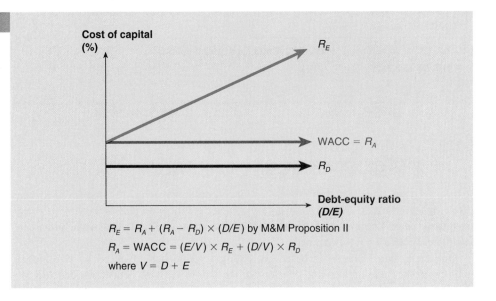

$$R_E = R_A + (R_A - R_D) \times (D/E) \text{ by M&M Proposition II}$$
$$R_A = \text{WACC} = (E/V) \times R_E + (D/V) \times R_D$$
$$\text{where } V = D + E$$

to a firm financed with debt and equity when the debt-equity ratio is changed. To simplify our analysis, we will continue to ignore taxes.

Based on our discussion in Chapter 12, if we ignore taxes, the weighted average cost of capital, WACC, is:

$$\text{WACC} = (E/V) \times R_E + (D/V) \times R_D$$

where $V = E + D$. We also saw that one way of interpreting the WACC is as the required return on the firm's overall assets. To remind us of this, we will use the symbol R_A to stand for the WACC and write:

$$R_A = (E/V) \times R_E + (D/V) \times R_D$$

If we rearrange this to solve for the cost of equity capital, we see that:

$$R_E = R_A + (R_A - R_D) \times (D/E) \qquad \text{[13.2]}$$

M&M Proposition II
A firm's cost of equity
capital is a positive
linear function of its
capital structure.

This is the famous **M&M Proposition II**, which tells us that the cost of equity depends on three things: the required rate of return on the firm's assets, R_A; the firm's cost of debt, R_D; and the firm's debt-equity ratio, D/E.

Figure 13.3 summarizes our discussion thus far by plotting the cost of equity capital, R_E, against the debt-equity ratio. As shown, M&M Proposition II indicates that the cost of equity, R_E, is given by a straight line with a slope of $(R_A - R_D)$. The y-intercept corresponds to a firm with a debt-equity ratio of zero, so $R_A = R_E$ in that case. Figure 13.3 shows that, as the firm raises its debt-equity ratio, the increase in leverage raises the risk of the equity and therefore the required return, or cost of equity (R_E).

Notice in Figure 13.3 that the WACC doesn't depend on the debt-equity ratio; it's the same no matter what the debt-equity ratio is. This is another way of stating M&M Proposition I: The firm's overall cost of capital is unaffected by its capital structure. As illustrated, the fact that the cost of debt is lower than the cost of equity is exactly offset by the increase in the cost of equity from borrowing. In other words, the change in the capital structure weights (E/V and D/V) is exactly offset by the change in the cost of equity (R_E), so the WACC stays the same.

The Cost of Equity Capital | **EXAMPLE 13.3**

The Ricardo Corporation has a weighted average cost of capital (ignoring taxes) of 12 percent. It can borrow at 8 percent. Assuming that Ricardo has a target capital structure of 80 percent equity and 20 percent debt, what is its cost of equity? What is the cost of equity if the target capital structure is 50 percent equity?

According to M&M Proposition II, the cost of equity, R_E, is:

$$R_E = R_A + (R_A - R_D) \times (D/E)$$

In the first case, the debt-equity ratio is $.2/.8 = .25$, so the cost of the equity is:

$$R_E = 12\% + (12\% - 8\%) \times .25$$
$$= 13\%$$

In the second case, verify that the debt-equity ratio is 1.0, so the cost of equity is 16 percent.

Business and Financial Risk

M&M Proposition II shows that the firm's cost of equity can be broken down into two components. The first component, R_A, is the required return on the firm's assets overall, and it depends on the nature of the firm's operating activities. The risk inherent in a firm's operations is called the **business risk** of the firm's equity. Referring back to Chapter 11, we see that this business risk depends on the systematic risk of the firm's assets. The greater a firm's business risk, the greater R_A will be, and, all other things being the same, the greater will be the firm's cost of equity.

> **business risk**
> The equity risk that comes from the nature of the firm's operating activities.

The second component in the cost of equity, $(R_A - R_D) \times (D/E)$, is determined by the firm's financial structure. For an all-equity firm, this component is zero. As the firm begins to rely on debt financing, the required return on equity rises. This occurs because the debt financing increases the risks borne by the stockholders. This extra risk that arises from the use of debt financing is called the **financial risk** of the firm's equity.

The total systematic risk of the firm's equity thus has two parts: business risk and financial risk. The first part (the business risk) depends on the firm's assets and operations and is not affected by capital structure. Given the firm's business risk (and its cost of debt), the second part (the financial risk) is completely determined by financial policy. As we have illustrated, the firm's cost of equity rises when it increases its use of financial leverage because the financial risk of the equity increases while the business risk remains the same.

> **financial risk**
> The equity risk that comes from the financial policy (i.e., capital structure) of the firm.

CONCEPT QUESTIONS

13.3a What does M&M Proposition I state?

13.3b What are the three determinants of a firm's cost of equity?

13.3c The total systematic risk of a firm's equity has two parts. What are they?

13.4 | CORPORATE TAXES AND CAPITAL STRUCTURE

Debt has two distinguishing features that we have not taken into proper account. First, as we have mentioned in a number of places, interest paid on debt is tax deductible. This is good for the firm, and it may be an added benefit to debt financing. Second, failure to meet debt obligations can result in bankruptcy. This is not good for the firm, and it may be an added cost of debt financing. Since we haven't explicitly considered either of these two features of debt, we may get a different answer about capital structure once we do. Accordingly, we consider taxes in this section and bankruptcy in the next one.

We can start by considering what happens when we consider the effect of corporate taxes. To do this, we will examine two firms, Firm U (unlevered) and Firm L (levered). These two firms are identical on the left-hand side of the balance sheet, so their assets and operations are the same.

We assume that EBIT is expected to be $1,000 every year forever for both firms. The difference between the two firms is that Firm L has issued $1,000 worth of perpetual bonds on which it pays 8 percent interest each year. The interest bill is thus .08 × $1,000 = $80 every year forever. Also, we assume that the corporate tax rate is 30 percent.

For our two firms, U and L, we can now calculate the following:

	Firm U	Firm L
EBIT	$1,000	$1,000
Interest	0	80
Taxable income	$1,000	$ 920
Taxes (30%)	300	276
Net income	$ 700	$ 644

The Interest Tax Shield

To simplify things, we will assume that depreciation is zero. We will also assume that capital spending is zero and that there are no additions to NWC. In this case, cash flow from assets is simply equal to EBIT − Taxes. For Firms U and L, we thus have:

Cash Flow from Assets	Firm U	Firm L
EBIT	$1,000	$1,000
−Taxes	300	276
Total	$ 700	$ 724

We immediately see that capital structure is now having some effect because the cash flows from U and L are not the same even though the two firms have identical assets.

To see what's going on, we can compute the cash flow to stockholders and bondholders.

Cash Flow	Firm U	Firm L
To stockholders	$700	$644
To bondholders	0	80
Total	$700	$724

What we are seeing is that the total cash flow to L is $24 more. This occurs because L's tax bill (which is a cash outflow) is $24 less. The fact that interest is deductible for tax purposes has generated a tax saving equal to the interest payment ($80) multiplied by the corporate tax rate (30 percent): $80 × .30 = $24. We call this tax saving the **interest tax shield**.

interest tax shield
The tax saving attained by a firm from the tax deductibility of interest expense.

Taxes and M&M Proposition I

Since the debt is perpetual, the same $24 shield will be generated every year forever. The aftertax cash flow to L will thus be the same $700 that U earns plus the $24 tax shield.

Since L's cash flow is always $24 greater, Firm L is worth more than Firm U by the value of this $24 perpetuity.

Because the tax shield is generated by paying interest, it has the same risk as the debt, and 8 percent (the cost of debt) is therefore the appropriate discount rate. The value of the tax shield is thus:

$$PV = \frac{\$24}{.08} = \frac{.30 \times \$1,000 \times .08}{.08} = .30 \times \$1,000 = \$300$$

As our example illustrates, the present value of the interest tax shield can be written as:

$$\text{Present value of the interest tax shield} = (T_C \times D \times R_D)/R_D$$
$$= T_C \times D \qquad \textbf{[13.3]}$$

We have now come up with another famous result, M&M Proposition I with corporate taxes. We have seen that the value of Firm L, V_L, exceeds the value of Firm U, V_U, by the present value of the interest tax shield, $T_C \times D$. M&M Proposition I with taxes therefore states that:

$$V_L = V_U + T_C \times D \qquad \textbf{[13.4]}$$

The effect of borrowing in this case is illustrated in Figure 13.4. We have plotted the value of the levered firm, V_L, against the amount of debt, D. M&M Proposition I with corporate taxes implies that the relationship is given by a straight line with a slope of T_C.

In Figure 13.4, we have also drawn a horizontal line representing V_U. As is shown, the distance between the two lines is $T_C \times D$, the present value of the tax shield.

As Figure 13.4 indicates, the value of the firm goes up by $.30 for every $1 in debt. In other words, the NPV *per dollar* of debt is $.30. It is difficult to imagine why any corporation would not borrow to the absolute maximum under these circumstances.

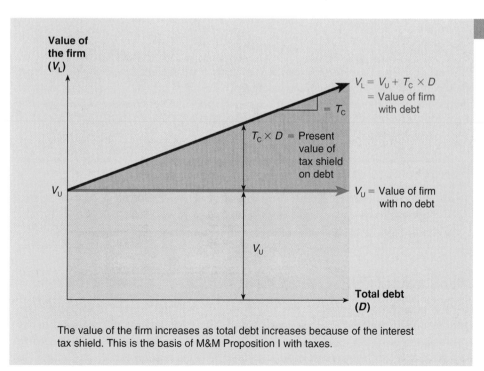

FIGURE 13.4

M&M Proposition I with taxes

The value of the firm increases as total debt increases because of the interest tax shield. This is the basis of M&M Proposition I with taxes.

TABLE 13.4

**Modigliani and Miller
summary**

I. The no-tax case

  A. Proposition I: The value of the firm levered (V_L) is equal to the value of the firm unlevered (V_U):

$$V_L = V_U$$

  B. Implications of Proposition I:

    1. A firm's capital structure is irrelevant.

    2. A firm's weighted average cost of capital, WACC, is the same no matter what mixture of debt and equity is used to finance the firm.

  C. Proposition II: The cost of equity, R_E, is:

$$R_E = R_A + (R_A - R_D) \times D/E$$

    where R_A is the WACC, R_D is the cost of debt, and D/E is the debt-equity ratio.

  D. Implications of Proposition II:

    1. The cost of equity rises as the firm increases its use of debt financing.

    2. The risk of the equity depends on two things: the riskiness of the firm's operations (*business risk*) and the degree of financial leverage (*financial risk*). Business risk determines R_A; financial risk is determined by D/E.

II. The tax case

  A. Proposition I with taxes: The value of the firm levered (V_L) is equal to the value of the firm unlevered (V_U) plus the present value of the interest tax shield:

$$V_L = V_U + T_C \times D$$

    where T_C is the corporate tax rate and D is the amount of debt.

  B. Implications of Proposition I with taxes:

    1. Debt financing is highly advantageous, and, in the extreme, a firm's optimal capital structure is 100 percent debt.

    2. A firm's weighted average cost of capital, WACC, decreases as the firm relies more heavily on debt financing.

Conclusion

The result of our analysis in this section is that, once we include taxes, capital structure definitely matters. However, we immediately reach the illogical conclusion that the optimal capital structure is 100 percent debt. Of course, we have not yet considered the impact of bankruptcy, so our story may change. For future reference, Table 13.4 contains a summary of the various M&M calculations and conclusions.

CONCEPT QUESTIONS

13.4a   What is the relationship between the value of an unlevered firm and the value of a levered firm once we consider the effect of corporate taxes?

13.4b   If we only consider the effect of taxes, what is the optimum capital structure?

13.5 | BANKRUPTCY COSTS

One limit to the amount of debt a firm might use comes in the form of *bankruptcy costs.* As the debt-equity ratio rises, so too does the probability that the firm will be unable to pay its bondholders what was promised to them. When this happens, ownership of the firm's assets is ultimately transferred from the stockholders to the bondholders.

In principle, a firm becomes bankrupt when the value of its assets equals the value of its debt. When this occurs, the value of equity is zero and the stockholders turn over control of the firm to the bondholders. At this point, the bondholders hold assets whose value is exactly equal to what is owed on the debt. In a perfect world, there are no costs associated with this transfer of ownership, and the bondholders don't lose anything.

This idealized view of bankruptcy is not, of course, what happens in the real world. Ironically, it is expensive to go bankrupt. As we discuss, the costs associated with bankruptcy may eventually offset the tax-related gains from leverage.

Direct Bankruptcy Costs

When the value of a firm's assets equals the value of its debt, then the firm is economically bankrupt in the sense that the equity has no value. However, the formal turning over of the assets to the bondholders is a *legal* process, not an economic one. There are legal and administrative costs to bankruptcy, and it has been remarked that bankruptcies are to lawyers what blood is to sharks.

Because of the expenses associated with bankruptcy, bondholders won't get all that they are owed. Some fraction of the firm's assets will "disappear" in the legal process of going bankrupt. These are the legal and administrative expenses associated with the bankruptcy proceeding. We call these costs **direct bankruptcy costs**.

Indirect Bankruptcy Costs

Because it is expensive to go bankrupt, a firm will spend resources to avoid doing so. When a firm is having significant problems in meeting its debt obligations, we say that it is experiencing financial distress. Some financially distressed firms ultimately file for bankruptcy, but most do not because they are able to recover or otherwise survive.

The costs of avoiding a bankruptcy filing incurred by a financially distressed firm are called **indirect bankruptcy costs**. We use the term **financial distress costs** to refer generically to the direct and indirect costs associated with going bankrupt and/or avoiding a bankruptcy filing.

The problems that come up in financial distress are particularly severe, and the financial distress costs are thus larger, when the stockholders and the bondholders are different groups. Until the firm is legally bankrupt, the stockholders control it. They, of course, will take actions in their own economic interests. Since the stockholders can be wiped out in a legal bankruptcy, they have a very strong incentive to avoid a bankruptcy filing.

The bondholders, on the other hand, are primarily concerned with protecting the value of the firm's assets and will try to take control away from the stockholders. They have a strong incentive to seek bankruptcy to protect their interests and keep stockholders from further dissipating the assets of the firm. The net effect of all this fighting is that a long, drawn-out, and potentially quite expensive legal battle gets started.

Meanwhile, as the wheels of justice turn in their ponderous way, the assets of the firm lose value because management is busy trying to avoid bankruptcy instead of running the business. Normal operations are disrupted, and sales are lost. Valuable employees leave, potentially fruitful programs are dropped to preserve cash, and otherwise profitable investments are not taken.

These are all indirect bankruptcy costs, or costs of financial distress. Whether or not the firm ultimately goes bankrupt, the net effect is a loss of value because the firm chose to use debt in its capital structure. It is this possibility of loss that limits the amount of debt that a firm will choose to use.

direct bankruptcy costs
The costs that are directly associated with bankruptcy, such as legal and administrative expenses.

indirect bankruptcy costs
The costs of avoiding a bankruptcy filing incurred by a financially distressed firm.

financial distress costs
The direct and indirect costs associated with going bankrupt or experiencing financial distress.

13.6 | OPTIMAL CAPITAL STRUCTURE

Our previous two sections have established the basis for an optimal capital structure. A firm will borrow because the interest tax shield is valuable. At relatively low debt levels, the probability of bankruptcy and financial distress is low, and the benefit from debt outweighs the cost. At very high debt levels, the possibility of financial distress is a chronic, ongoing problem for the firm, so the benefit from debt financing may be more than offset by the financial distress costs. Based on our discussion, it would appear that an optimal capital structure exists somewhere in between these extremes.

The Static Theory of Capital Structure

static theory of capital structure
Theory that a firm borrows up to the point where the tax benefit from an extra dollar in debt is exactly equal to the cost that comes from the increased probability of financial distress.

The theory of capital structure that we have outlined is called the **static theory of capital structure**. It says that firms borrow up to the point where the tax benefit from an extra dollar in debt is exactly equal to the cost that comes from the increased probability of financial distress. We call this the static theory because it assumes that the firm is fixed in terms of its assets and operations and it only considers possible changes in the debt-equity ratio.

The static theory is illustrated in Figure 13.5, which plots the value of the firm, V_L, against the amount of debt, D. In Figure 13.5, we have drawn lines corresponding to three

---

FIGURE 13.5

The static theory of capital structure: The optimal capital structure and the value of the firm

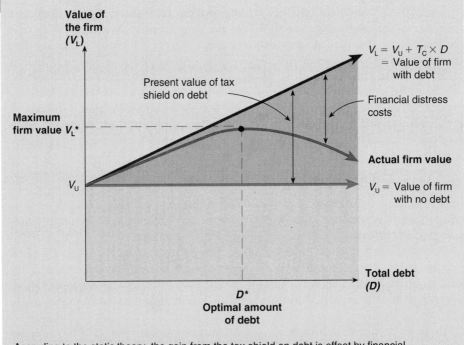

According to the static theory, the gain from the tax shield on debt is offset by financial distress costs. An optimal capital structure exists that just balances the additional gain from leverage against the added financial distress costs.

different stories. The first is M&M Proposition I with no taxes. This is the horizontal line extending from V_U, and it indicates that the value of the firm is unaffected by its capital structure. The second case, M&M Proposition I with corporate taxes, is given by the upward-sloping straight line. These two cases are exactly the same as the ones we previously illustrated in Figure 13.4.

The third case in Figure 13.5 illustrates our current discussion: The value of the firm rises to a maximum and then declines beyond that point. This is the picture that we get from our static theory. The maximum value of the firm, V_L^*, is reached at a debt level of D^*, so this is the optimal amount of borrowing. Put another way, the firm's optimal capital structure is composed of D^*/V_L^* in debt and $(1 - D^*/V_L^*)$ in equity.

The final thing to notice in Figure 13.5 is that the difference between the value of the firm in our static theory and the M&M value of the firm with taxes is the loss in value from the possibility of financial distress. Also, the difference between the static theory value of the firm and the M&M value with no taxes is the gain from leverage, net of distress costs.

Optimal Capital Structure and the Cost of Capital

As we discussed earlier, the capital structure that maximizes the value of the firm is also the one that minimizes the cost of capital. With the help of Figure 13.6, we can illustrate this point and tie together our discussion of capital structure and cost of capital. As we have seen, there are essentially three cases. We will use the simplest of the three cases as a starting point and then build up to the static theory of capital structure. Along the way, we will pay particular attention to the connection between capital structure, firm value, and cost of capital.

Figure 13.6 illustrates the original Modigliani and Miller, M&M, no-tax, no-bankruptcy argument in Case I. This is the most basic case. In the top part, we have plotted the value of the firm, V_L, against total debt, D. When there are no taxes, bankruptcy costs, or other real-world imperfections, we know that the total value of the firm is not affected by its debt policy, so V_L is simply constant. The bottom part of Figure 13.6 tells the same story in terms of the cost of capital. Here, the weighted average cost of capital, WACC, is plotted against the debt-to-equity ratio, D/E. As with total firm value, the overall cost of capital is not affected by debt policy in this basic case, so the WACC is constant.

Next, we consider what happens to the original M&M arguments once taxes are introduced. As Case II illustrates, the firm's value now critically depends on its debt policy. The more the firm borrows, the more it is worth. From our earlier discussion, we know that this happens because interest payments are tax deductible, and the gain in firm value is just equal to the present value of the interest tax shield.

In the bottom part of Figure 13.6, notice how the WACC declines as the firm uses more and more debt financing. As the firm increases its financial leverage, the cost of equity does increase, but this increase is more than offset by the tax break associated with debt financing. As a result, the firm's overall cost of capital declines.

To finish our story, we include the impact of bankruptcy, or financial distress, costs to get Case III. As is shown in the top part of Figure 13.6, the value of the firm will not be as large as we previously indicated. The reason is that the firm's value is reduced by the present value of the potential future bankruptcy costs. These costs grow as the firm borrows more and more, and they eventually overwhelm the tax advantage of debt financing. The optimal capital structure occurs at D^*, the point at which the tax saving from an additional dollar in debt financing is exactly balanced by the increased bankruptcy costs associated with the additional borrowing. This is the essence of the static theory of capital structure.

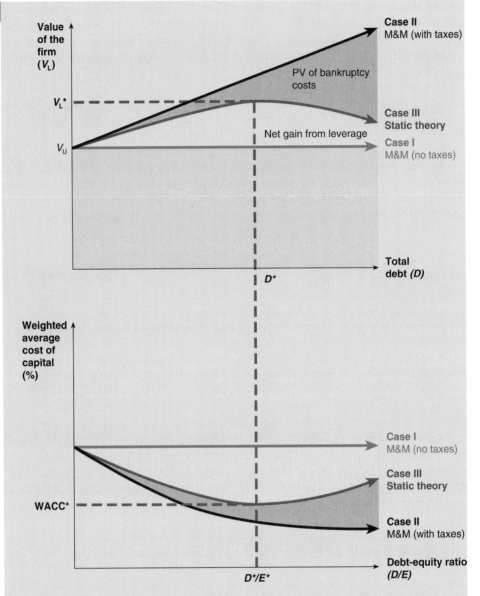

Case II
With corporate taxes and no bankruptcy costs, the value of the firm increases and the
weighted average cost of capital decreases as the amount of debt goes up.

Case III
With corporate taxes and bankruptcy costs, the value of the firm, V_L, reaches a maximum
at D^*, the optimal amount of borrowing. At the same time, the weighted average cost of
capital, WACC, is minimized at D^*/E^*.

The bottom part of Figure 13.6 presents the optimal capital structure in terms of the cost of capital. Corresponding to D^*, the optimal debt level, is the optimal debt-to-equity ratio, D^*/E^*. At this level of debt financing, the lowest possible weighted average cost of capital, **WACC***, occurs.

Capital Structure: Some Managerial Recommendations

The static model that we have described is not capable of identifying a precise optimal capital structure, but it does point out two of the more relevant factors: taxes and financial distress. We can draw some limited conclusions concerning these.

Taxes   First of all, the tax benefit from leverage is obviously only important to firms that are in a tax-paying position. Firms with substantial accumulated losses will get little value from the interest tax shield. Furthermore, firms that have substantial tax shields from other sources, such as depreciation, will get less benefit from leverage.

Also, not all firms have the same tax rate. The higher the tax rate, the greater the incentive to borrow.

Financial Distress   Firms with a greater risk of experiencing financial distress will borrow less than firms with a lower risk of financial distress. For example, all other things being equal, the greater the volatility in EBIT, the less a firm should borrow.

In addition, financial distress is more costly for some firms than for others. The costs of financial distress depend primarily on the firm's assets. In particular, financial distress costs will be determined by how easily ownership of those assets can be transferred.

For example, a firm with mostly tangible assets that can be sold without great loss in value will have an incentive to borrow more. For firms that rely heavily on intangibles, such as employee talent or growth opportunities, debt will be less attractive since these assets effectively cannot be sold.

CONCEPT QUESTIONS

13.6a   Can you describe the trade-off that defines the static theory of capital structure?

13.6b   What are the important factors in making capital structure decisions?

13.7 | OBSERVED CAPITAL STRUCTURES

No two firms have identical capital structures. Nonetheless, there are some regular elements that we see when we start looking at actual capital structures. We discuss a few of these next.

The most striking thing we observe about capital structures is their wide variation across industries. To illustrate, Table 13.5 presents debt-equity ratios for various Canadian industries in the fourth quarter of 2006. The use of debt ranges from $.20 per one dollar of equity for insurance companies to $4.92 for non-depository credit intermediaries, such as credit card companies.

Different industries have different operating characteristics in terms of, for example, EBIT volatility and asset types, and there does appear to be some connection between

Capital structures for
Canadian companies

Industries	Debt to equity ratio
Total, all industries	**0.89**
Total, non-financial industries	**0.96**
Primary industries	
Agriculture, forestry, fishing and hunting	1.33
Oil and gas extraction and support activities	0.85
Mining (except oil and gas)	0.48
Utilities	0.96
Construction	1.54
Manufacturing	0.59
Wholesale trade	0.79
Retail trade	1.16
Service industries	
Transportation and warehousing	1.70
Information and cultural industries	1.37
Real estate and rental and leasing	1.96
Professional, scientific and technical services	0.79
Administrative and support, waste management and remediation services	1.13
Educational, healthcare and social assistance services	0.81
Arts, entertainment and recreation	2.82
Accommodation and food services	3.28
Repair, maintenance and personal services	0.93
Total, finance and insurance industries	**0.70**
Non-depository credit intermediation	4.92
Insurance carriers and related activities	0.20
Activities related to credit intermediation	0.52
Depository credit intermediation	0.41
Securities, commodity contracts, and other financial investments and related activities	0.63

Source: Statistics Canada, Quarterly Financial Statistics for Enterprises, Fourth quarter 2006.

these characteristics and capital structure. For instance, accommodation and food service companies carry four times more debt than professional, scientific, and technical services companies. This disparity can be explained by the different costs of financial distress. Accommodation and food service companies have a much larger portion of tangible assets than professional services companies, which depend more on intangibles such as employee talent.

Our story involving tax savings and financial distress costs undoubtedly supplies part of the reason, but, to date, there is no fully satisfactory theory that explains observed capital structures. Take a look at our nearby *Work the Web* box for more on actual capital structures.

CONCEPT QUESTIONS

13.7a   Do Canadian corporations rely heavily on debt financing?

13.7b   What regularities do we observe in capital structures?

WORK THE WEB

When it comes to capital structure, all companies (and industries) are not created equal. To illustrate, we looked up some capital structure information on TransCanada Corporation (TRP), the natural gas utility company based in Calgary, Alberta, and Biovail (BVF), the biotechnology company headquartered in Mississauga, Ontario, using the ratio area of **investor.reuters.com**. TransCanada's capital structure looks like this:

FINANCIAL STRENGTH

	Company	Industry	Sector	S&P 500
Quick Ratio (MRQ)	0.53	0.50	0.55	1.23
Current Ratio (MRQ)	0.64	0.98	1.00	1.75
LT Debt to Equity (MRQ)	1.64	1.33	1.53	0.60
Total Debt to Equity (MRQ)	1.78	1.51	1.79	0.75
Interest Coverage (TTM)	3.19	3.48	5.18	13.73

For every dollar of equity, TransCanada has long-term debt of $1.64 and total debt of $1.78. Compare this result to Biovail:

FINANCIAL STRENGTH

	Company	Industry	Sector	S&P 500
Quick Ratio (MRQ)	3.09	3.07	2.01	1.23
Current Ratio (MRQ)	3.39	3.76	2.71	1.74
LT Debt to Equity (MRQ)	0.32	0.41	0.37	0.60
Total Debt to Equity (MRQ)	0.33	0.45	0.43	0.75
Interest Coverage (TTM)	4.76	14.26	15.56	13.78

For every dollar of equity, Biovail has only $0.32 of long-term debt and total debt of $0.33. When we examine the industry and sector averages, the differences are again apparent. The natural gas utilities industry, on average, has $1.33 of long-term and $1.51 of total debt for every dollar of equity. By comparison, the biotechnology industry, on average, has only $0.41 of long-term debt and $0.45 of total debt for every dollar of equity. Thus, we see that choice of capital structure is a management decision, but it is clearly also influenced by industry characteristics.

13.8 | A QUICK LOOK AT THE BANKRUPTCY PROCESS

As we have discussed, one of the consequences of using debt is the possibility of financial distress, which can be defined in several ways:

1. *Business failure.* This term is usually used to refer to a situation in which a business has terminated with a loss to creditors, but even an all-equity firm can fail.

2. *Legal bankruptcy.* Firms or creditors bring petitions to a federal court for bankruptcy. **Bankruptcy** is a legal proceeding for liquidating or reorganizing a business.

3. *Technical insolvency.* Technical insolvency occurs when a firm is unable to meet its financial obligations.

4. *Accounting insolvency.* Firms with negative net worth are insolvent on the books. This happens when the total book liabilities exceed the book value of the total assets.

We now very briefly discuss some of the terms and more relevant issues associated with bankruptcy and financial distress.

bankruptcy
A legal proceeding for liquidating or reorganizing a business.

The Office of the Superintendent of Bankruptcy provides information on bankruptcies and insolvencies in Canada. See **www.osb-bsf.gc.ca**.

Liquidation and Reorganization

liquidation
Termination of the firm as a going concern.

reorganization
Financial restructuring of a failing firm to attempt to continue operations as a going concern.

You can find the BIA and the CCAA at **laws.justice.gc.ca.**

Firms that cannot or choose not to make contractually required payments to creditors have two basic options: liquidation or reorganization. **Liquidation** means termination of the firm as a going concern, and it involves selling off the assets of the firm. The proceeds, net of selling costs, are distributed to creditors in order of established priority. **Reorganization** is the option of keeping the firm a going concern; it often involves issuing new securities to replace old securities. Liquidation or reorganization is the result of a bankruptcy proceeding. Which occurs depends on whether the firm is worth more "dead or alive."

In Canada, two federal laws govern bankruptcy liquidation and reorganization—the *Bankruptcy and Insolvency Act (BIA)* and the *Companies' Creditors Arrangement Act (CCAA)*. Both laws are administered by the Office of the Superintendent of Bankruptcy.

The BIA was enacted in 1919 and then amended in 1949, 1992, and 1997. Both individuals and businesses can seek creditor protection under the BIA. The BIA must be used by companies with under $5 million of debt. Companies with more than $5 million of debt can use either the BIA or the CCAA.

The CCAA was introduced in 1933 in response to the harsh economic conditions of the Great Depression. In 1997 it was revised to make it more consistent with the BIA. To apply for protection under the CCAA, the debtor's debts must exceed $5 million.

The CCAA is attractive to insolvent companies because its guidelines are much less specific and more flexible than those of the BIA. However, reorganization under the CCAA is more costly, because all proceedings are directed by the Court. Thus, the CCAA is usually used as an instrument for the reorganization of very large companies. For example, in January 29, 2004, Stelco, the second-largest steel maker in Canada, applied for creditor protection under the CCAA to reorganize the company and keep it as a going concern. In Canada, most reorganizations occur under the BIA. Our discussion below is based on the BIA of 1997.

Bankruptcy Liquidation   Liquidation takes places when a firm is terminated as a going concern and the trustee orders the sale of the assets of the firm. The following sequence of events is typical:

1. A petition is filed in a federal court. A corporation may file a voluntary petition, or involuntary petitions may be filed against the corporation by several of its creditors.
2. A trustee-in-bankruptcy is elected by the creditors to take over the assets of the debtor corporation. The trustee will attempt to liquidate the assets.
3. When the assets are liquidated, after payment of the bankruptcy administration costs, the proceeds are distributed among the creditors.
4. If any proceeds remain, after expenses and payments to creditors, they are distributed to the shareholders.

The distribution of the proceeds of the liquidation occurs according to the following priority list. The higher a claim is on this list, the more likely it is to be paid. In many of these categories, there are various limitations and qualifications that we omit for the sake of brevity.

1. Administrative expenses associated with the bankruptcy.
2. Other expenses arising after the filing of an involuntary bankruptcy petition but before the appointment of a trustee.
3. Wages, salaries, and commissions.

4. Contributions to employee benefit plans.

5. Consumer claims.

6. Government tax claims.

7. Payment to unsecured creditors.

8. Payment to preferred stockholders.

9. Payment to common stockholders.

Two qualifications to this list are in order. The first concerns secured creditors. Such creditors are entitled to the proceeds from the sale of the security and are outside this ordering. However, if the secured property is liquidated and provides cash insufficient to cover the amount owed, the secured creditors join with unsecured creditors in dividing the remaining liquidated value. In contrast, if the secured property is liquidated for proceeds greater than the secured claim, the net proceeds are used to pay unsecured creditors and others. The second qualification to the priority list is that, in reality, what happens, and who gets what in the event of bankruptcy, is subject to much negotiation, and, as a result, the priority list is frequently not followed.

Bankruptcy Reorganization   Corporate reorganization takes place under Part III of the BIA of 1997. Its general objective is to restructure the corporation with some provision for the repayment of creditors. A typical sequence of events follows:

1. A voluntary petition can be filed by the corporation, or an involuntary petition can be filed by creditors.

2. A federal judge either approves or denies the petition. If the petition is approved, a time for filing proofs of claims is set.

3. In most cases, the corporation (the "debtor in possession") continues to run the business.

4. The corporation (and, in certain cases, the creditors) submits a reorganization plan.

5. Creditors and shareholders are divided into classes. A class of creditors accepts the plan if a majority of the class agrees to the plan.

6. After its acceptance by creditors, the plan is confirmed by the court.

7. Payments in cash, property, and securities are made to creditors and shareholders. The plan may provide for the issuance of new securities.

8. For some fixed length of time, the firm operates according to the provisions of the reorganization plan.

The corporation may wish to allow the old stockholders to retain some participation in the firm. Needless to say, this may involve some protest by the holders of unsecured debt.

To give you some idea of the costs associated with a bankruptcy, consider the case of the energy giant Enron, which filed for bankruptcy in December 2001. The company wanted to reorganize through the bankruptcy process, but complications soon arose. In fact, the company filed at least six reorganization plans. By the end of 2004, lawyers, consultants, accountants, and other professionals had earned nearly $1 *billion* in fees, and the company was still in bankruptcy. The next largest fees appear to have been paid to those involved in the WorldCom bankruptcy. The fees in that case reached a mere $600 million.

It is not easy for a financially troubled company to earn approval for a reorganization plan from its creditors. For example, the Montreal-based discount airliner Jetsgo stopped all operations on March 11, 2005, leaving tens of thousands of travellers holding useless tickets. Two months later, as its court protection under the CCAA was expiring, Jetsgo had a reorganization plan to start operations as a charter airline. Jetsgo's largest creditor, Moneris Solutions Corp., however, rejected the plan. Without Moneris's support, Jetsgo could not get the approval of the majority of its creditors. Shortly after, the trustee proceeded with the sale of the company's assets and distribution of the money.

In some cases, the bankruptcy procedure is needed to invoke the "cram-down" power of the bankruptcy court. Under certain circumstances, a class of creditors can be forced to accept a bankruptcy plan even if they vote not to approve it, hence the remarkably apt description "cram down." For example, when Air Canada was operating under the protection of the CCAA in 2003, some of its creditors wanted to cease business operations with the company, but were required to continue under court order. Specifically, Global Payments was ordered to continue processing credit card transactions for Air Canada, despite Global's objection to doing so.

Financial Management and the Bankruptcy Process

For comprehensive information about bankruptcy visit **www.bankruptcy canada.com.**

It may seem a little odd, but the right to go bankrupt is very valuable. There are several reasons why this is true. First of all, from an operational standpoint, when a firm files for bankruptcy, there is an immediate "stay" on creditors, usually meaning that payments to creditors will cease, and creditors will have to await the outcome of the bankruptcy process to find out if and how much they will be paid. This stay gives the firm time to evaluate its options, and it prevents what is usually termed a "race to the courthouse steps" by creditors and others.

Beyond this, some bankruptcy filings are actually strategic actions intended to improve a firm's competitive position. Returning to our Air Canada example, in 2003 the company did not generate enough cash to pay its debts following the September 11 terrorist attack, the Toronto SARS outbreak, and the start of the war in Iraq. As a result, Air Canada decided to seek creditor protection under the CCAA in order to restructure its assets and escape formal bankruptcy liquidation. The company was able to terminate its existing labour agreements, lay off large numbers of workers, and slash wages for the remaining employees. In other words, at least in the eyes of its critics, Air Canada essentially used the bankruptcy process as a vehicle to reduce labour costs.

Bankruptcies usually bring large losses to investors, employees, customers, and vendors. As of early 2007, the largest bankruptcies ever, in terms of assets, were the 2001 flameout of energy giant Enron (with $63.4 billion in assets) and the 2002 collapse of telecommunications giant WorldCom (with $107 billion in assets). The 2003 bankruptcy filing of Italian dairy company Parmalat may have topped them both in terms of relative importance. This company, by itself, represented 1.5 percent of the Italian gross national product! Given the huge losses associated with bankruptcies, the ability to predict them could save a lot of money. The accompanying *Reality Bytes* box presents one tool for bankruptcy prediction.

Agreements to Avoid Bankruptcy

When a firm defaults on an obligation, it can avoid a bankruptcy filing. Because the legal process of bankruptcy can be lengthy and expensive, it is often in everyone's best interest to devise a "workout" that avoids a bankruptcy filing. Much of the time, creditors can work with the management of a company that has defaulted on a loan contract. Voluntary arrangements to restructure, or "reschedule," the company's debt can be and often are

REALITY BYTES

The Z-score—A Crystal Ball For Bankruptcy Prediction

More than 8,000 businesses went bankrupt in Canada in 2006. Will your investment be next? An important customer? Your employer? We would avoid many headaches and sleepless nights, if we could only predict bankruptcies before they occur. Fortunately, this magic prediction tool exists. It is called the Z-score.

About 40 years ago, Edward Altman, a finance professor at New York University, developed the Z-score model for predicting the financial distress of companies. He used the statistical technique of multiple discriminant analysis to identify the financial ratios and their weights that can be used for determining whether a company will go bankrupt or not. The final model is a linear equation of five financial ratios:

$$Z = 1.2 \frac{Working\ Capital}{Total\ Assets} + 1.4 \frac{Retained\ Earnings}{Total\ Assets} + 3.3 \frac{EBIT}{Total\ Assets} + 0.6 \frac{MV\ of\ Equity}{Total\ Liabilities} + 1.0 \frac{Sales}{Total\ Assets}$$

These ratios can be easily computed using companies' financial statements and their market stock prices. If a company's Z-score is above 2.99, then it is financially sound. If it has a Z-score between 1.81 and 2.99, the company is in the grey area. If the company's Z-score is below 1.81, it is in financial distress. The Z-score has proven its viability in the real business world in different time periods and in different countries. It correctly predicts 95 percent of bankruptcies one year and 70 percent of bankruptcies two years prior to the event.

Despite widespread adoption in the business community, the last two ratios of the equation limit the applicability of the original Z-score model. Specifically, how can we calculate the Z-score for private firms, which do not have a market value of equity (the fourth ratio)? How do we allow for considerable

variation in total assets turnover (the last ratio) across different industries? To address these problems, Altman developed two modified versions of the original Z-score model. While the original model calculates the Z-score for public manufacturing companies, two modified versions compute the Z-score for private manufacturers and all non-manufacturing firms. The Z-score for private manufacturing companies:

$$Z = .717 \frac{Working\ Capital}{Total\ Assets} + .847 \frac{Retained\ Earnings}{Total\ Assets} + 3.107 \frac{EBIT}{Total\ Assets} + 0.420 \frac{BV\ of\ Equity}{Total\ Liabilities} + .998 \frac{Sales}{Total\ Assets}$$

The Z-score for non-manufacturing companies:

$$Z = 6.56 \frac{Working\ Capital}{Total\ Assets} + 3.26 \frac{Retained\ Earnings}{Total\ Assets} + 6.72 \frac{EBIT}{Total\ Assets} + 1.05 \frac{BV\ of\ Equity}{Total\ Liabilities}$$

Note the use of the book value of equity in the fourth ratio and the changed coefficients. The cut-off Z-scores for the modified models changed as well. For example, for financially sound private manufacturing firms the Z-score is above 2.9, and for financially sound non-manufacturing firms it is above 2.6.

Availability of all the required information and ease of use have contributed to the wide use of the three Z-score models among practitioners. A quick calculation of the Z-score can be done in Excel, and several Web sites offer Z-score calculators. For example, visit an online Z-score calculator at www.jaxworks.com/calcpage.htm and calculate the Z-score for a large Canadian company. How can you interpret this score?

made. This may involve *extension,* which postpones the date of payment, or *composition,* which allows a reduced payment.

CONCEPT QUESTIONS

13.8a What are the differences between the CCAA and BIA?

13.8b What is the difference between liquidation and reorganization?

KEY EQUATIONS:

I. Symbols

V_L = the value of the levered firm
V_U = the value of the unlevered firm
R_A = the WACC
R_D = the cost of debt
R_E = the cost of equity
D = the market value of debt
E = the market value of equity
T_C = the corporate tax rate

II. Modigliani-Miller Propositions (No Taxes):

Proposition I:
$$\mathbf{V_L = V_U} \tag{13.1}$$

Proposition II:
$$\mathbf{R_E = R_A + (R_A - R_D) \times (D/E)} \tag{13.2}$$

III. Modigliani-Miller Propositions (With Taxes):

Present value of the interest tax shield
$$\begin{aligned} &= (T_C \times D \times R_D)/R_D \\ &= T_C \times D \end{aligned} \tag{13.3}$$

Proposition I:
$$\mathbf{V_L = V_U + T_C \times D} \tag{13.4}$$

SUMMARY AND CONCLUSIONS

The ideal mixture of debt and equity for a firm—its optimal capital structure—is the one that maximizes the value of the firm and minimizes the overall cost of capital. If we ignore taxes, financial distress costs, and any other imperfections, we find that there is no ideal mixture. Under these circumstances, the firm's capital structure is simply irrelevant.

If we consider the effect of corporate taxes, we find that capital structure matters a great deal. This conclusion is based on the fact that interest is tax deductible and thus generates a valuable tax shield. Unfortunately, we also find that the optimal capital structure is 100 percent debt, which is not something we observe in healthy firms.

We next introduced costs associated with bankruptcy, or, more generally, financial distress. These costs reduce the attractiveness of debt financing. We concluded that an optimal capital structure exists when the net tax saving from an additional dollar in interest just equals the increase in expected financial distress costs. This is the essence of the static theory of capital structure.

When we examine actual capital structures, we find a wide variation in the use of debt across industries. This variation suggests that the nature of a firm's assets and operations is an important determinant of its capital structure.

CHAPTER REVIEW AND SELF-TEST PROBLEMS

13.1 **EBIT and EPS.** Suppose the Grand Prairie Corporation has decided in favour of a capital restructuring that involves increasing its existing $5 million in debt to $25 million. The interest rate on the debt is 12 percent and is not expected to change. The firm currently has one million shares outstanding, and the price per share is $40. If the restructuring is expected to increase the ROE, what is the minimum level for EBIT that Grand Prairie's management must be expecting? Ignore taxes in your answer.

13.2 **M&M Proposition II (no taxes).** The Pro Bono Corporation has a WACC of 20 percent. Its cost of debt is 12 percent. If Pro Bono's debt-equity ratio is 2, what is its cost of equity capital? Ignore taxes in your answer.

13.3 **M&M Proposition I (with corporate taxes).** Suppose TransGlobal Co. currently has no debt and its equity is worth $20,000. If the corporate tax rate is 30 percent, what will the value of the firm be if TransGlobal borrows $6,000 and uses the proceeds to buy up stock?

◼ Answers to Chapter Review and Self-Test Problems

13.1 To answer, we can calculate the break-even EBIT. At any EBIT above this, the increased financial leverage will increase EPS. Under the old capital structure, the interest bill is $5 million × .12 = $600,000. There are one million shares of stock, so, ignoring taxes, EPS is (EBIT − $600,000)/1 million.

Under the new capital structure, the interest expense will be $25 million × .12 = $3 million. Furthermore, the debt rises by $20 million. This amount is sufficient to repurchase $20 million/40 = 500,000 shares of stock, leaving 500,000 outstanding. EPS is thus (EBIT − $3 million)/500,000.

Now that we know how to calculate EPS under both scenarios, we set the two expressions for EPS equal to each other and solve for the break-even EBIT:

$$(EBIT − \$600,000)/1 \text{ million} = (EBIT − \$3 \text{ million})/500,000$$
$$EBIT − \$600,000 = 2 × (EBIT − \$3 \text{ million})$$
$$EBIT = \$5,400,000$$

Verify that, in either case, EPS is $4.80 when EBIT is $5.4 million.

13.2 According to M&M Proposition II (no taxes), the cost of equity is:

$$R_E = R_A + (R_A − R_D) × (D/E)$$
$$= 20\% + (20\% − 12\%) × 2$$
$$= 36\%$$

13.3 After the debt issue, TransGlobal will be worth the original $20,000 plus the present value of the tax shield. According to M&M Proposition I with taxes, the present value of the tax shield is $T_C × D$, or .30 × $6,000 = $1,800, so the firm is worth $20,000 + 1,800 = $21,800.

CRITICAL THINKING AND CONCEPTS REVIEW

13.1 **Capital Structure Goal.** What is the basic goal of financial management with regard to capital structure?

13.2 Financial Leverage.   Why is the use of debt financing referred to as using financial "leverage"?

13.3 Homemade Leverage.   What is homemade leverage?

13.4 Business Risk versus Financial Risk.   Explain what is meant by business and financial risk. Suppose Firm A has greater business risk than Firm B. Is it true that Firm A also has a higher cost of equity capital? Explain.

13.5 M&M Propositions.   How would you answer in the following debate?

Q: Isn't it true that the riskiness of a firm's equity will rise if the firm increases its use of debt financing?

A: Yes, that's the essence of M&M Proposition II.

Q: And isn't it true that, as a firm increases its use of borrowing, the likelihood of default increases, which increases the risk of the firm's debt?

A: Yes.

Q: In other words, increased borrowing increases the risk of the equity *and* the debt?

A: That's right.

Q: Well, given that the firm uses only debt and equity financing, and given that the risk of both is increased by increased borrowing, does it not follow that increasing debt increases the overall risk of the firm and therefore decreases the value of the firm?

A: ??

13.6 Optimal Capital Structure.   Is there an easily identifiable debt-equity ratio that will maximize the value of a firm? Why or why not?

13.7 Observed Capital Structures.   Refer to the observed capital structures given in Table 13.5 of the text. What do you notice about the types of industries with respect to their average debt-equity ratios? Are certain types of industries more likely to be highly leveraged than others? What are some possible reasons for this observed segmentation? Do the operating results and tax history of the firms play a role? How about their future earnings prospects? Explain.

13.8 Bankruptcy and Corporate Ethics.   Firms sometimes use the threat of a bankruptcy filing to force creditors to renegotiate terms. Critics argue that in such cases, the firm is using bankruptcy laws "as a sword rather than a shield." Is this an ethical tactic?

13.9 Bankruptcy and Corporate Ethics.   As mentioned in the text, Air Canada filed for bankruptcy, at least in part, as a means of reducing labour costs. Is this a proper use of the bankruptcy process?

QUESTIONS AND PROBLEMS

Basic
(Questions 1–15)

1. **EBIT and Leverage.**   Iroquois, Inc., has no debt outstanding and a total market value of $90,000. Earnings before interest and taxes, EBIT, are projected to be $15,000 if economic conditions are normal. If there is strong expansion in the economy, then EBIT will be 20 percent higher. If there is a recession, then EBIT will be 30 percent lower. Iroquois is considering a $45,000 debt issue with a 5 percent interest rate. The proceeds will be used to repurchase shares of stock. There are currently 4,500 shares outstanding. Ignore taxes for this problem.

   a. Calculate earnings per share, EPS, under each of the three economic scenarios before any debt is issued. Also, calculate the percentage changes in EPS when the economy expands or enters a recession.

b. Repeat part (*a*) assuming that Iroquois goes through with recapitalization. What do you observe?

2. **EBIT, Taxes, and Leverage.** Repeat parts (*a*) and (*b*) in Problem 1 assuming Iroquois has a tax rate of 35 percent.

3. **ROE and Leverage.** Suppose the company in Problem 1 has a market-to-book ratio of 1.0.

   a. Calculate return on equity, ROE, under each of the three economic scenarios before any debt is issued. Also, calculate the percentage changes in ROE for economic expansion and recession, assuming no taxes.

   b. Repeat part (*a*) assuming the firm goes through with the proposed recapitalization.

   c. Repeat parts (*a*) and (*b*) of this problem assuming the firm has a tax rate of 35 percent.

4. **Break-Even EBIT.** Inuvic Corporation is comparing two different capital structures, an all-equity plan (Plan I) and a levered plan (Plan II). Under Plan I, Inuvic would have 800,000 shares of stock outstanding. Under Plan II, there would be 320,000 shares of stock outstanding and $10 million in debt outstanding. The interest rate on the debt is 10 percent, and there are no taxes.

   a. If EBIT is $1.5 million, which plan will result in the higher EPS?

   b. If EBIT is $5 million, which plan will result in the higher EPS?

   c. What is the break-even EBIT?

5. **M&M and Stock Value.** In Problem 4, use M&M Proposition I to find the price per share of equity. What is the value of the firm under each of the two proposed plans?

6. **Break-Even EBIT and Leverage.** Betts Co. is comparing two different capital structures. Plan I would result in 2,000 shares of stock and $40,000 in debt. Plan II would result in 4,000 shares of stock and $20,000 in debt. The interest rate on the debt is 10 percent.

   a. Ignoring taxes, compare both of these plans to an all-equity plan assuming that EBIT will be $5,000. The all-equity plan would result in 6,000 shares of stock outstanding. Which of the three plans has the highest EPS? The lowest?

   b. In part (*a*), what are the break-even levels of EBIT for each plan as compared to that for an all-equity plan? Is one higher than the other? Why?

   c. Ignoring taxes, when will EPS be identical for Plans I and II?

   d. Repeat parts (*a*), (*b*), and (*c*) assuming that the corporate tax rate is 38 percent. Are the break-even levels of EBIT different from before? Why or why not?

7. **Leverage and Stock Value.** Ignoring taxes in Problem 6, what is the price per share of equity under Plan I? Plan II? What principle is illustrated by your answers?

8. **Homemade Leverage.** Igloo, Inc., a prominent consumer products firm, is debating whether or not to convert its all-equity capital structure to one that is 30 percent debt. Currently, there are 1,200 shares outstanding and the price per share is $90. EBIT is expected to remain at $3,000 per year forever. The interest rate on new debt is 8 percent, and there are no taxes.

   a. Melanie, a shareholder of the firm, owns 100 shares of stock. What is her cash flow under the current capital structure, assuming the firm has a dividend payout rate of 100 percent?

   b. What will Melanie's cash flow be under the proposed capital structure of the firm? Assume that she keeps all 100 of her shares.

c.   Suppose Igloo does convert, but Melanie prefers the current all-equity capital structure. Show how she could unlever her shares of stock to recreate the original capital structure.

d.   Using your answer to part (*c*), explain why Igloo's choice of capital structure is irrelevant.

9.   **Homemade Leverage.**   Buffett Enterprises is considering a change from its current capital structure. Buffett currently has an all-equity capital structure and is considering a capital structure with 40 percent debt. There are currently 2,000 shares outstanding at a price per share of $100. EBIT is expected to remain constant at $29,000. The interest rate on new debt is 7 percent and there are no taxes.

a.   Rebecca owns $16,000 worth of stock in Buffett Enterprises. If the firm has a 100 percent payout, what is her cash flow?

b.   What would her cash flow be under the new capital structure, assuming that she keeps all of her shares?

c.   Suppose the company does convert to the new capital structure. Show how Rebecca can maintain her current cash flow.

d.   Under your answer to part (*c*), explain why Buffett's choice of capital structure is irrelevant.

10. **M&M and Taxes.**   Great Expectations uses no debt. The weighted average cost of capital is 12 percent. The current market value of the company is $45 million. The corporate tax rate is 40 percent. What is the value of the company if Great Expectations converts to debt-equity ratio of 1? What if the debt-equity ratio is 2?

11. **M&M and Taxes.**   In the previous question, suppose the corporate tax rate was 30 percent. What is the value of the firm under each of the three debt-equity scenarios? What does this tell you about corporate tax rates and the value of the firm?

12. **Calculating WACC.**   North Star Industries has a debt-equity ratio of 1.5. Its WACC is 11 percent, and its cost of debt is 6 percent. There is no corporate tax.

a.   What is North Star's cost of equity capital?

b.   What would the cost of equity be if the debt-equity ratio were 2.0? What if it were 0.5? What if it were zero?

13. **Calculating WACC.**   Saskatoon Corp. has no debt but can borrow at 7 percent. The firm's WACC is currently 10 percent, and there is no corporate tax.

a.   What is Saskatoon's cost of equity?

b.   If the firm converts to 30 percent debt, what will its cost of equity be?

c.   If the firm converts to 60 percent debt, what will its cost of equity be?

d.   What is Saskatoon's WACC in part (*b*)? In part (*c*)?

14. **M&M and Taxes.**   Strauss & Co. can borrow at 8 percent. Strauss currently has no debt, and the cost of equity is 15 percent. The current value of the firm is $480,000. What will the value be if Strauss borrows $90,000 and uses the proceeds to repurchase shares? The corporate tax rate is 35 percent.

15. **Interest Tax Shield.**   Green Gables Co. has a 38 percent tax rate. Its total interest payment for the year just ended was $28 million. What is the interest tax shield? How do you interpret this amount?

**Intermediate
(Questions 16–19)**

16. **M&M.**   Power Enterprises has no debt. Its current total value is $120 million. Ignoring taxes, what will Power's value be if it sells $35 million in debt? Suppose now that Power's tax rate is 40 percent. What will its overall value be if it sells $35 million in debt? Assume debt proceeds are used to repurchase equity.

17. **M&M.**   In the previous question, what is the debt-equity ratio in both cases?

18. **M&M.** Rebellion Co. has no debt. Its cost of capital is 12 percent. Suppose Rebellion converts to a debt-equity ratio of 1.0. The interest rate on the debt is 6.5 percent. Ignoring taxes, what is Rebellion's new cost of equity? What is its new WACC?

19. **Firm Value.** Wind Runner Corporation expects an EBIT of $23,000 every year forever. Wind Runner currently has no debt, and its cost of equity is 16 percent. The firm can borrow at 9 percent. If the corporate tax rate is 38 percent, what is the value of the firm? What will the value be if Wind Runner converts to 50 percent debt? To 100 percent debt?

20. **Bankruptcy process.** Moose Jaw, Inc., has filed a bankruptcy petition in bankruptcy court. The trustee estimates the liquidation value of the firm to be $17 million. If the firm is reorganized, it is expected to generate an annual cash flow of $4 million in perpetuity. The discount rate is 18.4 percent. Should Moose Jaw, Inc., be liquidated or reorganized?

Challenge (Questions 20–21)

21. **M&M and Taxes.** The Bluenose Corporation has no debt outstanding and a total market value of $3 million. EBIT is projected to be $400,000. The firm's WACC is currently 15 percent, and the corporate tax rate is 34 percent. The firm is considering a change from its current capital structure by borrowing $500,000 at 7 percent and using the proceeds to repurchase shares. For both the current and proposed capital structures:

a. What are the cash flows to stockholders and bondholders?

b. What is the total value of the firm?

c. What is the value of the shareholders' equity?

WHAT'S ON THE WEB?

13.1 **Capital Structure.** Go to **investor.reuters.com** and enter the ticker symbol CLS for Celestica Inc., an information technology company based in Toronto. Follow the "Ratios" link and find long-term debt-to-equity and total debt-to-equity ratios. How does Celestica compare to the industry, sector, and S&P 500 in these areas? Now answer the same question for George Weston Limited (WN), the food processing company, which is also based in Toronto. How do the capital structures of Celestica and George Weston compare? Can you think of possible explanations for the difference between these two companies?

13.2 **Capital Structure.** Go to **finance.yahoo.com** and find the stock screener. Use the Java stock screener to answer the following questions. How many companies have debt-to-equity ratios greater than 2? Greater than 5? Greater than 10? What company has the highest debt-to-equity ratio? What is the ratio? Now find how many companies have a negative debt-to-equity ratio. What is the lowest debt-to-equity ratio? What does it mean if a company has a negative debt-to-equity ratio?

13.3 **The Z-score.** Go to **www.sedar.com** and find the most recent financial statements for Nortel Networks. Find the numbers necessary for the calculation of the Z-score. Go to **ca.financeyahoo.com** and get the latest market price of Nortel's stock. Find an insolvency predictor at **www.creditguru.com** and calculate a Z-score for Nortel. Repeat the previous steps and calculate a Z-score for the National Bank of Canada. Which company has a higher Z-score? Why? Which of the financial ratios in the Z-score model has the largest difference between these companies? What does this ratio measure?

Dividends and Dividend Policy **14**

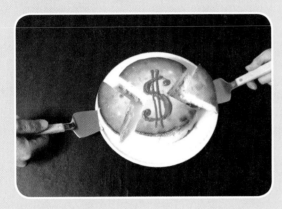

This chapter will pay you significant dividends if you study it closely. When you are finished, you should have a good understanding of:

14.1 Dividend types and how dividends are paid.

14.2 The issues surrounding dividend policy decisions.

14.3 The approaches to establishing a dividend policy.

14.4 Why share repurchases are an alternative to dividends.

14.5 The essentials of stock dividends and stock splits.

On October 31, 2006, Alcan, the world's second largest aluminum producer, headquartered in Montreal, and Rogers Communications, the telecommunications and media company based in Toronto, released their third-quarter results. Although announced on Hallowe'en, these results were like sweet treats, not scary tricks, to their investors.

The streak of consecutive record earnings for the first two quarters of the year was followed by a record cash flow of $803 million for Alcan. On the strength of its earnings, earlier in October Alcan had increased its dividends by 33 percent to US$0.20 per share and announced a share repurchase program of up to 5 percent of the company's 376 million common shares outstanding.

Rogers Communications reported a threefold increase in profits, and its quarterly revenue soared to a record level of $2.3 billion. Given this rise in profits, Rogers more than doubled its annual dividend to $0.32 from $0.15 a share and moved from semi-annual to quarterly dividend payments. In addition, Rogers announced a two-for-one split of its shares.

How did these companies make decisions about the size of their dividend payments? Why did Rogers decide to split its stock, while Alcan chose to repurchase its shares? These decisions depend on a company's dividend policy, which is discussed in this chapter. Going back to Chapter 7, we saw that the value of a share of stock depends on all the future dividends that will be paid to shareholders. In that analysis, we took the future stream of dividends as given. What we now examine is how corporations decide on the size and timing of dividend payments. What we would like to find out is how to establish an optimal dividend policy, meaning a dividend policy that maximizes the stock price. What we discover, among other things, is that it is not at all clear how to do this, or even if there is such a thing as an optimal dividend policy!

D ividend policy is an important subject in corporate finance, and dividends are a major cash outlay for many corporations. At first glance, it may seem obvious that a firm would always want to give as much as possible back to its shareholders by paying dividends. It might seem equally obvious, however, that a firm can always invest the money for its shareholders instead of paying it out. The heart of the dividend policy question is just this: Should the firm pay out money to its shareholders, or should the firm take that money and invest it for its shareholders?

It may seem surprising, but much research and economic logic suggest that dividend policy doesn't matter. In fact, it turns out that the dividend policy issue is much like the capital structure question. The important elements are not difficult to identify, but the interactions between those elements are complex and no easy answer exists.

Dividend policy is controversial. Many implausible reasons are given for why dividend policy might be important, and many of the claims made about dividend policy are economically illogical. Even so, in the real world of corporate finance, determining the most appropriate dividend policy is considered an important issue. It could be that financial managers who worry about dividend policy are wasting time, but it could also be true that we are missing something important in our discussions.

In part, all discussions of dividends are plagued by the "two-handed lawyer" problem. Former U.S. President Truman, while discussing the legal implications of a possible presidential decision, asked his staff to set up a meeting with a lawyer. Supposedly Mr. Truman said, "But I don't want one of those two-handed lawyers." When asked what a two-handed lawyer was, he replied, "You know, a lawyer who says, 'On the one hand I recommend you do so and so because of the following reasons, but on the other hand I recommend that you don't do it because of these other reasons.' "

Unfortunately, any sensible treatment of dividend policy will appear to have been written by a two-handed lawyer (or, in fairness, several two-handed financial economists). On the one hand, there are many good reasons for corporations to pay high dividends, but, on the other hand, there are also many good reasons to pay low dividends.

We will cover three broad topics that relate to dividends and dividend policy in this chapter. First, we describe the various kinds of dividends and how dividends are paid. Second, we consider an idealized case in which dividend policy doesn't matter. We then discuss the limitations of this case and present some real-world arguments for both high- and low-dividend payouts. Finally, we conclude the chapter by looking at some strategies that corporations might employ to implement a dividend policy, and we discuss share repurchases as an alternative to dividends.

14.1 | CASH DIVIDENDS AND DIVIDEND PAYMENT

The term **dividend** usually refers to cash paid out of earnings. If a payment is made from sources other than current or accumulated retained earnings, the term **distribution**, rather than *dividend*, is used. However, it is acceptable to refer to a distribution from earnings as a dividend and a distribution from capital as a liquidating dividend. More generally, any direct payment by the corporation to the shareholders may be considered a dividend or a part of dividend policy.

Dividends come in several different forms. The basic types of cash dividends are:

1. Regular cash dividends
2. Extra dividends
3. Special dividends
4. Liquidating dividends

Later in the chapter, we discuss dividends paid in stock instead of cash, and we also consider an alternative to cash dividends, stock repurchase.

dividend
Payment made out of a firm's earnings to its owners, in the form of either cash or stock.

distribution
Payment made by a firm to its owners from sources other than current or accumulated retained earnings.

Cash Dividends

The most common type of dividend is a cash dividend. Commonly, public companies pay **regular cash dividends** four times a year. As the name suggests, these are cash payments made directly to shareholders, and they are made in the regular course of business. In other words, management sees nothing unusual about the dividend and no reason why it won't be continued.

Sometimes firms will pay a regular cash dividend and an *extra cash dividend*. By calling part of the payment "extra," management is indicating that that part may or may not be repeated in the future. A *special dividend* is similar, but the name usually indicates that this dividend is viewed as a truly unusual or one-time event and it won't be repeated. Finally, the payment of a *liquidating dividend* usually means that some or all of the business has been liquidated, that is, sold off.

However it is labelled, a cash dividend payment reduces corporate cash and retained earnings, except in the case of a liquidating dividend (where paid-in capital may be reduced).

Of course, there are other types of dividends. In 2004, 24 percent of the companies listed on the Japanese Nikkei stock market gave shareholders alternative dividends in the form of food items, prepaid phone cards, and so forth. For example, McDonald's Holdings Company (Japan) gave its shareholders coupon books for free hamburgers.

Standard Method of Cash Dividend Payment

The decision to pay a dividend rests in the hands of the board of directors of the corporation. When a dividend has been declared, it becomes a liability of the firm and cannot be rescinded easily. Sometime after it has been declared, a dividend is distributed to all shareholders as of some specific date.

Commonly, the amount of the cash dividend is expressed in terms of dollars per share (*dividends per share*). As we have seen in other chapters, it is also expressed as a percentage of the market price (the *dividend yield*) or as a percentage of net income or earnings per share (the *dividend payout*).

Many Canadian corporations offer Dividend Reinvestment Plans (DRIPs or DRPs) that permit shareholders to automatically reinvest some or all of their cash dividends in shares of stock without paying brokerage fees. In some cases, shareholders actually receive a discount on the stock, which makes such plans very attractive. For example, Nexen and Agnico-Eagle Mines give a 5 percent discount in the cost of shares when the dividends are reinvested.

Dividend Payment: A Chronology

The mechanics of a cash dividend payment can be illustrated by the example in Figure 14.1 and the following description:

1. **Declaration date**. On January 15, the board of directors passes a resolution to pay a dividend of $1 per share on February 16 to all holders of record as of January 30.
2. **Ex-dividend date**. To make sure that dividend checks go to the right people, brokerage firms and stock exchanges establish an *ex-dividend date*. This date is two business days before the date of record (discussed next). If you buy the stock before this date, then you are entitled to the dividend. If you buy on this date or after, then the previous owner will get the dividend.

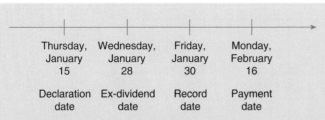

FIGURE **14.1**

Example of the procedure for dividend payment

1. *Declaration date:* The board of directors declares a payment of dividends.
2. *Ex-dividend date:* A share of stock goes ex dividend on the date the seller is entitled to keep the dividend; under TSX and NYSE rules, shares are traded ex dividend on and after the second business day before the record date.
3. *Record date:* The declared dividends are distributable to those who are shareholders of record as of this specific date.
4. *Payment date:* The dividend cheques are mailed to shareholders of record.

In Figure 14.1, Wednesday, January 28, is the ex-dividend date. Before this date, the stock is said to trade "with dividend," or "cum dividend." Afterwards, the stock trades "ex dividend."

The ex-dividend date convention removes any ambiguity about who is entitled to the dividend. Since the dividend is valuable, the stock price will be affected when the stock goes "ex." We examine this effect below.

3. **Date of record**. Based on its records, the corporation prepares a list on January 30 of all individuals believed to be stockholders. These are the *holders of record,* and January 30 is the *date of record* (or record date). The word *believed* is important here. If you bought the stock just before this date, the corporation's records might not reflect that fact because of mailing or other delays. Without some modification, some of the dividend cheques would get mailed to the wrong people. This is the reason for the ex-dividend day convention.

4. **Date of payment**. The dividend cheques are mailed on February 16.

Figure 14.2 shows Alcan's dividend notice, which we mentioned at the beginning of the chapter. Given that this dividend was declared on October 25, 2006, can you identify the remaining three key dividend payment dates from this notice?

More on the Ex-Dividend Date

The ex-dividend date is important and is a common source of confusion. We examine what happens to the stock when it goes ex, meaning that the ex-dividend date arrives. To illustrate, suppose we have a stock that sells for $10 per share. The board of directors declares a dividend of $1 per share, and the record date is Tuesday, June 12. Based on our discussion above, we know that the ex date will be two business (not calendar) days earlier, on Friday, June 8.

If you buy the stock on Thursday, June 7, right as the market closes, you'll get the $1 dividend because the stock is trading cum dividend. If you wait and buy the stock right as the market opens on Friday, you won't get the $1 dividend. What will happen to the value of the stock overnight?

If you think about it, the stock is obviously worth about $1 less on Friday morning, so its price will drop by this amount between close of business on Thursday and the Friday opening. In general, we expect that the value of a share of stock will go down by about the dividend amount when the stock goes ex dividend. The key word here is *about*. Since dividends are taxed, the actual price drop might be closer to some measure of the aftertax

Information on upcoming dividends is available at **www.earnings.com**.

date of record
Date by which holders must be on record in order to receive a dividend.

date of payment
Date that the dividend cheques are mailed.

FIGURE 14.2

**An example of a
dividend notice**

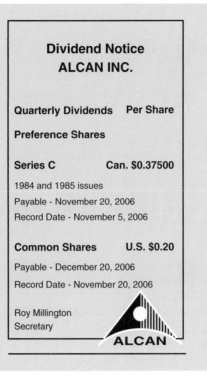

Source: Appeared in November 1, 2006 edition of *National Post.* Used with permission of Alcan.

FIGURE 14.3

**Price behaviour
around the
ex-dividend date for
a $1 cash dividend**

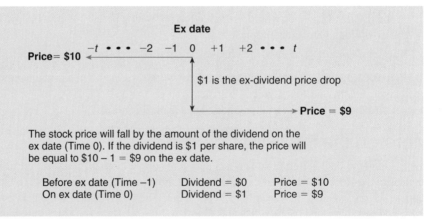

value of the dividend. Determining this value is complicated because of the different tax rates and tax rules that apply for different buyers. The series of events described here is illustrated in Figure 14.3.

As an example of the price drop on the ex-dividend date, consider a special dividend that was paid by Microsoft to its shareholders in December 2004. The stock went ex-dividend on November 15, 2004 with a total dividend of US$3.08 per share, consisting of a US$3 special dividend and a US$0.08 regular dividend. The stock price chart below shows the change in Microsoft's stock price on the four days prior to the ex-dividend date and on the ex-dividend date.

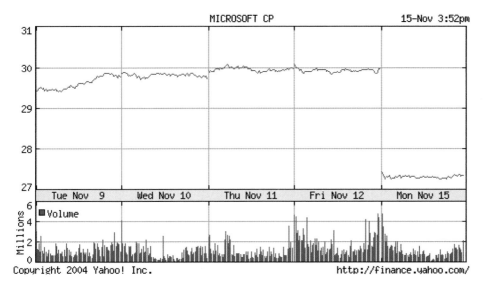

The stock closed at US$29.97 on November 12 (a Friday) and opened at US$27.34 on November 15, a drop of US$2.63. With a maximum tax rate on dividends of 15 percent in the United States, we would have expected a drop of US$2.62. Thus, the actual price drop was almost exactly what we expected.

"Ex" Marks the Day **EXAMPLE 14.1**

The board of directors of Divided Airlines has declared a dividend of $2.50 per share payable on Tuesday, May 30, to shareholders of record as of Tuesday, May 9. Cal Icon buys 100 shares of Divided on Tuesday, May 2, for $150 per share. What is the ex date? Describe the events that will occur with regard to the cash dividend and the stock price.

The ex date is two business days before the date of record, Tuesday, May 9, so the stock will go ex on Friday, May 5. Cal buys the stock on Tuesday, May 2, so Cal purchases the stock cum dividend. In other words, Cal will get $2.50 × 100 = $250 in dividends. The cheque will be mailed on Tuesday, May 30. When the stock does go ex on Friday, its value will drop overnight by about $2.50 per share.

CONCEPT QUESTIONS

14.1a What are the different types of cash dividends?

14.1b What are the mechanics of the cash dividend payment?

14.1c How should the price of a stock change when the stock goes ex dividend?

14.2 | DOES DIVIDEND POLICY MATTER?

To decide whether or not dividend policy matters, we first have to define what we mean by dividend *policy*. All other things being the same, of course dividends matter. Dividends are paid in cash, and cash is something that everybody likes. The question we will be discussing here is whether the firm should pay out cash now or invest the cash and pay it out later. Dividend policy, therefore, is the time pattern of dividend payout. In particular, should the firm pay out a large percentage of its earnings now or a small (or even zero) percentage? This is the dividend policy question.

An Illustration of the Irrelevance of Dividend Policy

A powerful argument can be made that dividend policy does not matter. We illustrate this by considering the simple case of Ryerson Corporation. Ryerson is an all-equity firm that has existed for 10 years. The current financial managers plan to dissolve the firm in two years. The total cash flows the firm will generate, including the proceeds from liquidation, are $10,000 in each of the next two years.

Current Policy: Dividends Set Equal to Cash Flow   At the present time, dividends at each date are set equal to the cash flow of $10,000. There are 100 shares outstanding, so the dividend per share will be $100. In Chapter 7, we showed that the value of the stock is equal to the present value of the future dividends. Assuming a 10 percent required return, the value of a share of stock today, P_0, is:

$$P_0 = \frac{D_1}{(1 + R)^1} + \frac{D_2}{(1 + R)^2}$$

$$= \frac{\$100}{1.10} + \frac{100}{1.10^2} = \$173.55$$

The firm as a whole is thus worth $100 \times \$173.55 = \$17,355$.

Several members of the board of Ryerson have expressed dissatisfaction with the current dividend policy and have asked you to analyze an alternative policy.

Alternative Policy: Initial Dividend Greater Than Cash Flow   Another policy is for the firm to pay a dividend of $110 per share on the first date (Date 1), which is, of course, a total dividend of $11,000. Because the cash flow is only $10,000, an extra $1,000 must somehow be raised. One way to do this is to issue $1,000 worth of bonds or stock at Date 1. Assume that stock is issued. The new stockholders will desire enough cash flow at Date 2 so that they earn the required 10 percent return on their Date 1 investment.

What is the value of the firm with this new dividend policy? The new stockholders invest $1,000. They require a 10 percent return, so they will demand $1,000 $\times$ 1.10 = $1,100 of the Date 2 cash flow, leaving only $8,900 to the old stockholders. The dividends to the old stockholders will be:

	Date 1	Date 2
Aggregate dividends to old stockholders	$11,000	$8,900
Dividends per share	110	89

The present value of the dividends per share is therefore:

$$P_0 = \frac{\$110}{1.10} + \frac{89}{1.10^2} = \$173.55$$

This is the same value we had before.

The value of the stock is not affected by this switch in dividend policy even though we had to sell some new stock just to finance the dividend. In fact, no matter what pattern of dividend payout the firm chooses, the value of the stock will always be the same in this example. In other words, for the Ryerson Corporation, dividend policy makes no difference. The reason is simple: Any increase in a dividend at some point in time is exactly offset by a decrease somewhere else, so the net effect, once we account for time value, is zero.

A Test

Our discussion to this point can be summarized by considering the following true-false test questions:

1. True or false: Dividends are irrelevant.
2. True or false: Dividend policy is irrelevant.

The first statement is surely false, and the reason follows from common sense. Clearly, investors prefer higher dividends to lower dividends at any single date if the dividend level is held constant at every other date. To be more precise regarding the first question, if the dividend per share at a given date is raised, while the dividend per share at every other date is held constant, the stock price will rise. The reason is that the present value of the future dividends must go up if this occurs. This action can be accomplished by management decisions that improve productivity, increase tax savings, strengthen product marketing, or otherwise improve cash flow.

The second statement is true, at least in the simple case we have been examining. Dividend policy by itself cannot raise the dividend at one date while keeping it the same at all other dates. Rather, dividend policy merely establishes the trade-off between dividends at one date and dividends at another date. Once we allow for time value, the present value of the dividend stream is unchanged. Thus, in this simple world, dividend policy does not matter, because managers choosing either to raise or to lower the current dividend do not affect the current value of their firm. However, we have ignored several real-world factors that might lead us to change our minds; we pursue some of these in subsequent sections.

Some Real-World Factors Favouring a Low Payout

The example we used to illustrate the irrelevance of dividend policy ignored taxes and flotation costs. We will now see that these factors might lead us to prefer a low-dividend payout.

Taxes Canadian tax laws are complex, and they affect dividend policy in a number of ways. The key tax feature has to do with the taxation of dividend income and capital gains. In Chapter 2 we saw that for individual shareholders, dividends from Canadian corporations and capital gains are taxed at lower rates than ordinary income. Specifically, individuals receive a dividend tax credit that decreases the payable tax on dividends, and only half of the capital gain is taxed at the individual's marginal rate. Moreover, the tax on a capital gain is deferred until the stock is sold, which makes the effective tax rate on capital gains much lower, because the present value of the tax is less. Taken together, capital gains are taxed at a lower rate than dividends.

A firm that adopts a low-dividend payout will reinvest the money instead of paying it out. This reinvestment increases the value of the firm and of the equity. All other things being equal, the net effect is that the expected capital gains portion of the return will be higher in the future. So the fact that capital gains are taxed favourably may lead us to prefer this approach.

Flotation Costs In our example illustrating that dividend policy doesn't matter, we saw that the firm could sell some new stock if necessary to pay a dividend. As we discuss in our next chapter, selling new stock can be very expensive. If we include the costs of selling stock ("flotation" costs) in our argument, then we will find that the value of the stock decreases if we sell new stock.

More generally, imagine two firms identical in every way except that one pays out a greater percentage of its cash flow in the form of dividends. Since the other firm plows back more, its equity grows faster. If these two firms are to remain identical, then the one with the higher payout will have to periodically sell some stock to catch up. Since this is expensive, a firm might be inclined to have a low payout.

Dividend Restrictions   In some cases, a corporation may face restrictions on its ability to pay dividends. For example, as we discussed in Chapter 6, a common feature of a bond indenture is a covenant prohibiting dividend payments above some level.

Some Real-World Factors Favouring a High Payout

In this section, we consider reasons why a firm might pay its shareholders higher dividends even if it means the firm must issue more shares of stock to finance the dividend payments.

Desire for Current Income   It has been argued that many individuals desire current income. The classic example is the group of retired people and others living on a fixed income, the proverbial "widows and orphans." It is argued that this group is willing to pay a premium to get a higher dividend yield.

It is easy to see, however, that this argument is not relevant in our simple case. An individual preferring high current cash flow but holding low-dividend securities could easily sell off shares to provide the necessary funds. Similarly, an individual desiring a low current cash flow but holding high-dividend securities could just reinvest the dividends. Thus, in a world of no transaction costs, a policy of high current dividends would be of no value to the stockholder.

The current-income argument may have relevance in the real world. Here the sale of low-dividend stocks would involve brokerage fees and other transaction costs. Such a sale might also trigger capital gains taxes. These direct cash expenses could be avoided by an investment in high-dividend securities. In addition, the expenditure of the stockholder's own time when selling securities and the natural (though not necessarily rational) fear of consuming out of principal might further lead many investors to buy high-dividend securities.

Tax and Legal Benefits from High Dividends   Earlier we saw that dividends were taxed more heavily than capital gains for individual investors. This fact is a powerful argument for a low payout. However, there are a number of other investors who do not receive unfavourable tax treatment from holding high-dividend yield, rather than low-dividend yield, securities.

Corporate investors   A significant tax break on dividends occurs when a Canadian corporation owns stock in another Canadian corporation. A corporate stockholder receiving either common or preferred dividends is granted a 100 percent dividend exclusion. Since the 100 percent exclusion does not apply to capital gains, this group is taxed unfavourably on capital gains.

As a result of the dividend exclusion, high-dividend, low-capital gains stocks may be more appropriate for corporations to hold. In fact, this is why corporations hold a substantial percentage of the outstanding preferred stock in the economy. This tax advantage of dividends also leads some corporations to hold high-yielding stocks instead of long-term bonds because there is no similar tax exclusion of interest payments to corporate bondholders.

Tax-exempt investors   We have pointed out both the tax advantages and the tax disadvantages of a low-dividend payout. Of course, this discussion is irrelevant to those in zero tax brackets. This group includes some of the largest investors in the economy, such as pension funds, endowment funds, and trust funds.

There are some legal reasons for large institutions to favour high-dividend yields. First, institutions such as pension funds and trust funds are often set up to manage money for the benefit of others. The managers of such institutions have a *fiduciary responsibility* to invest the money prudently. It has been considered imprudent in courts of law to buy stock in companies with no established dividend record.

Second, institutions such as university endowment funds and trust funds are frequently prohibited from spending any of the principal. Such institutions might therefore prefer high-dividend yield stocks so they have some ability to spend. Like widows and orphans, this group thus prefers current income. Unlike widows and orphans, this group is very large in terms of the amount of stock owned.

Overall, individual investors (for whatever reason) may have a desire for current income and may thus be willing to pay the dividend tax. In addition, some very large investors such as corporations and tax-free institutions may have a very strong preference for high-dividend payouts.

Clientele Effects: A Resolution of Real-World Factors?

In our earlier discussion, we saw that some groups (wealthy individuals, for example) have an incentive to pursue low-payout (or zero payout) stocks. Other groups (corporations, for example) have an incentive to pursue high-payout stocks. Companies with high payouts will thus attract one group, and low-payout companies will attract another.

These different groups are called *clienteles,* and what we have described is a **clientele effect**. The clientele effect argument states that different groups of investors desire different levels of dividends. When a firm chooses a particular dividend policy, the only effect is to attract a particular clientele. If a firm changes its dividend policy, then it just attracts a different clientele.

What we are left with is a simple supply and demand argument. Suppose 40 percent of all investors prefer high dividends, but only 20 percent of the firms pay high dividends. Here the high-dividend firms will be in short supply; thus, their stock prices will rise. Consequently, low-dividend firms will find it advantageous to switch policies until 40 percent of all firms have high payouts. At this point, the *dividend market* is in equilibrium. Further changes in dividend policy are pointless because all of the clienteles are satisfied. The dividend policy for any individual firm is now irrelevant.

To see if you understand the clientele effect, consider the following statement: In spite of the theoretical argument that dividend policy is irrelevant or that firms should not pay dividends, many investors like high dividends; because of this fact, a firm can boost its share price by having a higher dividend payout ratio. True or false?

The answer is "false" if clienteles exist. As long as enough high-dividend firms satisfy the dividend-loving investors, a firm won't be able to boost its share price by paying high dividends. An unsatisfied clientele must exist for this to happen, and there is no evidence that this is the case.

clientele effect
Argument that stocks attract particular groups based on dividend yield and the resulting tax effects.

CONCEPT QUESTIONS

14.2a Are dividends irrelevant?

14.2b What are some of the reasons for a low payout?

14.2c What are the implications of dividend clienteles for payout policies?

14.3 | ESTABLISHING A DIVIDEND POLICY

In this section, we focus on a particular approach to establishing a dividend policy that reflects many of the attitudes and objectives of financial managers as well as observed corporate dividend policies.

Residual Dividend Approach

Earlier, we noted that firms with higher dividend payouts will have to sell stock more often. As we have seen, such sales are not very common and they can be very expensive. Consistent with this, we will assume that the firm wishes to minimize the need to sell new equity. We will also assume that the firm wishes to maintain its current capital structure.

If a firm wishes to avoid new equity sales, then it will have to rely on internally generated cash flow to finance new, positive NPV projects.[1] Dividends can only be paid out of what is left over. This leftover is called the *residual,* and such a dividend policy is called a **residual dividend approach**.

residual dividend approach
Policy under which a firm pays dividends only after meeting its investment needs while maintaining a desired debt-equity ratio.

With a residual dividend policy, the firm's objective is to meet its investment needs and maintain its desired debt-equity ratio before paying dividends. Given this objective, we expect those firms with many investment opportunities to pay a small percentage of their earnings as dividends and other firms with fewer opportunities to pay a high percentage of their earnings as dividends. This result appears to occur in the real world. Young, fast-growing firms commonly employ a low payout ratio, whereas older, slower-growing firms in more mature industries use a higher ratio.

EXAMPLE 14.1 **Residual Dividend Policy**

King Inc. uses a residual dividend policy. The firm has $1,000 in earnings and a debt-equity ratio of .50, which is considered optimal. What is the maximum amount of capital spending possible without selling new equity? If planned capital spending is $900, will King pay a dividend?

Because King has a debt-equity ratio of .50, it can raise $.50 in debt for every $1 of equity. The firm's capital structure is thus 1/3 debt and 2/3 equity. If King reinvests the entire $1,000 and pays no dividend, then equity will increase by $1,000. To keep the debt-equity ratio at .50, King must borrow an additional $500. Thus, the maximum capital spending possible with no new equity is $1,000 + $500 = $1,500.

To decide whether or not a dividend will be paid, we compare the total amount that can be generated without selling new equity ($1,500 in this case) to the planned capital spending of $900. Because funds generated exceed funds needed, a dividend will be paid. To maintain the firm's capital structure, this $900 must be financed by 2/3 equity and 1/3 debt. So, the firm will actually borrow 1/3 × $900 = $300. The firm will spend 2/3 × $900 = $600 of the $1,000 in equity available. There is a $1,000 − 600 = $400 residual, so the dividend will be $400.

Dividend Stability

The key point of the residual dividend approach is that dividends are paid only after all profitable investment opportunities are exhausted. Of course, a strict residual approach might lead to a very unstable dividend payout. If investment opportunities in one period are quite high, dividends will be low or zero. Conversely, dividends might be high in the next period if investment opportunities are considered less promising.

---

[1]Our discussion of sustainable growth in Chapter 3 is relevant here. We assumed there that a firm has a fixed capital structure, profit margin, and capital intensity. If the firm raises no new external equity and wishes to grow at some target rate, then there is only one payout ratio consistent with these assumptions.

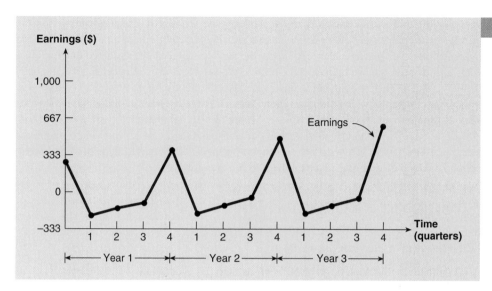

FIGURE 14.4

Earnings for Big Department Stores, Inc.

Consider the case of Big Department Stores, Inc., a retailer whose annual earnings are forecast to be equal from year to year but whose quarterly earnings change throughout the year. They are low in each year's first quarter because of the post-Christmas business slump. Although earnings increase only slightly in the second and third quarters, they advance greatly in the fourth quarter as a result of the Christmas season. A graph of this firm's earnings is presented in Figure 14.4.

The firm can choose between at least two types of dividend policies. First, each quarter's dividend can be a fixed fraction of that quarter's earnings. Here, dividends will vary throughout the year. This is a *cyclical dividend policy*. Second, each quarter's dividend can be a fixed fraction of yearly earnings, implying that all dividend payments would be equal. This is a *stable dividend policy*. These two types of dividend policies are displayed in Figure 14.5.

Most financial managers would agree that a stable dividend policy is in the best interests of the firm and its stockholders. Dividend cuts in particular are viewed as

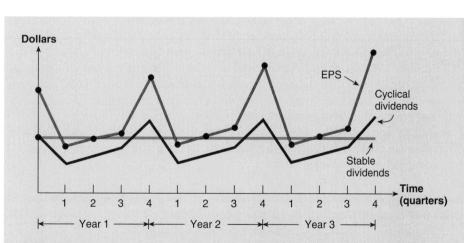

Cyclical dividend policy: Dividends are a constant proportion of earnings at each pay date.
Stable dividend policy: Dividends are a constant proportion of earnings over an earnings cycle.

highly undesirable because such cuts are often interpreted as a sign of financial distress. Consequently, most companies will try to maintain a steady dividend through time, increasing the dividend only when management is confident the new dividend can be sustained indefinitely.

To show how important dividend stability and increases are, consider that by the end of 2006, 54 TSX-listed companies had paid cash dividends for at least 25 consecutive years. Two companies with particularly long histories of successive dividend payments are Bank of Montreal and Bank of Nova Scotia. Bank of Montreal has paid cash dividends for 178 consecutive years, and Bank of Nova Scotia has paid its dividends for 174 consecutive years. In 2006, 168 of 1,598 companies listed on the TSX increased their dividend payments. Dividend cuts or omissions totalled 28 for the same year.

A Compromise Dividend Policy

In practice, many firms appear to follow what amounts to a compromise dividend policy. Such a policy is based on five main goals:

1. Avoid cutting back on positive NPV projects to pay a dividend.
2. Avoid dividend cuts.
3. Avoid the need to sell equity.
4. Maintain a target debt-equity ratio.
5. Maintain a target dividend payout ratio.

These goals are ranked more or less in order of their importance. In our strict residual approach, we assume that the firm maintains a fixed debt-equity ratio. Under the compromise approach, the debt-equity ratio is viewed as a long-range goal. It is allowed to vary in the short run if necessary to avoid a dividend cut or the need to sell new equity.

target payout ratio
A firm's long-term desired dividend-to-earnings ratio.

In addition to showing a strong reluctance to cut dividends, financial managers tend to think of dividend payments in terms of a proportion of income, and they also tend to think investors are entitled to a "fair" share of corporate income. This share is the long-run **target payout ratio**, and it is the fraction of the earnings the firm expects to pay as dividends under ordinary circumstances. Again, this is viewed as a long-range goal, so dividends might vary in the short run if this is needed. In the long run, earnings growth is followed by dividend increases, but only with a lag.

One can minimize the problems of dividend instability by creating two types of dividends: regular and extra. For companies using this approach, the regular dividend would most likely be a relatively small fraction of permanent earnings, so that it could be sustained easily. Extra dividends would be granted when an increase in earnings was expected to be temporary.

Since investors look at an extra dividend as a bonus, there is relatively little disappointment when an extra dividend is not repeated. This makes the extra dividend approach quite sensible, and companies frequently use it in practice. For example, 102 extra dividends were paid by the TSX-listed companies in 2006.

A cash dividend is not the only option for a corporation to distribute cash to its shareholders. Another alternative, which does much the same thing with some extra advantages, is a share repurchase. We discuss it next.

CONCEPT QUESTIONS

14.3a What is a residual dividend policy?

14.3b What is the chief drawback to a strict residual policy? What do many firms do in practice?

14.4 | STOCK REPURCHASE: AN ALTERNATIVE TO CASH DIVIDENDS

When a firm wants to pay cash to its shareholders, it normally pays a cash dividend. Another way is to **repurchase** its own stock. Stock repurchasing has been a major financial activity in recent years, and it appears that it will continue to be one.

repurchase
Refers to a firm's purchase of its own stock.

Cash Dividends versus Repurchase

Imagine an all-equity company with excess cash of $300,000. The firm pays no dividends, and its net income for the year just ended is $49,000. The market value balance sheet at the end of the year is represented below.

Market Value Balance Sheet
(before paying out excess cash)

Excess cash	$ 300,000	Debt	$ 0
Other assets	700,000	Equity	1,000,000
Total	$1,000,000	Total	$1,000,000

There are 100,000 shares outstanding. The total market value of the equity is $1 million, so the stock sells for $10 per share. Earnings per share, EPS, are $49,000/100,000 = $.49, and the price-earnings ratio, PE, is $10/.49 = 20.4.

One option the company is considering is a $300,000/100,000 = $3 per share extra cash dividend. Alternatively, the company is thinking of using the money to repurchase and cancel $300,000/10 = 30,000 shares of stock.

If commissions, taxes, and other imperfections are ignored in our example, the stockholders shouldn't care which option is chosen. Does this seem surprising? It shouldn't, really. What is happening here is that the firm is paying out $300,000 in cash. The new balance sheet is represented below.

Market Value Balance Sheet
(after paying out excess cash)

Excess cash	$ 0	Debt	$ 0
Other assets	700,000	Equity	700,000
Total	$700,000	Total	$700,000

If the cash is paid out as a dividend, there are still 100,000 shares outstanding, so each is worth $7.

The fact that the per-share value fell from $10 to $7 isn't a cause for concern. Consider a stockholder who owns 100 shares. At $10 per share before the dividend, the total value is $1,000.

After the $3 dividend, this same stockholder has 100 shares worth $7 each, for a total of $700, plus 100 × $3 = $300 in cash, for a combined total of $1,000. This just illustrates what we saw early on: A cash dividend doesn't affect a stockholder's wealth if there are no imperfections. In this case, the stock price simply fell by $3 when the stock went ex dividend.

Also, since total earnings and the number of shares outstanding haven't changed, EPS is still 49 cents. The price-earnings ratio, however, falls to $7/.49 = 14.3. Why we are looking at accounting earnings and PE ratios will be apparent just below.

Alternatively, if the company repurchases and cancels 30,000 shares, there will be 70,000 left outstanding. The balance sheet looks the same.

Market Value Balance Sheet
(after share purchase)

Excess cash	$ 0	Debt	$ 0	
Other assets	700,000	Equity	700,000	
Total	$700,000	Total	$700,000	

The company is worth $700,000 again, so each remaining share is worth $700,000/70,000 = $10. Our stockholder with 100 shares is obviously unaffected. For example, if they were so inclined, they could sell 30 shares and end up with $300 in cash and $700 in stock, just as they have if the firm pays the cash dividend.

In this second case, EPS goes up since total earnings stay the same while the number of shares goes down. The new EPS will be $49,000/70,000 = $.70 per share. However, the important thing to notice is that the PE ratio is $10/.70 = 14.3, just as it was following the dividend.

This example illustrates the important point that, if there are no imperfections, a cash dividend and a share repurchase are essentially the same thing. This is just another illustration of dividend policy irrelevance when there are no taxes or other imperfections.

Real-World Considerations in a Repurchase

The example we have just described shows that a repurchase and a cash dividend are the same thing in a world without taxes and transaction costs. In the real world, there are some accounting differences between a share repurchase and a cash dividend, but the most important difference is in the tax treatment.

Under current tax law, a repurchase has a significant tax advantage over a cash dividend. A dividend is taxed, and a shareholder has no choice about whether or not to receive the dividend. In a repurchase, a shareholder pays taxes only if (1) the shareholder actually chooses to sell and (2) the shareholder has a taxable capital gain on the sale.

Some corporations have engaged in massive repurchases in recent years. For example, consider Alcan's "buyback" (another word for repurchase) program of up to 5 percent of the company's common shares, which we discussed at the beginning of the chapter. At the then-current market value of the stock, this repurchase would amount to over $823 million of the company's stock.

One cautionary note is in order concerning share repurchases, or buybacks. A company announcing plans to buy back some of its stock has no legal obligation to actually do it, and it turns out that many announced repurchases are never completed. Nonetheless, as the accompanying *Reality Bytes* box indicates, share buybacks are very big business, and they seem to be getting bigger and more common all the time.

Share Repurchase and EPS

You may read in the popular financial press that a share repurchase is beneficial because earnings per share increase. As we have seen, this will happen. The reason is simply that a share repurchase reduces the number of outstanding shares, but it has no effect on total earnings. As a result, EPS rises.

However, the financial press may place undue emphasis on EPS figures in a repurchase agreement. In our example above, we saw that the value of the stock wasn't affected by the EPS change. In fact, the price-earnings ratio was exactly the same when we compared a cash dividend to a repurchase.

Since the increase in earnings per share is exactly tracked by the increase in the price per share, there is no net effect. Put another way, the increase in EPS is just an accounting adjustment that reflects (correctly) the change in the number of shares outstanding.

In the real world, to the extent that repurchases benefit the firm, we would argue that they do so primarily because of the tax considerations we discussed above.

CONCEPT QUESTIONS

14.4a Why might a stock repurchase make more sense than an extra cash dividend?

14.4b Why don't all firms use stock repurchases instead of cash dividends?

14.5 | STOCK DIVIDENDS AND STOCK SPLITS

Another type of dividend is paid out in shares of stock. This type of dividend is called a **stock dividend**. A stock dividend is not a true dividend because it is not paid in cash. The effect of a stock dividend is to increase the number of shares that each owner holds. Since there are more shares outstanding, each is simply worth less.

stock dividend
Payment made by a firm to its owners in the form of stock, diluting the value of each share outstanding.

A stock dividend is commonly expressed as a percentage; for example, a 20 percent stock dividend means that a shareholder receives one new share for every five currently owned (a 20 percent increase). Since every shareholder owns 20 percent more stock, the total number of shares outstanding rises by 20 percent. As we will see in a moment, the result is that each share of stock is worth about 20 percent less. For example, if a firm's stock price before the stock dividend, P_{Before}, was $20, the price of the stock after the stock dividend can be calculated as:

$$P_{After} = \frac{P_{Before}}{1 + Percentage\ Stock\ Dividend\ Rate} \qquad [14.1]$$

$$= \frac{\$20}{1 + 0.20}$$

$$= \$16.67$$

A **stock split** is essentially the same thing as a stock dividend, except that a split is expressed as a ratio instead of a percentage. When a split is declared, each share is split up to create additional shares. For example, in the two-for-one stock split by Rogers Communications that we discussed at the beginning of the chapter, each old share would split into two new shares.

stock split
An increase in a firm's shares outstanding without any change in owners' equity.

The stock price after a stock split is defined as:

$$P_{After} = \frac{P_{Before}}{Stock\ Split\ Ratio} \qquad [14.2]$$

Thus, if a stock price before a stock split, P_{Before}, is $30 and a stock split ratio is 4-for-1, the stock price after the split will be:

$$P_{After} = \frac{\$30}{4/1}$$
$$= \$7.50$$

By convention, stock dividends of less than 20 to 25 percent are called *small stock dividends*. A stock dividend greater than this 20 to 25 percent is called a *large stock dividend*. Large stock dividends are not uncommon. For example, in March 2006, the Royal Bank of Canada announced a 100 percent stock dividend, which had the same effect as a 2-for-1 stock split. One week earlier, SNC-Lavalin Group Inc., a group of engineering and construction companies based in Montreal, announced a 3-for-1 stock split in the form of a stock dividend.

REALITY BYTES

Stock Buybacks: No End in Sight

Usually companies repurchase their shares on the open market. If these announced purchases do not exceed 5 percent of the outstanding shares in a 12-month period, they are called "normal course issuer bids" in Canada. A normal course issuer bid cannot extend for more than one year from the date on which share repurchases may start. Companies frequently issue new notices of share repurchases to replace the ones that are about to expire.

Share repurchases have continued to grow. In March 2007, there were about 390 normal course issuer bids outstanding announced by TSX listed companies.

Some companies appear to have become serial repurchasers. Take EnCana, the Calgary-based natural gas producer, for example. In November 2006, the company announced a plan to complete the purchase of 10 percent of its outstanding shares by the end of the year. At the then-current market value of the stock, this repurchase would cost the company nearly $4.2 billion. But this buyback was nothing new to EnCana shareholders. The company had been increasing its share repurchases every year for the previous three years, starting from $868 million in 2003, and reaching almost $2 billion in 2005.

Stock buybacks have evolved to the point where they are used for other purposes. For example, in January 2005 consumer products giant Procter & Gamble (P&G) announced that it was purchasing razor manufacturer Gillette for $54 billion. The purchase was paid for entirely by stock in P&G. This is important because if a company acquires another company for cash, the shareholders of the acquired company are forced to pay taxes.

If shareholders receive stock, no taxes are due. What made the deal unique was that P&G announced at the same time that it would repurchase from $18 to $22 billion in stock. Thus, P&G essentially paid about 60 percent in stock and 40 percent in cash, but the way the deal was structured made it look like a 100 percent stock acquisition to Gillette's stockholders.

Stock buybacks are not limited to North America. In August 2004, Matsushita Electric, manufacturer of Panasonic electronics products, announced a stock buyback of up to 80 million shares, or about 3.5 percent of the company stock outstanding. The dollar amount of the buyback could be up to 100 billion yen, or about a billion dollars. In January 2005, the Brazilian phone company Tele Norte Leste Participacoes SA, or Telemar, announced a stock buyback of 3.46 million shares of common stock and 20.4 million shares of preferred stock. And in December 2004, South Korean tobacco company KT&G announced that it had bought back 10 million shares of its stock.

We haven't discussed what happens to the stock when a company does a buyback. There are actually several things the company can do. Many companies keep the stock and use the shares for employee stock option plans. When employee stock options are exercised by the employees, new shares are created, which increases the number of shares of stock outstanding. By using the repurchased shares, the company does not need to issue any new shares. A company can also keep the re-purchased stock for itself as Treasury stock. Finally, the company can cancel the stock completely. In essence, it destroys the shares repurchased, which reduces the number of shares outstanding.

Accounting Treatment of Stock Dividends and Stock Splits

Stock splits and stock dividends both have essentially the same impact on the corporation: they increase the number of shares outstanding and reduce the value per share. The accounting treatment is not the same, though.

Suppose Toonie Corporation, a brokerage firm, has 100,000 common shares outstanding, each selling at $15. The equity portion of Toonie's balance sheet might look like this:

Owners' Equity	
Common stock (100,000 shares outstanding)	$ 400,000
Retained earnings	600,000
Total owners' equity	$1,000,000

Accounting for Stock Dividends   With a 10 percent stock dividend, each stockholder receives one additional share for each 10 that they own, and the total number of shares outstanding after the stock dividend is 110,000. Because 10,000 new shares are issued, the common stock account is increased by $150,000 (10,000 shares at $15 each), for a total of $150,000 + $400,000 = $550,000.

Total owners' equity is unaffected by the stock dividend because no cash has come in or out, so retained earnings is reduced by the entire $150,000, leaving $450,000. The net effect of these machinations is that Toonie's equity accounts now look like this:

Post-Stock Dividend: Owners' Equity	
Common stock (110,000 shares outstanding)	$ 550,000
Retained earnings	450,000
Total owners' equity	$1,000,000

Accounting for Stock Splits   The accounting treatment of a stock split is a little different from (and simpler than) that of a stock dividend. Suppose Toonie decides to declare a two-for-one stock split. The number of shares outstanding will double to 200,000, while all other figures stay the same. Thus, the only change with the stock split is an increase in the number of shares outstanding:

Post-Stock Split: Owners' Equity	
Common stock (200,000 shares outstanding)	$ 400,000
Retained earnings	600,000
Total owners' equity	$1,000,000

Value of Stock Splits and Stock Dividends

The laws of logic tell us that stock splits and stock dividends can (1) leave the value of the firm unaffected, (2) increase its value, or (3) decrease its value. Unfortunately, the issues are complex enough that one cannot easily determine which of the three relationships holds.

The Benchmark Case   A strong case can be made that stock dividends and splits do not change either the wealth of any shareholder or the wealth of the firm as a whole. The reason is that they are just paper transactions and simply alter the number of shares outstanding. For example, if a firm declares a two-for-one split, all that happens is that the number of shares is doubled, with the result that each share is worth half as much. The total value is not affected.

Although this simple conclusion is relatively obvious, there are reasons that are often given to suggest that there may be some benefits to these actions. The typical financial manager is aware of many real-world complexities, and, for that reason, the stock split or stock dividend decision is not treated lightly in practice.

Popular Trading Range   Proponents of stock dividends and stock splits frequently argue that a security has a proper **trading range**. When the security is priced above this level, many investors do not have the funds to buy the common trading unit of 100 shares, called a *round lot*. Although securities can be purchased in *odd-lot* form (fewer than 100 shares), the commissions are greater. Thus, firms will split the stock to keep the price in this trading range.

Although this argument is a popular one, its validity is questionable for a number of reasons. Mutual funds, pension funds, and other institutions have steadily increased their trading

Information on upcoming stock splits is available at **www.earnings.com** and on the "Splits Calendar" at **www.investment-house.com**.

trading range
Price range between highest and lowest prices at which a stock is traded.

activity since the Second World War and now handle a sizable percentage of total trading volume (over half the trading volume on both the TSX and NYSE). Because these institutions buy and sell in huge amounts, the individual share price is of little concern.

Furthermore, we sometimes observe share prices that are quite large without appearing to cause problems. For example, consider the Swiss chocolatier Lindt. In May 2007, Lindt shares were selling for around 34,600 Swiss francs each, or about C$30,700. A round lot would have cost a cool C$3.07 million. This is fairly expensive, but not when compared to Berkshire-Hathaway, the U.S. company run by legendary investor Warren Buffett. In May 2007, each share of the company's class A stock sold for US$108,350, or about C$118,000 (the class B stock was much cheaper at US$3,600 per share).

Finally, there is evidence that stock splits may actually decrease the liquidity of the company's shares. Following a two-for-one split, the number of shares traded should more than double if liquidity is increased by the split. This doesn't appear to happen, and the opposite is sometimes observed.

Reverse Splits

reverse split

Stock split under which a firm's number of shares outstanding is reduced.

A less frequently encountered financial manoeuvre is the **reverse split**. In a 1-for-10 reverse split, each investor exchanges 10 old shares for one new share. The par value is increased tenfold in the process. For example, on December 1, 2006, Nortel Networks implemented a 1-for-10 reverse stock split, which reduced its number of outstanding shares from about 4.3 billion to 433 million and increased its stock price from $2.44 to about $24. As with stock splits and stock dividends, a case can be made that a reverse split has no real effect.

Given real-world imperfections, three related reasons are cited for reverse splits. First, transaction costs to shareholders may be less after the reverse split. Second, the liquidity and marketability of a company's stock might be improved when its price is raised to the popular trading range. Third, stocks selling at prices below a certain level are not considered respectable, meaning that investors underestimate these firms' earnings, cash flow, growth, and stability. Some financial analysts argue that a reverse split can achieve instant respectability. As was the case with stock splits, none of these reasons is particularly compelling, especially not the third one.

There are two other reasons for reverse splits. First, stock exchanges have minimum price per share requirements. A reverse split may bring the stock price up to such a minimum. For example, NYSE and Nasdaq can delist companies whose stock price drops below $1 per share for 30 days. Following the collapse of the Internet boom in 2001–2002, a large number of Internet-related companies found themselves in danger of being delisted and used reverse splits to boost their stock prices. For example, in April 2003, Nortel Networks shareholders gave management the option of a reverse stock split ranging from 1-for-5 to 1-for-10 for one year. The management asked for this after Nortel's share price fell below US$1, in violation of a NYSE listing requirement in the fall of 2002. But the share price recovered, and management did not implement a reverse stock split in that year. Second, companies sometimes perform reverse splits and, at the same time, buy out any stockholders who end up with less than a certain number of shares.

For example, in May 2004, Detwiler, Mitchell & Co., a Boston-based investment bank, completed a 1-for-600 reverse stock split, followed by a cash purchase of all holdings less than one share in order to buy out all shareholders who held less than one hundred shares to save in mailing and other administrative costs. The company ultimately repurchased about 64,000 shares from some 500 stockholders. What made the proposal especially imaginative was that immediately after the reverse stock split, the company underwent a 600-for-1 split to restore the stock to its original cost!

CONCEPT QUESTIONS

14.5a What is the effect of a stock split on stockholder wealth?

14.5b What is a reverse split?

KEY EQUATIONS:

I. Symbols

P_{Before} = Stock price before a stock dividend or a stock split

P_{After} = Stock price after a stock dividend or a stock split

II. Stock Price after a Stock Dividend

$$P_{After} = \frac{P_{Before}}{1 + \textit{Percentage Stock Dividend Rate}} \qquad [14.1]$$

III. Stock Price after a Stock Split

$$P_{After} = \frac{P_{Before}}{\textit{Stock Split Ratio}} \qquad [14.2]$$

SUMMARY AND CONCLUSIONS

In this chapter, we first discussed the types of dividends and how they are paid. We then defined dividend policy and examined whether or not dividend policy matters. Next, we illustrated how a firm might establish a dividend policy and described an important alternative to cash dividends, a share repurchase. Finally, we discussed stock dividends and stock splits, and their impact on the value of the firm.

In covering these subjects, we saw that:

1. Dividend policy is irrelevant when there are no taxes or other imperfections.

2. Individual shareholder income taxes and new issue flotation costs are real-world considerations that favour a low-dividend payout. With taxes and new issue costs, the firm should pay out dividends only after all positive NPV projects have been fully financed.

3. There are groups in the economy that may favour a high payout. These include many large institutions such as pension plans. Recognizing that some groups prefer a high payout and some prefer a low payout, the clientele effect supports the idea that dividend policy responds to the needs of stockholders. For example, if 40 percent of the stockholders prefer low dividends and 60 percent of the stockholders prefer high dividends, approximately 40 percent of companies will have a low-dividend payout, while 60 percent will have a high payout. This sharply reduces the impact of any individual firm's dividend policy on its market price.

4. A firm wishing to pursue a strict residual dividend payout will have an unstable dividend. Dividend stability is usually viewed as highly desirable. We therefore

discussed a compromise strategy that provides for a stable dividend and appears to be quite similar to the dividend policies many firms follow in practice.

5. A stock repurchase acts much like a cash dividend, but has a significant tax advantage. Stock repurchases are therefore a very useful part of overall dividend policy.

6. Stock dividends and stock splits increase the number of shares that each shareholder owns and decrease a share price. While a strong case can be made that stock dividends and stock splits do not change either the wealth of any shareholder or the wealth of the firm, a popular trading range argument suggests some benefits to these actions.

To close out our discussion of dividends, we emphasize one last time the difference between dividends and dividend policy. Dividends are important, because the value of a share of stock is ultimately determined by the dividends that will be paid. What is less clear is whether or not the time pattern of dividends (more now versus more later) matters. This is the dividend policy question, and it is not easy to give a definitive answer to it.

CHAPTER REVIEW AND SELF-TEST PROBLEM

14.1   Repurchase versus Cash Dividend. Trantor Corporation is deciding whether to pay out $300 in excess cash in the form of an extra dividend or to use the money for repurchasing and cancelling its shares. Current earnings are $1.50 per share, and the stock sells for $15. The market value balance sheet before paying out the $300 is as follows:

Market Value Balance Sheet
(before paying out excess cash)

Excess cash	$ 300	Debt	$ 400
Other assets	1,600	Equity	1,500
Total	$1,900	Total	$1,900

Evaluate the two alternatives in terms of the effect on the price per share of the stock, the EPS, and the PE ratio.

■ Answer to Chapter Review and Self-Test Problem

14.1   The market value of the equity is $1,500. The price per share is $15, so there are 100 shares outstanding. The cash dividend would amount to $300/100 = $3 per share. When the stock goes ex dividend, the price will drop by $3 per share to $12. Put another way, the total assets decrease by $300, so the equity value goes down by this amount to $1,200. With 100 shares, the new stock price is $12 per share. After the dividend, EPS will be the same, $1.50, but the PE ratio will be $12/1.50 = 8 times.

With a repurchase, $300/15 = 20 shares will be bought up and cancelled, leaving 80. The equity will again be worth $1,200 total. With 80 shares, this is $1,200/80 = $15 per share, so the price doesn't change. Total earnings for Trantor must be $1.50 × 100 = $150. After the repurchase, EPS will be higher at $150/80 = $1.875. The PE ratio, however, will still be $15/1.875 = 8 times.

CRITICAL THINKING AND CONCEPTS REVIEW

14.1 Dividend Policy Irrelevance. How is it possible that dividends are so important, but, at the same time, dividend policy is irrelevant?

14.2 Stock Repurchases. What is the impact of a stock repurchase on a company's debt ratio? Does this suggest another use for excess cash?

14.3 Dividend Policy. What is the chief drawback to a strict residual dividend policy? Why is this a problem? How does a compromise policy work? How does it differ from a strict residual policy?

14.4 Dividend Chronology. On Tuesday, December 8, Hometown Power Co.'s board of directors declares a dividend of 75 cents per share payable on Wednesday, January 17, to shareholders of record as of Wednesday, January 3. When is the ex-dividend date? If a shareholder buys stock before that date, who gets the dividends on those shares, the buyer or the seller?

14.5 Alternative Dividends. Some corporations, like one British company that offers its large shareholders free crematorium use, pay dividends in kind (that is, offer their services to shareholders at below-market cost). Should mutual funds invest in stocks that pay these dividends in kind? (The fundholders do not receive these services.)

14.6 Dividends and Stock Price. If increases in dividends tend to be followed by (immediate) increases in share prices, how can it be said that dividend policy is irrelevant?

14.7 Dividends and Stock Price. Last month, Central Ontario Power Company, which had been having trouble with cost overruns on a nuclear power plant that it had been building, announced that it was "temporarily suspending payments due to the cash flow crunch associated with its investment program." The company's stock price dropped from $28.50 to $25 when this announcement was made. How would you interpret this change in the stock price (that is, what would you say caused it)?

14.8 Dividend Reinvestment Plans. The DRK Corporation has recently developed a dividend reinvestment plan (DRIP). The plan allows investors to reinvest cash dividends automatically in DRK in exchange for new shares of stock. Over time, investors in DRK will be able to build their holdings by reinvesting dividends to purchase additional shares of the company.

Over 1,000 companies offer dividend reinvestment plans. Most companies with DRIPs charge no brokerage or service fees. In fact, the shares of DRK will be purchased at a 10 percent discount from the market price.

A consultant for DRK estimates that about 75 percent of DRK's shareholders will take part in this plan. This is somewhat higher than the average.

Evaluate DRK's dividend reinvestment plan. Will it increase shareholder wealth? Discuss the advantages and disadvantages involved here.

14.9 Dividend Policy. During 2006, 108 companies went public with common stock offerings on the TSX raising a combined total of $9.9 billion. Relatively few of these 108 companies involved paid cash dividends. Why do you think most chose not to pay dividends?

14.10 Investment and Dividends. The Phew Charitable Trust pays no taxes on its capital gains or on its dividend income or interest income. Would it be irrational for it to have low-dividend, high-growth stocks in its portfolio? Would it be irrational for it to have preferred stocks in its portfolio? Explain.

QUESTIONS AND PROBLEMS

**Basic
(Questions 1–15)**

1. **Dividends and Stock Prices.**   Your portfolio is 200 shares of Manitoba, Inc. The stock currently sells for $87 per share. The company has announced a dividend of $1.40 per share with an ex-dividend date of April 19. Assuming no taxes, how much will your stock be worth on April 19?

2. **Dividends and Stock Prices.**   It is April 19. Using the information in the previous problem, what is your total portfolio value?

3. **Dividends and Taxes.**   Ride On, Inc., has declared a $4.60 per share dividend. Suppose capital gains are not taxed, but the effective tax rate on dividends is 15 percent. Ride On sells for $105 per share, and the stock is about to go ex-dividend. What do you think the ex-dividend price will be?

4. **Stock Dividends.**   The owners' equity accounts for Robyn International are shown here:

Common stock (10,000 shares outstanding)	$ 170,000
Retained earnings	485,000
Total owners' equity	$655,000

a. If Robyn stock currently sells for $10 per share and a 10 percent stock dividend is declared, how many new shares will be distributed? Show how the equity accounts would change.

b. If Robyn declared a 25 percent stock dividend, how would the accounts change?

5. **Stock Splits.**   For the company in Problem 4, show how the equity accounts will change if:

a. Robyn declares a two-for-one stock split. How many shares are outstanding now?

b. Robyn declares a one-for-four reverse stock split. How many shares are outstanding now?

6. **Stock Splits and Stock Dividends.**   Bermuda Triangle Corporation (BTC) currently has 500,000 shares of stock outstanding that sell for $85 per share. Assuming no market imperfections or tax effects exist, what will the share price be after:

a. BTC has a five-for-three stock split?

b. BTC has a 15 percent stock dividend?

c. BTC has a 42.5 percent stock dividend?

d. BTC has a four-for-seven reverse stock split?

e. Determine the new number of shares outstanding in parts (*a*) through (*d*).

7. **Regular Dividends.**   The balance sheet for Magic Carpet, Inc., is shown here in market value terms. There are 20,000 shares of stock outstanding.

Market Value Balance Sheet

Cash	$ 50,000		
Fixed assets	250,000	Equity	$300,000
Total	$300,000	Total	$300,000

The company has declared a dividend of $1.10 per share. The stock goes ex-dividend tomorrow. Ignoring any tax effects, what is the stock selling for today? What will it sell for tomorrow? What will the balance sheet look like after the dividends are paid?

8. **Share Repurchase.**   In the previous problem, suppose the company has announced it is going to repurchase and cancel $22,000 worth of stock instead of paying a dividend. What effect will this transaction have on the equity of the firm? How many shares will be outstanding? What will the price per share be after the repurchase? Ignoring tax effects, show how the share repurchase is effectively the same as a cash dividend.

9. **Stock Dividends.**   The market value balance sheet for Nash Manufacturing is shown here. Nash has declared a 20 percent stock dividend. The stock goes ex-dividend tomorrow (the chronology for a stock dividend is similar to that for a cash dividend). There are 10,000 shares of stock outstanding. What will the ex-dividend price be?

Market Value Balance Sheet

Cash	$130,000	Debt	$120,000
Fixed assets	480,000	Equity	490,000
Total	$610,000	Total	$610,000

10. **Stock Dividends.**   The company with the common equity accounts shown here has declared a 10 percent stock dividend at a time when the market value of its stock is $25 per share. What effects will the distribution of the stock dividend have on the equity accounts?

Common stock (500,000 shares outstanding)	$ 1,000,000
Retained earnings	3,000,000
Total owners' equity	$ 4,000,000

11. **Stock Splits.**   In the previous problem, suppose the company instead decides on a two-for-one stock split. The firm's 60-cent-per-share cash dividend on the new (postsplit) shares represents an increase of 10 percent over last year's dividend on the presplit stock. What effect does this have on the equity accounts? What was last year's dividend per share?

12. **Residual Dividend Policy.**   Pete and Repete, a litter recycling company, uses a residual dividend policy. A debt-equity ratio of .70 is considered optimal. Earnings for the period just ended were $2,900, and a dividend of $350 was declared. How much in new debt was borrowed? What were total capital outlays?

13. **Residual Dividend Policy.**   Atlantic Corporation has declared an annual dividend of $1.40 per share. For the year just ended, earnings were $6.20 per share.

   a.   What is Atlantic's payout ratio?

   b.   Suppose Atlantic has seven million shares outstanding. Borrowing for the coming year is planned at $13 million. What are planned investment outlays assuming a residual dividend policy? What target capital structure is implicit in these calculations?

14. **Residual Dividend Policy.**   Canadian Idol Corporation follows a strict residual dividend policy. Its debt-equity ratio is 1.5.

   a.   If earnings for the year are $1.9 million, what is the maximum amount of capital spending possible with no new equity?

   b.   If planned investment outlays for the coming year are $6 million, will Canadian Idol pay a dividend? If so, how much?

   c.   Does Canadian Idol maintain a constant dividend payout? Why or why not?

15. **Residual Dividend Policy.**   Carmen, Inc., predicts that earnings in the coming year will be $30 million. There are six million shares, and Carmen maintains a debt-equity ratio of .9.

   a.   Calculate the maximum investment funds available without issuing new equity and the increase in borrowing that goes along with it.

   b.   Suppose the firm uses a residual dividend policy. Planned capital expenditures total $40 million. Based on this information, what will the dividend per share be?

   c.   In part (*b*), how much borrowing will take place? What is the addition to retained earnings?

   d.   Suppose Carmen plans no capital outlays for the coming year. What will the dividend be under a residual policy? What will new borrowing be?

Intermediate (Questions 16–18)

16. **Homemade Dividends.**   You own 1,000 shares of stock in Billy Bob Communications. You will receive a $3 per share dividend in one year. In two years, Billy Bob will pay a liquidating dividend of $40 per share. The required return on Billy Bob stock is 15 percent. What is the current share price of your stock (ignoring taxes)? If you would rather have equal dividends in each of the next two years, show how you can accomplish this by creating homemade dividends. (Hint: Dividends will be in the form of an annuity.)

17. **Homemade Dividends.**   In the previous problem, suppose you want only $2,000 total in dividends the first year. What will your homemade dividend be in two years?

18. **Stock Repurchase.**   Klondike Corporation is evaluating an extra dividend versus a share repurchase. In either case, $13,000 would be spent. Current earnings are $2.60 per share, and the stock currently sells for $60 per share. There are 800 shares outstanding. Ignore taxes and other imperfections in answering the first two questions.

   a.   Evaluate the two alternatives in terms of the effect on the price per share of the stock and shareholder wealth.

   b.   What will be the effect on Klondike's EPS and PE ratio under the two different scenarios?

   c.   In the real world, which of these actions would you recommend? Why?

Challenge (Question 19)

19. **Dividend Policies.**   The Mississauga Corporation has a debt-equity ratio of 1.5 and anticipates the following earnings and capital spending for the next year:

Quarter	Earnings	Capital Spending
1	$15 million	$10 million
2	9 million	7 million
3	8 million	6 million
4	4 million	12 million

a. Suppose the firm follows a residual dividend policy, how much will be paid in cash dividends over the next year?

b. Suppose the firm follows a 40 percent cyclical dividend policy, how much will be paid in cash dividends over the next year?

c. Suppose the firm follows a 40 percent stable dividend policy, how much will be paid in cash dividends over the next year?

WHAT'S ON THE WEB?

14.1 **Dividend Reinvestment Plans.** Dividend reinvestment plans (DRIPs or DRPs) permit shareholders to automatically reinvest cash dividends in the company. To find out more about DRPs, go to the Stingy Investor Web site at **www.ndir.com** and follow the "DRPs" link. What are the advantages Stingy Investor lists for DRPs? What is a Share Purchase Plan (SPP)? How does a SPP differ from a DRP? Click on the "Canadian DRPs" link and find which Canadian companies offer a discount in the cost of shares when the dividends are reinvested.

14.2 **Dividends.** Go to **www.earnings.com** and scroll down until you see the section titled Today's Highlighted Dividends and follow the "Full List" link. How many companies went "ex" on this day? What is the largest declared dividend? For the stocks going "ex" today, what is the longest time until the payable date?

14.3 **Stock Splits.** Go to **www.earnings.com** and scroll down until you see the section titled Today's Highlighted Splits and follow the "Full List" link. How many stock splits are listed? How many are reverse splits? What is the largest split and the largest reverse split in terms of shares? Pick a company and follow the link. What type of information do you find?

14.4 **Dividend Yields.** Which stock has the highest dividend yield? To answer this (and more), go to **www.globeinvestor.com** and locate the "Filters" link. Use the minimum value box for "Dividend Yield" to find out how many stocks have a dividend yield above 5 percent. Above 10 percent. Which company has the highest dividend yield?

14.5 **Stock Splits.** How many times has the Bank of Montreal split its stock? Go to the Bank of Montreal's Web page at **www.bmo.com** and click on the "Investor Relations" link. Follow the "Stock Split History" link in the "Shareholder Centre" section. When did the Bank of Montreal first split its stock? What was the split? When was the most recent stock split? If you owned 100 shares of the Bank of Montreal on January 1, 1960, and never sold any shares, how many shares would you own today?

Raising Capital

On November 17, 2006, in an eagerly awaited initial public offering (IPO), the largest Canadian airline, Air Canada, went public. It became the second emergence of the airline, which had just come out of bankruptcy protection a little more than two years earlier, as a public company. The IPO was priced at $21 per share for 25 million shares. The airline planned to use the proceeds for general purposes, including the renewal of its aircraft fleet. Air Canada raised $200 million through the IPO, while its parent company, ACE Aviation Holdings, raised another $325 million for itself through the sale of shares it owned. With a total of $525 million, this issue became the largest corporate IPO in 2006 and surpassed the $400 million underwriters were originally planning to raise. While this IPO was heavily oversubscribed, which meant that investors wanted more shares than were available, it was not very successful for investors. Air Canada shares fell about 6 percent on the first day of trading, and were still below their offering price three months later. In this chapter, we will examine the process by which companies such as Air Canada sell stock to the public, the costs of doing so, and the role of investment banks in the process.

Businesses large and small have one thing in common: They need long-term capital. The chapter describes how they get it. We pay particular attention to what is probably the most important stage in a company's financial life cycle, the initial public offering. Such offerings are the process by which companies convert from being privately owned to being publicly owned. For many, starting a company, growing it, and taking it public is the ultimate entrepreneurial dream.

After venturing through this chapter, you should understand:

15.1 The venture capital market and its role in the financing of new, high-risk ventures.

15.2 How securities are sold to the public.

15.3 The role of underwriters in the sale of securities.

15.4 The underpricing of initial public offerings and why it exists.

15.5 The impact of seasoned equity offerings on the value of the firm.

15.6 The different costs of issuing securities.

15.7 How long-term debt is issued.

All firms must, at varying times, obtain capital. To do so, a firm must either borrow the money (debt financing), sell a portion of the firm (equity financing), or both. How a firm raises capital depends a great deal on the size of the firm, its life cycle stage, and its growth prospects.

In this chapter, we examine some of the ways in which firms actually raise capital. We begin by looking at companies in the early stages of their lives and the importance of venture capital for such firms. We then look at the process of going public and the role of investment banks. Along the way, we discuss many of the issues associated with selling securities to the public and their implications for all types of firms. We close the chapter with a discussion of sources of debt capital.

15.1 | THE FINANCING LIFE CYCLE OF A FIRM: EARLY-STAGE FINANCING AND VENTURE CAPITAL

One day, you and a friend have a great idea for a new computer software product that helps users communicate using the next generation Meganet. Filled with entrepreneurial zeal, you christen the product MegaComm and set about bringing it to market.

Working nights and weekends, you are able to create a prototype of your product. It doesn't actually work, but at least you can show it around to illustrate your idea. To actually develop the product, you need to hire programmers, buy computers, rent office space, and so on. Unfortunately, because you are both university students, your combined assets are not sufficient to fund a pizza party, much less a start-up company. You need what is often referred to as OPM—other people's money.

Your first thought might be to approach a bank for a loan. You would probably discover, however, that banks are generally not interested in making loans to start-up companies with no assets (other than an idea) run by fledgling entrepreneurs with no track record. Instead, your search for capital would very likely lead you to the **venture capital (VC)** market.

venture capital (VC)
Financing for new, often high-risk ventures.

Venture Capital

The term *venture capital* does not have a precise meaning, but it generally refers to financing for new, often high-risk ventures. For example, before it went public, Research In Motion, the manufacturer of the famous BlackBerry wireless devices, was venture capital financed. Individual venture capitalists invest their own money, whereas venture capital firms specialize in pooling funds from various sources and investing them. The underlying sources of funds for such firms include individuals, pension funds, insurance companies, large corporations, and even university endowment funds. The broad term *private equity* is often used to label the rapidly growing area of equity financing for nonpublic companies.[1]

For a list of well-known VC firms, see www.vfinance.com.

Venture capitalists and venture capital firms recognize that many or even most new ventures will not fly, but the occasional one will. The potential profits are enormous in such cases. To limit their risk, venture capitalists generally provide financing in stages. At each stage, enough money is invested to reach the next milestone or planning stage. For example, the *first-stage* (or first round) *financing* might be enough to get a prototype built and a manufacturing plan completed. Based on the results, the *second-stage financing* might be a major investment needed to actually begin manufacturing, marketing, and distribution.

---

[1]So-called "vulture" capitalists specialize in high-risk investments in established, but financially distressed, firms.

There might be many such stages, each of which represents a key step in the process of growing the company.

Venture capital firms often specialize in different stages. Some specialize in very early "seed money," or ground floor financing. In contrast, financing in the later stages might come from venture capitalists specializing in so-called mezzanine level financing, where *mezzanine level* refers to the level just above the ground floor.

The fact that financing is available in stages and is contingent on specified goals being met is a powerful motivating force for the firm's founders. Often, the founders receive relatively little in the way of salary and have substantial portions of their personal assets tied up in the business. At each stage of financing, the value of the founder's stake grows and the probability of success rises. If goals are not met, the venture capitalist will withhold further financing, thereby limiting future losses.

In addition to providing financing, venture capitalists generally will actively participate in running the firm, providing the benefit of experience with previous start-ups as well as general business expertise. This is especially true when the firm's founders have little or no hands-on experience in running a company.

The Internet is a tremendous source of venture capital information, for both suppliers and demanders of capital. For example, the site **www.angelinvestment network.ca** helps entrepreneurs and venture capitalists (i.e., Angel Investors) find each other.

Some Venture Capital Realities

Although there is a large venture capital market, the truth is that access to venture capital is really very limited. Venture capital companies receive huge numbers of unsolicited proposals, the vast majority of which end up in the circular file (the waste basket). Venture capitalists rely heavily on informal networks of engineers, scientists, lawyers, accountants, bankers, and other venture capitalists to help identify potential investments. As a result, personal contacts are important in gaining access to the venture capital market; it is very much an "introduction" market.

Another simple fact about venture capital is that it is incredibly expensive. In a typical deal, the venture capitalist will demand (and get) 40 percent or more of the equity in the company. The venture capitalist will frequently hold voting convertible preferred stock, which gives various priorities in the event that the company is sold or liquidated. The venture capitalist will typically demand (and get) several seats on the company's board of directors and may even appoint one or more members of senior management.

Visit the Canada's Venture Capital & Private Equity Association site at **www.cvca.ca** for useful resources on venture capital.

Choosing a Venture Capitalist

Some start-up companies, particularly those headed by experienced, previously successful entrepreneurs, will be in such demand that they will have the luxury of looking beyond the money in choosing a venture capitalist. There are some key considerations in such a case, some of which can be summarized as follows:

For the latest venture capital news for different provinces visit the "Venture Capital" link at **www.canadait.com**.

1. Financial strength is important. The venture capitalist needs to have the resources and financial reserves for additional financing stages should they become necessary. This doesn't mean that bigger is necessarily better, however, because of our next consideration.

2. Style is important. Some venture capitalists will wish to be very much involved in day-to-day operations and decision making, whereas others will be content with monthly reports. Which is better depends on the firm and also on the venture capitalists' business skills. In addition, a large venture capital firm may be less flexible and more bureaucratic than a smaller "boutique" firm.

3. References are important. Has the venture capitalist been successful with similar firms? Of equal importance, how has the venture capitalist dealt with situations that didn't work out?

4. Contacts are important. A venture capitalist may be able to help the business in ways other than helping with financing and management by providing introductions to potentially important customers, suppliers, and other industry contacts. Venture capitalist firms frequently specialize in a few particular industries, and such specialization could prove quite valuable.

5. Exit strategy is important. Venture capitalists are generally not long-term investors. How and under what circumstances the venture capitalist will "cash out" of the business should be carefully evaluated.

> For news about venture capital and public financing, visit **www.techfinance.ca**.

Conclusion

If a start-up succeeds, the big payoff frequently comes when the company is sold to another company or goes public. Either way, investment bankers are often involved in the process. We discuss the process of selling securities to the public in the next several sections, paying particular attention to the process of going public.

CONCEPT QUESTIONS

15.1a What is venture capital?

15.1b Why is venture capital often provided in stages?

15.2 | SELLING SECURITIES TO THE PUBLIC

Regulation

There are many rules and regulations surrounding the process of selling securities. The Canadian Securities Administrators (CSA) organization co-ordinates and harmonizes the regulation of Canadian capital markets. The CSA operates as a forum for the 13 securities regulators of Canada's 10 provinces and 3 territories. Each province and territory regulates the capital markets located inside its borders through provincial acts. In contrast, in the United States, a single federal body, the Securities and Exchange Commission (SEC), regulates the capital markets across the country. The Canadian regulatory system is expected to offer a more efficient service because each regulator is closer to its local investors and market participants.

> Find out about new company listings in the "Market Activity" menu at **www.tsx.com**.

Ontario, Alberta, British Columbia, and Quebec securities commissions are the most notable regulators due to the number of companies and investors under their jurisdictions. For example, the Ontario Securities Commission (OSC) regulates all companies listed on the TSX, while the Alberta Securities Commission and the British Columbia Securities Commission jointly regulate the TSX Venture Exchange.

The Basic Procedure

There is a series of steps involved in issuing securities to the public. In general terms, the basic procedure is as follows:

1. Management's first step in issuing any securities to the public is to obtain approval from the board of directors. In some cases, the number of authorized shares of common stock must be increased. This requires a vote by the shareholders.

prospectus
A legal document describing details of the issuing corporation and the proposed offering to potential investors.

2. The firm must prepare a preliminary **prospectus** and file it with the OSC or another appropriate provincial regulator. Normally, a preliminary prospectus contains many pages of financial information, including a financial history, details of the existing business, proposed financing, and plans for the future. It is important to note that the regulator does not consider the economic merits of the proposed sale; it merely makes sure that various rules and regulations are followed. Also, the regulator generally does not check the accuracy or truthfulness of the information in the prospectus.

red herring
A preliminary prospectus distributed to prospective investors in a new issue of securities.

3. While the firm is waiting for regulatory approval, it may distribute copies of the preliminary prospectus to potential investors. The preliminary prospectus is sometimes called a **red herring,** in part because bold red letters are printed on the cover. The preliminary prospectus does not contain the price of the new issue, and the company cannot sell these securities during this period. However, verbal offers can be made.

tombstone
An advertisement announcing a public offering.

Tombstone advertisements (or, simply, tombstones) are used by underwriters to publicize the issue. Named after their black border and heavy black print, the tombstones provide investors with "bare bones," basic information about the issue and a list of the investment banks (the underwriters) involved with selling the issue.

4. Once regulatory approval is obtained, a price is determined upon and a full-fledged selling effort gets under way. A final prospectus must accompany the delivery of securities or confirmation of sale, whichever comes first.

Alternative Issue Methods

general cash offer
An issue of securities offered for sale to the general public on a cash basis.

rights offer
A public issue of securities in which securities are first offered to existing shareholders. Also, *rights offering.*

initial public offering
A company's first equity issue made available to the public. Also called an *unseasoned new issue* or an *IPO.*

seasoned equity offering (SEO)
A new equity issue of securities by a company that has previously issued securities to the public.

When a company decides to issue a new security, it can sell it as a public issue or a private issue. In the case of a public issue, the firm is required to register the issue with the appropriate provincial regulator. However, if the issue is to be sold to a small number of institutional investors or wealthy individuals, the sale can be carried out privately. In this case, registration is not required.

For equity sales, there are two kinds of public issues: a **general cash offer** and a **rights offer** (or *rights offering*). With a cash offer, securities are offered to the general public on a first come, first served basis. With a rights offer, securities are initially offered only to existing owners. Rights offers are fairly common in other countries, but they are relatively rare in Canada. We therefore focus on cash offers in this chapter.

The first public equity issue that is made by a company is referred to as an **initial public offering**, an IPO, or an *unseasoned new issue.* This issue occurs when a company decides to go public. Obviously, all initial public offerings are cash offers. If the firm's existing shareholders wanted to buy the shares, the firm wouldn't have to sell them publicly in the first place.

A **seasoned equity offering (SEO)** is a new issue for a company with securities that have been previously issued. The terms *secondary* and *follow-on offering* are also commonly used. A seasoned equity offering of common stock can be made by using a cash offer or a rights offer.

These methods of issuing new securities are shown in Table 15.1. They are discussed in sections 15.3 through 15.7.

Method	Type	Definition
Public		
Traditional negotiated cash offer	Firm commitment cash offer	Company negotiates an agreement with an investment banker to underwrite and distribute the new shares. A specified number of shares are bought by underwriters and sold at a higher price.
	Bought deal cash offer	Company has investment bankers buy an entire issue outright. Net proceeds to the company are known at the time of filing a preliminary prospectus or earlier. The underwriters resell the issue publicly or privately at a preset price.
	Best efforts cash offer	Company has investment bankers sell as many of the new shares as possible at the agreed-upon price. There is no guarantee concerning how much cash will be raised. Some best efforts offerings do not use an underwriter.
	Dutch auction cash offer	Company has investment bankers auction shares to determine the highest offer price obtainable for a given number of shares to be sold.
Privileged subscription	Direct rights offer	Company offers the new stock directly to its existing shareholders.
	Standby rights offer	Like the direct rights offer, this contains a privileged subscription arrangement with existing shareholders. The net proceeds are guaranteed by the underwriters.
Nontraditional cash offer	Competitive firm cash offer	Company can elect to award the underwriting contract through a public auction instead of negotiation.
Private	Direct placement	Securities are sold directly to a small number of investors.

TABLE 15.1

The methods of issuing new securities

CONCEPT QUESTIONS

15.2a What are the basic procedures in selling a new issue?

15.2b What is the difference between a rights offer and a cash offer?

15.3 | UNDERWRITERS

If the public issue of securities is a cash offer, **underwriters** are usually involved. Underwriters perform services such as the following for corporate issuers:

1. Formulating the method used to issue the securities.
2. Pricing the new securities.
3. Selling the new securities.

Typically, the underwriter buys the securities for less than the offering price and accepts the risk of not being able to sell them. The difference between the underwriter's buying price and the offering price is called the **spread**, or discount. It is the basic compensation

underwriters
Investment firms that act as intermediaries between a company selling securities and the investing public.

spread
Compensation to the underwriter: the difference between the underwriter's buying price and offering price.

received by the underwriter. Sometimes the underwriter will get noncash compensation in the form of warrants and stock in addition to the spread.[2]

Underwriters combine to form an underwriting group called a **syndicate** to share the risk and to help sell the issue. In a syndicate, one or more managers arrange the offering. This manager is designated as the lead manager, or principal manager. The lead manager typically has the responsibility of pricing the securities. The other underwriters in the syndicate serve primarily to distribute the issue.

A firm can offer its securities to the highest bidding underwriter on a *competitive offer* basis, or it can negotiate directly with an underwriter. In most cases, companies usually do new issues of debt and equity on a *negotiated offer* basis.

Types of Underwriting

Three basic types of underwriting are involved in a cash offer: firm commitment, bought deal, and best efforts.

Firm Commitment Underwriting   In **firm commitment underwriting**, the issuer sells the entire issue to the underwriters, who then attempt to resell it. This is really just a purchase-resale arrangement, and the underwriter's fee is the spread. For a new issue of seasoned equity, the underwriters can look at the market price to determine what the issue should sell for.

If the underwriter cannot sell all of the issue at the agreed-upon offering price, it may have to lower the price on the unsold shares. Nonetheless, with firm commitment underwriting, the issuer receives the agreed-upon amount, and all the risk associated with selling the issue is transferred to the underwriter.

Because the offering price usually isn't set until the underwriters have investigated how receptive the market is to the issue, this risk is usually minimal. The underwriters' risk is further reduced by a frequently included "market out" clause, which lets the underwriters walk away from the issue if some special circumstances arise. Examples are a sudden large market decline or governmental action that restricts the trading of the issuer's securities.

Bought Deal Underwriting   In **bought deal** underwriting, the underwriter buys an entire issue outright from the issuing company. Typically, the underwriter provides a portion of its own capital and borrows the rest. Then the underwriter resells the issue publicly or privately at a pre-set price.

Bought deal underwriting is closely related to firm commitment underwriting, but has at least two main differences. First, with firm commitment underwriting the offering price usually is not set until just before selling commences. In contrast, with bought deal underwriting the offering price is set much earlier, specifically before or at the time of filing a preliminary prospectus. Second, unlike firm commitments, a "market out" clause is not included in most bought deals. Taken together, the underwriter faces larger risk in bought deal underwriting than in firm commitment underwriting. On the other hand, for the issuer, a bought deal is a more attractive form of underwriting than a firm commitment because the issuer's exact net proceeds will be known earlier.

A bought deal is used primarily for underwriting seasoned equity offerings, which carry much less risk to the underwriter than IPOs. The existence of a secondary market for the shares of the issuing company makes it easier for the underwriter to assess investor interest in the issue and to set a price. Unlike other types of underwriting, bought deals can be completed in a matter of several days.

syndicate
A group of underwriters formed to share the risk and to help sell an issue.

firm commitment underwriting
The type of underwriting in which the underwriter buys the entire issue, assuming full financial responsibility for any unsold shares.

bought deal
The type of underwriting in which the underwriter buys an entire issue outright from the issuing company and commits to an offering price at the time of filing a preliminary prospectus, or earlier.

---

[2]Warrants are essentially options to buy stock at a fixed price for some fixed period of time.

Bought deals have become the most commonly used type of underwriting in Canada. Their popularity has been helped by the **prompt offering prospectus (POP)** system, which allows large, well-known companies to receive regulatory approval on short notice. Under the POP system, companies file financial statements annually regardless of whether they issue securities or not. Thus, the regulator has practically all the required information for a prospectus. When companies decide to issue securities, only a short-form prospectus is required, which can be approved in a matter of days, rather than weeks. A similar system, called **shelf registration** exists in the United States. Shelf registration, permits a corporation to register an offering that it reasonably expects to sell within the next two years and then sell the issue whenever it wants during that two-year period. To qualify for shelf registration, companies have to meet several requirements. For example, the company must be rated investment grade, and the market value of the company's outstanding stock must be more than $150 million.

Best Efforts Underwriting In **best efforts underwriting**, the underwriter is legally bound to use "best efforts" to sell the securities at the agreed-upon offering price. Beyond this, the underwriter does not guarantee any particular amount of money to the issuer. This form of underwriting has become very uncommon in recent years.

Dutch Auction Underwriting With **Dutch auction underwriting**, the underwriter does not set a fixed price for the shares to be sold. Instead, the underwriter conducts an auction in which investors bid for shares. The offer price is determined based on the submitted bids. A Dutch auction is also known by the more descriptive name *single price auction*. This approach to selling securities to the public is relatively new in the IPO market and has not been widely used there. It was much in the news in 2004, when Web search company Google elected to use a Dutch auction for its IPO. This approach is more common in the bond markets, though. For example, it is used by the Government of Canada to sell Real Return bonds, and it is the sole procedure used by the U.S. Treasury to sell enormous quantities of notes, bonds, and bills to the public. In addition, Canadian firms frequently use Dutch auctions for share buyback programs. For example, Mississauga-based MDS and Toronto-based ING Canada planned to repurchase up to $500-million of their common shares in a Dutch auction in 2007.

The best way to understand a Dutch or single price auction is to consider a simple example. Suppose the Rial Company wants to sell 400 shares to the public. The company receives five bids as follows:

Bidder	Quantity	Price
A	100 shares	$16
B	100 shares	14
C	200 shares	12
D	100 shares	12
E	200 shares	10

Thus, bidder A is willing to buy 100 shares at $16 each, bidder B is willing to buy 100 shares at $14, and so on. The Rial Company examines the bids to determine the highest price that will result in all 400 shares being sold. So, for example, at $14, A and B would buy only 200 shares, so that price is too high. Working our way down, all 400 shares won't

---

prompt offering prospectus (POP) system
The registration system that allows qualified companies to access capital markets more quickly by using a short-form prospectus.

shelf registration
Registration permitted in the United States that allows a company to register all issues it expects to sell within two years at one time, with subsequent sales at any time within those two years.

best efforts underwriting
The type of underwriting in which the underwriter sells as much of the issue as possible, but can return any unsold shares to the issuer without financial responsibility.

Dutch auction underwriting
The type of underwriting in which the offer price is set based on competitive bidding by investors. Also known as a *single price auction*.

Learn all about Dutch auction IPOs at www. wrhambrecht .com.

be sold until we hit a price of $12, so $12 will be the offer price in the IPO. Bidders A through D will receive shares; bidder E will not.

There are two additional important points to observe in our example: First, all the winning bidders will pay $12, even bidders A and B, who actually bid a higher price. The fact that all successful bidders pay the same price is the reason for the name "single price auction." The idea in such an auction is to encourage bidders to bid aggressively by providing some protection against bidding a price that is too high.

Second, notice that at the $12 offer price, there are actually bids for 500 shares, which exceeds the 400 shares Rial wants to sell. Thus, there has to be some sort of allocation. How this is done varies a bit, but, in the IPO market, the approach has been to simply compute the ratio of shares offered to shares bid at the offer price or better, which, in our example, is 400/500 = .8, and allocate bidders that percentage of their bids. In other words, bidders A through D would each receive 80 percent of the shares they bid at a price of $12 per share.

The Overallotment Option

overallotment option

A contract provision giving the underwriter the option to purchase additional shares from the issuer at the offering price less the underwriter's spread. Also called the *Green Shoe provision.*

Many underwriting contracts contain an **overallotment option** (sometimes called the Green Shoe provision), which gives the members of the underwriting group the option to purchase additional shares from the issuer at the offering price less the underwriter's discount.[3] Many IPOs and SEOs include this provision, but ordinary debt offerings generally do not. The stated reason for the overallotment option is to cover excess demand and **oversubscriptions**. Overallotment options usually last for about 30 days and involve no more than 15 percent of the newly issued shares.

The Aftermarket

oversubscription

A situation related to a new securities issue, in which investors want more securities (stocks or bonds) than are available.

The period after a new issue is initially sold to the public is referred to as the *aftermarket*. The lead underwriter frequently will "stabilize," or support, the market price for a relatively short time following the offering. This is done by actually selling 115 percent of the issue. If the price rises in the aftermarket, the underwriter will exercise the overallotment option to purchase the extra 15 percent needed. If the price declines, however, the underwriter will step in and buy the stock in the open market, thereby supporting the price. In this second case, the underwriter allows the overallotment option to expire.[4]

CONCEPT QUESTIONS

15.3a What do underwriters do?

15.3b What is the overallotment option?

---

[3]The term *Green Shoe provision* sounds quite exotic, but the origin is relatively mundane. The term comes from the name of the Green Shoe Manufacturing Company, which, in 1963, was the first issuer to grant such an option.

[4]Occasionally, the price of a security falls dramatically when the underwriter ceases to stabilize the price. In such cases, Bay Street humourists (the ones who didn't buy any of the stock) have referred to the period following the aftermarket as the aftermath.

15.4 | IPOS AND UNDERPRICING

Determining the correct offering price is the most difficult thing an underwriter must do for an initial public offering. The issuing firm faces a potential cost if the offering price is set too high or too low. If the issue is priced too high, it may be unsuccessful and have to be withdrawn. If the issue is priced below the true market value, the issuer's existing shareholders will experience an opportunity loss when they sell their shares for less than they are worth. Issuing securities at less than their market value is called **underpricing**.

Underpricing is fairly common. It obviously helps new shareholders earn a higher return on the shares they buy. However, the existing shareholders of the issuing firm are not helped by underpricing. To them, it is an indirect cost of issuing new securities. For example, in March 2006, Tim Hortons, the Oakville, Ontario, based coffee and doughnut chain, went public. On the first day of trading, the stock was as hot as the company's freshly brewed coffee. There were 29 million shares offered at $27 per share, raising $783 million. At the end of the first day, the stock sold for $33.10 per share, up 22.6 percent. Based on these numbers, Tim Hortons shares were apparently underpriced by $6.10 each, which meant that the company missed out on an additional $176.9 million.

Dutch auctions are supposed to eliminate this kind of "pop" in first day prices. For example, Google sold 19.6 million shares at a price of US$85 in a Dutch auction IPO. However, the stock closed at US$100.34 on the first day, an increase of 18 percent, so Google missed out on an additional US$300 million.

One of the biggest dollar amounts "left on the table" occurred in 1999 when eToys went public, offering 8.2 million shares. The stock jumped US$57 dollars above the offer price on the first day, which meant eToys left about half a billion dollars on the table! eToys could have used the money; it filed for bankruptcy less than two years later. In May 2002, the company sued its lead underwriter, claiming the offer price was deliberately set too low. In May 2004, a judge upheld the complaint, and as this is being written, the case is still in the courts.

underpricing
Issuing securities at less than their market value.

IPO information is ubiquitous on the World Wide Web. For Canadian IPOs visit **ipo.investcom.com,** and for U.S. IPOs go to **www.ipohome.com**.

Evidence on Underpricing

Figure 15.1 provides a more general illustration of the underpricing phenomenon. What is shown is the month-by-month history of underpricing for SEC-registered IPOs.[5] The period covered is 1960 through 2004. Figure 15.2 presents the number of offerings in each month for the same period.

Figure 15.1 shows that underpricing can be quite dramatic, exceeding 100 percent in some months. In such months, the average IPO more than doubled in value, sometimes in a matter of hours. Also, the degree of underpricing varies through time, and periods of severe underpricing ("hot issue" markets) are followed by periods of little underpricing ("cold issue" markets). For example, in the 1960s, the average IPO was underpriced by 21.25 percent. In the 1970s, the average underpricing was much smaller (8.95 percent), and the amount of underpricing was actually very small or even negative for much of that time. For 1990–1999, IPOs were underpriced by 20.9 percent on average, and for 2000–2004, average underpricing was 33.2 percent.

---

[5]The discussion in this section draws on Jay R. Ritter, "Initial Public Offerings," *Contemporary Finance Digest* 2 (Spring 1998).

FIGURE 15.1   **Average first-day returns by month for SEC-registered initial public offerings: 1960–2004**

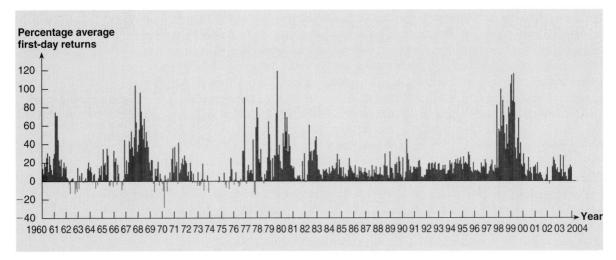

Source: Roger G. Ibbotson, Jody L. Sindelar, and Jay R. Ritter, "The Market's Problems with the Pricing of Initial Public Offerings," *Journal of Applied Corporate Finance* 7 (Spring 1994), as updated by the authors.

FIGURE 15.2   **Number of offerings by month for SEC-registered initial public offerings: 1960–2004**

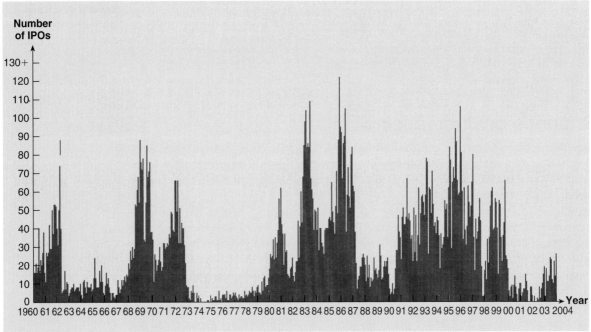

Source: Roger G. Ibbotson, Jody L. Sindelar, and Jay R. Ritter, "The Market's Problems with the Pricing of Initial Public Offerings," *Journal of Applied Corporate Finance* 7 (Spring 1994), as updated by the authors.

From Figure 15.2, it is apparent that the number of IPOs is also highly variable through time. Further, there are pronounced cycles in both the degree of underpricing and the number of IPOs. Comparing Figures 15.1 and 15.2, we see that increases in the number of new

REALITY BYTES

IPO Underpricing around the World

The phenomenon of initial public offering (IPO) underpricing exists in every country with a stock market, although the extent of underpricing varies from country to country.

In general, countries with developed capital markets have more moderate underpricing than in emerging markets. During the Internet bubble of 1999–2000, however, underpricing in the developed capital markets increased dramatically. In the United States, for example, the average first-day return during 1999–2000 was 65 percent. At the same time that under-pricing in the developed capital markets increased, the under-pricing of IPOs sold to residents of China moderated. The Chinese average

has come down to a mere 257 percent, which is lower than it had been in the early and mid-1990s. After the bursting of the Internet bubble in mid-2000, the level of underpricing in the United States, Germany, and other developed capital markets has returned to more traditional levels.

The table below gives a summary of the average first-day returns on IPOs in a number of countries around the world, with the figures collected from a number of studies by various authors. Note that the 7.0 percent underpricing of Canadian IPOs is one of the lowest in the table and is about 2.6 times smaller than the 18.1 percent underpricing of U.S. IPOs.

Country	Sample Size	Time Period	Average First-Day Return	Country	Sample Size	Time Period	Average First-Day Return
Australia	381	1976–1995	12.1%	Malaysia	401	1980–1998	104.1%
Austria	83	1984–2002	6.3	Mexico	37	1987–1990	33.0
Belgium	93	1984–2004	14.2%	Netherlands	143	1982–1999	10.2
Brazil	62	1979–1990	78.5	New Zealand	201	1979–1999	23.0
Canada	540	1971–2002	7.0	Nigeria	63	1989–1993	19.1
Chile	55	1982–1997	8.8	Norway	68	1984–1996	12.5
China	432	1990–2000	256.9	Philippines	104	1987–1997	22.7
Denmark	117	1984–1998	5.4	Poland	140	1991–1998	27.4
Finland	99	1984–1997	10.1	Portugal	21	1992–1998	10.6
France	571	1983–2000	11.6	Singapore	441	1973–2001	29.6
Germany	545	1978–2001	31.1	South Africa	118	1980–1991	32.7
Greece	363	1976–2005	25.1	Spain	99	1986–1998	10.7
Hong Kong	857	1980–2001	17.3	Sweden	332	1980–1998	30.5
India	2,713	1990–2004	95.4	Switzerland	120	1983–2000	34.9
Indonesia	265	1989–2003	20.2	Taiwan	293	1986–1998	31.1
Israel	285	1990–1994	12.1	Thailand	292	1987–1997	46.7
Italy	181	1985–2001	21.7	Turkey	282	1990–2004	10.8
Japan	1,689	1970–2001	28.4	United Kingdom	3,122	1959–2001	17.4
Korea	477	1980–1996	74.3	United States	15,333	1960–2005	18.1

Source: Jay R. Ritter, Cordell Professor of Finance, University of Florida.

offerings tend to follow periods of significant underpricing by roughly 6 to 12 months. This probably occurs because companies decide to go public when they perceive that the market is highly receptive to new issues. The *Reality Bytes* box above shows that IPO underpricing is not just confined to the United States. In fact, it exists in Canada as well, and seems to be a global phenomenon.

Why Does Underpricing Exist?

Based on the evidence we've examined, an obvious question is, Why does underpricing continue to exist? As we discuss, there are various explanations, but, to date, there is a lack of complete agreement among researchers as to which is correct.

We present some pieces of the underpricing puzzle by stressing two important caveats to our preceding discussion. First, the average figures we have examined tend to obscure the fact that much of the apparent underpricing is attributable to the smaller, more highly speculative issues. These firms tend to be young firms, and such young firms can be very risky investments. Arguably, they must be significantly underpriced, on average, just to attract investors, and this is one explanation for the underpricing phenomenon.

The second caveat is that relatively few IPO buyers will actually get the initial high average returns observed in IPOs, and many will actually lose money. Although it is true that, on average, IPOs have positive initial returns, a significant fraction of them have price drops. Furthermore, when the price is too low, the issue is often "oversubscribed." This means investors will not be able to buy all of the shares they want, and the underwriters will allocate the shares among investors.

The average investor will find it difficult to get shares in a "successful" offering (one in which the price increases) because there will not be enough shares to go around. On the other hand, an investor blindly submitting orders for IPOs tends to get more shares in issues that go down in price.

To illustrate, consider this tale of two investors. Smith knows very accurately what the Bonanza Corporation is worth when its shares are offered. She is confident that the shares are underpriced. Jones knows only that IPOs are usually underpriced. Armed with this information, Jones decides to buy 1,000 shares of every IPO. Does he actually earn an abnormally high return on the initial offering?

The answer is no, and at least one reason is Smith. Knowing about the Bonanza Corporation, Smith invests all her money in its IPO. When the issue is oversubscribed, the underwriters have to somehow allocate the shares between Smith and Jones. The net result is that when an issue is underpriced, Jones doesn't get to buy as much of it as he wanted.

Smith also knows that the Blue Sky Corporation IPO is overpriced. In this case, she avoids its IPO altogether, and Jones ends up with a full 1,000 shares. To summarize this tale, Jones gets fewer shares when more knowledgeable investors swarm to buy an underpriced issue and gets all he wants when the smart money avoids the issue.

This is an example of a "winner's curse," and it is thought to be another reason why IPOs have such a large average return. When the average investor "wins" and gets the entire allocation, it may be because those who knew better avoided the issue. The only way underwriters can counteract the winner's curse and attract the average investor is to underprice new issues (on average) so that the average investor still makes a profit.

A final reason for underpricing is that the underpricing is a kind of insurance for the investment banks. Conceivably, an investment bank could be sued successfully by angry customers if it consistently overpriced securities. Underpricing guarantees that, at least on average, customers will come out ahead.

CONCEPT QUESTIONS

15.4a Why is underpricing a cost to the issuing firm?

15.4b Suppose a stockbroker calls you up out of the blue and offers to sell you "all the shares you want" of a new issue. Do you think the issue will be more or less underpriced than average?

15.5 | NEW EQUITY SALES AND THE VALUE OF THE FIRM

We now turn to a consideration of seasoned equity offerings (SEOs), which, as we discussed earlier, are offerings by firms that already have outstanding securities. It seems reasonable to believe that new long-term financing is arranged by firms after positive net present value projects are put together. As a consequence, when the announcement of external financing is made, the firm's market value should go up. Interestingly, this is not what happens. Stock prices tend to decline following the announcement of a new equity issue, although they tend to not change much following a debt announcement. A number of researchers have studied this issue. Plausible reasons for this strange result include the following:

1. **Managerial information.** If management has superior information about the market value of the firm, it may know when the firm is overvalued. If it does, it will attempt to issue new shares of stock when the market value exceeds the correct value. This will benefit existing shareholders. However, the potential new shareholders are not stupid, and they will anticipate this superior information and discount it in lower market prices at the new issue date.

2. **Debt usage.** A company's issuing new equity may reveal that the company has too much debt or too little liquidity. One version of this argument says that the equity issue is a bad signal to the market. After all, if the new projects are favourable ones, why should the firm let new shareholders in on them? It could just issue debt and let the existing shareholders have all the gain.

3. **Issue costs.** As we discuss next, there are substantial costs associated with selling securities.

The drop in value of the existing stock following the announcement of a new issue is an example of an indirect cost of selling securities. This drop might typically be on the order of 3 percent for an industrial corporation (and somewhat smaller for a public utility), so, for a large company, it can represent a substantial amount of money. We label this drop the *abnormal return* in our discussion of the costs of new issues that follows.

CONCEPT QUESTIONS

15.5a What are some possible reasons why the price of stock drops on the announcement of a new equity issue?

15.5b Explain why we might expect a firm with a positive NPV investment to finance it with debt instead of equity.

15.6 | THE COST OF ISSUING SECURITIES

Issuing securities to the public isn't free, and the costs of different methods are important determinants of which is used. These costs associated with *floating* a new issue are generically called *flotation costs*. In this section, we take a closer look at the flotation costs associated with equity sales to the public.

The costs of selling stock are classified in the following table and fall into six categories: (1) the spread, (2) other direct expenses, (3) indirect expenses, (4) abnormal returns (discussed previously), (5) underpricing, and (6) the overallotment option.

The Costs of Issuing Securities	
1. Spread	The spread consists of direct fees paid by the issuer to the underwriting syndicate—the difference between the price the issuer receives and the offer price.
2. Other direct expenses	These are direct costs incurred by the issuer that are not part of the compensation to underwriters. These costs include filing fees, legal fees, and taxes—all reported on the prospectus.
3. Indirect expenses	These costs are not reported on the prospectus and include the cost of management time spent working on the new issue.
4. Abnormal returns	In a seasoned issue of stock, the price of the existing stock drops on average by 3 percent upon the announcement of the issue. This drop is called the abnormal return.
5. Underpricing	For initial public offerings, losses arise from selling the stock below the true value.
6. Overallotment option	The overallotment option gives the underwriters the right to buy additional shares at the offer price to cover overallotments.

Table 15.2 reports direct and indirect costs as percentages of the gross amount raised for IPOs sold by Canadian companies from 1997 to 1999. Expenses not included are the cost of the overallotment option and abnormal returns (for SEOs).

As Table 15.2 shows, direct costs alone can be very large, particularly for smaller issues (less than US$10 million). For a smaller IPO, for example, the total direct costs amount to 15.98 percent of the amount raised. This means that if a company sells $10 million in stock, it will only net about $8.4 million; the other $1.6 million would go to cover the underwriter spread and other direct expenses. Typical underwriter spreads on an IPO range from about 5 percent for large offerings to 8 percent for small offerings, and the average spread is about 7 percent.

As we have discussed, the underpricing of IPOs is an additional cost to the issuer. To get a better idea of the total cost of going public, Table 15.2 also shows the underpricing for IPOs (in the last column on the right). Comparing the total direct costs to the underpricing, we see that the direct costs are only about half of the underpricing for small issues (less than US$10 million), and they are roughly the same size for large issues (US$100 and more). Overall, across all size groups, the total direct costs amount to 12 percent of the amount raised and underpricing amounts to 19 percent.

In general, two clear patterns emerge from Table 15.2. First, there are substantial economies of scale. The underwriter spreads are smaller on larger issues, and the other direct costs fall sharply as a percentage of the amount raised, a reflection of the mostly fixed nature of such costs. Second, indirect expenses, such as underpricing, represent a significant portion of the cost of issuing securities and exceed total direct expenses, especially

TABLE 15.2 Direct and indirect costs as a percentage of gross proceeds for IPOs offered by Canadian companies: 1997–1999	Size of Offering (US$ millions)	Number of IPOs	Gross Spread	Other Direct Expenses	Total Direct Costs	Underpricing
	1–9.99	53	8.12%	7.86%	15.98%	30.61%
	10–49.99	49	6.14	3.31	9.45	11.30
	50–99.99	10	6.00	2.00	8.00	10.76
	100 and up	16	5.53	1.75	7.28	8.88
	Average		6.88	4.90	11.78	18.95

Source: Based on Maher Kooli and Jean-Marc Suret, "How Cost-Effective Are Canadian IPO Markets?" *Canadian Investment Review* (Winter 2003).

REALITY BYTES

Anatomy of an IPO

On February 2, 2007, Universal Energy Group, Ltd., a Toronto-based seller of electricity and natural gas, and ethanol producer, went public via an IPO. Universal Energy Group issued 11.4 million shares of stock at a price of $11.00 each. The underwriting syndicate for the offering was led by National Bank Financial Inc. and included CIBC World Markets, GMP Securities, and HSBC Securities.

Even though the IPO raised a gross sum of $125 million, Universal Energy Group only got to keep about $117.5 million after the underwriters' fee. The underwriters' fee was paid through the 6 percent underwriter spread, which is very standard for an offering of this size. Universal Energy Group sold each of the 11.4 million shares to the underwriters for $10.34, and the underwriters in turn sold the shares to the public for $11.00 each. Thus, of the $125 million investors paid for the shares, Universal Energy Group received $117.5 million.

But wait, there's more. In addition to the underwriters' fee, other direct expenses, which included filing, auditing, and legal fees, were approximately $2.5 million. In the end, Universal's expenses totalled $10 million, of which $7.5 million went to the underwriters and $2.5 million went to other parties. The total direct costs to Universal Energy Group were 8.5 percent of the issue proceeds.

However, this was still not the end of Universal's expenses. Underpricing and the overallotment option could bring IPO costs even higher. Specifically, on the first day of trading the stock was up $1.55 to close at $12.55. In other words, $17.6 million was "left on the table" by the company due to the 14 percent IPO underpricing. Universal Energy Group also granted the underwriters the overallotment option to purchase up to 1.7 million additional shares at the offering price less the underwriters' fees for a period of 30 days. If it was exercised in full, the option would increase the underwriters' fee to $8.6 million.

Taken together, the total cost of issuing securities could reach $28.7 million for the company, and we even ignored the cost of management time spent working on the issue. As Universal Energy Group's expenses show, an IPO can be a costly undertaking!

for smaller issues. The *Reality Bytes* box above provides a detailed example of the cost of issuing securities for a particular Canadian company.

Unlike equity sales, the costs of selling debt include only three categories: (1) the spread, (2) other direct expenses, and (3) indirect expenses. Table 15.3 shows the spread

| Proceeds ($ in millions) | Straight Bonds | | | | | |
| | Investment Grade | | | Noninvestment Grade | | |
	Number of Issues	Gross Spread	Total Direct Cost	Number of Issues	Gross Spread	Total Direct Cost
2–9.99	40	0.62%	1.90%	0	—	—
10–19.99	68	0.50	1.35	2	2.74%	4.80%
20–39.99	119	0.58	1.21	13	3.06	4.36
40–59.99	132	0.39	0.86	12	3.01	3.93
60–79.99	68	0.57	0.97	43	2.99	4.07
80–99.99	100	0.66	0.94	56	2.74	3.66
100–199.99	341	0.55	0.80	321	2.71	3.39
200–499.99	173	0.50	0.81	156	2.49	2.90
500 and up	97	0.28	0.38	20	2.45	2.71
Average		0.51	0.85		2.68	3.35

TABLE 15.3

Average gross spreads and total direct costs for U.S. bond issues: 1990–2003

Source: Inmoo Lee, Scott Lochhead, Jay Ritter, and Quanshui Zhao, "The Costs of Raising Capital," *Journal of Financial Research* 1 (Spring 1996), calculations and updates by the authors.

and total direct costs for bond issues of U.S. companies from 1990 to 2003. Recall from Chapter 6 that bonds carry different credit ratings. Higher-rated bonds are said to be investment grade, whereas lower-rated bonds are noninvestment grade.

Table 15.3 clarifies three things regarding debt issues. First, there are substantial economies of scale here as well. Second, investment-grade issues have much lower direct costs. Finally, there are relatively few non-investment-grade issues in the smaller size categories, reflecting the fact that such issues are more commonly handled as private placements, which we discuss in our next section.

CONCEPT QUESTIONS

15.6a   What are the different costs associated with security offerings?

15.6b   What lessons do we learn from studying issue costs?

15.7 | ISSUING LONG-TERM DEBT

The general procedures followed in a public issue of bonds are the same as those for stocks. The issue must be registered with the OSC or any other relevant provincial or territorial commission, there must be a prospectus, and so on. The registration statement for a public issue of bonds, however, is different from the one for common stock. For bonds, the registration statement must indicate an indenture.

Another important difference is that more than 50 percent of all debt is issued privately. There are two basic forms of direct private long-term financing: term loans and private placement.

Term loans are direct business loans. These loans have maturities of between one year and five years. Most term loans are repayable during the life of the loan. The lenders include chartered banks, insurance companies, and other lenders that specialize in corporate finance. **Private placements** are very similar to term loans except that the maturity is longer.

The important differences between direct private long-term financing and public issues of debt are:

1.   A direct long-term loan avoids the cost of OSC registration.

2.   Direct placement is likely to have more restrictive covenants.

3.   It is easier to renegotiate a term loan or a private placement in the event of a default. It is harder to renegotiate a public issue because hundreds of holders are usually involved.

4.   Life insurance companies and pension funds dominate the private-placement segment of the bond market. Chartered banks are significant participants in the term-loan market.

5.   The costs of distributing bonds are lower in the private market.

The interest rates on term loans and private placements are often higher than those on an equivalent public issue. This difference may reflect the trade-off between a higher interest rate and more flexible arrangements in the event of financial distress, as well as the lower costs associated with private placements.

An additional, and very important, consideration is that the flotation costs associated with selling debt are much less than the comparable costs associated with selling equity.

term loans
Direct business loans of, typically, one to five years.

private placements
Loans, usually long-term in nature, provided directly by a limited number of investors.

CONCEPT QUESTIONS

15.7a What is the difference between private and public bond issues?

15.7b A private placement is likely to have a higher interest rate than a public issue. Why?

SUMMARY AND CONCLUSIONS

This chapter has looked at how corporate securities are issued. The following are the main points:

1. The venture capital market is the primary source of financing for new high-risk companies. To limit their risk, venture capitalists generally provide financing in stages. Venture capital is incredibly expensive, and important considerations in choosing a venture capitalist include the venture capitalist's financial strength, style, references, contacts, and exit strategy.

2. Selling securities to the public requires several steps, such as obtaining approval from the board of directors, preparing preliminary and final prospectuses, and obtaining regulatory approval. When a company's stock is sold to the public for the first time, it is called an initial public offering. In contrast, a new issue for a company with securities that have been previously issued is called a seasoned equity offering.

3. Bought deal underwriting, in which the underwriter buys an entire issue outright from the issuing company, has become a more commonly used type of underwriting than firm commitment or best efforts underwriting in Canada. The popularity of bought deals has been helped by the prompt offering prospectus system, which allows large, well-known companies to receive regulatory approval on short notice.

4. Issuing securities at less than their market value is called underpricing. It results in an opportunity loss for the issuer's existing shareholders and can be quite large. Underpricing of IPOs exists at different degrees in every country with a stock market. While several explanations have been offered for underpricing, researchers disagree on which is correct.

5. Stock prices tend to drop on the announcement of a new equity issue, but they usually do not change much following a debt announcement. Possible explanations for this result include managerial information, debt usage, and issue costs.

6. The direct and indirect costs of issuing securities can be substantial. However, the costs are much lower (as a percentage) for larger issues.

7. Unlike stocks, the majority of all debt is issued privately. Two basic forms of direct private long-term financing are term loans and private placement.

CHAPTER REVIEW AND SELF-TEST PROBLEM

15.1 Flotation Costs. The L5 Corporation is considering an equity issue to finance a new space station. A total of $10 million in new equity is needed. If the direct costs are estimated at 6 percent of the amount raised, how large does the issue need to be? What is the dollar amount of the flotation cost?

■ Answer to Chapter Review and Self-Test Problem

15.1   The firm needs to net $10 million after paying the 6 percent flotation costs. So the amount raised is given by:

Amount raised $\times$ (1 − .06) = $10 million
Amount raised = $10/.94   = $10.638 million

The total flotation cost is thus $638,000.

CRITICAL THINKING AND CONCEPTS REVIEW

15.1   **Debt versus Equity Offering Size.**   In the aggregate, debt offerings are much more common than equity offerings and typically much larger as well. Why?

15.2   **Debt versus Equity Flotation Costs.**   Why are the costs of selling equity so much larger than the costs of selling debt?

15.3   **Bond Ratings and Flotation Costs.**   Why do noninvestment-grade bonds have much higher direct costs than investment-grade issues?

15.4   **Underpricing in Debt Offerings.**   Why is underpricing not a great concern with bond offerings?

Use the following information to answer the next three questions. Eyetech Pharmaceuticals, Inc., a company that develops treatments for eye problems, went public in January 2004. Assisted by the investment bank Merrill Lynch, Eyetech sold 6.5 million shares at $21 each, thereby raising a total of $136.5 million. At the end of the first day of trading, the stock sold for $32.40 per share. Based on the end-of-day numbers, Eyetech shares were apparently underpriced by $11.40 each, meaning that the company missed out on an additional $74.1 million.

15.5   **IPO Pricing.**   The Eyetech IPO was underpriced by about 54 percent. Should Eyetech be upset at Merrill Lynch over the underpricing?

15.6   **IPO Pricing.**   In the previous question, would it affect your thinking to know that the company was incorporated less than four years earlier, had only $30 million in revenues for the first nine months of 2003, and had never earned a profit. Additionally, the company had only one product, Macugen, which had won fast-track status from the FDA, but still did not have approval to be sold.

15.7   **IPO Pricing.**   In the previous two questions, how would it affect your thinking to know that in addition to the 6.5 million shares offered in the IPO, Eyetech had an additional 32 million shares outstanding? Of those 32 million shares, 10 million shares were owned by pharmaceutical giant Pfizer, and 12 million shares were owned by the 13 directors and executive officers.

15.8   **IPO Underpricing.**   In 1980, a certain assistant professor of finance bought 12 initial public offerings of common stock. He held each of these for approximately one month and then sold. The investment rule he followed was to submit a purchase order for every firm commitment initial public offering of oil and gas exploration companies. There were 22 of these offerings, and he submitted a purchase order for approximately $1,000 in stock for each of the companies. With 10 of these, no shares were allocated to this assistant professor. With five of the 12 offerings that were purchased, fewer than the requested number of shares were allocated.

The year 1980 was very good for oil and gas exploration company owners: on average, for the 22 companies that went public, the stocks were selling for 80 percent above the offering price a month after the initial offering date. The assistant professor looked at his performance record and found that the $8,400 invested in the 12 companies had grown to $10,000, representing a return of only about 20 percent (commissions were negligible). Did he have bad luck, or should he have expected to do worse than the average initial public offering investor? Explain.

15.9 IPO Pricing.   The following material represents the cover page and summary of the prospectus for the initial public offering of the Pest Investigation Control Corporation (PICC), which is going public tomorrow with a firm commitment initial public offering managed by the investment banking firm of Erlanger and Ritter. Answer the following questions:

a. Assume that you know nothing about PICC other than the information contained in the prospectus. Based on your knowledge of finance, what is your prediction for the price of PICC tomorrow? Provide a short explanation of why you think this will occur.

b. Assume that you have several thousand dollars to invest. When you get home from class tonight, you find that your stockbroker, whom you have not talked to for weeks, has called. She has left a message that PICC is going public tomorrow and that she can get you several hundred shares at the offering price if you call her back first thing in the morning. Discuss the merits of this opportunity.

PROSPECTUS   PICC

200,000 shares
PEST INVESTIGATION CONTROL CORPORATION

Of the shares being offered hereby, all 200,000 are being sold by the Pest Investigation Control Corporation, Inc. ("the Company"). Before the offering there has been no public market for the shares of PICC, and no guarantee can be given that any such market will develop.

These securities have not been approved or disapproved by the OSC nor has the commission passed upon the accuracy or adequacy of this prospectus. Any representation to the contrary is a criminal offense.

	Price to Public	**Underwriting Discount**	**Proceeds to Company***
Per share	$ 11.00	$ 1.10	$ 9.90
Total	$2,200,000	$220,000	$1,980,000

*Before deducting expenses estimated at $27,000 and payable by the Company.

This is an initial public offering. The common shares are being offered, subject to prior sale, when, as, and if delivered to and accepted by the Underwriters and subject to approval of certain legal matters by their Counsel and by Counsel for the Company. The Underwriters reserve the right to withdraw, cancel, or modify such offer and to reject offers in whole or in part.

Erlanger and Ritter, Investment Bankers
July 12, 2007

Prospectus Summary

The Company	The Pest Investigation Control Corporation (PICC) breeds and markets toads and tree frogs as ecologically safe insect-control mechanisms.
The Offering	200,000 shares of common stock, no par value.
Listing	The Company will seek listing on the TSX.
Shares Outstanding	As of June 30, 2007, 400,000 shares of common stock were outstanding. After the offering, 600,000 shares of common stock will be outstanding.
Use of Proceeds	To finance expansion of inventory and receivables and general working capital, and to pay for country club memberships for certain finance professors.

Selected Financial Information
(amounts in thousands except per-share data)

	Fiscal Year Ended June 30		
	2005	**2006**	**2007**
Revenues	$60.00	$120.00	$240.00
Net earnings	3.80	15.90	36.10
Earnings per share	.01	.04	.09

	As of June 30, 2007	
	Actual	**As Adjusted for This Offering**
Working capital	$ 8	$1,961
Total assets	511	2,464
Stockholders' equity	423	2,376

QUESTIONS AND PROBLEMS

Basic
(Questions 1–4)

1. **IPO Underpricing.** The Sun Co. and the Moon Co. have both announced IPOs at $40 per share. One of these is undervalued by $8, and the other is overvalued by $4, but you have no way of knowing which is which. You plan on buying 1,000 shares of each issue. If an issue is underpriced, it will be rationed, and only half your order will be filled. If you *could* get 1,000 shares in Sun and 1,000 shares in Moon, what would your profit be? What profit do you actually expect? What principle have you illustrated?

2. **Calculating Flotation Costs.** The W. W. Corporation needs to raise $90 million to finance its expansion into new markets. The company will sell new shares of equity via a general cash offering to raise the needed funds. If the offer price is $65 per share and the company's underwriters charge an 8 percent spread, how many shares need to be sold?

3. **Calculating Flotation Costs.** In the previous problem, if the OSC filing fee and associated administrative expenses of the offering are $450,000, how many shares need to be sold now?

4. **Dutch Auction.** The Dream Team Corporation wants to sell 500 shares to the public in a Dutch auction. The company received the following four bids from investors:

Bidder	Quantity	Price
A	300 shares	$40
B	150 shares	38
C	350 shares	35
D	400 shares	34

  a. What is the offer price of this IPO?

  b. How many shares will be allocated to bidder A?

5. **Dutch Auction.** Monarchy Inc., decided to go public and to use a Dutch auction for the sale of its 1,000 shares. The company received the following six bids from investors:

Intermediate
(Questions 5–9)

Bidder	Quantity	Price
A	300 shares	$20
B	350 shares	18
C	150 shares	17
D	200 shares	17
E	200 shares	17
F	325 shares	16

  a. What is the offer price of this IPO?

  b. How many shares will be allocated to each bidder?

6. **Calculating Flotation Costs.** The ZZ Bottom Co. has just gone public. Under a firm commitment agreement, ZZ Bottom received $28 for each of the 3.8 million shares sold. The initial offering price was $31 per share, and the stock rose to $37 per share in the first few minutes of trading. ZZ Bottom paid $625,000 in legal and other direct costs, and $250,000 in indirect costs. What was the flotation cost as a percentage of funds raised?

7. **Calculating Flotation Costs.** The Regent Corporation needs to raise $65 million to finance its expansion into new markets. The company will sell new shares of equity via a general cash offering to raise the needed funds. If the offer price is $53 per share and the company's underwriters charge a 6 percent spread, how many shares need to be sold?

8. **Calculating Flotation Costs.** In the previous problem, if the OSC filing fee and associated administrative expenses of the offering are $575,000, how many shares need to be sold now?

9. **Calculating Flotation Costs.** The Verbatim Co. has just gone public. Under a firm commitment agreement, Verbatim received $17 for each of the 4.1 million shares sold. The initial offering price was $18.75 per share, and the stock rose to $24 per share in the first few minutes of trading. Verbatim paid $400,000 in legal and other direct costs, and $175,000 in indirect costs. What was the flotation cost as a percentage of funds raised?

WHAT'S ON THE WEB?

15.1 Venture Capital.   What is the current state of Canada's venture capital industry? Go to **www.canadavc.com,** follow the "VC Resources" link, the "Stats" link, and follow the link for the most recent VC industry overview. How many companies were funded last year? What was the average amount invested per company? Which industry received the largest amount of venture capital financing? Which province had the largest share of the venture capital market in Canada?

15.2 Initial Public Offerings.   What companies are going forward with an IPO in the near future? Go to **ipo.investcom.com** and search by "Date of Filing" to find out how many companies are ready to go public. What industries are these companies from? What industry has the largest number of companies represented?

15.3 IPO Filings.   Look at the most recent initial public offering filed with SEDAR. Go to **www.techfinance.ca** and follow the "IPOs" link in the "Main Menu" section. Find the most recent IPO. What is the name of the company? What does this company do? What is the ticker symbol for the company? Next go to **www.sedar. com** and search for that company's documents. What is the name of the document filed with SEDAR for the IPO? Now view the document. For what purpose does the company propose to use the funds raised by the IPO?

15.4 IPO Pricing.   What is the largest recent IPO? Go to **ipo.investcom.com** and search by "Offering Size" to find the largest Canadian IPO listed. What company has the largest IPO? What is the offering price per share? What business is the company in? What is the size of the offering?

PART EIGHT

16 Short-Term Financial Planning

On January 1, 2005, retailing giant Wal-Mart began requiring its 100 largest suppliers to put radio-frequency identification (RFID) tags on cases and pallets shipped to three of its distribution centres and 100 of its stores. By October 2005, the company expanded the requirement to three additional distribution centres and 900 more stores. The next 200 largest suppliers also had to begin adding the RFID tags.

RFID tags are essentially high-tech replacements for bar codes. The advantage is that they can be read from a distance, so an entire warehouse can be scanned in seconds. RFID tag sales are expected to grow from about $1 billion in 2003 to about $4.6 billion in 2007.

So why the rapid growth in high-tech bar codes? Look no further than Wal-Mart for the answer. Specifically, the company thought it would save $6.7 billion in labour costs by eliminating individual scans, $600 million by reducing out-of-stock items, $575 million by reducing theft, $300 million with better tracking, and $180 million by reducing inventory. Thus, the total cost savings for Wal-Mart are estimated at $8.35 billion per year! As this example suggests, proper management of inventory can have a significant impact on the profitability of a company and the value investors place on it.

Short-term financial planning is one activity that concerns everyone in business. As this chapter illustrates, such planning requires, among other things, sales projections from marketing, cost numbers from accounting, and inventory requirements from operations. Perhaps a particularly good reason to study this chapter for many is that short-term planning and management are frequently where new hires start out in a corporation, especially in finance and accounting. Also, such planning is especially important for small businesses, and a lack of adequate short-term financial resources is a frequently cited reason for small business failure.

After more than a short-term studying effort, you should understand:

16.1 The short-term sources and uses of cash.

16.2 The operating and cash cycles and why they are important.

16.3 The different types of short-term financial policy.

16.4 How to use the cash budget for identifying short-term financial needs.

16.5 How to prepare a short-term financial plan.

16.6 Short-term borrowing options.

To this point, we have described many of the decisions of long-term finance, for example, capital budgeting, dividend policy, and financial structure. In this chapter, we begin to discuss short-term finance. Short-term finance is primarily concerned with the analysis of decisions that affect current assets and current liabilities.

Frequently, the term *net working capital* is associated with short-term financial decision making. As we describe in Chapter 2 and elsewhere, net working capital is the difference between current assets and current liabilities. Often, short-term financial management is called *working capital management*. These mean the same thing.

There is no universally accepted definition of short-term finance. The most important difference between short-term and long-term finance is the timing of cash flows. Short-term financial decisions typically involve cash inflows and outflows that occur within a year or less. For example, short-term financial decisions are involved when a firm orders raw materials, pays in cash, and anticipates selling finished goods in one year for cash. In contrast, long-term financial decisions are involved when a firm purchases a special machine that will reduce operating costs over, say, the next five years.

What types of questions fall under the general heading of short-term finance? To name just a very few:

Interested in a career in short-term finance? Visit the Treasury Management Association of Canada at **www.tmac.ca.**

1. What is a reasonable level of cash to keep on hand (in a bank) to pay bills?
2. How much should the firm borrow in the short term?
3. How much credit should be extended to customers?

This chapter introduces the basic elements of short-term financial decisions. First, we discuss the short-term operating activities of the firm. We then identify some alternative short-term financial policies. Finally, we outline the basic elements in a short-term financial plan and describe short-term financing instruments.

16.1 | TRACING CASH AND NET WORKING CAPITAL

In this section, we examine the components of cash and net working capital as they change from one year to the next. We have already discussed various aspects of this subject in Chapters 2 and 3. We briefly review some of that discussion as it relates to short-term financing decisions. Our goal is to describe the short-term operating activities of the firm and their impact on cash and working capital.

To begin, recall that *current assets* are cash and other assets that are expected to convert to cash within the year. Current assets are presented on the balance sheet in order of their liquidity—the ease with which they can be converted to cash and the time it takes to convert them. Four of the most important items found in the current asset section of a balance sheet are cash and cash equivalents, marketable securities, accounts receivable, and inventories.

Analogous to their investment in current assets, firms use several kinds of short-term debt, called *current liabilities.* Current liabilities are obligations that are expected to require cash payment within one year. Three major items found as current liabilities are accounts payable; expenses payable, including accrued wages and taxes; and notes payable.

Because we want to focus on changes in cash, we start off by defining cash in terms of the other elements of the balance sheet. This lets us isolate the cash account and explore the impact on cash from the firm's operating and financing decisions. The basic balance sheet identity can be written as:

Net working capital + Fixed assets = Long-term debt + Equity   **[16.1]**

Net working capital is cash plus other current assets, less current liabilities; that is,

Net working capital = (Cash + Other current assets) − Current liabilities   **[16.2]**

If we substitute this for net working capital in the basic balance sheet identity and rearrange things a bit, we see that cash is:

$$\text{Cash} = \text{Long-term debt} + \text{Equity} + \text{Current liabilities}$$
$$- \text{Current assets other than cash} - \text{Fixed assets} \qquad \textbf{[16.3]}$$

This tells us in general terms that some activities naturally increase cash and some activities decrease it. We can list these along with an example of each as follows:

Activities That Increase Cash

Increasing long-term debt (borrowing over the long term)

Increasing equity (selling some stock)

Increasing current liabilities (getting a 90-day loan)

Decreasing current assets other than cash (selling some inventory for cash)

Decreasing fixed assets (selling some property)

Activities That Decrease Cash

Decreasing long-term debt (paying off a long-term debt)

Decreasing equity (repurchasing some stock)

Decreasing current liabilities (paying off a 90-day loan)

Increasing current assets other than cash (buying some inventory for cash)

Increasing fixed assets (buying some property)

Notice that our two lists are exact opposites. For example, floating a long-term bond issue increases cash (at least until the money is spent). Paying off a long-term bond issue decreases cash.

Activities that increase cash are called *sources of cash*. Those activities that decrease cash are called *uses of cash*. Looking back at our list, we see that sources of cash always involve increasing a liability (or equity) account or decreasing an asset account. This makes sense because increasing a liability means we have raised money by borrowing it or by selling an ownership interest in the firm. A decrease in an asset means that we have sold or otherwise liquidated an asset. In either case, there is a cash inflow.

Uses of cash are just the reverse. A use of cash involves decreasing a liability by paying it off, perhaps, or increasing assets by purchasing something. Both of these activities require that the firm spend some cash.

Sources and Uses   EXAMPLE 16.1

Here is a quick check of your understanding of sources and uses: If accounts payable go up by $100, is this a source or a use? If accounts receivable go up by $100, is this a source or a use?

Accounts payable are what we owe our suppliers. This is a short-term debt. If it rises by $100, we have effectively borrowed the money, so this is a *source* of cash. Receivables are what our customers owe to us, so an increase of $100 in accounts receivable means that we have loaned the money; this is a *use* of cash.

CONCEPT QUESTIONS

16.1a What is the difference between net working capital and cash?

16.1b Will net working capital always increase when cash increases?

16.1c List five potential uses of cash.

16.1d List five potential sources of cash.

16.2 | THE OPERATING CYCLE AND THE CASH CYCLE

The primary concerns in short-term finance are the firm's short-run operating and financing activities. For a typical manufacturing firm, these short-run activities might consist of the following sequence of events and decisions:

Events	Decisions
1. Buying raw materials	1. How much inventory to order
2. Paying cash	2. Whether to borrow or draw down cash balances
3. Manufacturing the product	3. What choice of production technology to use
4. Selling the product	4. Whether credit should be extended to a particular customer
5. Collecting cash	5. How to collect

These activities create patterns of cash inflows and cash outflows. These cash flows are both unsynchronized and uncertain. They are unsynchronized because, for example, the payment of cash for raw materials does not happen at the same time as the receipt of cash from selling the product. They are uncertain because future sales and costs cannot be precisely predicted.

Defining the Operating and Cash Cycles

We can start with a simple case. One day, call it Day 0, you purchase $1,000 worth of inventory on credit. You pay the bill 30 days later, and, after 30 more days, someone buys the $1,000 in inventory for $1,400. Your buyer does not actually pay for another 45 days. We can summarize these events chronologically as follows:

Day	Activity	Cash Effect
0	Acquire inventory on credit	None
30	Pay for inventory	−$1,000
60	Sell inventory on credit	None
105	Collect on sale	+$1,400

operating cycle
The time period between the acquisition of inventory and the collection of cash from receivables.

inventory period
The time it takes to acquire and sell inventory.

accounts receivable period
The time between sale of inventory and collection of the receivable.

The Operating Cycle   There are several things to notice in our example. First, the entire cycle, from the time we acquire some inventory to the time we collect the cash, takes 105 days. This is called the **operating cycle**.

As we illustrate, the operating cycle is the length of time it takes to acquire inventory, sell it, and collect for it. This cycle has two distinct components. The first part is the time it takes to acquire and sell the inventory. This period, a 60-day span in our example, is called the **inventory period**. The second part is the time it takes to collect on the sale, 45 days in our example. This is called the **accounts receivable period**, or, simply, the receivables period.

Based on our definitions, the operating cycle is obviously just the sum of the inventory and receivables periods:

Operating cycle = Inventory period + Accounts receivable period   **[16.4]**
105 days = 60 days + 45 days

What the operating cycle describes is how a product moves through the current asset accounts. It begins life as inventory, it is converted to a receivable when it is sold, and it is finally converted to cash when we collect from the sale. Notice that, at each step, the asset is moving closer to cash.

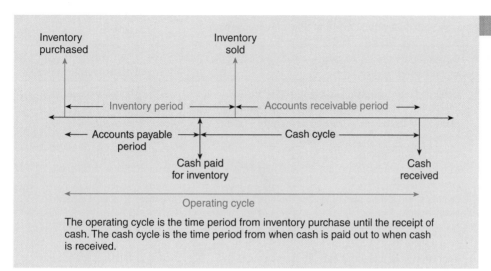

FIGURE 16.1

Cash flow time line and the short-term operating activities of a typical manufacturing firm

The operating cycle is the time period from inventory purchase until the receipt of cash. The cash cycle is the time period from when cash is paid out to when cash is received.

The Cash Cycle   The second thing to notice is that the cash flows and other events that occur are not synchronized. For example, we don't actually pay for the inventory until 30 days after we acquire it. The intervening 30-day period is called the **accounts payable period**. Next, we spend cash on Day 30, but we don't collect until Day 105. Somehow, we have to arrange to finance the $1,000 for 105 − 30 = 75 days. This period is called the **cash cycle**.

The cash cycle, therefore, is the number of days that pass until we collect the cash from a sale, measured from when we actually pay for the inventory. Notice that, based on our definitions, the cash cycle is the difference between the operating cycle and the accounts payable period:

$$\text{Cash cycle} = \text{Operating cycle} - \text{Accounts payable period} \qquad \textbf{[16.5]}$$
$$75 \text{ days} = 105 \text{ days} - 30 \text{ days}$$

Figure 16.1 depicts the short-term operating activities and cash flows for a typical manufacturing firm by looking at the cash flow time line. As is shown, the **cash flow time line** is made up of the operating cycle and the cash cycle. In Figure 16.1, the need for short-term financial management is suggested by the gap between the cash inflows and the cash outflows. This is related to the length of the operating cycle and the accounts payable period.

The gap between short-term inflows and outflows can be filled either by borrowing or by holding a liquidity reserve in the form of cash or marketable securities. Alternatively, the gap can be shortened by changing the inventory, receivable, and payable periods. These are all managerial options that we discuss below and in subsequent chapters.

The Operating Cycle and the Firm's Organizational Chart

Before we examine the operating and cash cycles in greater detail, it is useful to take a look at the people involved in managing a firm's current assets and liabilities. As Table 16.1 illustrates, short-term financial management in a large corporation involves a number of different financial and nonfinancial managers.[1] Examining Table 16.1, we see that selling on credit involves at least three different individuals: the credit manager, the

accounts payable period
The time between receipt of inventory and payment for it.

cash cycle
The time between cash disbursement and cash collection.

cash flow time line
Graphical representation of the operating cycle and the cash cycle.

---

[1]Our discussion draws on N. C. Hill and W. L. Sartoris, *Short-Term Financial Management,* 2nd ed. (New York: Macmillan, 1992), Chapter 1.

TABLE 16.1   **Managers who deal with short-term financial problems**

Title of Manager	Duties Related to Short-Term Financial Management	Assets/Liabilities Influenced
Cash manager	Collection, concentration, disbursement; short-term investments; short-term borrowing; banking relations	Cash, marketable securities, short-term loans
Credit manager	Monitoring and control of accounts receivable; credit policy decisions	Accounts receivable
Marketing manager	Credit policy decisions	Accounts receivable
Purchasing manager	Decisions on purchases, suppliers; may negotiate payment terms	Inventory, accounts payable
Production manager	Setting of production schedules and materials requirements	Inventory, accounts payable
Payables manager	Decisions on payment policies and on whether to take discounts	Accounts payable
Controller	Accounting information on cash flows; reconciliation of accounts payable; application of payments to accounts receivable	Accounts receivable, accounts payable

Source: Ned C. Hill and William L. Sartoris, *Short-Term Financial Management,* 2nd ed. (New York: Macmillan, 1992), p. 15.

marketing manager, and the controller. Of these three, only two are responsible to the vice president of finance (the marketing function is usually associated with the vice president of marketing). Thus, there is the potential for conflict, particularly if different managers only concentrate on part of the picture. For example, if marketing is trying to land a new account, it may seek more liberal credit terms as an inducement. However, this may increase the firm's investment in receivables or its exposure to bad-debt risk, and conflict can result.

Calculating the Operating and Cash Cycles

In our example, the lengths of time that made up the different periods were obvious. If all we have is financial statement information, we will have to do a little more work. We illustrate these calculations next.

To begin, we need to determine various things such as how long it takes, on average, to sell inventory and how long it takes, on average, to collect. We start by gathering some balance sheet information such as the following (in thousands):

Item	Beginning	Ending	Average
Inventory	$2,000	$3,000	$2,500
Accounts receivable	1,600	2,000	1,800
Accounts payable	750	1,000	875

Also, from the most recent income statement, we might have the following figures (in thousands):

Net sales	$11,500
Cost of goods sold	8,200

We now need to calculate some financial ratios. We discussed these in some detail in Chapter 3; here we just define them and use them as needed.

The Operating Cycle   First of all, we need the inventory period. We spent $8.2 million on inventory (our cost of goods sold). Our average inventory was $2.5 million. We thus turned our inventory over $8.2/2.5 times during the year:[2]

$$\text{Inventory turnover} = \frac{\text{Cost of goods sold}}{\text{Average inventory}}$$

$$= \frac{\$8.2 \text{ million}}{2.5 \text{ million}} = 3.28 \text{ times}$$

Loosely speaking, this tells us that we bought and sold off our inventory 3.28 times during the year. This means that, on average, we held our inventory for:

$$\text{Inventory period} = \frac{365 \text{ days}}{\text{Inventory turnover}}$$

$$= \frac{365}{3.28} = 111.3 \text{ days}$$

So, the inventory period is about 111 days. On average, in other words, inventory sat for about 111 days before it was sold.[3]

Similarly, receivables averaged $1.8 million, and sales were $11.5 million. Assuming that all sales were credit sales, the receivables turnover is:[4]

$$\text{Receivables turnover} = \frac{\text{Credit sales}}{\text{Average accounts receivable}}$$

$$= \frac{\$11.5 \text{ million}}{1.8 \text{ million}} = 6.4 \text{ times}$$

If we turn over our receivables 6.4 times, then the receivables period is:

$$\text{Receivables period} = \frac{365 \text{ days}}{\text{Receivables turnover}}$$

$$= \frac{365}{6.4} = 57 \text{ days}$$

The receivables period is also called the *days' sales in receivables* or the *average collection period*. Whatever it is called, it tells us that our customers took an average of 57 days to pay.

The operating cycle is the sum of the inventory and receivables periods:

$$\text{Operating cycle} = \text{Inventory period} + \text{Accounts receivable period}$$
$$= 111 \text{ days} + 57 \text{ days} = 168 \text{ days}$$

This tells us that, on average, 168 days elapse between the time we acquire inventory and, having sold it, collect for the sale.

---

[2]Notice that in calculating inventory turnover here, we used the *average* inventory instead of using the ending inventory as we did in Chapter 3. Both approaches are used in the real world. To gain some practice using average figures, we will stick with this approach in calculating various ratios throughout this chapter.

[3]This measure is conceptually identical to the days' sales in inventory we discussed in Chapter 3.

[4]If less than 100 percent of our sales are credit sales, then we just need a little more information, namely, credit sales for the year. See Chapter 3 for more discussion of this measure.

The Cash Cycle   We now need the payables period. From the information given above, average payables were $875,000, and cost of goods sold was again $8.2 million. Our payables turnover is:

$$\text{Payables turnover} = \frac{\text{Cost of goods sold}}{\text{Average payables}}$$

$$= \frac{\$8.2 \text{ million}}{.875 \text{ million}} = 9.4 \text{ times}$$

The payables period is:

$$\text{Payables period} = \frac{365 \text{ days}}{\text{Payables turnover}}$$

$$= \frac{365}{9.4} = 39 \text{ days}$$

Thus, we took an average of 39 days to pay our bills.

Finally, the cash cycle is the difference between the operating cycle and the payables period:

$$\text{Cash cycle} = \text{Operating cycle} - \text{Accounts payable period}$$
$$= 168 \text{ days} - 39 \text{ days} = 129 \text{ days}$$

So, on average, there is a 129-day delay from the time we pay for merchandise to the time we collect on the sale.

EXAMPLE 16.2 | **The Operating and Cash Cycles**

You have collected the following information for the Slowpay Company.

Item	Beginning	Ending
Inventory	$5,000	$7,000
Accounts receivable	1,600	2,400
Accounts payable	2,700	4,800

Credit sales for the year just ended were $50,000, and cost of goods sold was $30,000. How long does it take Slowpay to collect on its receivables? How long does merchandise stay around before it is sold? How long does Slowpay take to pay its bills?

We can first calculate the three turnover ratios:

Inventory turnover = $30,000/6,000 = 5 times
Receivables turnover = $50,000/2,000 = 25 times
Payables turnover = $30,000/3,750 = 8 times

We use these to get the various periods:

Inventory period = 365/5 = 73 days
Receivables period = 365/25 = 14.6 days
Payables period = 365/8 = 45.6 days

All told, Slowpay collects on a sale in 14.6 days, inventory sits around for 73 days, and bills get paid after about 46 days. The operating cycle here is the sum of the inventory and receivables periods: 73 + 14.6 = 87.6 days. The cash cycle is the difference between the operating cycle and the payables period: 87.6 − 45.6 = 42 days.

REALITY BYTES

Cash Cycle Comparison

In 2006 *CFO* magazine published its survey of working capital for various U.S. industries. The results of this survey highlight the differences in cash and operating cycles across industries. The table below shows four different industries and the operating and cash cycles for each. Of these, the restaurant industry has the lowest operating cycle and cash cycle. Moreover, its cash cycle is negative, which means the industry receives payments from customers before paying to suppliers. Looking at other components for the restaurant industry, it is not surprising that the receivables period is as short as 5 days (most customers either pay in cash or else use debit/credit cards).

Restaurants also have a short inventory period (we are happy to see this since we don't like spoiled food).

In contrast to the restaurant business, the medical devices industry has a much longer operating cycle; the long receivables period is the major cause. However, this does not necessarily mean the medical device industry is less efficient. Most, if not all, of the receivables in this industry are receivables that will be paid by medical insurance companies and U.S. government medical insurers such as Medicare, but these entities have relatively long payables periods.

	Receivables Period (days)	Inventory Period (days)	Operating Cycle (days)	Payables Period (days)	Cash Cycle (days)
Computer makers	49	18	67	39	28
Drug retailers	18	36	54	27	27
Medical devices firms	83	44	127	17	110
Restaurants	5	6	11	13	−2

We've seen that operating and cash cycles can vary quite a bit across industries, but these cycles can also be different for companies within the same industry. Below you will find the operating and cash cycles for selected companies within the computer makers industry. As you can see, there are major

differences. Dell and Apple Computer have the best operating cycles and cash cycles in the industry. In fact, Dell's cash cycle is an incredible negative 24 days. Dell has excelled at managing its inventory. Computer assembly does not start until an order arrives, and the order is then filled in a short period of time.

	Receivables Period (days)	Inventory Period (days)	Operating Cycle (days)	Payables Period (days)	Cash Cycle (days)
Dell	36	4	40	64	−24
Apple Computer	23	4	27	46	−19
Maxtor	35	21	56	60	− 4
IBM	93	11	104	29	75

By examining all parts of the cycle and the operating cash cycle, you can see where a company is performing well or poorly, as the case may be. For example, IBM's operating cycle is almost twice as long at Maxtor's cycle. This difference, however, is primarily due to IBM's very long receivables period. In contrast, IBM's inventory period is half as long as Maxtor's period.

When you look at the operating cycle and cash cycle, consider that each is really a financial ratio. As with any financial ratio,

firm and industry characteristics will have an effect, so take care in your interpretation. For example, in looking at IBM's, we note its seemingly long receivables period. Is that a bad thing? Maybe not. Many businesses encourage customers to open (and use) charge accounts. By extending credit in this way, companies can increase sales and also earn interest on consumer's outstanding balances. Of course, such an operation results in increased receivables, but, properly managed, it can be a good thing.

Interpreting the Cash Cycle

Our examples show that the cash cycle depends on the inventory, receivables, and payables periods. The cash cycle increases as the inventory and receivables periods get longer. It decreases if the company is able to defer payment of payables and thereby lengthen the payables period.

Most firms have a positive cash cycle, and they thus require financing for inventories and receivables. The longer the cash cycle, the more financing is required. Also, changes in the firm's cash cycle are often monitored as an early-warning measure. A lengthening cycle can indicate that the firm is having trouble moving inventory or collecting on its receivables. Such problems can be masked, at least partially, by an increased payables cycle, so both should be monitored.

We can easily see the link between the firm's cash cycle and its profitability by recalling that one of the basic determinants of profitability and growth for a firm is its total asset turnover, which is defined as Sales/Total assets. In Chapter 3, we saw that the higher this ratio is, the greater are the firm's accounting return on assets, ROA, and return on equity, ROE. Thus, all other things being the same, the shorter the cash cycle is, the lower is the firm's investment in inventories and receivables. As a result, the firm's total assets are lower, and total turnover is higher.

To see how important the cash cycle is, consider the case of General Electric. At the end of 2005 the company had a cash cycle of 53 days, 4 days less than a year earlier. As a result, the company freed up more than US$1 billion in cash. The nearby *Reality Bytes* box discusses the cash cycles and operating cycles for several industries, as well as for some specific companies.

CONCEPT QUESTIONS

16.2a   What does it mean to say that a firm has an inventory turnover ratio of 4?

16.2b   Describe the operating cycle and cash cycle. What are the differences?

16.2c   Explain the connection between a firm's accounting-based profitability and its cash cycle.

16.3 | SOME ASPECTS OF SHORT-TERM FINANCIAL POLICY

The short-term financial policy that a firm adopts will be reflected in at least two ways:

1. *The size of the firm's investment in current assets.* This is usually measured relative to the firm's level of total operating revenues. A *flexible,* or accommodative, short-term financial policy would maintain a relatively high ratio of current assets to sales. A *restrictive* short-term financial policy would entail a low ratio of current assets to sales.[5]

2. *The financing of current assets.* This is measured as the proportion of short-term debt (that is, current liabilities) and long-term debt used to finance current assets. A restrictive short-term financial policy means a high proportion of short-term debt relative to long-term financing, and a flexible policy means less short-term debt and more long-term debt.

If we take these two areas together, we see that a firm with a flexible policy would have a relatively large investment in current assets. It would finance this investment with relatively less in short-term debt. The net effect of a flexible policy is thus a relatively high level of net working capital. Put another way, with a flexible policy, the firm maintains a larger overall level of liquidity.

---

[5]Some people use the term *conservative* in place of *flexible* and the term *aggressive* in place of *restrictive.*

The Size of the Firm's Investment in Current Assets

Flexible short-term financial policies with regard to current assets include such actions as:

1. Keeping large balances of cash and marketable securities.
2. Making large investments in inventory.
3. Granting liberal credit terms, which results in a high level of accounts receivable.

Restrictive short-term financial policies would be just the opposite of the ones above:

1. Keeping low cash balances and little investment in marketable securities.
2. Making small investments in inventory.
3. Allowing few or no credit sales, thereby minimizing accounts receivable.

Determining the optimal level of investment in short-term assets requires an identification of the different costs of alternative short-term financing policies. The objective is to trade off the cost of a restrictive policy against the cost of a flexible one to arrive at the best compromise.

Current asset holdings are highest with a flexible short-term financial policy and lowest with a restrictive policy. So, flexible short-term financial policies are costly in that they require a greater investment in cash and marketable securities, inventory, and accounts receivable. However, we expect that future cash inflows will be higher with a flexible policy. For example, sales are stimulated by the use of a credit policy that provides liberal financing to customers. A large amount of finished inventory on hand ("on the shelf") provides a quick delivery service to customers and may increase sales. Similarly, a large inventory of raw materials may result in fewer production stoppages because of inventory shortages.

A more restrictive short-term financial policy probably reduces future sales levels below those that would be achieved under flexible policies. It is also possible that higher prices can be charged to customers under flexible working capital policies. Customers may be willing to pay higher prices for the quick delivery service and more liberal credit terms implicit in flexible policies.

Managing current assets can be thought of as involving a trade-off between costs that rise and costs that fall with the level of investment. Costs that rise with increases in the level of investment in current assets are called **carrying costs**. The larger the investment a firm makes in its current assets, the higher its carrying costs will be. Costs that fall with increases in the level of investment in current assets are called **shortage costs**.

In a general sense, carrying costs are the opportunity costs associated with current assets. The rate of return on current assets is very low when compared to that on other assets. For example, the rate of return on Treasury bills is usually well below 10 percent. This is very low compared to the rate of return firms would like to achieve overall. (Treasury bills are an important component of cash and marketable securities.)

Shortage costs are incurred when the investment in current assets is low. If a firm runs out of cash, it will be forced to sell marketable securities. Of course, if a firm runs out of cash and cannot readily sell marketable securities, it may have to borrow or default on an obligation. This situation is called a *cash-out*. A firm may lose customers if it runs out of inventory (a *stock-out*) or if it cannot extend credit to customers.

More generally, there are two kinds of shortage costs:

1. *Trading, or order, costs.* Order costs are the costs of placing an order for more cash (brokerage costs, for example) or more inventory (production setup costs, for example).
2. *Costs related to lack of safety reserves.* These are costs of lost sales, lost customer goodwill, and disruption of production schedules.

The top part of Figure 16.2 illustrates the basic trade-off between carrying costs and shortage costs. On the vertical axis, we have costs measured in dollars, and, on the horizontal axis, we have the amount of current assets. Carrying costs start out at zero when current assets are zero

carrying costs
Costs that rise with increases in the level of investment in current assets.

shortage costs
Costs that fall with increases in the level of investment in current assets.

FIGURE **16.2**	**Carrying costs and shortage costs**

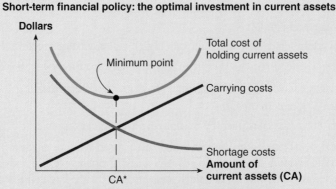

Short-term financial policy: the optimal investment in current assets

CA* represents the optimal amount of current assets.
Holding this amount minimizes total costs.

Carrying costs increase with the level of investment in current assets. They include
the costs of maintaining economic value and opportunity costs. Shortage costs
decrease with increases in the level of investment in current assets. They include
trading costs and the costs related to being short of the current asset (for example,
being short of cash). The firm's policy can be characterized as flexible or restrictive.

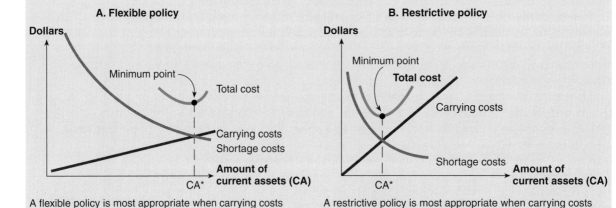

A. Flexible policy

A flexible policy is most appropriate when carrying costs
are low relative to shortage costs.

B. Restrictive policy

A restrictive policy is most appropriate when carrying costs
are high relative to shortage costs.

and then climb steadily as current assets grow. Shortage costs start out very high and then decline
as we add current assets. The total cost of holding current assets is the sum of the two. Notice
how the combined costs reach a minimum at CA*. This is the optimal level of current assets.

Optimal current asset holdings are highest under a flexible policy. This policy is one in which
the carrying costs are perceived to be low relative to shortage costs. This is Case A in Figure 16.2.
In comparison, under restrictive current asset policies, carrying costs are perceived to be high relative to shortage costs, resulting in lower current asset holdings. This is Case B in Figure 16.2.

Alternative Financing Policies for Current Assets

In previous sections, we looked at the basic determinants of the level of investment in current assets, and we thus focused on the asset side of the balance sheet. Now we turn to the
financing side of the question. Here we are concerned with the relative amounts of short-
term and long-term debt, assuming the investment in current assets is constant.

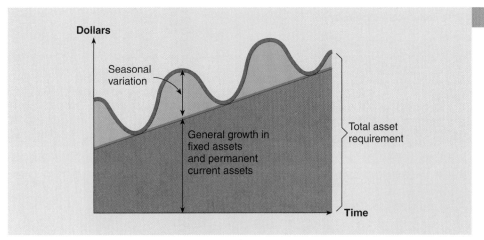

FIGURE 16.3

The total asset requirement over time

A growing firm can be thought of as having a total asset requirement consisting of the current assets and long-term assets needed to run the business efficiently. The total asset requirement may exhibit change over time for many reasons, including (1) a general growth trend, (2) seasonal variation around the trend, and (3) unpredictable day-to-day and month-to-month fluctuations. This situation is depicted in Figure 16.3. (We have not tried to show the unpredictable day-to-day and month-to-month variations in the total asset requirement.)

The peaks and valleys in Figure 16.3 represent the firm's total asset needs through time. For example, for a lawn and garden supply firm, the peaks might represent inventory buildups prior to the spring selling season. The valleys come about because of lower off-season inventories. There are two strategies such a firm might consider to meet its cyclical needs. First, the firm could keep a relatively large pool of marketable securities. As the need for inventory and other current assets begins to rise, the firm sells off marketable securities and uses the cash to purchase whatever is needed. Once the inventory is sold and inventory holdings begin to decline, the firm reinvests in marketable securities. This approach is the flexible policy illustrated in Figure 16.4 as Policy F. Notice that the firm essentially uses a pool of marketable securities as a buffer against changing current asset needs.

At the other extreme, the firm could keep relatively little in marketable securities. As the need for inventory and other assets begins to rise, the firm simply borrows the needed cash on a short-term basis. The firm repays the loans as the need for assets cycles back down. This approach is the restrictive policy illustrated in Figure 16.4 as Policy R.

In comparing the two strategies illustrated in Figure 16.4, notice that the chief difference is the way in which the seasonal variation in asset needs is financed. In the flexible case, the firm finances internally, using its own cash and marketable securities. In the restrictive case, the firm finances externally, borrowing the needed funds on a short-term basis. As we discussed above, all else being the same, a firm with a flexible policy will have a greater investment in net working capital.

Which Financing Policy Is Best?

What is the most appropriate amount of short-term borrowing? There is no definitive answer. Several considerations must be included in a proper analysis:

1. *Cash reserves.* The flexible financing policy implies surplus cash and little short-term borrowing. This policy reduces the probability that a firm will experience financial distress. Firms may not have to worry as much about meeting recurring short-run obligations. However, investments in cash and marketable securities are zero net present value investments at best.

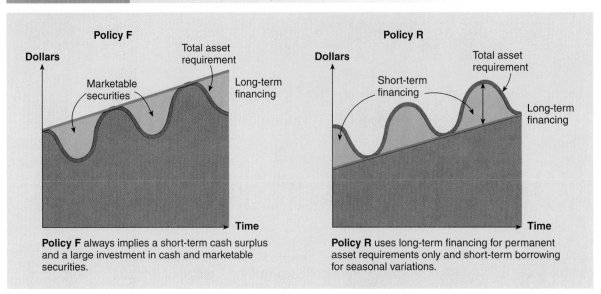

FIGURE 16.4   **Alternative asset financing policies**

Policy F always implies a short-term cash surplus and a large investment in cash and marketable securities.

Policy R uses long-term financing for permanent asset requirements only and short-term borrowing for seasonal variations.

2. *Maturity hedging.* Most firms attempt to match the maturities of assets and liabilities. They finance inventories with short-term bank loans and fixed assets with long-term financing. Firms tend to avoid financing long-lived assets with short-term borrowing. This type of maturity mismatching would necessitate frequent refinancing and is inherently risky because short-term interest rates are more volatile than longer-term rates.

3. *Relative interest rates.* Short-term interest rates are usually lower than long-term rates. This implies that it is, on the average, more costly to rely on long-term borrowing as compared to short-term borrowing.

The two policies, F and R, that we discuss above are, of course, extreme cases. With F, the firm never does any short-term borrowing, and, with R, the firm never has a cash reserve (an investment in marketable securities). Figure 16.5 illustrates these two policies along with a compromise, Policy C.

With this compromise approach, the firm borrows in the short term to cover peak financing needs, but it maintains a cash reserve in the form of marketable securities during slow periods. As current assets build up, the firm draws down this reserve before doing any short-term borrowing. This allows for some run-up in current assets before the firm has to resort to short-term borrowing.

Current Assets and Liabilities in Practice

The cash cycle is longer in some industries than in others because of different products and industry practices. Table 16.2 illustrates this point by comparing the current asset and liability percentages for three different companies. Of the three, Indigo has the highest level of inventory. Does this mean Indigo is less efficient? Probably not; instead, the relatively high inventory levels are consistent with the industry. Indigo needs a higher level of inventory on hand to satisfy customers who walk into its book and music stores. In contrast, Research In Motion mainly makes BlackBerry wireless devices to order, so its inventory levels are lower. In addition, Research In Motion generates its revenue by licensing software and providing service to its carrier partners, and these operations require practically no inventory at all. What might seem surprising is Bombardier's relatively low level of inventory,

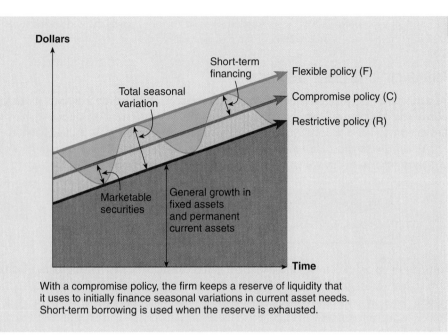

FIGURE 16.5

A compromise
financing policy

With a compromise policy, the firm keeps a reserve of liquidity that
it uses to initially finance seasonal variations in current asset needs.
Short-term borrowing is used when the reserve is exhausted.

	Bombardier	Indigo Books & Music	Research In Motion
Cash and cash equivalents	10.00	1.49	22.83
Short-term investments	0.00	0.00	6.82
Accounts receivable	11.24	1.42	17.44
Inventories	26.68	59.41	5.51
Other current assets	6.88	3.40	4.89
Total current assets	54.81	65.72	57.48
Accounts payable	39.90	52.11	3.12
Short-term borrowings	0.00	8.50	0.00
Other short-term liabilities	15.62	9.20	7.52
Total current liabilities	55.52	69.81	10.64

TABLE 16.2

**Current assets and
current liabilities as
a percentage of total
assets for selected
companies: 2006**

given that much of its inventory consists of aircraft and trains under construction. However,
notice that current assets for Bombardier are only 54.8 percent of total assets, implying that
fixed assets are large, as you would expect from such a capital-intensive company.

CONCEPT QUESTIONS

16.3a   What considerations determine the optimal size of the firm's investment in current assets?

16.3b   What considerations determine the optimal compromise between flexible and restrictive
net working capital policies?

16.4 | THE CASH BUDGET

The **cash budget** is a primary tool in short-run financial planning. It allows the financial
manager to identify short-term financial needs and opportunities. Importantly, the cash
budget will help the manager explore the need for short-term borrowing. The idea of the

cash budget
A forecast of cash
receipts and
disbursements for the
next planning period.

cash budget is simple: It records estimates of cash receipts (cash in) and disbursements (cash out). The result is an estimate of the cash surplus or deficit.

Sales and Cash Collections

We start with an example for the Fun Toys Corporation. We will prepare a quarterly cash budget. We could just as well use a monthly, weekly, or even daily basis. We choose quarters for convenience and also because a quarter is a common short-term business planning period.

All of Fun Toys's cash inflows come from the sale of toys. Cash budgeting for Fun Toys must therefore start with a sales forecast for the coming year, by quarter:

	Q1	Q2	Q3	Q4
Sales (in millions)	$200	$300	$250	$400

Note that these are predicted sales, so there is forecasting risk here; actual sales could be more or less. Also, Fun Toys started the year with accounts receivable equal to $120.

Fun Toys has a 45-day receivables, or average collection, period. This means that half of the sales in a given quarter will be collected the following quarter. This happens because sales made during the first 45 days of a quarter will be collected in that quarter. Sales made in the second 45 days will be collected in the next quarter. Note that we are assuming that each quarter has 90 days, so the 45-day collection period is the same as a half-quarter collection period.

Based on the sales forecasts, we now need to estimate Fun Toys's projected cash collections. First, any receivables that we have at the beginning of a quarter will be collected within 45 days, so all of them will be collected sometime during the quarter. Second, as we discussed, any sales made in the first half of the quarter will be collected, so total cash collections are:

$$\text{Cash collections} = \text{Beginning accounts receivable} + \tfrac{1}{2} \times \text{Sales} \qquad \text{[16.6]}$$

For example, in the first quarter, cash collections would be the beginning receivables of $120 plus half of sales, $\tfrac{1}{2} \times \$200 = \$100$, for a total of $220.

Since beginning receivables are all collected along with half of sales, ending receivables for a particular quarter would be the other half of sales. First-quarter sales are projected at $200, so ending receivables will be $100. This will be the beginning receivables in the second quarter. Cash collections in the second quarter will thus be $100 plus half of the projected $300 in sales, or $250 total.

Continuing this process, we can summarize Fun Toys's projected cash collections as shown in Table 16.3.

In Table 16.3, collections are shown as the only source of cash. Of course, this might not be the case. Other sources of cash could include asset sales, investment income, and receipts from planned long-term financing.

TABLE 16.3		Q1	Q2	Q3	Q4
Cash collections for Fun Toys (in millions)	Beginning receivables	$120	→ $100	→ $150	→ $125
	Sales	200	300	250	400
	Cash collections	220	250	275	325
	Ending receivables	100	150	125	200

Collections = Beginning receivables + $^1\!/_2$ × Sales
Ending receivables = Beginning receivables + Sales − Collections
= ½ × Sales

Cash Outflows

Next, we consider the cash disbursements, or payments. These come in four basic categories:

1. *Payments of accounts payable.* These are payments for goods or services rendered by suppliers, such as raw materials. Generally, these payments will be made sometime after purchases.

2. *Wages, taxes, and other expenses.* This category includes all other regular costs of doing business that require actual expenditures. Depreciation, for example, is often thought of as a regular cost of business, but it requires no cash outflow and is not included.

3. *Capital expenditures.* These are payments of cash for long-lived assets.

4. *Long-term financing expenses.* This category, for example, includes interest payments on long-term debt outstanding and dividend payments to shareholders.

   Fun Toys's purchases from suppliers (in dollars) in a quarter are equal to 60 percent of the next quarter's predicted sales. Fun Toys's payments to suppliers are equal to the previous quarter's purchases, so the accounts payable period is 90 days. For example, in the quarter just ended, Fun Toys ordered .60 × $200 = $120 in supplies. This will actually be paid in the first quarter (Q1) of the coming year.

   Wages, taxes, and other expenses are routinely 20 percent of sales; interest and dividends are currently $20 per quarter. In addition, Fun Toys plans a major plant expansion (a capital expenditure) of $100 in the second quarter. If we put all this information together, the cash outflows are as shown in Table 16.4.

The Cash Balance

The predicted *net cash inflow* is the difference between cash collections and cash disbursements. The net cash inflow for Fun Toys is shown in Table 16.5. What we see immediately is that there is a net cash inflow in the first and third quarters and a net outflow in the second and fourth.

We will assume that Fun Toys starts the year with a $20 cash balance. Furthermore, Fun Toys maintains a $10 minimum cash balance to guard against unforeseen contingencies and forecasting errors. So we start the first quarter with $20 in cash. This rises by $40 during the quarter, and the ending balance is $60. Of this, $10 is reserved as a minimum, so we subtract it out and find that the first-quarter surplus is $60 − 10 = $50.

Fun Toys starts the second quarter with $60 in cash (the ending balance from the previous quarter). There is a net cash inflow of −$110, so the ending balance is $60 − 110 = −$50.

	Q1	Q2	Q3	Q4
Payment of accounts (60% of sales)	$120	$180	$150	$240
Wages, taxes, other expenses	40	60	50	80
Capital expenditures	0	100	0	0
Long-term financing expenses (interest and dividends)	20	20	20	20
Total cash disbursements	$180	$360	$220	$340

TABLE 16.4

Cash disbursements for Fun Toys (in millions)

	Q1	Q2	Q3	Q4
Total cash collections	$220	$250	$275	$325
Total cash disbursements	180	360	220	340
Net cash inflow	$ 40	− $110	$ 55	− $ 15

TABLE 16.5

Net cash inflow for Fun Toys (in millions)

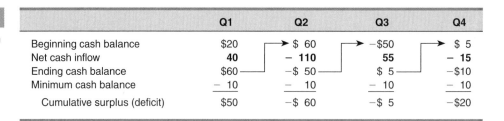

	Q1	Q2	Q3	Q4
Beginning cash balance	$20	$ 60	−$50	$ 5
Net cash inflow	40	− 110	55	− 15
Ending cash balance	$60	−$ 50	$ 5	−$10
Minimum cash balance	− 10	− 10	− 10	− 10
Cumulative surplus (deficit)	$50	−$ 60	−$ 5	−$20

We need another $10 as a buffer, so the total deficit is −$60. These calculations and those for the last two quarters are summarized in Table 16.6.

Beginning in the second quarter, Fun Toys has a cash shortfall of $60. This occurs because of the seasonal pattern of sales (higher towards the end of the second quarter), the delay in collections, and the planned capital expenditure.

The cash situation at Fun Toys is projected to improve to a $5 deficit in the third quarter, but, by year's end, Fun Toys is showing a $20 deficit. Without some sort of financing, this deficit will carry over into the next year. We explore this subject in the next section.

You can find a cash
flow calculator in the
"Small Business"
section at
**www.reporton
business.com.**

For now, we can make the following general comments on Fun Toys's cash needs:

1. Fun Toys' large outflow in the second quarter is not necessarily a sign of trouble. It results from delayed collections on sales and a planned capital expenditure (presumably a worthwhile one).

2. The figures in our example are based on a forecast. Sales could be much worse (or better) than the forecast figures.

CONCEPT QUESTIONS

16.4a How would you do a sensitivity analysis (discussed in Chapter 9) for Fun Toys net cash balance?

16.4b What could you learn from such an analysis?

16.5 | A SHORT-TERM FINANCIAL PLAN

To illustrate a completed short-term financial plan, we will assume that Fun Toys arranges to borrow any needed funds on a short-term basis. The interest rate is 20 percent APR, and it is calculated on a quarterly basis. From Chapter 5, we know that the rate is 20%/4 = 5% per quarter. We will assume that Fun Toys starts the year with no short-term debt.

From Table 16.6, we see that Fun Toys has a second-quarter deficit of $60 million. We will have to borrow this amount. Net cash inflow in the following quarter is $55 million. We now have to pay $60 × .05 = $3 million in interest out of that, leaving $52 million to reduce the borrowing.

We still owe $60 − 52 = $8 million at the end of the third quarter. Interest in the last quarter will thus be $8 × .05 = $.4 million. In addition, net inflows in the last quarter are −$15 million, so we have to borrow a total of $15.4 million, bringing our total borrowing up to $15.4 + 8 = $23.4 million. Table 16.7 extends Table 16.6 to include these calculations.

Notice that the ending short-term debt is just equal to the cumulative deficit for the entire year, $20 million, plus the interest paid during the year, $3 + .4 = $3.4 million, for a total of $23.4 million.

Our plan is very simple. For example, we ignored the fact that the interest paid on the short-term debt is tax deductible. We also ignored the fact that the cash surplus in the first quarter would earn some interest (which would be taxable). We could add on a number of refinements.

	Q1	Q2	Q3	Q4	
					TABLE 16.7
Beginning cash balance	$20	$ 60	$10	$10.0	**Short-term financial**
Net cash inflow	40	− 110	55	− 15.0	**plan for Fun Toys**
New short-term borrowing	—	60	—	15.4	**(in millions)**
Interest on short-term borrowing	—	—	− 3	− .4	
Short-term borrowing repaid	—	—	− 52	—	
Ending cash balance	$60	$ 10	$10	$10.0	
Minimum cash balance	− 10	− 10	− 10	− 10.0	
Cumulative surplus (deficit)	$50	$0	$ 0	$ .0	
Beginning short-term borrowing	0	0	60	8.0	
Change in short-term debt	0	60	− 52	15.4	
Ending short-term debt	$ 0	$ 60	$ 8	$23.4	

Even so, our plan highlights the fact that in about 90 days Fun Toys will need to borrow $60 million or so on a short-term basis. It's time to start lining up the source of the funds.

Our plan also illustrates that financing the firm's short-term needs will cost about $3.4 million in interest (before taxes) for the year. This is a starting point for Fun Toys to begin evaluating alternatives to reduce this expense. For example, can the $100 million planned expenditure be postponed or spread out? At 5 percent per quarter, short-term credit is expensive.

Also, if Fun Toys's sales are expected to keep growing, then the $20 million plus deficit will probably also keep growing, and the need for additional financing is permanent. Fun Toys may wish to think about raising money on a long-term basis to cover this need.

CONCEPT QUESTIONS

16.5a In Table 16.7, does Fun Toys have a projected deficit or surplus?

16.5b In Table 16.7, what would happen to Fun Toys deficit or surplus if the minimum cash balance was reduced to $5?

16.6 | SHORT-TERM BORROWING

Fun Toys has a short-term financing problem. It cannot meet the forecast cash outflows in the second quarter from internal sources. How it will finance the shortfall depends on its financial policy. With a very flexible policy, Fun Toys might seek up to $60 million in long-term debt financing.

In addition, note that much of the cash deficit comes from the large capital expenditure. Arguably, this is a candidate for long-term financing. Nonetheless, because we have discussed long-term financing elsewhere, we will concentrate here on two short-term borrowing options: (1) unsecured borrowing and (2) secured borrowing.

Unsecured Loans

The most common way to finance a temporary cash deficit is to arrange a short-term, unsecured bank loan. Firms that use short-term bank loans often arrange a line of credit. A **line of credit** is an agreement under which a firm is authorized to borrow up to a specified amount. To ensure that the line is used for short-term purposes, the borrower will sometimes be required to pay the line down to zero and keep it there for some period during the year, typically 60 days (called a *cleanup period*).

Short-term lines of credit are classified as either *committed* or *noncommitted.* The latter is an informal arrangement that allows firms to borrow up to a previously specified limit without

line of credit
A formal (committed) or informal (noncommitted) prearranged, short-term bank loan.

going through the normal paperwork (much as you would with a credit card). A *revolving credit arrangement* (or just *revolver*) is similar to a line of credit, but it is usually open for two or more years, whereas a line of credit would usually be evaluated on an annual basis.

Committed lines of credit are more formal legal arrangements and often involve a commitment fee paid by the firm to the bank. The interest rate on the line of credit will usually float. A firm that pays a commitment fee for a committed line of credit is essentially buying insurance to guarantee that the bank can't back out of the agreement (absent some material change in the borrower's status).

compensating balance
Money kept by a firm with a bank in low-interest or non-interest-bearing accounts as part of a loan agreement.

As a part of a credit line or other lending arrangement, banks may require that the firm keep some amount of money on deposit. This is called a compensating balance. Under the Bank Act, which governs banks in Canada, the borrower must agree to the compensating balance requirement; the banks cannot arbitrarily demand it. A **compensating balance** is some of the firm's money kept by the bank in low-interest or non-interest-bearing accounts. By leaving these funds with the bank and receiving little or no interest, the firm further increases the effective interest rate earned by the bank on the line of credit, thereby "compensating" the bank.

EXAMPLE 16.3 **Cost of a Compensating Balance**

Suppose you have a $100,000 line of credit with a 10 percent compensating balance requirement. This means that 10 percent of the amount actually used must be left on deposit in a non-interest-bearing account. The quoted interest rate on the credit line is 16 percent. If you need $54,000 to purchase some inventory, how much do you have to borrow? What interest rate are you effectively paying?

If you need $54,000, you have to borrow enough so that $54,000 is left over after you take out the 10 percent compensating balance. The amount borrowed is thus $54,000/(1 − .10) = $60,000.

The interest on the $60,000 for one year at 16 percent is $60,000 × .16 = $9,600. You're actually only getting $54,000 to use, so the effective interest rate is $9,600/54,000 = 17.78%. Notice that what effectively happens here is that you pay 16 cents in interest on every 90 cents you borrow because you don't get to use the 10 cents tied up in the compensating balance. The interest rate is thus .16/.90 = 17.78%, as calculated.

Secured Loans

Banks and other finance companies often require security for a short-term loan just as they do for a long-term loan. Security for short-term loans usually consists of accounts receivable, inventories, or both.

accounts receivable financing
A secured short-term loan that involves either the assignment or factoring of receivables.

Accounts Receivable Financing **Accounts receivable financing** involves either *assigning* receivables or *factoring* receivables. Under assignment, the lender has the receivables as security, but the borrower is still responsible if a receivable can't be collected. With *conventional factoring,* the receivable is discounted and sold to the lender (the factor). Once it is sold, collection is the factor's problem, and the factor assumes the full risk of default on bad accounts. With *maturity factoring,* the factor forwards the money on an agreed-upon future date.

EXAMPLE 16.4 **Cost of Factoring**

For the year just ended, LuLu's Pies had an average of $50,000 in accounts receivable. Credit sales were $500,000. LuLu's factors its receivables by discounting them 3 percent, in other words, by selling them for 97 cents on the dollar. What is the effective interest rate on this source of short-term financing?

(continued)

To determine the interest rate, we first have to know the accounts receivable, or average collection, period. During the year, LuLu's turned over its receivables $500,000/50,000 = 10 times. The average collection period is therefore 365/10 = 36.5 days.

The interest paid here is a form of "discount interest." In this case, LuLu's is paying 3 cents in interest on every 97 cents of financing. The interest rate per 36.5 days is thus .03/.97 = 3.09%. The APR is 10 × 3.09% = 30.9%, but the effective annual rate is:

$$EAR = 1.0309^{10} - 1 = 35.6\%$$

The factoring is a relatively expensive source of money in this case.

We should note that if the factor takes on the risk of default by a buyer, then the factor is providing insurance as well as immediate cash. More generally, the factor essentially takes over the firm's credit operations. This can result in a significant saving. The interest rate we calculated is therefore overstated, particularly if default is a significant possibility.

Inventory Loans **Inventory loans**, short-term loans to purchase inventory, come in three basic forms: blanket inventory liens, trust receipts, and field warehouse financing:

inventory loan
A secured short-term loan to purchase inventory.

1. *Blanket inventory lien.* A blanket lien gives the lender a lien against all the borrower's inventories (the blanket "covers" everything).

2. *Trust receipt.* A trust receipt is a device by which the borrower holds specific inventory in "trust" for the lender. Automobile dealer financing, for example, is done by use of trust receipts. This type of secured financing is also called *floor planning,* in reference to inventory on the showroom floor. However, it is somewhat cumbersome to use trust receipts for, say, wheat grain.

3. *Field warehouse financing.* In field warehouse financing, a public warehouse company (an independent company that specializes in inventory management) acts as a control agent to supervise the inventory for the lender.

Other Sources

There are a variety of other sources of short-term funds employed by corporations. Two of the most important are *commercial paper* and *trade credit.*

Commercial paper consists of short-term notes issued by large and highly rated firms. Typically, these notes are of short maturity, ranging up to 365 days (beyond that limit, the firm must file a registration statement with the OSC or another relevant provincial or territorial commission). Because the firm issues these directly, the interest rate the borrowing firm obtains can be significantly below the rate a bank would charge for a direct loan.

Another option available to a firm is to increase the accounts payable period; in other words, it may take longer to pay its bills. This amounts to borrowing from suppliers in the form of trade credit. This is an extremely important form of financing for smaller businesses in particular. As we discuss in Chapter 17, a firm using trade credit may end up paying a much higher price for what it purchases, so this can be a very expensive source of financing.

CONCEPT QUESTIONS

16.6a What are the two basic forms of short-term financing?

16.6b Describe two types of secured loans.

KEY EQUATIONS:

I. Net Working Capital and Cash

Net working capital + Fixed assets = Long-term debt + Equity   [16.1]

Net working capital = (Cash + Other current assets) − Current liabilities [16.2]

Cash = Long-term Debt + Equity + Current liabilities
    − Current assets other than cash − Fixed assets   [16.3]

II. The Operating Cycle and the Cash Cycle

Operating cycle = Inventory period + Accounts receivable period   [16.4]

Cash cycle = Operating cycle − Accounts payable period   [16.5]

SUMMARY AND CONCLUSIONS

1. This chapter has introduced the management of short-term finance. Short-term finance involves short-lived assets and liabilities. We traced and examined the short-term sources and uses of cash as they appear on the firm's financial statements. We saw how current assets and current liabilities arise in the short-term operating activities and the cash cycle of the firm.

2. Managing short-term cash flows involves the minimizing of costs. The two major costs are carrying costs, the returns foregone by keeping too much invested in short-term assets such as cash, and shortage costs, the costs of running out of short-term assets. The objective of managing short-term finance and doing short-term financial planning is to find the optimal trade-off between these two costs.

3. In an "ideal" economy, the firm could perfectly predict its short-term uses and sources of cash, and net working capital could be kept at zero. In the real world we live in, cash and net working capital provide a buffer that lets the firm meet its ongoing obligations. The financial manager seeks the optimal level of each of the current assets.

4. The financial manager can use the cash budget to identify short-term financial needs. The cash budget tells the manager what borrowing is required or what lending will be possible in the short run. The firm has available to it a number of possible ways of acquiring funds to meet short-term shortfalls, including the use of unsecured and secured loans.

CHAPTER REVIEW AND SELF-TEST PROBLEMS

16.1 The Operating and Cash Cycles. Consider the following financial statement information for the Glory Road Company:

Item	Beginning		Ending
Inventory	$1,543		$1,669
Accounts receivable	4,418		3,952
Accounts payable	2,551		2,673
Net sales		$11,500	
Cost of goods sold		8,200	

Calculate the operating and cash cycles.

16.2 **Cash Balance for Huron Corporation.** The Huron Corporation has a 60-day average collection period and wishes to maintain a $5 million minimum cash balance. Based on this and the information below, complete the following cash budget. What conclusions do you draw?

HURON CORPORATION Cash Budget (in millions)				
	Q1	Q2	Q3	Q4
Beginning receivables	$120			
Sales	90	$120	$150	$120
Cash collections				
Ending receivables				
Total cash collections				
Total cash disbursements	80	160	180	160
Net cash inflow				
Beginning cash balance	$ 5			
Net cash inflow				
Ending cash balance				
Minimum cash balance				
Cumulative surplus (deficit)				

■ Answers to Chapter Review and Self-Test Problems

16.1 We first need the turnover ratios. Note that we use the average values for all balance sheet items and that we base the inventory and payables turnover measures on cost of goods sold.

$$\text{Inventory turnover} = \$8,200/[(1,543 + 1,669)/2]$$
$$= 5.11 \text{ times}$$
$$\text{Receivables turover} = \$11,500/[(4,418 + 3,952)/2]$$
$$= 2.75 \text{ times}$$
$$\text{Payables turnover} = \$8,200/[(2,551 + 2,673)/2]$$
$$= 3.14 \text{ times}$$

We can now calculate the various periods:

$$\text{Inventory period} = 365 \text{ days}/5.11 \text{ times} = 71.43 \text{ days}$$
$$\text{Receivables period} = 365 \text{ days}/2.75 \text{ times} = 132.73 \text{ days}$$
$$\text{Payables period} = 365 \text{ days}/3.14 \text{ times} = 116.24 \text{ days}$$

So, the time it takes to acquire inventory and sell it is about 71 days. Collection takes another 133 days, and the operating cycle is thus 71 + 133 = 204 days. The cash cycle is this 204 days less the payables period, 204 − 116 = 88 days.

16.2 Since Huron has a 60-day collection period, only those sales made in the first 30 days of the quarter will be collected in the same quarter. Total cash collections in the first quarter will thus equal 30/90 = ⅓ of sales plus beginning receivables, or $120 + ⅓ × 90 = $150. Ending receivables for the first quarter (and the second-quarter beginning receivables) are the other ⅔ of sales, or ⅔ × $90 = $60. The remaining calculations are straightforward, and the completed budget follows.

HURON CORPORATION Cash Budget (in millions)				
	Q1	Q2	Q3	Q4
Beginning receivables	$120	$ 60	$ 80	$100
Sales	90	120	150	120
Cash collections	150	100	130	140
Ending receivables	$ 60	$ 80	$100	$ 80
Total cash collections	$150	$100	$130	$140
Total cash disbursements	80	160	180	160
Net cash inflow	$ 70	−$ 60	−$ 50	−$ 20
Beginning cash balance	$ 5	$ 75	$ 15	−$ 35
Net cash inflow	70	− 60	− 50	− 20
Ending cash balance	$ 75	$ 15	−$ 35	−$ 55
Minimum cash balance	−$ 5	−$ 5	−$ 5	−$ 5
Cumulative surplus (deficit)	$ 70	$ 10	−$ 40	−$ 60

The primary conclusion from this schedule is that, beginning in the third quarter, Huron's cash surplus becomes a cash deficit. By the end of the year, Huron will need to arrange for $60 million in cash beyond what will be available.

CRITICAL THINKING AND CONCEPTS REVIEW

16.1   Sources and Uses.   For the year just ended, you have gathered the following information on the Holly Corporation:

a.   A $200 dividend was paid.

b.   Accounts payable increased by $500.

c.   Fixed asset purchases were $900.

d.   Inventories increased by $625.

e.   Long-term debt decreased by $1,200.

Label each item as a source or use of cash and describe its effect on the firm's cash balance.

16.2   Operating Cycle.   What are some of the characteristics of a firm with a long operating cycle?

16.3   Cash Cycle.   What are some of the characteristics of a firm with a long cash cycle?

16.4   Cost of Current Assets.   Waterloo Manufacturing, Inc., has recently decided to minimize inventory holdings. Describe the effect this is likely to have on the company's carrying costs, shortage costs, and operating cycle.

16.5   Cycles.   Is it possible for a firm's cash cycle to be longer than its operating cycle? Explain why or why not.

Use the following information to answer Questions 16.6–16.10. Last month, BlueSky Airline announced that it would stretch out its bill payments to 45 days from 30 days. The reason given was that the company wanted to "control costs and optimize cash flow." The increased payables period will be in effect for all of the company's 4,000 suppliers.

16.6 Operating and Cash Cycles. What impact did this change in payables policy have on BlueSky's operating cycle? Its cash cycle?

16.7 Operating and Cash Cycles. What impact did the announcement have on BlueSky's suppliers?

16.8 Corporate Ethics. Is it ethical for large firms to unilaterally lengthen their payables periods, particularly when dealing with smaller suppliers?

16.9 Payables Period. Why don't all firms simply increase their payables periods to shorten their cash cycles?

16.10 Payables Period. BlueSky lengthened its payables period to "control costs and optimize cash flow." Exactly what is the cash benefit to BlueSky from this change?

QUESTIONS AND PROBLEMS

1. **Changes in the Cash Account.** Indicate the impact of the following corporate actions on cash, using the letter *I* for an increase, *D* for a decrease, or *N* when no change occurs.

Basic
(Questions 1–14)

   a. A dividend is paid with funds received from a sale of debt.

   b. Real estate is purchased and paid for with short-term debt.

   c. Inventory is bought on credit.

   d. A short-term bank loan is repaid.

   e. Next year's taxes are prepaid.

   f. Preferred stock is repurchased.

   g. Sales are made on credit.

   h. Interest on long-term debt is paid.

   i. Payments for previous sales are collected.

   j. The accounts payable balance is reduced.

   k. A dividend is paid.

   l. Production supplies are purchased and paid for with a short-term note.

   m. Utility bills are paid.

   n. Cash is paid for raw materials purchased for inventory.

   o. Marketable securities are purchased.

2. **Cash Equation.** Nunavut Company has a book value of equity of $38,000. Long-term debt is $6,500. Net working capital, other than cash, is $4,300. Fixed assets are $32,500. How much cash does the company have? If current liabilities are $7,200, what are current assets?

3. **Changes in the Operating Cycle.** Indicate the effect that the following will have on the operating cycle. Use the letter *I* to indicate an increase, the letter *D* for a decrease, and the letter *N* for no change.

   a. Average receivables go up.

   b. Credit payment times for customers are increased.

   c. Inventory turnover goes from 3 times to 7 times.

   d. Payables turnover goes from 6 times to 11 times.

   e. Receivables turnover goes from 7 times to 9 times.

   f. Payments to suppliers are accelerated.

4. **Changes in Cycles.** Indicate the impact of the following on the cash and operating cycles, respectively. Use the letter *I* to indicate an increase, the letter *D* for a decrease, and the letter *N* for no change.

    a. The terms of cash discounts offered to customers are made less favourable.

    b. The cash discounts offered by suppliers are increased; thus, payments are made earlier.

    c. An increased number of customers begin to pay in cash instead of with credit.

    d. Fewer raw materials than usual are purchased.

    e. A greater percentage of raw material purchases are paid for with credit.

    f. More finished goods are produced for inventory instead of for order.

 5. **Calculating Cash Collections.** The Crazy Train Company has projected the following quarterly sales amounts for the coming year:

	Q1	Q2	Q3	Q4
Sales	$490	$610	$780	$830

a. Accounts receivable at the beginning of the year are $300. Crazy Train has a 45-day collection period. Calculate cash collections in each of the four quarters by completing the following:

	Q1	Q2	Q3	Q4
Beginning receivables				
Sales				
Cash collections				
Ending receivables				

b. Rework (*a*) assuming a collection period of 60 days.

c. Rework (*a*) assuming a collection period of 30 days.

6. **Calculating Cycles.** Consider the following financial statement information for the Pawlonia Corporation:

Item	Beginning		Ending
Inventory	$6,118		$7,302
Accounts receivable	3,764		4,483
Accounts payable	4,986		5,327
Net sales		$65,351	
Cost of goods sold		41,654	

Assume all sales are on credit. Calculate the operating and cash cycles. How do you interpret your answer?

7. **Factoring Receivables.** Your firm has an average collection period of 46 days. Current practice is to factor all receivables immediately at a 1.5 percent discount. What is the effective cost of borrowing in this case? Assume that default is extremely unlikely.

8. **Calculating Payments.**   Hockeyville Products has projected the following sales for the coming year:

	Q1	Q2	Q3	Q4
Sales	$690	$650	$790	$840

Sales in the year following this one are projected to be 15 percent greater in each quarter.

   a.   Calculate payments to suppliers assuming that Hockeyville places orders during each quarter equal to 30 percent of projected sales for the next quarter. Assume that Hockeyville pays immediately. What is the payables period in this case?

	Q1	Q2	Q3	Q4
Payment of accounts				

   b.   Rework (*a*) assuming a 90-day payables period.

   c.   Rework (*a*) assuming a 60-day payables period.

9. **Calculating Payments.**   The Nordique Corporation's purchases from suppliers in a quarter are equal to 75 percent of the next quarter's forecast sales. The payables period is 60 days. Wages, taxes, and other expenses are 30 percent of sales, and interest and dividends are $30 per quarter. No capital expenditures are planned. Projected quarterly sales are:

	Q1	Q2	Q3	Q4
Sales	$700	$840	$780	$910

Sales for the first quarter of the following year are projected at $1,040. Calculate Nordique's cash outlays by completing the following:

	Q1	Q2	Q3	Q4
Payment of accounts				
Wages, taxes, other expenses				
Long-term financing expenses				
(interest and dividends)				
Total				

10. **Calculating Cash Collections.**   The following is the sales budget for Medicine Head, Inc., for the first quarter of 2008:

	January	February	March
Sales budget	$138,000	$165,000	$195,000

Credit sales are collected as follows:

65 percent in the month of the sale

20 percent in the month after the sale

15 percent in the second month after the sale

The accounts receivable balance at the end of the previous quarter was $68,000 ($49,000 of which was uncollected December sales).

a. Compute the sales for November.

b. Compute the sales for December.

c. Compute the cash collections from sales for each month from January through March.

11. **Calculating the Cash Budget.** Here are some important figures from the budget of Red River, Inc., for the second quarter of 2008:

	April	May	June
Credit sales	$440,000	$370,000	$510,000
Credit purchases	210,000	185,000	240,000
Cash disbursements			
Wages, taxes, and expenses	94,000	86,000	105,000
Interest	10,000	10,000	10,000
Equipment purchases	30,000	60,000	190,000

The company predicts that 5 percent of its credit sales will never be collected, 35 percent of its sales will be collected in the month of the sale, and the remaining 60 percent will be collected in the following month. Credit purchases will be paid in the month following the purchase.

In March 2008, credit sales were $380,000. Using this information, complete the following cash budget:

	April	May	June
Beginning cash balance	$185,000		
Cash receipts			
Cash collections from credit sales			
Total cash available			
Cash disbursements			
Purchases	190,000		
Wages, taxes, and expenses			
Interest			
Equipment purchases			
Total cash disbursements			
Ending cash balance			

12. **Calculating Cash Collections.** The Sail Away Company has projected the following quarterly sales amounts for the coming year:

	Q1	Q2	Q3	Q4
Sales	$4,900	$5,700	$5,100	$6,400

a. Accounts receivable at the beginning of the year are $2,200. Sail Away has a 45-day collection period. Calculate cash collections in each of the four quarters by completing the following:

	Q1	Q2	Q3	Q4
Beginning receivables				
Sales				
Cash collections				
Ending receivables				

b. Rework (*a*) assuming a collection period of 60 days.

c. Rework (*a*) assuming a collection period of 30 days.

13. Factoring Receivables. Your firm has an average collection period of 28 days. Current practice is to factor all receivables immediately at a 2 percent discount. What is the effective cost of borrowing in this case? Assume that default is extremely unlikely.

14. Calculating Payments. The Grizzly Corporation's purchases from suppliers in a quarter are equal to 60 percent of the next quarter's forecast sales. The payables deferral period is 45 days. Wages, taxes, and other expenses are 25 percent of sales, while interest and dividends are $15 per quarter. No capital expenditures are planned.

Projected quarterly sales are:

	Q1	Q2	Q3	Q4
Projected sales	$520	$540	$600	$680

Sales in the first quarter of the following year are projected at $750. Calculate Grizzly's cash outlays by completing the following:

	Q1	Q2	Q3	Q4
Payment of accounts				
Wages, taxes, other expenses				
Long-term financing expenses (interest and dividends)				
Total				

15. Costs of Borrowing. You've worked out a line of credit arrangement that allows you to borrow up to $70 million at any time. The interest rate is .480 percent per month. In addition, 5 percent of the amount that you borrow must be deposited in a noninterest-bearing account. Assume that your bank uses compound interest on its line-of-credit loans.

Intermediate (Questions 15–18)

a. What is the effective annual interest rate on this lending arrangement?

b. Suppose you need $15 million today and you repay it in six months. How much interest will you pay?

16. **Costs of Borrowing.** A bank offers your firm a revolving credit arrangement for up to $60 million at an interest rate of 1.24 percent per quarter. The bank also requires you to maintain a compensating balance of 6 percent against the *unused* portion of the credit line, to be deposited in a noninterest-bearing account. Assume you have a short-term investment account at the bank that pays 0.60 percent per quarter, and assume that the bank uses compound interest on its revolving credit loans.

   a. What is your effective annual interest rate (an opportunity cost) on the revolving credit arrangement if your firm does not use it during the year?

   b. What is your effective annual interest rate on the lending arrangement if you borrow $40 million immediately and repay it in one year?

   c. What is your effective annual interest rate if you borrow $60 million immediately and repay it in one year?

17. **Cash and Operating Cycles.** Fast Lane, Inc., has a cash cycle of 32 days, an operating cycle of 49 days, and an inventory period of 27 days. The company reported cost of goods sold in the amount of $325,000, and credit sales were $508,000. What is the company's average balance in accounts payable and accounts receivable?

18. **Cash Budget.** Too Late, Inc., has a 40-day average collection period and wants to maintain a minimum cash balance of $10 million, which is what the company currently has on hand. The company currently has a receivables balance of $110 million and has developed the following sales and cash disbursement budgets in millions:

	Q1	Q2	Q3	Q4
Sales	$210	$280	$260	$330
Total cash disbursement	190	240	350	220

Complete the following cash budget for the company. What conclusions do you draw?

TOO LATE, INC.
Cash Budget
(in millions)

	Q1	Q2	Q3	Q4
Beginning receivables				
Sales				
Cash collections				
Ending receivables				
Total cash collections				
Total cash disbursements				
Net cash inflow				
Beginning cash balance				
Net cash inflow				
Ending cash balance				
Minimum cash balance				
Cumulative surplus (deficit)				

19. **Costs of Borrowing.** Centennial Corp. has arranged a committed line of credit with a bank. This line of credit allows the firm to borrow up to $500 million at an interest rate of 2.3 percent per quarter. Centennial, however, has to pay an up-front commitment fee of .5 percent of the amount of the line. The bank also requires the firm to maintain a 4 percent compensating balance of the amount actually borrowed in a non-interest bearing account. Assume that the bank uses compound interest on its line-of-credit loans.

Challenge
(Questions 19–20)

    a. Ignoring the commitment fee, what is the effective annual interest rate on this lending arrangement?

    b. What is the effective rate on this lending arrangement if Centennial borrows $400 million immediately and repays it in one year?

    c. Assume the bank requires a 4 percent compensating balance, not on the amount borrowed but on the unused portion of the credit line. What is the effective rate on this lending arrangement if Centennial Corp. borrows $300 million immediately and repays it in one year?

20. **Cash Budget.** Dalhousie Corporation forecasts its sales to be $600 million for the first quarter, and then sales are expected to grow at 10 percent for the next four quarters. Accounts receivable at the beginning of the year are $200 million. Dalhousie has a 50-day collection period. Dalhousie's purchases from suppliers in a quarter are equal to 60 percent of the next quarter's forecast sales. The payables period is 60 days. Wages, taxes, and other expenses are 20 percent of sales, while interest and dividends are $20 million per quarter. Dalhousie plans a capital expenditure of $150 million in the third quarter. The corporation has a cash balance of $50 million and wants to maintain it in the coming year.

    a. Complete the following cash budget for Dalhousie.

DALHOUSIE CORPORATION Cash Budget (in millions)				
	Q1	Q2	Q3	Q4
Beginning receivables				
Sales				
Cash collections				
Ending receivables				
Total cash collections				
Payment of accounts				
Wages, taxes, other expenses				
Capital expenditures				
Long-term financing expenses				
Total cash disbursements				
Net cash inflow				
Beginning cash balance				
Net cash inflow				
Ending cash balance				
Minimum cash balance				
Cumulative surplus (deficit)				

    b. Assume that Dalhousie Corporation can borrow any needed funds on a short-term basis at a rate of 2.5 percent per quarter. Complete the following short-term financial plan for Dalhousie.

DALHOUSIE CORPORATION Short-Term Financial Plan (in millions)				
	Q1	Q2	Q3	Q4
Beginning cash balance				
Net cash inflow				
New short-term borrowing				
Interest on new short-term borrowing				
Short-term borrowing repaid				
Ending cash balance				
Minimum cash balance				
Cumulative surplus (deficit)				
Beginning short-term borrowing				
Change in short-term debt				
Ending short-term debt				

WHAT'S ON THE WEB?

16.1   **Sources and Uses of Cash.**   Find the two most recent balance sheets for Talisman Energy, an oil and gas company headquartered in Calgary, Alberta, at the "Analysis & Investors" link on the Web site **www.talisman-energy.com**. For each account in the balance sheet, show the change during the most recent year and note whether this was a source or use of cash. Do your numbers add up and make sense? Explain your answer for total assets as compared to your answer for total liabilities and owners' equity.

16.2   **Operating Cycle.**   Go to **www.sedar.com** and find the most recent annual income statement and the two most recent balance sheets for Biovail and Agnico-Eagle Mines. Both companies are in the S&P/TSX 60 Index. Biovail is involved in pharmaceuticals, while Agnico-Eagle Mines is a gold mining company. Calculate the operating cycle for each company and comment on any similarities or differences.

16.3   **Cash Cycle.**   Using the information you gathered in the previous problem, calculate the cash cycle for each company. What are the similarities or differences? Is this what you would expect from companies in each of these industries?

17 Working Capital Management

Most often, when news breaks about a firm's cash position, it's because the company's cash is running low. That wasn't the case for many companies in late 2006. The Bank of Montreal (BMO) had one of the largest cash reserves for a company its size. Its cash balance reached $19.7 billion, which works out to about $39 per share. The stock was trading at about $68 per share, so cash made up more than half of the company's value. In contrast, the Royal Bank of Canada (RBC), the country's largest bank, had only $4.4 billion in cash, which was equal to less than 7 percent of the company's value. Why would the Bank of Montreal hold such a large amount of cash reserve, while the Royal Bank of Canada had considerably less? To find out, this chapter examines cash management, which is just one of the important topics we consider under the general heading of working capital management.

This chapter considers various aspects of working capital management. Commonly, responsibility for working capital is spread across several different disciplines. Accounting is frequently responsible for payables and receivables; operations is in charge of inventory; and finance handles cash management. Marketing also plays a key role because sales forecasts are a key determinant of working capital needs. So, an understanding of working capital management is important for just about everyone in the firm.

Once you have made your way through this chapter, you should have a working knowledge of:

17.1 Why firms hold cash and the role of float in cash management.

17.2 How firms accelerate cash collections, manage disbursements, and invest idle cash in short-term marketable securities.

17.3 How firms manage their receivables and the basic components of a firm's credit policies.

17.4 The types of inventory and the costs associated with it.

17.5 Inventory management techniques and what determines the optimal inventory level.

This chapter examines working capital management. Recall from Chapter 1 that working capital management deals with a firm's short-term, or current, assets and liabilities. A firm's current liabilities consist largely of short-term borrowing. We discussed short-term borrowing in our previous chapter, so this chapter mainly focuses on current assets, in particular, cash, accounts receivable, and inventory.

17.1 | FLOAT AND CASH MANAGEMENT

We begin our analysis of working capital management by looking at how firms manage cash. The basic objective in cash management is to keep the investment in cash as low as possible while still operating the firm's activities efficiently and effectively. This goal usually reduces to the dictum "Collect early and pay late." Accordingly, we discuss ways of accelerating collections and managing disbursements.

In addition, firms must invest temporarily idle cash in short-term marketable securities. As we discuss in various places, these securities can be bought and sold in the financial markets. As a group, they have very little default risk, and most are highly liquid. There are different types of these so-called money market securities, and we discuss a few of the most important ones a bit later.

Reasons for Holding Cash

John Maynard Keynes, in his great work *The General Theory of Employment, Interest, and Money,* identified three reasons why liquidity is important: the speculative motive, the precautionary motive, and the transaction motive. We discuss these next.

speculative motive
The need to hold cash to take advantage of additional investment opportunities, such as bargain purchases.

The Speculative and Precautionary Motives   The **speculative motive** is the need to hold cash in order to be able to take advantage of, for example, bargain purchase opportunities that might arise, attractive interest rates, and (in the case of international firms) favourable exchange rate fluctuations.

For most firms, reserve borrowing ability and marketable securities can be used to satisfy speculative motives. Thus, for a modern firm, there might be a speculative motive for liquidity, but not necessarily for cash per se. Think of it this way: If you have a credit card with a very large credit limit, then you can probably take advantage of any unusual bargains that come along without carrying any cash.

precautionary motive
The need to hold cash as a safety margin to act as a financial reserve.

This is also true, to a lesser extent, for precautionary motives. The **precautionary motive** is the need for a safety supply to act as a financial reserve. Once again, there probably is a precautionary motive for liquidity. However, given that the value of money market instruments is relatively certain and that instruments such as T-bills are extremely liquid, there is no real need to hold substantial amounts of cash for precautionary purposes.

transaction motive
The need to hold cash to satisfy normal disbursement and collection activities associated with a firm's ongoing operations.

The Transaction Motive   Cash is needed to satisfy the **transaction motive**, the need to have cash on hand to pay bills. Transaction-related needs come from the normal disbursement and collection activities of the firm. The disbursement of cash includes the payment of wages and salaries, trade debts, taxes, and dividends.

Cash is collected from sales, the selling of assets, and new financing. The cash inflows (collections) and outflows (disbursements) are not perfectly synchronized, and some level of cash holdings is necessary to serve as a buffer. Perfect liquidity is the characteristic of cash that allows it to satisfy the transaction motive.

As electronic funds transfers and other high-speed, "paperless" payment mechanisms continue to develop, even the transaction demand for cash may all but disappear. Even if it does, however, there will still be a demand for liquidity and a need to manage it efficiently.

Costs of Holding Cash When a firm holds cash in excess of some necessary minimum, it incurs an opportunity cost. The opportunity cost of excess cash (held in currency or bank deposits) is the interest income that could be earned in the next best use, such as investment in marketable securities.

Given the opportunity cost of holding cash, why would a firm hold excess cash? The answer is that a cash balance must be maintained to provide the liquidity necessary for transaction needs—paying bills. If the firm maintains too small a cash balance, it may run out of cash. If this happens, the firm may have to raise cash on a short-term basis. This could involve, for example, selling marketable securities or borrowing.

Activities such as selling marketable securities and borrowing involve various costs. As we've discussed, holding cash has an opportunity cost. To determine the appropriate cash balance, the firm must weigh the benefits of holding cash against these costs. We discuss this subject in more detail in the sections that follow.

Understanding Float

As you no doubt know, the amount of money you have according to your chequebook can be very different from the amount of money that your bank thinks you have. The reason is that some of the cheques you have written haven't yet been presented to the bank for payment. The same thing is true for a business. The cash balance that a firm shows on its books is called the firm's *book,* or *ledger, balance.* The balance shown in its bank account as available to spend is called its *available,* or *collected, balance.* The difference between the available balance and the ledger balance is called the **float**, and it represents the net effect of cheques in the process of *clearing* (moving through the mail and the banking system).

float
The difference between the book or ledger cash balance and the available or collected balance, representing the net effect of cheques in the process of clearing.

Disbursement Float Cheques written by a firm generate *disbursement float,* causing a decrease in the firm's book balance but no change in its available balance. For example, suppose General Mechanics, Inc. (GMI), currently has $100,000 on deposit with its bank. On June 8, it buys some raw materials and puts a cheque in the mail for $100,000. The company's book balance is immediately reduced by $100,000 as a result.

GMI's bank, however, will not find out about this cheque until it is presented to GMI's bank for payment on, say, June 14. Until the cheque is presented, the firm's available balance is greater than its book balance by $100,000. In other words, before June 8, GMI has a zero float:

$$\text{Float} = \text{Firm's available balance} - \text{Firm's book balance}$$
$$= \$100,000 - 100,000$$
$$= \$0$$

GMI's position from June 8 to June 14 is:

$$\text{Disbursement float} = \text{Firm's available balance} - \text{Firm's book balance}$$
$$= \$100,000 - 0$$
$$= \$100,000$$

During this period of time while the cheque is clearing, GMI has a balance with the bank of $100,000. It can obtain the benefit of this cash while the cheque is clearing. For example, the available balance could be temporarily invested in marketable securities and thus earn some interest. We will return to this subject a little later.

Collection Float and Net Float Cheques received by the firm create *collection float.* Collection float increases book balances but does not immediately change available balances. For example, suppose GMI receives a cheque from a customer for $100,000 on October 8. Assume, as before, that the company has $100,000 deposited at its bank and a zero float. It processes the cheque and increases its book balance by $100,000, to $200,000. However, the additional cash is not available to GMI until the cheque is deposited in the firm's bank. This occurs on, say, October 9, the next day. In the meantime, the cash position at GMI reflects a collection float of $100,000. We can summarize these events. Before October 8, GMI's position is:

$$\text{Float} = \text{Firm's available balance} - \text{Firm's book balance}$$
$$= \$100,000 - 100,000$$
$$= \$0$$

GMI's position from October 8 to October 9 is:

$$\text{Collection float} = \text{Firm's available balance} - \text{Firm's book balance}$$
$$= \$100,000 - 200,000$$
$$= -\$100,000$$

In general, a firm's payment (disbursement) activities generate disbursement float, and its collection activities generate collection float. The net effect, that is, the sum of the total collection and disbursement floats, is the *net float*. The net float at any point in time is simply the overall difference between the firm's available balance and its book balance. If the net float is positive, then the firm's disbursement float exceeds its collection float and its available balance exceeds its book balance. If the available balance is less than the book balance, then the firm has a net collection float.

A firm should be concerned with its net float and available balance more than its book balance. If a financial manager knows that a cheque written by the company will not clear for several days, that manager will be able to keep a lower cash balance at the bank than might be true otherwise. This can generate a great deal of money.

For example, take the case of Toronto-based food processing and distribution giant George Weston. The average daily sales for George Weston were about $86 million in 2005. If George Weston's collections could have been speeded up by a single day, then George Weston could have freed up $86 million for investing. At a relatively modest .01 percent daily rate, the interest earned would have been on the order of $8,600 *per day*.

EXAMPLE 17.1 **Staying Afloat**

Suppose you have $5,000 on deposit. One day you write and mail a cheque for $1,000 to pay for textbooks. The same day you receive a cheque for $2,000 and put it in your backpack to deposit the next time you use a bank machine. What are your disbursement, collection, and net floats?

After you write the $1,000 cheque, you show a balance of $4,000 on your books, but the bank still shows $5,000 while the cheque is in the mail. This means you have a disbursement float of $1,000.

After you receive the $2,000 cheque, you show a balance of $6,000. Your available balance doesn't rise until you deposit the cheque. This means you have a collection float of −$2,000. Your net float is the sum of the collection and disbursement floats, or −$1,000.

Overall, you show $6,000 on your books, but the bank only shows a $5,000 balance. The discrepancy between your available balance and your book balance is the net float (−$1,000), and it is bad for you. If you write another cheque for $5,500, there may not be sufficient available funds to cover it, and it might bounce. This is the reason that the financial manager has to be more concerned with available balances than book balances.

Float Management Float management involves controlling the collection and disbursement of cash. The objective in cash collection is to speed up collections and reduce the lag between the time customers pay their bills and the time the cash becomes available. The objective in cash disbursement is to control payments and minimize the firm's costs associated with making payments.

Total collection or disbursement times can be broken down into three parts: mailing time, processing delay, and availability delay:

1. *Mailing time* is the part of the collection and disbursement process during which cheques are trapped in the postal system.
2. *Processing delay* is the time it takes the receiver of a cheque to process the payment and deposit it in a bank for collection.
3. *Availability delay* refers to the time required to clear a cheque through the banking system. This is the least important part, because in the Canadian banking system the availability delay is usually one day or less.

Speeding up collections involves reducing one or more of these components. Slowing up disbursements involves increasing one or more of them. We will describe some procedures for managing collection and disbursement times below.

Ethical and Legal Questions The cash manager must work with collected bank cash balances and not the firm's book balance (which reflects cheques that have been deposited but not collected). If this is not done, a cash manager could be drawing on uncollected cash as a source of funds for short-term investing. Most banks charge a penalty rate for the use of uncollected funds. However, banks may not have good enough accounting and control procedures to be fully aware of the use of uncollected funds. This raises some ethical and legal questions for the firm.

For example, in May 1998, the Canadian Imperial Bank of Commerce (CIBC) filed a lawsuit against Douglas Walls, who ran a car dealership in Prince George, British Columbia, and his controller, certified general accountant Michael Millard. The lawsuit claimed that Walls and Millard had been writing cheques against insufficient funds back and forth between their accounts at CIBC and Spruce Credit Union. Taking advantage of the time required for a cheque to clear through the banking system, the scheme resulted in overstated account balances by showing the same amount on deposit simultaneously in two bank accounts. The managers used this cheque-swapping scheme to obtain unauthorized credit. This type of systematic overdrafting of accounts (or cheque *kiting,* as it is sometimes called) is neither legal nor ethical. According to the CIBC, it suffered a loss of more than $1.5 million due to the alleged kiting scheme. This case dragged on for almost nine years. Eventually both men pleaded guilty and were given conditional sentences of two years on March 8, 2007. We should note that the key issue in the case against Walls and Millard was not their float management *per se,* but, rather, their practice of writing cheques for no economic reason other than to exploit float.

Electronic Data Interchange and Cheque Imaging: The End of Float? *Electronic data interchange* (EDI) is a general term that refers to the growing practice of direct, electronic information exchange between all types of businesses. One important use of EDI, often called financial EDI, or FEDI, is to electronically transfer financial information and funds between parties, thereby eliminating paper invoices, paper cheques, mailing, and handling. For example, it is possible to arrange to have your chequing account directly debited each month to pay many types of bills, and corporations now routinely directly

Visit **www. checkfreesoftware. com** for examples of the extensive electronic resources available for managing float.

Try **www.cfoasia.com** for an international view on cash management.

deposit paycheques into employee accounts. More generally, EDI allows a seller to send a bill electronically to a buyer, thereby avoiding the mail. The buyer can then authorize payment, which also occurs electronically. Its bank then transfers the funds to the seller's account at a different bank. The net effect is that the length of time required to initiate and complete a business transaction is shortened considerably, and much of what we normally think of as float is sharply reduced or eliminated. As the use of FEDI increases (which it will), float management will evolve to focus much more on issues surrounding computerized information exchange and funds transfers.

The Canadian Payments Association is leading an industry-wide project to modernize the Canadian cheque clearing system and enhance its efficiency through image technology. In this project, which will begin in January 2008, images of the front and back of cheques will be captured electronically and then transmitted, or "cleared," between banks, rather than delivering the actual paper documents. This image-based processing of cheques will not only significantly reduce float, but will also allow banks to offer new services. For example, customers will have online access to the cheque image within hours of the debit being posted to their accounts, instead of waiting for monthly statements to arrive in the mail.

To learn more about the clearing system visit the Canadian Payments Association site at www.cdnpay.ca.

CONCEPT QUESTIONS

17.1a What is the transaction motive for holding cash?

17.1b What is the cost to the firm of holding excess cash?

17.1c Which of these would a firm be more interested in reducing: collection float or disbursement float? Why?

17.1d What is the benefit from reducing or eliminating float?

17.2 | CASH MANAGEMENT: COLLECTION, DISBURSEMENT, AND INVESTMENT

As a part of managing its cash, a firm must make arrangements to collect from its customers, pay its suppliers, and invest any excess cash on hand. We begin by examining how firms collect and concentrate cash.

Cash Collection and Concentration

From our previous discussion, we know that collection delays work against the firm. All other things being the same, then, a firm will adopt procedures to speed up collections and thereby decrease collection times. In addition, even after cash is collected, firms need procedures to funnel, or concentrate, that cash where it can be best used. We discuss some common collection and concentration procedures next.

Components of Collection Time   Based on our discussion above, we can depict the basic parts of the cash collection process as follows: The total time in this process is made up of mailing time, cheque-processing delay, and the bank's availability delay.

The amount of time that cash spends in each part of the cash collection process depends on where the firm's customers and banks are located and how efficient the firm is at collecting cash.

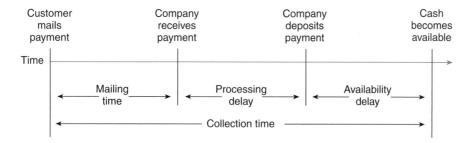

Cash Collection   How a firm collects from its customers depends in large part on the nature of the business. The simplest case would be a business such as a restaurant chain. Most of its customers will pay with cash, cheque, or credit card at the point of sale (this is called *over-the-counter collection*), so there is no problem with mailing delay. Normally, the funds would be deposited in a local bank, and the firm would have some means (discussed next) of gaining access to the funds.

When some or all of the payments a company receives are cheques that arrive through the mail, all three components of collection time become relevant. The firm may choose to have all the cheques mailed to one location, or, more commonly, the firm might have a number of different mail collection points to reduce mailing times. Also, the firm may run its collection operation itself or might hire an outside firm that specializes in cash collection. We discuss these issues in more detail below.

Other approaches to cash collection exist. One that is becoming more common is the preauthorized payment system. With this arrangement, the payment amounts and payment dates are fixed in advance. When the agreed-upon date arrives, the amount is automatically transferred from the customer's bank account to the firm's bank account, sharply reducing or even eliminating collection delays. The same approach is used by firms that have online terminals, meaning that when a sale is rung up, the money is immediately transferred to the firm's accounts.

Lockboxes   When a firm receives its payments by mail, it must decide where the cheques will be mailed and how the cheques will be picked up and deposited. Careful selection of the number and locations of collection points can greatly reduce collection times. Many firms use special post office boxes called **lockboxes** to intercept payments and speed cash collection.

lockboxes
Special post office boxes set up to intercept and speed up accounts receivable collections.

Figure 17.1 illustrates a lockbox system. The collection process is started by customers mailing their cheques to a post office box instead of sending them to the firm. The lockbox is maintained by a local bank. A large corporation may actually have many lockboxes, one in each major market area.

In the typical lockbox system, the local bank collects the lockbox cheques from the post office several times a day. The bank deposits the cheques directly to the firm's account. Details of the operation are recorded (in some computer-usable form) and sent to the firm.

A lockbox system reduces mailing time because cheques are received at a nearby post office instead of at corporate headquarters. Lockboxes also reduce the processing time because the corporation doesn't have to open the envelopes and deposit cheques for collection. In all, a bank lockbox should enable a firm to get its receipts processed, deposited, and cleared faster than if it were to receive cheques at its headquarters and deliver them itself to the bank for deposit and clearing.

For an example of payment services, including lockboxes and EDI, visit **www.scotiabank.com** and select "Business Services."

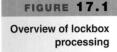

FIGURE **17.1**

Overview of lockbox processing

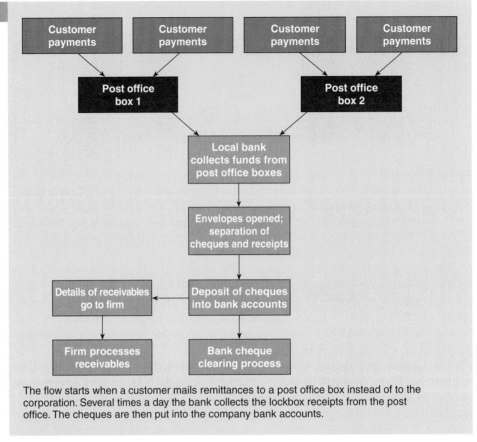

The flow starts when a customer mails remittances to a post office box instead of to the corporation. Several times a day the bank collects the lockbox receipts from the post office. The cheques are then put into the company bank accounts.

Cash Concentration　As we discussed earlier, a firm will typically have a number of cash collection points, and, as a result, cash collections may end up in many different banks and bank accounts. From here, the firm needs procedures to move the cash into its main accounts. This is called **cash concentration**. By routinely pooling its cash, the firm greatly simplifies its cash management by reducing the number of accounts that must be tracked. Also, by having a larger pool of funds available, a firm may be able to negotiate a better rate on any short-term investments.

cash concentration
The practice of and procedures for moving cash from multiple banks into the firm's main accounts.

In setting up a concentration system, firms will typically use one or more *concentration banks*. A concentration bank pools the funds obtained from local banks contained within some geographic region. Concentration systems are often used in conjunction with lockbox systems. Figure 17.2 illustrates how an integrated cash collection and cash concentration system might look.

Cash concentration can result in significant savings. For example, Lucent Technologies implemented a cash concentration program in 2004 that reduced the number of transfers among Lucent's various subsidiaries by 97 percent and reduced the dollar volume of transfers by 67 percent. This cash concentration is expected to save the company US$4 million per year. Sun Microsystems followed the same approach. It moved US$412 million from its subsidiaries in a cash concentration program and gained US$4.9 million on its short-term investments for the year.

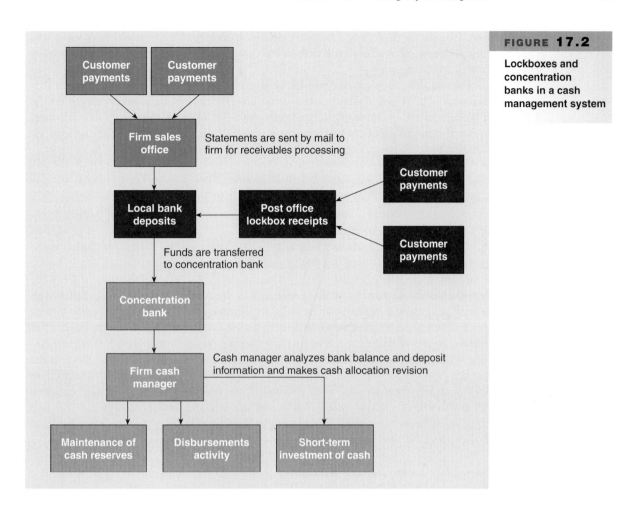

Managing Cash Disbursements

From the firm's point of view, disbursement float is desirable, so the goal in managing disbursement float is to slow down disbursements as much as possible. To do this, the firm may develop strategies to *increase* mail float, processing float, and availability float on the cheques it writes. Beyond this, firms have developed procedures for minimizing cash held for payment purposes. We discuss the most common of these below.

Increasing Disbursement Float   As we have seen, float in terms of slowing down payments comes from the time involved in mail delivery, cheque processing, and collection of funds. In the United States, disbursement float can be increased by writing a cheque on a geographically distant bank. In Canada, where cheque deposits receive same-day availability regardless of where they are drawn, this technique will not work. One way to slow down disbursement in Canada is to mail cheques from remote post offices so that the mailing time might be extended.

  Tactics for maximizing disbursement float are debatable on both ethical and economic grounds. First, as we discuss later, payment terms very frequently offer a substantial discount for early payment. The discount is usually much larger than any possible savings

For a free cash budgeting spreadsheet, go to **www.toolkit.com/ tools.**

from "playing the float game." In such cases, increasing mailing time will be of no benefit if the recipient dates payments based on the date received (as is common) as opposed to the postmark date.

Beyond this, suppliers are not likely to be fooled by attempts to slow down disbursement. The negative consequences from poor relations with suppliers can be costly. In broader terms, intentionally delaying payments by taking advantage of mailing times or unsophisticated suppliers may amount to avoiding paying bills when they are due, an unethical business procedure.

Controlling Disbursements We have seen that maximizing disbursement float is probably poor business practice. However, a firm will still wish to tie up as little cash as possible in disbursements. Firms have therefore developed systems for efficiently managing the disbursement process. The general idea in such systems is to have no more than the minimum amount necessary to pay bills on deposit in the bank. We discuss some approaches to accomplishing this goal next.

zero-balance account
A disbursement account in which the firm maintains a zero balance, transferring funds in from a master account only as needed to cover cheques presented for payment.

Zero-balance accounts With a **zero-balance account**, the firm, in co-operation with its bank, maintains a master account and a set of subaccounts. When a cheque written on one of the subaccounts must be paid, the necessary funds are transferred in from the master account. Figure 17.3 illustrates how such a system might work. In this case, the firm maintains two disbursement accounts, one for suppliers and one for payroll. As is shown, if the firm does not use zero-balance accounts, then each of these accounts must have a safety stock of cash to meet unanticipated demands. If the firm does use zero-balance accounts, then it can keep one safety stock in a master account and transfer the funds to the two subsidiary accounts as needed. The key is that the total amount of cash held as a buffer is smaller under the zero-balance arrangement, which frees up cash to be used elsewhere.

controlled disbursement account
A disbursement account to which the firm transfers an amount that is sufficient to cover demands for payment.

Controlled disbursement accounts Almost all payments that must be made in a given day are known in the morning. With a **controlled disbursement account**, the bank informs the firm of the day's total, and the firm transfers (usually by wire) the amount needed.

FIGURE 17.3 Zero-balance accounts

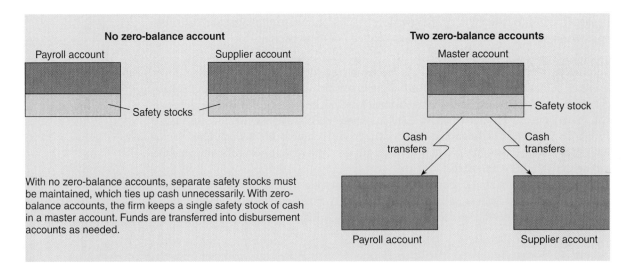

No zero-balance account

Payroll account   Supplier account
Safety stocks

Two zero-balance accounts

Master account
Safety stock
Cash transfers   Cash transfers
Payroll account   Supplier account

With no zero-balance accounts, separate safety stocks must be maintained, which ties up cash unnecessarily. With zero-balance accounts, the firm keeps a single safety stock of cash in a master account. Funds are transferred into disbursement accounts as needed.

Investing Idle Cash

If a firm has a temporary cash surplus, it can invest in short-term securities. As we have mentioned at various times, the market for short-term financial assets is called the *money market*. The maturity of short-term financial assets that trade in the money market is one year or less.

Most large firms manage their own short-term financial assets, transacting through banks and dealers. Some large firms and many small firms use money market mutual funds. These are funds that invest in short-term financial assets for a management fee. The management fee is compensation for the professional expertise and diversification provided by the fund manager.

Among the many money market mutual funds, some specialize in corporate customers. In addition, Canadian chartered banks offer arrangements in which the bank takes all excess available funds at the close of each business day and invests them for the firm.

Temporary Cash Surpluses   Firms have temporary cash surpluses for various reasons. Two of the most important are the financing of seasonal or cyclical activities of the firm and the financing of planned or possible expenditures.

Seasonal or cyclical activities   Some firms have a predictable cash flow pattern. They have surplus cash flows during part of the year and deficit cash flows the rest of the year. For example, Toys "Я" Us, a retail toy firm, has a seasonal cash flow pattern influenced by Christmas.

A firm such as Toys "Я" Us may buy marketable securities when surplus cash flows occur and sell marketable securities when deficits occur. Of course, bank loans are another short-term financing device. The use of bank loans and marketable securities to meet temporary financing needs is illustrated in Figure 17.4. In this case, the firm is following a compromise working capital policy in the sense we discussed in the previous chapter.

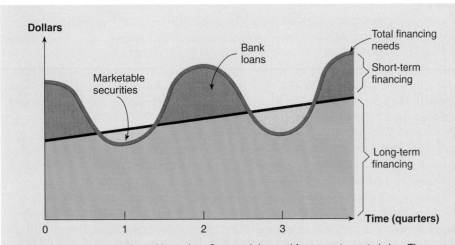

FIGURE 17.4

Seasonal cash demands

Time 1: A surplus cash position exists. Seasonal demand for current assets is low. The surplus is invested in short-term marketable securities.

Time 2: A deficit cash position exists. Seasonal demand for current assets is high. The financial deficit is financed by selling marketable securities and by bank borrowing.

Planned or possible expenditures   Firms frequently accumulate temporary investments in marketable securities to provide the cash for a plant construction program, dividend payment, or other large expenditure. Thus, firms may issue bonds and stocks before the cash is needed, investing the proceeds in short-term marketable securities and then selling the securities to finance the expenditures. Also, firms may face the possibility of having to make a large cash outlay. An obvious example would be the possibility of losing a large lawsuit. Firms may build up cash surpluses against such a contingency.

Characteristics of Short-Term Securities

Given that a firm has some temporarily idle cash, there are a variety of short-term securities available for investing. The most important characteristics of these short-term marketable securities are their maturity, default risk, and marketability.

Maturity   Maturity refers to the time period over which interest and principal payments are made. From Chapter 6, we know that for a given change in the level of interest rates, the prices of longer-maturity securities will change more than those of shorter-maturity securities. As a consequence, firms often limit their investments in marketable securities to those maturing in less than 90 days to avoid the risk of losses in value from changing interest rates.

Default risk   Default risk refers to the probability that interest and principal will not be paid in the promised amounts on the due dates (or not paid at all). Of course, some securities have negligible default risk, such as Canada Treasury bills. Given the purposes of investing idle corporate cash, firms typically avoid investing in marketable securities with significant default risk.

Marketability   Marketability refers to how easy it is to convert an asset to cash; so, marketability and liquidity mean much the same thing. Some money market instruments are much more marketable than others. At the top of the list are Canada Treasury bills, which can be bought and sold very cheaply and very quickly.

Some Different Types of Money Market Securities

Money market securities are generally highly marketable and short term. They usually have low risk of default. They are issued by the federal government (for example, Treasury bills), domestic and foreign banks (for example, certificates of deposit), and business corporations (for example, commercial paper). There are many types in all, and we only illustrate a few of the most common here.

Treasury bills are obligations of the federal government that mature in 1, 2, 3, 6, or 12 months. They are sold at bi-weekly auctions and actively traded in the secondary market through investment dealers.

Commercial paper refers to short-term debt notes issued by large, well-known companies. Maturities range from several days to 365 days. Typically, commercial paper is unsecured. Commercial paper can carry a credit rating similar to the bond ratings, which we discussed in Chapter 6.

There is no especially active secondary market in commercial paper. As a consequence, the marketability can be low; however, firms that issue commercial paper will often repurchase it directly before maturity. The default risk of commercial paper depends on the financial strength of the issuer.

Bankers' Acceptance refers to short-term securities issued by corporations with payment guaranteed by a chartered bank. Usually they are issued as a credit instrument in international trade, which is discussed in more detail in the next section. The holder of the bankers' acceptance may collect the payment from the bank at maturity or sell it at a discount in the market. Given the bank's guarantee, bankers' acceptances have low default risk and are highly liquid.

Certificates of deposit (CDs) are short-term loans to chartered banks. These are normally jumbo CDs – those in excess of $100,000. While there is an active secondary market in CDs in the United States, CDs are not transferable in Canada.

Because 100 percent of the dividends received by one Canadian corporation from another are exempt from taxation, the relatively high dividend yields on preferred stock provide a strong incentive for investment. The only problem is that the dividend is fixed with ordinary preferred stock, so the price can fluctuate more than is desirable in a short-term investment. So-called floating rate preferred stock is a recent innovation featuring a floating dividend. The dividend is reset fairly often (usually every 49 days), so this type of preferred has much less price volatility than ordinary preferred, and it has become a popular short-term investment.

> Check out short-term rates online at **www.bankofcanada. ca/en/rates/digest. html.**

CONCEPT QUESTIONS

17.2a What is a lockbox? What purpose does it serve?

17.2b What is a concentration bank? What purpose does it serve?

17.2c Is maximizing disbursement float a sound business practice?

17.2d What are some types of money market securities?

17.3 | CREDIT AND RECEIVABLES

When a firm sells goods and services, it can demand cash on or before the delivery date or it can extend credit to customers and allow some delay in payment.

Why would firms grant credit? The obvious reason is that offering credit is a way of stimulating sales. The costs associated with granting credit are not trivial. First, there is the chance that the customer will not pay. Second, the firm has to bear the costs of carrying the receivables. The credit policy decision thus involves a trade-off between the benefits of increased sales and the costs of granting credit.

From an accounting perspective, when credit is granted, an account receivable is created. These receivables include credit to other firms, called *trade credit,* and credit granted consumers, called *consumer credit,* and they represent a major investment of financial resources by Canadian businesses. Furthermore, trade credit is a very important source of financing for corporations. However we look at it, receivables and receivables management are very important aspects of a firm's short-term financial policy.

Components of Credit Policy

If a firm decides to grant credit to its customers, then it must establish procedures for extending credit and collecting. In particular, the firm will have to deal with the following components of credit policy:

1. **Terms of sale**. The terms of sale establish how the firm proposes to sell its goods and services. If the firm grants credit to a customer, the terms of sale will specify (perhaps implicitly) the credit period, the cash discount and discount period, and the type of credit instrument.

> **terms of sale**
> Conditions under which a firm sells its goods and services for cash or credit.

credit analysis
The process of determining the probability that customers will not pay.

2. Credit analysis. In granting credit, a firm determines how much effort to expend trying to distinguish between customers who will pay and customers who will not pay. Firms use a number of devices and procedures to determine the probability that customers will not pay, and, put together, these are called credit analysis.

collection policy
Procedures followed by a firm in collecting accounts receivable.

3. Collection policy. After credit has been granted, the firm has the potential problem of collecting the cash when it becomes due, for which it must establish a collection policy.

In the next several sections, we will discuss these components of credit policy that collectively make up the decision to grant credit.

Terms of the Sale

As we described above, the terms of a sale are made up of three distinct elements:

1. The period for which credit is granted (the credit period).
2. The cash discount and the discount period.
3. The type of credit instrument.

Within a given industry, the terms of sale are usually fairly standard, but these terms vary quite a bit across industries. In many cases, the terms of sale are remarkably archaic and literally date to previous centuries. Organized systems of trade credit that resemble current practice can be easily traced to the great fairs of medieval Europe, and they almost surely existed long before then.

The Basic Form   The easiest way to understand the terms of sale is to consider an example. For bulk candy, terms of 2/10, net 60 might be quoted. This means that customers have 60 days from the invoice date (discussed next) to pay the full amount. However, if payment is made within 10 days, a 2 percent cash discount can be taken.

Consider a buyer who places an order for $1,000, and assume that the terms of the sale are 2/10, net 60. The buyer has the option of paying $1,000 × (1 − .02) = $980 in 10 days, or paying the full $1,000 in 60 days. If the terms were stated as just net 30, then the customer would have 30 days from the invoice date to pay the entire $1,000, and no discount would be offered for early payment.

In general, credit terms are interpreted in the following way:

(take this discount off the invoice price)/(if you pay in this many days),
(else pay the full invoice amount in this many days)

Thus, **5**/10, net 45 means take a 5 percent discount from the full price if you pay within 10 days, or else pay the full amount in 45 days.

credit period
The length of time for which credit is granted.

The Credit Period   The **credit period** is the basic length of time for which credit is granted. The credit period varies widely from industry to industry, but it is almost always between 30 and 120 days. If a cash discount is offered, then the credit period has two components: the net credit period and the cash discount period.

The net credit period is the length of time the customer has to pay. The cash discount period, as the name suggests, is the time during which the discount is available. With 2/10, net 30, for example, the net credit period is 30 days and the cash discount period is 10 days.

The invoice date The invoice date is the beginning of the credit period. An **invoice** is a written account of merchandise shipped to the buyer. For individual items, by convention, the invoice date is usually the shipping date or the billing date, *not* the date that the buyer receives the goods or the bill.

invoice
Bill for goods or services provided by the seller to the purchaser.

Length of the credit period A number of factors influence the length of the credit period. Two of the most important are the *buyer's* inventory period and operating cycle. All other things being equal, the shorter these are, the shorter the credit period will normally be.

Based on our discussion in Chapter 16, the operating cycle has two components: the inventory period and the receivables period. The inventory period is the time it takes the buyer to acquire inventory (from us), process it, and sell it. The receivables period is the time it then takes the buyer to collect on the sale. Note that the credit period that we offer is effectively the buyer's payables period.

By extending credit, we finance a portion of our buyer's operating cycle and thereby shorten the buyer's cash cycle. If our credit period exceeds the buyer's inventory period, then we are financing not only the buyer's inventory purchases, but part of the buyer's receivables as well.

Furthermore, if our credit period exceeds our buyer's operating cycle, then we are effectively providing financing for aspects of our customer's business beyond the immediate purchase and sale of our merchandise. The reason is that the buyer effectively has a loan from us even after the merchandise is resold, and the buyer can use that credit for other purposes. For this reason, the length of the buyer's operating cycle is often cited as an appropriate upper limit to the credit period.

There are a number of other factors that influence the credit period. Many of these also influence our customers' operating cycles; so, once again, these are related subjects. Among the most important are:

For more on the credit process for small businesses, see **www.newyorkfed. org/education/ addpub/credit.html**.

1. *Perishability and collateral value.* Perishable items have relatively rapid turnover and relatively low collateral value. Credit periods are thus shorter for such goods.

2. *Consumer demand.* Products that are well established generally have more rapid turnover. Newer or slow-moving products will often have longer credit periods associated with them to entice buyers.

3. *Cost, profitability, and standardization.* Relatively inexpensive goods tend to have shorter credit periods. The same is true for relatively standardized goods and raw materials. These all tend to have lower markups and higher turnover rates, both of which lead to shorter credit periods.

4. *Credit risk.* The greater the credit risk of the buyer, the shorter the credit period is likely to be (assuming that credit is granted at all).

5. *The size of the account.* If the account is small, the credit period may be shorter, because small accounts are more costly to manage, and the customers are less important.

6. *Competition.* When the seller is in a highly competitive market, longer credit periods may be offered as a way of attracting customers.

7. *Customer type.* A single seller might offer different credit terms to different buyers. A food wholesaler, for example, might supply groceries, bakeries, and restaurants. Each group would probably have different credit terms. More generally, sellers often have both wholesale and retail customers, and they frequently quote different terms to the two types.

cash discount
A discount given to induce prompt payment. Also, *sales discount.*

Cash Discounts   As we have seen, **cash discounts** are often part of the terms of sale. The practice of granting discounts for cash purchases has a long history and is widespread today. One reason discounts are offered is to speed up the collection of receivables. This will have the effect of reducing the amount of credit being offered, and the firm must trade this off against the cost of the discount.

Notice that when a cash discount is offered, the credit is essentially free during the discount period. The buyer only pays for the credit after the discount expires. With 2/10, net 30, a rational buyer either pays in 10 days to make the greatest possible use of the free credit or pays in 30 days to get the longest possible use of the money in exchange for giving up the discount. So, by giving up the discount, the buyer effectively gets $30 - 10 = 20$ days' credit.

Another reason for cash discounts is that they are a way of charging higher prices to customers that have had credit extended to them. In this sense, cash discounts are a convenient way of charging for the credit granted to customers.

In our examples, it might seem that the discounts are rather small. With 2/10, net 30, for example, early payment only gets the buyer a 2 percent discount. Does this provide a significant incentive for early payment? The answer is yes because the implicit interest rate is extremely high.

Visit the Credit Institute of Canada at **www.creditinstitute .org.**

To see why the discount is important, we will calculate the cost to the buyer of not paying early. To do this, we will find the interest rate that the buyer is effectively paying for the trade credit. Suppose the order is for $1,000. The buyer can pay $980 in 10 days or wait another 20 days and pay $1,000. It's obvious that the buyer is effectively borrowing $980 for 20 days and that the buyer pays $20 in interest on the "loan." What is the interest rate?

With $20 in interest on $980 borrowed, the rate is $20/980 = 2.0408\%$. This is relatively low, but remember that this is the rate per 20-day period. There are $365/20 = 18.25$ such periods in a year, so, by not taking the discount, the buyer is paying an effective annual rate of:

$$EAR = 1.020408^{18.25} - 1 = 44.6\%$$

From the buyer's point of view, this is an expensive source of financing!

Given that the interest rate is so high here, it is unlikely that the seller benefits from early payment. Ignoring the possibility of default by the buyer, the decision by a customer to forgo the discount almost surely works to the seller's advantage.

EXAMPLE 17.2   What's the Rate?

Ordinary tiles are often sold with terms of 3/30, net 60. What effective annual rate does a buyer pay by not taking the discount? What would the APR be if one were quoted?

Here we have 3 percent discount interest on $60 - 30 = 30$ days' credit. The rate per 30 days is $.03/.97 = 3.093\%$. There are $365/30 = 12.17$ such periods in a year, so the effective annual rate is:

$$EAR = 1.03093^{12.17} - 1 = 44.9\%$$

The APR, as always, would be calculated by multiplying the rate per period by the number of periods:

$$APR = .03093 \times 12.17 = 37.6\%$$

An interest rate calculated like this APR is often quoted as the cost of the trade credit, and, as this example illustrates, this can seriously understate the true cost.

Credit Instruments   The **credit instrument** is the basic evidence of indebtedness. Most trade credit is offered on *open account*. This means that the only formal instrument of credit is the invoice, which is sent with the shipment of goods and which the customer signs as evidence that the goods have been received. Afterwards, the firm and its customers record the exchange on their books of account.

credit instrument
The evidence of indebtedness.

At times, the firm may require that the customer sign a *promissory note*. This is a basic IOU and might be used when the order is large or when the firm anticipates a problem in collections. Promissory notes are not common, but they can eliminate possible controversies later about the existence of debt.

One problem with promissory notes is that they are signed after delivery of the goods. One way to obtain a credit commitment from a customer before the goods are delivered is to arrange a *commercial draft*. Typically, the firm draws up a commercial draft calling for the customer to pay a specific amount by a specified date. The draft is then sent to the customer's bank with the shipping invoices.

If immediate payment on the draft is required, it is called a *sight draft*. If immediate payment is not required, then the draft is a *time draft*. When the draft is presented and the buyer "accepts" it, meaning that the buyer promises to pay it in the future, then it is called a *trade acceptance* and is sent back to the selling firm. The seller can then keep the acceptance or sell it to someone else. If a bank accepts the draft, meaning that the bank is guaranteeing payment, then the draft becomes a *banker's acceptance*. This arrangement is common in international trade.

Optimal Credit Policy

In principle, the optimal amount of credit is determined by the point at which the incremental cash flows from increased sales are exactly equal to the incremental costs of carrying the increased investment in accounts receivable.

The Total Credit Cost Curve   The trade-off between granting credit and not granting credit isn't hard to identify, but it is difficult to quantify precisely. As a result, we can only describe an optimal credit policy.

To begin, the carrying costs associated with granting credit come in three forms:

1.   The required return on receivables.
2.   The losses from bad debts.
3.   The cost of managing credit and credit collections.

We have already discussed the first and second of these. The third cost, the cost of managing credit, is the expense associated with running the credit department. Firms that don't grant credit have no such department and no such expense. These three costs will all increase as credit policy is relaxed.

If a firm has a very restrictive credit policy, then all of the above costs will be low. In this case, the firm will have a "shortage" of credit, so there will be an opportunity cost. This opportunity cost is the extra potential profit from credit sales that is lost because credit is refused. This forgone benefit comes from two sources: the increase in quantity sold and, potentially, a higher price. These costs go down as credit policy is relaxed.

The sum of the carrying costs and the opportunity costs of a particular credit policy is called the total **credit cost curve**. We have drawn such a curve in Figure 17.5. As Figure 17.5 illustrates, there is a point, C^*, where the total credit cost is minimized. This point corresponds to the optimal amount of credit, or, equivalently, the optimal investment in receivables.

credit cost curve
Graphical representation of the sum of the carrying costs and the opportunity costs of a credit policy.

FIGURE 17.5

The costs of granting credit

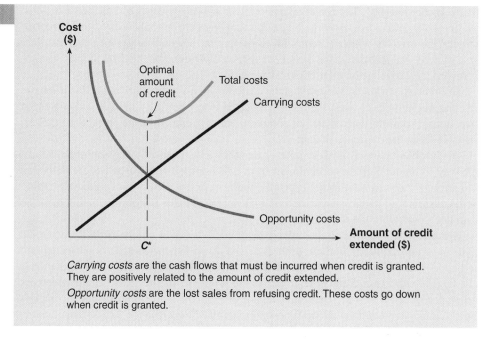

Carrying costs are the cash flows that must be incurred when credit is granted. They are positively related to the amount of credit extended.

Opportunity costs are the lost sales from refusing credit. These costs go down when credit is granted.

If the firm extends more credit than this amount, the additional net cash flow from new customers will not cover the carrying costs of the investment in receivables. If the level of receivables is below this amount, then the firm is forgoing valuable profit opportunities.

In general, the costs and benefits from extending credit will depend on characteristics of particular firms and industries. All other things being equal, for example, it is likely that firms with (1) excess capacity, (2) low variable operating costs, and (3) repeat customers will extend credit more liberally than other firms. See if you can explain why each of these contributes to a more liberal credit policy.

Organizing the Credit Function   Firms that grant credit have the expense of running a credit department. In practice, firms often choose to contract out all or part of the credit function to a factor, an insurance company, or a captive finance company. Chapter 16 discussed factoring, an arrangement in which the firm sells its receivables. Depending on the specific arrangement, the factor may have full responsibility for credit checking, authorization, and collection. Smaller firms may find such an arrangement cheaper than running a credit department.

Firms that manage internal credit operations are self-insured against default, meaning that they bear all the risk of nonpayment. An alternative is to buy credit insurance through an insurance company. The insurance company offers coverage up to a preset dollar limit for accounts. As you would expect, accounts with a higher credit rating merit higher insurance limits. This type of insurance is particularly important for exporters, and government insurance is available for certain types of exports.

captive finance company

A wholly owned subsidiary that handles the credit function for the parent company.

Large firms often extend credit through a **captive finance company**, which is simply a wholly owned subsidiary that handles the credit function for the parent company. Ford Motor Credit Company, or FMCC, is a well-known example. Ford Motor sells to car dealers, who in turn sell to customers. FMCC finances the dealer's inventory of cars and also finances customers who buy the cars.

Credit Analysis

Thus far, we have focused on establishing credit terms. Once a firm decides to grant credit to its customers, it must then establish guidelines for determining who will and who will not be allowed to buy on credit. *Credit analysis* refers to the process of deciding whether or not to extend credit to a particular customer. It usually involves two steps: gathering relevant information and determining creditworthiness.

Credit Information If a firm does want credit information on customers, there are a number of sources. Information sources commonly used to assess creditworthiness include the following:

1. *Financial statements.* A firm can ask a customer to supply financial statements such as balance sheets and income statements. Minimum standards and rules of thumb based on financial ratios like the ones we discussed in Chapter 3 can then be used as a basis for extending or refusing credit.

2. *Credit reports on the customer's payment history with other firms.* Quite a few organizations sell information on the credit strength and credit history of business firms. Dun & Bradstreet Canada provides subscribers with a credit reference book and credit reports on individual firms. Experian is another well-known credit-reporting firm. Ratings and information are available for a huge number of firms, including very small ones. Equifax Canada, Trans Union Canada, and Experian are the major suppliers of consumer credit information.

> For business credit reports, visit Dun & Bradstreet Canada at **www.dnb.ca.**

3. *Banks.* Banks will generally provide some assistance to their business customers in acquiring information on the creditworthiness of other firms.

4. *The customer's payment history with the firm.* The most obvious way to obtain information about the likelihood of a customer's not paying is to examine whether they have settled past obligations and how quickly they have met these obligations.

Credit Evaluation and Scoring There are no magical formulas for assessing the probability that a customer will not pay. In very general terms, the classic **five Cs of credit** are the basic factors to be evaluated:

> **five Cs of credit**
> The five basic credit factors to be evaluated: character, capacity, capital, collateral, and conditions.

1. *Character.* The customer's willingness to meet credit obligations.
2. *Capacity.* The customer's ability to meet credit obligations out of operating cash flows.
3. *Capital.* The customer's financial reserves.
4. *Collateral.* Assets pledged by the customer for security in case of default.
5. *Conditions.* General economic conditions in the customer's line of business.

Credit scoring refers to the process of calculating a numerical rating for a customer based on information collected; credit is then granted or refused based on the result. For example, a firm might rate a customer on a scale of 1 (very poor) to 10 (very good) on each of the five *C*s of credit using all the information available about the customer. A credit score could then be calculated based on the total. From experience, a firm might choose to grant credit only to customers with a score above, say, 30.

> **credit scoring**
> The process of quantifying the probability of default when granting consumer credit.

Firms such as credit card issuers have developed elaborate statistical models for credit scoring. Usually, all of the legally relevant and observable characteristics of a large pool of customers are studied to find their historic relation to default rates. Based on the results, it is possible to determine the variables that best predict whether or not a customer will pay and then calculate a credit score based on those variables.

> To obtain a copy of your credit report from Equifax Canada, go to "Consumer Information Centre" at **www.equifax.com/ EFX_Canada.**

Because credit-scoring models and procedures determine who is and who is not credit-worthy, it is not surprising that they have been the subject of government regulation. In particular, the kinds of background and demographic information that can be used in the credit decision are limited.

Collection Policy

Collection policy is the final element in credit policy. Collection policy involves monitoring receivables to spot trouble and obtaining payment on past-due accounts.

Monitoring Receivables   To keep track of payments by customers, most firms will monitor outstanding accounts. First, a firm will normally keep track of its average collection period, ACP, through time. If a firm is in a seasonal business, the ACP will fluctuate during the year, but unexpected increases in the ACP are a cause for concern. Either customers in general are taking longer to pay, or some percentage of accounts receivable is seriously overdue.

aging schedule
A compilation of accounts receivable by the age of each account.

The **aging schedule** is a second basic tool for monitoring receivables. To prepare one, the credit department classifies accounts by age.[1] Suppose a firm has $100,000 in receivables. Some of these accounts are only a few days old, but others have been outstanding for quite some time. The following is an example of an aging schedule.

Aging Schedule		
Age of Account	**Amount**	**Percentage of Total Value of Accounts Receivable**
0–10 days	$ 50,000	50%
11–60 days	25,000	25
61–80 days	20,000	20
Over 80 days	5,000	5
	$100,000	100%

If this firm has a credit period of 60 days, then 25 percent of its accounts are late. Whether or not this is serious depends on the nature of the firm's collections and customers. It is often the case that accounts beyond a certain age are almost never collected. Monitoring the age of accounts is very important in such cases.

Firms with seasonal sales will find the percentages on the aging schedule changing during the year. For example, if sales in the current month are very high, then total receivables will also increase sharply. This means that the older accounts, as a percentage of total receivables, become smaller and might appear less important. Some firms have refined the aging schedule so that they have an idea of how it should change with peaks and valleys in their sales.

Collection Effort   A firm usually goes through the following sequence of procedures for customers whose payments are overdue:

1. It sends out a delinquency letter informing the customer of the past-due status of the account.
2. It makes a telephone call to the customer.

---

[1]Aging schedules are used elsewhere in business. For example, aging schedules are often prepared for inventory items.

3. It employs a collection agency.

4. It takes legal action against the customer.

At times, a firm may refuse to grant additional credit to customers until arrears are cleared up. This may antagonize a normally good customer, and it points to a potential conflict of interest between the collections department and the sales department.

CONCEPT QUESTIONS

17.3a What are the basic components of credit policy?

17.3b Explain what terms of "3/45, net 90" mean. What is the effective interest rate?

17.3c What are the five *C*s of credit?

17.4 | INVENTORY MANAGEMENT

Like receivables, inventories represent a significant investment for many firms. For a typical manufacturing operation, inventories will often exceed 15 percent of assets. For a retailer, inventories could represent more than 25 percent of assets. From our discussion in Chapter 16, we know that a firm's operating cycle is made up of its inventory period and its receivables period. This is one reason for considering credit and inventory policy in the same chapter. Beyond this, both credit policy and inventory policy are used to drive sales, and the two must be co-ordinated to ensure that the process of acquiring inventory, selling it, and collecting on the sale proceeds smoothly. For example, changes in credit policy designed to stimulate sales must be simultaneously accompanied by planning for adequate inventory.

Visit the Society for Inventory Management Benchmarking Analysis at **www.simba.org.**

The Financial Manager and Inventory Policy

Despite the size of a typical firm's investment in inventories, the financial manager of a firm will not normally have primary control over inventory management. Instead, other functional areas such as purchasing, production, and marketing will usually share decision-making authority. Inventory management has become an increasingly important specialty in its own right, and financial management will often only have input into the decision. However, as the accompanying *Reality Bytes* box describes, inventory policy can have dramatic financial effects. We will therefore survey some basics of inventory and inventory policy in the sections ahead.

Inventory Types

For a manufacturer, inventory is normally classified into one of three categories. The first category is *raw material*. This is whatever the firm uses as a starting point in its production process. Raw materials might be something as basic as iron ore for a steel manufacturer or something as sophisticated as disk drives for a computer manufacturer.

The second type of inventory is *work-in-progress,* which is just what the name suggests—unfinished product. How big this portion of inventory is depends in large part on the length of the production process. For an airframe manufacturer, for example, work-in-progress can be substantial. The third and final type of inventory is *finished goods,* that is, products ready to ship or sell.

REALITY BYTES

Inventory Management: From Chips to Cars to Groceries

So you want to be a CEO? We suggest you learn working capital management and pay particular attention to inventory. Consider the case of United Microelectronics (UMC), a Taiwanese computer chip manufacturer. In February 2005, the company announced that its fourth-quarter profits had fallen 80 percent, and, as a result, it planned to make drastic cuts in capital spending in 2005. All of this occurred despite a 10 percent rise in revenues. UMC blamed the drop on a glut of inventory in the computer chip market and also explained how the glut had hurt operations. The production facility utilization rate, which shows current production as a percentage of full production capabilities, fell from 94 percent to 72 percent. Shipments fell by 17 percent during the quarter, and UMC expected shipments to fall by another 17 percent in the next quarter.

Proper inventory levels are important in every industry, but perhaps none more so than in the automobile industry. In the fall of 2004, GM scored a marketing coup when it gave 100 of its new Pontiac G6s to studio audience members on Oprah Winfrey's talk show. The giveaway resulted in widespread coverage by television, print media, and online media. Even so, the car didn't sell as well as GM expected, and the same was true for another GM model, the new Buick LaCrosse. As a result, in January 2005, the company had 71 days of inventory for each

model, which was higher than the industry average of about 60 days. In contrast, at about the same time, DaimlerChrysler had no such problem with its new (and cool) Chrysler 300C. The 300Cs flew off dealer lots, leaving DaimlerChrysler with only 28 days' inventory on hand.

Inventory problems at GM grew worse quickly. By February 2005, inventory levels of the G6 had grown to 123 days, and inventory levels of the LaCrosse had grown to 122 days. As a result, the company scaled back production of the G6 and delayed the start of a second shift of production on the car. Worse, GM had to offer significant discounts to sell these models. The company began offering $1,500 to $2,000 in rebates, 0 percent financing, and a further $1,000 for buyers who traded in a car made by a competing manufacturer.

Unfortunately, inventory management is sometimes used for unethical purposes. In late 2004, grocery wholesaler Fleming Company agreed to settle SEC charges regarding widespread accounting fraud. One of the charges levelled by the SEC was that Fleming inflated earnings by buying too much inventory near the end of quarters. These orders generated cash and volume discounts, which the company booked as earnings. What made the situation worse was that the orders included outdated and perishable goods.

There are three things to keep in mind concerning inventory types. First, the names for the different types can be a little misleading because one company's raw materials could be another's finished goods. For example, going back to our steel manufacturer, iron ore would be a raw material, and steel would be the final product. An auto body panel stamping operation will have steel as its raw material and auto body panels as its finished goods, and an automobile assembler will have body panels as raw materials and automobiles as finished products.

The second thing to keep in mind is that the various types of inventory can be quite different in terms of their liquidity. Raw materials that are commodity-like or relatively standardized can be easy to convert to cash. Work-in-progress, on the other hand, can be quite illiquid and have little more than scrap value. As always, the liquidity of finished goods depends on the nature of the product.

Finally, a very important distinction between finished goods and other types of inventories is that the demand for an inventory item that becomes a part of another item is usually termed *derived* or *dependent demand* because the firm's need for these inventory types depends on its need for finished items. In contrast, the firm's demand for finished goods is not derived from demand for other inventory items, so it is sometimes said to be *independent*.

Inventory Costs

As we discussed in Chapter 16, there are two basic types of costs associated with current assets in general and with inventory in particular. The first of these are *carrying costs*. Here, carrying costs represent all of the direct and opportunity costs of keeping inventory on hand. These include:

1. Storage and tracking costs.
2. Insurance and taxes.
3. Losses due to obsolescence, deterioration, or theft.
4. The opportunity cost of capital for the invested amount.

The sum of these costs can be substantial, roughly ranging from 20 to 40 percent of inventory value per year.

The other types of costs associated with inventory are *shortage costs*. These are costs associated with having inadequate inventory on hand. The two components of shortage costs are restocking costs and costs related to safety reserves. Depending on the firm's business, order or restocking costs are either the costs of placing an order with suppliers or the cost of setting up a production run. The costs related to safety reserves are opportunity losses such as lost sales and loss of customer goodwill that result from having inadequate inventory.

A basic trade-off in inventory management exists because carrying costs increase with inventory levels while shortage or restocking costs decline with inventory levels. The basic goal of inventory management is thus to minimize the sum of these two costs. We consider ways to reach this goal in the next section.

CONCEPT QUESTIONS

17.4a What are the different types of inventory?

17.4b What are three things to remember when examining inventory types?

17.4c What is the basic goal of inventory management?

17.5 | INVENTORY MANAGEMENT TECHNIQUES

As we described earlier, the goal of inventory management is usually framed as cost minimization. Three techniques are discussed in this section, ranging from the relatively simple to the very complex.

The ABC Approach

The ABC approach is a simple approach to inventory management where the basic idea is to divide inventory into three (or more) groups. The underlying rationale is that a small portion of inventory in terms of quantity might represent a large portion in terms of inventory value. For example, this situation would exist for a manufacturer that uses some relatively expensive, high-tech components and some relatively inexpensive basic materials in producing its products.[2]

---

[2]The ABC approach to inventory should not be confused with activity-based costing, a common topic in managerial accounting.

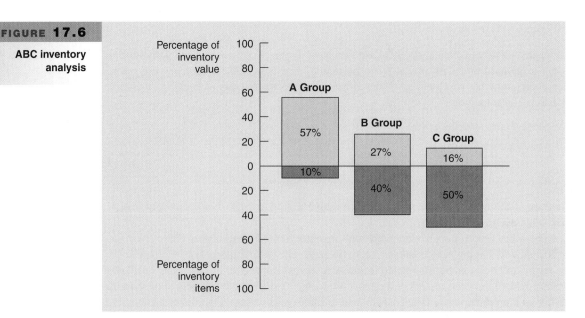

Figure 17.6 illustrates an ABC comparison of items in terms of the percentage of inventory value represented by each group versus the percentage of items represented. As Figure 17.6 shows, the A Group constitutes only 10 percent of inventory by item count, but it represents over half of the value of inventory. The A Group items are thus monitored closely, and inventory levels are kept relatively low. At the other end, basic inventory items, such as nuts and bolts, will also exist, but because these are crucial and inexpensive, large quantities are ordered and kept on hand. These would be C Group items. The B Group is made up of in-between items.

The Economic Order Quantity Model

The economic order quantity (EOQ) model is the best-known approach to explicitly establishing an optimal inventory level. The basic idea is illustrated in Figure 17.7, which plots the various costs associated with holding inventory (on the vertical axis) against inventory levels (on the horizontal axis). As is shown, inventory carrying costs rise and restocking costs decrease as inventory levels increase. From our discussion of the total credit cost curve in this chapter, the general shape of the total inventory cost curve is familiar. With the EOQ model, we will attempt to specifically locate the minimum total cost point, Q^*.

In our discussion below, an important point to keep in mind is that the actual cost of the inventory itself is not included. The reason is that the *total* amount of inventory the firm needs in a given year is dictated by sales. What we are analyzing here is how much the firm should have on hand at any particular time. More precisely, we are trying to determine what order size the firm should use when it restocks its inventory.

Inventory Depletion   To develop the EOQ, we will assume that the firm's inventory is sold off at a steady rate until it hits zero. At that point, the firm restocks its inventory back to some optimal level. For example, suppose the Eyssell Corporation starts out today with 3,600 units of a particular item in inventory. Annual sales of this item are 46,800 units, which is about 900 per week. If Eyssell sells off 900 units in inventory each week, then, after four weeks, all the available inventory will be sold, and Eyssell will restock by ordering (or manufacturing) another 3,600 and start over. This selling and restocking

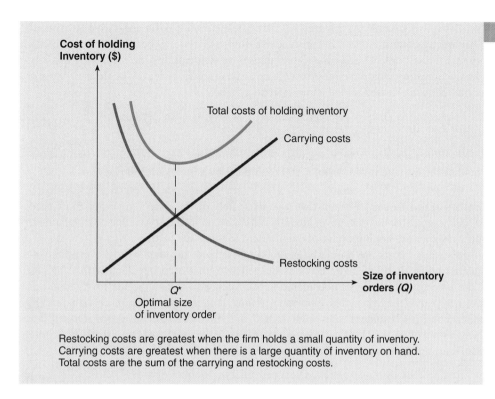

FIGURE 17.7

Costs of holding inventory

Restocking costs are greatest when the firm holds a small quantity of inventory.
Carrying costs are greatest when there is a large quantity of inventory on hand.
Total costs are the sum of the carrying and restocking costs.

process produces a sawtooth pattern for inventory holdings; this pattern is illustrated in Figure 17.8. As the figure shows, Eyssell always starts with 3,600 units in inventory and ends up at zero. On average, then, inventory is half of 3,600, or 1,800 units.

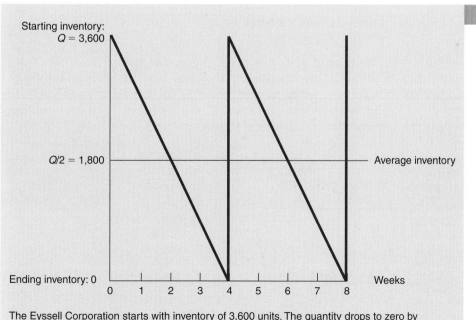

FIGURE 17.8

Inventory holdings for the Eyssell Corporation

The Eyssell Corporation starts with inventory of 3,600 units. The quantity drops to zero by the end of the fourth week. The average inventory is $Q/2 = 3,600/2 = 1,800$ over the period.

The Carrying Costs   As Figure 17.7 illustrates, carrying costs are normally assumed to be directly proportional to inventory levels. Suppose we let Q be the quantity of inventory that Eyssell orders each time (3,600 units); we will call this the restocking quantity. Average inventory would then just be $Q/2$, or 1,800 units. If we let CC be the carrying cost per unit per year, Eyssell's total carrying costs will be:

$$\text{Total carrying costs} = \text{Average inventory} \times \text{Carrying costs per unit}$$
$$= (Q/2) \times \text{CC} \qquad\qquad \text{[17.1]}$$

In Eyssell's case, if carrying costs were \$.75 per unit per year, then total carrying costs would be the average inventory of 1,800 multiplied by \$.75, or \$1,350 per year.

The Shortage Costs   For now, we will focus only on the restocking costs. In essence, we will assume that the firm never actually runs short on inventory, so that costs relating to safety reserves are not important. We will return to this issue below.

Restocking costs are normally assumed to be fixed. In other words, every time we place an order, there are fixed costs associated with that order (remember that the cost of the inventory itself is not considered here). Suppose we let T be the firm's total unit sales per year. If the firm orders Q units each time, then it will need to place a total of T/Q orders. For Eyssell, annual sales were 46,800, and the order size was 3,600. Eyssell thus places a total of $46,800/3,600 = 13$ orders per year. If the fixed cost per order is F, the total restocking costs for the year would be:

$$\text{Total restocking costs} = \text{Fixed cost per order} \times \text{Number of orders}$$
$$= F \times (T/Q) \qquad\qquad \text{[17.2]}$$

For Eyssell, order costs might be \$50 per order, so the total restocking costs for 13 orders would be $\$50 \times 13 = \$650$ per year.

The Total Costs   The total costs associated with holding inventory are the sum of the carrying costs and the restocking costs:

$$\text{Total costs} = \text{Carrying costs} + \text{Restocking costs}$$
$$= (Q/2) \times \text{CC} + F \times (T/Q) \qquad\qquad \text{[17.3]}$$

Our goal is to find the value of Q, the restocking quantity, that minimizes this cost. To see how we might go about this, we can calculate total costs for some different values of Q. For the Eyssell Corporation, we had carrying costs (CC) of \$.75 per unit per year, fixed costs (F) of \$50 per order, and total unit sales (T) of 46,800 units. With these numbers, some possible total costs are (check some of these for practice):

Restocking Quantity (Q)	Total Carrying Costs (Q/2 × CC)	+	Restocking Costs (F × T/Q)	=	Total Costs
500	\$ 187.5		\$4,680.0		\$4,867.5
1,000	375.0		2,340.0		2,715.0
1,500	562.5		1,560.0		2,122.5
2,000	750.0		1,170.0		1,920.0
2,500	**937.5**		**936.0**		**1,873.5**
3,000	1,125.0		780.0		1,905.0
3,500	1,312.5		668.6		1,981.1

Inspecting the numbers, we see that total costs start out at almost $5,000, and they decline to just under **$1,900.** The cost-minimizing quantity appears to be approximately **2,500.**

To find the precise cost-minimizing quantity, we can take a look back at Figure 17.7. What we notice is that the minimum point occurs right where the two lines cross. At this point, carrying costs and restocking costs are the same. For the particular types of costs we have assumed here, this will always be true, so we can find the minimum point just by setting these costs equal to each other and solving for Q^*:

Carrying costs = Restocking costs
$(Q^*/2) \times \text{CC} = F \times (T/Q^*)$

With a little algebra, we get:

$$(Q^*)^2 = \frac{2T \times F}{\text{CC}}$$

To solve for Q^*, we take the square root of both sides to find:

$$Q^* = \sqrt{\frac{2T \times F}{\text{CC}}} \qquad\qquad \text{[17.4]}$$

This reorder quantity, which minimizes the total inventory cost, is called the **economic order quantity**, or **EOQ**. For the Eyssell Corporation, the EOQ is:

$$
\begin{aligned}
Q^* &= \sqrt{\frac{2T \times F}{\text{CC}}} \\
&= \sqrt{\frac{(2 \times 46{,}800) \times \$50}{.75}} \\
&= \sqrt{6{,}240{,}000} \\
&= 2{,}498 \text{ units}
\end{aligned}
$$

economic order quantity (EOQ)
The restocking quantity that minimizes the total inventory costs.

Thus, for Eyssell, the economic order quantity is actually 2,498 units. At this level, verify that the restocking costs and carrying costs are identical (they're both $936.75).

Carrying Costs | EXAMPLE 17.3

Thiewes Shoes begins each period with 100 pairs of hiking boots in stock. This stock is depleted each period and reordered. If the carrying cost per pair of boots per year is $3, what are the total carrying costs for the hiking boots?

Inventories always start at 100 items and end up at 0, so average inventory is 50 items. At an annual cost of $3 per item, total carrying costs are $150.

Restocking Costs | EXAMPLE 17.4

In our previous example (Example 17.3), suppose Thiewes sells a total of 600 pairs of boots in a year. How many times per year does Thiewes restock? Suppose the restocking cost is $20 per order. What are total restocking costs?

Thiewes orders 100 items each time. Total sales are 600 items per year, so Thiewes restocks six times per year, or about every two months. The restocking costs would be 6 orders × $20 per order = $120.

EXAMPLE 17.5   **The EOQ**

Based on our previous two examples, what size orders should Thiewes place to minimize costs? How often will Thiewes restock? What are the total carrying and restocking costs? The total costs?

We have that the total number of pairs of boots ordered for the year (T) is 600. The restocking cost (F) is $20 per order, and the carrying cost (CC) is $3. We can calculate the EOQ for Thiewes as follows:

$$
\begin{aligned}
\text{EOQ} &= \sqrt{\frac{2T \times F}{\text{CC}}} \\
&= \sqrt{\frac{(2 \times 600) \times \$20}{3}} \\
&= \sqrt{8{,}000} \\
&= 89.44 \text{ units}
\end{aligned}
$$

Since Thiewes sells 600 pairs per year, it will restock 600/89.44 = 6.71 times. The total restocking costs will be $20 × 6.71 = $134.16. Average inventory will be 89.44/2 = 44.72. The carrying costs will be $3 × 44.72 = $134.16, the same as the restocking costs. The total costs are thus $268.33.

Extensions to the EOQ Model

Thus far, we have assumed that a company will let its inventory run down to zero and then reorder. In reality, a company will wish to reorder before its inventory goes to zero for two reasons. First, by always having at least some inventory on hand, the firm minimizes the risk of a stock-out and the resulting losses of sales and customers. Second, when a firm does reorder, there will be some time lag before the inventory arrives. Thus, to finish our discussion of the EOQ, we consider two extensions, safety stocks and reorder points.

Safety Stocks   A *safety stock* is the minimum level of inventory that a firm keeps on hand. Inventories are reordered whenever the level of inventory falls to the safety stock level. Part A of Figure 17.9 illustrates how a safety stock can be incorporated into an EOQ model. Notice that adding a safety stock simply means that the firm does not run its inventory all the way down to zero. Other than this, the situation here is identical to that considered in our earlier discussion of the EOQ.

Reorder Points   To allow for delivery time, a firm will place orders before inventories reach a critical level. The *reorder points* are the times at which the firm will actually place its inventory orders. These points are illustrated in Part B of Figure 17.9. As is shown, the reorder points simply occur some fixed number of days (or weeks or months) before inventories are projected to reach zero.

One of the reasons that a firm will keep a safety stock is to allow for uncertain delivery times. We can therefore combine our reorder point and safety stock discussions in Part C of Figure 17.9. The result is a generalized EOQ model in which the firm orders in advance of anticipated needs and also keeps a safety stock of inventory to guard against unforeseen fluctuations in demand and delivery times.

Managing Derived-Demand Inventories

The third type of inventory management technique is used to manage derived-demand inventories. As we described previously, demand for some inventory types is derived from, or dependent on, other inventory needs. A good example is given by the auto manufacturing

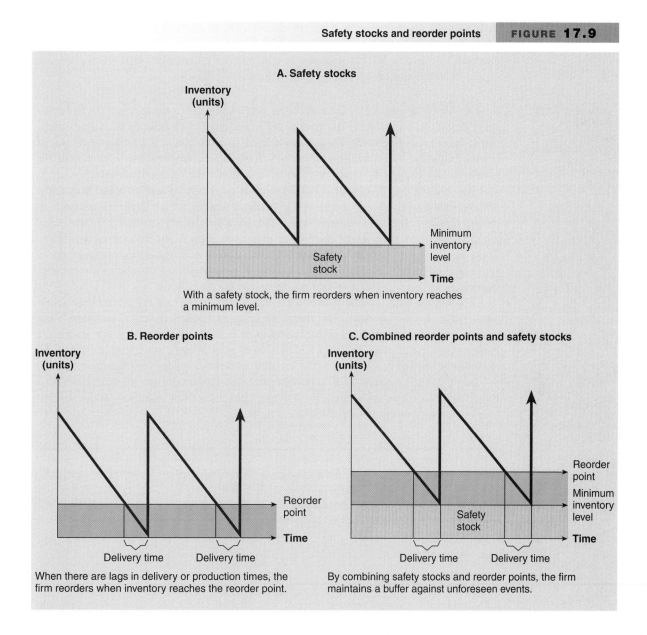

Safety stocks and reorder points   **FIGURE 17.9**

A. Safety stocks

With a safety stock, the firm reorders when inventory reaches a minimum level.

B. Reorder points

When there are lags in delivery or production times, the firm reorders when inventory reaches the reorder point.

C. Combined reorder points and safety stocks

By combining safety stocks and reorder points, the firm maintains a buffer against unforeseen events.

industry, where the demand for finished products derives from consumer demand, marketing programs, and other factors related to projected unit sales. The demand for inventory items such as tires, batteries, headlights, and other components is then completely determined by the number of autos planned. Materials requirements planning and just-in-time inventory management are two methods for managing demand-dependent inventories.

Materials Requirements Planning   Production and inventory specialists have developed computer-based systems for ordering and/or scheduling production of demand-dependent types of inventories. These systems fall under the general heading of **materials requirements planning (MRP)**. The basic idea behind MRP is that, once finished goods inventory levels are set, it is possible to determine what levels of work-in-progress inventories must exist to meet the need for finished goods. From there, it is possible to calculate

materials requirements planning (MRP)
A set of procedures used to determine inventory levels for demand-dependent inventory types, such as work-in-progress and raw materials.

the quantity of raw materials that must be on hand. This ability to schedule backwards from finished goods inventories stems from the dependent nature of work-in-progress and raw materials inventories. MRP is particularly important for complicated products for which a variety of components is needed to create the finished product.

just-in-time (JIT) inventory
A system for managing demand-dependent inventories that minimizes inventory holdings.

Just-in-Time Inventory   **Just-in-time**, or **JIT**, **inventory** is a modern approach to managing dependent inventories. The goal of JIT is essentially to minimize such inventories, thereby maximizing turnover. The approach began in Japan, and it is a fundamental part of much of Japanese manufacturing philosophy. As the name suggests, the basic goal of JIT is to have only enough inventory on hand to meet immediate production needs.

The result of the JIT system is that inventories are reordered and restocked frequently. Making such a system work and avoiding shortages requires a high degree of cooperation among suppliers. Japanese manufacturers often have a relatively small, tightly integrated group of suppliers with whom they work closely to achieve the needed co-ordination. These suppliers are a part of a large manufacturer's (such as Toyota's) industrial group, or *keiretsu*. Each large manufacturer tends to have its own *keiretsu*. It also helps to have suppliers located nearby, a situation that is common in Japan.

The *kanban* is an integral part of a JIT inventory system, and JIT systems are sometimes called *kanban systems*. The literal meaning of *kanban* is "card" or "sign," but, broadly speaking, a kanban is a signal to a supplier to send more inventory. For example, a kanban could literally be a card attached to a bin of parts. When a worker pulls that bin, the card is detached and routed back to the supplier, who then supplies a replacement bin.

A JIT inventory system is an important part of a larger production planning process. A full discussion of it would necessarily shift our focus away from finance to production and operations management, so we will leave it here.

CONCEPT QUESTIONS

17.5a   What does the EOQ model determine for the firm?

17.5b   Which cost component of the EOQ model does JIT inventory minimize?

KEY EQUATIONS:

I. Symbols

Q = Order size in units
CC = Carrying cost per unit
F = Fixed cost per order
T = Total unit sales

II. The Economic Order Quantity Model

$$\text{Total carrying costs} = \text{Average inventory} \times \text{Carrying costs per unit}$$
$$= (Q/2) \times \text{CC} \qquad \text{[17.1]}$$

$$\text{Total restocking costs} = \text{Fixed cost per order} \times \text{Number of orders}$$
$$= F \times (T/Q) \qquad \text{[17.2]}$$

Total costs = Carrying costs + Restocking costs
$$= (Q/2) \times CC + F \times (T/Q) \qquad \text{[17.3]}$$

The optimal order size Q^*:

$$Q^* = \sqrt{\frac{2T \times F}{CC}} \qquad \text{[17.4]}$$

SUMMARY AND CONCLUSIONS

This chapter has covered cash, receivables, and inventory management. Along the way, we have touched on a large number of subjects. Some of the more important issues we examined are:

1. There are, at least, three reasons for firms to hold cash: to take advantage of investment opportunities, to act as a financial reserve, and to conduct transactions. Firms seek to manage their cash by keeping no more on hand than is needed. The reason is that holding cash has an opportunity cost, namely, the returns that could be earned by investing the money.

   The difference between a firm's available balance and its book balance is the firm's net float. Float is an important consideration in cash management, and firms seek to manage collections and disbursements in ways designed to optimize the firm's net float.

2. The firm can make use of a variety of procedures to manage the collection and disbursement of cash in such a way as to speed up the collection of cash and slow down the payments. Some methods to speed up the collection are the use of lockboxes and cash concentration.

   Because of seasonal and cyclical activities, to help finance planned expenditures, or as a contingency reserve, firms temporarily hold a cash surplus. The money market offers a variety of possible vehicles for "parking" this idle cash.

3. A firm's credit policy includes the terms of sale, credit analysis, and collection policy. The terms of sale cover three related subjects: the credit period, cash discount, and credit instrument.

   The optimal credit policy for a firm depends on many specific factors, but generally involves trading off the costs of granting credit, such as the carrying costs of receivables and the possibility of nonpayment, against the benefits in terms of increased sales.

4. There are different types of inventories that differ greatly in their liquidity and management. The basic trade-off in inventory management is the cost of carrying inventory versus the cost of restocking.

5. Firms use different inventory management techniques; we described a few of the better known, including the ABC approach and the famous EOQ model, which balances the carrying costs against the restocking costs. We also touched briefly on materials requirements planning, MRP, and just-in-time, or JIT, inventory management.

CHAPTER REVIEW AND SELF-TEST PROBLEMS

17.1 Calculating Float. You have $10,000 on deposit with no outstanding cheques or uncleared deposits. One day you write and mail a cheque for $4,000 and then receive a cheque for $3,000. What are your disbursement, collection, and net floats?

17.2   The EOQ.   Heusen Computer Manufacturing starts each period with 4,000 central processing units (CPUs) in stock. This stock is depleted each month and reordered. If the carrying cost per CPU is $1 and the fixed order cost is $10, is Heusen following an economically advisable strategy?

■ Answers to Chapter Review and Self-Test Problems

17.1   First, after you write the cheque for $4,000, you show a balance of $6,000. However, while the cheque is moving through the mail, your bank shows a balance of $10,000. This is a $4,000 disbursement float, and it is good for you. Next, when you receive the $3,000, you show a balance of $9,000, but your account will not be credited for the $3,000 until it is deposited. This is a −$3,000 collection float, and it is bad for you.

   The sum of the disbursement float and the collection float is your net float of $1,000. In other words, on a net basis, you show a balance of $9,000, but your bank shows a $10,000 balance, so, in net terms, you are benefiting from the float.

17.2   We can answer by first calculating Heusen's carrying and restocking costs. The average inventory is 2,000 CPUs, and, since the carrying costs are $1 per CPU, total carrying costs are $2,000. Heusen restocks every month at a fixed order cost of $10, so the total restocking costs are $120. What we see is that carrying costs are large relative to reorder costs, so Heusen is carrying too much inventory.

   To determine the optimal inventory policy, we can use the EOQ model. Because Heusen orders 4,000 CPUs 12 times per year, total needs (T) are 48,000 CPUs. The fixed order cost is $10, and the carrying cost per unit (CC) is $1. The EOQ is therefore:

$$
\begin{aligned}
\text{EOQ} &= \sqrt{\frac{2T \times F}{\text{CC}}} \\
&= \sqrt{\frac{(2 \times 48,000) \times \$10}{\$1}} \\
&= \sqrt{960,000} \\
&= 979.80 \text{ units}
\end{aligned}
$$

We can check this by noting that the average inventory is about 490 CPUs, so the carrying cost is $490. Heusen will have to reorder 48,000/979.8 = 49 times. The fixed order cost is $10, so the total restocking cost is also $490.

CRITICAL THINKING AND CONCEPTS REVIEW

17.1   Cash Management.   Is it possible for a firm to have too much cash? Why would shareholders care if a firm accumulates large amounts of cash?

17.2   Cash Management.   What options are available to a firm if it believes it has too much cash? How about too little?

17.3   Agency Issues.   Are stockholders and creditors likely to agree on how much cash a firm should keep on hand?

17.4   Motivations for Holding Cash.   In the chapter opening, we discussed a large cash balance held by the Bank of Montreal. Automobile manufacturers also have enormous cash reserves. At the end of 2006, Ford Motor Co. had 13.5 billion U.S. dollars in cash, General Motors had 17.8 billion U.S. dollars, and Toyota had about 1.4 trillion Japanese yen. Why would firms such as these hold such large quantities of cash?

17.5 Short-Term Investments. Why is a preferred stock with a dividend tied to short-term interest rates an attractive short-term investment for corporations with excess cash?

17.6 Collection and Disbursement Floats. Which would a firm prefer: a net collection float or a net disbursement float? Why?

17.7 Float. Suppose a firm has a book balance of $2 million. At the automatic banking machine (ABM), the cash manager finds out that the bank balance is $2.5 million. What is the situation here? If this is an ongoing situation, what ethical dilemma arises?

17.8 Short-Term Investments. For each of the short-term marketable securities given here, provide an example of the potential disadvantages the investment has for meeting a corporation's cash management goals.

   a. Treasury bills

   b. Ordinary preferred stock

   c. Certificates of deposit (CDs)

   d. Commercial paper

17.9 Agency Issues. It is sometimes argued that excess cash held by a firm can aggravate agency problems (discussed in Chapter 1) and, more generally, reduce incentives for shareholder wealth maximization. How would you frame the issue here?

17.10 Use of Excess Cash. One option a firm usually has with any excess cash is to pay its suppliers more quickly. What are the advantages and disadvantages of this use of excess cash?

17.11 Use of Excess Cash. Another option usually available for dealing with excess cash is to reduce the firm's outstanding debt. What are the advantages and disadvantages of this use of excess cash?

17.12 Float. An unfortunately common practice goes like this (Warning: don't try this at home): Suppose you are out of money in your chequing account; however, your local grocery store will, as a convenience to you as a customer, cash a cheque for you. So you cash a cheque for $200. Of course, this cheque will bounce unless you do something. To prevent this, you go to the grocery the next day and cash another cheque for $200. You take this $200 and deposit it. You repeat this process every day, and, in doing so, you make sure that no cheques bounce. Eventually, manna from heaven arrives (perhaps in the form of money from home) and you are able to cover your outstanding cheques.

    To make it interesting, suppose you are absolutely certain that no cheques will bounce along the way. Assuming this is true, and ignoring any question of legality (what we have described is probably illegal cheque kiting), is there anything unethical about this? If you say yes, then why? In particular, who is harmed?

17.13 Credit Instruments. Describe each of the following:

   a. Sight draft

   b. Time draft

   c. Banker's acceptance

   d. Promissory note

   e. Trade acceptance

17.14 Trade Credit Forms. In what form is trade credit most commonly offered? What is the credit instrument in this case?

17.15 Receivables Costs. What are the costs associated with carrying receivables? What are the costs associated with not granting credit? What do we call the sum of the costs for different levels of receivables?

17.16 Five Cs of Credit. What are the five Cs of credit? Explain why each is important.

17.17 Credit Period Length. What are some of the factors that determine the length of the credit period? Why is the length of the buyer's operating cycle often considered an upper bound on the length of the credit period?

17.18 Credit Period Length. In each of the following pairings, indicate which firm would probably have a longer credit period and explain your reasoning.

    a. Firm A sells a miracle cure for baldness; Firm B sells toupees.

    b. Firm A specializes in products for landlords; Firm B specializes in products for renters.

    c. Firm A sells to customers with an inventory turnover of 10 times; Firm B sells to customers with an inventory turnover of 20 times.

    d. Firm A sells fresh fruit; Firm B sells canned fruit.

    e. Firm A sells and installs carpeting; Firm B sells rugs.

17.19 Inventory Types. What are the different inventory types? How do the types differ? Why are some types said to have dependent demand whereas other types are said to have independent demand?

17.20 Just-in-Time Inventory. If a company moves to a JIT inventory management system, what will happen to inventory turnover? What will happen to total asset turnover? What will happen to return on equity, ROE? (Hint: Remember the Du Pont equation from Chapter 3.)

QUESTIONS AND PROBLEMS

**Basic
(Questions 1–10)**

1. **Calculating Float.** You have $190,000 on deposit with no outstanding cheques or uncleared deposits. One day you write a cheque for $76,000. Does this create a disbursement float or a collection float? What is your available balance? Book balance?

2. **Calculating Float.** You have $18,000 on deposit with no outstanding cheques or uncleared deposits. If you receive a cheque for $7,000, does this create a disbursement float or a collection float? What is your available balance? Book balance?

3. **Calculating Float.** You have $50,000 on deposit with no outstanding cheques or uncleared deposits. One day you write a cheque for $6,000 and then receive a cheque for $13,000. What are your disbursement, collection, and net floats?

4. **Cash Discounts.** You place an order for 750 units of Good X at a unit price of $65. The supplier offers terms of 1/15, net 40.

    a. How long do you have to pay before the account is overdue? If you take the full period, how much should you remit?

    b. What is the discount being offered? How quickly must you pay to get the discount? If you do take the discount, how much should you remit?

    c. If you don't take the discount, how much interest are you paying implicitly? How many days' credit are you receiving?

5. **Calculating Float.** In a typical month, the Curfman Corporation receives 100 cheques totalling $75,000. These are delayed four days on average. What is the average daily float?

6. **Calculating Net Float.** Each business day, on average, a company writes cheques totaling $39,000 to pay its suppliers. The usual clearing time for the cheques is four days. Meanwhile, the company is receiving payments from its customers each day, in the form of cheques, totalling $63,000. The cash from the payments is available to the firm after two days.

   a. Calculate the company's disbursement float, collection float, and net float.

   b. How would your answer to part (*a*) change if the collected funds were available in one day instead of two?

7. **Size of Accounts Receivable.** Essence of Skunk Fragrances, Ltd., sells 4,000 units of its perfume collection each year at a price per unit of $400. All sales are on credit with terms of 2/15, net 40. The discount is taken by 60 percent of the customers. What is the amount of the company's accounts receivable? In reaction to sales by its main competitor, Sewage Spray, Essence of Skunk is considering a change in its credit policy to terms of 4/10, net 30 to preserve its market share. How will this change in policy affect accounts receivable?

8. **Size of Accounts Receivable.** The Real Deal Corporation has annual credit sales of $45 million. The average collection period is 38 days. What is Real Deal's average investment in accounts receivable as shown on the balance sheet?

9. **ACP and Accounts Receivable.** Miyagi Data, Inc., sells earnings forecasts for Japanese securities. Its credit terms are 2/10, net 30. Based on experience, 65 percent of all customers will take the discount.

   a. What is the average collection period for Miyagi?

   b. If Miyagi sells 1,200 forecasts every month at a price of $2,200 each, what is its average balance sheet amount in accounts receivable?

10. **Size of Accounts Receivable.** Two Doors Down, Inc., has weekly credit sales of $51,000, and the average collection period is 27 days. What is TDD's average accounts receivable figure?

11. **Terms of Sale.** A firm offers terms of 2/9, net 40. What effective annual interest rate does the firm earn when a customer does not take the discount? Without doing any calculations, explain what will happen to this effective rate if:

    Intermediate **(Questions 11–17)**

    a. The discount is changed to 3 percent.

    b. The credit period is increased to 60 days.

    c. The discount period is increased to 15 days.

    What is the EAR for each scenario?

12. **ACP and Receivables Turnover.** Now or Never, Inc., has an average collection period of 43 days. Its average daily investment in receivables is $82,000. What are annual credit sales? What is the receivables turnover?

13. **EOQ.** Clap Off Manufacturing uses 1,800 switch assemblies per week and then reorders another 1,800. If the relevant carrying cost per switch assembly is $2 and the fixed order cost is $650, is Clap Off's inventory policy optimal? Why or why not?

14. **EOQ.** The Trektronics store begins each month with 800 phasers in stock. This stock is depleted each month and reordered. If the carrying cost per phaser is $34 per year and the fixed order cost is $480, what is the total carrying cost? What is the restocking cost? Should Trektronics increase or decrease its order size? Describe an optimal inventory policy for Trektronics in terms of order size and order frequency.

15. **EOQ.**   Kryptonite Manufacturing uses 5,100 subframes per week and then reorders another 5,100. If the relevant carrying cost per subframe is $95, and the fixed order cost is $4,200, is Kryptonite's inventory policy optimal? Why or why not?

16. **EOQ.**   The Wheeling Pottery Store begins each month with 1,600 pots in stock. This stock is depleted each month and reordered. If the carrying cost per pot is $9 per year and the fixed order cost is $900, what is the total carrying cost? What is the restocking cost? Should Wheeling increase or decrease its order size? Describe an optimal inventory policy for Wheeling in terms of order size and order frequency.

17. **EOQ, Safety Stocks and Reorder Points.**   The Magnificent Ice store sells a total of 400 pairs of skates in a year. The carrying cost per pair is $4 and the fixed order cost is $60. It takes 10 days to receive a shipment after an order is placed, and the store wishes to hold a safety stock of skates equal to four days' sales. What is the EOQ for pairs of skates? If the store is open 320 days per year, what is the safety stock? What should be the reorder point for skates?

Challenge (Questions 18–19)

18. **Disbursement Float.**   The Mad Cow Corporation disburses cheques every week that average $50,000 and take four days to clear. The company decides to delay transfer of funds from an interest-bearing account that pays .03 percent daily for these four days.

   a.   How much simple interest can the company earn per year because of the delay?

   b.   How much compound interest can the company earn per year?

19. **Safety Stocks and Reorder Points.**   Hockey Paradise, Ltd., expects to sell 140 hockey sticks every week. The store is open seven days a week and expects to sell the same number of sticks every day. The company has an EOQ of 100 sticks and a safety stock of 20 sticks. Once an order is placed, it takes three days for Hockey Paradise to get the sticks in. How many orders does the company place per year? Assume that it is Monday morning before the store opens, and a shipment of hockey sticks has just arrived. When will Hockey Paradise place its next order?

WHAT'S ON THE WEB?

17.1   **Commercial Paper.**   Ontario-based Hydro One sells commercial paper to interested institutional investors. Go to the Hydro One Web site at **www. hydroone.com/en/**, click on the "Investor Centre" link, and select "Debt Information" in the pull-down menu. What is the credit rating for Hydro One's commercial paper? What companies provided the ratings? Now follow the "Short Term Promissory Note Information Memorandum" link. What are the minimum size and increments in which Hydro One will sell its commercial paper? What is the longest maturity?

17.2   **Commercial Paper Rates.**   What were the highest and lowest historical interest rates for commercial paper? Go to the Bank of Canada Web site at **www. bankofcanada.ca** and select "Interest Rates" in the "Rates and Statistics" menu at the top of the home page. By clicking on "Selected Historical Interest Rates," you will find a list of links for different historical interest rates. What were the highest and lowest interest rates for one month and three-month prime corporate paper? When did they occur? What implications do these rates have for short-term financial management?

MINI-CASE

PIEPKORN MANUFACTURING
WORKING CAPITAL MANAGEMENT

You have recently been hired by Piepkorn Manufacturing to work in its newly established treasury department. Piepkorn Manufacturing is a small company that produces cardboard boxes in a variety of sizes. Gary Piepkorn, the owner of the company, works primarily in the sales and production areas. Currently, the company puts all receivables in one shoe box and all payables in another. Because of the disorganized system, the finance area needs work, and that's what you've been brought in to do.

The company currently has a cash balance of $164,000 and plans to purchase new box folding machinery in the fourth quarter at a cost of $240,000. The purchase of the machinery will be made with cash because of the discount offered. The company's policy is to maintain a target cash balance of $100,000. All sales and all purchases are made on credit.

Gary Piepkorn has projected the following gross sales for each of the next four quarters:

	Q1	Q2	Q3	Q4
Gross sales	$695,000	$708,000	$741,000	$757,000

Also, gross sales for the first quarter of next year are projected at $784,000. Piepkorn currently has an accounts receivable period of 57 days and an accounts receivable balance of $426,000. Ten percent of the accounts receivable balance is from a company that has just entered bankruptcy, and it is likely this portion of the accounts receivable will never be collected.

Piepkorn typically orders 50 percent of next quarter's projected gross sales in the current quarter, and suppliers are typically paid in 53 days. Wages, taxes, and other costs run about 25 percent of gross sales. The company has a quarterly interest payment of $85,000 on its long-term debt.

The company uses a chartered bank for its short-term financial needs. It pays 1.5 percent per quarter on all short-term borrowing and maintains a money market account that pays 1 percent per quarter on all short-term deposits.

Gary has asked you to prepare a cash budget and short-term financial plan for the company under the current policies. He has also asked you to prepare additional plans based on changes in several inputs.

1. Use the numbers given to complete the cash budget and short-term financial plan.

2. Rework the cash budget and short-term financial plan assuming Piepkorn changes to a target balance of $80,000.

3. You have looked at the credit policy offered by your competitors and have determined that the industry standard credit policy is 1/10, net 45. The discount will begin to be offered on the first day of the year. You want to examine how this credit policy would affect the cash budget and short-term financial plan. If this credit policy is implemented, you believe that 25 percent of all customers will take advantage of it, and that the accounts receivable period will decline to 38 days. Rework the cash budget and short-term financial plan under the new credit policy and a target cash balance of $80,000. What interest rate are you effectively offering customers?

4. You have talked to the company's suppliers about the credit terms Piepkorn receives. Currently, the company receives terms of net 45. The suppliers have stated that they would offer new credit terms of 2/25, net 40. The discount would begin to be offered on the first day of the year. What interest rate are the suppliers offering the company? Rework the cash budget and short-term financial plan, assuming you take the credit terms on all orders and the minimum cash balance is $80,000. Assume the sales discount is offered as well.

(continued)

PIEPKORN MANUFACTURING
Cash Budget

	Q1	Q2	Q3	Q4
Beginning cash balance				
Net cash inflow				
Ending cash balance				
Minimum cash balance				
Cumulative surplus (deficit)				

PIEPKORN MANUFACTURING
Short-Term Financial Plan

	Q1	Q2	Q3	Q4
Target cash balance				
Net cash inflow				
New short-term investments				
Income from short-term investments				
Short-term investments sold				
New short-term borrowing				
Interest on short-term borrowing				
Short-term borrowing repaid				
Ending cash balance				
Minimum cash balance				
Cumulative surplus (deficit)				
Beginning short-term investments				
Ending short-term investments				
Beginning short-term debt				
Ending short-term debt				

18 International Aspects of Financial Management

In early 2002, major currencies such as the German mark, Italian lira, and French franc became footnotes in history, replaced by the euro (€). In an extraordinary turn of events, 12 of the 15 countries that comprised the European Economic and Monetary Union (EMU) turned over their sovereign currencies and much of the control of their monetary policies to the new European Central Bank.

Some of the major proponents of the new system were businesses in these 12 countries; many business leaders believed the union was necessary to enhance competitiveness with such countries as the United States. And the euro will continue to grow. In January 2007, the euro became the official currency of Slovenia. Nine more countries are currently in the process that leads to the adoption of the euro. As the euro spreads, it will become more widely used than the U.S. dollar and will play an increasingly important role in the global economy. In this chapter, we will explore the role played by currencies and exchange rates, along with a number of other key topics in international finance.

As businesses of all types have increased their reliance on international operations, all areas of business have been strongly affected. Human resources, production, marketing, accounting, and strategy, for example, all become much more complex when nondomestic considerations come into play. This chapter discusses one of the most important aspects of international business: the impact of shifting exchange rates and what companies (and individuals) can do to protect themselves against adverse exchange rate movements.

After reading this chapter, you should have a good understanding of:

18.1 Some basic terminology of international finance.

18.2 How exchange rates are quoted, what they mean, and the difference between spot and forward exchange rates.

18.3 Two forms of purchasing power parity.

18.4 Relationship between exchange rates and interest rates.

18.5 The different types of exchange rate risk and ways firms manage exchange rate risk.

18.6 The impact of political risk on international business investing.

Companies with significant foreign operations are often called *international corporations* or *multinationals*. Such companies must consider many financial factors that do not directly affect purely domestic firms. These include foreign exchange rates, differing interest rates from country to country, complex accounting methods for foreign operations, foreign tax rates, and foreign government intervention.

The basic principles of corporate finance still apply to international corporations; like domestic companies, they seek to invest in projects that create more value for the shareholders (or owners) than they cost and to arrange financing that raises cash at the lowest possible cost. In other words, the net present value principle holds for both foreign and domestic operations, but it is usually more complicated to apply the NPV rule to foreign investments.

We won't have much to say here about the role of cultural and social differences in international business. We also will not be discussing the implications of differing political and economic systems. These factors are of great importance to international businesses, but it would take another book to do them justice. Consequently, we will focus only on some purely financial considerations in international finance and some key aspects of foreign exchange markets.

18.1 | TERMINOLOGY

A common buzzword for the student of business finance is *globalization*. The first step in learning about the globalization of financial markets is to conquer the new vocabulary. As with any specialty, international finance is rich in jargon. Accordingly, we get started on the subject with a highly eclectic vocabulary exercise.

The terms that follow are presented alphabetically, and they are not all of equal importance. We choose these particular ones because they appear frequently in the financial press or because they illustrate some of the colourful language of international finance.

American Depositary Receipt (ADR)
Security issued in the U.S. representing shares of a foreign stock, allowing that stock to be traded in the U.S.

See
www.adr.com
for more.

cross-rate
The implicit exchange rate between two currencies quoted in some third currency (usually the U.S. dollar).

Eurobonds
International bonds issued in multiple countries but denominated in a single currency (usually the issuer's currency).

Eurocurrency
Money deposited in a financial centre outside the country whose currency is involved.

1. An **American Depositary Receipt**, or **ADR**, is a security issued in the United States that represents shares of a foreign stock, allowing that stock to be traded in the United States. Foreign companies use ADRs, which are issued in U.S. dollars, to expand the pool of potential U.S. investors. ADRs are available in two forms: company sponsored, which are listed on an exchange, and unsponsored, which are usually held by the investment bank that deals in the ADR. Both forms are available to individual investors, but only company-sponsored issues are quoted daily in newspapers.

2. The **cross-rate** is the implicit exchange rate between two currencies when both are quoted in some third currency, usually the U.S. dollar.

3. A **Eurobond** is a bond issued in multiple countries, but denominated in a single currency, usually the issuer's home currency. Such bonds have become an important way to raise capital for many international companies and governments. Eurobonds are issued outside the restrictions that apply to domestic offerings and are syndicated and traded mostly from London. Trading can and does take place anywhere there is a buyer and a seller.

4. **Eurocurrency** is money deposited in a financial centre outside the country whose currency is involved. For instance, Eurodollars—the most widely used Eurocurrency—are U.S. dollars deposited in banks outside the U.S. banking system.

5. **Foreign bonds**, unlike Eurobonds, are issued in a single country and are usually denominated in that country's currency. Often, the country in which these bonds are issued will draw distinctions between them and bonds issued by domestic issuers, including different tax laws, restrictions on the amount issued, and tougher disclosure rules.

   Foreign bonds often are nicknamed for the country where they are issued: Maple Bonds (Canada), Yankee bonds (United States), Samurai bonds (Japan), Rembrandt bonds (the Netherlands), and Bulldog bonds (Britain). Partly because of tougher regulations and disclosure requirements, the foreign-bond market hasn't grown in past years with the vigour of the Eurobond market. A substantial portion of all foreign bonds are issued in Switzerland.

6. **Gilts**, technically, are British and Irish government securities, although the term also includes issues of local British authorities and some overseas public-sector offerings.

7. The **London Interbank Offer Rate (LIBOR)** is the rate that most international banks charge one another for loans of Eurodollars overnight in the London market. LIBOR is a cornerstone in the pricing of money market issues and other debt issues by both government and corporate borrowers. Interest rates are frequently quoted as some spread over LIBOR, and they then float with the LIBOR rate.

8. There are two basic kinds of **swaps:** interest rate and currency. An interest rate swap occurs when two parties exchange a floating-rate payment for a fixed-rate payment or vice versa. Currency swaps are agreements to deliver one currency in exchange for another. Often both types of swaps are used in the same transaction when debt denominated in different currencies is swapped.

> **foreign bonds**
> International bonds issued in a single country, usually denominated in that country's currency.
>
> **gilts**
> British and Irish government securities.
>
> **London Interbank Offer Rate (LIBOR)**
> The rate most international banks charge one another for overnight Eurodollar loans.
>
> For current LIBOR rates, see www.economagic.com/libor.htm.
>
> **swaps**
> Agreements to exchange two securities or currencies.

CONCEPT QUESTIONS

18.1a What are the differences between a Eurobond and a foreign bond?

18.1b What are Eurodollars?

18.2 | FOREIGN EXCHANGE MARKETS AND EXCHANGE RATES

The **foreign exchange market** is undoubtedly the world's largest financial market. It is the market where one country's currency is traded for another's. Most of the trading takes place in a few currencies such as the U.S. dollar ($), the British pound sterling (£), the Japanese yen (¥), and the euro (€). Table 18.1 lists some of the more common currencies and their symbols.

The foreign exchange market is an over-the-counter market, so there is no single location where traders get together. Instead, market participants are located in the major commercial and investment banks around the world. They communicate using computer terminals, telephones, and other telecommunications devices. For example, one communications network for foreign transactions is the Society for Worldwide Interbank Financial Telecommunications (SWIFT), a Belgian not-for-profit co-operative. Using data transmission lines, a bank in New York can send messages to a bank in London via SWIFT regional processing centres.

> **foreign exchange market**
> The market in which one country's currency is traded for another's.
>
> Visit SWIFT at www.swift.com.

	TABLE 18.1

International currency symbols

Country	Currency	Symbol
Australia	Dollar	A$
Brazil	Real	R$
Canada	Dollar	Can$
China	Yuan (Renminbi)	元
Denmark	Kroner	DKr
EMU (Eurozone)	Euro	€
India	Rupee	Rs
Iran	Rial	RI
Japan	Yen	¥
Kuwait	Dinar	KD
Mexico	Peso	Ps
New Zealand	Dollar	NZ$
Norway	Kroner	NKr
Russia	Rouble	Руб
Saudi Arabia	Riyal	SR
Singapore	Dollar	S$
South Africa	Rand	R
South Korea	Won	₩
Sweden	Krona	Skr
Switzerland	Franc	SF
Thailand	Baht	฿
Turkey	Lira	£
United Kingdom	Pound	£
United States	Dollar	$

The many different types of participants in the foreign exchange market include the following:

1. Importers who pay for goods in foreign currencies.
2. Exporters who receive foreign currency and may want to convert to their domestic currency.
3. Portfolio managers who buy or sell foreign stocks and bonds.
4. Foreign exchange brokers who match buy and sell orders.
5. Traders who "make a market" in foreign currencies.
6. Speculators who try to profit from changes in exchange rates.
7. Individuals who buy foreign currencies to travel abroad or make purchases in foreign countries.

Exchange Rates

exchange rate
The price of one country's currency expressed in terms of another country's currency.

An **exchange rate** is simply the price of one country's currency expressed in terms of another country's currency. In practice, almost all trading of currencies takes place in terms of the U.S. dollar. For example, both the Swiss franc and the Japanese yen are traded with their prices quoted in U.S. dollars. Exchange rates are constantly changing. Our nearby *Work the Web* box shows you how to get up-to-the-minute rates.

For current and historical exchange rates, go to **fx.sauder.ubc.ca.**

Exchange Rate Quotations   Figure 18.1 reproduces exchange rate quotations as they appear in the *National Post.* The left portion (labelled "Per US$") of the "Foreign Exchange" table shows how much it takes to buy one U.S. dollar in different currencies. For example, the Canadian dollar is quoted at 1.0585, which means that you can buy one U.S. dollar with 1.0585 Canadian dollars.

WORK THE WEB

You just returned from your dream vacation to Jamaica and feel rich since you have 10,000 Jamaican dollars left over. You now need to convert this to Canadian dollars. How much will you have? You can look up the current exchange rate and do the conversion yourself, or simply work the Web. We went to **www.xe.com** and used the currency converter on the site to find out. This is what we found:

Universal Currency Converter™ Results   Using live mid-market rates. More currencies...

Live rates at 2007.06.02 05:19:53 UTC

10,000.00 JMD = 155.724 CAD
Jamaica Dollars   Canada Dollars
1 JMD = 0.0155724 CAD   1 CAD = 64.2163 JMD

New! XE.com Forex Speculation. Click here*!!*

Looks like you left Jamaica just before you ran out of money.

FOREIGN EXCHANGE

Supplied by Reuters. Listings indicative of late afternoon rates. Charts based on close.

Per US$	Latest	Prev day	4 wks ago	Day %ch	Wk %ch	4wk %ch	Per C$	Latest	Prev day	4 wks ago	Day %ch	Wk % ch	4wk %ch
Canada $	1.0585	1.0609	1.1019	-0.2	-2.0	-3.9	US $	0.9448	0.9426	0.9075	+0.2	+2.1	+4.1
euro*	1.349	1.3444	1.3603	+0.3	+0.3	-0.8	euro*	1.4274	1.4258	1.4984	+0.1	-1.7	-4.7
Japan yen	121.78	122.09	120.09	-0.3	nil	+1.4	Japan yen	115.01	115.05	108.95	nil	+2.1	+5.6
UK pound*	1.9912	1.9821	1.993	+0.5	+0.4	-0.1	UK pound*	2.107	2.1021	2.1952	+0.2	-1.6	-4.0
Swiss franc	1.2236	1.2301	1.2112	-0.5	-0.4	+1.0	Swiss franc	1.1557	1.1592	1.0987	-0.3	+1.6	+5.2
Australia $*	0.8341	0.8325	0.8254	+0.2	+1.8	+1.1	Australia $*	0.8825	0.8828	0.9089	nil	-0.3	-2.9
Mexico peso	10.7566	10.7173	10.8367	+0.4	-0.2	-0.7	Mexico peso	10.1601	10.0985	9.8296	+0.6	+1.8	+3.4
Hong Kong	7.8066	7.811	7.8197	-0.1	-0.2	-0.2	Hong Kong	7.3741	7.3615	7.0944	+0.2	+1.9	+3.9
Singapore $	1.5303	1.5314	1.5149	-0.1	+0.1	+1.0	Singapore $	1.4451	1.4431	1.3739	+0.1	+2.2	+5.2
China renminbi	7.6465	7.6461	7.705	nil	nil	-0.8	China renminbi	7.2242	7.2075	6.9925	+0.2	+2.1	+3.3
India rupee	40.21	40.27	40.56	-0.1	-0.5	-0.9	India rupee	37.99	37.96	36.81	+0.1	+1.6	+3.2
Russia rouble	25.8608	25.8955	25.7378	-0.1	-0.1	+0.5	Russia rouble	24.4401	24.415	23.3511	+0.1	+2.0	+4.7
Brazil real	1.9271	1.9049	2.0202	+1.2	-0.8	-4.6	Brazil real	1.8208	1.7937	1.8332	+1.5	+1.2	-0.7

FORWARD EXCHANGE

PerUS$	1 mo	3 mo	6 mo	1 yr	2 yr	3 yr	4 yr	5 yr
C$	1.0581	1.0573	1.0550	1.0496	1.0403	1.0328	1.0286	1.0291
euro	1.3495	1.3516	1.3558	1.3661	1.3863	1.4041	1.4198	1.4393
Yen	121.75	121.74	121.73	121.71	121.67	121.64	121.60	121.57
£	1.9876	1.9813	1.9736	1.9621	1.9479	1.9398	1.9293	1.9264

Per C$	1 mo	3 mo	6 mo	1 yr	2 yr	3 yr	4 yr	5 yr
US$	0.9451	0.9458	0.9479	0.9527	0.9613	0.9682	0.9722	0.9717
euro	1.4277	1.4284	1.4295	1.4313	1.4421	1.4502	1.4604	1.4812
Yen	114.79	114.36	113.76	112.45	109.48	106.53	103.43	100.17
£	2.1031	2.0948	2.0821	2.0594	2.0264	2.0035	1.9845	1.9825

CURRENCY CROSS RATES

	C$	US$	euro	Yen	£	Sw.fr.	A$
C$	-----	1.0585	1.4274	0.0087	2.1070	0.8653	0.8832
US$	0.9448	-----	1.3490	0.0082	1.9912	0.8173	0.8341
euro	0.7006	0.7413	-----	0.6086	1.4757	0.6057	0.6181
Yen	115.01	121.78	164.22	-----	242.39	99.49	101.53
£	0.4746	0.5022	0.6773	0.4123	-----	0.4104	0.4188
SW. fr.	1.1557	1.2236	1.6501	1.0044	2.4357	-----	1.0202
A$	1.1323	1.1989	1.6167	0.9841	2.3863	0.9795	-----
Gold	711.38	672.00	498.11	81850	337.45	822.33	805.47

inverted

FIGURE 18.1

Exchange rate quotations

Source: The National Post, June 5, 2007.

The right portion of the "Foreign Exchange" table (labelled "Per C$) gives the number of units of foreign currency it takes to buy one Canadian dollar. The U.S. dollar is quoted here at 0.9448, so you can get 0.9448 U.S. dollars for one Canadian dollar. Naturally, this second exchange rate is just the reciprocal of the first one; 1/1.0585 = 0.9448, allowing for a rounding error. Note that four weeks ago you would get less U.S. dollars, .9075 to be exact, for one Canadian dollar. Thus, as the last column shows, the Canadian dollar had appreciated by 4.1 percent during this four-week period.

Notice the asterisk next to the euro, British pound, and Australian dollar. It indicates that, by convention, exchange rates for these currencies are quoted as the number of units of foreign currency needed to buy one euro, British pound, or Australian dollar. For example, the right portion of the "Foreign Exchange" table shows that it takes 2.107 Canadian dollars to buy one British pound, not vice versa.

Forward exchange rates ranging from one month to five years are shown in the "Forward Exchange" table (we will discuss forward exchange rates later in this section). The "Currency Cross Rates" table displays exchange rates between seven major currencies and gold. For example, the first row shows the number of Canadian dollars it takes to buy one unit of foreign currency. You will need 1.4274 Canadian dollars to buy one euro, but you can buy one yen with only 0.87 Canadian cents.

EXAMPLE 18.1   **A Yen for Euros**

Get up-to-the-minute exchange rates at **www.xe.com** and **www.exchangerate .com.**

Suppose you have $1,000. Based on the rates in Figure 18.1, how many Japanese yen can you get? Alternatively, if a Porsche costs € 200,000 (€ is the symbol for the euro), how many dollars will you need to buy it?

The exchange rate in terms of yen per Canadian dollar is 115.01. Your $1,000 will thus get you:

$1,000 × 115.01 yen per $1 = 115,010 yen

Since the exchange rate in terms of Canadian dollars per euro is 1.4274, you will need:

€ 200,000 × 1.4274 $ per euro = $285,480

Cross-Rates and Triangle Arbitrage   Using the U.S. dollar or the euro as the common denominator in quoting exchange rates greatly reduces the number of necessary cross-currency quotes. For example, with five major currencies, there would potentially be 10 exchange rates instead of just four. Also, the fact that the dollar is used throughout cuts down on inconsistencies in the exchange rate quotations.

Earlier, we defined the cross-rate as the exchange rate for a non-U.S. currency expressed in terms of another non-U.S. currency. For example, suppose we observed the following for the Mexican peso (Ps) and the Swiss franc (SF):

Ps per US$1 = 10.00
SF per US$1 = 2.00

Suppose the cross-rate is quoted as:

Ps per SF = 4.00

What do you think?

The cross-rate here is inconsistent with the exchange rates. To see this, suppose you have US$100. If you convert this to Swiss francs, you will receive:

US$100 × SF 2 per US$1 = SF 200

If you convert this to pesos at the cross-rate, you will have:

SF 200 × Ps 4 per SF 1 = Ps 800

However, if you just convert your dollars to pesos without going through francs, you will have:

US$100 × Ps 10 per US$1 = Ps 1,000

What we see is that the peso has two prices, Ps 10 per US $1 and Ps 8 per US $1, depending on how we get the pesos.

To make money, we want to buy low, sell high. The important thing to note is that pesos are cheaper if you buy them with U.S. dollars because you get 10 pesos instead of just 8. You should proceed as follows:

For international news and events, visit **www.ft.com.**

1. Buy 1,000 pesos for US$100.
2. Use the 1,000 pesos to buy Swiss francs at the cross-rate. Since it takes four pesos to buy a franc, you will receive Ps 1,000/4 = SF 250.
3. Use the SF 250 to buy U.S. dollars. Since the exchange rate is SF 2 per dollar, you receive SF 250/2 = US$125, for a round-trip profit of US$25.
4. Repeat Steps 1 through 3.

This particular activity is called *triangle arbitrage* because the arbitrage involves moving through three different exchange rates:

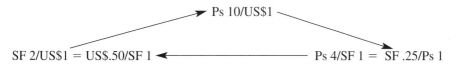

To prevent such opportunities, it is not difficult to see that since a dollar will buy you either 10 pesos or two francs, the cross-rate must be:

(Ps 10/US$1)/(SF 2/US $1) = Ps 5/SF 1

That is, five pesos per franc. If it were anything else, there would be a triangle arbitrage opportunity.

Shedding Some Pounds **EXAMPLE 18.2**

Suppose the exchange rates for the British pound and Swiss franc are:

Pounds per US$1 = .60
SF per US$1 = 2.00

The cross-rate is three francs per pound. Is this consistent? Explain how to go about making some money.

The cross-rate should be SF 2.00/£ .60 = SF 3.33 per pound. You can buy a pound for SF 3 in one market, and you can sell a pound for SF 3.33 in another. So we want to first get some francs, then use the francs to buy some pounds, and then sell the pounds. Assuming you had US$100, you could:

1. Exchange U.S. dollars for francs: US$100 × 2 = SF 200.
2. Exchange francs for pounds: SF 200/3 = £66.67.
3. Exchange pounds for U.S. dollars: £66.67/.60 = US$111.12.

This would result in an US$11.12 round-trip profit.

Types of Transactions

spot trade
An agreement to trade currencies based on the exchange rate today for settlement within two business days.

There are two basic types of trades in the foreign exchange market: spot trades and forward trades. A **spot trade** is an agreement to exchange currency "on the spot," which actually means that the transaction will be completed, or settled, within two business days. The exchange rate on a spot trade is called the **spot exchange rate.** Implicitly, all of the exchange rates and transactions we have discussed so far have referred to the spot market.

spot exchange rate
The exchange rate on a spot trade.

A **forward trade** is an agreement to exchange currency at some time in the future. The exchange rate that will be used is agreed upon today and is called the **forward exchange rate.** A forward trade will normally be settled sometime in the next 12 months but some forward exchange rates can be quoted up to five years into the future.

forward trade
Agreement to exchange currency at some time in the future.

If you look back at Figure 18.1, you will see forward exchange rates quoted for some of the major currencies. For example, the spot exchange rate between Canadian and U.S. dollars is C$1.0585 = US$1. The one-year forward exchange rate is C$1.0496 = US$1. This means that you can buy a U.S. dollar today for C$1.0585, or you can agree to take delivery of a U.S. dollar in one year and pay C$1.0496 at that time.

forward exchange rate
The agreed-upon exchange rate to be used in a forward trade.

Notice that the U.S. dollar is cheaper in the forward market (C$1.0496 versus C$1.0585). Since the U.S. dollar is cheaper in the future than it is today, it is said to be selling at a *discount* relative to the Canadian dollar. For the same reason, the Canadian dollar is said to be selling at a *premium* relative to the U.S. dollar.

Why does the forward market exist? One answer is that it allows businesses and individuals to lock in a future exchange rate today, thereby eliminating any risk from unfavourable shifts in the exchange rate.

EXAMPLE 18.3   **Looking Forward**

Suppose you are expecting to receive a million British pounds in six months, and you agree to a forward trade to exchange your pounds for Canadian dollars. Based on Figure 18.1, how many dollars will you get in six months? Is the pound selling at a discount or a premium relative to the dollar?

In Figure 18.1, the spot exchange rate and the six-month forward rate in terms of Canadian dollars per pound are $2.107 = £1 and $2.0821 = £1, respectively. (Note that the British pound is quoted as the number of units of foreign currency per one British pound in the "Foreign Exchange" and "Forward Exchange" tables). If you expect £1 million in six months, then you will get £1 million × $2.0821 per £ = $2.0821 million. Since it is less expensive to buy a pound in the forward market than in the spot market ($2.0821 versus $2.107), the pound is selling at a discount relative to the dollar.

As we showed earlier, an exchange rate can be quoted in two ways: as the number of dollars it takes to buy one unit of foreign currency and as the number of units of foreign currency it takes to buy one dollar. For the remainder of this chapter, we will quote rates as the amount of foreign currency per Canadian dollar. Things can get extremely confusing if you forget this. Thus, when we say things like "the exchange rate is expected to rise," it is important to remember that we are talking about the exchange rate quoted as units of foreign currency per Canadian dollar.

CONCEPT QUESTIONS

18.2a   What is triangle arbitrage?

18.2b   What do we mean by the three-month forward exchange rate?

18.2c   If we say that the exchange rate is SF 1.90, what do we mean?

18.3 | PURCHASING POWER PARITY

Now that we have discussed what exchange rate quotations mean, we can address an obvious question: What determines the level of the spot exchange rate? In addition, we know that exchange rates change through time. A related question is thus: What determines the rate of change in exchange rates? At least part of the answer in both cases goes by the name of **purchasing power parity (PPP),** and it is the idea that the exchange rate adjusts to keep purchasing power constant among currencies. As we discuss next, there are two forms of PPP: *absolute* and *relative.*

purchasing power parity (PPP)
The idea that the exchange rate adjusts to keep purchasing power constant among currencies.

Absolute Purchasing Power Parity

The basic idea behind *absolute purchasing power parity* is that a commodity costs the same regardless of what currency is used to purchase it or where it is selling. This is a very straightforward concept. If a beer costs £2 in London, and the exchange rate is £.60 per dollar, then a beer costs £2/.60 = $3.33 in Toronto. In other words, absolute PPP says that $1 will buy you the same number of, say, cheeseburgers, anywhere in the world.

More formally, let S_0 be the spot exchange rate between the British pound and the Canadian dollar today (Time 0), and remember that we are quoting exchange rates as the amount of foreign currency per dollar. Let P_{CAN} and P_{UK} be the current Canadian and British prices, respectively, on a particular commodity, say, apples. Absolute PPP simply says that:

$$P_{UK} = S_0 \times P_{CAN}$$

This tells us that the British price for something is equal to the Canadian price for that same something, multiplied by the exchange rate.

According to PPP, if we let P_{FC} be the price of a commodity in a foreign country, the exchange rate between the Canadian dollar and any other foreign currency can be defined as:

$$S_0 = P_{FC}/P_{CAN} \qquad\qquad \text{[18.1]}$$

The rationale behind PPP is similar to that behind triangle arbitrage. If PPP did not hold, arbitrage would be possible (in principle) if apples were moved from one country to another. For example, suppose apples in Toronto are selling for $4 per bushel, while in London the price is £2.40 per bushel. Absolute PPP implies that:

$$\begin{aligned} S_0 &= P_{UK}/P_{CAN} \\ &= £2.40/\$4 = £.60 \end{aligned}$$

That is, the implied spot exchange rate is £.60 per dollar. Equivalently, a pound is worth $1/£.60 = $1.67.

Suppose, instead, that the actual exchange rate is £.50. Starting with $4, a trader could buy a bushel of apples in Toronto, ship it to London, and sell it there for £2.40. Our trader could then convert the £2.40 into dollars at the prevailing exchange rate, $S_0 = £.50$, yielding a total of £2.40/.50 = $4.80. The round-trip gain is 80 cents.

Because of this profit potential, forces are set in motion to change the exchange rate and/or the price of apples. In our example, apples would begin moving from Toronto to London. The reduced supply of apples in Toronto would raise the price of apples there, and the increased supply in Britain would lower the price of apples in London.

In addition to moving apples around, apple traders would be busily converting pounds back into dollars to buy more apples. This activity increases the supply of pounds and simultaneously increases the demand for dollars. We would expect the value of a pound to fall. This means that the dollar is getting more valuable, so it will take more pounds to buy one dollar. Since the exchange rate is quoted as pounds per dollar, we would expect the exchange rate to rise from £.50.

For absolute PPP to hold absolutely, several things must be true:

1. The transaction costs of trading apples—shipping, insurance, spoilage, and so on—must be zero.

2. There must be no barriers to trading apples, such as tariffs, taxes, or other political barriers such as VRAs (voluntary restraint agreements).

3. Finally, an apple in Toronto must be identical to an apple in London. It won't do for you to send red apples to London if the English eat only green apples.

Given the fact that the transaction costs are not zero and that the other conditions are rarely exactly met, it is not surprising that absolute PPP is really applicable only to traded goods, and then only to very uniform ones.

For this reason, absolute PPP does not imply that a Mercedes costs the same as a Ford or that a nuclear power plant in France costs the same as one in Ontario. In the case of the cars, they are not identical. In the case of the power plants, even if they were identical, they are expensive and very difficult to ship. On the other hand, we would be very surprised to see a significant violation of absolute PPP for gold. See our nearby *Reality Bytes* box for an interesting example of PPP violations.

Relative Purchasing Power Parity

As a practical matter, a relative version of purchasing power parity has evolved. *Relative purchasing power parity* does not tell us what determines the absolute level of the exchange rate. Instead, it tells what determines the *change* in the exchange rate over time.

The Basic Idea   Suppose the British pound–Canadian dollar exchange rate is currently $S_0 = £.50$. Further suppose that the inflation rate in Britain is predicted to be 10 percent over the coming year and (for the moment) the inflation rate in Canada is predicted to be zero. What do you think the exchange rate will be in a year?

If you think about it, a dollar currently costs .50 pound in Britain. With 10 percent inflation, we expect prices in Britain to generally rise by 10 percent. So we expect that the price of a dollar will go up by 10 percent, and the exchange rate should rise to £.50 × 1.1 = £.55.

If the inflation rate in Canada is not zero, then we need to worry about the *relative* inflation rates in the two countries. For example, suppose the Canadian inflation rate is predicted to be 4 percent. Relative to prices in Canada, prices in Britain are rising at a rate of 10% − 4% = 6% per year. So we expect the price of the dollar to rise by 6 percent, and the predicted exchange rate is £.50 × 1.06 = £.53.

The Result   In general, relative PPP says that the change in the exchange rate is determined by the difference in the inflation rates of the two countries. To be more specific, we will use the following notation:

S_0 = Current (Time 0) spot exchange rate (foreign currency per dollar)
$E(S_t)$ = Expected exchange rate in t periods
h_{CAN} = Inflation rate in Canada
h_{FC} = Foreign country inflation rate

Based on our discussion just above, relative PPP says that the expected percentage change in the exchange rate over the next year, $[E(S_1) − S_0]/S_0$, is:

$$[E(S_1) − S_0]/S_0 = h_{FC} − h_{CAN} \qquad \text{[18.2]}$$

REALITY BYTES

McPricing

As we discussed in the chapter, absolute purchasing power parity (PPP) does not seem to hold in practice. One of the more famous violations of absolute PPP is the Big Mac Index constructed by *The Economist*. To construct the index, prices for a Big Mac in different countries are gathered from McDonald's. Below you will find the December 2004 Big Mac index from www.economist.com (we will leave it to you to find the most recent index).

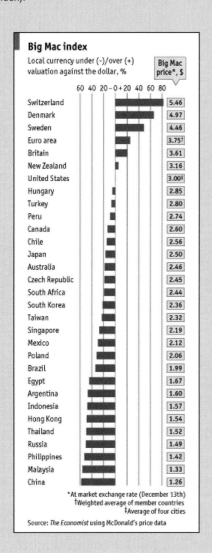

Big Mac index

Local currency under (–)/over (+) valuation against the dollar, %

Big Mac price*, $

60 40 20 – 0 + 20 40 60 80

Country	Big Mac price*, $
Switzerland	5.46
Denmark	4.97
Sweden	4.46
Euro area	3.75†
Britain	3.61
New Zealand	3.16
United States	3.00‡
Hungary	2.85
Turkey	2.80
Peru	2.74
Canada	2.60
Chile	2.56
Japan	2.50
Australia	2.46
Czech Republic	2.45
South Africa	2.44
South Korea	2.36
Taiwan	2.32
Singapore	2.19
Mexico	2.12
Poland	2.06
Brazil	1.99
Egypt	1.67
Argentina	1.60
Indonesia	1.57
Hong Kong	1.54
Thailand	1.52
Russia	1.49
Philippines	1.42
Malaysia	1.33
China	1.26

*At market exchange rate (December 13th)
†Weighted average of member countries
‡Average of four cities

Source: *The Economist* using McDonald's price data

As you can see from the index, absolute PPP does not seem to hold, at least for the Big Mac. In fact, in only four of the 29 currencies surveyed by *The Economist* is the exchange rate within 10 percent of that predicted by absolute PPP. The largest disparity is in Switzerland, where the currency is apparently overvalued by 80 percent. And 12 of the 29 currencies are "incorrectly" priced by more than 40 percent. Why?

There are several reasons. First, a Big Mac is not really transportable. Yes, you can load a ship with Big Macs and send it to Denmark where the currency is supposedly overvalued by more than 60 percent. But do you really think people would buy your Big Macs? Probably not. Even though it is relatively easy to transport a Big Mac, it would be relatively expensive, and the hamburger would suffer in quality along the way.

Also, if you look, the price of the Big Mac in the United States is the average price from New York, Chicago, San Francisco, and Atlanta. The reason is that the Big Mac does not sell for the same price in different parts of the United States, where presumably they are all purchased with the dollar. The cost of living and competition are only a few of the factors that will affect the price of a Big Mac in the United States. Since Big Macs are not all priced the same even in the same currency, would we expect absolute PPP to hold across currencies?

Finally, differing tastes can account for the apparent discrepancy. In the United States, hamburgers and fast food have become a staple of the American diet. In other countries, hamburgers have not become as entrenched. We would expect the price of the Big Mac to be lower in the United States since there is more fast food competition.

While the above reasons prevent the Big Mac index from being a good measure of PPP, the index did a decent job in predicting the change in value of the Canadian dollar over the last two years. In December 2004, the Canadian dollar was undervalued by 13 percent according to the Big Mac index and was trading at 1.2413 per U.S. dollar. Consistent with the prediction of the Big Mac index, the Canadian dollar has appreciated and was trading at 1.0585 per U.S. dollar in June 2007.

Having examined the Big Mac prices, we should say that absolute PPP should hold more closely for more easily transportable items. For instance, there are many companies with stock listed on both the NYSE and the stock exchange of another country. If you examine the share prices on the two exchanges, you will find that the price of the stock is almost exactly what absolute PPP would predict. The reason is that a share of stock in a particular company is (usually) the same wherever you buy it and whatever currency is used.

In words, relative PPP simply says that the expected percentage change in the exchange rate is equal to the difference in inflation rates. If we rearrange this slightly, we get:

$$E(S_1) = S_0 \times [1 + (h_{FC} - h_{CAN})] \tag{18.3}$$

This result makes a certain amount of sense, but care must be used in quoting the exchange rate.

In our example involving Britain and Canada, relative PPP tells us that the exchange rate will rise by $h_{FC} - h_{CAN} = 10\% - 4\% = 6\%$ per year. Assuming that the difference in inflation rates doesn't change, the expected exchange rate in two years, $E(S_2)$, will therefore be:

$$\begin{aligned} E(S_2) &= E(S_1) \times (1 + .06) \\ &= .53 \times 1.06 \\ &= .562 \end{aligned}$$

Notice that we could have written this as:

$$\begin{aligned} E(S_2) &= .53 \times 1.06 \\ &= (.50 \times 1.06) \times 1.06 \\ &= .50 \times 1.06^2 \end{aligned}$$

In general, relative PPP says that the expected exchange rate at some time in the future, $E(S_t)$, is:

$$E(S_t) = S_0 \times [1 + (h_{FC} - h_{CAN})]^t \tag{18.4}$$

Because we don't really expect absolute PPP to hold for most goods, we will focus on relative PPP in any future discussion. Henceforth, when we refer to PPP without further qualification, we mean relative PPP.

EXAMPLE 18.4   **It's All Relative**

Suppose the Japanese exchange rate is currently 105 yen per dollar. The inflation rate in Japan over the next three years will run, say, 2 percent per year, while the Canadian inflation rate will be 6 percent. Based on relative PPP, what will the exchange rate be in three years?

Since the Canadian inflation rate is higher, we expect that a dollar will become less valuable. The exchange rate change will be $2\% - 6\% = -4\%$ per year. Over three years, the exchange rate will fall to:

$$\begin{aligned} E(S_3) &= S_0 \times [1 + (h_{FC} - h_{CAN})]^3 \\ &= 105 \times [1 + (-.04)]^3 \\ &= 92.90 \text{ yen per dollar} \end{aligned}$$

Currency Appreciation and Depreciation   We frequently hear things like "the dollar strengthened (or weakened) in financial markets today" or "the dollar is expected to appreciate (or depreciate) relative to the pound." When we say that the dollar strengthens, or appreciates, we mean that the value of a dollar rises, so it takes more foreign currency to buy a dollar.

What happens to the exchange rates as currencies fluctuate in value depends on how exchange rates are quoted. Since we are quoting them as units of foreign currency per dollar, the exchange rate moves in the same direction as the value of the dollar: It rises as the dollar strengthens, and it falls as the dollar weakens.

Relative PPP tells us that the exchange rate will rise if the Canadian inflation rate is lower than the foreign country's. This happens because the foreign currency depreciates in value and therefore weakens relative to the dollar.

CONCEPT QUESTIONS

18.3a What does absolute PPP say? Why might it not hold for many types of goods?

18.3b According to relative PPP, what determines the change in exchange rates?

18.4 | EXCHANGE RATES AND INTEREST RATES

The next issue we need to address is the relationship between spot exchange rates, forward exchange rates, and nominal interest rates. To get started, we need some additional notation:

$$F_t = \text{Forward exchange rate for settlement at time } t$$
$$R_{CAN} = \text{Canadian nominal risk-free interest rate}$$
$$R_{FC} = \text{Foreign country nominal risk-free interest rate}$$

As before, we will use S_0 to stand for the spot exchange rate. You can take the Canadian nominal risk-free rate, R_{CAN}, to be the T-bill rate.

Covered Interest Arbitrage

Suppose we observe the following information about Canadian and Swiss currency in the market:

$$S_0 = \text{SF } 2.00 \qquad R_{CAN} = 10\%$$
$$F_1 = \text{SF } 1.90 \qquad R_S = 5\%$$

where R_S is the nominal risk-free rate in Switzerland. The period is one year, so F_1 is the one-year forward rate.

Do you see an arbitrage opportunity here? There is one. Suppose you have $1 to invest, and you want a riskless investment. One option you have is to invest the $1 in a riskless Canadian investment such as a one-year T-bill. We will call this Strategy 1. If you do this, then, in one period, your $1 will be worth:

$$\$ \text{ value in 1 period} = \$1(1 + R_{CAN})$$
$$= \$1.10$$

Alternatively, you can invest in the Swiss risk-free investment. To do this, you need to convert your $1 to francs and simultaneously execute a forward trade to convert francs back to dollars in one year. We will call this Strategy 2. The necessary steps would be as follows:

1. Convert your $1 to $1 $\times S_0 = $ SF 2.00.

2. At the same time, enter into a forward agreement to convert francs back to dollars in one year. Since the forward rate is SF 1.90, you get $1 for every SF 1.90 that you have in one year.

3. Invest your SF 2.00 in Switzerland at R_S. In one year, you will have:

$$\text{SF value in 1 year} = \text{SF } 2.00 \times (1 + R_S)$$
$$= \text{SF } 2.00 \times 1.05$$
$$= \text{SF } 2.10$$

4. Convert your SF 2.10 back to dollars at the agreed-upon rate of SF 1.90 = $1. You end up with:

$$\$ \text{ value in 1 year} = \text{SF } 2.10/1.90$$
$$= \$1.1053$$

For exchange rates and even pictures of currencies, see www.travlang.com/money.

Notice that the value in one year from this strategy can be written as:

$$\$ \text{ value in 1 year} = \$1 \times S_0 \times (1 + R_S)/F_1$$
$$= \$1 \times 2.00 \times 1.05/1.90$$
$$= \$1.1053$$

The return on this investment is apparently 10.53 percent. This is higher than the 10 percent we get from investing in Canada. Since both investments are risk-free, there is an arbitrage opportunity.

To exploit the difference in interest rates, you need to borrow, say, $5 million at the lower Canadian rate and invest it at the higher Swiss rate. What is the round-trip profit from doing this? To find out, we can work through the steps above:

For news on global markets, go to www.bloomberg.com/markets and www.marketwatch.com/news/globalmarkets.

1. Convert the $5 million at SF 2.00 = $1 to get SF 10 million.
2. Agree to exchange francs for dollars in one year at SF 1.90 to the dollar.
3. Invest the SF 10 million for one year at R_S = 5%. You end up with SF 10.5 million.
4. Convert the SF 10.5 million back to dollars to fulfill the forward contract. You receive SF 10.5 million/1.90 = $5,526,316.
5. Repay the loan with interest. You owe $5 million plus 10 percent interest, for a total of $5.5 million. You have $5,526,316, so your round-trip profit is a risk-free $26,316.

The activity that we have illustrated here goes by the name of *covered interest arbitrage*. The term *covered* refers to the fact that we are covered in the event of a change in the exchange rate since we lock in the forward exchange rate today.

Interest Rate Parity

If we assume that significant covered interest arbitrage opportunities do not exist, then there must be some relationship between spot exchange rates, forward exchange rates, and relative interest rates. To see what this relationship is, note that, in general, Strategy 1 above, investing in a riskless Canadian investment, gives us $(1 + R_{CAN})$ for every dollar we invest. Strategy 2, investing in a foreign risk-free investment, gives us $S_0 \times (1 + R_{FC})/F_1$ for every dollar we invest. Since these have to be equal to prevent arbitrage, it must be the case that:

$$1 + R_{CAN} = S_0 \times (1 + R_{FC})/F_1$$

interest rate parity (IRP)
The condition stating that the interest rate differential between two countries is equal to the percentage difference between the forward exchange rate and the spot exchange rate.

Rearranging this a bit gets us the famous **interest rate parity (IRP)** condition:

$$F_1/S_0 = (1 + R_{FC})/(1 + R_{CAN}) \qquad \textbf{[18.5]}$$

There is a very useful approximation for IRP that illustrates very clearly what is going on and is not difficult to remember. If we define the percentage forward premium or discount as $(F_1 - S_0)/S_0$, then IRP says that this percentage premium or discount is *approximately* equal to the difference in interest rates:

$$(F_1 - S_0)/S_0 = R_{FC} - R_{CAN} \qquad \textbf{[18.6]}$$

Very loosely, what IRP says is that any difference in interest rates between two countries for some period is just offset by the change in the relative value of the currencies, thereby eliminating any arbitrage possibilities. Notice that we could also write:

$$F_1 = S_0 \times [1 + (R_{FC} - R_{CAN})] \qquad \text{[18.7]}$$

In general, if we have t periods instead of just one, the IRP approximation will be written as:

$$F_t = S_0 \times [1 + (R_{FC} - R_{CAN})]^t \qquad \text{[18.8]}$$

Parity Check   **EXAMPLE 18.5**

Suppose the exchange rate for Japanese yen, S_0, is currently ¥120 = \$1. If the interest rate in Canada is R_{CAN} = 10% and the interest rate in Japan is R_J = 5%, then what must the one-year forward rate be to prevent covered interest arbitrage?

From IRP, we have:

$$
\begin{aligned}
F_1 &= S_0 \times [1 + (R_J - R_{CAN})] \\
&= ¥120 \times [1 + (.05 - .10)] \\
&= ¥120 \times .95 \\
&= ¥114
\end{aligned}
$$

Notice that the yen will sell at a premium relative to the dollar (why?).

CONCEPT QUESTIONS

18.4a   What is interest rate parity?

18.4b   Do you expect that interest rate parity will hold more closely than purchasing power parity? Why?

18.5 | EXCHANGE RATE RISK

Exchange rate risk is the natural consequence of international operations in a world where relative currency values move up and down. As we discuss next, there are three different types of exchange rate risk, or exposure: short-run exposure, long-run exposure, and translation exposure.

exchange rate risk
The risk related to having international operations in a world where relative currency values vary.

Short-Run Exposure

The day-to-day fluctuations in exchange rates create short-run risks for international firms. Most such firms have contractual agreements to buy and sell goods in the near future at set prices. When different currencies are involved, such transactions have an extra element of risk.

For example, imagine that you are importing pasta from Italy and reselling it in Canada under the Itpasta brand name. Your largest customer has ordered 10,000 cases of Itpasta. You place the order with your supplier today, but you won't pay until the goods arrive in 60 days. Your selling price is \$6 per case. Your cost is €4.48 per case, and the exchange rate is currently €0.80, so it takes €0.80 to buy \$1.

At the current exchange rate, your cost in dollars from filling the order is €4.48/€0.80 = $5.60 per case, so your pretax profit on the order is $10,000 \times (\$6 - 5.60) =$ $4,000. However, the exchange rate in 60 days will probably be different, so your profit will depend on what the exchange rate in the future turns out to be.

For example, if the rate goes to €0.85, your cost is €4.48/€0.85 = $5.27 per case. Your profit goes to $7,294. If the exchange rate goes to, say, €0.747, then your cost is €4.48/€0.747 = $6 per case, and your profit is zero.

The short-run exposure in our example can be reduced or eliminated in several ways. The most obvious way is to enter a forward exchange agreement to lock in an exchange rate. For example, suppose the 60-day forward rate is €0.82. What will your profit be if you hedge?

If you hedge, you lock in an exchange rate of €0.82. Your cost in dollars will thus be €4.48/€0.82 = $5.46 per case, so your profit will be $10,000 \times (\$6 - 5.46) = \$5,400$.

Long-Run Exposure

For a great source of information about exporting, go to **exportsource.ca.**

In the long run, the value of a foreign operation can fluctuate because of unanticipated changes in relative economic conditions. For example, imagine that we own a labour-intensive assembly operation located in another country to take advantage of lower wages. Through time, unexpected changes in economic conditions can raise the foreign wage levels to the point where the cost advantage is eliminated or even becomes negative.

Hedging long-run exposure is more difficult than hedging short-term risks. For one thing, organized forward markets don't exist for such long-term needs. Instead, the primary option that firms have is to try to match up foreign currency inflows and outflows. The same thing goes for matching foreign currency–denominated assets and liabilities. For example, a firm that sells in a foreign country might try to concentrate its raw material purchases and labour expense in that country. That way, the dollar values of its revenues and costs will move up and down together.

Similarly, a firm can reduce its long-run exchange risk by borrowing in the foreign country. Fluctuations in the value of the foreign subsidiary's assets will then be at least partially offset by changes in the value of the liabilities.

One of the more common methods used to reduce long-term exchange rate exposure is to build a plant in the country that imports the products. This method is often used in the automotive industry. Honda, Toyota, and General Motors, to name a few, have built plants in Canada. In total, in 2005, about 2.7 million cars were produced in Canada by U.S. and Japanese car manufacturers.

Translation Exposure

When a Canadian company calculates its accounting net income and EPS for some period, it must "translate" everything into dollars. This can create some problems for the accountants when there are significant foreign operations. In particular, two issues arise:

1. What is the appropriate exchange rate to use for translating each balance sheet account?

2. How should balance sheet accounting gains and losses from foreign currency translation be handled?

To illustrate the accounting problem, suppose that we started a small foreign subsidiary in Lilliputia a year ago. The local currency is the gulliver, abbreviated GL. At the beginning of the year, the exchange rate was GL 2 = $1, and the balance sheet in gullivers looked like this:

Assets	GL 1,000	Liabilities	GL 500
		Equity	500

At two gullivers to the dollar, the beginning balance sheet in dollars was:

Assets	$500	Liabilities	$250
		Equity	250

Lilliputia is a quiet place, and nothing at all actually happened during the year. As a result, net income was zero (before consideration of exchange rate changes). However, the exchange rate did change to 4 gullivers = $1, perhaps because the Lilliputian inflation rate is much higher than the Canadian inflation rate.

Since nothing happened, the accounting ending balance sheet in gullivers is the same as the beginning one. However, if we convert it to dollars at the new exchange rate, we get:

Assets	$250	Liabilities	$125
		Equity	125

Notice that the value of the equity has gone down by $125, even though net income was exactly zero. Despite the fact that absolutely nothing really happened, there is a $125 accounting loss. How to handle this $125 loss has been a controversial accounting question.

One obvious and consistent way to handle this loss is simply to report the loss on the parent's income statement. During periods of volatile exchange rates, this kind of treatment can dramatically impact an international company's reported EPS. This is purely an accounting phenomenon, but, even so, such fluctuations are disliked by some financial managers.

The current accounting approach to translation gains and losses is based on rules set out in Section 1650, "Foreign Currency Translation," of the *Canadian Institute of Chartered Accountants (CICA) Handbook.* The rules classify a firm's foreign subsidiary as integrated or self-sustaining. An integrated foreign subsidiary has cash flows and business operations highly interconnected with those of the parent company. In such a case, non-monetary assets and liabilities, and income statement items are translated into Canadian dollars at the exchange rate at the time of the original transactions. Any translation gains or losses are carried directly to the consolidated income statement of the parent company.

A self-sustaining foreign subsidiary operates independently from the parent company. In this case, all assets and liabilities are translated from the subsidiary's currency into the parent's currency using the exchange rate in effect at the balance sheet date. Any translation gains and losses that occur are accumulated in a special account within the shareholders' equity section of the balance sheet. This account might be labelled something like "unrealized foreign exchange gains (losses)." These gains and losses are not reported on the income statement. As a result, the impact of translation gains and losses will not be recognized explicitly in net income until the underlying assets and liabilities are sold or otherwise liquidated.

Managing Exchange Rate Risk

Information on doing business globally can be found at **www. internationalist.com/ business.**

For a large multinational firm, the management of exchange rate risk is complicated by the fact that there can be many different currencies involved for many different subsidiaries. It is very likely that a change in some exchange rate will benefit some subsidiaries and hurt others. The net effect on the overall firm depends on its net exposure.

For example, suppose a firm has two divisions. Division A buys goods in Canada for dollars and sells them in Britain for pounds. Division B buys goods in Britain for pounds and sells them in Canada for dollars. If these two divisions are of roughly equal size in terms of their inflows and outflows, then the overall firm obviously has little exchange rate risk.

In our example, the firm's net position in pounds (the amount coming in less the amount going out) is small, so the exchange rate risk is small. However, if one division, acting on its own, were to start hedging its exchange rate risk, then the overall firm's exchange rate risk would go up. The moral of the story is that multinational firms have to be conscious of the overall position that the firm has in a foreign currency. For this reason, management of exchange rate risk is probably best handled on a centralized basis.

CONCEPT QUESTIONS

18.5a   What are the different types of exchange rate risk?

18.5b   How can a firm hedge short-run exchange rate risk? Long-run exchange rate risk?

18.6 | POLITICAL RISK

political risk
Risk related to changes in value that arise because of political actions.

One final element of risk in international investing is **political risk.** Political risk is related to changes in value that arise as a consequence of political actions. This is not a problem faced only by international firms. For example, changes in Canadian tax laws and regulations may benefit some Canadian firms and hurt others, so political risk exists nationally as well as internationally. For example, in October 31, 2006, federal finance minister Jim Flaherty announced that the Canadian government would impose a tax on income trust distributions. This was bad news for income trusts, and the trust sector lost $19 billion of its value the following day. In contrast, the same news made dividend-paying stocks, such as the Royal Bank of Canada and the Bank of Montreal, more attractive to investors, and both stocks rose to 52-week highs.

Some countries do have more political risk than others, however. When firms have operations in these riskier countries, the extra political risk may lead them to require higher returns on overseas investments to compensate for the risk that funds will be blocked, critical operations interrupted, and contracts abrogated. In the most extreme case, the possibility of outright confiscation may be a concern in countries with relatively unstable political environments.

Export Development Canada (EDC) offers political risk insurance to Canadian exporters. To learn more about EDC's services, go to **www.edc.ca.**

Political risk also depends on the nature of the business; some businesses are less likely to be confiscated because they are not particularly valuable in the hands of a different owner. An assembly operation supplying subcomponents that only the parent company uses would not be an attractive "takeover" target, for example. Similarly, a manufacturing operation that requires the use of specialized components from the parent is of little value without the parent company's co-operation.

Natural resource developments, such as copper mining or oil drilling, are just the opposite. Once the operation is in place, much of the value is in the commodity. The political risk for such investments is much higher for this reason. Also, the issue of exploitation is more pronounced with such investments, again increasing the political risk.

Political risk can be hedged in several ways, particularly when confiscation or nationalization is a concern. The use of local financing, perhaps from the government of the foreign country in question, reduces the possible loss because the company can refuse to pay on the debt in the event of unfavourable political activities. Based on our discussion above, structuring the operation in such a way that it requires significant parent company involvement to function is another way to reduce political risk.

CONCEPT QUESTIONS

18.6a What is political risk?

18.6b What are some ways of hedging political risk?

KEY EQUATIONS:

I. Symbols

S_0 = Current (Time 0) spot exchange rate (foreign currency per dollar)
P_{CAN} = Price of a good in Canada
P_{FC} = Price of a good in a foreign country
$E(S_t)$ = Expected exchange rate in t periods (foreign currency per dollar)
F_t = Forward exchange rate for settlement at time t
h_{CAN} = Canadian inflation rate
h_{FC} = Foreign country inflation rate
R_{CAN} = Canadian nominal risk-free interest rate
R_{FC} = Foreign country nominal risk-free interest rate

II. Absolute Purchasing Power Parity

$$S_0 = P_{FC}/P_{CAN} \qquad [18.1]$$

III. Relative Purchasing Power Parity

$$[E(S_1) - S_0]/S_0 = h_{FC} - h_{CAN} \qquad [18.2]$$
$$E(S_1) = S_0 \times [1 + (h_{FC} - h_{CAN})] \qquad [18.3]$$
$$E(S_t) = S_0 \times [1 + (h_{FC} - h_{CAN})]^t \qquad [18.4]$$

IV. Interest Rate Parity

Exact formula:
$$F_1/S_0 = (1 + R_{FC})/(1 + R_{CAN}) \qquad [18.5]$$

Approximation:
$$(F_1 - S_0)/S_0 = R_{FC} - R_{CAN} \qquad [18.6]$$
$$F_1 = S_0 \times [1 + (R_{FC} - R_{CAN})] \qquad [18.7]$$
$$F_t = S_0 \times [1 + (R_{FC} - R_{CAN})]^t \qquad [18.8]$$

SUMMARY AND CONCLUSIONS

The international firm has a more complicated life than the purely domestic firm. Management must understand the connection between interest rates, foreign currency exchange rates, and inflation, and it must become aware of a large number of different financial market regulations and tax systems. This chapter was intended to be a concise introduction to some of the financial issues that come up in international investing.

Our coverage was necessarily brief. The main topics we discussed included:

1. Some basic vocabulary. We briefly defined some exotic terms such as *LIBOR* and *Eurocurrency.*
2. The basic mechanics of exchange rate quotations. We discussed the spot and forward markets and how exchange rates are interpreted.
3. The fundamental relationships between international financial variables:
   a. Absolute and relative purchasing power parity, or PPP.
   b. Interest rate parity, or IRP.

   Absolute purchasing power parity states that $1 should have the same purchasing power in each country. This means that an orange costs the same whether you buy it in Ottawa or in Tokyo.

   Relative purchasing power parity means that the expected percentage change in exchange rates between the currencies of two countries is equal to the difference in their inflation rates.

   Interest rate parity implies that the percentage difference between the forward exchange rate and the spot exchange rate is equal to the interest rate differential. We showed how covered interest arbitrage forces this relationship to hold.
4. Exchange rate and political risk. We described the various types of exchange rate risk and discussed some commonly used approaches to managing the effect of fluctuating exchange rates on the cash flows and value of the international firm. We also discussed political risk and some ways of managing exposure to it.

CHAPTER REVIEW AND SELF-TEST PROBLEMS

18.1   Relative Purchasing Power Parity.   The inflation rate in Canada is projected at 6 percent per year for the next several years. The Australian inflation rate is projected to be 2 percent during that time. The exchange rate is currently A$ 2.2. Based on relative PPP, what is the expected exchange rate in two years?

18.2   Covered Interest Arbitrage.   The spot and one-year forward rates on the Swiss franc are SF 1.8 and SF 1.7, respectively. The risk-free interest rate in Canada is 8 percent, and the risk-free rate in Switzerland is 5 percent. Is there an arbitrage opportunity here? How would you exploit it?

■ Answers to Chapter Review and Self-Test Problems

18.1   From relative PPP, the expected exchange rate in two years, $E(S_2)$, is:

$$E(S_2) = S_0 \times [1 + (h_A - h_{CAN})]^2$$

where h_A is the Australian inflation rate. The current exchange rate is A$ 2.2, so the expected exchange rate is:

$$E(S_2) = \text{A\$ } 2.2 \times [1 + (.02 - .06)]^2$$
$$= \text{A\$ } 2.2 \times .96^2$$
$$= \text{A\$ } 2.03$$

18.2 From interest rate parity, the forward rate should be (approximately):

$$F_1 = S_0 \times [1 + (R_S - R_{CAN})]$$
$$= 1.8 \times [1 + .05 - .08]$$
$$= 1.75$$

Since the forward rate is actually SF 1.7, there is an arbitrage opportunity.

To exploit the arbitrage opportunity, we first note that dollars are selling for SF 1.7 each in the forward market. From IRP, this is too cheap because they should be selling for SF 1.75. So, we want to arrange to buy dollars with Swiss francs in the forward market. To do this, we can:

1. Today: Borrow, say, $10 million for one year. Convert it to SF 18 million in the spot market, and buy a forward contract at SF 1.7 to convert it back to dollars in one year. Invest the SF 18 million at 5 percent.

2. In one year: Your investment has grown to SF 18 × 1.05 = SF 18.9 million. Convert this to dollars at the rate of SF 1.7 = $1. You will have SF 18.9 million/1.7 = $11,117,647. Pay off your loan with 8 percent interest at a cost of $10 million × 1.08 = $10,800,000 and pocket the difference of $317,647.

CRITICAL THINKING AND CONCEPTS REVIEW

18.1   **Spot and Forward Rates.**   Suppose the exchange rate for the Swiss franc is quoted as SF 1.50 in the spot market and SF 1.53 in the 90-day forward market.

   a.   Is the dollar selling at a premium or a discount relative to the franc?

   b.   Does the financial market expect the franc to strengthen relative to the dollar? Explain.

   c.   What do you suspect is true about relative economic conditions in Canada and Switzerland?

18.2   **Purchasing Power Parity.**   Suppose the rate of inflation in Russia will run about 3 percent higher than the Canadian inflation rate over the next several years. All other things being the same, what will happen to the rouble versus dollar exchange rate? What relationship are you relying on in answering?

18.3   **Exchange Rates.**   The exchange rate for the Australian dollar is currently A$1.40. This exchange rate is expected to rise by 10 percent over the next year.

   a.   Is the Australian dollar expected to get stronger or weaker?

   b.   What do you think about the relative inflation rates in Canada and Australia?

   c.   What do you think about the relative nominal interest rates in Canada and Australia? Relative real rates?

18.4   **Maple Bonds.**   Which of the following most accurately describes a Maple bond?

   a.   A bond issued by Bell Canada in Japan with the interest payable in Canadian dollars.

   b.   A bond issued by Bell Canada in Japan with the interest payable in yen.

   c.   A bond issued by Sony in Canada with the interest payable in yen.

   d.   A bond issued by Sony in Canada with the interest payable in Canadian dollars.

   e.   A bond issued by Sony worldwide with the interest payable in Canadian dollars.

18.5   Exchange Rates.   Are exchange rate changes necessarily good or bad for a particular company?

18.6   International Risks.   In January 2005, South Korea's Hynix Semiconductor, Inc., the world's second largest producer of dynamic random access memory, or DRAM, chips announced an alliance with Taiwan's ProMOS Technologies, Inc., to produce computer chips. For ProMOS, the alliance was needed to provide the company with a steady supply of chips. For Hynix, the motive for the alliance was tariffs placed on computer chips manufactured in South Korea. In 2004, both the United States and the European Union had enacted steep tariffs on computer chips from that country. What advantages might Hynix see from the alliance? What are some of the risks to Hynix?

18.7   Multinational Corporations.   Given that many multinationals based in many countries have much greater sales outside their domestic markets than within them, what is the particular relevance of their domestic currency?

18.8   Exchange Rate Movements.   Are the following statements true or false? Explain why.

   a.   If the general price index in Great Britain rises faster than that in Canada, we would expect the pound to appreciate relative to the dollar.

   b.   Suppose you are a German machine tool exporter and you invoice all of your sales in foreign currency. Further suppose that the European monetary authorities begin to undertake an expansionary monetary policy. If it is certain that the easy money policy will result in higher inflation rates in "Euroland" relative to those in other countries, then you should use the forward markets to protect yourself against future losses resulting from the deterioration in the value of the euro.

   c.   If you could accurately estimate differences in the relative inflation rates of two countries over a long period of time while other market participants were unable to do so, you could successfully speculate in spot currency markets.

18.9   Exchange Rate Movements.   Some countries encourage movements in their exchange rate relative to those of some other country as a short-term means of addressing foreign trade imbalances. For each of the following scenarios, evaluate the impact the announcement would have on a Canadian importer and a Canadian exporter doing business with the foreign country.

   a.   Officials in the Canadian government announce that they are comfortable with a rising Mexican peso relative to the dollar.

   b.   British monetary authorities announce that they feel the pound has been driven too low by currency speculators relative to the dollar.

   c.   The Brazilian government announces that it will print billions of new reals and inject them into the economy in an effort to reduce the country's 40 percent unemployment rate.

QUESTIONS AND PROBLEMS

**Basic
(Questions 1–10)**

1.   Using Exchange Rates.   Take a look back at Figure 18.1 to answer the following questions:

   a.   If you have $100, how many Russian roubles can you get?

   b.   How much is one euro worth?

c. If you have five million euros, how many dollars do you have?

d. Which is worth more, an Australian dollar or a Singapore dollar?

e. How many Swiss francs can you get for a euro? What do you call this rate?

f. Has the Indian rupee appreciated or depreciated against the Canadian dollar in the last four weeks?

g. Against which currency has the Canadian dollar appreciated the most in the last week?

h. Per unit, what is the most valuable currency of those listed? The least valuable?

2. **Using the Cross-Rate.** Use the information in Figure 18.1 to answer the following questions:

a. Which would you rather have, $100 or £100? Why?

b. Which would you rather have, €100 or £100? Why?

c. What is the cross-rate for euros in terms of British pounds? For British pounds in terms of euros?

3. **Forward Exchange Rates.** Use the information in Figure 18.1 to answer the following questions:

a. What is the six-month forward rate for the Japanese yen in yen per Canadian dollar? Is the yen selling at a premium or a discount? Explain.

b. What is the three-month forward rate for the British pound in Canadian dollars per British pound? Is the dollar selling at a premium or a discount? Explain.

c. What do you think will happen to the value of the dollar relative to the yen and the British pound, based on the information in the figure? Explain.

4. **Using Spot and Forward Exchange Rates.** Suppose the spot exchange rate for the U.S. dollar is US$.91 and the six-month forward rate is US$.87.

a. Which is worth more, a U.S. dollar or a Canadian dollar?

b. Assuming absolute PPP holds, what is the cost in Canada of an Elkhead beer if the price in the United States is US$2.82? Why might the beer actually sell at a different price in Canada?

c. Is the Canadian dollar selling at a premium or a discount relative to the U.S. dollar?

d. Which currency is expected to appreciate in value?

e. Which country do you think has higher interest rates—the United States or Canada? Explain.

5. **Cross-Rates and Arbitrage.** Suppose the Japanese yen exchange rate is ¥105 = $1, and the British pound exchange rate is £1 = $1.86.

a. What is the cross-rate in terms of yen per pound?

b. Suppose the cross-rate is ¥190 = £1. Is there an arbitrage opportunity here? If there is, explain how to take advantage of the mispricing.

6. **Interest Rate Parity.** Use Figure 18.1 to answer the following questions. Suppose interest rate parity holds, and the current risk-free rate in Canada is 3 percent per six months. What must the six-month risk-free rate be in the United States? In Japan? In Great Britain?

7. **Interest Rates and Arbitrage.** The treasurer of a major Canadian firm has $30 million to invest for three months. The annual interest rate in Canada is .34 percent per month. The interest rate in Great Britain is .24 percent per month. The spot

exchange rate is £.54, and the three-month forward rate is £.51. Ignoring transaction costs, in which country would the treasurer want to invest the company's funds? Why?

8. **Inflation and Exchange Rates.**   Suppose the current exchange rate for the Russian ruble is rouble 28.13. The expected exchange rate in three years is rouble 30.04. What is the difference in the annual inflation rates for Canada and Russia over this period? Assume that the anticipated rate is constant for both countries. What relationship are you relying on in answering?

9. **Exchange Rate Risk.**   Suppose your company imports computer motherboards from Singapore. The exchange rate is given in Figure 18.1. You have just placed an order for 30,000 motherboards at a cost to you of 210 Singapore dollars each. You will pay for the shipment when it arrives in 90 days. You can sell the motherboards for $160 each. Calculate your profit if the exchange rate goes up or down by 10 percent over the next 90 days. What is the break-even exchange rate? What percentage rise or fall does this represent in terms of the Singapore dollar versus the Canadian dollar?

10. **Exchange Rates and Arbitrage.**   Suppose the spot and six-month forward rates on the won are won 1029.55 and won 1034.42, respectively. The annual risk-free rate in Canada is 5 percent, and the annual risk-free rate in South Korea is 7 percent.

   a.   Is there an arbitrage opportunity here? If so, how would you exploit it?

   b.   What must the six-month forward rate be to prevent arbitrage?

Intermediate (Questions 11–15)

11. **Spot versus Forward Rates.**   Suppose the spot and three-month forward rates for the yen are ¥112.53 and ¥111.61, respectively.

   a.   Is the yen expected to get stronger or weaker?

   b.   What would you estimate is the difference between the inflation rates of Canada and Japan?

12. **Expected Spot Rates.**   Suppose the spot exchange rate for the Hungarian forint is HUF 191. Interest rates in Canada are 4.8 percent per year. They are 10.6 percent in Hungary. What do you predict the exchange rate will be in one year? In two years? In five years? What relationship are you using?

13. **Calculating Cross-Rates.**   Calculate the ¥/€ cross-rate given ¥104.944 = $1 and €0.78426 = $1.

14. **Cross-Rates and Arbitrage.**   The £ trades at $1.8561 in London and $1.8436 in Toronto. How much profit could you earn on each trade with $10,000?

15. **Purchasing Power Parity and Exchange Rates.**   According to purchasing power parity, if a Big Mac sells for $2.39 in the United States and kronur 155 in Iceland, what is the kronur/$ exchange rate?

Challenge (Question 16)

16. **Cross-Rates and Arbitrage.**   Suppose you are a currency trader and observe the following foreign exchange rates:
Toronto: $1.540/€ and $.009/¥; Paris: €1.449/£; London: £.448/$; Sidney: A$1.125/$; Tokyo: ¥102.500/A$.

   a.   Is there an arbitrage opportunity here? If there is, explain how to take advantage of the mispricing.

   b.   How much profit could you earn on each trade with $100,000?

   c.   What would be the impact of your arbitrage trading on the exchange rates in each city?

WHAT'S ON THE WEB?

18.1 **Purchasing Power Parity.** One of the more famous examples of a violation of absolute purchasing power parity is the Big Mac index calculated by *The Economist*. This index calculates the U.S. dollar price of a McDonald's Big Mac in different countries. You can find the Big Mac index by going to **www.economist.com**, following the "Markets & Data" link and then the "Big Mac index" link. Using the most recent index, which country has the most expensive Big Macs? Which country has the cheapest Big Macs? Why is the price of a Big Mac not the same in every country?

18.2 **Inflation and Exchange Rates.** Go to **www.marketvector.com** and follow the "Exchange Rates" link. Select the "Canadian Dollar" link. Is the Canadian dollar expected to appreciate or depreciate compared to the U.S. dollar over the next six months? What is the difference in the annual inflation rates for Canada and the United States over this period? Assume that the anticipated rate is constant for both countries. What relationship are you relying on in answering?

18.3 **Interest Rate Parity.** Go to the Pacific Exchange Rate Service Web site at **fx.sauder.ubc.ca** and find the current exchange rate between the Canadian dollar and the euro. Next, go to **www.economagic.com,** click on the "LIBOR" link and find the Canadian dollar LIBOR and the Euro LIBOR interest rates. What must the one-year forward rate be to prevent arbitrage? What principle are you relying on in your answer?

18.4 **Exchange Rate Risk.** You can find annual reports of many multinational corporations at **www.annualreports.com.** Find an annual report for a Canadian company and look for statements that discuss the company's exchange rate risk. Does this risk arise from short-run exposure, long-run exposure, or translation exposure? Summarize the company's exposures based on information from the annual report.

18.5 **Political Risk.** Go to the Export Development Canada (EDC) site at **www.edc.ca,** click on the "Our Services" link and select "Insurance" in the pull-down menu. Examine the political risk insurance (PRI) offered by EDC. What types of political risk are covered by PRI? What do transfer risk and conversion risk mean? What are the qualification criteria for PRI? What additional coverage does EDC's PRI provide for banks?

CANADIAN AIR GOES INTERNATIONAL

Mark Sexton and Todd Story, the owners of Canadian Air, have been in discussions with an aircraft dealer in Europe about selling the company's Eagle airplane. The Eagle sells for $78,000 and has a variable cost of $60,000 per airplane. Amalie Diefenbaker, the dealer, wants to add the Eagle to her current retail line. Amalie has told Mark and Todd that she feels she will be able to sell 30 airplanes per month in Europe. All sales will be made in euros, and Amalie will pay the company €65,000 for each plane. Amalie proposes that she order 30 aircraft today for the first month's sales. She will pay for all 30 aircraft in 90 days. This order and payment schedule will continue each month.

Mark and Todd are confident they can handle the extra volume with their existing facilities, but they are unsure about the potential financial risks of selling their aircraft in Europe. In their discussion with Amalie, they found out that the current exchange rate is $1.20/€. This means that they can convert the €65,000 per airplane paid by Amalie to $78,000. Thus, the profit on the international sales is the same as the profit on dollar-denominated sales.

Mark and Todd decided to ask Chris Guthrie, their financial analyst, to prepare an analysis of the proposed international sales. Specifically, they ask Chris to answer the following questions.

QUESTIONS

1. What are the pros and cons of the international sales? What additional risks will the company face?

2. What happens to the company's profits if the dollar strengthens? What if the dollar weakens?

3. Ignoring taxes, what are Canadian Air's projected gains or losses from this proposed arrangement at the current exchange rate of $1.20/€? What happens to profits if the exchange rate changes to $1.30/€? At what exchange rate will the company break even?

4. How could the company hedge its exchange rate risk? What are the implications for this approach?

5. Taking all factors into account, should the company pursue the international sales deal further? Why or why not?

Photo Credits

Mathematical Tables

Future value of $1 at the end of t periods $= (1 + r)^t$

Number of Periods	Interest Rate								
	1%	2%	3%	4%	5%	6%	7%	8%	9%
1	1.0100	1.0200	1.0300	1.0400	1.0500	1.0600	1.0700	1.0800	1.0900
2	1.0201	1.0404	1.0609	1.0816	1.1025	1.1236	1.1449	1.1664	1.1881
3	1.0303	1.0612	1.0927	1.1249	1.1576	1.1910	1.2250	1.2597	1.2950
4	1.0406	1.0824	1.1255	1.1699	1.2155	1.2625	1.3108	1.3605	1.4116
5	1.0510	1.1041	1.1593	1.2167	1.2763	1.3382	1.4026	1.4693	1.5386
6	1.0615	1.1262	1.1941	1.2653	1.3401	1.4185	1.5007	1.5869	1.6771
7	1.0721	1.1487	1.2299	1.3159	1.4071	1.5036	1.6058	1.7138	1.8280
8	1.0829	1.1717	1.2668	1.3686	1.4775	1.5938	1.7182	1.8509	1.9926
9	1.0937	1.1951	1.3048	1.4233	1.5513	1.6895	1.8385	1.9990	2.1719
10	1.1046	1.2190	1.3439	1.4802	1.6289	1.7908	1.9672	2.1589	2.3674
11	1.1157	1.2434	1.3842	1.5395	1.7103	1.8983	2.1049	2.3316	2.5804
12	1.1268	1.2682	1.4258	1.6010	1.7959	2.0122	2.2522	2.5182	2.8127
13	1.1381	1.2936	1.4685	1.6651	1.8856	2.1329	2.4098	2.7196	3.0658
14	1.1495	1.3195	1.5126	1.7317	1.9799	2.2609	2.5785	2.9372	3.3417
15	1.1610	1.3459	1.5580	1.8009	2.0789	2.3966	2.7590	3.1722	3.6425
16	1.1726	1.3728	1.6047	1.8730	2.1829	2.5404	2.9522	3.4259	3.9703
17	1.1843	1.4002	1.6528	1.9479	2.2920	2.6928	3.1588	3.7000	4.3276
18	1.1961	1.4282	1.7024	2.0258	2.4066	2.8543	3.3799	3.9960	4.7171
19	1.2081	1.4568	1.7535	2.1068	2.5270	3.0256	3.6165	4.3157	5.1417
20	1.2202	1.4859	1.8061	2.1911	2.6533	3.2071	3.8697	4.6610	5.6044
21	1.2324	1.5157	1.8603	2.2788	2.7860	3.3996	4.1406	5.0338	6.1088
22	1.2447	1.5460	1.9161	2.3699	2.9253	3.6035	4.4304	5.4365	6.6586
23	1.2572	1.5769	1.9736	2.4647	3.0715	3.8197	4.7405	5.8715	7.2579
24	1.2697	1.6084	2.0328	2.5633	3.2251	4.0489	5.0724	6.3412	7.9111
25	1.2824	1.6406	2.0938	2.6658	3.3864	4.2919	5.4274	6.8485	8.6231
30	1.3478	1.8114	2.4273	3.2434	4.3219	5.7435	7.6123	10.063	13.268
40	1.4889	2.2080	3.2620	4.8010	7.0400	10.286	14.974	21.725	31.409
50	1.6446	2.6916	4.3839	7.1067	11.467	18.420	29.457	46.902	74.358
60	1.8167	3.2810	5.8916	10.520	18.679	32.988	57.946	101.26	176.03

10%	12%	14%	15%	16%	18%	20%	24%	28%	32%	36%
1.1000	1.1200	1.1400	1.1500	1.1600	1.1800	1.2000	1.2400	1.2800	1.3200	1.3600
1.2100	1.2544	1.2996	1.3225	1.3456	1.3924	1.4400	1.5376	1.6384	1.7424	1.8496
1.3310	1.4049	1.4815	1.5209	1.5609	1.6430	1.7280	1.9066	2.0972	2.3000	2.5155
1.4641	1.5735	1.6890	1.7490	1.8106	1.9388	2.0736	2.3642	2.6844	3.0360	3.4210
1.6105	1.7623	1.9254	2.0114	2.1003	2.2878	2.4883	2.9316	3.4360	4.0075	4.6526
1.7716	1.9738	2.1950	2.3131	2.4364	2.6996	2.9860	3.6352	4.3980	5.2899	6.3275
1.9487	2.2107	2.5023	2.6600	2.8262	3.1855	3.5832	4.5077	5.6295	6.9826	8.6054
2.1436	2.4760	2.8526	3.0590	3.2784	3.7589	4.2998	5.5895	7.2058	9.2170	11.703
2.3579	2.7731	3.2519	3.5179	3.8030	4.4355	5.1598	6.9310	9.2234	12.166	15.917
2.5937	3.1058	3.7072	4.0456	4.4114	5.2338	6.1917	8.5944	11.806	16.060	21.647
2.8531	3.4785	4.2262	4.6524	5.1173	6.1759	7.4301	10.657	15.112	21.199	29.439
3.1384	3.8960	4.8179	5.3503	5.9360	7.2876	8.9161	13.215	19.343	27.983	40.037
3.4523	4.3635	5.4924	6.1528	6.8858	8.5994	10.699	16.386	24.759	36.937	54.451
3.7975	4.8871	6.2613	7.0757	7.9875	10.147	12.839	20.319	31.691	48.757	74.053
4.1772	5.4736	7.1379	8.1371	9.2655	11.974	15.407	25.196	40.565	64.359	100.71
4.5950	6.1304	8.1372	9.3576	10.748	14.129	18.488	31.243	51.923	84.954	136.97
5.0545	6.8660	9.2765	10.761	12.468	16.672	22.186	38.741	66.461	112.14	186.28
5.5599	7.6900	10.575	12.375	14.463	19.673	26.623	48.039	85.071	148.02	253.34
6.1159	8.6128	12.056	14.232	16.777	23.214	31.948	59.568	108.89	195.39	344.54
6.7275	9.6463	13.743	16.367	19.461	27.393	38.338	73.864	139.38	257.92	468.57
7.4002	10.804	15.668	18.822	22.574	32.324	46.005	91.592	178.41	340.45	637.26
8.1403	12.100	17.861	21.645	26.186	38.142	55.206	113.57	228.36	449.39	866.67
8.9543	13.552	20.362	24.891	30.376	45.008	66.247	140.83	292.30	593.20	1178.7
9.8497	15.179	23.212	28.625	35.236	53.109	79.497	174.63	374.14	783.02	1603.0
10.835	17.000	26.462	32.919	40.874	62.669	95.396	216.54	478.90	1033.6	2180.1
17.449	29.960	50.950	66.212	85.850	143.37	237.38	634.82	1645.5	4142.1	10143.
45.259	93.051	188.88	267.86	378.72	750.38	1469.8	5455.9	19427.	66521.	*
117.39	289.00	700.23	1083.7	1670.7	3927.4	9100.4	46890.	*	*	*
304.48	897.60	2595.9	4384.0	7370.2	20555.	56348.	*	*	*	*

*The factor is greater than 99,999.

APPENDIX A.2   Present value of $1 to be received after t periods $= 1/(1 + r)^t$

Number of Periods	Interest Rates								
	1%	2%	3%	4%	5%	6%	7%	8%	9%
1	0.9901	0.9804	0.9709	0.9615	0.9524	0.9434	0.9346	0.9259	0.9174
2	0.9803	0.9612	0.9426	0.9246	0.9070	0.8900	0.8734	0.8573	0.8417
3	0.9706	0.9423	0.9151	0.8890	0.8638	0.8396	0.8163	0.7938	0.7722
4	0.9610	0.9238	0.8885	0.8548	0.8227	0.7921	0.7629	0.7350	0.7084
5	0.9515	0.9057	0.8626	0.8219	0.7835	0.7473	0.7130	0.6806	0.6499
6	0.9420	0.8880	0.8375	0.7903	0.7462	0.7050	0.6663	0.6302	0.5963
7	0.9327	0.8706	0.8131	0.7599	0.7107	0.6651	0.6227	0.5835	0.5470
8	0.9235	0.8535	0.7894	0.7307	0.6768	0.6274	0.5820	0.5403	0.5019
9	0.9143	0.8368	0.7664	0.7026	0.6446	0.5919	0.5439	0.5002	0.4604
10	0.9053	0.8203	0.7441	0.6756	0.6139	0.5584	0.5083	0.4632	0.4224
11	0.8963	0.8043	0.7224	0.6496	0.5847	0.5268	0.4751	0.4289	0.3875
12	0.8874	0.7885	0.7014	0.6246	0.5568	0.4970	0.4440	0.3971	0.3555
13	0.8787	0.7730	0.6810	0.6006	0.5303	0.4688	0.4150	0.3677	0.3262
14	0.8700	0.7579	0.6611	0.5775	0.5051	0.4423	0.3878	0.3405	0.2992
15	0.8613	0.7430	0.6419	0.5553	0.4810	0.4173	0.3624	0.3152	0.2745
16	0.8528	0.7284	0.6232	0.5339	0.4581	0.3936	0.3387	0.2919	0.2519
17	0.8444	0.7142	0.6050	0.5134	0.4363	0.3714	0.3166	0.2703	0.2311
18	0.8360	0.7002	0.5874	0.4936	0.4155	0.3503	0.2959	0.2502	0.2120
19	0.8277	0.6864	0.5703	0.4746	0.3957	0.3305	0.2765	0.2317	0.1945
20	0.8195	0.6730	0.5537	0.4564	0.3769	0.3118	0.2584	0.2145	0.1784
21	0.8114	0.6598	0.5375	0.4388	0.3589	0.2942	0.2415	0.1987	0.1637
22	0.8034	0.6468	0.5219	0.4220	0.3418	0.2775	0.2257	0.1839	0.1502
23	0.7954	0.6342	0.5067	0.4057	0.3256	0.2618	0.2109	0.1703	0.1378
24	0.7876	0.6217	0.4919	0.3901	0.3101	0.2470	0.1971	0.1577	0.1264
25	0.7798	0.6095	0.4776	0.3751	0.2953	0.2330	0.1842	0.1460	0.1160
30	0.7419	0.5521	0.4120	0.3083	0.2314	0.1741	0.1314	0.0994	0.0754
40	0.6717	0.4529	0.3066	0.2083	0.1420	0.0972	0.0668	0.0460	0.0318
50	0.6080	0.3715	0.2281	0.1407	0.0872	0.0543	0.0339	0.0213	0.0134

10%	12%	14%	15%	16%	18%	20%	24%	28%	32%	36%
0.9091	0.8929	0.8772	0.8696	0.8621	0.8475	0.8333	0.8065	0.7813	0.7576	0.7353
0.8264	0.7972	0.7695	0.7561	0.7432	0.7182	0.6944	0.6504	0.6104	0.5739	0.5407
0.7513	0.7118	0.6750	0.6575	0.6407	0.6086	0.5787	0.5245	0.4768	0.4348	0.3975
0.6830	0.6355	0.5921	0.5718	0.5523	0.5158	0.4823	0.4230	0.3725	0.3294	0.2923
0.6209	0.5674	0.5194	0.4972	0.4761	0.4371	0.4019	0.3411	0.2910	0.2495	0.2149
0.5645	0.5066	0.4556	0.4323	0.4104	0.3704	0.3349	0.2751	0.2274	0.1890	0.1580
0.5132	0.4523	0.3996	0.3759	0.3538	0.3139	0.2791	0.2218	0.1776	0.1432	0.1162
0.4665	0.4039	0.3506	0.3269	0.3050	0.2660	0.2326	0.1789	0.1388	0.1085	0.0854
0.4241	0.3606	0.3075	0.2843	0.2630	0.2255	0.1938	0.1443	0.1084	0.0822	0.0628
0.3855	0.3220	0.2697	0.2472	0.2267	0.1911	0.1615	0.1164	0.0847	0.0623	0.0462
0.3505	0.2875	0.2366	0.2149	0.1954	0.1619	0.1346	0.0938	0.0662	0.0472	0.0340
0.3186	0.2567	0.2076	0.1869	0.1685	0.1372	0.1122	0.0757	0.0517	0.0357	0.0250
0.2897	0.2292	0.1821	0.1625	0.1452	0.1163	0.0935	0.0610	0.0404	0.0271	0.0184
0.2633	0.2046	0.1597	0.1413	0.1252	0.0985	0.0779	0.0492	0.0316	0.0205	0.0135
0.2394	0.1827	0.1401	0.1229	0.1079	0.0835	0.0649	0.0397	0.0247	0.0155	0.0099
0.2176	0.1631	0.1229	0.1069	0.0930	0.0708	0.0541	0.0320	0.0193	0.0118	0.0073
0.1978	0.1456	0.1078	0.0929	0.0802	0.0600	0.0451	0.0258	0.0150	0.0089	0.0054
0.1799	0.1300	0.0946	0.0808	0.0691	0.0508	0.0376	0.0208	0.0118	0.0068	0.0039
0.1635	0.1161	0.0829	0.0703	0.0596	0.0431	0.0313	0.0168	0.0092	0.0051	0.0029
0.1486	0.1037	0.0728	0.0611	0.0514	0.0365	0.0261	0.0135	0.0072	0.0039	0.0021
0.1351	0.0926	0.0638	0.0531	0.0443	0.0309	0.0217	0.0109	0.0056	0.0029	0.0016
0.1228	0.0826	0.0560	0.0462	0.0382	0.0262	0.0181	0.0088	0.0044	0.0022	0.0012
0.1117	0.0738	0.0491	0.0402	0.0329	0.0222	0.0151	0.0071	0.0034	0.0017	0.0008
0.1015	0.0659	0.0431	0.0349	0.0284	0.0188	0.0126	0.0057	0.0027	0.0013	0.0006
0.0923	0.0588	0.0378	0.0304	0.0245	0.0160	0.0105	0.0046	0.0021	0.0010	0.0005
0.0573	0.0334	0.0196	0.0151	0.0116	0.0070	0.0042	0.0016	0.0006	0.0002	0.0001
0.0221	0.0107	0.0053	0.0037	0.0026	0.0013	0.0007	0.0002	0.0001	*	*
0.0085	0.0035	0.0014	0.0009	0.0006	0.0003	0.0001	*	*	*	*

*The factor is zero to four decimal places.

APPENDIX A.3   Present value of an annuity of $1 per period for t periods $= [1 - 1/(1 + r)^t]/r$

Number of Periods	Interest Rate								
	1%	2%	3%	4%	5%	6%	7%	8%	9%
1	0.9901	0.9804	0.9709	0.9615	0.9524	0.9434	0.9346	0.9259	0.9174
2	1.9704	1.9416	1.9135	1.8861	1.8594	1.8334	1.8080	1.7833	1.7591
3	2.9410	2.8839	2.8286	2.7751	2.7232	2.6730	2.6243	2.5771	2.5313
4	3.9020	3.8077	3.7171	3.6299	3.5460	3.4651	3.3872	3.3121	3.2397
5	4.8534	4.7135	4.5797	4.4518	4.3295	4.2124	4.1002	3.9927	3.8897
6	5.7955	5.6014	5.4172	5.2421	5.0757	4.9173	4.7665	4.6229	4.4859
7	6.7282	6.4720	6.2303	6.0021	5.7864	5.5824	5.3893	5.2064	5.0330
8	7.6517	7.3255	7.0197	6.7327	6.4632	6.2098	5.9713	5.7466	5.5348
9	8.5660	8.1622	7.7861	7.4353	7.1078	6.8017	6.5152	6.2469	5.9952
10	9.4713	8.9826	8.5302	8.1109	7.7217	7.3601	7.0236	6.7101	6.4177
11	10.3676	9.7868	9.2526	8.7605	8.3064	7.8869	7.4987	7.1390	6.8052
12	11.2551	10.5753	9.9540	9.3851	8.8633	8.3838	7.9427	7.5361	7.1607
13	12.1337	11.3484	10.6350	9.9856	9.3936	8.8527	8.3577	7.9038	7.4869
14	13.0037	12.1062	11.2961	10.5631	9.8986	9.2950	8.7455	8.2442	7.7862
15	13.8651	12.8493	11.9379	11.1184	10.3797	9.7122	9.1079	8.5595	8.0607
16	14.7179	13.5777	12.5611	11.6523	10.8378	10.1059	9.4466	8.8514	8.3126
17	15.5623	14.2919	13.1661	12.1657	11.2741	10.4773	9.7632	9.1216	8.5436
18	16.3983	14.9920	13.7535	12.6593	11.6896	10.8276	10.0591	9.3719	8.7556
19	17.2260	15.6785	14.3238	13.1339	12.0853	11.1581	10.3356	9.6036	8.9501
20	18.0456	16.3514	14.8775	13.5903	12.4622	11.4699	10.5940	9.8181	9.1285
21	18.8570	17.0112	15.4150	14.0292	12.8212	11.7641	10.8355	10.0168	9.2922
22	19.6604	17.6580	15.9369	14.4511	13.1630	12.0416	11.0612	10.2007	9.4424
23	20.4558	18.2922	16.4436	14.8568	13.4886	12.3034	11.2722	10.3741	9.5802
24	21.2434	18.9139	16.9355	15.2470	13.7986	12.5504	11.4693	10.5288	9.7066
25	22.0232	19.5235	17.4131	15.6221	14.0939	12.7834	11.6536	10.6748	9.8226
30	25.8077	22.3965	19.6004	17.2920	15.3725	13.7648	12.4090	11.2578	10.2737
40	32.8347	27.3555	23.1148	19.7928	17.1591	15.0463	13.3317	11.9246	10.7574
50	39.1961	31.4236	25.7298	21.4822	18.2559	15.7619	13.8007	12.2335	10.9617

10%	12%	14%	15%	16%	18%	20%	24%	28%	32%
0.9091	0.8929	0.8772	0.8696	0.8621	0.8475	0.8333	0.8065	0.7813	0.7576
1.7355	1.6901	1.6467	1.6257	1.6052	1.5656	1.5278	1.4568	1.3916	1.3315
2.4869	2.4018	2.3216	2.2832	2.2459	2.1743	2.1065	1.9813	1.8684	1.7663
3.1699	3.0373	2.9137	2.8550	2.7982	2.6901	2.5887	2.4043	2.2410	2.0957
3.7908	3.6048	3.4331	3.3522	3.2743	3.1272	2.9906	2.7454	2.5320	2.3452
4.3553	4.1114	3.8887	3.7845	3.6847	3.4976	3.3255	3.0205	2.7594	2.5342
4.8684	4.5638	4.2883	4.1604	4.0386	3.8115	3.6046	3.2423	2.9370	2.6775
5.3349	4.9676	4.6389	4.4873	4.3436	4.0776	3.8372	3.4212	3.0758	2.7860
5.7590	5.3282	4.9464	4.7716	4.6065	4.3030	4.0310	3.5655	3.1842	2.8681
6.1446	5.6502	5.2161	5.0188	4.8332	4.4941	4.1925	3.6819	3.2689	2.9304
6.4951	5.9377	5.4527	5.2337	5.0286	4.6560	4.3271	3.7757	3.3351	2.9776
6.8137	6.1944	5.6603	5.4206	5.1971	4.7932	4.4392	3.8514	3.3868	3.0133
7.1034	6.4235	5.8424	5.5831	5.3423	4.9095	4.5327	3.9124	3.4272	3.0404
7.3667	6.6282	6.0021	5.7245	5.4675	5.0081	4.6106	3.9616	3.4587	3.0609
7.6061	6.8109	6.1422	5.8474	5.5755	5.0916	4.6755	4.0013	3.4834	3.0764
7.8237	6.9740	6.2651	5.9542	5.6685	5.1624	4.7296	4.0333	3.5026	3.0882
8.0216	7.1196	6.3729	6.0472	5.7487	5.2223	4.7746	4.0591	3.5177	3.0971
8.2014	7.2497	6.4674	6.1280	5.8178	5.2732	4.8122	4.0799	3.5294	3.1039
8.3649	7.3658	6.5504	6.1982	5.8775	5.3162	4.8435	4.0967	3.5386	3.1090
8.5136	7.4694	6.6231	6.2593	5.9288	5.3527	4.8696	4.1103	3.5458	3.1129
8.6487	7.5620	6.6870	6.3125	5.9731	5.3837	4.8913	4.1212	3.5514	3.1158
8.7715	7.6446	6.7429	6.3587	6.0113	5.4099	4.9094	4.1300	3.5558	3.1180
8.8832	7.7184	6.7921	6.3988	6.0442	5.4321	4.9245	4.1371	3.5592	3.1197
8.9847	7.7843	6.8351	6.4338	6.0726	5.4509	4.9371	4.1428	3.5619	3.1210
9.0770	7.8431	6.8729	6.4641	6.0971	5.4669	4.9476	4.1474	3.5640	3.1220
9.4269	8.0552	7.0027	6.5660	6.1772	5.5168	4.9789	4.1601	3.5693	3.1242
9.7791	8.2438	7.1050	6.6418	6.2335	5.5482	4.9966	4.1659	3.5712	3.1250
9.9148	8.3045	7.1327	6.6605	6.2463	5.5541	4.9995	4.1666	3.5714	3.1250

APPENDIX A.4   Future value of an annuity of $1 per period for t periods $= [(1 + r)^t - 1]/r$

Number of Periods	Interest Rate								
	1%	2%	3%	4%	5%	6%	7%	8%	9%
1	1.0000	1.0000	1.0000	1.0000	1.0000	1.0000	1.0000	1.0000	1.0000
2	2.0100	2.0200	2.0300	2.0400	2.0500	2.0600	2.0700	2.0800	2.0900
3	3.0301	3.0604	3.0909	3.1216	3.1525	3.1836	3.2149	3.2464	3.2781
4	4.0604	4.1216	4.1836	4.2465	4.3101	4.3746	4.4399	4.5061	4.5731
5	5.1010	5.2040	5.3091	5.4163	5.5256	5.6371	5.7507	5.8666	5.9847
6	6.1520	6.3081	6.4684	6.6330	6.8019	6.9753	7.1533	7.3359	7.5233
7	7.2135	7.4343	7.6625	7.8983	8.1420	8.3938	8.6540	8.9228	9.2004
8	8.2857	8.5830	8.8932	9.2142	9.5491	9.8975	10.260	10.637	11.028
9	9.3685	9.7546	10.159	10.583	11.027	11.491	11.978	12.488	13.021
10	10.462	10.950	11.464	12.006	12.578	13.181	13.816	14.487	15.193
11	11.567	12.169	12.808	13.486	14.207	14.972	15.784	16.645	17.560
12	12.683	13.412	14.192	15.026	15.917	16.870	17.888	18.977	20.141
13	13.809	14.680	15.618	16.627	17.713	18.882	20.141	21.495	22.953
14	14.947	15.974	17.086	18.292	19.599	21.015	22.550	24.215	26.019
15	16.097	17.293	18.599	20.024	21.579	23.276	25.129	27.152	29.361
16	17.258	18.639	20.157	21.825	23.657	25.673	27.888	30.324	33.003
17	18.430	20.012	21.762	23.698	25.840	28.213	30.840	33.750	36.974
18	19.615	21.412	23.414	25.645	28.132	30.906	33.999	37.450	41.301
19	20.811	22.841	25.117	27.671	30.539	33.760	37.379	41.446	46.018
20	22.019	24.297	26.870	29.778	33.066	36.786	40.995	45.762	51.160
21	23.239	25.783	28.676	31.969	35.719	39.993	44.865	50.423	56.765
22	24.472	27.299	30.537	34.248	38.505	43.392	49.006	55.457	62.873
23	25.716	28.845	32.453	36.618	41.430	46.996	53.436	60.893	69.532
24	26.973	30.422	34.426	39.083	44.502	50.816	58.177	66.765	76.790
25	28.243	32.030	36.459	41.646	47.727	54.865	63.249	73.106	84.701
30	34.785	40.568	47.575	56.085	66.439	79.058	94.461	113.28	136.31
40	48.886	60.402	75.401	95.026	120.80	154.76	199.64	259.06	337.88
50	64.463	84.579	112.80	152.67	209.35	290.34	406.53	573.77	815.08
60	81.670	114.05	163.05	237.99	353.58	533.13	813.52	1253.2	1944.8

10%	12%	14%	15%	16%	18%	20%	24%	28%	32%	36%
1.0000	1.0000	1.0000	1.0000	1.0000	1.0000	1.0000	1.0000	1.0000	1.0000	1.0000
2.1000	2.1200	2.1400	2.1500	2.1600	2.1800	2.2000	2.2400	2.2800	2.3200	2.3600
3.3100	3.3744	3.4396	3.4725	3.5056	3.5724	3.6400	3.7776	3.9184	4.0624	4.2096
4.6410	4.7793	4.9211	4.9934	5.0665	5.2154	5.3680	5.6842	6.0156	6.3624	6.7251
6.1051	6.3528	6.6101	6.7424	6.8771	7.1542	7.4416	8.0484	8.6999	9.3983	10.146
7.7156	8.1152	8.5355	8.7537	8.9775	9.4420	9.9299	10.980	12.136	13.406	14.799
9.4872	10.089	10.730	11.067	11.414	12.142	12.916	14.615	16.534	18.696	21.126
11.436	12.300	13.233	13.727	14.240	15.327	16.499	19.123	22.163	25.678	29.732
13.579	14.776	16.085	16.786	17.519	19.086	20.799	24.712	29.369	34.895	41.435
15.937	17.549	19.337	20.304	21.321	23.521	25.959	31.643	38.593	47.062	57.352
18.531	20.655	23.045	24.349	25.733	28.755	32.150	40.238	50.398	63.122	78.998
21.384	24.133	27.271	29.002	30.850	34.931	39.581	50.895	65.510	84.320	108.44
24.523	28.029	32.089	34.352	36.786	42.219	48.497	64.110	84.853	112.30	148.47
27.975	32.393	37.581	40.505	43.672	50.818	59.196	80.496	109.61	149.24	202.93
31.772	37.280	43.842	47.580	51.660	60.965	72.035	100.82	141.30	198.00	276.98
35.950	42.753	50.980	55.717	60.925	72.939	87.442	126.01	181.87	262.36	377.69
40.545	48.884	59.118	65.075	71.673	87.068	105.93	157.25	233.79	347.31	514.66
45.599	55.750	68.394	75.836	84.141	103.74	128.12	195.99	300.25	459.45	700.94
51.159	63.440	78.969	88.212	98.603	123.41	154.74	244.03	385.32	607.47	954.28
57.275	72.052	91.025	102.44	115.38	146.63	186.69	303.60	494.21	802.86	1298.8
64.002	81.699	104.77	118.81	134.84	174.02	225.03	377.46	633.59	1060.8	1767.4
71.403	92.503	120.44	137.63	157.41	206.34	271.03	469.06	812.00	1401.2	2404.7
79.543	104.60	138.30	159.28	183.60	244.49	326.24	582.63	1040.4	1850.6	3271.3
88.497	118.16	158.66	184.17	213.98	289.49	392.48	723.46	1332.7	2443.8	4450.0
98.347	133.33	181.87	212.79	249.21	342.60	471.98	898.09	1706.8	3226.8	6053.0
164.49	241.33	356.79	434.75	530.31	790.95	1181.9	2640.9	5873.2	12941.	28172.3
442.59	767.09	1342.0	1779.1	2360.8	4163.2	7343.9	22729.	69377.	*	*
1163.9	2400.0	4994.5	7217.7	10436.	21813.	45497.	*	*	*	*
3034.8	7471.6	18535.	29220.	46058.	*	*	*	*	*	*

*The factor is greater than 99,999.

Answers to Selected End-of-Chapter Problems

CHAPTER 2

1. Equity = $3,400
   NWC = $1,500

3. $91,500

5. Book value of assets = $4,075,000
   Market value of assets = $6,200,000

7. Average tax rate = 38.87%
   Marginal tax rate = 50%

9. $690,000

11. −$135,000

13. $305,000

15. $4,455

17. $800; $0

19. Net new long-term debt = $25,000

21. *a.* $4,572; $3,967
   b. −$245
   c. Fixed assets sold = $1,080
      Cash flow from assets = $6,898
   d. Debt retired = $360
      Cash flow to creditors = −$331

23. *a.* $25,508; $27,009
   b. $390; $360

25. *a.* $3,000,800; $16,368
   b. $3,410; $1,860

CHAPTER 3

1. Current ratio = 1.26 times
   Quick ratio = 0.88 times

3. Receivables turnover = 8.32 times
   Days' sales in receivables = 43.88 days

5. Debt/equity ratio = 1.22
   Equity multiplier = 2.22

7. 22.19%

9. 78.08 days

11. 9.89%

13. ROE = 20.30%
   Sustainable growth rate = 18.67%

17. 36.87%

19. 7.67%

21. 23.83%

23. 13.86%

25. 4.21%

27. $6,131.76

29. Profit margin = 9.57%
   Total asset turnover = 1.57 times
   ROE = 27.12%

31. 2.27 times

33. Profit margin = −8.24%
   Net income = −$26,167

35. 40.65%

41. ROA = 9.38%
   Sustainable growth rate = 12.28%

43. Maximum sustainable growth rate = 10.65%

CHAPTER 4

1. $1,602.91

3. $10,856; $32,765; $36,789; $11,959

5. 25.50 years; 14.09 years; 22.13 years; 7.10 years

7. 10.24 years; 20.49 years

9. 37.44 years

11. $113.44

13. 8.53%; $21,428,377

15. −4.46%

17. $50,430

19. $20,629

21. $29,703; $27,953

23. 163.81 months

25. $9,130; $111,297

27. $16,880

CHAPTER 5

1. $3,151.36; $2,626.48; $2,318.96

3. $4,984.95; $5,138.26; $5,862.05

5. $1,939.17

7. $145,131.04; $887,047.61

9. $5,960.72

11. 7.41%

13. 11.66%; 16.67%; 6.77%; 10.44%

15. 15.70%

17. $7,291.79; $8,861.70; $13,088.29

19. APR = 300.00%
   EAR = 1,355.19%

21. 41.71 months
23. Monthly return = 1.71%
  APR = 20.57%
  EAR = 22.63%
25. $666,480.02
27. $2,227.10
29. 6.63%
31. $728.43
33. $1.15; $1.33
35. $137,085.37; $138,341.66
37. 8.15%; 8.24%
39. 125.90 payments
41. $35,802,654
43. APR = 7.51%
  EAR = 7.78%
45. 12.36%
47. $7,453.30
49. $5,241.05
51. $151,812.58
53. APR = 23.19%
  EAR = 25.82%
55. Third year = $1,824.87
  Life of loan = $10,243.76
57. $912.03
59. a. $941.40
  c. $105,710.67
61. $50.67

CHAPTER 6

3. $1,052.06
5. 7.77%
7. 8.85%
9. 3.20%; 3.11%
11. 2.73%
13. Coupon rate = 8%
  Bid price = $1,454.20
  Yield = 4.59%
19. 8.25%
21. $883.00
23. $982.85
25. a. 25,000; 96,742
  b. $26,750,000; $96,742,112
27. 5.37%
29. 9.53%
31. 9.57%
33. $1,120.79

CHAPTER 7

1. $43.75; $50.65; $90.95
3. Dividend yield = 3.83%
  Capital gains yield = 6.50%
5. 10.10%

7. $77.19
9. $5,625,045; $2,250,045
11. 5.93%
13. $37.50; $75.00
15. $72.27
17. $54.47
19. $5.55
21. Dividend yields: 8%; 18%; 23%; 5.6%
  Capital gains yields: 10%; 0%; −5%; 12.4%
25. −5.57%
27. $18.92
29. 19.39%

CHAPTER 8

1. 2.75 years
3. A: 2.44 years;   B: 3.06 years
5. 19.03%
7. $2,296.27; −$921.40; 17.79%
9. $15,000; $7,683.70; $2,231.48; −$1,948.57
11. Crossover rate = 13.28%
13. 1.101; 1.021; 0.926
17. a. 1.12; 1.11
  b. $5,544.98; $6,987.50
19. 0%; <0%
21. a. F: 2.13 years; G: 3.14 years
  b. F: $100,689.53; G: $110,147.47
23. 13.16%; −$1,051.02; −$14,000.00; $8,588.97
27. a. $50,000
  b. 12%
  c. 3%

CHAPTER 9

1. $23,850,000
3. $44,200
7. $97,250.48; $105,000
9. $11,652,500
11. $131,190.41
13. $277,885.64
15. 21.03%
19. a. OCF = $448,333.33
  NPV = $306,709.74
  ΔNPV/ΔS = $34.44
  b. ΔOCF/Δv = −$71,500
21. 3.26 years; −$45,869.27; 8.69%
23. NPV = $3,767,853.21
25. a. Base-case NPV = $447,155.04
  Best-case NPV = $1,146,210.76
  Worst-case NPV = −$158,371.60
  b. ΔNPV/ΔFC = −$1.86
27. Best-case NPV = $30,890,102.07
  Worst-case NPV = −$18,253,871.39

CHAPTER 10

1. 11.33%

3. Total return = −6.75%
Dividend yield = 1.69%
Capital gains yield = −8.43%

5. a. 11.70%
   b. 7.51%

7. X: 10.00%; 0.01685; 12.98%
Y: 16.20%; 0.06167; 24.83%

9. a. 8.80%
   b. 0.02357; 15.35%

11. 0.86%; 3.55%

13. 7.31%

15. 34.88%; 39.71%

17. −2.0% to 16.80%;   −11.4% to 26.2%

19. 38.00%; 22.15%

21. 11.13%; 10.62%

23. 4.62%

25. 2.5%;   0.8% to 9.0%;   −7.4% to 17.2%

CHAPTER 11

1. A: 0.6656; B: 0.3344

3. 13.30%

5. 15.20%

7. A: 8.60%; 3.54%
   B: 14.05%; 16.80%

9. a. 11.77%
   b. 0.00665

11. 1.36

13. 14.60%

15. 13.76%

17. a. 10.25%
   b. 0.3846
   c. 0.889
   d. −100.00%

19. Y: 0.0767
Z: 0.0625
SML: 0.0750

21. 9.55%; 9.45%

23. a. 10.10%
   b. 3.32%

25. J: 0.5556
$E(R_P)$ = 13.44%

27. $31,250

31. −$7,407

CHAPTER 12

1. 11.80%

3. 11.88%

5. 8.06%

7. a. 8.61%
   b. 5.60%

9. 9.49%

11. 0.56

13. 11.08%

15. 9.39%

19. 9.72%

21. Arithmetic = 11.27%
Geometric = 11.22%

23. 11.99%

25. $1,308,601

27. a. 6.17%
   b. 12.40%

CHAPTER 13

1. a. $2.33, $3.33; $4.00
   b. $3.67; $5.67; $7.00

3. a. 11.67%; 16.67%; 20.00%
   b. 18.33%; 28.33%; 35.00%
   c. 7.58%; 10.83%; 13.00%
      11.92%; 18.42%; 22.75%

5. Price = $20.83
I = II = $16,666,667

7. $10 per share

9. a. $2,320
   b. $3,120
   c. Sell 64 shares

11. $45 million; $52.94 million; $56.25 million

13. a. 10.00%
   b. 11.29%
   c. 14.50%
   d. 10.00%; 10.00%

15. $10,640,000

17. 0.41; 0.35

19. $89,125.00; $110,030.86; $143,750.00

21. a. Cash flow to stockholders: $264,000; $240,900
      Cash flow to bondholders: $0; $35,000
   b. $1,760,000; $1,930,000
   c. $1,760,000; $1,430,000

CHAPTER 14

1. $17,120

3. $101.09

5. a. 20,000   **b.** 2,500

7. $15.00; $13.90

9. $40.83

11. New shares outstanding = 1,000,000; $1.09

13. a. 22.58%
   b. 0.387

15. a. $57,000,000; $27,000,000
   b. $1.49
   c. $18,947,368; $21,052,632
   d. $5.00; $0

17. $41,150

19. a. $22,800,000
   b. $14,400,000
   c. $14,400,000

CHAPTER 15

1. $4,000; $0

3. 1,512,542

5. *a.* $17
   b. 250; 291.7; 125.0; 166.7; 166.7; 0

7. 1,304,697

9. 42.35%

CHAPTER 16

2. Cash = $7,700; CA = $19,200

6. Operating cycle = 81.83 days
   Cash cycle = 36.64 days

7. 12.74%

9. $800; $897; $882; $1,018

11. $243,000; $270,500; $181,000

13. 30.13%

15. *a.* 6.23%
   b. $460,228.73

17. Payables = $15,136.99
   Receivables = $30,619.18

19. *a.* 9.92%
   b. 9.98%
   c. 9.87%

CHAPTER 17

1. $190,000; $114,000

3. $6,000; −$13,000; −$7,000

5. $10,000

7. $109,589.04

9. *a.* 17.00 days
   b. $1,475,507

11. 26.85%;
   a. 43.14%;
   b. 15.56%;
   c. 34.31%

13. Carrying costs = $1,800
   Restocking costs = $33,800
   EOQ = 7,800

15. Carrying costs = $242,250
   Restocking costs = $218,400
   EOQ = 4,842

17. EOQ = 110
   Safety stock = 5
   Reorder point = 18

19. 73; Wednesday morning

CHAPTER 18

1. *a.* 2,444.01
   b. $1.4274
   c. $7,137,000

5. *a.* ¥195.30/£1
   b. $0.028 per dollar

7. Canada: $30,307,041.58
   Britain: $31,993,961.10

9. Break-even rate = S$1.3125/$1

11. *b.* −3.23%

13. ¥133.813/€1

15. 64.8536 kronur/$

Using the HP-10B and TI BA II Plus Financial Calculators

This appendix is intended to help you use your Hewlett-Packard HP-10B or Texas Instruments BA II Plus financial calculator to solve problems encountered in the introductory finance course. It describes the various calculator settings and provides keystroke solutions for nine selected problems from this book. Please see your owner's manual for more complete instructions.

CALCULATOR SETTINGS

Most calculator errors in the introductory finance course are the result of inappropriate settings. Before beginning a calculation, you should ask yourself the following questions:

1. Did I clear the financial registers?
2. Is the compounding frequency set to once per period?
3. Is the calculator in END mode?
4. Did I enter negative numbers using the **+/−** key?

Clearing the Registers

All calculators have areas of memory, called registers, where variables and intermediate results are stored. There are two sets of financial registers, the time value of money (TVM) registers and the cash flow (CF) registers. These must be cleared before beginning a new calculation. On the Hewlett-Packard HP-10B, pressing {CLEAR ALL} clears both the TVM and the CF registers.[1] To clear the TVM registers on the BA II Plus, press **2nd** {CLR TVM}. Press **2nd** {CLR Work} from within the cash flow worksheet to clear the CF registers.

Compounding Frequency

Both the HP-10B and the BA II Plus are hardwired to assume monthly compounding, that is, compounding 12 times per period. Because very few problems in the introductory finance course make this assumption, you should change this default setting to once per period. On the HP-10B, press 1 {P/YR}. To verify that the default has been changed, press the key, then press and briefly hold the **INPUT** key.[2] The display should read "1 P_Yr".

On the BA II Plus, you can specify both payment frequency and compounding frequency, although they should normally be

set to the same number. To set both to once per period, press the key sequence **2nd** {P/Y} 1 **ENTER**, then press ↓ 1 **ENTER**. Pressing **2nd** {QUIT} returns you to standard calculator mode.

END Mode and Annuities Due

In most problems, payment is made at the end of a period, and this is the default setting (end mode) for both the HP-10B and the BA II Plus. *Annuities due* assume payments are made at the *beginning* of each period (begin mode). On the HP-10B, pressing {BEG/END} toggles between begin and end mode. Press the key sequence **2nd** {BGN} **2nd** {SET} **2nd** {QUIT} to accomplish the same task on the BA II Plus. Both calculators will indicate on the display that your calculator is set for begin mode.

Sign Changes

Sign changes are used to identify the direction of cash inflows and outflows. Generally, cash inflows are entered as positive numbers and cash outflows are entered as negative numbers. To enter a negative number on either the HP-10B or the BA II Plus, first press the appropriate digit keys and then press the change sign key, **+/−**. Do *not* use the minus sign key, **−**, as its effects are quite unpredictable.

SAMPLE PROBLEMS

This section provides keystroke solutions for selected problems from the text illustrating the nine basic financial calculator skills.

1. Future Value or Present Value of a Single Sum

Compute the future value of $2,250 at a 17 percent annual rate for 30 years.

HP-10B		BA II PLUS	
−2,250.00 **PV**		−2,250.00 **PV**	
30.00 **N**		30.00 **N**	
17.00 **I/YR**		17.00 **I/Y**	
FV 249,895.46		**CPT** **FV** 249,895.46	

The future value is $249,895.46.

---

[1]The key is coloured orange and serves as a Shift key for the functions in curly brackets.

[2]This is the same keystroke used to clear all registers; pretty handy, eh?

2. Present Value or Future Value of an Ordinary Annuity

Betty's Bank offers you a $20,000, seven-year term loan at 11 percent annual interest. What will your annual loan payment be?

HP-10B		BA II PLUS	
−20,000.00	**PV**	−20,000.00	**PV**
7.00	**N**	7.00	**N**
11.00	**I/YR**	11.00	**I/Y**
PMT	4,244.31	**CPT PMT**	4,244.31

Your annual loan payment will be $4,244.31.

3. Finding an Unknown Interest Rate

Assume that the total cost of a college education will be $75,000 when your child enters college in 18 years. You presently have $7,000 to invest. What rate of interest must you earn on your investment to cover the cost of your child's college education?

HP-10B		BA II PLUS	
−7,000.00	**PV**	−7,000.00	**PV**
18.00	**N**	18.00	**N**
75,000.00	**FV**	75,000.00	**FV**
I/YR	14.08	**CPT I/Y**	14.08

You must earn an annual interest rate of at least 14.08 percent to cover the expected future cost of your child's education.

4. Finding an Unknown Number of Periods

One of your customers is delinquent on his accounts payable balance. You've mutually agreed to a repayment schedule of $374 per month. You will charge 1.4 percent per month interest on the overdue balance. If the current balance is $12,000, how long will it take for the account to be paid off?

HP-10B		BA II PLUS	
−12,000.00	**PV**	−12,000.00	**PV**
1.40	**I/YR**	1.40	**I/Y**
374.00	**PMT**	374.00	**PMT**
N	42.90	**CPT N**	42.90

The loan will be paid off in 42.90 months.

5. Simple Bond Pricing

Mullineaux Co. issued 11-year bonds one year ago at a coupon rate of 8.25 percent. The bonds make semiannual payments. If the YTM on these bonds is 7.10 percent, what is the current bond price?

HP-10B		BA II PLUS	
41.25	**PMT**	41.25	**PMT**
1,000.00	**FV**	1,000.00	**FV**
20.00	**N**	20.00	**N**
3.55	**I/YR**	3.55	**I/Y**
PV	−1,081.35	**CPT PV**	−1,081.35

Because the bonds make semiannual payments, we must halve the coupon payment (8.25 ÷ 2 = 4.125 ==> $41.25), halve the YTM (7.10 ÷ 2 ==> 3.55), and double the number of periods (10 years remaining × 2 = 20 periods). Then, the current bond price is $1,081.35.

6. Simple Bond Yields to Maturity

Vasicek Co. has 12.5 percent coupon bonds on the market with eight years left to maturity. The bonds make annual payments. If one of these bonds currently sells for $1,145.68, what is its YTM?

HP-10B		BA II PLUS	
−1,145.68	**PV**	−1,145.68	**PV**
125.00	**PMT**	125.00	**PMT**
1,000.00	**FV**	1,000.00	**FV**
8.00	**N**	8.00	**N**
I/YR	9.79	**CPT I/Y**	9.79

The bond has a yield to maturity of 9.79 percent.

7. Cash Flow Analysis

What are the IRR and NPV of the following set of cash flows? Assume a discount rate of 10 percent.

Year	Cash Flow
0	−$1,300
1	400
2	300
3	1,200

HP-10B		BA II PLUS	
−1,300.00	**CFj**	**CF**	
400.00	**CFj**	**2nd**	{CLR Work}
1.00	{Nj}	−1,300.00	**ENTER** ↓
300.00	**CFj**	400.00	**ENTER** ↓
1.00	{Nj}	1.00	**ENTER** ↓
1,200.00	**CFj**	300.00	**ENTER** ↓
1.00	{Nj}	1.00	**ENTER** ↓
{IRR/YR}	17.40	1,200.00	**ENTER** ↓
10.00	**I/YR**	1.00	**ENTER** ↓
{NPV}	213.15	**IRR CPT**	17.40
		NPV	
		10.00	**ENTER**
		↓ **CPT**	213.15

The project has an IRR of 17.40 percent and an NPV of $213.15.

8. Loan Amortization

Prepare an amortization schedule for a three-year loan of $24,000. The interest rate is 16 percent per year, and the loan calls for equal annual payments. How much interest is paid in the third year? How much total interest is paid over the life of the loan?

To prepare a complete amortization schedule, you must amortize each payment one at a time:

HP-10B	BA II PLUS

HP-10B			BA II PLUS
−24,000.00 **PV**			−24,000.00 **PV**
16.00 **I/YR**			16.00 **I/Y**
3.00 **N**			3.00 **N**
PMT 10,686.19			**CPT** **PMT** 10,686.19
1.00 **INPUT** {AMORT} = 3,840.00 <== Interest			**2nd** {AMORT} **2nd** {CLR Work}
= 6,846.19 <== Principal			1.00 **ENTER** ↓
= −17,153.81 <== Balance			1.00 **ENTER** ↓ −17,153.81 <== Balance
2.00 **INPUT** {AMORT} = 2,744.61 <== Interest			↓ 6,846.19 <== Principal
= 7,941.58 <== Principal			↓ 3,840.00 <== Interest
= −9,212.23 <== Balance			↓
3.00 **INPUT** {AMORT} = 1,473.96 <== Interest			2.00 **ENTER** ↓
= 9,212.23 <== Principal			2.00 **ENTER** ↓ −9,212.23 <== Balance
= 0.00 <== Balance			↓ 7,941.58 <== Principal
			↓ 2,744.61 <== Interest
			↓
			3.00 **ENTER** ↓
			3.00 **ENTER** ↓ 0.00 <== Balance
			↓ 9,212.23 <== Principal
			↓ 1,473.96 <== Interest
			↓

Interest of $1,473.96 is paid in the third year.

Enter both a beginning and an ending period to compute the total amount of interest or principal paid over a particular period of time.

HP-10B	BA II PLUS

HP-10B		BA II PLUS
−24,000.00 **PV**		−24,000.00 **PV**
16.00 **I/YR**		16.00 **I/Y**
3.00 **N**		3.00 **N**
PMT 10,686.19		**CPT** **PMT** 10,686.19
1.00 **INPUT**		**2nd** {AMORT} **2nd** {CLR Work}
3.00 {AMORT} = 8,058.57 <== Interest		1.00 **ENTER** ↓
= 24,000.00 <== Principal		3.00 **ENTER** ↓ 0.00 <== Balance
= 0.00 <== Balance		↓ 24,000.00 <== Principal
		↓ 8,058.57 <== Interest

Total interest of $8,058.57 is paid over the life of the loan.

9. Interest Rate Conversions

Find the effective annual rate, EAR, corresponding to a 7 percent annual percentage rate, APR, compounded quarterly.

HP-10B	BA II PLUS
4.00 {P/YR}	**2nd** {IConv}
7.00 {NOM%}	7.00 **ENTER**
{EFF%} 7.19	↓ ↓
	4.00 **ENTER**
	↑ **CPT** 7.19

The effective annual rate equals 7.19 percent.

Glossary

accounts payable period The time between receipt of inventory and payment for it. (487)

accounts receivable financing A secured short-term loan that involves either the assignment or factoring of receivables. (502)

accounts receivable period The time between sale of inventory and collection of the receivable. (486)

adjusted cost of disposal The amount subtracted from the asset class's undepreciated capital cost when an asset is sold; equal to the sale price of the asset or its original cost, whichever is less. (271)

agency problem The possibility of conflict of interest between the owners and management of a firm. (14)

aging schedule A compilation of accounts receivable by the age of each account. (534)

American Depositary Receipt (ADR) Security issued in the United States representing shares of a foreign stock, allowing that stock to be traded in the United States. (554)

annual percentage rate (APR) The interest rate charged per period multiplied by the number of periods per year. (144)

annuity A level stream of cash flows for a fixed period of time. (134)

annuity due An annuity for which the cash flows occur at the beginning of the period. (140)

arithmetic average return The return earned in an average year over a multiyear period. (319)

asset-specific risk A risk that affects at most a small number of assets. Also *unique* or *unsystematic risk.* (343)

average tax rate Total taxes paid divided by total taxable income. (41)

balance sheet Financial statement showing a firm's accounting value on a particular date. (24)

bankruptcy A legal proceeding for liquidating or reorganizing a business. (423)

bearer form The form of bond issue in which the bond is issued without record of the owner's name; payment is made to whoever holds the bond. (179)

benefit-cost ratio The present value of an investment's future cash flows divided by its initial cost. Also *profitability index.* (248)

best efforts underwriting The type of underwriting in which the underwriter sells as much of the issue as possible, but can return any unsold shares to the issuer without financial responsibility. (467)

beta coefficient Amount of systematic risk present in a particular risky asset relative to that in an average risky asset. (348)

bid price The price a dealer is willing to pay for a security. (191)

bought deal The type of underwriting in which the underwriter buys an entire issue outright from the issuing company and commits to an offering price at the time of filing a preliminary prospectus, or earlier. (466)

broker An agent who arranges security transactions among investors. (18)

business risk The equity risk that comes from the nature of the firm's operating activities. (413)

call premium The amount by which the call price exceeds the par value of the bond. (181)

call protected bond A bond that currently cannot be redeemed by the issuer. (181)

call provision An agreement giving the corporation the option to repurchase the bond at a specific price prior to maturity. (181)

Canada Yield Curve A plot of the yields on Government of Canada bonds relative to maturity. (196)

capital asset pricing model (CAPM) Equation of the security market line showing the relationship between the expected return and the beta. (357)

capital budgeting The process of planning and managing a firm's long-term investments. (7)

capital cost allowance (CCA) The deduction allowed for income tax purposes in respect to the decline in the value of assets that occurs through their use. (269)

capital gains yield The dividend growth rate, or the rate at which the value of an investment grows. (215)

capital rationing The situation that exists if a firm has positive net present value projects but cannot obtain the necessary financing. (287)

capital structure The mixture of debt and equity maintained by a firm. (7)

captive finance company A wholly owned subsidiary that handles the credit function for the parent company. (532)

carrying costs Costs that rise with increases in the level of investment in current assets. (493)

carryover of losses A tax provision allowing corporations with capital or operating losses to apply these losses to earlier or future years. (44)

cash budget A forecast of cash receipts and disbursements for the next planning period. (497)

cash concentration The practice of and procedures for moving cash from multiple banks into the firm's main accounts. (522)

cash cycle The time between cash disbursement and cash collection. (487)

cash discount A discount given to induce prompt payment. Also, *sales discount.* (530)

cash flow from assets The total of cash flow to creditors and cash flow to stockholders, consisting of the following: operating cash flow, capital spending, and changes in net working capital. (33)

cash flow time line Graphical representation of the operating cycle and the cash cycle. (487)

cash flow to creditors A firm's interest payments to creditors less net new borrowings. (36)

cash flow to stockholders Dividends paid out by a firm less net new equity raised. (36)

clean price The price of a bond net of accrued interest; this is the price that is typically quoted. (191)

clientele effect Argument that stocks attract particular groups based on dividend yield and the resulting tax effects. (443)

collection policy Procedures followed by a firm in collecting accounts receivable. (528)

common stock Equity without priority for dividends or in bankruptcy. (216)

common-size statement A standardized financial statement presenting all items in percentage terms. Balance sheet items are shown as a percentage of assets and income statement items as a percentage of sales. (58)

compensating balance Money kept by a firm with a bank in low-interest or non-interest-bearing accounts as part of a loan agreement. (502)

compound interest Interest earned on both the initial principal and the interest reinvested from prior periods. (101)

compound value The amount an investment is worth after one or more periods. Also *future value.* (100)

compounding The process of accumulating interest in an investment over time to earn more interest. (101)

consol A type of perpetuity. (140)

contingency planning Taking into account the managerial options implicit in a project. (285)

controlled disbursement account A disbursement account to which the firm transfers an amount that is sufficient to cover demands for payment. (524)

corporation A business created as a distinct legal entity owned by one or more individuals or entities. (9)

cost of capital The minimum required return on a new investment. (360)

cost of debt The return that lenders require on the firm's debt. (379)

cost of equity The return that equity investors require on their investment in the firm. (375)

coupon Stated interest payment made on a bond. (168)

coupon rate The annual coupon divided by the face value of a bond. (168)

credit analysis The process of determining the probability that customers will not pay. (528)

credit cost curve Graphical representation of the sum of the carrying costs and the opportunity costs of a credit policy. (531)

credit instrument The evidence of indebtedness. (531)

credit period The length of time for which credit is granted. (528)

credit scoring The process of quantifying the probability of default when granting consumer credit. (533)

cross-rate The implicit exchange rate between two currencies quoted in some third currency (usually the U.S. dollar). (554)

cumulative voting A procedure in which a shareholder may cast all votes for one member of the board of directors. (217)

current yield A bond's annual coupon divided by its price. (173)

date of payment Date that the dividend cheques are mailed. (437)

date of record Date by which holders must be on record in order to receive a dividend. (437)

dealer An agent who buys and sells securities from inventory. (18)

debenture An unsecured debt, usually with a maturity of 10 years or more. (180)

declaration date Date on which the board of directors passes a resolution to pay a dividend. (436)

default risk premium The portion of a nominal interest rate or bond yield that represents compensation for the possibility of default. (197)

deferred call provision A call provision prohibiting the company from redeeming the bond prior to a certain date. (181)

depreciation tax shield The tax saving that results from the depreciation deduction, calculated as depreciation multiplied by the corporate tax rate. (267)

direct bankruptcy costs The costs that are directly associated with bankruptcy, such as legal and administrative expenses. (417)

dirty price The price of a bond including accrued interest, also known as the *full* or *invoice price*. This is the price the buyer actually pays. (191)

discount Calculate the present value of some future amount. (107)

discount rate The rate used to calculate the present value of future cash flows. (108)

discounted cash flow (DCF) valuation (a) Valuation calculating the present value of a future cash flow to determine its value today, (b) The process of valuing an investment by discounting its future cash flows. (109, 233)

distribution Payment made by a firm to its owners from sources other than current or accumulated retained earnings. (435)

dividend Payment made out of a firm's earnings to its owners, in the form of either cash or stock. (435)

dividend discount model A model that determines the current price of a stock as the present value of all the future dividends. (209)

dividend growth model A model that determines the current price of a stock as its dividend next period divided by the discounted rate less the dividend growth rate. (211)

dividend tax credit A tax credit on dividends earned on shares of Canadian companies by individuals. (42)

dividend yield A stock's expected cash dividend divided by its current price. (215)

dividends Payments by a corporation to shareholders, made in either cash or stock. (219)

Du Pont identity A way of breaking ROE into three parts: profit margin, total asset turnover, and financial leverage. (70)

Dutch auction underwriting The type of underwriting in which the offer price is set based on competitive bidding by investors. Also known as a *single price auction*. (467)

economic order quantity (EOQ) The restocking quantity that minimizes the total inventory costs. (541)

effective annual rate (EAR) The interest rate expressed as if it were compounded once per year. (142)

efficient capital market Market in which security prices reflect available information. (322)

efficient markets hypothesis (EMH) The hypothesis that actual capital markets, such as the TSX, are efficient. (322)

erosion The cash flows of a new project that come at the expense of a firm's existing projects. (263)

estimation risk The possibility that errors in projected cash flows will lead to incorrect decisions. Also, *forecasting risk*. (279)

Eurobonds International bonds issued in multiple countries but denominated in a single currency (usually the issuer's currency). (554)

Eurocurrency Money deposited in a financial centre outside the country whose currency is involved. (554)

ex-dividend date Date two business days before the date of record, establishing those individuals entitled to a dividend. (436)

exchange rate The price of one country's currency expressed in terms of another country's currency. (556)

exchange rate risk The risk related to having international operations in a world where relative currency values vary. (567)

expected return Return on a risky asset expected in the future. (334)

face value The principal amount of a bond that is repaid at the end of the term. Also, *par value*. (168)

financial distress costs The direct and indirect costs associated with going bankrupt or experiencing financial distress. (417)

financial ratios Relationships that are determined from a firm's financial information and used for comparison purposes. (61)

financial risk The equity risk that comes from the financial policy (i.e., capital structure) of the firm. (413)

firm commitment underwriting The type of underwriting in which the underwriter buys the entire issue, assuming full financial responsibility for any unsold shares. (466)

Fisher effect The relationship between nominal returns, real returns, and inflation. (193)

five Cs of credit The five basic credit factors to be evaluated: character, capacity, capital, collateral, and conditions. (533)

float The difference between the book or ledger cash balance and the available or collected balance, representing the net effect of cheques in the process of clearing. (517)

forecasting risk The possibility that errors in projected cash flows will lead to incorrect decisions. Also, *estimation risk*. (279)

foreign bonds International bonds issued in a single country, usually denominated in that country's currency. (555)

foreign exchange market The market in which one country's currency is traded for another's. (555)

forward exchange rate The agreed-upon exchange rate to be used in a forward trade. (560)

forward trade   Agreement to exchange currency at some time in the future. (560)

free cash flow   Another name for cash flow from assets. (35)

future value (FV)   The amount an investment is worth after one or more periods. (100)

general cash offer   An issue of securities offered for sale to the general public on a cash basis. (464)

Generally Accepted Accounting Principles (GAAP)   The common set of standards and procedures by which audited financial statements are prepared. (27)

geometric average return   The average compound return earned per year over a multiyear period. (319)

gilts   British and Irish government securities. (555)

half-year rule   Only one-half of the purchase cost of an asset is eligible for CCA in the first year of use. (270)

hard rationing   The situation that occurs when a business cannot raise financing for a project under any circumstances. (287)

homemade leverage   The use of personal borrowing to change the overall amount of financial leverage to which the individual is exposed. (409)

income statement   Financial statement summarizing a firm's performance over a period of time. (28)

incremental cash flows   The difference between a firm's future cash flows with a project and those without the project. (261)

indenture   The written agreement between the corporation and the lender detailing the terms of the debt issue. (179)

indirect bankruptcy costs   The costs of avoiding a bankruptcy filing incurred by a financially distressed firm. (417)

inflation premium   The portion of a nominal interest rate that represents compensation for expected future inflation. (196)

initial public offering (IPO)   A company's first equity issue made available to the public. Also called an *unseasoned new issue* or an *IPO*. (464)

interest on interest   Interest earned on the reinvestment of previous interest payments. (101)

interest rate parity (IRP)   The condition stating that the interest rate differential between two countries is equal to the percentage difference between the forward exchange rate and the spot exchange rate. (566)

interest rate risk premium   The compensation investors demand for bearing interest rate risk. (196)

interest tax shield   The tax saving attained by a firm from the tax deductibility of interest expense. (414)

internal growth rate   The maximum possible growth rate for a firm that relies only on internal financing. (73)

internal rate of return (IRR)   The discount rate that makes the net present value of an investment zero. (240)

inventory loan   A secured short-term loan to purchase inventory. (503)

inventory period   The time it takes to acquire and sell inventory. (486)

invoice   Bill for goods or services provided by the seller to the purchaser. (529)

just-in-time (JIT) inventory   A system for managing demand-dependent inventories that minimizes inventory holdings. (544)

line of credit   A formal (committed) or informal (non-committed) prearranged, short-term bank loan. (501)

liquidation   Termination of the firm as a going concern. (424)

liquidity premium   The portion of a nominal interest rate or bond yield that represents compensation for lack of liquidity. (198)

lockboxes   Special post office boxes set up to intercept and speed up accounts receivable collections. (521)

London Interbank Offer Rate (LIBOR)   The rate most international banks charge one another for overnight Eurodollar loans. (555)

M&M Proposition I   The value of the firm is independent of its capital structure. (411)

M&M Proposition II   A firm's cost of equity capital is a positive linear function of its capital structure. (412)

managerial options   Opportunities that managers can exploit if certain things happen in the future. Also known as "real" options. (285)

marginal tax rate   Amount of tax payable on the next dollar earned. (41)

market risk   A risk that influences a large number of assets. Also *systematic risk*. (343)

market risk premium   Slope of the security market line, the difference between the expected return on a market portfolio and the risk-free rate. (357)

materials requirements planning (MRP)   A set of procedures used to determine inventory levels for demand-dependent inventory types, such as work-in-progress and raw materials. (543)

maturity   Date on which the principal amount of a bond is paid. (168)

mortgage   A loan collateralized with real estate. (149)

multiple rates of return   The possibility that more than one discount rate makes the net present value of an investment zero. (244)

mutually exclusive investment decisions   A situation where taking one investment prevents the taking of another. (245)

net present value (NPV) The difference between an investment's market value and its cost. (233)

net present value profile A graphical representation of the relationship between an investment's net present values and various discount rates. (241)

net working capital Current assets less current liabilities. (25)

nominal rates Interest rates or rates of return that have not been adjusted for inflation. (192)

noncash items Expenses charged against revenues that do not directly affect cash flow, such as depreciation. (30)

normal distribution A symmetric, bell-shaped frequency distribution that is completely defined by its average and standard deviation. (313)

North American Industry Classification System (NAICS) North American code used to classify a firm by its type of business operations. (78)

note An unsecured debt, usually with a maturity under 10 years. (180)

operating cash flow Cash generated from a firm's normal business activities. (33)

operating cycle The time period between the acquisition of inventory and the collection of cash from receivables. (486)

opportunity cost The most valuable alternative that is given up if a particular investment is undertaken. (262)

overallotment option A contract provision giving the underwriter the option to purchase additional shares from the issuer at the offering price less the underwriter's spread. Also called the *Green Shoe provision*. (468)

oversubscription A situation related to a new securities issue, in which investors want more securities (stocks or bonds) than are available. (468)

par value The principal amount of a bond that is repaid at the end of the term. Also, *face value*. (168)

partnership A business formed by two or more individuals or entities. (8)

payback period The amount of time required for an investment to generate cash flows sufficient to recover its initial cost. (236)

perpetuity An annuity in which the cash flows continue forever. (140)

political risk Risk related to changes in value that arise because of political actions. (570)

portfolio Group of assets such as stocks and bonds held by an investor. (337)

portfolio weight Percentage of a portfolio's total value in a particular asset. (337)

precautionary motive The need to hold cash as a safety margin to act as a financial reserve. (516)

preferred stock Stock with dividend priority over common stock, normally with a fixed dividend rate, sometimes without voting rights. (219)

present value (PV) The current value of future cash flows discounted at the appropriate discount rate. (107)

primary market The market in which new securities are originally sold to investors. (17)

principle of diversification Spreading an investment across a number of assets will eliminate some, but not all, of the risk. (345)

private placements Loans, usually long-term in nature, provided directly by a limited number of investors. (476)

pro forma financial statements Financial statements projecting future years' operations. (264)

profitability index (PI) The present value of an investment's future cash flows divided by its initial cost. Also *benefit-cost ratio*. (248)

prompt offering prospectus (POP) system The registration system that allows qualified companies to access capital markets more quickly by using a short-form prospectus. A similar system is known in the U.S. as *shelf registration*. (467)

prospectus A legal document describing details of the issuing corporation and the proposed offering to potential investors. (464)

protective covenant A part of the indenture limiting certain actions that might be taken during the term of the loan, usually to protect the lender. (182)

proxy A grant of authority by a shareholder allowing another individual to vote that shareholder's shares. (218)

purchasing power parity (PPP) The idea that the exchange rate adjusts to keep purchasing power constant among currencies. (561)

pure play approach Use of a weighted average cost of capital that is unique to a particular project, based on companies in similar lines of business. (387)

quoted interest rate The interest rate expressed in terms of the interest payment made each period. Also, *stated interest rate*. (142)

real rates Interest rates or rates of return that have been adjusted for inflation. (192)

recapture The taxable amount created when an asset is sold; equal to the excess of the adjusted cost of disposal over the asset class's undepreciated capital cost. (271)

red herring A preliminary prospectus distributed to prospective investors in a new issue of securities. (464)

registered form The form of bond issue in which the registrar of the company records ownership of each bond; payment is made directly to the owner of record. (179)

regular cash dividend   Cash payment made by a firm to its owners in the normal course of business, usually made four times a year. (436)

reorganization   Financial restructuring of a failing firm to attempt to continue operations as a going concern. (424)

repurchase   Refers to a firm's purchase of its own stock. (447)

residual dividend approach   Policy under which a firm pays dividends only after meeting its investment needs while maintaining a desired debt-equity ratio. (444)

reverse split   Stock split under which a firm's number of shares outstanding is reduced. (452)

rights offer   A public issue of securities in which securities are first offered to existing shareholders. Also, *rights offering.* (464)

risk premium   The excess return required from an investment in a risky asset over that required from a risk-free investment. (310)

sales discount   A discount given to induce prompt payment. Also, *cash discount.* (530)

scenario analysis   The determination of what happens to net present value estimates when we ask what-if questions. (282)

seasoned equity offering (SEO)   A new equity issue of securities by a company that has previously issued securities to the public. (464)

secondary market   The market in which previously issued securities are traded among investors. (18)

security market line (SML)   Positively sloped straight line displaying the relationship between expected return and beta. (357)

sensitivity analysis   Investigation of what happens to net present value when only one variable is changed. (283)

shelf registration   Registration permitted in the U.S. that allows a company to register all issues it expects to sell within two years at one time, with subsequent sales at any time within those two years. (467)

shortage costs   Costs that fall with increases in the level of investment in current assets. (493)

simple interest   Interest earned only on the original principal amount invested. (101)

sinking fund   An account managed by the bond trustee for early bond redemption. (181)

soft rationing   The situation that occurs when units in a business are allocated a certain amount of financing for capital budgeting. (287)

sole proprietorship   A business owned by a single individual. (8)

speculative motive   The need to hold cash to take advantage of additional investment opportunities, such as bargain purchases. (516)

spot exchange rate   The exchange rate on a spot trade. (560)

spot trade   An agreement to trade currencies based on the exchange rate today for settlement within two business days. (560)

spread   Compensation to the underwriter: the difference between the underwriter's buying price and offering price. (465)

stakeholder   Someone who potentially has a claim on the cash flows of the firm. (16)

stand-alone principle   The assumption that evaluation of a project may be based on the project's incremental cash flows. (261)

standard deviation   The positive square root of the variance. (311)

stated interest rate   The interest rate expressed in terms of the interest payment made each period. Also, *quoted interest rate.* (142)

static theory of capital structure   Theory that a firm borrows up to the point where the tax benefit from an extra dollar in debt is exactly equal to the cost that comes from the increased probability of financial distress. (418)

stock dividend   Payment made by a firm to its owners in the form of stock, diluting the value of each share outstanding. (449)

stock split   An increase in a firm's shares outstanding without any change in owners' equity. (449)

straight voting   A procedure in which a shareholder may cast all votes for each member of the board of directors. (217)

strategic options   Options for future, related business products or strategies. (286)

strip bond/zero coupon bond   A bond that makes no coupon payments, and thus is initially priced at a deep discount. (185)

sunk cost   A cost that has already been incurred and cannot be recouped and therefore should not be considered in an investment decision. (262)

sustainable growth rate   The maximum possible growth rate for a firm that maintains a constant debt ratio and doesn't sell new stock. (75)

swaps   Agreements to exchange two securities or currencies. (555)

syndicate   A group of underwriters formed to share the risk and to help sell an issue. (466)

systematic risk   A risk that influences a large number of assets. Also *market risk.* (343)

systematic risk principle   The expected return on a risky asset depends only on that asset's systematic risk. (347)

target payout ratio   A firm's long-term desired dividend-to-earnings ratio. (446)

taxability premium   The portion of a nominal interest rate or bond yield that represents compensation for unfavourable tax status. (190)

term loans   Direct business loans of, typically, one to five years. (476)

term structure of interest rates   The relationship between nominal interest rates on default-free, pure discount securities and time to maturity; that is, the pure time value of money. (194)

terminal loss   The tax deductible amount created when an asset class is terminated; equal to the excess of the asset class's undepreciated capital cost over the adjusted cost of disposal. (271)

terms of sale   Conditions under which a firm sells its goods and services for cash or credit. (527)

tombstone   An advertisement announcing a public offering. (464)

trading range   Price range between highest and lowest prices at which a stock is traded. (451)

transaction motive   The need to hold cash to satisfy normal disbursement and collection activities associated with a firm's ongoing operations. (516)

undepreciated capital cost (UCC)   The asset class's balance of the capital cost available for CCA. (270)

underpricing   Issuing securities at less than their market value. (469)

underwriters   Investment firms that act as intermediaries between a company selling securities and the investing public. (465)

unique risk   A risk that affects at most a small number of assets. Also *unsystematic* or *asset-specific risk.* (343)

unseasoned new issue   A company's first equity issue made available to the public. Also *initial public offering.* (464)

unsystematic risk   A risk that affects at most a small number of assets. Also *unique* or *asset-specific risk.* (343)

variance   The average squared difference between the actual return and the average return. (311)

venture capital (VC)   Financing for new, often high-risk ventures. (461)

weighted average cost of capital (WACC)   The weighted average of the cost of equity and the aftertax cost of debt. (382)

working capital   A firm's short-term assets and liabilities. (7)

yield to maturity (YTM)   The rate required in the market on a bond. (168)

zero coupon bond   A bond that makes no coupon payments, and thus is initially priced at a deep discount. (185)

zero-balance account   A disbursement account in which the firm maintains a zero balance, transferring funds in from a master account only as needed to cover cheques presented for payment. (524)

Name Index

Subject Index